Beyond the Written Word

Beyond the Written Word

Oral Aspects of Scripture in the History of Religion

William A. Graham

CAMBRIDGE UNIVERSITY PRESS

Cambridge
New York New Rochelle Melbourne Sydney

Published by the Press Syndicate of the University of Cambridge
The Pitt Building, Trumpington Street, Cambridge CB2 1RP
32 East 57th Street, New York, NY 10022, USA
10 Stamford Road, Oakleigh, Melbourne 3166, Australia

First published 1987

Printed in Canada

Library of Congress Cataloging-in-Publication Data
Graham, William A. (William Albert), 1943–
Beyond the Written Word
Bibliography: p.
Includes index.
1. Sacred books – History and criticism. I. Title.
BL71.G7 1987 291.8′2 87–18310

British Library Cataloguing-in-Publication Data
Graham, William A.
Beyond the Written Word : Oral Aspects of
Scripture in the History of Religion.
1. Sacred books – Language, style
I. Title
291.8′2 BL71

ISBN 0 521 33176 5

For

Barbara

and

in memory of

Kendall Wayne Folkert (1942–1985)

Contents

Preface	*page ix*
Acknowledgments	*xiii*
Introduction	**1**
Part I Of Written and Spoken Words	**9**
1 Writing and Written Culture	11
2 The Print Textuality of Modern Culture	19
3 Books, Reading, and Literacy in the Premodern West	30
Part II Of Written and Spoken Scripture	**45**
4 Scripture in Judeo-Christian Perspective	49
5 Holy Writ and Holy Word	58
6 Scripture as Spoken Word: The Indian Paradigm	67
Part III "An Arabic Reciting": Qur'ān as Spoken Book	**79**
7 Revelation and Recitation	81
8 Muslim Scripture as Spoken Word	96
9 Voicing the Qur'ān: Questions of Meaning	110
Part IV "The Lively Oracles of God": Bible as Spoken Word	**117**
10 The Spoken Word of Christian Holy Writ	119
11 God's Word in the Desert	126
12 Hearing and Seeing: The Rhetoric of Martin Luther	141
Conclusion	**155**
Notes	*173*
Abbreviations	*239*
Bibliography	*244*
Index of Names	*285*
Index of Subjects	*296*

If all the seas were of ink, and all ponds planted with reeds, if the sky and the earth were parchments and if all humankind practiced the art of writing - they would not exhaust the Torah I have learned, just as the Torah itself would not be diminished any more than is the sea when the tip of a paintbrush is dipped in it.

– attributed to Rabbi Eliezer

For Books are not absolutely dead things, but do contain a potency of life in them to be as active as that soul was whose progeny they are.

– John Milton, *Areopagitica*

Preface

This is a book about the fundamental orality of scripture; that is, about the significant oral roles of written sacred texts in the history of religion.

In discussing this work with others, I have found repeatedly that the topic strikes most initially as odd or even hard to understand. Focus on the oral dimension of written texts does not come naturally, and perhaps least of all to the book-bound scholar. We live in a world increasingly dominated by the printed word – a world, as the novelist Italo Calvino has put it, "dense with writing that surrounds us on all sides," whether in newsprint, magazines, and paperbacks or on billboards. As written texts, scriptural books form part of the printed background of our entire culture. In the academy, as well as more widely in the modern world – in particular the high-literacy world of the contemporary West – the accepted understanding of scripture has been focused all but exclusively on scriptural texts as written documents or artifacts: that is, as physical objects, as "sacred books" in the most trivial, objectified sense of the term. Scripture is widely understood today to be the antithesis of a community's oral tradition. It is conceived as the tangible document that fixes the fluid sacred word and gives it substance and permanence. The idea hardly even occurs that a sacred text could exist for long *without* being written; nor does the recognition come easily that virtually every scripture has traditionally functioned in large measure as vocal, not silent discourse. Our current Western notions of "holy writ" too easily take for granted the written text as the focus of piety and faith in scriptural communities. Too often lost to us is the central place of the scriptural word recited, read aloud, chanted, sung, quoted in debate, memorized in childhood, meditated upon in murmur and full voice, or consciously and unconsciously used as the major building block of public and private discourse. Our attitudes in this regard derive from the natural tendency for a community to venerate physical copies of their scriptural text, but it is especially the ubiquity of printed copies of the Bible and most other sacred books, from the Qur'ān to the Lotus Sūtra, that has reinforced our notion of scripture as a concrete and often commonplace object belonging to the physical paraphernalia of religious life and practice.

Religionists, philologists, and textual historians have tacitly encouraged such a reified understanding of sacred texts by concentrating attention almost exclusively on their written form and textual history as documentary codices. Yet such restricted use of the term "scripture" to refer only or principally to the tangible, physical book constrains unnecessarily the scope of the idea of scripture. It emphasizes the undeniable importance of the orthographic text, but it does so at the expense of the many uses of scripture that do not center on the tangible document. In particular, it obscures the vocal presence of the holy book in individual and collective piety. This presence is the focus of what follows here, for I believe that it offers us access to a much-neglected dimension of sacred texts – a dimension that extends the range of scripture's historical significance beyond the written word alone.

The circuitous path that led to the present work had its beginning at least two decades ago when, on my first stay of any length in Egypt, I was fortunate to be in Cairo during the month of Ramaḍān, which fell that year in December. It was there, walking the streets of the old city amidst the animated bustle of the nocturnal crowds of men, women, and children, that I first heard at length the compelling chanting of the professional Qur'ān reciters. It seemed that wherever I wandered in the old city, from Bāb Zuwaylah to Bāb al-Futūḥ, the drawn-out, nuanced cadences of the sacred recitations gave the festive nights a magical air as the reciters' penetrating voices sounded over radios in small, open shops, or wafted into the street from the doorways of mosques and from under the canvas marquees set up specially for this month of months in the Muslim calendar. If it was only an impressionistic introduction to the living tradition of Qur'ān recitation, it was also an unforgettable one.

A more intimate acquaintance with qur'anic recitation came through a summer spent in Damascus a few years later, an experience that put me for a time in the hands of an amiable amateur reciter and *ḥāfiẓ*, 'Abd al-Raḥmān Shalabī. Under his patient direction, I spent many a hot afternoon in Qur'ān reading and learned firsthand how vividly alive the sacred text could be for a faithful reciter. At the same time, my friend Rafīq Ḥamdān saw to it that I was exposed to different kinds of recitation in local mosques and at local *dhikr*-sessions.

It was, however, back here in Cambridge, in 1977, while searching Muslim texts to trace the early use of the verbal noun *qur'ān*, that I began to understand just how fundamentally the Muslim scripture was first a "recitation" and only second a written or printed "book". This and my subsequent inquiry into the role of the Qur'ān in Muslim life led me inexorably into a wider study of scripture as a general phenomenon in the history of religion, a study that benefited greatly from the challenge of preparing the article on scripture for Macmillan's new *Encyclopedia of Religion* and especially from working among an increasing number of colleagues and students here at Harvard who were also interested in one or another aspect of scripture and scriptural piety around the globe.

My own pursuit of the problem now took me far afield from qur'anic studies, but the problem of scripture's various oral functions continued to intrigue me. As I became more and more convinced that a major reason for the dearth of material on oral dimensions of scripture lay in our own modern Western cultural biases, I was pushed inexorably into the history of textuality in the pre- and post-Gutenberg history of Western culture. Concurrently, I wanted to compare the decidedly oral focus of qur'anic piety with scriptural attitudes and usages in other major religious communities. I went first to the obvious primacy of oral treatment of scripture in both Vedic and non-Vedic traditions in India. I also turned to Buddhist *sūtra* recitation and concepts of the Buddha-word, to Torah cantillation and other Judaic traditions of scriptural piety, and especially to Christian Bible-piety. The last of these proved of special interest, and within the Christian context my reading soon had two contrasting foci: first, on early Christian treatment of the Hebrew scriptures and the emerging gospel and epistle literature; second, by way of contrast, on the post-Gutenberg, European Protestant tradition. The former led me eventually into early Christian monasticism, one of the major sources of all forms of Christian biblical piety. The latter sent me to the scripturally saturated writings of major reformers and Protestant thinkers like Martin Luther, Martin Bucer, John Bunyan, and John Donne, since I was convinced that, even in the heart of Protestant "book religion", the importance of the oral aspects of scripture would be significant, if also hard to extrapolate from the written page alone. In the end, I settled on the Pachomian monastic tradition and the work of Martin Luther as two diverse and important subjects for more detailed study.

This, then, is a rough sketch of the intellectual odyssey that lies behind the disparate but organically related discussions of the present book. If I have any regret about this study, it is largely that I had to curtail its originally intended scope and could not treat fully the significant Judaic, Buddhist, Chinese, Sikh, and other traditions of scriptural orality. What is offered here is far from a survey of scriptural orality. My only hope is that it may be useful as an essay into relatively poorly demarcated territory, one that might serve as a starting point for work in areas I have not touched upon or was forced to pass over with minimal reference.

This book has been written with as wide an audience as possible in mind. I wanted to provide the general reader and especially the student interested in the study of religion with a readable discussion of scripture set in a comparative context. However, my purpose in trying to suggest different ways of thinking about scripture and, by extension, other religious phenomena, was especially to speak to specialists in the separate traditions who might take up in their own fields some of the lines of inquiry broached and pursued for only a few cases here. Therefore, I have tried in both the notes and bibliography not only to lay out the immediate sources for my arguments, but to include those materials that I have found helpful and that would be needed to pursue particular points beyond where I have taken them.

These considerations have dictated also a format that involves a relatively "clean" and nontechnical text bought at the price of what can only be termed (acronymically, with respects to Robert K. Merton for his incomparable *On the Shoulders of Giants*) an "otsogian" critical apparatus lodged in the notes. Indeed, the extensive notes are a fair indication of the gigantic and the lesser shoulders whose support afforded me vistas on territories I could never have surveyed without them. Furthermore, since some of what I argue here may be not only controversial but dependent on widely scattered sources, I have tried to document my points as completely as reasonable limits of space and endurance allowed. The abbreviations and bibliography, together with the index, should enable anyone to find their way through the notes with, I trust, minimal inconvenience and maximal clarity. The specialist can follow in detail my route through the sources and the scholarship in his or her field on which I have relied; on the other hand, the reader primarily interested in the general exposition, arguments, and conclusions of the book should be able to follow these with little recourse to the notes (although I must confess to the scholar's conceit that some of the most fascinating elements of the whole will be lost by ignoring the notes).

Finally, a brief discussion of the treatment of foreign-language materials is in order. The nature of the inquiry has demanded reliance on primary and secondary materials in a variety of languages. To facilitate access to the materials, I have provided English translations of important passages in the text, relegating original-text citations to the notes. All foreign languages have been transliterated into the Latin script according to generally standard systems. All foreign-language citations in English are my own translations, unless an English-translation source is explicitly indicated (as, for example, in the case of most of the Pachomian texts cited in Chapter 11, where I have always consulted the original texts but cited Vielleux's excellent translations from his *Pachomian Koinonia*). In a few cases, where I differ with an existing English translation on a given passage or have a potentially controversial interpretation of it, or where the context makes the source of the translation unclear, I have explicitly noted that the translation is my own.

Cambridge, Massachusetts
August 1986

Acknowledgments

Much of the basic research for this book was made possible by the exemplary generosity of the John Simon Guggenheim Foundation and the Alexander von Humboldt Stiftung, which together underwrote a year of work in Cambridge, Bonn, and India during 1982–83. Support from the Faculty of Arts and Sciences and the Center for the Study of World Religions at Harvard allowed me to complete most of the text in 1985. A particular note of gratitude goes to the staff of the various libraries in which I spent so many fruitful hours, especially the main library and seminar collections of the University of Bonn, the Andover–Harvard Library, and, most of all, the incomparable collection of Harvard's Widener Library. The Cambridge University Press sought out and encouraged the project in its early stages and passed on helpful comments from scholars whom I do not know by name, but for whose support and suggestions I am very grateful. David Emblidge and Michael Gnat, as the editors primarily responsible for the finished product, were always helpful and a pleasure to work with – as was everyone at the Press. The book was start to finish a Macintosh-computer product, and the finish was only possible because Zack Deal at Harvard's Office of Information Technology helped me secure the considerable computer expertise of John Cheng. To the latter I owe special thanks for solving the unusual character and font problems, enabling the printing of the rather complicated manuscript directly from disk.

A study such as this is only possible because of the more detailed work of experts in the many fields on which it touches. At every turn I have been dependent in substantial ways upon not only the published work of past and present scholars, but also the living knowledge of many of the latter and their willingness to share some of it with me. The following list of my scholarly indebtedness is long, yet inevitably incomplete – those whom I have omitted will, I hope, accept my apologies. To all who helped, my gratitude is none the less great for the length of time that has elapsed since they gave their assistance.

Muslim friends and teachers at home and in the Arab world have provided me with invaluable insights into Qur'ān-piety. Besides those named in the Preface, I owe special gratitude to my old friend, Mahmoud Ayoub, and my Harvard colleague, Ali Asani, as well as Shaykh Naṣr al-Dīn al-Albānī and his scholarly circle in Damascus. Other friends and colleagues read part or the whole of the first draft and offered encouragement as well as advice. From the inception of the project, Wilfred Cantwell Smith was an interested and, as ever, incisive and inspiring respondent to diverse issues and ideas. Because he, too, has been at work on the general problem of scripture over the past eight years or so, his counsel was especially helpful. Richard Niebuhr was always generous in his willingness to listen when problems arose. David Eckel was a favorite sounding board and thoughtful critic in the tougher moments of writing. James Engell, John Carman, Giles Constable, Gary Tubb, Wolfhart Heinrichs, Muhsin Mahdi, and Albert Henrichs suffered with early chapter or full drafts and passed on helpful criticism, references, and suggestions. Other scholars who contributed substantially at various times and in diverse ways include J. L. Mehta, Thomas Coburn, Stephen Ozment, Zeph Stewart, Hans-Joachim Klimkeit, Monika Thiel-Horstmann, Albrecht Noth, Miriam Levering, Douglas Langston, Thomas Head, Mary McGee, Wendy O'Flaherty, Raoul Birnbaum, Marilyn Waldman, Frederick Denny, Richard Martin, Margaret Miles, and Philip Lutgendorf. I was helped and heartened several times by the responses of those students in graduate seminars who read and discussed preliminary studies toward the book. During the actual writing, my Harvard office colleagues - Wei-Ming Tu, Diana Eck, and Carol Zaleski - were the nearest patient scholarly ears, and each proffered suggestions both specific and general. At the office also, Diane Dana tried nobly to protect my working time, and Alice Colwell proved an exceptional proofreader of the complex welter of text, notes, and bibliography that comprised the manuscript in its later versions. Anne Marie Crowley and Irit Averbuch also helped with the final proofs. The enthusiastic and astute work of graduate research assistants - Birgitta Mehdi, Henry Simoni, and Brian Hatcher - saved me innumerable hours of library time. The quality of the indexes also owes much to Mr. Hatcher's careful work. To all the aforementioned, and others mentioned in specific notes, I am indebted. They are not, however, to blame for any inadequacies or errors that follow; these remain my responsibility.

Finally, a word about the dedication page of this volume. The first entry there can only feebly suggest how much this book owes to the patient and loving presence of my wife Barbara. The second testifies to how much I would like to have shared the pleasure of publication with my late friend, Kendall W. Folkert. It means a great deal that, before his untimely death, I was able to share with him not only more than two decades of stimulating interchange on every topic conceivable, but many hours of discussion specifically on the subject of scripture, with which he was also engaged both as a Jain specialist and a general historian of religion.

Introduction

If any domain of the history of man and of his thought seems to us quite straightforward, we may be fairly certain that we are ill-informed about it or view it from a partisan standpoint.

- Arthur Darby Nock

Probably no major concept or phenomenon in the history of religion appears more self-evident or unproblematic than scripture. One need only look at the treatment of the term in an average dictionary or encyclopedia to illustrate how blithely confident we are about its fundamental simplicity and straightforwardness. "Scripture" was once all but exclusively reserved for the Christian or Jewish Bible, and this remains its primary signification. Today, however, "scripture" or "the scriptures" is readily and increasingly employed as a generic term for "any sacred or religious writings or books" in any cultural or religious setting. We know so well, we presume, what our paradigm for a scripture is – namely, the printed book of the Bible[1] – that treating sacred texts in other traditions as scripture by analogy with it seems hardly to present any serious interpretive problems. At least since 1879, when Max Müller initiated the great series of translations of sacred texts that he called "The Sacred Books of the East," there has been scant objection raised to the wider application of terms such as "sacred text", "holy book", or "[holy] scripture" to any of those texts that are sacrosanct and authoritative for a particular community of faith.

The apparent straightforwardness of scripture as a generic religious phenomenon may suggest that it has little to offer as a focus of study that would repay intensive investigation. More than that, it may even make scripture appear to be a basically one-dimensional and therefore essentially boring subject for discussion. When compared to myth or ritual, mysticism or totemism, holy places or sacred images, scripture seems scarcely the kind of exotic or exciting topic that promises new interpretive possibilities to the student of religion. Once the philological work of establishing the most authentic text of a particular scriptural book has been completed, we are inclined to feel that any remaining problems have primarily to do with using that text and its history to reconstruct the history of the community in which it came into being – again by analogy with the way in which the Bible has been studied and used in modern scholarship to reconstruct the early Hebrew or Christian milieu. Any wider study of scripture as a general phenomenon or concept appears doomed to take one of two basic forms: either a phenomenological catalog of recurring characteristics of scriptural texts (canonical definition, authoritativeness, divine origin, and the like) or a comparative survey of the content, form, and extent of the various "sacred books" or "scriptural canons" of East and West. The relatively few studies that have been devoted to scripture as a general phenomenon tend to bear out this supposition, whatever their individual quality.[2]

Scripture as Problem

Despite its apparent simplicity and the seemingly obvious treatment it requires, scripture is by no means a dead issue. In at least some sectors of the scholarly community concerned with the study of religion, there is growing interest in the active roles and significance of scriptural texts in the years or centuries after their original appearance and codification or canonization.[3] This is not a wholly new development: the study of the varied strands of scriptural interpretation in particular traditions has long proven an attractive field of investigation.[4] Moreover, as the study of the postredactional history of scriptural texts in the world's diverse religious communities progresses, the ambiguity and complexity of scripture as a general concept and recurring form become more and more evident. Questions of redaction, canonization, oral and written tradition, and exegetical forms and techniques push the specialist in one field to look abroad to other fields for new methods, models, questions, and hypotheses. In addition, scripture attracts the student of religion now as before simply because of its central importance in so many different religious traditions.

For all of the interest of scripture, much work remains to be done if it is to be understood adequately as a recurring phenomenon around the world. The time has come to give more careful scrutiny to this major element of religious life, not only because of its interest and importance, but also because our assumptions about its straightforwardness and simplicity need considerable revision. In the study of scripture in a worldwide context, as in all comparative ventures, what begins with perceived similarities and continuities proceeds rapidly to recognition of contrasts and disparities among differing traditions. At a still later stage, ever greater complexity and nuance enter where first analogies and correspondences and then emerging differences had seemed relatively clear-cut. Scripture, not unlike religion, or ritual, or any other significant element of human life and society, proves finally ambiguous and elusive of simple definition or easy delineation.

At the most basic level, there is the fact of radical diversity in form and content among the notable scriptures of world religion and, indeed, often within the same scriptural text or corpus. Myth and legend, historical narratives, ritual books, legal codes, ecstatic or mystical poetry, apocalyptic visions, utterances of prophets and teachers, divine revelations, and hymns and prayers to a deity have all found a place in one or another scripture. The love lyrics of The Song of Songs in the Hebrew Bible, the talismanic prayers against evil in the last two *sūrah*s of the Qur'ān, Kṛṣṇa's self-revelation in chapter 11 of the Bhagavadgītā, Kabīr's poetry in the Ādi Granth of the Sikhs, and the Buddha's parable of the burning house in chapter 3 of the Lotus Sūtra have each played a significant role as scripture in its respective context, yet they share little or nothing common in their style, form, subject matter, meaning, or purpose. Such disparity makes any reasonably comprehensive yet still straightforward and manageable definition of scripture a will-o'-the-wisp.[5]

A second ambiguity of scripture as a conceptual category is evident in the problem of texts that might seem only peripherally "religious", yet whose functions still can be classified as "scriptural" in many cultural contexts. A key instance involves those "classic" texts in literate cultures that have many cultural, social, and spiritual functions usually associated with more overtly "religious" texts.[6] The instances that come first to mind for most Westerners are the *Iliad* and *Odyssey*. Thus Gibbon could say of the Romans that "[Homer's] works and those of his successors were the scriptures of the nation."[7] Examples from other cultures also abound: the five (or six, nine, twelve, or thirteen) "classics" (*ching*) and the four "books" (*shu*) in Chinese traditional culture;[8] the great Sanskrit epics, the *Mahābhārata* and *Rāmāyaṇa,* in India; or the *Nihongi* (*Chronicles of Japan*) and *Kojiki* (*Records of Ancient Matters*) in Japan. These texts have some clearly "scriptural" qualities, such as the veneration and reverence they inspire, the faith, morals, and values they sustain, and the authority they command, although none is so closely tied to liturgy and other more traditional "religious" contexts as are the Bible, Zend-Avesta, or Qur'ān. As a result, there can be little argument that such texts might be treated as scripture in certain contexts, even if not in others.

A further difficulty in delimiting scripture is to distinguish the primary sacred text or texts of a religious tradition from others that are also sacred but secondarily so. Such distinction between a community's preeminent scripture and the rest of its sacred texts is helpful in understanding many religious traditions, but others not at all: in some cases, the panoply of texts revered is so great and the relative distinctions of authority and sacrality among them so unclear or unimportant that all have some legitimate claim to the title "scripture". In Mahāyāna Buddhist tradition as a whole, the number of texts treated as sacred is so vast that it is impossible to single out some as more deserving of being termed "scripture" than others, save in particular segments of the tradition where one *sūtra* is given extraordinary status – as, for example, in Nichiren Buddhist veneration of the Lotus Sūtra in Japan. Yet the "canonical" traditions regarding *sūtra*s, and the concept of *āgama,* or sacred text, are crucial ones for Mahāyāna faith and practice in all of its various forms. Even in a community with a scriptural book or canon that is clearly *more* sacrosanct than other revered texts, the decision to reserve the status of scripture only for the former can be a debatable one. For example, the Purāṇas function scripturally across a wide spectrum of Indian society even though they are not accorded the "scriptural" status of "what is heard", or *śruti* (see Chapter 6); and in Theravāda Buddhist traditions, texts such as Buddhaghosa's *Visuddhimagga* are greatly revered even though they do not report the "word of the Buddha" (*buddhavacana*) in the strict sense. Nor would it be out of place to refer here to Rabbinic Jewish tradition, in which the Mishnah is held to be the oral Torah also revealed at Sinai; or to Islamic tradition, in which the Ḥadīth serve not only to clarify and to explain, but to supplement the Qur'ān as a religious authority, especially in matters of practice. In each tradition, the uniqueness of the texts and the diversity of their functions are strong enough that we are finally left with few if any external criteria for separating "primary" and "secondary" sacred texts across the wide range of scriptural traditions.

Yet a fourth obstacle to simple delineation of the phenomenon of scripture, and the one that most concerns us in the present investigation, is its medium of expression. The term "scripture" is usually reserved for religious texts that have been committed to the written or printed page, as the word itself and its common equivalents, such as "holy writ", suggest (see Chapter 4). Yet in most major religious traditions, sacred texts were transmitted orally in the first place and written down only relatively recently. Nor do written sacred books exhaust the full range of texts that function clearly as scripture. It may be argued, for example, that nonliterate communities – the so-called "little" or "extracivilizational" societies – have oral texts that function in similar ways to written sacred texts in literate societies, insofar as these cultures use traditional recitations in cultic practice or hold certain myths or other oral texts sufficiently sacred to be worthy of transmission over generations. It is, however, the Hindu tradition in particular that presents a major problem for defining scripture in terms of the written word. Its holiest texts, the Vedas, have been orally transmitted for three millennia or more – for the majority of that time not because writing was unknown, but rather by choice, in explicit preference to writing them down. Despite their great length, they have been committed to the page only in comparatively recent centuries. Nor is the Hindu tradition alone in insistence upon the primacy of the oral text. We cannot ignore the prominent but rarely emphasized oral function – in ritual, reading, recitation, devotions, and song – of *all* religious texts, written as well as unwritten. For example, in the case of Islam, unlike that of traditional India, the oral, recited Qur'ān has retained its primacy despite being written down as well as transmitted orally. Even in Jewish and especially Christian "book religion", the oral dimension of the scriptures has been much stronger than is usually recognized. For all these reasons, a descriptive distinction between oral and written scriptures, or oral and written uses of the same scripture, is on occasion necessary, even though etymologically "oral scripture" is an oxymoron and "written scripture" a redundancy.

Scripture as a Relational Concept

These considerations underscore not only the difficulty of finding a satisfactory "simple" definition of scripture in a generic sense, but also the axiom that neither form nor content can serve to distinguish or identify scripture as a general phenomenon or category. It is true that the form, content, or other specific attributes of a text may be perceived by the faithful as the guarantee of the extraordinary character of their major scripture (e.g., Muslim faith in the literary "matchlessness" [*i'jāz*] of the qur'anic style as a proof of the Qur'ān's divine origin). Nevertheless, from the historian's perspective, the sacrality or holiness of a book is not an a priori attribute of a text but one that is realized historically in the life of communities who respond to it as something sacred or holy. A text becomes "scripture" in active, subjective relationship to persons, and as part of a cumulative communal tradition. No text, written or oral or both, is sacred or authoritative in isolation from a community. One does not have to be a proponent of contemporary fads in literary criticism to recognize that there is no absolute "meaning" in a scriptural text apart from the interpreting community that finds it meaningful. This is one of the reasons that it is seldom if ever enough simply to open a sacred book and read, as one would read the instructions on a package; rather one must hear it read and expounded in a special context to grasp its meaning. A book is only "scripture" insofar as a group of persons perceive it to be sacred or holy, powerful and portentous, possessed of an exalted authority, and in some fashion transcendent of, and hence distinct from, all other speech and writing.

Conversely, what is scripture for one group may be a perfectly ordinary, or even a meaningless, nonsensical, or perversely false text for another. Much of the dark side of the history of religion has been characterized by one community's vehement rejection of the validity of another's claim to possess a sacred scripture: So Jews reject the Christian New Testament, Christians the Qur'ān, Muslims the writings of Bahā'ullāh, Buddhists the Vedas, and so on. Such rejection postulates normally the absolute validity of only one scripture or body of scriptures - one's own. It ignores what the historian of religion cannot: the relational character of scriptural texts when viewed as particular instances of a common and widespread historical phenomenon.

This relational quality - or, if one prefers, contextual or functional quality - is of paramount importance for the study of scripture in the history of religion. Recognition of it is recognition that the significant "scriptural" characteristics of a text belong not only to the text itself but also to its role in a community and in individual lives. The historian does not have to prove or disprove claims of ultimacy or transcendence for a given text, but he or she does have to address seriously its significant mundane importance: the historical fact that men and women of faith have found ultimacy, have encountered trancendence, in its text. This, after all, is why we call it "scripture". Furthermore, this recognition means that scripturality arises not from the formal acts of religious leaders or church councils, however important their eventual roles in confirming the sacrality and boundaries of scripture, but rather in the interaction of persons and groups of persons with a text or texts. In other words, there is, historically speaking, no text that in and of itself can be called "scripture"; in Aristotelian terms, "scripturality" is an accidental, not an essential characteristic. The study of a text as a document focuses on the historical background and the origin and growth of the text. The study of a text as scripture, on the other hand, focuses upon its contextual meaning, interpretation, and use - that is, the ongoing role the text has played in a tradition, not only in formal exegesis, but in every sector of life. To put it succinctly, "scripture" is not a literary genre but a religiohistorical one, and it must be understood as such.

The Sensual Dimension

If we attempt to treat scripture in this relational fashion, we are driven directly to consideration of the affective realm of religious life, that sphere of meaning that involves what I term the "sensual" aspects of religiousness. I use this word not so much to refer in a technical way to the five senses, but rather to suggest that seeing, hearing, and touching in particular are essential elements in religious life as we can observe it. Even if they do not admit of easy or exact analysis, they deserve greater attention than our bias in favor of the mental and emotional aspects of religion (in the case of scripture, toward the "original message" or "theological meaning" of the text) typically allows. A sacred text can be read laboriously in silent study, chanted or sung in unthinking repetition, copied or illuminated in loving devotion, imaginatively depicted in art or drama, solemnly processed in ritual pagentry, or devoutly touched in hope of luck and blessing. In each instance, in very diverse and not always predictable but still very real ways, such contact with scripture can elicit in reader, hearer, onlooker, or worshiper diverse responses: a surge of joy or sorrow; a feeling of belonging or even of alienation; a sense of guidance or consolation (or the want of either); or a feeling of intimacy with or awesome distance from the divine. These kinds of religious response are important to an adequate understanding of what it means to encounter a text as scripture. Such aspects are difficult, perhaps finally impossible, for the scholar to get at in any systematic way, but to ignore them entirely is to omit a substantial portion of their reality. Ideally, our knowledge of the textual history, doctrinal interpretation, ritual and devotional use, and political and social roles of a scriptural book should be joined to an awareness of these sensual elements in the response of the faithful to their sacred text. Only in this way can our understanding of scripture as a relational phenomenon begin to be adequate.

The Problem of Scriptural Orality

The present investigation is an attempt to contribute to such understanding by focusing specifically on one dimension of the relation between religious communities and their scriptures – that of the oral function and use of these texts. "Orality" itself is a loaded, or at least ambiguous term, and when it is treated as a functional dimension of a written text, it can be especially problematic. The orality at issue in this work is not the "primary orality" of illiterate or preliterate cultures. We are not interested here in the often-discussed dichotomies of "oral culture" versus "literate culture" and "oral tradition" versus "written tradition"; nor are we concerned with the question of oral and written stages in the developmental history of sacred texts. The former of these problems is usually treated through study of "nonliterate" societies, and the latter through inquiry into the origins of the sacred written texts of the major literate traditions of world religion.[9] Our attention will be directed instead to the ongoing function of scriptural texts as oral phenomena. *It is the specifically oral dimension of the written scriptural text that is at issue here.* Our special concern will be the important, often primary, ways in which scripture has been a significantly vocal as well as visual fact: how individuals and groups have understood and dealt with their sacred scriptures not only as holy books to be calligraphed and illuminated, preserved and revered, paraded and displayed, but also as texts to be memorized, sung and chanted, read aloud, recited, retold, and woven into the texture of their language, thought, and being as auditory facts.

The immense importance of the oral aspects of scriptural piety and practice to an adequate understanding of scripture is belied by the relative paucity of scholarly work devoted to them. Because the issue of orality has received so little attention, it is important to see it in the context of our modern Western intellectual world as well as in that of the history of particular scriptural traditions. In what follows, we shall explore the neglected oral dimension through a consideration of, first, the issue of the oral dimension of written texts generally; then the written and oral character of scripture in particular; and, finally, specific instances in which the scriptures of two major "book religions" have functioned as oral texts in significant ways. The breakdown of the remainder of the book is as follows.

In Parts I and II, I discuss how the biases and presuppositions of modern Western book and print culture have diminished our capacity to grasp the meaning of scripture as an active, vocal presence in the lives of individuals and communities everywhere. Here I argue that the contemporary Western conception of books as silent written documents has skewed our perception of the special kind of book that we call "scripture", especially as regards its important oral functions. Part I (Chapters 1–3) is devoted to the general problem of our attitudes to written text and the history behind these attitudes in the Western world since the Greeks. Part II deals with the specific problem of written and oral aspects of scripture: whence we derive our conception of scripture (Chapter 4), some of the functions of both sacred spoken and sacred written word in the history of religion (Chapter 5), and the uniquely oral character of scriptural texts in India (Chapter 6).

The Indian case treated in Chapter 6 clearly demonstrates that our notion of scripture as only a written or printed book cannot do justice to scripture in a global context. The Hindu emphasis on sacred word as spoken word is, however, only the most extreme example of a significant oral dimension to scripture in all major religious traditions. To document this, I examine in Parts III and IV (Chapters 7–12) some specific historical cases of the central, yet today unfamiliar or inadequately emphasized orality of scripture in Islam and Christianity, two traditions known particularly for their focus on the sacred book. These provide the critical cases in which to see just how much is lost when our notion of scripture fails to include the significant oral functions of the written text.

PART I

Of Written and Spoken Words

Had the *Iliad* been written, it would have been sung much less.
- Jean-Jacques Rousseau

Of course the very best writing is an attempt to convey in printed words some of those overtones which are sounded by the voice and emanated from the physical personality.
- Alfred North Whitehead

Our current understanding of scripture rests in significant degree upon the more general notion in contemporary Western culture of what constitutes a book of any kind, secular or religious. In our minds, a book is a written or printed document of reasonable length to which the basic access is through an individual's private, silent reading and study. For most if not all of us, the fixed, visible page of print is the fundamental medium of both information and demonstration or proof. If anything is truly important, we have to "get it in writing", be it an idea, a report, a directive, or an agreement. We want tangible evidence of "documentation"; we need things of importance "signed and sealed". To a degree unknown in any other culture of history, knowledge for us is "book-learning";[1] and no orally communicated word carries the kind of legal, scholarly, or administrative authority for us that a written or printed document does. Ours is not only a literate, but a book and print culture – what Northrop Frye has called a postliterate culture.

Still more: For us the written word has become the basic form of language, not a secondary vehicle for its communication, not a mere "graphic representation of language" (de Saussure). So tied are we to the written or printed page that we have lost any awareness of the essential orality of language, let alone of reading.[2] Not only do we want everything of moment "in black and white", but we presume that that is the fundamental medium of language. There seems to be a basic human tendency for the visual to replace the aural, for writing to become more important than speech,[3] and print seems to accelerate this tendency. "The speaker or writer can now hardly conceive of language, except in printed or written form; . . . his idea of language is irrevocably modified by his experience of printed matter."[4]

In historical perspective, our current conception of the book (and therefore of the reading process and literacy as well) proves to be quite limited and limiting. This limitation exercises particularly pernicious influence upon our attempts to understand the functional historical role of texts in other times and places, for it involves a series of assumptions about the nature of a written "composition" that are both relatively recent in date and quite culture-specific. These assumptions have skewed our understanding of the ways in which books – and by "books" I mean written texts in general – have actually functioned through most of history since the inception of writing. Because they bear directly upon our understanding of scripture, these assumptions have to be confronted at the outset. In what follows, I shall take up, first, our notion of the importance of writing for culture and history (Chapter 1); second, the influence of printing on our modern attitudes toward books and other texts (Chapter 2); and, third, the degree to which premodern society even in our own Western tradition has been orally rather than visually oriented in its treatment of texts (Chapter 3). Only against this background can we begin to understand more clearly what a book of scripture is and has been for most peoples in most cultures throughout history.

CHAPTER 1

Writing and Written Culture

I cannot see that lectures can do so much good as reading the books from which the lectures are taken.

- Samuel Johnson

Access to phonetic writing constitutes at once a supplementary degree of representativity and a total revolution in the structure of representation. Direct or hieroglyphic pictography represents the thing or the signified. . . . Phonetic writing . . . . uses, through the analysis of sounds, signifiers that are in some way non-signifying.

- Jacques Derrida

The close linkage in literate culture between writing and textuality is axiomatic. Our common identification of "book" (or of "text" in general) with "written document" proceeds naturally from the documentary revolution that the advent of writing in a culture inevitably brings in its wake. This identification is vividly evident in the derivations of our common words for written texts. The very word "book" in English and its cognates in other Germanic languages (as the German *Buch,* Dutch *Boek,* or Swedish and Danish *Bok*) have commonly been linked etymologically with the name for beech tree (Old Norse *bók,* Old English *bóc*), the bark or wood of which may have been the earliest form of writing material among Germanic peoples.[1] Similarly, the Greek words for "book", *biblos* and *biblion,* are taken from the word for the Egyptian papyrus, *byblos* or *biblos,* the premier writing material of the ancient world.[2] Many other Greco-Latinate terms for verbal texts, from "letter" to "inscription" to "monograph", are also connected etymologically with the act of writing, as we shall see later in the case of specific interest to us: "scripture", *Schrift, scrittura,* and so on.

Writing as the Measure of Civilization

It is hard to overestimate the perceived significance of writing to a literate culture. Virtually every culture that has mastered the art of writing, or even only come into direct contact with scribal or chirographic culture,[3] has assigned immense importance and prestige to the written word. Where only a small priestly or other élite have commanded the art of writing, mystery and reverence have typically surrounded the book; where writing has been more widely disseminated, its prestige has been tied up with the economic or social advantage that it confers on those who can master it; and where moveable-type printing has joined with other forces to help expand the literate population, writing and reading have become necessities for full participation in the larger society.

Thus it is not surprising how important a place writing occupies in our valuation of progress in every society of history.[4] We have made it a major yardstick, if not the prime one, for gauging civilized culture. The Egyptologist Alan Gardiner has remarked that "man's successive discoveries, at very great intervals, of the respective techniques of Speech and Writing, have been the two main stages passed by him on his long road to civilization." Oswald Spengler puts it even more succinctly: "The word is a possession of man generally, whereas writing belongs exclusively to the cultured [*Kulturmenschen*]." Such dicta express well our sense of the momentous character of the breakthrough to the written word for the onset of true civilization. We commonly use, as Robert Redfield notes, "absence of literacy and literature . . . as a criterion of primitive as contrasted with civilized living." We not only take it as a given that purely oral communication is eventually "unable to meet the demands of progressive cultural development" (Hans Jensen), but our very definition of cultural progress depends upon the rather facile idea that "only phonetic writing has the power to translate man from the tribal to the civilized sphere" (Marshall McLuhan). It is even argued that writing is a key factor in political progress, allowing humans, in the words of Carl Becker, to "unite small communities into large states, and by the conquest and consolidation of many states create great empires."[5] In general, there is much evidence to support our widespread association of writing with civilization, although this should not be used to support either the once fashionable assumption that preliterates are "simpler" or have lesser intellectual capacities than literates, or the argument that literacy automatically conveys new intellectual capacities.[6]

Writing as the Basis for Historical Inquiry

These ideas have decisive consequences also for our present-day understanding of the history of civilizations past and present. To begin with, history as written narrative normally demands written records to give any real access to the course of particular events. We divide "prehistory" from "history" by the same principle by which we distinguish uncivilized from civilized culture: namely, that of the absence or presence of writing, and hence of written records. It is not that so-called preliterate cultures of the past have no history in the absolute sense of existence over time, nor that archaeology cannot give us clues about many facets of those cultures that have left no written artifacts. Rather, it is simply that history as investigation of past events – as "learning by inquiry", in the literal sense of the Greek *historia* – is ineluctably tied to the critical ordering and evaluation of human affairs in their continuity and change over time. Since these activities are largely dependent upon written records, to speak of a "chapter" or "page" of history is not so idle a use of metaphor as it might appear.

There is considerable justice in this view. In those eras for which we have no written evidence, archaeological investigations, especially in conjunction with anthropological findings, can tell us a surprising amount about material culture, trade and industry, demographics, and even, on occasion, the occurrence of major catastrophes such as floods, famines, or wars. They can often provide us with a basis for reasonable deductions or at least educated guesses about the economic, governmental, and social organization of vanished societies. However, about crucial aspects of human affairs such as events and personages, religious convictions, legal and political theories, cultural values, or even power structures, archaeology can rarely offer more than the most tentative of hypotheses unless its findings can be correlated with written evidence.[7] George Steiner suggests this when he describes history as "a speech-act" and remarks that

> even substantive remains such as buildings and historical sites must be 'read', i.e. located in a context of verbal recognition and placement, before they assume real presence. What material reality has history outside language, outside our interpretative belief in essentially linguistic records (silence knows no history)? Where worms, fires of London, or totalitarian régimes obliterate such records, our consciousness of past being comes on a blank space.[8]

Such, for example, remains the state of our study of the so-called Harappan civilization of the ancient Indus valley. However interesting the information produced by new excavations, so long as the seal inscriptions of this widely dispersed and long-lived culture cannot be deciphered (and perhaps not even then, if no more extensive texts are found), we can know about it only a fraction of what we know about contemporaneous civilizations in Mesopotamia and Egypt.

In his study of the written book, David Diringer gives an unusually apodictic statement of the historian's basic need for written sources in a section he entitles "Real History is Based on Written Documents":

> To write real history, we require something very different [from oral tradition] – apart from the special qualities of the historian, . . . we require actual and reliable record. . . . There is no doubt that we cannot entirely rely on a purely oral tradition, fostered as this would normally be by tribal feeling and pride, rather than by a concern for historical accuracy. At the very least, we require contemporary *written* documents.[9]

Although we may be allowed considerable skepticism about Diringer's total confidence in the absolute, qualitative differences between all oral and written traditions (not to mention the "special qualities" of the historian), the kind of historical inquiry that written sources make possible is rarely if ever possible with other kinds of evidence alone.

This is not to deny that the capacities of oral transmission to record past events, genealogies, biographical information, and other traditions in nonliterate cultures are much greater than earlier generations of historians wanted to recognize. Increasing recognition of the diversity of oral cultures alone has led to recognition of similar variance in both the "historical consciousness" that characterizes them and the genres of oral tradition they have preserved.[10] Once the bias against use of strictly oral tradition for historical purposes was overcome, oral history proved fruitful not only in the study of contemporary nonliterate or newly literate societies, but also in that of our own society within the span of living memory. Nevertheless, without written sources of some kind, the historian has no substantial access to human affairs except in those extant societies in which oral traditions can be consulted directly – and even in these, the nature of such traditions demands that the historian handle them with great caution and, if possible, supplement their use with other kinds of data.[11]

Writing and the Reorientation of Thought

Even where there are differing evaluations of whether there is "progress" involved in the shift from oral to written communication in a given context, few would deny that it brings important cultural changes with it.[12] At the very least, it is one element in a complex of forces that have figured prominently in the cultural heydays of the major world civilizations. The "literate revolution"[13] that alphabetic culture introduces helps to open new vistas on both the substance and the shape of knowledge, even if it does so only very gradually.

M. T. Clanchy remarks that "the intellectual act of remembering is essentially different from the act of referring to a written record,"[14] and this difference is mirrored in changed ways of dealing with the transmission of information and ideas once writing takes hold. In terms of the quantity of material that can be retained, even the most astounding human memories cannot compete finally with documents. As writing penetrates a society, mnemonic systems for preserving its traditions give way to physical texts that can be referred to independently of individual human transmitters and need no special devices such as versification or visual-image associative systems to record and transmit extensive bodies of discourse.[15] It may be that the earliest use of the written text is simply as an *aide-mémoire,* although documents tend rapidly to replace rather than to support memory.[16] In any case, the written record makes fixing the chronology of events, disseminating literary works, or recording agreements and treaties much more certain than can ever be the case with oral tradition alone, especially over any span of more than one generation.

Still more: The use of written records eventually stimulates or coincides with new concerns and purposes for verbal narrative that are qualitatively as well as quantitatively different from those of primary oral cultures. Speaking involves interaction with an audience; writing necessitates distancing of the writer from his or her readers. The inclination of modern hermeneuts such as Paul Ricoeur to see the written text as utterly independent of its author is an extreme but logical expression of the autonomy of the written word. Fixing a text visually objectifies its discourse as symbols on the page and makes it possible to treat it as something abstract and impersonal, an object of analysis apart from the specific, always contextual situations of oral speech. This point has been emphasized by a variety of scholars, notably Jack Goody:

> . . . writing, and more especially alphabetic literacy, made it possible to scrutinise discourse in a different kind of way by giving oral communication a semi-permanent form; this scrutiny favoured the increase in scope of critical activity . . . . writing laid out discourse before one's eyes in a different kind of way . . . .[17]

This may be seen in the rise of new genres and linguistically more elaborate types of text. It has been suggested, for example, that the literary possibilities offered by writing made possible the creation of the great Mesopotamian epic of *Gilgamesh* out of a number of earlier and, in some cases, unrelated oral legends or legend-cycles.[18] The qualitative differences of written from oral texts are especially evident in the treatment of ideas, which are subject to different kinds and levels of analysis once they have been reduced to fixed words on a page.[19] As Walter J. Ong puts it, literacy makes "study" possible, and with it, the "abstractly sequential, classificatory, explanatory examination of phenomena or of stated truths" that is "impossible without writing and reading."[20]

In other words, writing changes not only the amounts and kinds of information and ideas a culture collects and generates, but its fundamental modes of assimilating and using them as well. Such change is especially evident in historical narratives. Where memory collapses time spans, writing tends to fix events temporally and heighten the sense of their distinctiveness as well as their "pastness", or separation from the present and the individual person. The sense of participation in the events narrated becomes more difficult. Something of this kind of perceptual shift is what we often try to get at by distinguishing (oral) "myth" from (written) "history" as narrative modes. The crux of the difference between the two is not their relative "truth", but their presentation of temporality – the one in a synchronic or atemporal frame of reference of "time out of time" (Mircea Eliade's *illud tempus*) and the other in a fundamentally diachronic, linear frame of temporal sequence and relation.

Oral retelling of the past, even by specialized guardians of a society's traditions, is not subject to the same repeated scrutiny over time (whether within a single transmitter's lifetime or over several generations) that a written record receives. Where the former is personal (which is to say, communal, in the most immediate sense) and directed to present concerns and situations, the latter has existence apart from its author, his or her "present" concerns, and those of the community, which will rarely be the same as those of a later time:[21]

> In oral societies the cultural tradition is transmitted almost entirely by face-to-face communication; and changes in its content are accompanied by the homeostatic process of forgetting or transforming those parts of the tradition that cease to be either necessary or relevant. Literate societies, on the other hand, cannot discard, absorb, or transmute the past in the same way. Instead, their members are faced with permanently recorded versions of the past and its beliefs; and because the past is thus set apart from the present, historical enquiry becomes possible.[22]

In other words, literacy changes the relationship between a society and its traditions, as well as that between individuals and their past, because it fixes those traditions and that past in a way that distances both from the present. This kind of distinction may be at work in Thucydides' statement that his own work is written as a permanent possession (*ktēma*), in contrast to the ephemeral words intended for an *agōnisma*, or public recitation contest. His contrast here is essentially one between the lasting written book of critical reflection and the momentary oral performance aimed at pleasing a particular audience.[23] In part, the contrast is between analytical historical prose and epic, dramatic, or poetic works. However, quite apart from this, it also points to different audiences with different perceptions: The private reader will demand of and find in a text very different things from the listening audience. What is appropriate for historical analysis in Thucydides' *History*, or, to give it its proper title, "Writing" (*Suggraphē*), would not be so in the *Iliad* or the *Medea* (although, once fixed in writing, the *Iliad* or the *Medea* itself becomes susceptible to new uses and analyses).

Such changes in modes of thinking and dealing with verbal text must not, however, be seen as the result of underlying differences between the mental capacities of oral peoples and literate peoples. They stem, rather, from a fundamental change in the tools available to each – in the case of writing, the introduction of a new technology.[24] As Goody argues, "the graphic representation of speech . . . is a tool" that "encourages reflection upon and the organisation of information" and "also changes the nature of the representations of the world" even for those in the culture who cannot write.[25]

In sum, then, the advent – or, more precisely, the entrenchment – of literacy in a society appears to result not only in new quantities, but new kinds of texts and new perceptions and uses of texts. These, in turn, change the way we understand the past and, therefore, ultimately the present. Many of the new perceptions and uses of texts have to do with the new possibilities for analysis that written texts offer and even stimulate. If Havelock and others are right, it is more than coincidence that the "literate revolution" in Greece – the oldest such revolution in terms of alphabetic script culture – coincided with the origins and efflorescence of Greek philosophy, science, and literature – to use Bruno Snell's term, "the discovery of the mind".

Some Qualifications

Even if the force of these arguments about the revolutionary impact of writing and book culture be admitted, significant questions nevertheless remain. For example, if a major role in developing new kinds of critical and historical consciousness be granted to scribal culture, it is still not clear that this is the motive force rather than simply one among a number of factors that produce (or accompany) civilization and historical awareness. Moreover, wholly aside from the counterarguments of someone like Robert Pattison, who would see writing as a technology with no particular power to change consciousness or to "give birth to history, skepticism, and science,"[26] any simple contrast of oral and written culture as embodiments of different modes of thinking ignores important continuities between the two.

In particular, two considerations give cause for caution in placing too much emphasis upon the disparities between oral and script culture. First, script culture remains highly oral in its use of language and texts. This raises serious question as to the degree to which, and how rapidly, orality can be displaced by writing, except under special conditions. Second, the advent and spread of printing in Europe may be the only available historical example in which the revolutionary potential of writing and a related shift away from oral modes of discourse have been realized in an extensive and ultimately radical way. In the West at least, the really major displacement of oral modes of thought and communication came only as a postprint phenomenon, in the ambit of the developments Marshall McLuhan called "the Gutenberg galaxy".

We may formulate these latter points as two related hypotheses: (1) Only with the culmination of the print revolution in the industrial society of nineteenth-century Western Europe have oral habits and modes of communication ever effectively died out, so that books have become silent repositories of information rather than vehicles by which writers might speak to absent audiences. (2) In the West as elsewhere, orality remained always a significant part of chirographic, or script culture, even for a considerable time after the coming of printing technology, so that most of human history has known texts primarily as oral/aural rather than written or printed realities. I want now to explore each of these in turn.

CHAPTER 2

The Print Textuality of Modern Culture

The reader of print . . . stands in an utterly different relation to the writer from the reader of manuscript. Print gradually made reading aloud pointless . . . . just as print was the first mass-produced thing, so it was the first uniform and repeatable "commodity".

- Marshall McLuhan

The existence of the book as a common, central fact of personal life depends on economic, material, educational preconditions which hardly predate the late sixteenth century in western Europe and in those regions of the earth under direct European influence.

- George Steiner

Whitehead may not have been far off when he remarked that "writing was an invention which took about two thousand years to make its effect felt."[1] The transition from oral orientations to script and eventually print orientations has been in most cultures a protracted one, even though in recent history the process has been significantly, if artificially compressed in cases of smaller oral societies engulfed all at once by modern technology and culture. The slower transitional processes that lie behind our present-day typographic culture in the Western world began with the development of alphabetic literacy among the Greeks from as early as the seventh century B.C. and continued through later antiquity and the European Middle Ages. As Michael Clanchy and others have shown, these processes speeded up considerably from the eleventh or twelfth century onward in Western Europe, and both anticipated and prepared the way for the print revolution.[2] Material factors, such as the production of paper or development of spectacles, and the demands of new fields and technologies, such as navigation, clock-making, and military gunnery, were also at work.[3] The processes of change accelerated sharply after the coming of age of print culture in the seventeenth and eighteenth centuries. It culminated in the highly literate, print-dominated, post-Enlightenment West, especially since the industrial revolution.

The modern Western cultural complex is discontinuous with earlier periods. This is particularly evident, although by no means intuitively or immediately obvious, in our relationship to texts, which is a key element of modern intellectual traditions and one that sets them apart from all earlier eras. Of primary importance are some key factors that have shaped these traditions, and, along with them, in varying degrees, more popular literate traditions. I refer especially to the development of a print-dominated society with a high rate of minimal literacy – something achieved in the European–American world as a whole only in the late nineteenth or early twentieth century, even if "minimal literacy" means only ability to write one's name and to read simple sentences. Whether these factors be seen as causes, results, or concomitants of much that is characteristic of modern Western culture, their importance is clear. They are of moment today in many societies and will continue to be prominent elements of "modernity" around the world, as they are in the West.

The Impact of Print: Typographic Attitudes

Moveable-type letterpress printing is the heir and successor to writing, and its advent has intensified the effects and magnified the importance of the written word. In China, where moveable-type, but not alphabetic-letter printing was developed in the eleventh century, the social, cultural, economic, and intellectual impact of printing has yet to be studied fully.[4] As for the impact of letterpress printing in Europe, there is a substantial body of scholarly argument to the effect that it has been the major factor in the decisive increase in literacy, availability of books, and the commonplace character of the written/printed word in modern society.[5] This argument seems to me to assign too great a causal power to print technology alone (which, for example, was long available to the Turkish and Arab world but not taken up until quite late, primarily for religious and cultural reasons). There can be no doubt, however, that the spread of printing meshed with and contributed substantially to these and other developments that have made contemporary Western society what it is today.

The print revolution in the modern West, and in modern high-literacy culture in general, has turned the book into one of the most common furnishings of our physical and mental worlds.[6] This has, in turn, resulted in more complete identification of books with physical documents than occurred in the earlier script revolution. The printed page is as ubiquitous a fixture of our culture as there is; cheaply and speedily produced on a mass scale, it still plays a major role in today's electronic age of telephone, film, radio, and telecommunications.

In addition, most electronic media continue to be alphabetic-print-based or to provide an interface with other visual-text media, even if they do not depend on paper copy. Displayed on a screen or printed as "hard copy", visual documentation has become the functional basis of every sector of life, from administration to business to entertainment. We cannot even imagine a complex society that could function without the printed (or displayed) word.

If the printed word has proven to be more decisive than the written word for the displacement of orality in almost all sectors of life over the past two or three centuries, nowhere has the displacement of oral modes of thought and textuality been more evident than in scholarship and intellectual culture generally. Because these sectors involve the greatest use of and influence from texts of all kinds, they deserve specific attention.

What Walter Ong calls "the relentless dominance of textuality in the scholarly mind"[7] has taken on new dimensions under the influence of print. Ong's own phrasing demonstrates his point: In typographic culture, "textuality" itself is presumed at some level to denote only script or print, not oral textuality as well, even though we have no separate term for the latter. Paul Ricoeur can even limit a "text" explicitly to "any discourse fixed by writing."[8] Thus the broader senses of the original Latin *textus* (from Indo-European *tek*) – "that which is woven", "tissue", "texture", "structure", "context" – are often lost.[9] The custodians of knowledge have always been especially prone to exalt the written over the spoken word, and they have seized with little or no reservation upon the printed word as the main bulwark of learning and progress. A telling index of this is provided in a thought-provoking essay by Fred Mauk, a musicologist, who examines "the focus upon music paper [notation] and other documents rather than upon sound [performance] . . . that has been maintained for long in the study of the Western musical tradition." Mauk's point that musicology has not "quite come to grips with the altogether revolutionary situation that recorded traditions constitute," applies still more to disciplines concerned with verbal discourse rather than musical scores.[10] Voice, like music, is much more subjective, and more ephemeral (even in the age of electronic recording), than the tangible page, and seems simply less real to modern scholarly minds. As a result, the page becomes the focus of attention and the necessary criterion of proof ("documentation") for any thesis. If it is true that this written and especially printed-text bias is dominant in humanistic scholarship and in modern intellectual culture generally, how much more is it the case in modern scientific and technological work, which would be all but inconceivable without printed or displayed data in words and diagrams.

The reassuring precision of print has come to embody symbolically as well as actually the highest standards of modern research and scholarly inquiry. The printed page goes hand in hand with the values of "scientific ' scholarship, these being (1) suspension of "subjective" emotions and personal *engagement* in favor of "objectivity" and visual verification – the values essential to experimental science; (2) observation and analysis of the data of sense perception rather than immersion in them – what George Steiner has summed up tellingly as "the cult of the positive, the exact, and the predictive," or "the mirage of mathematical exactitude and predictability"; and (3) rapid and easy access to "raw data" – a response to the "growing thirst for quantitative information" that John Nef describes as a key element in the rise of industrial civilization and Elizabeth Eisenstein suggests was a thirst that printing helped to slake.[11]

Of all scholarly and scientific values, objectivity has been especially important in modern Western thought, and supremely so since the scientific revolution and the Enlightenment era. With scientific detachment have come, however, other kinds of detachment and increased objectification of the world around us. These have been hastened on by the printed word of the modern book. Ashley Montagu has observed that "the more 'literate' people become, the more they tend to become detached from the world in which they live,"[12] and certainly our modern typographic literacy far exceeds any previous kind of literacy in terms of both facility with and dependence upon alphabetic script. The all but endless replicability made possible by the printing press adds greatly to the sense of the reliability and "objective" neutrality of the words on a page.[13] This new replicability has also had very concrete results: Printing led directly, for example, to the use of accurate citations because of the invariance of pagination and page-by-page content in all copies of a given edition set in type.[14] Similarly, the visual quantification (in tables and lists) or pictorial representation (in pictures, graphs, and diagrams) of information that printing made possible on a large scale and with high precision also increased reliance on the printed word (and the engraved drawing) in diverse sectors of society – whether among businessmen, craftsmen, builders, technicians, engineers, or scientists.[15] From our vantage point, we can recognize the prophetic quality of the words of Thomas Elyot in 1531, regarding education in geometry, astronomy, and cosmography: "I dare affirm a man shall more profit, in one week, by figures and charts, well and perfectly made, than he shall by the only reading or hearing the rules of that science by the space of half a year at the least."[16]

With the new functions that print gives to documents of all kinds, words and books lose their dynamism and personal quality and become themselves things – that is to say, mass-produced, impersonal objects. Carothers has argued that "when words are written . . . , they become static things and lose, as such, the dynamism which is so characteristic of the auditory world in general, and of the spoken word in particular."[17] What is true of the written word is a fortiori true of the printed word, for "print suggests that words are things far more than writing ever did."[18] Printed words are particularly well suited to their roles as neutral bearers of objective content accessible to any literate person who can understand that content. A social reflex of this may have been a shift away from public speeches and toward dissemination of printed tracts as the best means of communicating ideas. Prerequisite to such a shift is the assumption that knowledge is an objective content most efficiently gained through private reading and study.[19] How much more sure, fixed, and unambiguous than the merely spoken or even the handwritten word is the printed word, or still more, the statistical list, schematic diagram, graphic table, or mathematical equation that can be exactly reproduced, widely distributed, and hence independently verified!

Print textuality of the kind I am describing may be especially the province of the scholar and intellectual, but in our modern, highly literate society, its influence permeates also popular literate attitudes toward books and other texts. The scholarly world is, at least in this regard, not alien to other sectors of modern society, where the authority of the printed word reigns supreme.[20] "Relentless textuality" is quite easy to document elsewhere today, whether in the proverbial mountains of paperwork of which our civil and military bureaucracies are built, or in the paper-lined labyrinths of the legal and financial worlds. Full participation in modern society demands at least minimal literacy, and with this comes the textual and visual orientation characteristic of the mainstream culture.

The foregoing indicates that it should be no cause for wonder that the whole trend of education in the post-Enlightenment West, especially in this century, has been away from memorization (in essence an oral activity), reading aloud (together with reciting by heart and declamation), and classical rhetoric (formerly the core discipline of literate education and culture).[21] In their place have come ever greater emphasis upon swifter, more efficient comprehension of printed texts by the silent, scanning reader, and increased reliance upon reference aids and massive information storage of all kinds, from encyclopedias to the computer data bases of the present day. The anonymous and impersonal, universally accessible, and "independently verifiable" word of the printed book, which was the first piece of goods in history to be truly mass-produced mechanically,[22] is the backbone of modern scholarship and of modern, literate, technological society as a whole. The printed book is at once a source of authority and so commonplace as to be taken for granted.

While the shift to almost total reliance upon the printed text (and eventually its electronic stepchildren) instead of oral communication and memory could be documented in a variety of ways,[23] brief consideration of two at once substantive and symbolic developments of the latter half of the typographic age in the West must suffice. These developments are (1) the disappearance of traditional rhetoric from the Western educational curriculum and (2) the attempts to organize rapidly expanding quantities of knowledge in massive printed encyclopedias in order to make more information more readily accessible. Both developments highlight the heightened visual and diminished oral orientation of modern print culture.

The Passing of Rhetoric

Rhetoric as a technique of oral argumentation and persuasion apparently arose in the fifth century B.C. The first *rhētōr*s may well have been, as Cicero reports on Aristotle's authority, those men of Sicily who argued their legal and political claims after the fall of the tyrants of Agrigentum and Syracuse. Its formal method, principles, and forms emerged most fully in the teaching of Gorgias of Leontini (d. ca. 375 B.C.), which focused upon the technique, or art, of speaking. The Greek Sophists of the late fifth century, and especially the slightly younger Isocrates (436–338 B.C.), established rhetoric as the central discipline of the classical curriculum by emphasizing the development of the ideal, virtuous orator. From the time of Isocrates forward, Western education was heavily dependent upon the tradition of literate oratorical culture associated with formal rhetoric. The public, civil lecture ceased to be the early rhetors' specimen of skillful oratory and became "an instrument of action, especially political action, a means whereby the thinker could put his ideas into circulation" and thus affect others – hence the common description of rhetoric as the art of persuasion. Although Isocrates' own speeches were written rather than oral discourses (the beginning of a major trend in rhetoric), his entire teaching was aimed at producing eloquent speakers: persons who could persuade, but also persons of ethical integrity who could be cultured and virtuous leaders.[24]

Classical rhetoric was not only an oratorical technique but an educational ideal. When, in the Greek world of the fourth century B.C., technical rhetoric won out over the philosophical tradition of rhetoric represented by Plato and Aristotle, it became a key element of Hellenistic educational method. "Education became first and foremost a training for public life; the arts of judicial, political, and panegyric oratory became central to the curriculum of the majority."[25] This state of affairs continued into the Roman period, and rhetoric, as a cornerstone of classical education, became such a fundamental basis of literate training throughout late antiquity that even Christianity appropriated rhetoric for its own purposes. (How well it did so is symbolized in the "standard" character for many centuries of Augustine's treatment of rhetoric in *De doctrina christiana,* book 4.) Roman rhetorical works became basic textbooks of Western education from the Middle Ages into the Renaissance, in some instances later: most notably, the anonymous *Rhetorica ad herennium* (ca. 84 B.C.), the *De inventione* of the master rhetorician, Cicero (d. 43 B.C.), and Quintilian's *Institutio oratoria* (ca. 95 C.E.). In these the five classical divisions or "offices" of rhetoric received systematic delineation: invention (*heuresis*/*inventio*), arrangement (*taxis*/*dispositio*), style or diction (*lexis/elocutio*), memory (*mnēmē/memoria*), and delivery (*hypocrisis/actio* [or *pronuntiatio*]).[26] In medieval times, grammar and rhetoric joined with dialectic to make up the *trivium* upon which secondary and higher education were based for hundreds of years.

One of the reasons for the enduring importance of rhetoric was its early and enduring adaptation to written as well as oral erudition. Rhetorical techniques of argumentation, organization, and style were applied not only to public speaking but also to literature. This phenomenon had already begun with Isocrates and the use of his written speeches as literary models and was to recur not only in later antiquity, but in the Middle Ages, Renaissance, and into the nineteenth century in Europe. This "repeated slippage of rhetoric into literary composition" has been dubbed *letteraturizzazione* by George Kennedy.[27] Yet while the application of rhetoric to writing was a constant through the long march of Western culture, it was upstaged at times by the pertinence of rhetoric in periods congenial to the resurgence of public speaking and oral debate – as, for example, in the Roman republic during its heyday, in the Italian city-states of the early Renaissance, and in eighteenth- and nineteenth-century England.

Once applied to literary composition, the rhetorical discipline became ever more closely intertwined with the written rather than the spoken word, a strategy for style in written prose and verse rather than in vocal speech. As Kennedy suggests, first the dominance of writing, then that of printing, diminished the importance of the spoken word increasingly down to the modern day (when the spoken word, albeit in different form and context, may again be becoming more important through radio and television).[28]

For all of its *letteraturizzazione* over the centuries in the West, rhetoric still played a role in an educational process and intellectual environment in which writings were penned with an ear to their sound and were memorized, declaimed, and *listened to* to a degree that we can no longer appreciate. The emphasis of Ramist rhetoric on style (elocution) and action (pronunciation) narrowed and fragmented the traditional range of rhetoric and reduced it to a system of literary conventions. Nevertheless, countermovements reemphasized oral delivery, the most famous being the eighteenth-century elocutionist movement involving such figures as Thomas Sheridan. However, this emphasis only showed, as Thomas O. Sloan and Chaim Perelman point out, that a "new, virtually irrevocable split had apparently occurred between spoken language and printed or written discourse."[29] With the Age of Reason, rhetoric lost more and more of its character as a public oral art and became increasingly a technique for written composition. For a century and more now, the term rhetoric itself has denoted training in the skills of written composition or, in a pejorative sense, affectation and flowery insincerity in speech. A symbol of this development is the shift in the subject area of the Boylston Professor of Rhetoric and Oratory at Harvard (the first of whom was

John Quincy Adams), from oratorical rhetoric to belles-lettres and then to poetry in the course of the nineteenth century.[30] The eventual decline and disappearance of the classical rhetorical discipline from the Western curriculum in the nineteenth century were but reflexes of developments already long under way, the last, most important of which was the development of print culture:

> More than the medieval logicians, more than Ramus, more than all Rationalist philosophers, more than even the new philosophies of science, it was probably the very momentum of the revolution begun by Johannes Gutenberg's invention of the printing press that caused traditional rhetoric, both as an educational principle and as a theory, to go under.[31]

The demise of rhetoric marks in many ways the dominance of typographic culture and the disappearance of once essential techniques, such as memorization and declamation, not only from the Western classroom, but also from public life.

The Pursuit of Encyclopedic Knowledge

The encyclopedia, in the special sense of a book attempting a comprehensive organization or survey of knowledge and the relationships among its branches, existed long before the printing press both in Western antiquity and in the non-Western world. Comprehensive writings aimed at providing a conspectus and systematic arrangement of current human knowledge were produced in Western, Chinese, and Arabic cultures over the period from classical antiquity through the European Renaissance. The encyclopedia came into its own, however, only after the advent of printing and especially after the scientific revolution in Western Europe. In doing so, it became less and less what it had traditionally been – a work aimed at a classification and an integrative survey of knowledge – and more and more an attempt to present an easily accessible compendium of the totality of human knowledge, or of one or more areas of that knowledge.[32]

The growing desire to systematize and to compress vast areas of human knowledge onto the printed page in order to make them available to a literate élite in the most efficient format possible was first visible in the "dictionary" works of the late seventeenth and early eighteenth centuries. The most famous of these is Pierre Bayle's *Dictionnaire historique et critique* (1697). In the eighteenth century, beginning already with the encyclopedias of Chambers in England (1728) and Zedler in Germany (1732–54), stimulated by the "big-name-contributor" approach of the famous *Encyclopédie* of Diderot and d'Alembert (1751–77), and culminating in the appearance in 1801 of the *Encyclopaedia Britannica, or Dictionary of Arts and Sciences,* the modern "lexicon" emerged to become what has been the standard form of encyclopedic compendium of knowledge ever since. The modern encyclopedia is characterized by a vast number of relatively brief, alphabetically arranged, methodically chosen and subdivided entries, massive indexing and cross-referencing, multiple prominent contributors, and universal scope. It offers a generally literate public not only a comprehensive reference work, but functions also as a symbolic token of modern progress: It expands our knowledge of the world and makes access to it available to everyone. One may speculate that a significant part of its appeal, and hence its success, is due to the pervasive illusion in our generally literate culture that books are the ultimate sources of wisdom, proof, and authority. The encyclopedia may come as close as is possible to everyman's idea of the book of knowledge par excellence – on top of which it is one that can be ready to hand in one's own home. With the democratization of literacy comes the democratization of knowledge.

A more concrete reason for the encyclopedia's success lies in the increasing difficulty of satisfying growing demand for comprehension of a hypothetical body of "common knowledge" by the ever more isolated specialist as well as the layperson, at whatever level of comprehension. The knowledge accumulated over the centuries has been increasing exponentially in recent times, and much of this increase can be attributed in the first instance to the print medium itself and the massive growth in volume of published material internationally. Once orally based memorization of material no longer sufficed, knowing how to utilize reference resources became a major skill needed by most professionals – scientists, scholars, engineers, technicians, doctors, lawyers, clergy, businesspersons, or whomever.

Today many much more sophisticated reference resources are on the way to displacing the encyclopedic book or set of books. Increasingly, the "knowledge explosion" demands recourse to new forms of information transmission, storage, and "retrieval" that allow for constant updating and manipulation for readers and users. What printed encyclopedias and books in general have done in handling information for at least the past two centuries, electronic publishing and new technologies that incorporate artificial intelligence and may soon allow development of "expert systems" are already on their way to doing for the present and coming generations. If oral forms of communication are being reintroduced in these postprint technologies, they will hardly herald a return to traditional orality; they may, however, signal new kinds of thinking as well as new kinds of communication.[33]

Speculation about these new forms of massive information storage and access takes us beyond the scope of our inquiry, but all were in some measure latent in the print, industrial, and scientific revolutions of Western Europe in recent centuries, of which the modern encyclopedia is only one minor product. All of these new forms could emerge only from a high-literacy, print-based society in which knowledge had become more and more impersonal and quantifiable and the demand for knowledge much more demographically dispersed, both of which characteristics are embodied in the idea and success of the printed universal encyclopedia.

Thus I venture that the modern encyclopedia can be seen as one symptom of changed and changing attitudes toward not only words and discourse, but knowledge itself (others abound: the development of systematic indexing, or even the simple convention of the book title page). These attitudes are characteristic of, if not possible only in, print culture over against either oral or scribal culture.[34] Since the age of reason, knowledge has come to be conceived of less and less either as wisdom and learning acquired from special persons or as the legacy of a cultural and historical tradition, and more and more as accumulation and mastery of objective data and "scientific" methodologies acquired through diverse means. Further, most of these means can be divorced from the personal relationship of teacher–student, master–disciple, or sometimes even author–reader. In the present day, "data transfer" seems to be displacing older notions of the learning process (including much "book-learning"), and in many ways the modern reference encyclopedia represents the major first stage of this transition in our conceptual frameworks. Whatever the good or bad aspects of such trends, they are here for the foreseeable future. They are also the particular legacy of the past two centuries of Western modernism.

Modern Literate Consciousness

The burden of the preceding considerations is that the truly decisive emphasis upon the written or printed page has come at the expense of the memorized, recited, and orally transmitted word. This emphasis has been closely tied to the circumstances of the modern technological age – an age that first came to maturity in Western Europe between about 1600 and 1900 and is beginning now to revolutionize most other societies in the world. These circumstances were presaged by the growth of lay literacy and learning in the late Middle Ages and Renaissance and inaugurated by the coming of moveable-type letterpress printing. They include increased industrialization and mechanization, the explosion of science and technology on all fronts, the spread of literacy and mass media, increased "populist" and "individualist" influences in religious and political thought, and the expansion of modern scholarship and education with their mixture of humanistic and scientific assumptions.

These circumstances are new in history, and thus have consequences for any effort to understand other societies past or present. When trying to talk about written texts of any kind, we speak from within a thought-world that is cut off in a variety of different ways from those of most if not all other places and times in history. One of the more important of these ways is in our relationship to the two basic media of verbal communication: documentary texts and human speech. As I have indicated in Chapter 1, we are accustomed to presuming that the most important experiential and material step in human progress from the most primitive to the most advanced communications capacities is that from primary orality to functional alphabetic literacy: the ability not only to speak but to put ideas into written symbols that record the basic elements of spoken language. This important milestone of development in communications proves on closer examination, however, to be in many ways less significant than the one that has followed in its wake in the past half-millennium; namely, that of cheap letterpress printing on mass-produced paper.

To summarize: In terms of changes in modes of consciousness as well as sheer material change, the great chasm in forms of communication turns out to be not that between literate societies and nonliterate societies, but that to which McLuhan's eccentric, often infuriating, but also often prescient *Gutenberg Galaxy* pointed – the gulf between our own modern Western, post-Enlightenment world of the printed page and *all* past cultures (including our own predecessors in the West), as well as most contemporary ones.[35] We stand on this side of the epochal transition accomplished to large degree by about 1800 in the urban culture of Western Europe, and now still in progress elsewhere, from a scribal or chirographic, and still significantly oral culture to a print-dominated or typographic, primarily visual culture.[36] Our alphabetic "book culture", like our "book religion", is not even the same as the "book culture" (or "book religion") of sixteenth- or seventeenth-century Europe, let alone that of classical antiquity, the Medieval or Renaissance West, or the great literary civilizations of Asia past and present.[37] It is essential to be aware of this if we are to escape falling into provincialism or anachronism in our understanding of other cultures and eras. To complete the picture, therefore, we must turn to the question of premodern "book culture" in the West.

CHAPTER 3

Books, Reading, and Literacy in the Premodern West

Körper und Stimme leiht die Schrift dem stummen Gedanken;
Durch der Jahrhunderte Strom trägt ihn das redende Blatt.
[Writing lends body and voice to mute thought, which
through the centuries' stream is borne by the speaking page.]
- Friedrich Schiller

The discrepancy between our common contemporary notions of speech, language, and text and those of both oral and chirographic cultures not conditioned as we are by almost exclusive dependence upon the printed page has not gone wholly unnoticed. It has been explicitly or implicitly highlighted in a variety of studies, each of which touches upon matters that suggest the historical novelty of our modern relationship to words and books.[1] Some of these overstate or underdocument their particular cases, and none are uncontroversial. In the aggregate, however, these studies offer strong arguments for the new and distinctive nature of recent Western attitudes to the written or printed word vis-à-vis the spoken word. When these arguments are joined to work on literacy, books, and scribal and print culture in specific periods of classical antiquity and European history, there is persuasive evidence that the preprint relationship to books and the written word, even in the West, has been significantly different from that which we know in our society today. It may even turn out that it is not as extravagant as it seems at first to argue that the typographic revolution brought with it what Walter Ong, following McLuhan, describes rather categorically as a basic alteration in the "ratio of the senses" - a fundamental shift in the "sensorium" of Western consciousness.

This is in no way intended to minimize the importance of script culture as a first stage in the decline of the power and importance of the spoken word and the modes of thinking congenial to it in the face of an emerging "literate consciousness" (Havelock). In the West, for example, the transition from oral culture to book culture, often associated at least symbolically with Aristotle and his library, was by no means an inconsequential one for progress in the communication of ideas.[2] Similarly, much later, in England and on the Continent, the centuries just before Gutenberg saw a substantial rise in lay literacy and the use of writing and books in various spheres of life, and this may have been a first stage in, or at least a necessary prerequisite for, the print revolution that followed.[3]

It is also necessary to recognize that any shift from oral to scribal or print mentalities was both a gradual and protracted as well as a fluctuating and uneven process. Havelock's work on the transition from oral to literate culture in ancient Greece is significant for the recognition that the cleft between preliteracy and literacy is not so sharp as we are usually inclined to think (see also Chapter 1, "Some Qualifications"). He even maintains that the writing down, or "alphabetization" of the Homeric epics reflects not simply "destruction" of oral culture, but the setting in of "a process of erosion of 'orality,' extending over centuries of the European experience, one which has left modern culture unevenly divided between oral and literate modes of expression, experience, and living."[4]

Certainly we have to imagine a temporal continuum of change stretching from the advent of literacy in Greece down to twentieth-century mass-literacy print culture. Over this long span of time, with some periods of stasis or recidivism (e.g., the sixth to eleventh centuries C.E.), visual literacy and facility with written language have progressively displaced oral literacy and facility with spoken language. In the West as elsewhere, scribal culture was still a significantly, even predominantly oral culture, in which reading was largely vocal and illiteracy the rule rather than the exception. In general, at least until a very late stage in the development of a script culture (and likely for a considerable while after the introduction of printing),[5] there obtains a "dynamic tension" between oral and written modes of expression, a situation "in which language managed acoustically on echo principles is met with competition from language managed visually on architectural principles."[6]

Vocal Reading

In the circumstances of semiliterate and literate cultures that I am describing, it is ultimately the functional differences between the manuscript book and the printed book that are decisive in the relative speed of the transition from a primarily oral/aural orientation to a primarily visual one. These differences are certainly related to material differences touched upon in the preceding chapter:

legibility, form of publication, ease of rapid reproduction, use of page numbering and exact references, cost per copy, and the like. At the most basic level, however, it is the reading process per se, in both its psychological and its physical aspects, that is today different from what it was in the West twenty-five hundred, and in considerable degree even 250 years ago - or from what it still is in more traditional cultures in the world today. The physical forms of books have varied greatly through history, and their functions have been equally diverse.

The considerable contrast between our experience and perception as "print-persons" and those of other persons in other places or times could be pointed up in a variety of ways. One of the most vivid examples of the conceptual gap that separates us from chirographic, but still nonprint societies can be seen in a papyrus from the Egyptian New Kingdom, a scribal culture that we associate automatically with passionate attachment to the written word and the production of diverse writings consciously intended for posterity. In the papyrus inscription in question, the ancient writer penned (or, more likely, dictated to his scribe) the following words:

> A human being perishes, and his body becomes dirt; all his fellows dissolve to dust. *But writings let him live on in the mouth of the reader.* A book is more useful than the house of a builder, than chapels in the west; it is better than a solidly walled castle and a monument in the temple. - Is there anyone here [today] like Jedef-Hor or another like Imhotep? . . . *What these wise men proclaimed, occurred, and what came from their mouths was realized. It was discovered as a saying, it was written in their books* . . . . They have gone, their names would have been forgotten, but writings keep their memory alive. [italics mine][7]

Writing for this author was inseparable from speaking. In turn, a written text was something conceived as realizable only in the vocal act of reading aloud: The *reader* was inevitably a *lector,* one who gives life to the written word by voicing it. The associations of writing in his mind were instinctively aural rather than visual in the first instance - exactly the opposite of our own ingrained response, which would be to think of the fixity of the "black and white" page, the calligraphed image, not the sound of the words of the text, as the enduring monument to the author's memory.

Reading for us today is a silent, apparently wholly mental process. "Our implicit model of written literature" is "the mode of communication to a silent reader through the eye alone, from a definitive written text."[8] We assume that reading is simply mental cognition of visual symbols on a page. Our usual training in reading, especially that in "speed-reading", is aimed at ridding us of vocalization and even subvocalization. For most of us, our naïve model for reading is virtually that of the operation of an encoding machine or computer: the brain as "processor" scanning and translating simultaneously the "code" of the printed page into information the brain can interpret. In this model, verbalization is supposed to have little, or, ideally, no part in the process. Human "language" is thus, for all practical purposes, popularly construed as but a communications medium analogous to an artificial "computer language", a symbolic notational system that can be "read" if one knows the meaning of the symbols. Optimally, speech is not involved. To us "sounding" a text aloud is an exercise for someone learning to read and to pronounce a language; it is associated with childhood, semiliteracy, reading disability, or a foreigner's difficulty in reading a strange tongue.

There is, however, much to be said for the contention that, whether we recognize it or not, reading is an oral process: "'reading' a text means converting it to sound, aloud, subvocally, or in the imagination, syllable-by-syllable in slow reading or sketchily in the rapid reading common to high-technology cultures."[9] Oral speech remains the intrinsic form of human communication, and for most literate peoples of history outside our society in recent times, reading has normally been a vocal, physical activity, even for the solitary reader. One normally "mouthed" the words of the text and preferably voiced them aloud, not only in reading them but even in composing or copying them into writing. Josef Balogh and G. L. Hendrickson especially have stressed the dominance of reading aloud from classical antiquity through the Western Middle Ages. Balogh argues further that reading aloud even in solitude remained common into the nineteenth century.[10] One wonders if Thomas Carlyle was not expressing a still strongly aural perception of reading when he wrote that "in Books lies the *soul* of the whole Past Time; the articulate audible voice of the Past . . . ."[11]

These essential facts appear to have been obscured by the particular kind of literacy that we have developed in the modern West, especially since the industrial revolution. Many authors, poets in particular, still do read their work aloud or even dictate it as they work; but in general, modern readers – especially highly literate ones – read primarily in silence and without moving their lips. Consequently, we have constantly to question our assumptions about books, reading, and writing, not only when dealing with non-Western cultures that are often still highly oral, but also when studying our own culture prior to the nineteenth century. The original and basic orality of reading is the key to the fundamentally oral function of written texts outside of the special context in which we live today. When we turn to the long march of Western culture, we find that the oral uses of language, including the language of the written word, have been not only present but dominant for much of the more than two-and-one-half millennia since the development of alphabetic writing among the Greeks. Although no extensive historical survey can be attempted here, a brief look at some specific examples from key periods of Western history can give a sense of the oral side of book-learning and script literacy that is usually forgotten or ignored.

Western Antiquity

Orality was certainly the norm in ancient Hellas. This is not to deny that writing and books had been known in Greece, not to mention elsewhere, long before the "golden age" of Athenian culture. Indeed, writing was increasing by this time according to a number of indicators; oral culture was beginning to share the stage with written culture.[12] While the circulation of written texts must have been limited in Athens in the late fifth century B.C., it is hard to conceive even of many orally performed and memorized works of the day, such as the great classical dramas, let alone the work of a Thucydides, as purely oral compositions.[13]

Writing and the book may have come to stay, but in the fifth century B.C. they had not yet won the day from oral texts. Eric Havelock has argued convincingly that education in Greece in this period revolved not around reading and writing but around "music, poetry, and recitation," and that literacy did not become widespread in Athens until at least the last third of the century.[14] Even then, it is debatable how "widespread" reading and writing really was. Even written texts would have been readable only with difficulty, unless one already knew the text well.[15] At issue here is not the persistence of the much-discussed techniques of oral composition and communication, whether of epic, dialectic and rhetoric, lyric poetry, or whatever,[16] but the ongoing necessity in a semiliterate society (and one that did not esteem the written word at all so highly as did some other ancient cultures)[17] for widespread oral use and transmission even of written texts. Literate as well as nonliterate discourse in ancient Greece was highly oral. As Hadas notes, "among the Greeks the regular method of publication was by public recitation . . . and public recitation continued to be the regular method of publication even after books and the art of reading had become common."[18] For classical Greece, we have reports of oral readings of not only the compositions of poets, but even those of an historian like Herodotus.[19] Completely aside from the traditional Greek bias against the written word, the much-quoted diatribe of Socrates on the dangers of the written word, as recorded in Plato's *Phaedrus,* underscores the continuing importance of memory and oral learning to an educated person even in an age of increasing alphabetic literacy.[20] So too does the report that, of the Athenians taken prisoner at Syracuse in 413, those who could recite Euripides for their captors were able to save their lives and gain their release by doing so.[21]

As I have noted, Aristotle (d. 322 B.C.) is often taken to represent the moment of transition from primarily oral to primarily literate book culture in the classical world. Although Strabo's report that Aristotle was the first to collect books is likely an exaggeration, his may in fact have been the first private library of any size and substance. If so, this is but one among other indications that by his day written texts had become permanent fixtures of the intellectual and perhaps the public scene.[22] Nevertheless, despite the spread of book culture and the development of libraries and academies in Hellenistic and antique times (third century B.C. to fifth century C.E.), oral treatment and transmission of texts continued to be basic, and not only for those genres like speeches and poetry that are by nature or by function orally oriented. Extensive memorization, the backbone of an oral-text orientation, remained an important part of the standard educational curriculum, and dictation, not writing by hand, was the author's standard method of "written" composition.[23] There is also ample evidence that not only poetic or dramatic, but even historical works continued to be read before audiences: "public readings either preceded or accompanied the diffusion of individual historical works in manuscript copies."[24] For the Roman period down to the time of Hadrian, the evidence that such public *lectiones* were a staple of social life is particularly plentiful: The recitations of poetry to a private circle of friends or a larger group gathered by formal invitation are referred to in diverse authors, from Horace (d. 8 B.C.) to Suetonius (d. ca. 140 C.E.).[25] Jérôme Carcopino has even argued that the practice of reading one's own works aloud or having them recited became such a ubiquitous and oppressively repetitive fixture of Roman social life in imperial times that "instead of promoting a love of literature, these public readings produced mental indigestion and must more often have deadened than stimulated the love of letters."[26]

Quite apart from the oral composition and publication of written works, classical and late antiquity knew little of silent reading in which the words of the text are not sounded automatically with the lips. This was remarked long ago by Nietzsche and emphasized by the philologist Eduard Norden.[27] The classic and most frequently cited example of this is from late antiquity, namely the passage in his *Confessions* in which the young Augustine registers his amazement at seeing the venerable Ambrose reading silently: "But when he read, his eyes swept across the pages, and his heart sought out the sense, but his voice and tongue were at rest."[28] A panoply of further examples from late antiquity, as well as medieval Europe and even the Renaissance have been adduced by Balogh; for classical antiquity, Hendrickson's article is the best source.[29]

All of the foregoing points to the fact that, in Havelock's words, "later antiquity never wholly discarded oral habit . . . . Even the solitary reader read aloud to himself, and writers still sought audiences."[30] Rhetoric's firm place in the center of the Hellenistic curriculum contributed also to the continuing prominence of oral techniques of composition, transmission, and delivery in later centuries.

The Medieval West

When we turn to medieval Europe, we are again concerned neither with issues of oral formulaic composition nor with wholly or principally oral traditions of epic, lyric poetry, *chanson,* or folk narrative, but rather with the oral/aural character of written texts themselves. The functional orality of written texts did not disappear with the passing of late antiquity. Whatever the expansion of "literate consciousness" after Aristotle, from classical times right through the European Middle Ages and even after the coming of printing the fundamental form of "publication" or dissemination of any text remained that of oral reading and recitation.[31]

At the most basic level, the oral text was the "base text", if only because reading a manuscript text virtually demanded prior knowledge of the text. Punctuation and abbreviation were intended to help the lector, not the silent reader.[32] The medieval reader confronted

> a manuscript often crabbed in script and full of contractions, and his instinctive question, when deciphering a text, was not whether he had seen, but whether he had heard this or that word before; he brought not a visual but an auditory memory to his task. Such was the result of his up-bringing; he had learnt to rely on the memory of spoken sounds, not upon the interpretation of written signs. And when he had deciphered a word, he pronounced it audibly.[33]

Thus we should not wonder that, in medieval England, King Alfred should write (ca. 891) in the "preface" to his English rendition of the *Pastoralis* that he translated it "as I learned it from Plegmund, my archbishop, from Asser, my bishop, from Grimbold, my priest, and from John, my priest. I translated it into English as soon as I had learned it and was able to state it most intelligibly."[34] One may have copied a manuscript when one studied it, but the important thing was that one memorized it by reciting it aloud, in much the way that this is done still today in traditional Muslim, Hindu, and other educational systems around the world.

Long after the time of Augustine and Ambrose, normal reading remained reading aloud. The very unremarkability of this fact is the main reason why we have so little comment on it in the sources.[35] Oblique evidence of it can be found nevertheless in a variety of places, as the examples assembled by Balogh and Ruth Crosby show.[36] Others can also be adduced. A passage from an early medieval Celtic prayer for dead souls underscores the automatic association of reading aloud with books: "these offerings . . . we give Thee for the souls of our dear brothers and sisters, *whose names we read forth, and for those whose names we do not read forth, but which will rather be read forth by Thee in the 'Book of Life'*" (italics mine).[37] Another example is Jocelin of Brakelond's report at the beginning of the thirteenth century that Abbot Samson, a graduate of Paris, who "was eloquent in French and Latin," was also able "to read literature (*scriptura*) written in English most elegantly (*elegantissime*)."[38] The Anglo-Norman writer, Master Thomas, begins his *Romance of Horn* with these words to his *audience:* "Gentlemen, you have heard the lines of parchment . . . ."[39]

The chief locus of learning and literacy into the high Middle Ages was the monastery, and for all of their bookishness, its readers read for the most part audibly. This is evident early on, for example, from the *Rule* of St. Benedict, which admonishes any monk who wants to read in his cell in the evening to "read to himself [that is, silently], so as not to disturb anyone else,"[40] clearly indicating that the norm in private reading was to voice the text aloud as one read. Along with his extensive collection of examples of vocal reading, Balogh stresses the fact that even writing was oral so long as the values of classical rhetoric held sway; where Christian opposition to these values and the slow copying of the monastic scriptorium held sway, silent writing probably first began to become common.[41] Nevertheless, Wattenbach cites one medieval copyist's vivid confirmation of the innately oral, as well as generally physical, nature of scribal labor: "Three fingers write, two eyes look [at the page]; one tongue speaks, the whole body works . . . ."[42]

The vexing question of literacy is also important to any consideration of the oral dimensions of medieval texts. In general, at least through the twelfth century, and likely four or more centuries beyond, the vast majority of the population could read little if at all, even in the vernaculars. Thus they had necessarily to "hear" their books read aloud by someone else. This was almost certainly the case among the laity of all ranks and not seldom so among clerics and monks as well.[43] Strictly speaking, based on the meaning of *litteratus* at the time as ability to read and write Latin, literacy was very restricted – primarily to clergy – for the better part of the Middle Ages (ca. sixth to twelfth century). However, if judged by more than the criterion of reading and writing Latin, literacy in the medieval period, especially later on, was not so rare, at least among the upper classes of the laity, as medievalists once commonly thought.[44]

The problem in discussing medieval literacy rates at all involves not only the question of vernacular as opposed to Latinate literacy and that of reading as opposed to writing as the measure of "literacy", but also that of the meaning of the dichotomies *litterati-illitterati/idiotae* and *clerici-laici*. For example, from a functional point of view, those "quasi-literates" who were dependent upon literates for needed access to written materials are, for many purposes, better classed with the literate than with the illiterate segment of the population (who could neither read nor needed to do so in order to perform their societal roles).[45] Nevertheless, such nonreading "literates" still could only know texts as aural facts. Further, even recognition of limited lay literacy at various times and in various places does not imply that scholars have been wrong to stress that most medieval people could not read and had to be auditors.[46]

More important was the oral orientation not only of illiterates, but also of literates. M. T. Clanchy points out that "medieval writing was mediated to the non-literate by the persistence of the habit of reading aloud and by the preference, even among the educated, for listening to a statement rather than scrutinizing it in script."[47] The substantial growth in use of documents from about the twelfth century onward did not quickly change this. As Brian Stock notes, "medieval society after the eleventh century was increasingly oriented towards the scribe, the written word, the literary text, and the document. . . . But the written did not supersede the oral."[48]

In a semiliterate society such as obtained not only before, but persisted well beyond the Middle Ages in Europe, there were thus many people, both fully literate and quasi-literate, who had much or all of their contact with written texts through the reading aloud of others, just as every wholly illiterate person did. The example of Baldwin II, Duke of Guines, near Calais, is instructive: He had a passion for learning, debated with scholars, and both collected books and had many translated into French. He did not, however, read them himself, but had them read aloud to him by his librarian, a layman he had had educated for the position, and he memorized the greater part of what he heard.[49] Similarly, the German ruler Otto IV (r. 1198–1215) evidently could not read, but probably "could understand simple Latin when it was read to him" – at least the dedication to him of the *Otia imperialia* by Gervase of Tilbury (b. ca. 1165) indicates that it was intended for him to hear: Gervase "deemed it fitting to present to the king's ears a book whose tales would serve to refresh and revive the royal mind in hours of weariness."[50] Books were meant for ears as much as or more than for eyes, and authors wrote them with that explicitly or implicitly in mind.[51]

The basis for expanded literacy and increasing use of books and written records was laid in the twelfth and thirteenth centuries, as work such as that of Clanchy and Stock has shown. By the fourteenth and fifteenth centuries, the ability to read and write in the vernaculars was decidedly on the rise – not only in church and secular administration, trades, and the law, but more widely, and enough so that "the rising demand for books quickly assumed commercial importance."[52] Yet written texts continued to be orally handled and disseminated through the later Middle Ages and well beyond. However much silent reading may have been increasing in later medieval times, the newest trends in education focused more and more on a literacy centered on rhetoric rather than scholastic logic. The humanists from Petrarch to Erasmus sought to return to "the rhetorical beauty of the literature of antiquity" and emphasized reading with the voice and oratorical eloquence on classical models.[53]

These were the scholarly élite, however. At a level much closer to the grass roots of society were people such as the "heretical" Lollards, followers of John Wyclif, who, from the late fourteenth into the sixteenth century, championed reading of scripture and other books in the vernacular for the common people.

Although the Lollards stimulated many to learn to read and write, the sources show that much of this reading was reading or reciting out loud to groups of presumably largely illiterate people who were hungry for the plain word of God in English. William Wakeham of Devizes, an accused heretic, admitted in 1434, "that I with other heretics and Lollards was accustomed and used to hear in secret places, in nooks and corners, the reading of the Bible in English, and to this reading gave attendance by many years."[54] Such "hearing" of the scriptures was often a stimulus that pushed men and women to acquire the ability to read – an ability that manifested itself in turn in the social rather than private act of reading to others.[55] Of this phenomenon, Margaret Aston writes that

> books themselves became voices. Wherever they existed they were heard as well as seen, and the reverberations of vocalized texts resounded outwards, with diminishing accuracy and immediacy, away from the readers and hearers who worked directly upon the page.[56]

After the Advent of Printing

Many persons have viewed the coming of printing as the decisive blow that felled the practice of oral, vocalized reading. One of McLuhan's dicta expresses this in typically vivid and apodictic fashion: "as the Gutenberg typography filled the world the human voice closed down. People began to read silently and passively as consumers."[57] This did not, however, happen overnight. Although the impact of print was decisive, it was dispersed over a number of centuries, even in the most advanced countries of Europe. What Virgil understood under "book" and what not only Bede or Dante, but even Luther or Edmund Spenser, and possibly Milton or Pascal, understood under the same term, are much closer to one another than any of these is to what we today conceive a book to be. Similarly, they are much closer to what persons in the other cultures of the world have conceived, and still today in many places conceive, a book to be: something to be read aloud or recited from, an *aide-mémoire* and repository of the vocal words of an author – in short, a transmitter of speech where voice cannot carry and memory cannot suffice.

The mind-set that associated the book and writing with aural rather than visual perception certainly continued well after the coming of print. In his engrossing study of the Jesuit China missionary, Matteo Ricci (d. 1610), Jonathan D. Spence cites a statement by Ricci that is telling in this regard. Ricci writes to the Peking publisher Cheng Dayue [Ch'eng Ta-yüeh] concerning the importance of books: "the whole point of writing something down is that your voice will then carry for thousands of miles, whereas in direct conversation it fades at a hundred paces."[58] His words reflect the degree to which writing was associated conceptually for him with speaking. It was a form of speech that might be heard by a distant auditor (the reader) as well as by one to whom one might speak face to face.

No one can deny that the centuries after Gutenberg saw a considerable rise in levels of literacy as well as in the availability and distribution of reading matter of all kinds. Most indications are that the Reformation in particular gave a large impetus to the spread of vernacular literacy and habits of reading.[59] Yet the new flow of books and the increased reading and literacy that can be documented for the sixteenth century[60] were not incompatible with continuing oral roles for written or printed texts. A variety of scholars have recognized the fact that, as Steven Ozment puts it, "the first half of the sixteenth century remained very much an oral age" for all the massive upsurge in print distribution.[61] Far more people had to hear read than could read for themselves the new outpouring of books, pamphlets, and flyers in the sixteenth century. One example of this from France is the statement of a Protestant linen-weaver in a heresy proceeding in 1566: "I was led to knowledge of the gospel by . . . my neighbor, who had a Bible printed at Lyon and who taught me the Psalms by heart."[62] Compare this with the frequently cited words of an English apprentice about what happened when Henry VIII ordered the English Bible placed in all churches: "imedyately after diveres pore men in the towne of Chelmsford . . . bought the Newe Testament of Jesus Christ, and on sundays dyd set redinge in the lower ende of the church, and many wolde floke about them to heare theyr redinge."[63]

Of the "sudden leap forward" in print publications in the sixteenth century, Robert Scribner notes that its scale and impact "can only be understood by bearing in mind that the Reformation emerged in a society still heavily dependent on oral communication. . . . Printing was, in fact, an addition to, not a replacement for, oral communication."[64] The clear dominance of sixteenth-century printing production by three texts – the Huguenot psalter and the Roman breviary and missal, all of which were intended to be read or sung aloud in worship – is at least a symbolic reminder of the truth of this assertion.[65] Printed texts did not destroy orality in the first instance, but employed and augmented it: "reading from printed books . . . . can give people something fresh to talk about. Learning from printed books does not suddenly replace learning by doing. It can provide people with new ways to relate their doings to authority, old and new."[66]

William Nelson has shown through a wide variety of examples that much of the literature written in the sixteenth and seventeenth centuries was penned with a listening audience rather than a solitary, silent reader in mind. Both the instructions in authors' prefaces directed to those who would read their works aloud and the episodic structuring of longer narratives reflect the orientation in this period to a listening audience and serial reading sessions.[67] Furthermore, readers of printed texts still worked even in the seventeenth century with a punctuation system designed "for the ear and not the eye."[68] Despite increases in printed texts, literacy, and private reading, reading aloud to others remained a fixture at different levels of society, whether at the court of Queen Elizabeth, in the homes of nobility or gentry, or even in village gatherings: "Not only the long narratives of the Renaissance but also books of every conceivable kind, whether in prose or in verse, were commonly read aloud, sometimes by the author himself, sometimes by members of a household taking turns, sometimes by a professional reader . . . ."[69]

At least through the seventeenth century, oral modes of communication, from announcements of town criers to diverse public readings, continued strong, especially in rural areas, and sufficed for the many who could not read. Documents were not only filed but read aloud, public notices were "proclaimed as well as posted," and letters were read to circles of family or friends: "occasions like these served to open the literate world to the uneducated and gave an extra dimension of voice and ceremony to those who needed such assistance."[70] Popular publications such as the cheap pamphlets of the popular *Bibliothèque bleue de Troyes* in seventeenth-century France penetrated the largely illiterate world of the peasantry.[71] The vernacular Bible and prayer book as well as romances or Aesop were peddled even in the French countryside, and reading aloud joined storytelling on social occasions such as the winter-evening gathering in the villages that was known as the *veillée.* Only one literate person in a village was needed to disseminate the relatively cheap printed texts that were increasingly available and sometimes specifically aimed at a peasant public. In the French towns, reading groups brought literates and illiterates together, workers read aloud to their colleagues in the shops, and clandestine Protestant meetings joined readers to listeners.[72]

Silent, private reading appears to have become dominant only with the advent of widespread literacy in much of Western Europe, which was largely a nineteenth-century phenomenon. The spread of silent reading in recent centuries deserves closer attention, as does the practice of reading or reciting literary works in public. The latter was something well-known in many places in Europe and America at least through the eighteenth and into the nineteenth century: Witness the "penny readings" of Thackeray and Dickens in England and the authors' readings in literary societies or smaller literary circles or salons such as those described by Mme. de Sévigne.[73] Vestiges of such venerable practices remain, to be sure, even now, perhaps most prominently in the academy. The tradition of the German *Vorlesung* as an oral "publication" of a forthcoming printed work continues to the present time, as does that of the academic "paper" that is read at scholarly conferences. In addition, one can even find contemporary novelists as well as poets who read on occasion from their works to public audiences today, but such events are scarcely a major part of the modern European or American literary scene. Whatever the cause-and-effect relationship, the silent reading practices of our present high-literacy societies go hand in hand with a modern decline in vocal reading of all kinds, private or public.

The Protestant emphasis on widespread education, to the end that the average person be able to read the Scriptures, prayer books, and catechisms, played a major role in shifting the preponderance of literacy from the Catholic south of Europe to its Protestant north and west over this period.[74] This influence can, to be sure, be overestimated, at least for Protestant England, especially with regard to seventeenth- and eighteenth-century literacy rates.[75] Yet it is hard to ignore the stunning success of church-driven literacy efforts in Sweden and Scotland in the seventeenth and eighteenth centuries or even the relatively higher levels of reading ability in nonconformist and especially Puritan areas of England, as compared to those of strongly Anglican areas, prior to the Civil War.[76]

Nevertheless, one should not overestimate the actual dispersion of literacy, especially in the sixteenth and seventeenth centuries, when it was still a substantially restricted capacity in European society as a whole.[77] Literacy and illiteracy coexisted well into the industrial revolution. It is now very hard for those of us raised in highly literate societies in the mid-twentieth century to recognize that historically, even in Europe, the majority of the population until the past hundred years or so have been unable to read and write and thus can only have known books or any other writings as vocal texts read aloud for them to hear. Even in early nineteenth-century England, in the workplace and public houses, reading aloud – often of news and politics rather than religion – continued to be an important means of dissemination of printed material to the illiterate or semiliterate (a function today of radio and television for the same groups).[78]

Accurate overall literacy statistics for the whole or even major areas of Europe are all but impossible to compile, not least because of the paucity of reliable and synchronic indicators and the many different kinds of statistics that have to be used. Many variations are hidden beneath all gross estimates: For example, religious affiliation, in good part because of differing schooling, affected literacy levels considerably, just as different professions demanded greater or lesser ability to read or write;[79] and literacy in the countryside appears to have lagged significantly behind that in urban centers, just as literacy among women lagged behind that of men.[80] Although this is not the place for discussion of even a fraction of the extensive literature on European literacy rates since the sixteenth century, a few exemplary statistics can indicate something of the general picture.

Whatever the stunning figures for print distribution in the sixteenth, seventeenth, and eighteenth centuries,[81] only in special cases are the statistics on growth of literacy equally impressive in terms of the net levels attained. Thus, although relative increases were often significant, absolute levels did not approach mass literacy outside of a few exceptional areas until well into the nineteenth century. For example, on the basis of marriage-register signatures only, literacy among adult males in France may have risen in the hundred years between 1686–90 and 1786–90 by some 62 percent (at the very best), but the 1688 level was only about 29 percent and the 1788 level still only about 47 percent.[82] The same adult-male, marriage-signature statistics for England (including Wales) in 1675 and 1775 yield about 45 and 56 percent, respectively.[83] Figures for Ireland, Spain, or Italy would be far below these relatively high estimates, even though those for Scotland, Prussia, Switzerland, or Sweden would be considerably higher.[84]

In general, the latter half of the nineteenth century was the period in Europe in which mass literacy replaced the restricted, élite literacy of previous eras. It is estimated that by 1930, no less than 90 percent of all European adults could read and write;[85] yet around 1850 as many as one-half of all European adults could neither read nor write (and this excludes Russia, where adult literacy is estimated to have been no more than 5–10 percent at that time).[86] In the 1840s in England as a whole, only about 70 percent of men and 50 percent of women could sign their names.[87] (If those who could read but not sign their name were added, these figures might be higher, but by how much is not certain.)[88] In France, the estimated adult literacy in 1851 was only 55–60 percent of the total population,[89] and in 1901, still only some 84 percent of French males and 76 percent of French women over twenty could read and write.[90] Meanwhile, in 1871, overall adult literacy in highly rural, Catholic Italy is reckoned to have been no more than about 31 percent and, by 1901, to have risen only to about 52 percent.[91]

What such statistical estimates indicate is that reading was hardly widespread enough among the population of Europe before the past 150 years to have given much more than half the population private access to books, newspapers, and other writings. At least for the illiterate half, the texts of books remained totally aural facts, if there was any contact with them at all. Those illiterates and semiliterates who knew lesser or greater parts of the Bible or other books had to have learned them by rote memorization of orally repeated passages, just as they learned songs, stories, poetry, or proverbs. For these at least, written texts were still repositories of spoken words.

Even with regard to the fully literate segment of the population, the triumph of the silent page and reader in the past one to two hundred years needs to be more precisely documented. It was probably not complete until at least the eighteenth century, if then.[92] The poet Schiller can still refer to "the speaking page" (*das redende Blatt*),[93] but a contemporary, Adam Müller, in his "Twelve Speeches on Eloquence" of 1812 can only lament the victory of the silent hand, eye, and page of contemporary literacy over the voice, ear, and word of days gone by:

Once speech has been transposed most unnaturally from the domain of the ear to the domain of the reading eye, from the domain of the voice to the province of the writing hand, it then dries up more and more, and shrivels away: the word shrinks into itself and becomes more and more a cipher.[94]

At least by Müller's time, in the literate sector of our Western, post-Enlightenment world, visual, typographic culture seems to have been well on its way to replacing oral, chirographic culture. The book had become, or was becoming, a document with silent pages.

PART II

Of Written and Spoken Scripture

Scripture . . . . The Sacred writings of the Old or New Testament, or (more usually) of both together; Holy Writ; the Bible. . . . Sacred writings or records. . . .

- *The Oxford English Dictionary*

But revelation . . . is not only meant to be transmitted by being written down in many copies . . . , rather the holy book should also be recited and taught, preferably by heart.

- Geo Widengren

We have seen the fallacy of the widespread presupposition that our modern Western relationship to texts is essentially the same as that of earlier ages, not to mention that of other cultures. The evidence is substantial that it is only in relatively recent history, and specifically in the modern West, that the book has become a silent object, the written word a silent sign, and the reader a silent spectator.

It is true that through the depersonalized transmissions of modern mass-communications media, the oral word does play a major role in today's individual and social psychology. It is, however, a subsidiary or ancillary role to that of the visual media in which it most often occurs – ". . . a major portion of print, as it is emitted daily, is, at least in the broad sense of the term, a caption. It accompanies, it surrounds, it draws attention to material which is essentially pictorial."[1] Consequently, the role of the spoken word is a very different one from that which it has played in previous centuries. It is a significant change that once-important oral arts such as reading aloud, declamation, forensics, and oratory no longer hold the dominant place in the everyday routine of our modern secular culture that they did in earlier Western society. The trivialized news broadcasts of prime-time radio and television cater largely to a level of comprehension requiring minimal verbal literacy. Apart from such media, the mass-produced book, paper, or magazine is the chief and most generally recognized vehicle of information and authority for the private, silent reading of the average "literate" person. The printed page has become the symbol of reliability and authority in communications.

If these circumstances have determined our attitudes toward books in general, they have figured even more decisively in determining our notions of scriptural books. Today both the secular, avowedly nonreligious person, and the average professing Christian (just as many a contemporary Jew) would assent to a simple definition of scripture as "holy book" and think thereby principally of a bound volume (or possibly a Torah scroll). Neither reading aloud nor hearing the scriptures read or recited aloud has remained the primary and pervasive mode of contact with the Word that it once was for most faithful Christians or even Jews. In comparison with contemporary Muslim or Buddhist practice, not to mention that of Hindus, the oral/aural roles of sacred texts are truly meager, whereas the written text of scripture plays today a singularly dominant role both in Western religious piety and practice and in the wider Western cultural context.

These relatively recent attitudes toward scripture go beyond a simple emphasis upon the written rather than the spoken use of the text. For example, something of the commonplace character of the modern book often attaches even to sacred texts. The casual familiarity with which we move among and handle books as a part of everyday routine has bred in us its own kind of contempt for, or at least carelessness of, the unremarkable and ubiquitous printed page. In the specific case of scripture, the cheap and easy availability of myriad versions of the Jewish or Christian scriptures has done much to reduce the special quality of the physical text as an object of reverence and devotion in and of itself. Scripture's presence as a bound volume in a living-room bookcase, a church pew, or a hotel-room drawer may conceivably encourage Bible reading, but it also reinforces the primary image of scripture as but another printed book. The tracing of manuscript traditions and collation of textual variants has improved our understanding of the growth of scriptural texts, but it has also taught us how to treat them only as simply historical documents. Consequently, we have some difficulty empathizing with persons for whom a copy of a sacred text was or is a seldom and wonderful thing, perhaps a magical and awesome thing, to be handled with solicitude and to which the proper response is reverential deference or even worshipful veneration.

Alongside such leveling of scripture to commonplace status in our collective life, an older and seemingly contradictory development or attitude is discernible. The common ascription of fixity, permanence, reliability, and authority to the printed page generally has applied also, and usually in much greater degree, to the scriptural page; yet such valuation of the printed word is finally as much a reduction of scripture to a "thing" as is the treatment of it as but another volume of paper and ink. The security of having divine revelation "in black and white" can be a tempting crutch to lean on. The fundamentalist Christian who points to the literal text of his or her Bible as the proof text for everything in every sphere of life objectifies Holy Writ as much as does the secular atheist who considers the Bible but one among other printed volumes of legend and nonsense.

Even where the Bible remains a powerful symbol of revelation and guidance according to its spirit rather than its letter, it is today much more easily conceived of as a documentary text than a voice of inspired utterance. It is more likely to occupy a visible and symbolic place such as the ark of the synagogue or a church altar, lectern, or home bookshelf than it is to occupy the time of the faithful in sustained reading, recitation, memorization, and study. The authority of Torah or Bible is as likely to stem from its status as a fixed, tangible, and visible book as from its theological status as the word of God. "It's in the Bible" comes more quickly to the tongue than "God says."

These developments need still to be more carefully studied and documented for particular religious groups and for Western society at large, but they are readily discernible in the scholarly world. In general academic usage, *scripture* is not only synonymous with *holy writ* in the restricted sense of a written text; it is, as a matter of course, objectified as a clear *factum* of more advanced religious development and set over against the ubiquitous religious *datum* of sacred spoken word or oral tradition that is exemplified in nonliterate societies. We take as axiomatic a view such as that expressed by Friedrich Heiler: "the creation of a holy scripture marks a deep divide in the history of religions; the scriptural religions rise far above the scriptureless religions."[2] On this basis we uncritically affirm and strengthen the valuation of the sacred written document as the primary source and most reliable index of what is normative in a given tradition.

On the other hand, the aforementioned "relentless dominance of textuality in the scholarly mind" has joined in the history of religion with the comparativist's passion for categorizing religious phenomena to relegate scripture as "holy book" to the status of one more item to be ticked off in listing the "essentials" of a given religious tradition or the "fundamental categories" of religious phenomena around the world. Analogously, the documentary, historical- and text-critical orientation that characterizes modern religious-text studies[3] reflects in the treatment of texts the wider contemporary conception of scripture as merely a particular kind of written text, perhaps special in many ways, but ultimately one among other genres of written or printed matter. While such approaches are perfectly legitimate in and of themselves, they share and promote more widely held notions of scripture that greatly limit our ability as scholars to grasp the functional roles of scripture in other historical contexts.

For such reasons, scripture, both as a concept in the study of religion and as a concrete historical form, presents problems of definition and identification when we try to extrapolate from our current usage or experience in order to interpret that of other times and places. Jewish and Christian, and especially Protestant Christian, emphasis upon the sacred book and its authority have combined with scholarly interests and techniques, as well as the broader developments in the modern West sketched in Part I, to fix in our minds today a rather narrow concept of scripture; a concept even more sharply culture-bound than that of "book" itself. In this regard, the literalist "book religion" of the Protestant fundamentalist, the conscious or unconscious image of the biblical text in the mind of the average person of whatever religious persuasion, and the liberal scholar's historical-critical understanding of the Bible's genesis are part of the same wider orientation. All are based on a notion of scripture as a written book put together in the first centuries of the Christian era as an authoritative "canon" for the faithful. Although this is correct as far as it goes, it nevertheless objectifies scripture as the tangible book of the Bible and for the most part leaves it at that.

The history of our modern ideas about books, writing, and reading rehearsed in Part I forms only a general backdrop for an understanding of contemporary notions of scripture and the role of scripture in religious life. The more immediate background for our current "model" of, and our restricted approaches to, scripture in the history of religion lies necessarily closer to the concept "scripture" itself. In particular, the historical factors behind modern Western use of "scripture" in both specific and generic senses offer concrete reasons for the eventual development of the largely unexamined assumptions about the nature of scriptural texts that characterize not only popular but even scholarly thinking today.

CHAPTER 4

Scripture in Judeo-Christian Perspective

. . . and as for the sacred Scriptures, or Bibles of mankind, who in this town can tell me even their titles? Most men do not know that any nation but the Hebrews have had a scripture.

– Henry David Thoreau

The predominance of the silent, written or printed form of scripture and its reduction to a commonplace of religious life in the modern West are not only the products of the general cultural and material developments sketched in Part I. They have also been reinforced, if not in some measure originally produced, by ways of thought and piety fully within the Judaic and Christian traditions. Of all the world's great religious traditions, with the possible exception of the classical Chinese, or "Confucian", the Judaic and Christian have been historically the ones most clearly defined by attachment to an authoritative written text – a holy writ,[1] even though especially in Christian tradition the actual importance of scripture has varied radically among its diverse subgroups.[2]

Thus our concept of scripture in the Western world has passed to us through the filter of Judeo-Christian "book religion", as well as through that of European cultural, scientific, and intellectual history more generally, just as it has come to us under some lesser influence also from the development in later antiquity of the notion of "the classics". Although I shall argue below that the "holy books" of the Christian Bible, like those of the Jewish scriptures, have historically been far more significantly oral in their actual function as religious texts than we commonly recognize, this by no means negates the fact that the idea of the written word and its importance to faith have been peculiarly central in these two traditions. History as well as etymology joins the concepts of scripture in both traditions inextricably to the written word and to the visible, physical page. Before we can explore the neglected oral and aural aspects of the holy book, it is important to delve at least briefly into some of the dominant written and visual connotations of scripture in Judaic and Christian tradition that lie behind our modern use of the term.

The Idea of a Heavenly Book

The development of the concept of a scriptural book in the great Western, or "Semitic", monotheisms has been often linked to the apparently older idea of a heavenly book. This idea is an ancient and persistent one that seems to be the legacy of the ancient Near Eastern–Mediterranean world – in other words, the cultural world in which writing probably began, and in which the first phonetic and alphabetic writing systems were developed. Jewish, Christian, and Islamic notions of a scriptural book rest at least in part upon the idea of a heavenly writ containing divine knowledge or decrees, and this idea is demonstrably much older than any one of the three great monotheistic traditions themselves, however great an impact each has had upon its ultimate development.

The concept of the heavenly book can take one of several forms, typically that of either the book of wisdom, book of destinies (or laws), book of works, or book of life.[3]

The motif of a celestial book or tablet of divine wisdom goes back to ancient Mesopotamia and Egypt and recurs in almost all subsequent Near Eastern traditions, apparently as an expression of divine omniscience. Geo Widengren has argued further that such a book was coupled in the ancient Near East, Judaism, and finally Islam to a messenger figure to whom the book is given in a personal encounter with God or who is verified through such an encounter (e.g., Moses at Sinai, Muhammad on his Ascension, or *Mi'rāj*). The related idea of a book of destinies or fates in which the allotted days and assigned end of human lives and human history are written down was known, as art and textual evidence shows, in ancient Babylonia, Egypt, Greece, Rome, and especially late antiquity. From Ps. 139.16 we can see that the Israelites also shared this idea: "Thy eyes beheld my unformed substance; / in thy book were written, every one of them, / the days that were formed for me, when as yet there was none of them." Similarly, when the author of Revelation (5.1,3) speaks of seeing "in the right hand of him who was seated on the throne a scroll written within and on the back, sealed with seven seals" and reports that "no one in heaven or on earth was able to open the scroll or to look into it," the sealed scroll here may well be a Christian recasting of the older Hebrew idea of a book of fates or divine foreknowledge, as the subsequent description of its contents (6.1–17, 8.1–10.11) indicates. This concept of a book of destiny is also prominent in the Qur'ān, as one can see from many passages, among them Sūrah 57.22: "No misfortune strikes on earth or in yourselves without its being [written] in a Book before We cause it to be. Truly, that is easy for God."[4]

The notion of a book of works in which a heavenly record of human deeds is kept for some future reckoning was also widely known of old. References to the writing down of good and bad deeds, typically in connection with a last judgment, are found among the ancient Babylonians, Egyptians, Persians, and Hebrews, as well as Greek, Roman, Jewish, and Christian writers of later antiquity. It appears also in Islamic tradition in Ḥadīth reports about the Day of Judgment, when each person, according to some traditions, will be given his or her "book" (*kitāb*) of earthly deeds, the just in the right hand, the evildoer in the left.[5]

However, it is in the Biblical traditions of Judaism and Christianity that the book of life, in which the names of God's elect are inscribed, finds a special place.[6] Compare, for example, Exodus 32.33, in which the Lord says to Moses, "Whoever has sinned against me, him will I blot out of my book," with Paul's reference in Philippians 4.3 to "Clement and the rest of my fellow workers, whose names are in the book of life." As Leo Koep has shown, this motif lived on in later, especially medieval, Christian tradition with particular vigor.[7]

Although the precise relationship of these concepts to that of a revealed, authoritative scriptural book needs to be clarified more satisfactorily, their role in developing and reinforcing the idea of an authoritative, even revealed, scripture is significant. The appearance of many elements of these ideas in Jewish, Christian, and Muslim scripture reflects the persistence and strength of the notion of a written book as the repository of divine, suprahuman knowledge or divine, heavenly decrees. The book emerges in these traditions as a physical symbol of divine as opposed to human knowledge, and hence as a tangible symbol of authority and truth.

The Idea of an Authoritative Revealed Book

The quintessential "book religions" of Judaic, Christian, and Muslim tradition trace their lineage in some fashion to the Hebrews, the prototypical "people of the book." What was understood under "book" was, in the Hebrew tradition and in its spiritual offspring, preeminently the word of God as revealed to human beings, by which God's laws were expressed. As such it was the chief authority for individual and collective existence, the divine ordinances by which all aspects of life, from morals to food, were to be regulated. Siegfried Morenz has astutely pointed out that the origin of "book religion" lay in the Hebrew "genius for hearing";[8] what the Israelites "heard" was preeminently God's imperative or command: His Law, His Torah. This has colored all subsequent notions of the scriptural word in all three traditions of monotheistic faith.

Yet it is also the case that the Torah was conceived of as an authoritative written unity relatively early on – certainly long before any "canon" of the

Hebrew scriptures was recognized. As Brevard Childs points out, the core of this conception was the notion both that God is the writer of the decalogue (Exod. 34.1; Deut. 4.13, 10.4) and that Moses "not only proclaims the 'words and ordinances' of God to the people [at Sinai] (Ex[od]. 24.3), but he is also commissioned to write them (34.4; cf. 34.27)." Exodus 31 formulates this latter idea most clearly in its emphasis on the written book of the law, and later scriptural references to the book of the law confirm it (Ezra 6.18; Neh. 13.1; 2 Chron. 25.2). Moses' writing of the Torah as depicted in the Exodus account thus served theologically as "part of the canonical witness." The last editors of the Pentateuchal material affirmed in their work, according to Childs, that with this writing down by Moses, "the law of God has now been transmitted for the future generations in the written form of scripture."[9] These Mosaic passages testify to the special authority of the *written* book of God's Law as the proper form for the divine word.

Other notions of sacred writings were also afoot throughout the ancient world in the same period in which Judaic "book religion" was codified, roughly the sixth to third centuries B.C. We do not, however, understand fully how Judaic ideas of a book of divine law, divinely revealed, joined historically with influences from Egyptian and other sectors of the ancient Near East and the growing status of the book in Hellenistic culture to set in motion the "book religion" that plays so large a role in Christianity, Manichaeism, and, most spectacularly and decisively, in Islam. Although Johannes Leipoldt and Siegfried Morenz have laid a solid general foundation upon which to build in trying to trace the development of this "book religion",[10] many connections, especially those showing lines of influence, remain to be clarified.

More recently, however, Wilfred Cantwell Smith has sought to pinpoint the specific emergence in the Mediterranean world of late antiquity of the scripture-idea as the centerpiece of religious life.[11] He points to the gathering strength in the period after Alexander the Great, and especially from the second century C.E., of the idea of a sacred book or "classic" – a text that carries ultimate or at least supreme authority. Thus, as Moses Hadas remarks, Homer and Hesiod had long been regarded by the Greeks "with reverence", and Alexander himself, perhaps under Aristotle's influence, virtually worshiped Homer. Alexander's veneration even went so far as to lead him to found a cult of Homer at Alexandria, which was to become the home of the study of "the classics" in the next two centuries.[12]

Christianity's increasing emphasis on authoritative writings, the point of departure for which was the Jew's cultic use of, reverence for, and identification with the Torah, was especially decisive in the development of the sacred-book idea. Mani's self-conscious effort to produce books of scriptural authority reflects the degree to which by his time (3rd C. C.E.) it was necessary for a religious movement to have its own scriptures in order to establish its legitimacy. The fourth century C.E. in particular seems to have been a time when scriptures, notably the Christian and Manichaean, were coming into their own. The oldest application of the noun *kanōn,* "canon" (originally, "rule, measure"; then "list"), to a body of writings is usually said to be that by Athanasius in the late fourth century, and from the time of Jerome the word became common.[13] However, it was only in the early seventh century C.E. that the Qur'ān's insistence upon the centrality of the divine book, conceived of now as the recited word taught from God's heavenly scripture, carried the development of book religion to its apogee. Later developments such as Sikh veneration of its "book" (*Granth*) have, as Smith remarks, to be seen as but new variations on a theme already fully articulated in Islam, the book religion par excellence.[14]

The Semantic Background

Whatever the roles of earlier ideas of heavenly books or divinely revealed writings in Judaic and Christian thinking, the most tangible evidence of the strong focus upon holy writ in these traditions is the conceptual and linguistic background of our modern terminology related to scripture. In traditional Judaic and Christian thinking and usage we can see with great clarity how closely "scripture", "sacred writings", "bible", and similar terms were linked semantically with writing and physical documents from relatively early on.

The most basic meaning of the word "scripture", as of its European-language cognates (Ger. *Schrift,* Ital. *scrittura,* Fr. *écriture,* etc.), is "a writing", "something written". It is derived from the Latin *scriptura,* "a writing" (pl.: *scripturae*). The Latin word translated the Greek word *graphē* (pl.: *graphai*), which corresponded in classical and Hellenistic usage to the postexilic Hebrew *k^etāb, k^etūb* (pl.: *k^etūvîm*) as a term for any piece of writing, whether a letter, an inscription, a written decree, or a holy writing. The Greek term could even refer, as in Plato, to written law, or, in the Septuagint, to the Mosaic law of Torah.[15] In the Mediterranean world of later antiquity, these words (or their plurals) were used for various kinds of written texts in the Hebrew Bible, the Greek Septuagint, and the Old Testament books of the Latin Vulgate, as well as in the writings of pagan, Jewish, and Christian authors.[16]

By the time of the Christian New Testament writers, however, these terms had come gradually to be used in particular for sacred books, above all to refer to the sum of the three divisions of the Hebrew scriptures, the Pentateuch (*Torāh*), Prophets (*N^evī'îm*), and (other) Writings (*K^etūvîm*) – which in later Jewish usage came to be known by the the acronym "Tanak", or "Tanakh" (formed by vocalization of the initial letters, *Tāw, Nūn, Kaf,* of the Hebrew words for these three groups of texts). In early Christian usage, the Greek *hai graphai* and Latin *scripturae,* "the writings/scriptures" were applied also to the Gospels, Pauline epistles, and other texts that eventually came to form the New

Testament. In Jewish as well as Christian use, the singular forms *kᵉtāb/kᵉtūb, graphē,* and *scriptura* referred primarily to a particular passage or particular writing, and their plurals were used in a collective sense for the whole. Some examples are Daniel 10.21: "in a true writing/scripture" (Heb.: *bi-kᵉtāb 'emet;* Septuagint: *en graphē alētheias;* Vulg.: *in scriptura veritatis*); Luke 4.21 (referring to Isa. 61.1f.): "this [passage of] scripture" (Gk.: *hē graphē autē;* Vulg.: *haec scriptura*); and Matthew 21.42, Acts 17.11, etc.: "the [Hebrew] Scriptures" (Gk.: *hai graphai;* Vulg.: *scripturae*). The Christian church fathers used both singular and plural forms collectively to refer to the Old and New Testament books.[17] Although in the New Testament these terms in singular or plural seem to refer uniformly to scriptural as opposed to other kinds of writings, there is some ambiguity as to whether the singular *hē graphē* (=*scriptura*) can refer collectively to the whole of the scriptures or only to one or a part of one of them, as, for example, in Romans 11.2: "Do you not know what the scripture/Scripture (*hē graphē*) says of Elijah . . . ?"[18] In other words, Paul may be referring either only to the one passage (1 Kings 19.10) that speaks of Elijah, or to Scripture as a unitary whole, the entire word of God.

Other terms, also associated normally with writing or books, were used in like fashion to refer to sacred, authoritative writings. In Greek, *grammata* (sing.: *gramma* [from the same root as *graphē*], "what is written, writing", =Lat.: *littera*), was used generally for literature or documents, as in the Septuagint, where it usually translates the Hebrew *sᵉfārîm,* the plural form of *sēfer,* "writing", "book". In Hellenistic times, in pagan as well as Jewish and Christian contexts, it came to refer especially to any sacred text. An example of this is the reference to "sacred writings" in 2 Timothy 3.15 (Gk.: *ta hiera grammata;* Vulg.: *sacras litteras*). Scriptural citations in the New Testament and early Christian writers are commonly introduced by the formula used in the Septuagint, "(as) it is written", (*kathōs*) *gegraptai* (compare the Talmudic equivalent, *ka-k-kᵉtūb*).[19]

Of special importance is the Greek *byblos* or *biblos* ("book"), or, more commonly in the Septuagint and New Testament, its diminutive form, *biblion* (pl.: *biblia*). This denoted originally any type of written document - scroll, codex, book, letter, and the like. In the Septuagint and subsequent Jewish and Christian Hellenistic Greek sources (for example, the Greek preface to the Wisdom of Ben Sirach, 1 and 2 Maccabees, 1 Clement, Philo, Josephus, and Origen), although not in New Testament writings, terms like *hiera biblos,* "sacred book", and (*hierai*) *bibloi,* "(sacred) books", were used for the Pentateuch or the entire Hebrew scriptures.[20] From the earliest days of the Christian church, in which "the books" (*ha-s-sᵉfārîm*) of Hebrew scripture were effectively "the Bible of the Church,"[21] the Greek neuter plural *ta biblia* and its derivative Latin *biblia* were used in Christian contexts to refer specifically to these scriptures. By the end of the second century, or at latest by the end of the fourth, the generally recognized writings of the emerging New Testament were also included in "the Books".[22] In the later Middle Ages (certainly from the thirteenth century and probably earlier)[23], the Latin *biblia* came to be treated commonly as a feminine singular rather than a neuter plural, whence we have the modern singular forms, "the Bible", *die Bibel, la Bibbia,* and other European-language equivalents.

In the New Testament and church fathers, and as well as in the Apocrypha, Philo, and Josephus, various adjectives were added to the words for "scripture(s)" and "book(s)" to emphasize their special, holy character. The most common were *hieros, hagios,* and *sanctus* ("holy"); *theios* and *divinus* ("divine"); *theopneustos* ("divinely inspired"); or *kuriakos* ("of the Lord").[24] Such usage had much earlier, pre-Christian, precedents. One of these was the use in Ptolemaic times of *ta hiera grammata,* "the holy writings", to refer to the sacred Egyptian hieroglyphic literature in contrast to the demotic writings (note that the English *hieroglyph* comes from the Greek *hiera glyphē,* "holy inscription/carving"). Another was the use of the Hebrew equivalent *kitvê ha-q-qodesh* ("the Holy Scriptures") in Rabbinic writings, even as early as the Tannaim, to designate the sacred scriptures (compare the use of *sifrê ha-q-qodesh,* "the Sacred Books", in medieval Jewish writings, a usage that occurs occasionally even in pre-Christian times).[25]

All of these usages reflect the direct and inseparable link of scriptural concepts with writing and written texts. In this linkage, as in the book concepts connected with scripture, we can see specific examples that reinforced for scriptural works the general tendency in the history of Western tradition toward reification of texts as written documents. With Jewish or Christian scripture, *the* book of books, there was an even stronger than usual impetus to concretization and objectification of the text. Thus it comes as no surprise that, whatever other uses a scripture might have, it has remained first and foremost a tangible book of holy writ, reassuring as well as venerable in its fixity and apparent permanence.

Generalization of the Concept

The gradual appropriation by Jews and Christians of terms like *scripture, holy scripture(s), books,* and *sacred books* was long limited to applying these as proper names for their own scriptures. In particular, as Christian culture and religion triumphed in the Mediterranean and southern Europe, *(sacred) scripture* came to mean specifically *the* sacred scripture of the Christian Bible. Such limitation of the idea of scripture to a proper noun referring only to the Old and New Testaments continues even today in many Christian circles. By contrast, the use of *scriptura(e)* or *scriptura(e) sancta(e)* and their European-language equivalents to refer to sacred texts in general was apparently uncommon until recently – chiefly in the past century or two. This has not, however, been studied closely and would likely repay systematic investigation. In the meanwhile, a few observations may be in order.

Scriptura could be also used in classical Latin as a neutral term for any piece of writing and, in later Latin, for a written law or a charter.[26] The German *Schrift* is still used simply to mean a writing or written text, and even the English *scripture* long retained this now obsolete secular meaning alongside the religious one.[27] It is not a giant step from such secular generic usage to a generalized concept of religious writings in other cultures. Peter the Venerable (d. 1156), for example, contrasts the Christian scriptures with the Muslim Qur'ān at one point by juxtaposing *sacra scriptura* with the *nefaria scriptura* of Muhammad.[28] *Scriptura* in this instance may be used in a strictly neutral, secular way as "a writing" – in the first occurrence a "sacred" one (the Bible) and in the other an "abominable" one (the Qur'ān). However, it might also already carry the connotation in both instances of a specifically religious book, no matter how true or false a book one judged it to be. In either event, this passage reflects the movement toward, if not the existence of, the use of *scriptura* as a generic term for a religious text in any community (on analogy, to be sure, with *the* scripture of the Bible).

An even clearer example of the notion of "scripture" as a religious phenomenon common to more than one culture can be found as early as the mid-thirteenth century. It occurs in William of Rubroek's description of one of his experiences in the inner Asian city of Karakorum, the Mongol capital, in the year 1254. A guest at the court of the Great Khan of the Mongols, William has left us engaging accounts of his trials and tribulations as an ambassador of God (and the Roman church) in what were to the Christian West of that day very distant reaches of the earth (1254 was, after all, roughly the year that the subsequently more famous European China-traveler and writer, Marco Polo, was born back in faraway Europe). On the occasion in question, the Great Khan had ordered an interreligious debate on religion among Buddhists, Muslims, and Christians (all of whom except Rubroek were Nestorians from Asia). In discussing the coming event with his fellow Christians, he (Rubroek) gave the following warning to the Nestorians about Christian debating tactics vis-à-vis the Buddhists and Muslims: "They do not have faith in [our] Scriptures; if you recite one [scripture], they will recite another."[29] Here William's, if not his Nestorian cousins', recognition of the conflicting authority claims of diverse sacred books, or *scripturae,* is manifest. Objectively, Christians are not the only people who give their allegiance and trust to a sacred text.

If one takes a global view of the matter, such Western Christian generalization of the scripture concept was hardly novel by this time. The rejection of the authority of the Veda by Buddhists and Jains had not made either group less aware that the Veda was authoritative and holy above all else for Hindus.

In particular, in the Muslim world, the concept of sacred "scripture" (*kitāb*) had already been explicitly generalized in the Qur'ān, where Jews and Christians are spoken of repeatedly as "scripture-folk" (*ahl al-kitāb;* lit.: "people of [the] scripture"). The term designates those communities that have previously received "books" (*kutub*)[30] sent by God, all of which were in time tampered with and faultily preserved, then ultimately eclipsed in the perfection of His final "sending" of *the* Book (*al-kitāb*), the Qur'ān, through Muhammad. *Ahl al-kitāb* status was early extended to Zoroastrians and Mandeans, and later even to Hindus.

There seems, however, to be no evidence of direct influence of the Muslim use of *kutub* on modern Western generic usage. It appears rather that it was the growing Western awareness in the eighteenth century of the Indian Veda in particular, and the Chinese "classics" to some degree also, that led in the Enlightenment and post-Enlightenment period to wider currency of the idea of other scriptures and books of wisdom that could claim great antiquity as well as importance in their cultures comparable to that of the Bible in the West.[31]

In English, clearly generic use of the word "scripture" for religious texts can be dated from at least the eighteenth century. The oldest instance that I have found is one from the pen of George Sale in 1734. In the introduction to his translation of the Islamic scripture, he speaks of what the Qur'ān shares with "other books of Scripture."[32] The earliest such use cited in the *Oxford English Dictionary* is from Edward Gibbon, in 1764, who remarks of Homer that "his works and those of his successors were the scriptures of the nation."[33] In the nineteenth century, the generic use of the term or of approximate equivalents like "sacred writings" became more common. The ambitious series of translations of the great scriptures of the world, *The Sacred Books of the East,* inaugurated in 1879 by Max Müller, reflects a clear recognition by this time in the modern West of the worldwide existence of texts that function as scripture in ways analogous to those of the Jewish or Christian Bible.

The extended use of "scripture" for any particularly sacred text is now common in modern Western usage and widely current internationally. Thus one hears and reads not seldom of "Buddhist scripture", "Taoist scriptures", and the like.[34] At times, even the word "bible" has been used, albeit less often, in a similarly general sense to refer to any sacred scripture. This can be found at least as early as 1873 in Monier Williams's description of the Ṛg Veda's collection of hymns as "the first bible of the Hindū religion, and the special bible of Vedism."[35] Another, more recent example is Franklin Edgerton's reference to the Gītā as "India's favorite Bible," or the title given an English anthology of Buddhist sacred texts, *A Buddhist Bible*.[36] Nevertheless, "scripture" is the term that today is most commonly and properly used as the generic term for especially sacred texts, and it is "scripture" in this sense that is our prime concern in what follows.

CHAPTER 5

Holy Writ and Holy Word

The most important source of knowledge for the general study of religion is still the Word. Above all, one must study how religions so diversely express themselves in speech and writ [*Rede und Schrift*] in order to penetrate to the essential nature of religion.
- Heinrich Frick

The fundamental contention of the present study is that any concept of "scripture" that is useful and meaningful for the study of religion must include recognition of its importance both as written and as spoken word. Such recognition requires, however, more than intellectual assent to the obvious facts that written texts are sometimes read aloud and usually have oral antecedents and that oral myths, hymns, or prayers can be written down as well as transmitted orally. The notion of a contrast, if not antithesis, between oral and written texts is deeply ingrained. In the light of what we have seen of the history of Western notions of books in general and scriptural books in particular, it will come as no surprise that students of religion have tended to separate holy writ from the spoken sacred word in largely dichotomous fashion. Even though no one would deny that each is closely related to the other, virtually every phenomenological study of religious data has perpetrated the word–writ, oral–written dichotomy as a given datum of religious history.

At the risk of further perpetuating this dichotomy, we need to review at least briefly the significance of the written text qua written text and the spoken word qua spoken word in the history of religion in order to pursue the oral dimension of scripture in any depth. It is essential to recognize the close connection of the written words of formal holy writ with the spoken words of ritual, myth, and devotion and, still more, the necessary oral and aural function of holy writ in religious life, for only in this way can much unnecessary and misleading dichotomization be reduced.

The Holy Writ of Scripture

If Western culture has assigned unusual importance to the written, and especially the printed, word, it is also the case that written texts have enjoyed a special status in virtually every literate society. Anyone would be foolish to deny or belittle the worldwide historical significance of writing and written texts, and, above all, sacred writing and holy writ. With the notable exceptions of classical Greece and India,[1] the writing down of a text, particularly a sacred text, has from ancient times lent it unique authority and made it often even the object of worshipful veneration.[2] The replacement of purely oral transmission by use of the written word has been the repeated and apparently uniform pattern of historical development across all geographical and cultural boundaries, even though the variation as to how long or late this occurs is quite large. Whenever writing does take hold, written fixation of the central religious texts of the society usually follows rapidly, if it has not occurred at the very introduction of the scribal art. This commonly enhances the status of religious texts as visible, lasting heritages of the sacred tradition handed down from the past and hence as tangible sources of guidance in the present. As we have seen in Part I, there is something about the written word that bespeaks authority and reliability in its very anonymity and independence of particular persons and individual memories. Even the writing itself, the fixed text on the page, apparently contributes to this authority: "reverence for the written Word, as expressing an independent authority, was a cultural possibility ever inherent in the very discovery of writing."[3] Beyond, or growing out of, the reverence inspired by the written word, written fixation can even affirm or create for the holy text, in the eyes of the faithful, what Karl Kerényi, borrowing from Thomas Mann, has called *Unsterblichkeitscharakter,* the quality of immortality.[4] The very permanence and fixity of the written page lends credence to the idea that its sacred word has always existed and always will exist: "The written holy word . . . is more than a magical formula, which works for the moment. It lends a religion immortality. . . ."[5] Ancient Egypt seems to be a textbook case for the development of such an idea.[6] Whether the sense of permanence or that of authority is primary is not of great consequence; they are mutually supportive and often indistinguishably mingled attributes.

Once written, the sacred text acquires typically a visible solidity or even immutability for the faithful. This can be documented repeatedly in world history. It is a process that can hardly be reversed, yet should not be taken as a necessarily progressive evolution in religious life, for it does not lead to uniformly positive developments in faith and piety. The fixing of the holy word in writing always carries with it potential threats to the original spontaneity and living quality of the scriptural text, for it places it ever in danger of becoming only a "dead letter" rather than the "living word".[7]

There are numerous examples of traditions in which the written fixation and transmission of unusually sacred or otherwise significant and authoritative texts have been crucial to the definition and sustenance of the traditions themselves. After the particularly striking case of Pharaonic Egypt,[8] classical China comes immediately to mind. There the written texts of the five classics (*ching*) were the basis as well as the overt symbols of all culture from at least the first century C.E., by which time the Confucian tradition (*Ju Chiao*) had become dominant.[9] In the Hellenistic world, as I noted in Chapter 4, we can follow a cumulative development of the importance of written texts of books that were considered to be "classics" or "scriptures" of various kinds. This can be documented for the Judaic tradition and its written Torah,[10] as well as in the Christian movement, with its eventual development of formal concepts of "bible" and "canon".[11] In traditions as diverse as the Rabbinic Jewish and the Theravāda Buddhist, the delineation and consensual recognition of a written corpus, or "canon", of scriptures is also evidence of how important to a tradition the fixation of "holy writ" can be, even when great emphasis is placed upon memorizing and reciting aloud the words of the writ.[12]

The elevated place of the written word of scripture in many cultures is dramatically demonstrated in the notion of a divine prototype for the earthly exemplar of holy writ (see Chapter 4). With respect to this, suffice it here to call attention again to Geo Widengren's argument that a leitmotif of religion in the Near Eastern world – the home of the *Schriftreligionen,* or "scriptural religions" – has been the notion of a divine revelation that is given to a human bearer of revelation (*Offenbarungsträger*) and subsequently fixed as holy writ (*heilige Schrift*). Widengren notes that even though the holy writ so revealed is in the usual course of things subsequently recited and orally taught, and written and oral transmission mutually reinforce one another, the written tradition is still considered to be "the normative one, the firm model, for it [written tradition] is scripture as the document of divine revelation, a copy of the sacred book that the bearer of revelation himself received from the divinity."[13] Scripturality in the specific sense of "writtenness" appears in such instances to be a crucial part of what makes the text special and authoritative. Although the degree of importance ascribed to this pattern by Widengren is perhaps exaggerated, the peculiar importance of the holy book as written document in the ancient Mediterranean and Near Eastern world is underscored by the widespread occurrence of the heavenly book motif there.[14] Even where this motif does not occur, the idea of the divine origin of holy writ usually does, and this idea is found as easily in South and East Asia as in the West, as examples from India, China, and Japan show.[15]

The most common explanation for the special treatment and status of the written word of scripture has been the common perception of writing and the written word as possessing an inherently magical power. Alfred Bertholet maintains, for example, that "respect particularly for what is written has penetrated deeply into the human soul . . . ," and G. van der Leeuw goes even farther: "Writing, then, is magic: – one method of gaining power over the living word. . . . Committing sacred texts to writing therefore . . . was . . . intended . . . to attain power, since with the written word man can do just what he will . . . ."[16] Certainly the magical or quasi-magical quality of the written word is abundantly visible in the popular use of written excerpts from or physical copies of sacred scriptures, be they Bible, Qur'ān, Ismā'īlī *ginān,* or Buddhist *sūtra*.. Such use is typically for purposes of divination or augury, sealing of oaths and contracts, or talismanic protection from evil or harm.[17] Certain forms of Jewish and Christian treatment of their scriptures involve not only reverence for the physical text but even magical or quasi-magical uses of it that can only be termed bibliolatry. Diverse folk practices can be cited, from the old European practice of laying a Bible under a sick or yet-to-be christened child,[18] to – in an example that I encountered recently in Boston – the placing of a Bible copy (one that is "not to be opened") in an automobile as a protection against car thieves. Even Augustine admitted to participating in a form of bibliomancy when he once used the Bible in divinatory fashion for help in making a difficult spiritual decision.[19] The continuing use today in America of a copy of the Bible for courtroom oaths, whether by Christians, Jews, or avowed atheists, also reflects a quasi-magical residue of feeling about the power of a sacred text in our modern secular society, and serves as a symbolic statement and reminder of our national roots in a particular tradition of faith.

The reverence for the written sacred word goes, however, beyond the magical, superstitious, or talismanic in the recurring veneration and even adoration shown to it around the world. We have today little access to the sense of awe and respect before the physical copy of *any* text that prevailed in ages (and even today in places) in which a book was (is) a rare thing, and a scriptural book often the *only* book. Such a sense of awe before a volume of text was still vivid for Shakespeare;[20] how much greater, then, the reverence of wholly illiterate folk (who have been the majority throughout history) in the presence of holy writ? Such reverence is evident in folk Buddhist reverence for copies of *sūtra*s and could have been the basis of the "cult of the book" that may once have existed in India alongside or even in competition with the more familiar relic cult in early Mahāyāna tradition.[21]

Yet it is not only among the "illiterate masses" that the veneration of holy writ has flourished. Instances of the profound regard and reverential treatment accorded scriptural texts in the public and private devotional life of religious communities around the world are everywhere to hand. The deep reverence of Jews for their magnificent, ritually prepared Torah scrolls and the liturgical centrality of these elaborate text-copies in the synagogue (as in the "lifting up of the Torah") provide familiar examples. No less striking is the Tibetan

Buddhist veneration for the physical copies of the *sūtras*, which is observable today in the daily circumambulation of the *sūtra* library in monastic compounds such as that of the Tibetan exile community in Dharamsala, India. Other vivid examples are to be found in Japanese Buddhist reverence, especially in Nichiren sects, for the scrolls of the Lotus Sūtra and in Muslims' formal and reverential treatment of copies of the Qur'ān.[22]

The natural and widespread reverence for the physical copies of sacred texts is also, at least in some degree, the result of the desire to set such texts apart from all other forms of written word in definitive, tangible ways.[23] This is seen in Judaic tradition in the Mishnaic term used to distinguish the holy scriptures from other texts as those that "defile the hands", or make ritual ablution necessary after touching them (lest their sacred power be communicated to profane objects).[24] This desire to set off scriptural texts from all others may have been a major motivation for the early Christians' appropriation of the otherwise little-used parchment codex, which they made their distinctive medium for sacred texts.[25] Similarly, both early and later Bible manuscripts testify to the elaborate care given to the copying, illustration, and illumination of the Bible as a holy object.[26] Such pious copying and illumination or illustration of sacred texts is widely attested in other traditions also. We need think only of Mani's illustrated books of scripture, the staggering variety and artistry of Qur'ān calligraphy and illumination, the massive, elegant block-print collections of the Tibetan Buddhist cannon, or the reverent liturgical zeal with which the physical copy of the Adi Granth is treated among the Sikhs.[27]

All of the preceding points us to the central importance of the written text for an understanding of scripture's historical functions. This aspect of scripture is the one with which we are most at home in our typographic culture, with its strong print orientation and book consciousness. The power of scripture as holy writ has been prominent in all traditions in which scripture has figured at all prominently. Nevertheless, this power is not at odds with the power of the scriptural word that is read aloud or recited. The written and spoken aspects of the text complement and augment each other, and hence to speak of competition between the two has little meaning. Any comprehension of what scripture is must include awareness of its role and function as written text, just as of its role and function as spoken text.

The Sacred Spoken Word

If some of the traditional forms of religious piety that revolve around holy writ seem foreign to modern culture because of our matter-of-factness about the written or printed word, they are, as I have suggested, still easier for us to grasp than are those forms of piety that center on the spoken word, and the spoken word of the written text in particular. If the sense of awe before the written copy of the Bible has waned for many modern Western Christians and for some Jews, it is still generally stronger than the awareness among these same persons of the power of the biblical text as a memorized and recited word that is "lived with" orally and aurally, not just in devotional and liturgical practice, but also in everyday life.

This is evident, for example, in the modern Christian, especially Protestant Christian, emphasis upon scripture as writ. Here the common reference to holy scripture as "the word of God" no longer reflects so much an aural sense of hearing God speak as it does a fixing or reification of "word" into a synonym for "Bible" in the sense of holy writ. The word is thought of primarily as something readily at hand in the pages of our Bibles, since so few of us any longer have much if any of the word ready to the tongue in our memories. Such reification masks in many instances the degree to which for Christians the "word" is theologically and functionally not a written text but the living, spoken message of the Gospel. The identity of this vocal message of the Gospel preaching with the vocal word of God that spoke from the pages of scripture was still vivid for Christians of earlier, more aurally oriented ages. As we shall see in Chapter 12, for all of the Protestant Reformers' emphasis upon scripture as *Schrift, écriture,* "writ", or the like, at the heart of their movement's "book religion" was a vivid sense of the living, spoken word of God that is communicated both in Christian preaching and in the reading of scripture.[28] The Christian was supposed to listen to this and to heed it as the one certain word of truth. *Sola scriptura* was not an idea fixed upon written word, but upon the authority of the word of God. In the words of Martin Luther, "it is after all not possible to comfort a soul, unless it hear the word of its God. But where is God's word in all books except Scripture? . . . Comfort can no book save Holy Scripture."[29]

We have seen that in modern, print-dominated culture such a sense of a written text as spoken word is no longer intuitive for most persons. In scholarly studies of culture, substantive recognition of the importance of oral speech, including the sacred utterance, is today limited largely to the work, primarily in anthropology and religion, that focuses upon nonliterate cultures of "extracivilizational" peoples or the preliterate or semiliterate beginnings of the great civilizations.[30] We are able to accept an oral/aural orientation as fundamental to prehistorical or nonliterate culture on the assumption that we moderns have put such an orientation well behind us. The evolutionary aspect of this is readily apparent. As Gustav Mensching put it, "the word that is heard precedes (not everywhere, but in many instances) the written word . . . ."[31] We seem to have taken this literally, and consequently we readily ignore the ongoing centrality of oral expression to religious and social life even in script and print culture.

Nevertheless, logically and historically the sacred word of holy writ is an extension of the oral sacred word. In oral or predominantly oral cultures, the transmission of sacred lore as well as the sustenance of ritual life are dependent upon the sacred spoken word. This centrality of the word of myth and ritual is commonly traced to the presence in such cultures of a feeling that the spoken word is something alive with magical or transcendent power.[32] Word and act here are not to be separated. There is no cleavage, as there is for most of us, save perhaps in moments of deepest *engagement* in vocal acts of worship, between *legomenon* and *drōmenon,* "what is said" and "what is done". Speech is action here, never merely Hamlet's "words, words, words."[33] Hence the oft-remarked bond between myth and ritual, story and rite.

"The word . . . is a decisive power: whoever utters words sets power in motion."[34] This recognition has led students of archaic and modern nonliterate cultures to see in the inherent power of the spoken word one of the primal elements in religious faith and practice. The oversimplified extreme in emphasis on the power of the word is the view of Hermann Usener, and following him, Ernst Cassirer, in which the identification of the word that names a deity with the deity itself is carried so far as to see in the naming the creation of a "momentary deity" (*Augenblicks-gott*).[35] As a hypothetical model of the "origin" of human personification of the transcendent, this view has at best heuristic value; but as a reminder of the power that words carry, it is instructive. There is much to be said for the perception that, especially in the cult-oriented world of wholly oral traditions, and to a lesser degree in any ritual activity, the act of naming makes present, or at least summons the power of, that which is named.[36] What J. F. Staal says of Vedic recitative transmission is probably applicable to the function of the oral sacred word in most cultic contexts, even if especially so in nonliterate cultures:

> There is no sharp distinction between word and meaning and between form and contents. In this "archaic" world lie the roots of the efficacy and power of mantra recitation, which is related to "magical" identification as well as to the creative force of the word in poetry, in divine and in human speech.[37]

The sense of word as power and as overt act is especially vivid in the cosmogonic myths of diverse peoples, ancient and modern, in all parts of the globe. Accounts of the origin of the world ascribe the initial creative act again and again to the generative divine word. Not only the opening of the Christian Gospel of John or the divine command of Genesis 1.3, "Let there be light," but also the creative word of the god Ptah described in the Memphite cosmogony of ancient Egypt[38] are eloquent testimony to this. Similarly striking is the role of *Vāc,* "Speech", as primordial being, creative word, or creator-goddess in the Ṛg Veda,[39] or the creative word of the gods in the mythology of the South American Witoto tribe and in that of the African Dogon tribe.[40] Not surprisingly, the Qur'ān also emphasizes God's eternal creative power: on whatever He decides, "He has only to say, 'Be!' and it is [*kun fa-yakun*]" (Sūrah 40.68). The generative power of the spoken word is apparently one of the most basic and widespread of religious themes.

In many of the major, literate traditions of history, the idea of the primordial word of power is linked to the power of scripture itself. This is most explicitly evident in theological formulations such as we find in Rabbinic Judaism and medieval Islam concerning the preexistence of the divine word of scripture.[41] Ideas of the eternality of the Buddha-word, the Qur'ān, or the sounds of the Veda also reflect the identification of the preserved scriptural texts with the primal power of the original word of truth.[42] Even in the aforementioned traditions of the heavenly book, we find more than once that the heavenly writ is said to have begun before time as the spoken word of God.[43]

Thus it bears repeating that, in many senses, speech always precedes writing, cosmically and anthropologically as well as historically. If there is anything that can be called protoscripture, it is surely the utterances of ecstatics, prophets, and seers, in which it is commonly held to be not they but the divinity who speaks through them as their chosen mouthpieces.[44] In societies in which transcendence is not wholly personified or anthropomorphically conceived, truth can be as easily or more easily a matter of audition as of vision: In Old Chinese, for example, the close linguistic connection between "sage" (*sheng*) and words for "ear" (the radical *er/erh*) and "sound" (the phonetic *ch'eng*) points to the probability that "hearing much" is what constituted knowledge for the ancient sages.[45] Furthermore, though the Vedic "seers", or *ṛṣi*s, are spoken of as "seeing" the truth of what is Veda, the auditory metaphor is used in India to designate the most sacred ancient Hindu texts, above all the Vedas. These most sacred of texts are *śruti,* "what is heard", as distinct from later, less sacred texts, which are *smṛti,* "what is remembered".

Whatever the primordial power and significance of the spoken word or formula, it does not evaporate with the coming of writing and reading, in religious or other spheres of life. The book, and none moreso than the holy book of scripture, is, or was, first the vehicle of the living, spoken word, then an object of veneration. Where spoken word and written word have met most fully was likely first in scripture, in holy texts that sought to fix and hold the spoken word of sacred truth and power in the most tangible way possible.[46] If "scripture" is etymologically inseparably linked to the written word, as an historical phenomenon it is experientially indissolubly tied to the spoken word.

Recitation or reading aloud of scripture is a common feature of piety in virtually every scriptural tradition. For example, as we shall see in Chapter 10, in the early synagogue and early Christian church, the reading aloud of scripture in worship was fundamental to communal life, just as it was in pagan cults of the Hellenistic Mediterranean such as that of Isis.[47] Many scriptures have primary or secondary schemes of division according to the needs of recitation or reading aloud in communal ritual or personal devotion (e.g., the 154 divisions of the Torah for synagogal reading over a three-year span). Important passages of scriptures are frequently collected in special works that serve the ritual and devotional needs of a community, as in the Christian breviary, psalter, lectionary, or evangeliary, or, in Buddhist tradition, the Pāṭimokkha selection from the Vinaya that is recited as a basic part of Theravāda monastic discipline; the *Paritta* ("Pirit") collection of sacred texts for recitation to ward off sickness or danger; or the Blue Sūtra, an abridgement of the Lotus Sūtra used in the ritual of the modern Reiyukai Buddhist sect in Japan.[48] Such recitative texts often become the functionally primary scriptures of entire communities, since these are the texts that are known best by heart and used in daily life and ritual practice.

Another point too easily neglected is that, even where writing exists and scripture carries great authority, oral transmission can be the preferred or exclusive means of preserving and using the sacred texts. For example, in the case of the Zoroastrian tradition, it appears that until the coming of Islam stimulated the writing down of the Avesta as a book, the most sacred Zoroastrian texts, those in Old Persian, were transmitted and used only orally, in recitation, whereas the less sacred commentaries (Zand) and other religious books in Pahlavi had long been written.[49] Here memory and the tongue, not the physical page, are seen as the proper vehicles for the holiest words of the community.

It is the Hindu tradition, however, that presents the most stunning case of a tradition in which scripture has been so fundamentally and completely conceived of and handled as recited, oral word that to speak of it as "scripture" in the sense of "sacred written text" must simply be rejected as an error. The unique Hindu case offers the one unassailable example of a highly developed scriptural tradition in which the importance of the oral word has been so central as to dominate and largely even to exclude the written word altogether over most of its long history. As a result, the Hindu treatment of sacred texts can provide a benchmark and a point of departure for consideration of the oral dimensions of scripture in other traditions that are more explicitly bound to the written word.

CHAPTER 6

Scripture as Spoken Word: The Indian Paradigm

> Vedic Tradition is in some respects the most remarkable in recorded history. From the entire Vedic period we have not one single piece of antiquarian or archæological material, not one bit of real property; not a building, nor a monument; not a coin, jewel, or utensil; – nothing but winged words.
>
> - Maurice Bloomfield

> Having admitted an aspiration to explore the notion of scripture in India . . . , one finds oneself immediately in that familiar position in comparative studies, where the terms in which the original question is asked turn out to be ill-suited for under-standing the data at hand. . . . It is necessary to conceptualize our venture here as a typology of the Word, rather than one of scripture, in Hindu life.
>
> - Thomas B. Coburn

By now it should be evident that the primacy and power of the oral word are not limited to nonliterate or archaic stages of culture and religion. In virtually every society, truth is bound up in significant ways with the spoken word, whether the word is that of a divinity or that of a human sage or teacher.[1] This is still true to a surprising degree even in modern typographic, technocentric culture. Here also, one still has to learn from others, and not insignificantly through oral means. The premium placed today upon finding and developing "communicators" and using their "human skills" in modern industrial hiring and business training bespeaks more than merely the presence of ambitious social scientists trying to justify a field of study such as "organizational behavior". It is a sign of how much more is needed to keep a highly developed society operating beyond simple "book-learning", or, for that matter, "computer-learning".

Nevertheless, it is especially in traditional cultures around the world that the fundamental link between the spoken word and truth is all but indissoluble – not because oral transmission and communication are practically or technically superior to written forms, but because most traditional cultures see the loci (but not necessarily the origins) of both truth and authority primarily in persons and their utterances, not in documents and records. In such contexts, the teacher who knows the sacred text by heart and has devoted his or her life to studying and explicating it is the one and only reliable guarantor of the sacred truth. The power of the holy word is realized only through the human word of the seer, prophet, or spiritual master, not through a manuscript, even where the latter is also important. However exalted its status in a particular tradition, the written text alone is typically worthless, or at least worth little, without a human teacher to transmit both it and the traditions of learning and interpretation associated with it.

To be reckoned as scripture, whether in its written or oral form, any text must be perceived in some sense as a prime locus of verbal contact with transcendent truth, or ultimate reality. In theocentric traditions, scripture is preeminently "the place where God speaks to men,"[2] and the historical tendency for this speech to be conceived of as a unitary whole, as a single text or "book", is especially strong in these contexts. On the other hand, in nontheistic or semitheistic traditions, scripture tends to be more readily conceived of as the cumulative record of the teachings of sages or holy persons, however unitary the truth of these teachings is ultimately perceived to be. It is in scripture that the primordial wisdom heard and taught by generations of prophets or spiritual teachers is preserved, and in the ongoing tradition of oral teaching, be it of the Buddha-word (*buddhavacana*) or of the Vedic *mantra*s, scripture comes alive only as the sacred word of truth spoken, and *only* spoken, by teacher to pupil. Here especially the role of scripture as oral word takes on central significance within the larger tradition.

Nowhere has this significance been more categorical, more dominant, than in India. The ancient Vedic tradition represents the paradigmatic instance of scripture as spoken, recited word. Moreover, in the subsequent Hindu tradition, for all of its massive internal diversity of sects and schools, the oral word has remained the only fully acceptable and authoritative form for sacred texts for over two, possibly over two and one-half, millennia *after* the implementation of writing.[3] In the Indian context, it is not the inability to write that has resulted in the supremacy of the oral form of religious texts, but the conscious choice of oral transmission as the only appropriate vehicle for holy utterance. Once developed, the use of writing was appropriate for the affairs of merchants, court officials, and the like, but not for the weightier matters of religious and philosophical truth. For the Hindus, "writing is a secondary function and has no standing reference in the religious tradition whose hermeneutical task lies rather in reconstructing the relationship between text and speaking."[4] Even if the highly developed Indian semantic studies of grammar and phonetics did make use of writing as early as the mid-first millennium B.C., they were still fundamentally oral sciences that grew up principally as means of accurately preserving the Vedic hymns, India's oldest and most authoritative scriptures, and employing them in ritual.[5]

The fundamentally oral nature of Hindu sacred texts, from the Veda to popular devotional compositions, has been noted and commented on by most students of the Hindu tradition, among them scholars of the stature of Georg Bühler, Moriz Winternitz, Louis Renou, J. A. B. van Buitenen, and Jan Gonda.[6] More significant for our interests, however, are the particularly thoughtful and perceptive discussions of the basic orality of Indian texts by J. F. Staal, Walther Eidlitz, and most recently Thomas Coburn.[7] These treatments of Hindu sacred books offer clear evidence that the pattern in India has been not merely one of prominent oral use of written texts, but one of almost exclusively oral use and transmission in preference to dealing with written texts at all – not only for the Vedic texts, but for all religious texts. Nor is the primacy of orality limited to Hindu traditions. The oral character of the scriptural roots of Buddhist tradition is clearly evident in the well-known formula that introduces a teaching of the Buddha in a Buddhist text: "Thus have I heard" (Pali: *evaṃ me sutam*).

The recitative, oral character of Hindu scripture can be seen not only in the specialized preservation, teaching, and transmission of religious texts, but also in every aspect and at every level of life. Recitation of sacred texts forms the indispensable core of Hindu ritual life. Whether in private devotion or temple ritual, acts of worship consist of or require at least some recitation of scriptural texts or scriptural phrases. This is evident to anyone who has spent any length of time in a Hindu environment, and modern Hindi linguistic usage corroborates it in interesting ways. For example, whereas the basic Sanskrit word for worship or devotion, *pūjā,* can serve also in Hindi to refer to personal worship, the more common term in popular use is the compound *pūjā-pāṭha.* *Pāṭha* means "recitation, recital, study (especially of sacred texts)", and, as one student of modern Hindu practice puts it, "its presence in the compound reflects the importance, for Hindus, of the oral/aural dimension of ritual, and the notion that it should ideally include recitation of the sacred word." In similar fashion, one telling Hindi term that indicates that a text has been "memorized" is *kaṇṭhastha,* which means literally "situated in the throat". Knowing a text means also to "place it in the heart" (Hindi: *hṛdaya meṃ dhāraṇa karnā*), much as in our English idiom; but such "by heart" (or "by throat") knowledge means especially having it ready to the tongue.[8]

Veda and Vedic Recitation

The prototypical sacred texts of the Hindus are called *Veda*, "what is known", or "knowledge", in the absolute sense of true knowledge or eternal wisdom that is itself transcendent (*apauruṣeya,* "not of personal origin").[9] The singular form of the word, *vedaḥ,* and its plural, *vedāḥ,* were given concreteness even as early as the first half of the first millenium B.C. in the later Vedic texts themselves (e.g., *Atharva Veda* 4.35.6),[10] where either could refer collectively to the texts of the Ṛg, Yajur, and Sāma collections (*saṁhitā*s). These collections were not, however, written but oral texts, and *veda* never lost its fundamental meaning of the knowledge of eternal reality originally perceived by the ancient seers (*ṛṣi*s, or *draṣṭṛ*s) and articulated in sound (*śabda*) or speech (*vāc*) through every generation.

The *ṛṣi*s' revelatory experience, their apprehension of ultimate truth, is described variously as "seeing" or "hearing" – metaphorical expressions that together convey, as Coburn aptly expresses it, "the holistic and supremely compelling nature" of the indescribable revelatory experience.[11] What the *ṛṣi*s "saw" and "heard", what "shone" and "sounded" forth, was not verbal text, but eternal truth, and the abiding and fundamental form that they gave to Vedic wisdom was the spoken word. Through their inspired utterances, which are the substance of *veda,* the human listener could (and can) make contact with transcendence and ultimacy.

This view is corroborated in the earlier and later Vedic literature, where the power of speech or the spoken word is clearly associated with ultimacy and transcendence. Viśvakarman, the "All-Maker", or creator of all, is called *Vācaspati,* "Lord of Speech", in Ṛg Veda 10.81.7.[12] *Vāc,* "speech", "utterance", is ascribed creative powers in the Ṛg Veda, and also personified as a goddess, albeit with minimal anthropomorphic qualities.[13] In Ṛg Veda 1.164, Vāc appears clearly as the creative principle and absolute force in the universe; she is described in Ṛg Veda 1.164.6 as "the One" (*ékam*) and in 1.164.46 as "the One Real" (*ékam sát*).[14] In Ṛg Veda 10.125, Vāc is similarly depicted as possessing or embodying creative power. The human priest/sacrificer who has gained knowledge of Vāc has attained the highest knowledge: Vāc loves him and makes him "powerful, a true knower of the mystical power, a seer, a successful sacrificer" (10.125.5).[15] Ṛg Veda 10.71 deals with the origin of *vāc* as speech or language and depicts it as a mighty, even elemental reality, but does not clearly personify or anthropomorphize it as a goddess.[16] In the later Brāhmaṇic literature, the goddess Vāc's cosmogonic aspect is further stressed, as is her relationship to Soma and her sanctity as the sacred utterance especially associated with the Vedic sacrifice.[17] By the time of the later Vedic literature, Vāc can even be called "the mother of the Vedas" (*Taittirīya Brāhmaṇa* 2.8.8.5).[18]

Speech or utterance is also identified with the supreme power or transcendent reality in many later Vedic texts. Vāc is equated with Brahman in this sense in *Śatapatha Brāhmaṇa* 2.1.4.10 and in *Bṛhadāranyaka Upaniṣad* 4.1.2.[19] The *Aitareya Āraṇyaka* (1.1.1) links the two in the symbolism of the opening formulas of the Māhāvrata rite and, in 1.3.8, explains the words of Ṛg Veda 10.114.8, "As far as *brahman* extends so far does Vāc" (*yāvadbrahma viṣṭhitaṃ tāvatī vāk*), as follows: "wherever there is *brahman,* there is Vāc, wherever Vāc, there is *brahman,* is what is meant."[20] *Brahman* itself apparently meant originally, in the Ṛg Veda, the "formulation" of the sacred utterance of truth, or magical word of power, by the inspired poet who, as one capable of such formulation, was known as a *brāhmaṇa.* Later, in the texts of the Brāhmaṇas and Upaniṣads, *brahman* came to refer to the ritual word of power and even the very ground of truth, or ultimate reality, itself (and *brāhmaṇa* to both the text that bore the Vedic formulation of truth and the priest who preserved the textual word).[21]

The special association of speech and sound with eternal reality or truth is reflected in other usages that became standard in many sectors of classical and later Hindu culture. Noteworthy here is the use of *śabda* (lit.: "sound") by the classical grammarians after Patañjali (d. ca. 150 C.E.) and by the thinkers of the Mīmāṁsā school to designate the eternal Word or Speech that underlies or is embodied in all language and discourse. Also significant is the further development of the notion of the eternal meaning or essence of word or speech (*śabda*), known as *sphoṭa,* which was also identified with the Absolute by the grammarians. These latter thinkers, foremost among them Bhartṛhari (d. 651 C.E.), saw the true nature of ultimate reality, or Brahman, as the eternal Word and expressed this notion with terms like *śabda-brahman,* "sound-Brahman", or *parā vāk,* the "supreme Word", the self-revelation of which is the Veda.[22] The idea of the eternal quality of sound or speech was also taken up and elaborated on extensively by theoreticians of Vedānta, Sāṁkhya-yoga, and Kashmiri Śaivism.[23]

All such speculative theories reflect the immense significance accorded the holy words of the Vedic texts in ancient, classical, and later Indian tradition. Nevertheless, still more indicative of the oral/aural orientation in Hindus' understanding of revealed truth and its textual expression is their standard and generally accepted categorization of all Vedic texts as *śruti,* "what is heard". *Śruti* as a concept emphasizes both the auditory character of Vedic truth and its transcendent, revealed nature. By contrast with later religious texts, which are often classified as *smṛti,* "what is remembered" (i.e., "tradition"), *śruti* is that which was "seen" and "heard" by those in closest touch with ultimate reality, or Brahman – the inspired Vedic seers.

For these reasons, it will come as no surprise that the Veda has been traditionally transmitted only as spoken word. It is the oral scripture par excellence. The manifold Vedic texts that have come down to the present in apparently highly accurate transmission, from perhaps as early as the end of the second millennium B.C. or even earlier, have been viewed as too holy to be committed to writing at all, save in relatively recent times.[24] Even the oldest Vedic manuscripts are of less use in establishing the most accurate text than the professional Vedic recitative tradition.[25] The manuscript text is, after all, literally a copy of oral recitation, and thus prone to all the errors of the copyist. In a real sense, it was only through the work of nineteenth-century European scholarship – specifically Max Müller's six-volume edition of the Ṛg Veda (1849–74), that this ancient text became conceptually or tangibly a "book" in any usual sense of the word in modern times (and Müller himself found that the only reliable tradition of text transmission was the oral one of the Vedic specialists).[26]

For centuries the Veda was meticulously and faithfully transmitted only as a sounded text by male Brahman reciters. Still today, although much diminished, the traditional recitative practice (*svādhyāya*) has been kept alive, especially in south India. Particular Brahman caste groups still specialize in the preservation and chanting of one or another of the Vedic *saṁhitā*s, and continue to learn and to transmit their texts verbatim through the most rigorous and intricate mnemonic techniques imaginable.[27] Specifically, the same text is normally memorized in its entirety in up to eleven different modes of recitation (*pāṭha*s) that require complex grammatical and recitative manipulation of the base text. The first three of these modes retain the normal word order of the text: the first (*saṁhitā-pāṭha*) being a full, connected reading of the words with all proper grammatical elisions (*a-b-c-d-e*, etc.); the second (*pada-pāṭha*) being a reading of the text with each word as an isolated unit, without elision between words (*a, b, c, d, e*, etc.); and the third (*krama-pāṭha*) involving repetition of the second of each pair of words (on the pattern *ab, bc, cd, de*, etc.). The remaining eight modes, or *vikṛti*s (lit., "alterations"), involve manipulation (through some kind of inversion, or *viloma*) of the basic word order: The *jaṭā-pāṭha*, for example, which is held to be the first and oldest of the *vikṛti*s, reverses the order and repeats each pair of words in the text three times (on the pattern *ab, ba, ab; bc, cb, bc;* etc.). Even more complex is the *vikṛti* known as *ghana-pāṭha: ab, ba, abc, cba, abc; bc, cb, bcd, dcb, bcd;* and so on. In these ways, together with strict traditions of accentuation and melodic rendering, the base text is mastered literally backward and forward in fully acoustic fashion as a hedge against faulty transmission of any word or syllable.[28]

It is therefore no exaggeration to say that a Vedic text is explicitly *not* a written text, but an oral one. This often-neglected fact is dramatically underscored by the answer that an eighteenth-century Indian pundit is said to have given a European Christian who inquired about "the Vedic books": "*Veda* is that which pertains to religion; books are not *veda*."[29] Veda is not a text received from a god and written down only in order that its divine words not be lost or altered: It is the verbalization of truth immemorial and unchangeable, and the subsequent memorization and oral transmission of it by teacher to pupil, from generation to generation, represent the effort to conserve, convey, and keep alive this truth in its exact original vocal form with all its pristine purity and power. Nowhere has this better or more eloquently articulated than in the recent formulation of J. L. Mehta, who is not only a philosopher steeped in the traditions of the Western academy, but also a Brahman:

> . . . the Ṛgveda is a text, consisting of "formulations" painstakingly composed by a number of seer-poets at different times and artfully put together to form a rounded whole. It is a sacred text, revealed in the sense that these "formulations" are a gift of the gods (*devattam brahma*) to the Rishis who "saw" them, and therefore regarded as not man-made, with its source in the "highest region" of transcendent truth and speech. Yet it is not a Book or Scripture; like all "knowledge", its paradigmatic mode of being is to exist in the minds of men (where *esse* and *legere* are at one) and to be recited and chanted by them. The textuality of this text, hence, cannot be understood in terms or categories proper to "the religions of the Book" but must rather be treated as *sui generis*.[30]

This transmission, and the elaborate cultus that it accompanied and sustained, have been, as I have indicated, the specialist responsibilities and prerogatives of Brahman males over many centuries. Until more modern times, "learning" in the Hindu context meant only Vedic learning (*vedavidyā*): "a man's education was not complete until he acquired a thorough knowledge of the Vedas."[31] This has always, even today, meant learning prodigious amounts of the sacred texts by heart. Sanskrit terminology reflects this primacy of oral memorization clearly: The word for study, and study of the Veda specifically, is *svādhyāya,* "going over by oneself", or memorizing through vocal repetition. Another term used similarly for study is *abhyāsa,* "tossing over", or repeating aloud a text to be learned.

Vedic recitation is also the essential element of daily worship for the Brahman. As the *Laws of Manu* make clear, a male Brahman is obligated to recite from the Veda, at least the Gāyatrī (or Sāvitrī) verse of Ṛg Veda 3.62.10, preceded by the holy syllable *om,* every day, morning and evening.[32] On the other hand, neither a woman nor any man who is not "twice-born" – that is, one who not by class (*varṇa*) either a *brāhmaṇa, kṣatriya,* or *vaiśya* – is even supposed to hear the sacred Vedic word recited, let alone study it.[33] (This latter abhorrence of profaning the sacred word by having it fall on unclean or unworthy ears is deeply ingrained and persists even today in many instances.)[34]

We should not underestimate the degree of sacrality of the Vedic word and its oral traditions of transmission. Through most of Indian history there has been a virtual taboo against writing down anything considered to be Veda. This is graphically seen in an anecdote related by Danish missionaries in the year 1737. They report that a south Indian Brahman scholar was willing to write down for them whole passages from non-Vedic, *śāstra* texts that he knew, but refused to write down any of the text of the "Yajur Veda" that he knew. He did agree to give them orally its "main contents", but as he recited for them, he would only write particular words from the recited text as the need arose to explain questions of orthography. Even then, he would "draw" the words with his finger on the table, or sometimes write them on a piece of paper (palm leaf), which he destroyed immediately afterward.[35] This kind of attitude, which has strong magical elements, goes back a long way in India. The *Aitareya Āraṇyaka,* a late Vedic text, speaks explicitly of writing as a ritually polluting activity , after which the student must purify himself before learning (through recitation of) the Vedic texts: "He [the *śiṣya*] should not learn when he has eaten flesh, or seen blood, or a dead body, or done what is unlawful, . . . or had intercourse, or written, or obliterated writing."[36]

Such a view of scriptural authority seems to us "strange", as Moriz Winternitz puts it, because we cannot grasp "that in India, from most ancient times down to the present day, the spoken word and not writing was authoritative for all literary and scholarly activity." In Max Müller's words, "manuscripts were never considered in India as of very high authority; they were always over-ruled by the oral traditions of certain schools."[37] Perhaps the most vivid expression of these scholarly and religious attitudes to the written as opposed to the oral, memorized word comes, however, from a traditional Sanskrit proverb repeated by countless generations of Hindu pandits to their students:

> As for the knowledge that is in books, it is like money placed in another's hand: When the time has come to use it, there is no knowledge, there is no money.[38]

A corollary of all of the aforementioned aspects of transmission and use of the Veda is that the teacher, and preeminently the teacher of the Veda, enjoys immensely high status in Hindu culture. The *Laws of Manu* can even say: "Of him who gives natural birth and him who gives the Veda, the giver of the Veda is the more venerable father."[39] Such a teacher is known as *ācārya* or *guru.* Both the liturgical texts of the four Vedic *saṁhitā*s ("collections") and their appendages, and the later philosophical Vedic texts (especially the Upaniṣads), have been passed from teacher (*guru*) to pupil (*śiṣya*) down the centuries in an unbroken oral transmission known as *saṃpradāya,* "handing down", or *guruparaṃparā,* the "succession of teachers (*guru*s)" stretching from the first great seers to the present day. This has established the *guru–śiṣya* relationship as the only model for true learning in India.

Written texts have been used, certainly, but a text without a teacher to teach it directly and orally to a pupil is only so many useless leaves or pages. This is in many ways the dimension of textuality in the Indian context that the modern Westerner finds hardest to grasp: the indissoluble link between the authoritative, oral transmission from a qualified teacher and the authoritativeness of one's own "possession", or appropriation and understanding, of a sacred text:

> From the earliest times, Indians have thought of the learned man, not as one who has read much, but as one who has been profoundly taught. It is much rather from a master than from any book that wisdom can be learned.[40]

Here, as in other traditions of textual learning around the world, the written or printed text, however graphically accurate, is, by itself, only an empty cipher, never a valid proof text. Knowledge or truth, especially salvific knowledge or truth, is tied to the living words of authentic persons, not authentic documents. Further, these living words can be valid only on the lips of one who has been given the authority from a valid teacher to use them.[41]

Non-Vedic Texts and Recitation

These attitudes toward the transmission of sacred texts have extended well beyond the Veda proper. While the *śruti* texts have retained their authority as holy sources for Brahmanic ritual, philosophical speculation, and recitative mantras, the functional scriptures of the masses in India have been other texts usually categorized as *smṛti* rather than *śruti*.[42] One could even argue that the popularity of such texts has relegated the Vedic texts, especially the liturgical books, almost to the status of a *scriptura abscondita* in Hindu life.[43] This is not, however, to denigrate the foundational importance of the Vedas to the Hindu tradition. Their almost exclusively oral use and transmission have provided the model for oral treatment of popular scriptural works. These latter include the Purāṇas and Tantras, the *Rāmāyaṇa,* the *Gītagovinda,* the Bhagavadgītā, and many other texts, of which, as van Buitenen notes, "it is widely believed or believed by particular religious groups that recitation and listening bestow a special merit."[44] Scripture of any description remains recited scripture.

This is strikingly evident in the case of the Purāṇas, whose multiform nature and rootedness in oral tradition has joined with popular reverence for and delight in their stories and lore to make them favorite texts for recitation on diverse occasions. They contain a wide spectrum of material that includes not only ancient stories and myths, but also Vedic verses and mantras. They are, in many respects, the most actively used of the scriptural texts of Hindus, and their recitation is an especially prominent part of Indian life. As Giorgio Bonazzoli notes, it is "through a public and solemn recitation that the purāṇa-s fulfill their scope."[45]

The Purāṇas themselves remind their listeners of the blessings of reciting their words, as, for example, the claim of the Nārada-Purāṇa (1.6.54): "Hari is present wherever purāṇas are recited."[46] It is, however, clear from the Purāṇas' own statements that their recitation could be from the written page of a book, and that, at least from the twelfth century onward, written transmission of their texts was common, in contradistinction to the Vedas. This written transmission never proceeded, however, without the necessary oral memorization and recitation that is the basis of text reading and study in India. The Purāṇas stand squarely within the tradition of religious texts going back to the Vedas: They "are not private books, but rather 'liturgical' texts, for the way of reading, reciting, listening to, singing, copying them etc. is regulated by the purāṇic texts themselves . . . not left to private initiative." There is a whole literature on the rules for reciting the Purāṇas. These pertain not only to the recitation itself, but also to matters such as the appropriate days and places for recitation and the ritual to be followed. Bonazzoli points out that these rules, or *vidhi*s, for recitation are very old and indicate that "from a certain moment in the purāṇic evolution – if not since the beginning – the purāṇa-s were meant to be recited in religious celebrations following fixed rules."[47]

Just as their forerunners, the Vedas, influenced the oral treatment of all later Indian texts, the recitation of the Purāṇas has served also as a model for the treatment of other popular Hindu texts. One among several possible examples of such a widely revered and recited text is the *Rāmacaritamānasa,* a Hindi retelling of the *Rāmāyaṇa* epic by the great poet Tulsīdās (d. 1623 C.E.). The important place of this much beloved text among north Indian Hindus of all classes has recently been studied, with special reference to Vārāṇasī (Banāras), by Philip Lutgendorf. The rich detail of this study makes the use of this text an especially valuable example of the kind of attitudes toward and treatment of popular "scriptures" to which I am referring.[48]

The increasing popularity of the *Rāmacaritamānasa* over the past two centuries has made it one of the most important religious texts of large segments of north Indian society. The popularity of the epic has given it a mediating or synthesizing role between Vaiṣṇava and Śaiva/Śākta groups. Its recitation has become both a staple religious exercise and a major form of entertainment across the whole spectrum of Hindu life, inasmuch as it tends to be, as Lutgendorf puts it, "the text of choice for filling any vacuum in popular religious practice."[49] The range of types of recitation session and recitative or even singing style in which the *Mānasa* is performed is truly vast. Although a "complete recitation" (*pārāyaṇa-pāṭha*) takes many hours, this is typically what is aspired to. It does not matter whether the epic is performed in one twenty-four-hour "unbroken recitation" (*akhaṇḍa-pāṭha*) by as many as one hundred and eight Brahman reciters at a special festival, a few stanzas a day for seven months by Brahman schoolboys in a classroom, or only a stanza a day together with commentarial study by a single student in the privacy of his home. The efficacy and blessing of the performance is assiduously sought by diverse kinds of people in diverse contexts.

Interestingly, the great popularity of the *Mānasa* recitation seems to be largely a product of the past two centuries and to have been greatly stimulated by the printing of text editions of the whole from as early as 1810 (in Calcutta). Availability of printed texts and increasing numbers of the literate élite stimulated interest in and knowledge of the text that widened the audience for its recitation – which was ever the fundamental mode in which the epic has been communicated and used. One edition alone from the Gita Press in Gorakhpur had gone through seventy-two printings by 1983, for a total of 5,695,000 copies, and in 1983 alone, two printings, each of 100,000, were made. These are staggering numbers in a country of extremely high illiteracy rates.[50]

Professional expounders of the text have to have the entire text of the *Rāmacaritamānasa* by heart, and not only as a matter of pride. Since any recitation of the text is a ritual event, it is important that the recitation be performed correctly. Similarly, ritual requirements such as ablution, special dress, and preliminary meditation and mantra recitation must be carried out for formal recitations. Lutgendorf points out that in this and other ways – notably the designation of major festival recitations of the *Mānasa* as *mahāyajña*s, or "great sacrifices", we can see the model of the Veda's recitation in Brahmanic ritual being appropriated for the popular epic much as it has been for the Purāṇas. On the other hand, the popularity of the *Mānasa* among rural and urban singing groups as the text of choice for entertainment indicates its integration, still in a decidedly oral form, into less ritually oriented aspects of everyday life.[51]

It would be possible to go on at length about the oral function and character of diverse scriptural texts in India: mantra recitation, public performances of the praise-compositions known as *māhātmyas* (e.g., the *Devī Māhātmya* or *Śrī Durga Saptaśatī)*[52] the singing of Bhakti hymns, festival recitations of the *Rāmāyaṇa* or *Bhāgavata Purāṇa*.[53] – the list could be long. The point, however, remains the same: For Hindus, scripture is, if not exclusively, then overwhelmingly, spoken word *rather than* holy writ. The diverse and numerous sacred texts of Indian history have all been written texts only in the second instance if at all; their authoritative as well as their functional form has always been that of the audibly recited word.[54]

Hindu insistence upon the sounded, recited holy text as the proper and sacred form of scripture may be an extreme case among scriptural traditions with regard to the balance between orality and chirography (or typography) as the dominant means through which sacred texts are known and used. Nevertheless, the Hindu reverence for and sensitivity to the spoken word of scripture still cannot be regarded as an aberration in the history of religion. This can be demonstrated, I am persuaded, by a closer look at the oral and aural functions of scripture in traditional religious communities elsewhere in the world. It is to this that the remainder of this book is devoted.

PART III

"An Arabic Reciting": *Qur'ān* as Spoken Book

God has said: "Whoever is so absorbed in reciting the Qur'ān that he is distracted from praying to Me and asking [things] of Me, him I shall give the best reward [that is granted to] those who are grateful."

– *Ḥadīth* of the Prophet

He who does not recite the Qur'ān melodiously is not one of us.

– *Ḥadīth* of the Prophet

The major importance of the written text of scripture in Islam is apparent even to the casual observer in any Islamic society. The centrality of the sacred book in Islam represents, as we have seen, in many respects the culmination of the long Near Eastern tradition of the divinely revealed, authoritative written book.[1] The importance of the book of scripture in Muslim faith and practice is especially closely related to, and in significant part derived from, the emphasis on holy writ in Islam's older sibling traditions of Judaic and Christian piety. Because Islam is not just one of the three major "book religions", but in many ways even the most radical of the three in the exalted place that it assigns to its book, both ritually and theologically, it is not amiss to speak of the Qur'ān as the prototypical "book of scripture".

In Muslim piety, however, the written word of its scripture has always been secondary to a strong tradition of oral transmission and aural presence of scripture that far surpasses that of Judaic or Christian usage. In Islam, the functions of the holy book as an oral text have predominated over its functions as a written or printed one. As an English Arabist put it long ago, "from first to last the Koran is essentially a book to be heard, not read."[2] For countless millions of Muslims over more than thirteen centuries of Islamic history, “scripture”, *al-kitāb,* has been a book learned, read, and passed on by vocal repetition and memorization. The written Qur’ān may “fix” visibly (and with supreme calligraphic artistry) the authoritative text of divine word in a way unknown in the history of the Vedic texts among Hindus; but like the Veda, the authoritativeness of the qur’anic text is only realized in its fullness and perfection when it is correctly recited aloud. In other words, the book of holy writ (*kitāb*) in Islam is ultimately not a written or printed document, but a holy “reciting”, or “recitation”, which is precisely what the Arabic word *qur’ān* means.

It was the dominant oral dimension of the Qur’ān as scripture that provided the original impetus to my investigation of the oral aspects of scripture more generally. The Hindus' treatment of their scriptures could always be dismissed as an anomaly – the exception that proves the rule that “sacred book” means written or printed book as we today normally understand the term. Yet because the Qur’ān (unlike the Veda or other Hindu texts) has been the object of *both* significant graphic/visual piety and attention *and also* intense oral/aural piety and attention, it is of special interest in the context of the present study. It offers the clearest, and therefore the pivotal example in which to consider the dimension of scripture that concerns us, namely, its capacity to function simultaneously both as spoken and as written word. Since the Qur’ān is characterized above all by its unusually strong oral treatment and function, the Muslims' scriptural orientation reminds us more of that of the Hindu tradition than that of Islam's near relation, the Christian tradition. Yet no one would deny the presence in Islam of a marked dependence upon scriptural authority reminiscent of those Christian traditions, such as the Puritan “movement of the Book”,[3] that assign greatest importance to the book of scripture.

It is the abiding and intrinsic orality of the Qur’ān as scriptural book of revelation and authority to which I want to direct our attention in the following three chapters. Here we shall see a paradigm of scripture that is remarkably like that of the Bible in numerous ways, yet also remarkably like that of the Veda in many others. For that reason, it is an excellent example in which to see vividly the oral dimensions of written scripture.

CHAPTER 7

Revelation and Recitation

Truly it is a clear Recitation [*qur'ān mubīn*] in a written [fixed, prescribed?] Book [*kitāb maktūb*], which none [may] touch except the purified – a revelation [*tanzīl*] from the Lord of all beings.

– Qur'ān, S. 56.77-80[1]

Had we sent down to you a writing [*kitāb*] on parchment so that they might touch it with their hands, those who do not have faith would say, "Truly, this is nothing but obvious magic."

– Qur'ān, S. 6.7

One could hardly imagine a tradition of religious thought and practice more categorically focused upon a sacred book of divinely revealed word than that initiated by Muhammad in the second and third decades of the seventh century. Yet the undeniable "book" orientation of Islam was from the outset joined to a notion of scripture that is founded and centered upon the active, spoken word of God given in its most perfect and its final form to humankind as a "reciting", or *qur'ān*. In what follows, we shall look first at the general notion of scripture in Islam, and then specifically at the early meaning of the word *qur'ān,* in order to provide the background to an understanding of the orality of the Qur'ān as scripture, which I shall address in Chapter 8.

The Conception of Scripture in Islam

As I have indicated (Chapter 4), the history of "book religion" in the Near Eastern–Mediterranean world apparently began in ancient Mesopotamia, took decisive shape in Exilic and post-Exilic Judaic tradition, and developed dramatically in late antiquity. The last-named period proved especially momentous for the consolidation and definition of scriptural religion, first at the hands of Christians, gnostics, Jewish sectarians, and subsequently the

Manichaeans. Mani (216–77 C.E.) seems to have been the first major religious leader who set out consciously to produce either a new "religion" or a "book" of scripture.[2] In doing so, he saw himself as the latest in a series of religious prophets and seers and his books as the scriptural foundation for a new tradition of faith. It remained, however, for Islam to appear on the scene to give a fully developed and theologically coherent interpretive framework along these lines to the phenomenon of a scriptural book claiming the authority of divine revelation.

Scripture and Heilsgeschichte

The notion of successive revelations to various nations, each in the form of a book transmitted through a prophet, appears with force and clarity in the Qur'ān. However one chooses to describe the gradual fleshing-out of the idea of successive revelation in the course of the original revelations to Muhammad,[3] it forms ultimately the backbone of the entire qur'anic (and hence the Islamic) *Heilsgeschichte*. In the qur'anic view, the leitmotiv of history (and history *is* "salvation-history" here) consists in God's having sent to nation after nation a prophet (*nabī;* pl.: *anbiyā'*) or apostle (*rasūl;* pl.: *rusul*) to lead its people aright. Where a distinction is occasionally implied between prophetic and apostolic status, the apostles in particular are mentioned as each having been given a divine revelation in the form of a book of scripture (*kitāb;* pl.: *kutub*), which he is charged to proclaim to his people.[4] These revealed books include the Psalms given to David, the Torah given Moses, and the Gospel sent to Jesus, as well as the Qur'ān revealed to Muhammad. What has followed God's revelation in each case is the creation of a new community of those who respond positively to God's revelation. However, in each previous case, this new community has strayed eventually from the right path and let its scripture be partially lost or its text changed and debased over time. Thus, the Qur'ān comes as a final divine revelation, the last in the scriptural series, sent through "the seal of the prophets", Muhammad, and intended to be taken to heart and preserved henceforward as the guide for true obedience to God. It is the culmination and completion of, as well as the replacement for, all earlier revelations: "And this is a blessed scripture that we sent down to you, confirming that which came before it . . ." (S. 6.92).[5]

Scripture as a Generic Idea

The notion that the Qur'ān is not the only *kitāb* given by God to humankind – in other words, that other peoples before the coming of Muhammad (d. 11/632)[6] had been given their own *kutub,* their own revealed scriptures – is thus not a secondary development of theological reflection in Islam, but a fundamental part of the qur'anic worldview itself. This distinguishes the history of the concept of scripture in Islam rather decisively from that in either Christian or Jewish tradition (although the Christians' appropriation of Hebrew scripture as their own presents certain analogies, particularly in the accompanying idea of a cumulative history of revelation).

Whereas the generic idea of scripture developed only relatively late in Christian, Judaic, and Western secular use, it was present from the beginning in Islam as part and parcel of the history of prophecy and revelation.[7] Correspondingly, Judaic and Christian ideas about their respective scriptures tended from the outset to be more exclusive, whereas the qur'anic and subsequent Muslim concept of scripture was inclusive – at least insofar as it ultimately allowed (as, e.g., with the Avesta and Veda) the recognition of more than only the Semitic book traditions as part of the divine plan of revelation leading up to the Qur'ān. (Needless to say, none of the three great monotheistic traditions has been so inclusive as to allow for new revelations coming *after* their own.) The Qur'ān's own words (S. 2.285) indicate just how clearly Muhammad and the Qur'ān were integrated into a larger *Heilsgeschichte:* ". . . and the faithful all have faith in God, His angels, His scriptures (*kutub*), and his apostles (*rusul*). We make no distinctions among His apostles . . . ."[8] Just as there had been prophets before Muhammad (see, e.g., S. 3.144), so had there been previous scriptural revelations (as mentioned in S. 3.38). The Qur'ān is indeed the culminating scripture that takes precedence over the inherited (and faulty) versions of previous revelations, but it belongs to the same genre as these, in that it, like them, has come from God through a chosen messenger.

The word for scripture in Arabic, *kitāb* (pl.: *kutub*), is also, both in classical and in modern Arabic, the common word for any kind of writing, even a letter (in much the same way that *Schrift* in German can refer not only to religious "scripture" but also to any piece of writing – a duality of meaning that the English word "scripture" also once had but now has lost).[9] In the Qur'ān itself, the word is used with several different meanings, but most generally and most often, it designates God's revealed scripture – preeminently the Qur'ān, but also any and (in the plural) all of His scriptures, as already described. Accordingly, Jews and Christians in particular are called "scripture folk", "people of scripture", or "people of the [heavenly] scripture" (*ahl al-kitāb*). In this world, however, the Qur'ān is *the* Scripture (*al-kitāb*), the "Book of books", the sacred word par excellence.[10]

The qur'anic use of *kitāb* reflects the obvious association of this term with not only the most common meaning of the root *K-T-B*, "to write", but also the related meaning, "to decree", "to prescribe", "to make [something] incumbent" (as in God's actions with respect to His creation).[11] The close association of writing down with laying down or impressing something in a lasting, authoritative way carries over in some, if not all, of the qur'anic meanings of *kitāb*. It is seen, for example, in the use of the word to refer to a heavenly book with God in which all events and the nature of all things are written beforetime (6.59; 11.6, 35.11, etc.), as well as a book of destiny, recording a person's good and evil deeds, that will be produced on the Day of Judgment (e.g., 17.71, 39.69). Furthermore, it is also possible to see the use of *kitāb* for that which is decreed, or for the preemptive knowledge of God, as basic to the idea of a written book of revelation; for after all, scripture contains that which God has laid down for or made incumbent upon humankind.[12]

The Qur'ān's generic concept of scripture appears to be based upon the idea of an original, heavenly scripture from which the discrete earthly scriptural revelations are drawn. One could interpret several occurrences of *kitāb* as references to this *Urschrift,* or divine prototype of all scripture. Note, for example, S. 10.37:

> This Recitation [*qur'ān*] is not such as could be invented save by God. Rather it is a confirmation of what came before it and an exposition of the Scripture [*kitāb*], about which there is no doubt, from the Lord of all beings.[13]

There are two still more specific qur'anic terms that seem to be used to designate this heavenly *Urschrift: umm al-kitāb,* literally “the mother of scripture,” in the sense of “the essence or prototype of scripture,” “the source of scripture,” or “the original scripture” (S. 13.39, 43.4);[14] and *lawḥ maḥfuẓ,* the “preserved tablet” (S. 3.7). A synonym in later Muslim usage for this heavenly text is *aṣl al-kitāb,* literally “the root or source of scripture.”[15]

Muslim Scripture: Some Comparisons and Contrasts

The qur'anic and later Muslim concept of scripture as a generic phenomenon (of which the Qur'ān is the last and best, but by no means the only earthly example) is the backdrop against which the Muslims' specific understanding and treatment of the Qur'ān as *the* scripture must be seen. The image and status accorded the Qur'ān among Muslims present some familiar, but still more unfamiliar characteristics to the person accustomed only to Judaic or Christian treatment of scripture. A few comparisons between Muslim notions about the Qur'ān and other peoples' concepts of their particular scriptures – in particular, Jewish or Christian ideas about the Bible – offer one means of clarifying the major elements of Muslims' understanding of their holy text, especially for those of us who have been schooled to take the Jewish Tanakh or the Christian Bible as the normative example of scripture.

Jews and Muslims share the sense of importance attached to the specific (Hebrew or Arabic) language of God's revelation; yet despite the presence in both traditions of an aversion to translation of holy scripture into vernacular tongues, Muslims have been much more categorical than Jews about rejecting such translation. Jews have, it is true, been exceedingly tenacious about study of the Hebrew language and exceedingly devout about reverential preservation and regular reading aloud of the Hebrew Torah scrolls in the synagogue. Nevertheless, they have also adjusted to the pragmatic need for the congregation (who may know little or no Hebrew) to understand the content of the Torah reading: hence the translation of the Hebrew text into Greek in the Septuagint and the development of the post-Exilic Targums (Aramaic paraphrases of the Torah), which were to be read in the synagogue after the reading of the Hebrew text.[16] Muslims, on the other hand, have insisted with remarkable consistency that every Muslim, whatever his or her linguistic or cultural background, must maintain the purely Arabic recitation of the Qur'ān in formal worship (*ṣalāt*), even if the only Arabic he or she knows is the memorized syllables of a few short *sūrah*s necessary to *ṣalāt*. In addition, there has historically been general opposition among Muslim scholars, save in one school of legal thought, to the translation of the Qur'ān into vernaculars.[17]

Why this fastidious fervor about the Arabic text? Because it is God's direct discourse, *ipsissima vox*. He sent his revelation as a clear "Arabic recitation" (*qur'ān 'arabī*) that was transmitted verbatim through His apostle. For humans to translate it amounts to unfounded and dangerous tampering with the very speech of the Almighty. Because of the fundamental holiness of the words of the Qur'ān, the classical Arabic language has taken on a sacrality felt in often quite visceral fashion by the Muslim who knows it as the sublimely beautiful and untranslatable language of God's perfect revealed word, even if he or she speaks no Arabic. It is not insignificant that where Christian theological disputation has focused on the divine-human nature of Jesus Christ and the virgin birth as a guarantee of his divine nature, Muslim discussion has centered on *i'jāz,* the "inimitability" or "matchlessness" of the divine word of the Qur'ān as proof of its divine character, and the "protection" (*'iṣmah*) of the Prophet Muhammad from sin as the additional guarantee of the unblemished transmission of the divine word from God to humankind.[18]

This importance of scriptural language can hardly be overemphasized. If this seems foreign to those raised in different traditions, it is well to remember that most scriptural traditions, from Jewish to Hindu to Theravāda Buddhist, exhibit some form of attachment and liturgical commitment to the original language, the *Ursprache,* of their own holy texts. Even the Christian tradition, for all of its long tradition of wholesale translation of scripture into every possible language, is not without parallel elements of such attachment to one linguistic form of the Bible. Here, however, the attachment has been usually not to the Hebrew or Greek *Urtext* but to a particular translation of these that time and tradition has hallowed in one particular sector of the Church as a whole - witness the long-standing Roman Catholic defense of the Vulgate as *the* sacred version of the scriptures and of Latin as *the* sacred liturgical language,[19] or the modern Anglo-American resistance to replacing the Authorized, or "King James" Version with a new translation ("If the King James Bible was good enough for Jesus, it's good enough for me!"). It may be that the sense of the sacrality of the original language of revelation is strongest in highly oral cultures such as the Indian or Islamic, but it is certainly not limited to these.

Another, and particularly revealing, comparison between Muslim and both Jewish and Christian treatment of scripture can be found in the attention lavished upon the physical text of the scriptural word, not only in the honor shown to it ritually, but also in its embellishment and ornamentation. Whereas Christian, Judaic, and Muslim calligraphic art all reached their respective pinnacles of perfection in the preparation of magnificently calligraphed and illuminated (and, for the Christian Bible, lavishly illustrated) copies of holy scripture, only in Islam has the calligraphic scriptural word become not merely the major expression of religious art, but the dominant visible motif in the art of the entire surrounding culture. The visual, public presence of the qur’anic word in virtually every part of the Islamic world is striking, even by contrast with the most iconic and visually oriented of Christian cultures (e.g., Byzantine or Latin Christian society in the late Middle Ages). Aniconic tendencies in Judaic and Christian tradition did not lead to anything like the compensating artistic exaltation of the written word of scripture that Muslim iconoclasm stimulated in the supremely developed arts of Islamic manuscript calligraphy and monumental epigraphy, the chief object of which has ever remained the text of “the noble Qur’ān”.

Still sharper contrasts between Muslim and Judaic or Christian ideas of scripture can be drawn. The concept of scriptural canon is one example. The notion of a canon of scriptures collected over time as a part of the ongoing record of God's dealing with His people is peculiar to Jews and Christians – albeit in different ways – and distinguishes their concepts of what scripture as divine word means from that of Muslims. For Muslims, revelation was sent one final, culminating time, in the course of one prophetic career, during which and immediately afterward it was collected with scrupulous care into book form. This collected text, as God's direct speech, has been explicitly recognized as scripture since the actual period of Muhammad's prophetic career during which it “came down.” Thus Muslims know nothing of a process of gradual communal canonization analogous to that of Judaic or Christian history.[20]

In some ways the theory of the authority of the word of the Buddha behind the various Buddhist canons of *sūtra*s comes closer than either Jewish or Christian theories of canon to the Muslim concept of an authoritative scriptural text fixed in and shortly after the founder's lifetime, though here too there is a vast distinction. Buddhist understandings of *sūtra* have emphasized their character as the “word of the Buddha” (*buddhavacana*), taught either exoterically or esoterically by Siddhartha Gautama; yet the sheer volume and variety of *sūtra* literature in all the various traditions gives it a wholly different character from the short, comparatively uniform qur’anic text with its significantly stronger historical claim to having attained roughly its present form in the Prophet's lifetime.

Another important and revealing divergence between Muslim and Christian or Muslim and Judaic ideas of scripture is in the theological place accorded holy scripture in the Islamic tradition and those of its two sibling traditions. Although all three have been characterized by the centrality of scripture in worship, piety, devotion, and faith, the Qur'ān stands more clearly alone as the transcendent focus of Muslim faith than does the Christian Bible or even the Jewish Tanakh in its tradition of faith.

On the one hand, it is true that Jews, Christians, and Muslims all hold that scripture contains the word of God. For this reason, all three sacred texts hold positions of major importance in their respective traditions. Indeed, in its most basic sense as the Law revealed at Sinai - as well as in the related sense of the Law as the totality of life for the observant Jew - the Torah plays a role in Judaic tradition that is akin in its ritual centrality and moral-theological significance to the notion of the Qur'ān as God's explicit and complete guidance for Muslim life. Similarly, attachment to the scriptural word of God has been almost as overwhelmingly important a determinant of piety in Christian, and especially Protestant, tradition as it has been in Islam.

On the other hand, for all of the similarities, the character of the Qur'ān as the verbatim speech of God given once and for all through a single chosen prophet sets it apart from the Bible in either of the other two traditions. To a degree unmatched in even the most book-bound Judaic or Christian piety, Muslim religious thought and practice has been relentlessly "scriptural" in its derivation and focus. For Jews, the prime medium of divine–human encounter is the Torah (literally "law", "teaching") - but *Torah* understood not simply as scriptural text but as divine will, cosmic order, and human responsibility, to which the scriptural Torah is the guide. For Christians the encounter comes first and foremost through the person and life of Christ (which are accessible, but not exclusively so, in scripture). In Islam, on the other hand, it is in the concrete text, the very words of the Qur'ān, that Muslims most directly experience God. Scripture for Muslims is itself the divine presence as well as the mediator of divine will and divine grace. In the Qur'ān, God speaks with his own voice, not through inspired human writers. Thus it is not an exaggeration to compare Qur'ān recitation with the Christian Eucharist,[21] nor to say that in chanting the words of the Qur'ān, one "chants not words about God, but of Him, and indeed, as those words are His essence, chants God himself."[22]

This immediacy of divine speech in the words of the Qur'ān leads to a last point of comparison regarding the primary medium of scriptural communication. Here we come to the question with which we are principally concerned in the present study: how sacred, divine word has been transmitted, preserved, and used in the form of scripture. In the Muslim instance, this is remarkably clear and unequivocal: The Qur'ān has functioned primarily as a vocally transmitted text. It has, for example, been itself the prayerbook and liturgical book of Islam - a function that neither the Jewish nor the Christian Bible, with the exception of the Psalter, has had.[23] Thus, although the Qur'ān does invite comparison in the first instance with the scripturality of Jewish, Christian, and other religious communities that give central importance to holy writ, it is the spoken, not the inscribed Qur'ān that has always taken precedence in the Islamic context. In this regard it suggests, as I have previously noted, distinct analogies to Hindu scriptures.

In Chapter 8, we shall look specifically at the major oral roles of the Qur'ān in Muslim piety and practice. First, however, we need to reevaluate the meaning of the word *qur'ān* in its original context, for it is there that the clear roots of the role and place of the Qur'ān in Muslim life can be found.

The Original Muslim Understanding of "Qur'ān"

The very name "al-Qur'ān" underscores the fact that the qur'anic revelations were originally wholly oral texts intended to be rehearsed and recited, first by Muhammad, then by the faithful; they were not sent as "a writing on parchment" (S. 6.7). The word *qur'ān* is a verbal noun derived from the Arabic root *Q-R-'*, the basic sense of which is "to recite, read aloud."[24] Accordingly, "al-Qur'ān" is most accurately translated as "the Reciting" or "the Recitation," and it is as a recited text that the Qur'ān, even after its codification as a single, composite book of revelations, has played its central role in Muslim piety and practice.

Muslims as well as orientalists customarily think of and use the Arabic word *qur'ān* primarily as a proper noun with the definite article: "al-Qur'ān," *the* Qur'ān.[25] With this they refer to the collected and written corpus of Muhammad's revelations from God, most specifically the written text that was codified during the reign of the third caliph, 'Uthmān (23–35/644–56) and orthographically improved about four decades later at the behest of al-Ḥajjāj, then-governor of Iraq. This corpus is widely held to have been assembled and arranged in essentially its present form by a few of the most respected original "transmitters of the recitation" (*ḥamalat al-qur'ān*), or "transmitters of the revelation" (*ḥamalat al-waḥy*) who were still alive at this time.[26] Some of these had been Muhammad's scribes during his lifetime and merited the title, "scribes of the revelation" (*kuttāb al-waḥy*); all were presumably "reciters" (*qurrā'*; pl. of *qāri'*), persons who knew greater or lesser portions of the revelations by heart.[27]

As a codified whole, the revelations have been known and thought of since these earliest days of Islam both as "al-Qur'ān" and simply as "the Book" or "the Scripture" (*al-kitāb*). This idea of a single scriptural codex is expressed also in traditional usage by referring to the Qur'ān as "that which is between the two boards."[28] It has been understood theologically by Muslims over the centuries as "the speech of God" (*kalām Allāh*) preserved from all eternity in God's heavenly scripture (*al-kitāb, umm al-kitāb, al-lawḥ al-maḥfūẓ*) and written down for human use in earthly exemplars or codices (*maṣāḥif;* sing.: *muṣḥaf*).

It is obvious that "al-Qur'ān" in the later, fixed meaning of God's word as written down in the *maṣāḥif* is necessarily a post-'Uthmānic, or at the very least a post-Muhammadan, usage. Until the codification of what has since served as the *textus receptus* – or at least until active revelation ceased with Muhammad's death – there could have been no use of "al-Qur'ān" to refer to the complete body of "collected revelations in written form."[29] This is not to deny that even in the Qur'ān there may be hints of a developing notion of the collective revelation in the use of the words *qur'ān* and *kitāb,* but rather to emphasize the fallacy involved in "reading back" the later, concretized meaning of these terms into all of their qur'anic or other traditional-text occurrences.

Nor is this to say that when the Qur'ān was revealed, it was necessarily limited to oral transmission and human memories simply because of lack of knowledge of writing – as, for example, was the case, we may presume, with the Veda among the original Indo-Aryans. We have clear epigraphic evidence of Arabic writing, especially Christian inscriptions, well before the time of Muhammad, and there are many terms in the Qur'ān that bespeak the presence of books and writing in the Arabian milieu in the early seventh century.[30] Traditional Islamic accounts tell how not only the qur'anic revelations but also missives to particular tribes or towns were written down at the Prophet's behest by various scribes (although how much trust can be placed in the historicity of these latter reports is open to question).[31] Technically, the scripture given Muhammad presumably *could* have been passed on from the outset primarily as a holy written text, but it was not, or at least only alongside and as an adjunct to its memorization and recitation. It is patent in the Qur'ān and borne out in the traditional sources that the word of God was specifically intended to live on the lips of the faithful. While the revelations were considered to be a part of God's "Arabic *kitāb*", this in no way conflicted with or detracted from their fundamental character as divine words meant to be learned by heart, chanted aloud, and orally transmitted.[32]

That this was the case is confirmed not merely by traditional stories or the compelling euphony of qur'anic language, but also by the many variant readings to the standard written text of the Qur'ān that have been preserved.[33] These variants are commonly synonymous words or differently voweled readings of the consonantal base text that obviously represent divergent oral rather than written traditions.[34] Fundamentally, the Qur'ān was what its name proclaimed it to be: the Recitation given by God for Muhammad, and after him, all of His worshipers, to recite (as S. 96.1ff. suggests), above all in worship of Him. Such chanting or reciting served as a "reminder" (*dhikr*) and a "criterion" (*furqān*) for human beings who are by nature "forgetful"; it proclaimed God's word and kept this word constantly before its intended hearers. In an earlier, detailed article on the earliest meaning of the word *qur'ān,* I have documented this original oral character of Muslim scripture from the Qur'ān and the Hadīth literature.[35] I want now to reiterate and add to some of the salient points of that study in order to sketch in broad strokes the contextual and textual evidence of this original oral character.

Contextual Evidence for the Original Meaning of "Qur'ān"

The very word *qur'ān* is not attested in any Arabic sources before the Qur'ān itself. This supports the strong linguistic probability that the use of this word for the new revelations to Muhammad would only have been intelligible to the Arabs at that time if analogous words were prominent in contemporary Christian or Jewish use. Before and after Muhammad's time, the Syriac cognate term *qeryānā,* "lection", "reading", was used by Syriac-speaking Christians (and presumably as a borrowing by Arabic-speaking Christians) both for the oral, liturgical reading from holy writ (=*lectio, anagnōsis*) and for the passage of scripture that is read aloud (=*lectio, periochē, anagnōsma,* etc.).[36] John Bowman in particular has rightly stressed the strong parallels in liturgical terminology and usage between eastern Christian liturgical use of a lectionary, or *ktābā d'qeryānā,* and what we can reconstruct of liturgical use of the qur'anic revelations from the Qur'ān itself.[37] Also of likely relevance is the additional parallel in both Muslim use of *qur'ān* and Syriac use of *qeryānā* to Rabbinic and later Jewish use of the Hebrew cognates *qerī'ā* and *miqrā'* as terms denoting the act of scripture reading and the passage read aloud, respectively.[38] *Miqrā'* is used also as a Talmudic term for the whole Bible, one that "serves to underline both the vocal manner of study and the central role that the public reading of the Scriptures played in the liturgy of the Jews."[39]

Such parallels in Christian and Jewish usage do not have to be taken as evidence of direct or conscious "influence on Muhammad" – a formulation that Muslims rightly find offensive, since it has been used to polemicize against the divine origin of the Qur'ān. What reasonable Muslims and non-Muslims should be able to agree on is that because the Qur'ān was revealed in Arabic (as a "clear" Arabic scripture, if you will), it could only have been proclaimed in terms that made sense in the linguistic and conceptual framework of the day and region. Otherwise, it would not have been intelligible to the Arabs. The Arabic of the day cannot have been devoid of echoes or direct use of Syriac and Hebrew terms nor of major ideas shared by Arab Christians and Jews, since these groups were, as the Qur'ān and other sources show, conspicuous parts of the Arabian scene. The linguistic parallels I have cited make it highly likely that *qur'ān* was understood by the Arabs to refer to texts intended for vocal proclamation, reading, and recitation such as Jews and Christians already practiced in the seventh-century Arabian milieu just as elsewhere.[40] Furthermore, not only were these two scriptural traditions very much in evidence in Arabia, but so also was that of the Zoroastrians, in which oral recitation of scripture figured even more prominently.[41] For all of these traditions, a "book" used in liturgy and devotions would not have been the silently read document that we today understand a "book" to be; rather, it would have been a sacred, divine word that was meant to be recited or read viva voce and listened to with reverence.

"Qur'ān" in the Qur'ān

The internal evidence of the qur'anic text itself supports the fundamentally oral/aural nature of the understanding of scripture among the first Muslims. That the qur'anic revelations were meant to be proclaimed aloud is immediately obvious in the recurring imperative "Qul!" ("Say!"), which introduces well over three hundred different passages of the text. Note, for example, the early *sūrah* known as "Unity" or "Purity": "Say, He is God, One! God is the Everlasting. He neither begets [offspring], nor is He begotten. To Him there is no equal, not one!" (S. 112). Here presumably Muhammad is addressed by the singular imperative, but so too is every person. Thus have Muslims of every generation heard in this ringing call to declare God's singularity and omnipotence one of the most important commands addressed to them in scripture – so much so that in Muslim worship and devotion only the opening *sūrah* is equally or more often recited than this succinct testimony of Muslim faith.[42]

Another indication of the originally oral form and intended oral use of the revelations is to be found in the frequent occurrence in the Qur'ān (sixty-three times) of the verb *talā,* "to recite, follow", with similar reference to reading the text aloud. This root occurs, for example, in many passages that link God's apostle to recitation of His word; for instance, in S. 62.2:

> [God] is He who has sent among the gentiles [lit.: "the unlettered"] an apostle from their own ranks to recite [*yatlū*] to them His wonders [or "verses", "signs"], to purify them, and to teach them scripture [*al-kitāb*] and wisdom, while before this they were in clear error.[43]

The verbal noun of *talā, tilāwah,* became a general term in Islamic usage (alongside *qirā'ah*) for recitation or chanting of the Qur'ān, and the qur'anic basis for this is clear even from the single occurrence of this form, in S. 2.121: "Those to whom We [God] have given the scripture [*kitāb*] and who recite it truly [*yatlūnahu ḥaqq*^{a} *tilāwat*^{i}*hi*][44] – those are they who have faith in it." The burden of such passages is clear: Scripture and recitation go together. They are, one may even say, inextricable.

The most impressive qur'anic evidence, however, for the oral character of the scripture given Muhammad comes from the many qur'anic passages in which the word *qur'ān* and the other forms of its root verb *qara'a* can best be understood in context if their verbal force is retained. Unfortunately, later, especially modern, students and interpreters of the Qur'ān have taken so to heart the reified, objectified sense of Qur'ān as both a physical volume of text and the proper name of the text that they have lost its original meaning as simply "reciting" (*qur'ān*). That this verbal force was still present in qur'anic usage can be demonstrated in many of its more than eighty occurrences.[45] It is most clearly manifest in the two indisputable qur'anic instances in which *qur'ān* functions as a true verbal noun denoting an activity, not an object:

> Observe the *ṣalāt* at the sinking of the sun until the darkening of night, and the dawn recital [*qur'ān al-fajr*]; truly, the dawn recital [*qur'ān al-fajr*] is attested [*mashhūd*]. (S. 17.78)

> Do not move your tongue with it so that you hurry too much! Ours it is to collect it and to recite it [*qur'ān*^{a}*hu*], and when We recite it, follow the recitation of it [*qur'ān*^{a}*hu*]. (S. 75.16-18)

Beyond those passages in which *qur'ān* can be read in a strictly verbal sense as the action of reciting, there are others in which it occurs, with or without the definite article, not as the proper name of the whole scripture revealed to Muhammad, but as a single revelation or as a generic term for a scriptural text. Two of the clearest examples follow:

> Neither are you involved in any affair, nor do you recite any recitation [*qur'ān*] from it [the scripture], nor do you perform any act, without Our being your witness when you undertake it. . . . (S. 10.61)[46]

> When Our revelations [*ayāt*] are recited [*tutlá*] as clear proofs to them, those who do not hope to meet Me say: "Bring a recitation [*qur'ān*] other than this, or change it" . . . . (S. 10.15)

All of these passages point us toward an understanding of both the active, verbal sense of the word *qur'ān* that underlies every other use of it, and also its nominal use, not only as a proper noun that names the collected book of Muslim scripture, but also as a common noun referring to a particular passage (of revelation) meant for recitation. In these uses, the parallels with both *qeryānā* and *qerī'ā*/*miqrā'* in Christian and Judaic usage are particularly evident.

"Qur'ān" in Non-Qur'anic Sources

Our earliest Islamic sources after the Qur'ān are the thousands of separate traditions or reports known individually and collectively as *ḥadīth*. An individual *ḥadīth* consists of a report, usually brief, about words and actions of Muhammad and his Companions. Such reports form the major content of not only the large "standard" Ḥadīth works compiled in the third/ninth century, but also the earlier and later works of history, Qur'ān-exegesis, jurisprudence, and theology. While some *ḥadīth*s do go back to the time of the Prophet or the first generations after him, others are certainly later forgeries (albeit usually pious, well-intended ones that often seek to put the stamp of his authority on later Islamic praxis). Nevertheless, as source materials at least as old as the third Islamic (ninth C.E.) century, they still offer material from a relatively early period of Islamic history.

In many and diverse *ḥadīth* reports we can find considerable evidence that the verbal-noun and common-noun force of the word *qur'ān* lasted well after the time of Muhammad, even in the face of the increasingly dominant use of "al-Qur'ān" as the proper name of the physical book exemplar (*muṣḥaf*). Of examples involving verbal usages, one of the clearest is a tradition that quotes from a verse ascribed to a famous poet and older companion of the Prophet, Ḥassān b. Thābit. In this, Ḥassān speaks with approval of "one who 'interrupts' the night[47] by praising [God] and reciting [*qur'ān*]"[48] – a clear adverbial use of *qur'ān* to denote the act of recitation. A second example is the *ḥadīth* that reports that Muhammad spoke highly of the person "who is constantly mindful of God in/during [his] reciting [*qur'ān*]."[49] A particularly striking *ḥadīth* tells how one of the Prophet's Companions came to him one morning and reported how, when he was reciting a *qur'ān* the night before (in some versions, specifically S. 18, "Kahf"), one of his animals tried to bolt from the courtyard. Although he looked around, he could not find what had frightened the animal. Muhammad, however, responded at once: "That was the divine aura [or "presence", *al-sakīnah*] that descended with the recitation [*al-qur'ān*]."[50]

Qur'ān as a common-noun term for any individual unit of the revelation is attested throughout the early sources, as well as in later ones. One *ḥadīth* reports Muhammad's saying that "in every ritual worship [*ṣalāt*] there is a recitation [*qur'ān*]."[51] Various of the Companions are said to have "feared that a *qur'ān* would be sent down about us/me" on a particular occasion.[52] Ibn 'Umar is even reported to have said that the Companions avoided joking publicly with their wives up until Muhammad's death for fear that a specific *qur'ān* would be revealed to prohibit that.[53] Various occasions are mentioned on which a particular *qur'ān* was revealed; thus one Companion could report to another that "a *qur'ān* was sent down to him [Muhammad] last night."[54]

Apart from *ḥadīth* reports, there is an amusing common-noun occurrence of *qur'ān* in the story told of how the wife of the Companion and poet 'Ābd Allāh b. Rawāḥah suspected him of making love to a slave girl. Confronting him as he left the girl's quarters, and knowing that he had once sworn never to recite the Qur'ān unless ritually clean, she asked him to recite from scripture for her in order to catch him out. The quick-witted poet promptly recited three lines of poetry that sounded enough like a qur'anic verse to satisfy his wife of his innocence, since "she thought this to be a *qur'ān*."[55] Later sources also continue to use *qur'ān* as an indefinite noun to refer to a unit of scripture. One example from the fifth century is from a comment by Ibn Ḥazm (d. 456/1064) that among those things that make a *ṣalāt* valid, no matter who performs it, is that he or she "recite the 'mother of the Qur'ān' [S. 1] and a[nother] *qur'ān* along with it."[56] Finally, Al-Qushayrī (d. 466/1074), in a discussion of God's word, says of the word *qur'ān:* "What is recited is called 'a recitation' [*qur'ān*], just as what is drunk is called 'a drink'."[57]

Implications

All of the foregoing examples testify to a more multifaceted understanding and use of the very term *qur'ān* than modern ideas of "al-Qur'ān" as the book of scripture would imply. The use of *qur'ān* both as an action - reciting - and as a unit of text meant to be recited underscores how seriously "al-Qur'ān" as the name of Muslim scripture is to be taken and how central the recited character of the book of revelation was from the beginning.

There is also a further aspect of the use of the term *qur'ān* in Qur'ān, *Ḥadīth,* and other early sources. The predominant context in which the word occurs is that of the performance of either the formal worship rite (*ṣalāt*) or personal devotion and prayer. As evidence of this beyond the citations already given, one need only mention the myriad *ḥadīth*s that were clearly meant to define or confirm the ritual obligations of Muslims vis-à-vis the *ṣalāt.* For example, one of these reports Muhammad to have said that any performance of the worship rite without "a *qur'ān*" in it is "deficient",[58] although another tells how the Prophet instructed a bedouin who had asked how to perform the *ṣalāt* as follows: "if you have a *qur'ān,* recite it; if not, then praise and magnify God."[59] Most aspects of the worship rite are covered in one or another prophetic tradition: Thus, for example, the manner in which one recites in *ṣalāt* may be governed by the report of how the Prophet "raised his voice with the Recitation [*qur'ān*]" in his *ṣalāt.*[60] With regard to personal devotional practice, there are also a vast number of traditions that encourage qur'anic chanting apart from the *ṣalāt* and make recitation a mark of individual piety.[61] In general, the sources make clear that, at a very basic level, the reciting of God's word is, as one *ḥadīth* has it, something "to be returned" to God as "the very best" of all that He has given humankind.[62]

This is not to deny that Muslims relied heavily on the revelations to address nonliturgical, nondevotional issues, from matters of inheritance to theology. According to the sources, they avidly sought *qur'ān*s from Muhammad and, later, each other, in order to gain guidance for individual and collective life. Thus, for example, Ibn 'Abbās answers another Muslim's question with "I shall recite for you a *qur'ān* about that."[63] Nevertheless, the recitative texts as a genre (for Muslims, *the* highest genre of all, namely revelation) seem to have had their original *Sitz im Leben* more in liturgical and devotional life than in the arenas of legal, social, political, or doctrinal matters. However, the latter concerns are in Muslim view virtually inextricable from worship: It is not without reason that, in the books of jurisprudence, the prescribed acts of worship and service (*'ibādāt*) precede the problems of social relations (*mu'āmalāt*). The heart of an Islamic society and of any branch of Islamic learning or other activity is conceived to be the piety of the faithful, the most tangible expression of which is the public cultus.

I emphasize this point about the early understanding and use of *qur'ān,* because later Islamic and much of modern orientalist scholarship has been generally more interested in the Qur'ān as the authority for Islamic institutions and ideas than as what has been often called "the prayerbook of the Muslims." We cannot remind ourselves too often that the chanting or reciting of God's word was the chief visible mark of being a Muslim from the outset.[64] Furthermore, the oral, recitative function of the Qur'ān that I have described for the early community did not cease after the initial generations of Muslims were gone. It has been evident across the broad spectrum of Muslim faith and practice, at all times and in all places where Muslims have formed a community. Knowledge and recitation of the Qur'ān have continued always to be the badges of the Muslim in a sociopolitical sense as well as in a personal, religious sense, as we shall see.

CHAPTER 8

Muslim Scripture as Spoken Word

Whenever a group gathers in a house of God to recite God's scripture [*kitāb allāh*] and to teach it to one another, there descends upon them the divine presence,[1] mercy covers them, angels spread their wings over them, and God mentions them to those close to Him.

- *Ḥadīth* of the Prophet

You can return to God nothing better than that which came from Him, namely the Recitation [*al-qur'ān*].

- *Ḥadīth* of the Prophet

The oral character of the Qur'ān is readily perceptible in almost any sector of Muslim life, today as in every previous age of Islamic history. Whatever the changes being wrought by rapid change in recent decades, the importance of the recited Qur'ān in Muslim societies is still a major element in the character of these societies. As I have adumbrated in Chapter 7, this recitative function of the Qur'ān has been of paramount importance especially in public ritual and private devotional life over the centuries. In the present chapter, we look at several aspects of this importance in Muslim communal and personal life. We need, however, to look first at how the recitative tradition itself has been sustained: namely, through the cultivation among Muslims of qur'anic recitation both as an art of considerable sophistication and as a science - indeed, the fundamental science - in traditional Islamic scholarship and education.

The Formal Tradition of Recitation (*Qirā'ah*)

The persistent orality of the Qur'ān is graphically reflected in the preparation at the beginning of this century of the now generally accepted "standard" qur'anic text known as the "Cairo" or "Egyptian" official version of 1342/1923–24.[2] This printed text was the result of over a decade of collaborative work by a group of outstanding Muslim Qur'ān specialists on a critical and authoritative printed edition of the Qur'ān. Although cognizant of the many very ancient Qur'ān manuscripts and manuscript fragments that are preserved, these scholars did not depend upon collation of the earliest texts to verify the most authoritative textual readings. Instead, they relied upon their extensive, largely orally acquired and orally sustained knowledge of the several most venerable traditions of Qur'ān readings (*qirā'āt;* pl. of *qirā'ah*) and of the literature that has grown out of and accompanied these traditions. Even the orthography of the edition they produced was based not upon manuscripts but upon the oral and written traditions of the "science of readings" (*'ilm al-qirā'āt*). Although this procedure went against many canons of Western text-critical scholarship, it produced a qur'anic text now all but universally recognized as the most authoritative version available. Indeed, not long after this new text appeared, one of the leading European Qur'ān scholars of the day, Gotthelf Bergsträsser, declared that all of the textual scholarship of the West could not have brought forth a more exact or critical edition than that produced by these leading exponents of the highly oral and highly mnemonic Islamic "science of readings."[3]

Qirā'ah as a Technical Discipline

The "science of readings" behind the modern standard Qur'ān text is a linchpin not simply of the scribal traditions of qur'anic orthography and calligraphy, but even more of the oral tradition of Qur'ān recitation, or *qirā'ah,* which has been the primary medium of transmission of the scriptural text.

What is *qirā'ah* in a technical sense? To begin with, it is, as I noted in Chapter 7, the common verbal noun of the verb *qara'a,* "to read aloud, recite". It is used technically to refer not only to (1) the specific act of reciting aloud part or the whole of the Qur'ān (and hence to the science or art of how one does this), but also to (2) a particular "reading" (i.e., pronouncing, "sounding out") of any word or group of words in the Qur'ān – in other words, a textual "variant" for a particular word or phrase in a manuscript text. This is the sense in which its plural, *qirā'āt,* is used, as already noted, for the various "readings" of the text of the Qur'ān. *Qirā'ah* is also used by extension to designate (3) an entire corpus or tradition of specific variant readings of the basic 'Uthmānic consonantal text (which can be pointed and voweled, and therefore pronounced, in a variety of ways at numerous points). In this third sense, it designates a particular "reading" of the entire qur'anic text according to one of the various historical traditions of oral text transmission. All such traditions are traced to prominent reciters or to local "schools" of recitation-readings in the first two centuries A.H. (seventh and eighth centuries C.E.).[4]

Thus one can speak of the *qirā'ah* of Ibn Kathīr, 'Āṣim, or "the people of Kūfa."

As a formal Islamic "science" (*'ilm*), *qirā'ah* encompasses both the study and transmission of the variant readings (*qirā'āt*) of the 'Uthmānic consonantal text – the written *muṣḥaf* – and also the actual art of oral recitation or cantillation, called *tajwīd* ("doing well by," "rendering excellent" [the Qur'ān]), with its various traditions of vocal performance. As a joint science, the *'ilm al-qirā'āt wal-tajwīd* represents the long Muslim tradition of qur'anic textual studies. These studies rely, to be sure, upon knowledge of various other sciences, from grammar (*nahw*) and philology (*lughah*) to rhetoric (*balāghah*), orthography (*rasm*), and especially exegesis (*tafsīr*). Like these other sciences, recitative studies have an extensive literary tradition of great scholastic complexity. Their purpose or focus is, however, a noble and religiously central one: the exact preservation and ongoing re-creation of the living divine word as it "came down" in oral, recited form to Muhammad.[5]

This is not to deny the necessary and significant role of the written text of the Qur'ān in these or other Muslim sciences, but to emphasize that the written text is always secondary. It exists as a support to the orally transmitted and recited text, not as a determinant of it. Because the written codification of the authoritative text under 'Uthmān took place before the development of an Arabic orthography that could indicate with true precision how a text actually is to be read, the written *muṣḥaf* could never stand alone. When 'Uthmān sent out copies of his new Qur'ān text to the major cities of the young empire, he sent them with knowledgeable reciters who could teach the text of the *muṣḥaf.* Its defective consonantal form allows for variant readings not only of vowels and inflectional endings, but even of many of the wholly unpointed consonants themselves. (The system of pointing – that is, using marks above or below in order to distinguish among consonants with the same shape in Arabic script and to show which vowel or inflectional ending is to be read after a consonant – has no real equivalent in Indo-European languages. The differences between "c" and "ç" in French, "a" and "ä" in German, or "o" and "ø" in Swedish suggest only in a very mild way the degree of change that pointing indicates in Arabic.) For these reasons, the Qur'ān had to be transmitted primarily as it had originally been given: as a recited, phonetic text. The base form of this oral text existed, after 'Uthmān's time, in a standard but rudimentary written form, and its details were noted, described, and preserved by tradition (the original manuscript and its copies have not survived). As such it could serve as an *aide-mémoire* but not a documentary text apart from the memorization and oral recitation of its content.[6] To read the bare, unpointed text, one had to know it already by heart, or very nearly so.

Qirā'āt and Qirā'ah

It seems to have been accepted from the outset that there could be various readings of the same divine text, whether because of dialectical differences among the first Arab Muslims or because even the Prophet is said to have recited the same passage in various ways at various times. The ‘Uthmānic reform had not even been able to do away entirely with what seems to have been the most important alternative written version of the qur'anic text – that of Ibn Mas‘ūd, which continued to be popular in Kūfa and among some Shī‘īs for a long time. How much more impossible must it have been that a single oral "reading" of even the "standard" written text could have won the day across the already vast Islamic empire. This was especially so because the defective script of the ‘Uthmānic *muṣḥaf* allowed for considerable variety in recitation of particular words and passages, even if almost none of these radically altered the content of the Qur'ān at any point.

In the end, if not from the outset, Muslims interpreted this variety of possible readings of the same text as a blessing, not a curse for the community, and all the accepted readings were deemed to have come ultimately from Muhammad himself.[7] The consensus eventually allowed for the "preference" of a capable scholar-reader in choosing to recite the text according to one *qirā'ah* from among the various ones generally recognized – such recognition eventually being based formally upon adherence to (1) linguistic correctness, (2) the accepted ‘Uthmānic text, and (3) a sound tradition of transmission from the earliest authorities.[8] In this acceptance of divergent readings and recitative practices, Muslims relied for their proof text upon the statement, ascribed to Muhammad, that "the Qur'ān was sent down according to seven *aḥruf* (lit.: "letters"; usually taken as "dialects" or "modes").[9]

As the traditional accounts of the preparation of the ‘Uthmānic written codex have it, both recitation, *qirā'ah,* and the individual *qirā'āt,* or variant readings of the qur'anic text, were of moment from the earliest decades after Muhammad's death because of the concern with accurate preservation of the revelations and exclusion of interpolated readings. However, although there are also references to and some manuscripts of treatises ascribed to experts on *qirā'ah* in the first two Islamic centuries, the crystallization of *qirā'ah* as a more formal science probably took place substantially only in the third/ninth century.[10] In any event, the culmination of this process came in the efforts of Abū Bakr Ibn Mujāhid (d. 324/936) of Baghdad to systematize and give rules for proper recitation.[11] He is identified as the person who effected the recognition of seven different "traditions" (*riwāyāt;* pl. of *riwāyah*) of recitation-readings as authentic modes of transmitting the Qur'ān.[12] Some later scholars added three further traditions of *qirā'āt* as permissible, or "authentic", variant systems, and still others have recognized these plus an additional four.

Accordingly, seven, ten, or fourteen traditions of "readings" are sometimes cited as "authentic" in the Muslim literature, and even these traditions have branched to form subtraditions. Thus the panoply of variant *riwāyāt* that the expert must master is quite large, even though the actual textual variations they represent are relatively minor and do not involve crucial differences in the literal meaning of the sacred text.[13]

The Art of Tajwīd

Within the general science of recitation, the study of the *qirā'āt* is, as I have indicated, inextricable from the science or art of *tajwīd,* the actual recitative practice or method of Qur'ān cantillation.[14] For Muslims, *tajwīd* is the attempt to preserve the living word of God in the full beauty and full range of meaning with which it was given to and faithfully transmitted by the Prophet. Chanting the Qur'ān is a reenactment of the revelatory act itself, and how the Qur'ān is vocally rendered not only matters, but matters ultimately. Thus it is no wonder that qur'anic cantillation has its own forms that set it forever apart from all other text recitation as well as all musical forms.

The traditional authority for *tajwīd* – "ornamenting" or "making beautiful" the sacred text, and hence cantillation of it – is taken from the Qur'ān itself, namely its exhortation (S. 73.4) to "chant the recitation in measured, clear chant" (*wa-rattil al-qur'āna tartīlan*).[15] Although the word used here is *tartīl,* which traditionally refers to carefully enunciated, measured chanting, the verse is widely interpreted as referring more broadly to *tajwīd* as the practice of cantillation according to the proper rules.

As the general art of vocal recitation or cantillation, *'ilm al-tajwīd* encompasses many traditions and types of oral recitation. The basic one of these is the *murattal,* or measured and precise, usually less melodic cantillation (as noted, sometimes called *tartīl;* both words are from the same Arabic root, *R-T-L*). As the style of reciting normally used in *ṣalāt,* personal devotion, and education, it has been and remains the fundamental form of the scriptural text in Islam.[16] At its most "ornamented" (*mujawwad* – from the same root as *tajwīd*), *tajwīd* includes more melodically modulated and musically cadenced forms of cantillation that are closer to singing. Such forms are more specifically referred to as "recitation with melodies" (*qirā'ah bil-alḥān*), and in some places, such as Cairo today, these are by far the most popular forms of recitation. Sometimes, however, *tajwīd* is even used in a narrower sense to refer specifically to such melodically embellished recitative modes, in which quality of voice and musical ability figure more prominently, as distinct from the more sober, less modulated *murattal* form of chant.[17]

Within the range of generally recognized recitational styles, there are differing opinions about what constitutes more and less acceptable forms of chanting. Some feel that only the melodic *mujawwad* styles render the full beauty of the sacred text and replicate the Prophet's (and Gabriel's!) recitation; others feel that such recitation slides too dangerously close to secular music, and hence one should keep to the *murattal* form. Be that as it may, none would deny that all forms of qur'anic chanting involve more than just the fundamentals of the recitative art necessary to *tartīl* or *murattal* chanting: accurate memorization, knowledgeable technique, careful comprehension, and sensitive interpretation of the whole Qur'ān.[18]

The chanting or cantillation of the Qur'ān is viewed as a vocal form sui generis: Its forms and possibilities come from the divine text itself, not from the minds or mouths of its human readers. In the more musical forms of *tajwīd* the beauty of a good voice is joined ideally to technical accuracy in what an outsider might well feel to be impressively modulated and melodically sophisticated song. Nevertheless, Muslim tradition rejects utterly the description of any accepted form of Qur'ān recitation as "music" in the sense of secular singing. The Qur'ān is "inimitable" (*mu'jiz*), and since it is preeminently a "recitation", this miraculous quality inheres not simply in its literal wording on a page, but even more so in its vocal rendering as divine speech. Perhaps the non-Muslim would find the Muslim theological doctrine of "inimitability" (*i'jāz*) much easier to grasp if he or she were to hear an accomplished reciter (*qāri'*) "perform" the sacred text. To judge from my own observation, listening, and reading, it is in the moving oral rendition of the text that the Qur'ān is realized and received as divine. The ontological "fencing off" of Qur'ān recitation from all other vocal recitation or singing is a reflection of the overwhelming Muslim sense of the sacrality of this text of texts – a sense closely linked to the chanted Qur'ān.

The Recitative Sciences in Muslim Society

On the basis of the foregoing, it should be easier to see how the conjoined sciences of *tajwīd* and *qirā'āt,* together with that of exegesis (*tafsīr*), have been the guardians and normative mediators of the qur'anic text as living scripture in the Muslim community. Because of its predominantly oral character, *tajwīd* has received even less modern scholarly attention than the *qirā'āt,* which themselves have hardly been dealt with exhaustively.[19] It is encouraging to note, however, that in recent years several scholars have done much to redress this deficiency.[20] As they have demonstrated through consideration of both the classical literature on *qirā'āt* and *tajwīd* and the living tradition of Qur'ān recitation in its contemporary center, Cairo, both Muslim study of the Qur'ān and Muslim popular involvement with it center on the spoken, recited, chanted word of its text.

Moreover, the science and art of the textual specialists are never isolated in the academy as, for example, modern biblical studies sometimes have been in the West (and, one might argue, the science and art of the Brahmanical reciters of the Veda are in India). The study of *qirā'āt* and *tajwīd* opens out automatically into the public domain in Muslim society. Here it finds practical application in the highly popular artistic and devotional forms of oral recitation that have been one of the hallmarks of Islamic culture wherever it has spread.[21] In turn, the formal and public recitation of the Qur'ān, whether as a pious act of worship or as artistic performance (and the two are never easily separated), is but one segment of the larger role of the Qur'ān as an oral/aural reality in Muslim life more generally. It is in consideration of this larger role that we come at last to the heart of the functional role of scripture as spoken word in Islam.

The Recited Qur'ān in Everyday Piety and Practice

An anonymous Muslim devotional pamphlet describes the Muslims as those "whose gospels are in their hearts while others read them from sacred volumes."[22] The formal sciences of readings and cantillation could not have been sustained as vibrantly as they have been over the centuries had not Qur'ān memorization, *ḥifẓ*, and recitation, *qirā'ah* or *tilāwah*,[23] always been central to the daily and seasonal round of life in Islamic societies. Here we can only touch briefly upon memorization and recitation and their place in Muslim life, but any discussion of the Qur'ān as scripture - especially with regard to its oral qualities - would be sorely deficient without some indication of its active recitative role among "average" Muslims of diverse times, places, and stations.

In Worship (Ṣalāt)

First and foremost, the Qur'ān has been the one absolute essential of Muslim ritual and devotional life. The qur'anic and other early evidence of the fundamental orality of the Qur'ān points, as we have seen, to the primary importance of this function of scripture in Islam. In a way that, for example, the Jewish or Christian Bible (with the notable exception of the Psalter) is not, the Qur'ān is prayerbook, lectionary, and hymnal rolled into one. Furthermore, unlike the Vedas, the qur'anic text (or at least some part of it) is the common property of all the faithful, whatever their social status or education, even those who do not speak Arabic; for in the formal worship of *ṣalāt* and also in individual devotional and prayer life, no Muslim can function without being able to recite a minimal amount of the Arabic scripture.[24]

An oblique but therefore perhaps all the more telling indication of the liturgical centrality of the Qur'ān occurs in the earliest extant work on the qur'anic sciences, the *Kitāb al-Mabānī* (425/1033). The passage in question attempts to distinguish specifically qur'anic words from the extra-qur'anic words of God reported in the so-called Divine Sayings - those *ḥadīth*s that relate non-qur'anic words of God. This passage characterizes the Divine Saying as a divinely revealed text, but then proceeds to differentiate it from the Qur'ān as follows:[25]

> It is not permissible to recite any of it [the Divine Saying] in the *ṣalāt,* for it was not sent down in the same form in which all of the Qur'ān was sent down – which [Qur'ān] we have been commanded to recite [*umirnā bi-tilāwatihi*], which is written in [our] copies [*al-maṣāḥif*], and the transmission of which has come to us generally attested in every generation [*mutawātir*].

The functional orientation of this distinction between qur'anic and other divine words is striking. Here it is the Qur'ān's form as a text intended for recitation in the daily ritual of worship that distinguishes it. Later theological distinctions of "inimitability" (*i'jāz*) or the like notwithstanding, it is above all the practical, ritual function of the Qur'ān as recited word in worship that sets it apart from any other text.

Indeed, the recitation of the Qur'ān is what one student of Muslim piety has called "the very heart of the prayer-rite."[26] No *ṣalāt* is valid without recitation of at least the Fātiḥah, or "Opening" (S. 1), and it is expected that one or more shorter *sūrah*s or verses will also be recited.[27] It is quite common to precede or to follow the *ṣalāt*-rite proper with substantial recitation from the Qur'ān,[28] just as most major Muslim festival and commemorative occasions (e.g., funerals)[29] involve recitation of shorter or longer segments of the divine word. Qur'ān recitation in general is a highly preferred form of religious devotion at any time – in many ways an extension of the *ṣalāt* into the other parts of the day for its practitioners.

The Sacrality of Recitation

As we have seen, the fact that the Qur'ān is the sacred word of God in the form of "an Arabic recitation" (*qur'ān*^an^ *'arabīy*^an^)[30] has deterred Muslims from translating it from the original Arabic. Conversely, it has spurred even Muslims who know no Arabic to memorize shorter or longer passages as they are able in order to be able to worship in *ṣalāt* and apart from *ṣalāt* by reciting the Qur'ān. Among many possible examples illustrative of this latter phenomenon is a delightful anecdote recounted by a French traveler to Singapore over a century ago. He tells of walking one day in the Malay quarter of the city and hearing children's voices apparently chanting a lesson from a nearby house. Going in, he found an old Malay with a white beard sitting on the floor together with over a dozen children and leading them in recitation – he from a book, they from pieces of paper. Questioned by the visitor as to what was being recited, the old man replied that it was the Qur'ān, in Arabic, which he admitted he did not understand, but could sound aloud from the script on the written page. The European found this intriguing or amusing and asked further why they would be learning words they could not understand. The old teacher replied at once that in reading them aloud, the children learn them by heart, and they do this because

> the sons of the Prophet ought to have this word in their memory so that they can repeat it often. These words are endowed with a special virtue. . . . In translating [them] we might alter the meaning, and that would be a sacrilege.[31]

Here the inherent sacrality of the original Arabic sounds – and of their meaning as well, even if that meaning is not understood in a literal, word-by-word or sentence-by-sentence fashion – is affirmed in no uncertain terms. The sense of the sacrality, or *barakah* ("blessing"), of the very sounds of the holy text is something that seems to penetrate into every corner of the Islamic world. The family of a longtime Ismā'īlī friend of mine begin each day in their East African home with the strains of Radio Pakistan's morning broadcast of qur'anic recitation filling the entire house. His explanation of the clearly understood purpose behind this is that *barakah* permeates the house from the Arabic recitation (which, in this instance, is carried by shortwave from an Urdu-speaking Islamic land to Gujarati and Swahili-speaking Muslims on another continent!). The sounded strains of the word of God – and they are only powerful when sounded with full voice – start everyone's day on the proper note, even before the performance of the day's first prayer-rite in the local mosque.

To dismiss the qur'anic presence in such situations as either the fulfillment of superstitions, or as merely "background noise", or even as only a taken-for-granted habit, is to miss the perceived power and genuine spriritual function of such recitation quite apart from an understanding of every word or sentence. Here we are up against a particularly intransigent and thorny problem of the meaning of scripture, one to which we shall return in Chapter 9.

Muslim Education

Beyond this issue, however, the story of the Malay recitation lesson points us to the role of qur'anic recitation as the backbone of Muslim education, in its earliest as well as its most advanced stages. In this we have a vivid expression of the enduring Muslim conviction that Muslims need to be able, as early in life as possible, to recite from the Qur'ān in its original form with some ease.[32] This conviction is succinctly expressed in the tradition, ascribed to the Prophet himself, that says "it is a grievous mistake to take the written page as your *shaykh*."[33]

Memorizing from the Qur'ān has always been basic to bringing up children in every Muslim society, and there are few sounds more constant in diverse parts of the Islamic world, from Morocco to Indonesia, than the mesmerizing singsong chant of tiny children as they recite the Qur'ān for their teacher in the neighborhood Qur'ān school known commonly as *kuttāb* or *maktab*. Even though only a small percentage of such children ever stay in school long enough (typically five to eight years) to memorize the whole Qur'ān or become literate in Arabic,[34] the learning of at least some part of the divine word by heart is the single most common early learning experience shared in some degree by all Muslims.

Ibn Khaldūn remarked long ago that "teaching the Qur'ān to children is one of the signs of (the) religion that Muslims profess and practice in all their cities."[35] More significantly, the universal presence of some kind of childhood "rote" learning of the Qur'ān – principally by boys, but also commonly by girls – has traditionally given to the participants in Islamic societies a common cultural heritage as well as a common religious training. Shared familiarity with some or all of the qur'anic text and especially its values and shared appreciation for the melodic cadences of its recitation have been not only signs of Muslim faith, but the essential common thread in the diverse fabric of the myriad different cultures of the Islamic world – the identifiable tie binding Muslims across barriers of language, color, and custom, as well as time and place.

The *kuttāb* has thus been traditionally a major part of the formative experience of Muslims. Whatever its shortcomings, it has been a key influence in the early stages of the "islamization" of the Muslim individual. In Islamic societies, "the Muslim does not put a child in a qur'anic school in order to teach him, but in order to form him according to the immutable tradition that was that of his own parents and that of theirs."[36] In his study of qur'anic schooling in Cameroon, Renaud Santerre has written of the role of this schooling as "a mechanism of total formation" of the person, which socializes the child in diverse ways.[37] Similarly, Dale Eickelman trenchantly observes that "a firm discipline in the course of learning the Quran is culturally regarded as an integral part of socialization. . . . the discipline of Quranic memorization is an integral part of learning to be human and Muslim."[38]

Ṭaha Ḥusayn (1889–1973), the great modern Egyptian educational reformer, gives particularly striking testimony in his autobiography to the centrality of qur'anic memorizing and recitation in the earliest experience of the children of rural Egypt some ninety years ago.[39] The picture he paints of his first education was still largely valid for most of the Islamic world until quite recently, when modern, state-sponsored school systems, most of them secularized to some degree, have begun to compete with or to replace the traditional *kuttāb* as the locus of primary education. Even today in Muslim countries, qur'anic education is often still offered alongside, as preschool preparation for, or even as a part of, government-sponsored public education based on more secular models.[40]

Memorization of the Qur'ān has traditionally been an accomplishment of great pride and status in Muslim communities. One of the most cherished honorifics a Muslim can earn is that of *ḥāfiẓ* (fem.: *ḥāfiẓah*), one who "has by heart" (lit.: "preserves", *ḥafiẓa*) the entire scripture. Sometimes the one who has learned the whole Qur'ān is even accorded the honor of being addressed as *shaykh,* or "master". Traditionally, complete mastery of the entire text has been the necessary prerequisite to becoming, through further study, an accomplished religious scholar (*'ālim;* pl.: *'ulamā'*) in any of the religious sciences (it is, needless to say, a sine qua non for entry into serious study of *tajwīd*). Of those children who stay more than a few months or years in school, some already manage this kind of mastery of scripture by the age of ten or twelve, a few earlier. Even those who never truly control the entire text nor aspire to become themselves schoolteachers or more advanced scholars can quote and recite substantial portions from it, if they have studied for a long time in the *kuttāb* and, especially, beyond it. Certainly it is not unusual for a "layperson" without advanced religious and legal education to be a *ḥāfiẓ* or *ḥāfiẓah;* one of my first Muslim Qur'ān teachers, and a creditable *ḥāfiẓ,* was a chemist from Medina, Saudi Arabia. The most accomplished members of a given local gathering of Qur'ān reciters may not be professionals, nor even very educated or literate persons.[41]

At higher levels of education, knowledge of the Qur'ān is essential and presumed. The correct contextual application of its verses is an art that one develops only over time, and its technical interpretation is a science that must be learned through laborious study.[42] Among religious scholars, the international language is not so much Arabic qua Arabic as the classical qur'anic Arabic, which is the ideal standard of Arabic literacy. The writing and the speech of scholarship in the traditional Islamic context is based to a degree that we can hardly imagine on the vocabulary, phraseology, and diction of the Arabic scripture. One does not have to read long in Muslim texts nor listen often to an *'ālim* speak to discover how the ring of the qur'anic text cadences the thinking, writing, and speaking of those who live with and by the Qur'ān. Mastery of the Qur'ān is a baseline for the scholar: Completely aside from knowledge of *tajwīd,* the *'ālim* has to be able to quote and to recite from the Qur'ān at will even to begin to hold his own among compatriots. It is by no means excessive to say that Muslim scholarship is based to a significant extent upon acceptance of the Prophetic adage from the *Ḥadith* that claims that "knowledge shall not perish so long as the Qur'ān is recited."[43]

Permeation of Communal Life

Anyone who has lived for a time in a Muslim society will have remarked also the degree to which the lilting refrain of qur'anic recitation occupies a prominent place in the public sphere, forming a significant part of the auditory "background" of everyday life. The virtual omnipresence of the sound of qur'anic cantillation has been, if anything, intensified by radio and other electronic media by comparison with earlier eras, although the competing sounds of the media and modern technology in general have flooded the aural universe of Muslim society with many distractions unknown in an earlier day. Apart from the many modern Muslims for whom the Qur'ānic word is *primarily* in the "background", there are also many others who cling to traditional piety and strive to preserve the lilting strains of the chanted Qur'ān as a prominent element in the "foreground" of their lives. When I think of my traditionalist, or *salafī,* Muslim friends in Damascus, my memories of time with them is inseparable from the sound of the Qur'ān – in their worship, their conversation, and their special efforts to recite for me and each other. It is safe to say that the *ḥadīth* that says, "the most excellent form of worship and devotion [*'ibādah*] among my people is reciting the Qur'ān,"[44] has been taken to heart in traditional Muslim practice.

In that most social and communal of all Muslim religious events, the month of fasting in Ramaḍān, the nights are filled with the sound of Qur'ān recitation in the mosques. Muslim interpretation has traditionally found in S. 96, "al-Qadr" ("The Power"), a specific description of the night in which the Qur'ān was first revealed – in part or all at once, depending upon the particular tradition followed. The text reads: "Truly, We have sent it down on the Night of Power. And what has revealed to you what the Night of Power is? The Night of Power is better than a thousand months. Peace! Until the breaking of the dawn." Various dates have been given to the "Night of Power" (*laylat al-qadr*), most commonly the 27th of Ramaḍān, but also variously any one of the odd-numbered days of that month from the 21st onward. As a result, the latter third of the month is counted an especially auspicious time for reciting. In general, recitation of the Qur'ān has been strongly linked to the observance of Ramaḍān, an observance that ranks at the top of Muslim holy days and rituals in personal and communal significance. The basic recitative division of the Qur'ān into thirty parts is sometimes said to be designed especially for the purpose of reciting one "part", or *juz'*, in each night of Ramaḍān.[45] In practice, the whole is often recited in shorter cycles ranging down even to a single night by unusually zealous individuals or groups who repair to the mosques for this purpose.[46] Anwarul Haq tells of an Indian Muslim woman, the mother of the Indian Sūfī leader Muhammad Ilyās (d. 1943), who not only knew the Qur'ān by heart, but used to recite the whole Qur'ān *plus* ten "parts" *each day* in Ramaḍān, for a total of forty complete recitations, or "completions" (*khatamāt;* pl. of *khatmah,* "sealing") of the holy book during the sacred month every year.[47]

Another popular form of public *tilāwah* is the group chanting associated both with the formal *dhikr*-sessions of the Sūfī brotherhoods and with the popular *dhikr*-sessions at certain mosques, especially tomb-mosques. *Dhikr,* the "remembrance" of God in litanies of devotion, involves the chanting of formulas and texts steeped in the language of the Qur'ān. Qur'ānic recitation itself commonly begins or is woven into such sessions.[48] I have witnessed one popular *dhikr* held each Friday after the evening prayer at the tomb in Damascus of "Sīdī Maḥyiddīn," the great mystical thinker Muḥyī' l-Dīn Ibn al-'Arabī (d. 638/1240). In this gathering, the men who crowd into the tomb chamber to sit on the floor all join in a singsong recitation in popular *dhikr* style, focusing at least in the first hour or so on favorite *sūrah*s of the Qur'ān.

In contrast to such group chanting is the session in which listeners and reciters come together to hear the Qur'ān recited by a series of individual practitioners of *tajwīd*. Cairo is especially well known for its varied forms of this kind of event, which is called a *maqra'*, or "recitation session" (from the root *Q-R-'*). Most of these are associated with particular mosques and take place regularly one or more times a week. The most prestigious are those at places like the Imām Shāfi'ī tomb-mosque and the Azhar University mosque, but there are many smaller, more private, or local-mosque settings for the *maqra'*.[49] Still another kind is the *nadwah*, or "gathering", a listening session held often in private homes and attended by cognoscenti of the recitative art.[50] In this latter type of session the musical aspects of recitation often receive special attention, although it is never easy to distinguish the aesthetic from the religious elements of Qur'ān recitation and listening. Thanks to the works of Nelson and Denny, we have interesting documentation of some of the inner dynamics of varied *maqra'*s in Cairo today. These studies point up the degree to which *tilāwah* is at once a demanding art form, a popular entertainment, and sometimes even a performing contest, as well as always an act of devotion and piety and a formal part of the transmission of the Qur'ān in its most perfect possible form.[51]

Permeation of Family and Personal Life

The foregoing reflects something of the variety of the ways in which the Qur'ān's vocal presence in the Muslim community is felt; yet the active role of the Qur'ān as spoken word among Muslims is still more pervasive than even these examples from ritual, devotional, and public life can adequately convey. From birth to death, virtually every action a Muslim makes, not to mention every solemn or festive event in his or her life, is potentially accompanied by spoken words of the Qur'ān, whether these be entire recited passages or simply discrete qur'anic words or phrases that have passed into everyday usage. Such a qur'anic word may be the simple *basmalah*, "In the name of God, the Merciful, the Compassionate" (*bism allāh al-raḥmān al-raḥīm*) that precedes countless daily acts such as drinking or eating, just as it precedes all but one *sūrah* of the Qur'ān. It may be the words of S. 2.156, "Truly, we are God's and, truly, unto him we are returning," which are uttered as a statement of resignation to fate and recognition of God's power over and guidance of all earthly affairs. Alternatively, it may be the ubiquitous *mā shā' llāh* ("whatever

God wills!") of S. 18.39 and *al-ḥamdu lillāh* ("Praise be to God!") of S. 1, both of which punctuate Muslim speech even outside of the Arabic-speaking world, as do qur'anic expressions invoking God's mercy (*raḥmah*) or forgiveness (*istighfār*).[52]

As an example of longer qur'anic passages heard in daily life, one thinks immediately of the *Fātiḥah,* S. 1, which every Muslim knows by heart and which is recited not only in every *ṣalāt* but on virtually every formal occasion, be it the signing of a wedding contract, closing of an agreement, or prayer at a tomb, not to mention at informal moments such as when one approaches a tomb.[53] There is also the powerful *sūrah* of "Unity", or "Purity", S. 112, which enters into most prayers and forms the basis of countless litanies of praise; or the final two *sūrah*s, S. 113 and 114 (*al-Mu'awwidhatān*), that "deliver from evil" and hence figure prominently as talismanic recitations; or the prayer for forgiveness in the final verses of S. 2, "The Cow" (*al-Baqarah*), which are known as "the seals of the Baqarah" and often are recited before going to sleep; or the powerful and moving strains of S. 36, *Yā Sīn,* which one recites at burials, on the approach of death, and also on the "Night of Quittance" (*laylat al-barā'ah,* a kind of Muslim All-Soul's Night, when life and death in the coming year and the deeds of the past year are popularly held to hang in the balance).[54] These are but a sampling of those that could be mentioned, as anyone knows who is aware of how popular the "Throne Verse" of S. 2.255 and the *sūrah* of "Light" (S. 24) also are.

What Ghazālī said of the Qur'ān nearly nine hundred years ago still holds today: "Much repetition cannot make it seem old and worn to those who recite it."[55] The powerful presence of the rhythmic cadence of qur'anic *tilāwah* is everywhere evident in traditional and much of modern Muslim society: ". . . the book lives on among its people, stuff of their daily lives, taking for them the place of a sacrament. For them these are not mere letters or mere words. They are the twigs of the burning bush, aflame with God."[56]

CHAPTER 9

Voicing the Qur'ān: Questions of Meaning

I saw God in my sleep, and I asked, "Lord, what is the best way by which those close to You draw [so] close?" God answered, "Through My word [*kalām*], Aḥmad." Then I asked, "O Lord, with or without understanding?" He said, "With and without understanding."

- ascribed to Ibn Ḥanbal

As I have previously indicated, my emphasis upon the oral function of the Qur'ān is not an effort to belittle the importance of the written form of the Qur'ān. The Qur'ān was early - perhaps as early as Muḥammad's own lifetime - put down in writing. It has been inscribed in countless volumes in magnificent fashion over the centuries: Its traditions of manuscript illumination and calligraphic artistry are among the true wonders of the Islamic artistic and cultural heritage. The written qur'anic word embellishes virtually every Muslim religious building as the prime form of decorative art. The reverence and honor shown the written Qur'ān text in Muslim piety are no less striking and impressive.

Instead of an argument for the displacement of the written Qur'ān by the spoken one, I am putting forward one for the functional primacy of the oral text over the written one - but always alongside it, not in competition with it. Both are dimensions of the same sacred reality for the Muslim: the presence and accessibility of God's very word in the created world. Both the visual and the auditory senses take pleasure in the beauty of the "Noble Qur'ān", which is for Muslim eyes or ears, without question or limitation, "the most beautiful of stories" (S. 12.3). The place of the Qur'ān in Muslim piety and practice is a particularly compelling demonstration that the scriptural word, even where its written form is most prominent, can be, and perhaps must be, also a spoken word, a recited word, a word that makes itself felt in personal and communal life in large part through its living quality as sacred sound. The facts of the Islamic treatment of scripture should at least cause us to question whether our easy dichotomization of oral word and written word is at all adequate as a way of talking about religious texts, let alone about stages of religious development. If the Muslim treatment of the Qur'ān – that clearest, even purest and most radical instance of "book religion" – presents us with a scripture that is oral as well as written, then certainly orality can characterize "scriptural" as well as "prescriptural" or "nonliterate" forms of religious life.

Yet the problem of the oral character of scripture does not end with demonstration of its ubiquity in Islamic tradition – or in any other, for that matter. With specific regard to Islam, for example, the European traveler's story of the Malay Qur'ān class in Singapore cited in the previous chapter poses in sharp definition the perplexing question broached in the same place: namely, that of the meaning of a text to someone who holds it sacred above all other texts but understands few specifics of its actual text because of ignorance of its language. This is a problem not only for the non-Arabic-speaking Muslim but also for the Arabic speaker whose spoken dialect and lack of formal education give him or her only marginally better access to the meaning of the classical language of the Qur'ān. Are such Muslims effectively cut off from penetrating the content? Is the meaning of the Qur'ān available only to the learned person who has added to the rote memorization of the holy text some years of additional study of the text and its interpretation?

The answer to this question must finally be "no". The discursive understanding, at whatever level, of qur'anic teaching is not the only access to meaning in the interaction of the faithful with the text. There is also a nondiscursive understanding or meaning that is part of the experience of overt encounter with the text itself – an encounter that is primarily oral/aural in character, rooted as it is in the recitation, or listening to the recitation, of the text. If the peculiarly strong orality of the Qur'ān or other sacred scriptures can reveal anything about the functional *meaning* of scriptural texts in religious life, it is that this meaning is not tied exclusively to the literal and intellectual content of the sacred texts, any more than it is to folk appropriation of such texts for divination, healing, or the like. Because we as modern students of religion typically invest most of our time and effort poring over precisely the linguistic meaning of the words of religious texts, we are least prepared to tackle the question of meaning when it seems to be divorced from, or at least in part independent of, the literal, word-by-word content of the text in a linguistic sense.

However, it will simply not do, in dealing with such a case as the Malayan anecdote above, to conclude that it has nothing to tell us about the meaning of the qur'anic text – or even that, as representative of countless similar situations across the Islamic world, it has less to tell us about that meaning historically than do, for example, the great works of Muslim exegesis (*tafsīr*). We must resolutely avoid dismissing the "blind" faith of the old teacher in the holiness of the Arabic words and their "special virtue" as merely uneducated superstition or a quasi-magical understanding of the efficacy of scripture recitation. The following is a good example of such dismissal by a non-Muslim scholar:

> [In the Qur'ān-school,] the Ḳur'ān is not studied to know and understand it. It is learned by heart for the reward promised in the next world to those who know it and to benefit by the virtue or *baraka* of the divine word. *This latter point of view is very much in keeping with the mentality of Muḥammadan peoples with a strong belief in magic.* [italics mine][1]

Any such reductionist analysis of the relationship between the faithful and their scriptural text is an effort to give an easy (and condescending) answer to a difficult problem: that of religious meaning that may exist apart from rational, discursive meaning – and, indeed, apart from mystical or esoteric meaning as well. Oddly enough, it is in such reductionism that orientalist rationalism and Muslim conservatism and literalism walk the same path, for both prefer the precise words of the text, on the page, as the only legitimate object of interpretive interest.

A more reflective and balanced response to this problem of textual meaning involves us in a less clear-cut explanation than we might like, but takes us closer to what I have termed the sensual arena of religion: the dimension of participation that involves not only affective states of the mind and subtle emotions such as those suggested by analyses along the lines of Friedrich Schleiermacher's *Über die Religion* and Rudolf Otto's classic *Das Heilige*, but those dependent upon the sheer physical and sensual aspects of religious practice and faith. By this I mean the encounter with the concrete world of the natural elements and the resulting visual, auditory, and tactile, or even olfactory, experiences and perceptions. As a student of religion, one is here "in the trenches" of the history of religion as it were – perhaps where one needs to be a trained anthropologist or sociologist as well as a psychologist in order to work most effectively. In any case, here one needs to be sensitive to how one approaches the role of the senses in religious life without reducing spirituality to mere "emotions" or, at the other extreme, underestimating the more intellectual side of faith that presents itself even at relatively low levels of sophistication. Yet if anything, the trend in the study of religion seems to have long been toward ever more symbolic interpretation of everyday religious piety and practice, which, for all of its ability to show that all human action is meaningful, often seems to have little to do with day-to-day experiences of individual religious persons and the more particular, even mundane meanings that they themselves attach to those experiences. Furthermore, labeling many of those meanings "magic" or "superstition" does little to move one toward a solution.

Thus it may not be a bad thing if the immensely important role of the recited Qur'ān in Muslim religiosity pushes us toward confrontation with the more physical or sensual elements of religious experience. Certainly the oral functions of scripture generally move us squarely into this sensual arena – the world of rituals, of pilgrimages and processions, hymnody and prayers, meditative and ascetic exercises, and specifically the recitation or cantillation of scripture as a distinct practice in and of itself. A story such as that of our French informant of so many years ago must be seen in this perspective. It is a perspective in which neither rational, systematic analysis of texts by theologians nor the mystical or esoteric interpretation of seers and saints need always occupy center stage. What does predominate are precisely activities such as those described throughout Chapters 7 and 8, especially the latter: *ṣalāt* recitations, Ramaḍān practices, *maqra'*s, *dhikr*-sessions, funerals, festivals, and Qur'ān lessons.

When we consider even the one small, but hardly atypical example of our Malay Qur'ān teacher, the fundamental conclusion to which it leads us is precisely that the meaning of the divine "Recitation", the Qur'ān, is often not simply either discursive or esoteric. (Although these it may be as well, as the centuries of elaborate *tafsīr* and *ta'wīl,* exoteric and esoteric Qur'ān interpretation, and the thought of Muslim legists and mystics sufficiently demonstrate.) It is also visceral and sensual, which is to say, nondiscursive, poetic, symbolic, or even aesthetic in nature. The content of an orally communicated, memorized, and recited text such as the Qur'ān always retains to a high degree what I am rather arbitrarily calling sensual meaning alongside, or in interaction with if not prior to, its discursive or esoteric sense. This is borne out in the immense and intense effect that recitation of the Qur'ān has on its Muslim (and not a few non-Muslim) hearers, as well as in the symbolic or iconic character of the text, which is such that even the smallest word or phrase from the Qur'ān – "understood" or not – refers in some degree to the whole and to the authority that the whole commands among Muslims.

Thomas Mann writes in his *Doktor Faustus* that music is the most demonic of the arts because in it form and content most completely merge and dissolve in one another. I would say of intensive oral repetition of texts such as that found in Muslim practice that this may be the most characteristically "religious" medium for the scriptural word because in it also form and content merge in a manner peculiarly congenial to conveying what William James called the experience of "the reality of the unseen"; what Rudolf Otto described as the prerational "Gefühl des *mysterium tremendum,* des schauervollen Geheimnisses" – the feeling of the dreadful and awesome Secret and Holy, the Numinous (*das Numinose*); and what Schleiermacher saw to be accessible primarily to those with "Sinn und Geschmack fürs Unendliche" – feeling and taste for the Infinite.[2] It is not at all incomprehensible even to us typographic folk that a scriptural truth that is read, recited, chanted, or sung aloud strikes the hearer with an immediacy and emotional potential that the silently read word on the page is much less likely to effect in and of itself – however important that written word may be to the person of faith.

As to meaning, I have little doubt that the old Malay and, in some degree, the little children around him, grasped some of the *meaning* of the Qur'ān – part of it wholly aside from the text itself, not to mention the recitation sessions, through the substantial education in qur'anic norms and concepts that a traditional Muslim environment impregnates in all who dwell in it; and part of it in the recitation proper, through the moving, lyric chanting of a text that each *knew* in his or her heart to be God's very speaking. At one level, the Qur'ān's meaning is to some significant degree available to anyone of any educational or literacy level in a Muslim community, because the Qur'ān is so strongly and explicitly the standard against which every aspect of life in an Islamic society is measured. Literate or not, it is virtually impossible for someone raised in a strongly Muslim environment not to imbibe the fundamental values and norms, let alone the aesthetics and sensibilities or the actual words and phrases, of the sacred text, simply because its presence is ubiquitous. A Muslim does not have to have progressed far either in piety or in his or her memorization of the text to be remarkably well acquainted with the qur'anic word and its general content.

Those who do know the text learn to apply particular phrases and passages to the widest imaginable range of circumstances, and those who do not know the text hear and necessarily absorb some of this constant referential application of the text with which they live. Whether in the Friday sermon in the mosque or family teaching in the home, the Muslim, young or old, learns weekly, daily, and hourly something of the Qur'ān as it is applied to life in the Muslim context. If such knowledge as is gained in this fashion is far less than that of the true *'ālim,* it nevertheless suffices to sustain individual Muslims as part of the larger Muslim community. Certainly it gives to the average Muslim a more than passing knowledge of scripture.

My own sense of how this can be is derived in good part from my adult experiences in a Qur'ān-saturated environment (albeit an Arabic-speaking one), and to some degree from my childhood in an American Protestant Christian environment that had its own analogies to traditional Muslim contexts as regards memorization and other aspects of the treatment of scripture. A text that is holy to a person is finally its own verification and justification; memorizing and repeating its words are exercises in appropriation of its meaning, but not always, and rarely *only,* at a discursive level. The symbolic and affective force of the recited scripture among Muslims of all ages, education, and cultural-linguistic backgrounds must not be underestimated. Meaning is carried by the recitation over and above the particular meaning of the literal passage recited, however deeply felt and understood that meaning may be on an intellectual plane. How to get at that meaning is a detailed project for another place, but unless we can recognize that it exists, the true import of the Qur'ān for the Muslim will remain inaccessible to the outsider, as will its recitational, oral aspect as scripture.

PART IV

"The Lively Oracles of God": Bible as Spoken Word

Consider by how many testimonies the word of the Lord urges us to recite the holy Scriptures that we may possess through faith what we have repeated with our mouth. . . .

– *Testament* of Horsiesius

The Bible [*die Biblia*] is the Holy Spirit's own special book, writ, and word.

– Martin Luther

The Islamic world is far from homogeneous, and the range of religious piety and practice is certainly large. Nevertheless, the Qur'ān's central and dominant place in Islam has ensured for it an unusually consistent status and role in Muslim faith and usage. Like other stable "pillars" of Muslim piety such as the prescribed daily worship in the *ṣalāt* and the fast in the month of Ramaḍān, the salient forms of qur'anic piety and practice exhibit far more continuities than divergences across the wide spectrum of Islamic life. Details of custom and interpretation may cause particular variances from place to place and group to group, as, for example, in which *sūrah*s, or chapters, of the holy text are recited on a given occasion or which legal interpretation of a qur'anic verse is followed; yet the basic roles and authority of the Qur'ān remain everywhere identifiable. Consequently, it is possible in treating scripture in Islam to draw upon evidence from diverse periods and places without doing violence to the experience and practice of the many and varied cultural, ethnic, linguistic, geographic, and sectarian traditions of the vast Muslim world.

Christianity, on the other hand, presents a much more diverse set of attitudes and usages with respect to scripture's place in faith and practice. This is hardly surprising since, as much as any other major religious tradition, Christianity encompasses a bewildering variety of confessional, liturgical, and organizational, not to mention cultural, linguistic, and institutional forms. This makes the problem of selection for any general investigation of Christian scriptural use a vexing one. An exhaustive study of the role of the Bible in Christendom is obviously an impossibility; yet a "representative" sampling is likely to be an equally elusive venture. With such a method, it would be only slightly less difficult to prove the absence than to prove the presence of significant scriptural orality across the tradition as a whole.

For this reason, I have not resorted to a broad sampling from the vast range of piety and practice in Christianity such as I have attempted with Islamic scripturality in Part III. Instead, I have chosen a different approach. What I propose in the ensuing three chapters is to look at the oral dimension of Christian scripturality with reference first to some salient aspects of scripture in the Christian tradition as a whole, but with particular attention to the early church; and then with regard to two specific, and very diverse, historical cases of biblical piety in which this oral dimension is clearly evident. In focusing on two concrete traditions and contexts within the larger Christian framework, I want to suggest that a rethinking of our common ideas about the function of scripture in many other, if not all sectors of Christian tradition may be in order.

The particular cases I have chosen are drawn from the disparate worlds of early monasticism and the Protestant Reformation. With the former, we shall look in detail at the oral role of scripture in the Pachomian discipline of upper Egypt in the third and fourth centuries. With the latter, we shall investigate the highly oral and aural orientation to the biblical word in the writings of the giant of the sixteenth-century reformers, Martin Luther. Although these two examples cannot establish a rule for all other cases in Christian experience, they do present compelling evidence for the centrality of the spoken word of holy writ in significant and significantly different historical and cultural phases of that experience. They suggest in different ways the lively and highly oral relationship to scripture that large numbers of Christians have known and cherished for many centuries (and in many, if fewer, instances still today). This relationship is belied by any simplistic notion of scripture as "only a book" in the sense of only a written codex or printed volume. Even though it is by no means "lively" only because of the oral dimension of scripture in Christian use, an appreciation of this particular dimension can do much to illuminate some of the richness and complexity of Christian scripturalism, or "book religion", as a whole.

CHAPTER 10

The Spoken Word of Christian Holy Writ

So faith is from hearing [*ex akoēs*], but hearing is through the word of Christ [*dia hrēmatos Christou*].
– Paul, Epistle to the Romans 10.17

Any discussion of Christian scripture must begin with the concept of the word of God before proceeding to that of holy writ. The traditional Christian emphasis upon the word of God and its use in many instances as a synonym for the Bible is such an all-embracing topic as to make it too amorphous and diverse to provide a focus or primary concern for our investigations here. Nevertheless, it does bear some comment at the outset, especially with regard to its specific relation to the Bible.

The Word of God and Holy Writ

To begin with, the understanding of Book and Word among any group of Christians is not a simple or monolithic one. It may appall as many Christians as it pleases when an American Protestant evangelist raises a copy of the Bible over his head and says to the crowds gathered in one of our latter-day amphitheaters, "Lift up your Bibles! Lift up your Bibles! The Spirit of God is moving here tonight in Madison Square Garden!" Yet whatever the religious judgment upon such an act, the preacher is making undeniably a time-honored call upon the central importance of Holy Writ in Christian faith. In addition, more is going on here than some kind of call upon either the magical power of the written/printed word of the Bible or the traditional authority of the bound, "canonical" volume containing the church's recognized text of divine revelation (although these factors may also be involved). In such a situation, the Book functions rather as an icon, a multifaceted symbol of Christian faith and divine revelation, not least to symbolize and presage the preaching of the word of God in what will follow the melodramatic initial gesture of the evangelist.

From the beginning, the word of God for Christians was expressed above all in the kerygma, the preached message of the Resurrection to the unconverted and to the faithful members of the nascent church. Even through much of the second Christian century, this preaching of the "good news" took precedence over any scriptural authority accorded to Jewish holy writ or early Christian writings as the prime vehicle of God's word. Put simply, the word of God was the gospel message of the risen Christ long before it was a book or collection of books.

Once the young Christian tradition became self-consciously a "religion of the Book", like the Judaic tradition out of which it came, the chief authority for its preaching of the word of God came to be sought in the words of scripture. The scriptures, however, were not merely written documents pored over only by the literate in the quiet of their own houses. The actual contents of the scriptural book (or, more correctly for the early Christian centuries, of the scriptural *books*) were transmitted largely through liturgical reading, catechetical instruction, and quotation and exegesis in sermons. This was especially true through the entire early medieval period, from the sixth to the tenth or eleventh century, when, if anything, literacy rates fell rather than rose from the levels that probably obtained in the Hellenistic–Roman culture of late antiquity.[1] Nor did these oral modes of transmission of scripture ever die out. However, in the Christianity of the Middle Ages, especially in Western Europe, the centrality of the bare scriptural word in liturgy, catechism, and sermon receded before the elaboration of the church liturgical tradition. This had presumably greatest effect upon the ordinary layperson, who, with few exceptions, no longer spoke or understood Latin, the language of liturgy and Bible in Western Christendom. Constant exposure to the biblical text, not to mention active scriptural study and use, came to be largely the preserve of the monk, the scholar, and, to a lesser degree, the cleric. Thus the Word was available to the rank and file mainly through the evolved forms of the liturgy, biblical storytelling, or biblically inspired art, and much less, if at all, through substantial reading, recitation, and study of the holy words themselves.

The Protestant Reformation in Europe was in many ways a conscious effort to recover the early Christian kerygmatic orientation – the direct preaching and teaching of the word of God to all who would listen. (Never mind that by this time it was a Word more firmly set in writing than ever before, not only in manuscript codices, but also in the new medium of the printed book.) "Reformation" in this regard meant submission to the authority of "scripture alone" (*sola scriptura*), but this was not so much a call to go "back to the Book" in the sense of the written/printed word as to return to the spirit and authority of the scriptures as texts containing the all-sufficient word of God.[2] In other words, to return to the imagined purity of early Christian obedience to the authority of the gospel word rather than the state of the corrupt medieval Western church in Rome. As we shall see in the case of Luther, the word of God was for him above all the preached word that conveyed and explained the scriptural word and ultimately was drawn from it. In general, the Word as such was the kerygma itself rather than a specific text or texts.

Nor did the reformers understand the scriptures only in the narrow sense of a volume with so and so many lines of divinely revealed, immutable text. Translation into the vernaculars was, after all, an important plank in the reformers' platforms (and humanist emphasis upon recovery of more accurate texts still did not militate against providing more accurate, intelligible translations). Furthermore, Luther, Calvin, Zwingli, and the other reformers were not working with an absolutely fixed "canon" of biblical "books". "Official" pronouncements about the exact books to be included and excluded from the canon, especially as regards the Apocrypha, would have to wait for the institutionalizing work of the Council of Trent in Roman Catholic Europe (1546) or the Westminster Confession in Protestant England (1647). The word of God in scripture was not a single, verbatim revelation but a message carried by writings deemed by the tradition to be divinely inspired and, in this sense, the revealed word of God.

These considerations suggest at least something of the conceptual and functional complexity of "the word of God" in the Christian tradition. Added to these is the identification of Jesus the Christ with the divine word (*ho logos*), which has made Christian thinking about the word of God particularly involved and Christian use of the concept often ambiguous. For example, Christian discussions of God's word and the word of scripture have been substantially less straightforward than Muslim treatments of the relation of the divine word (*kalām Allāh*) to the Qur'ān. As we have seen above, for the Muslim the Qur'ān is the earthly form of God's word not simply as a scriptural record of revelation analogous to the Bible for the Christian, but specifically as the tangible embodiment of divine revelation analogous to the saving mediator, Christ.[3] As such there is little room for any identification of the Word with anything other than the Qur'ān, whereas in the Christian case, the Christ was conceived to be the Word incarnate.

Thus, while we shall focus here on functional roles of the scriptural word of God among Christians, we must not forget the deeper structures of symbolization associated with the notion of the Word itself: This Word can be the preached kerygma of the risen Christ, the revealed words of the biblical text, or the Christ himself. The symbolic and sacramental interpenetration of these three senses of the Word cannot be ignored any more than can the interpenetration of the qur'anic word and the active speaking of God to the individual in Muslim perspective or of the speech of God and God's holy law in Judaic thought. While all three Western monotheistic traditions affirm the indissoluble link between the divine word set forth in scripture and the historical experience of encounter with the divine, it is the Christian tradition that presents unusual complexity and even ambiguity in its treatment of the divine word.

Scripture in the Early Church

To understand the oral or any other role of Christian scripture in either early monasticism or the Reformation, it is necessary to understand something of the place accorded scripture in the formative development of the larger tradition – that is, in roughly its first two to three centuries. This period was ever after a normative one for Christian practice and faith, whether among the desert monks of fourth-century Egypt and Syria, the reformers of sixteenth-century Europe, or whatever far-flung segment of the Christian tradition one chooses. If this period has often been misunderstood, misinterpreted, even misappropriated in very different later circumstances so as to authorize particularist interpretations and practices, it remains still the undeniable foundation upon which the whole Christian venture in all its diverse strands has rested. Thus it is here we must begin.

The early Christian relationship to the texts that would gradually become "the Bible" was based, at least with regard to the Hebrew scriptures, on the Christians' understanding of the practice of Jesus himself. Because he was a Jew in a largely Judaic religious and social context, his ministry drew naturally upon the authority of the Judaic holy writings that were eventually to become the "Old Testament" of the Christian movement. The writer of Acts (17.10-11) and the apostle Paul (at least in his four major epistles: see, e.g., Rom. 15.4) also testify to the authority of the Hebrew scriptures for the earliest Christian followers of Jesus.[4] For over a century, the only sacred books, or "bible" (*ta biblia*), available to the Christians were the Hebrew scriptures (whether in Hebrew, Greek, Syriac, or other versions).[5] They were cited as authorities not only by New Testament writers, but also by the earliest of the so-called Apostolic Fathers, the author of the *First Epistle of Clement,* Ignatius of Antioch, and the author of the *Epistle of Barnabas*.[6]

These scriptures were important primarily as sources of moral norms and as prophetic proof texts confirming the new kerygma of the risen Christ.[7] If the Christians' eventual development of a bipartite corpus of holy writings through the addition of their own "new testament" was novel, the fundamental idea of the divine inspiration and authority of sacred written books was not: It grew naturally out of the Judaic matrix in which the Christian community took shape in its first three centuries.[8] In addition, the Judaic notion of the authoritativeness of the written word was reinforced for the early Christians by the Hellenistic tradition of Greek and Latin scholarship, education, and reading, to which literate Christian thought and practice also fell heir in later antiquity.

Christianity did not, to be sure, begin (as did Islam) by being a religion of the sacred book; but by the middle or late second century, true to its Judaic background,[9] it had become one to a degree unknown in any other tradition in the Hellenistic milieu.[10] It is not an exaggeration to speak even of "an addiction to literacy" in the early Christian movement;[11] certainly it appears that even in the face of attacks by outsiders and heretics who themselves cited scripture as proof text, the young church never resorted to attempts to limit study and circulation of scripture among the laity.[12]

The Oral Dimension

An appreciation of the Christians' unusually strong emphasis on having and reading a written scripture does not diminish the importance of the audible presence of the biblical word in the early church. On the contrary, such emphasis should be a confirmation of the prominence of the vocal word of scripture in both individual and communal life. Let us pause briefly to examine why this is so.

In the first place, a written text was still an oral phenomenon. As we have seen in Chapter 3, reading by oneself and even copying were vocal, not silent activities in these centuries. Revelation 1.3 shows us that written texts were conceived of as things to be read forth and attended: "Blessed is he who reads aloud the words of the prophecy, and blessed are those who hear, and who keep what is written therein . . . ." The sacred books carried both the special authority of the written page and the living immediacy of oral reading and recitation. Oral reading and recitation were the primary means through which the written word was apprehended and reflected upon, as well as communicated, not only among the illiterate but also among the educated members of the community.

In the second place, the formal public reading or lesson (Lat.: *lectio*; Gr.: *anagnōsis*) from the Hebrew scriptures became a basic part of Christian worship and education relatively early.[13] Although it is unlikely that this reading was a regular part of Christian congregational observances in the Apostolic age, by the mid-second century it had become customary. The author of the First Epistle to Timothy (ca. 120–60 C.E.) exhorts the latter: "Till I come, attend to the public reading of scripture [*proseche tē anagnōsei*], to preaching, to teaching" (1 Tim. 4.13). Equally clear are the references to the public reading of scripture in Justin Martyr's *First Apology* (ca. 150) and the probably slightly earlier Christian homily known as the *Second Epistle of Clement*.[14]

By this time, the liturgy of the Word had come to include also readings not only from the Hebrew scriptures (the Prophets, in particular), but also from the writings of the Apostles[15] – presumably the Gospels and Pauline epistles.[16] Indeed, in the view of the "Muratorian Canon" (ca. 200 C.E.), the accepted use of particular books in the public, liturgical *lectio* (as opposed to private reading) seems to be the acid test of the scripturality or "apostolicity" of the still fluid body of "New Covenant" writings.[17] Thus the public *lectio* would be a key sector of Christian practice in which to trace the emergence of the idea of a two-testament grouping and, later, an actual two-part written collection of Christian scriptures, had we sufficiently detailed descriptions of worship in the apostolic and early patristic periods.

The early sources, however, give us only very occasional and brief glimpses of the details of Christian worship before the fourth century. As a result, it is difficult to judge how formally the liturgy of the Word was developed in the second and third centuries. References to the "reader", or "lector" (Gk: *anagnōstēs, anagignōskonta*), indicate that by the middle or later part of the third century this was becoming a formally recognized position in the early church order.[18] There is also evidence from at least as early as the mid-third century that the liturgy of the Word had come to accompany the Eucharist on at least some occasions in the practice of various Christian communities.[19]

Alongside, and normally in connection with the liturgical reading, the scriptural word was also constantly spoken and heard in the sermon, which most often took the form of either a cento from scripture or exegesis of a scriptural passage.[20] The scriptural word was also vividly present in worship through the preeminent liturgical role of the Psalms in chant and song,[21] not to mention their dominance of the language of homiletic and theological discourse.[22] The later development in East and West of collections of scriptural passages specifically arranged for oral recitation in divine service and daily devotional use points also to the major role of the spoken scriptural word in traditional Christian piety. These collections include, in addition to the psalter, the lectionaries – such as the Gospel reader, or evangeliary (Gk.: *euangelion;* Lat.: *evangeliarium*), and epistolary (Gk.: *apostolos* or *epistolarē;* Lat.: *epistolarium*), containing the Acts and Epistles – and the later breviary, or *breviarium* (Ger.: *Stundenbuch*), which contains a variety of texts for use in the Mass.[23]

We must also not forget the practical necessity for memorization and reading aloud of the scriptures in ages in which all copies of texts were hand-copied and not so easily or cheaply placed in the hands of every Christian as Gideon Bibles are today – and in times when there must have been a significant percentage, presumably a majority, of Christians who could not read and write at all.[24] Even as early as the end of the third century, it has been argued, many laypersons knew "the major portions" of scripture by heart.[25] Augustine, for example, gives us at least oblique testimony to widespread lay familiarity with the (read or recited) scriptural word. In a letter to Jerome, he criticizes the reading in divine service of the book of Jonah in Jerome's new Latin translation: The new version, he complains, differs from the text "which had been rooted in the affection and memories of all the people and repeated in so many succeeding generations."[26] On another occasion he asserts that, rather than for him to give a sermon, it is better for the congregation to whom he was to preach to be put instead into immediate contact with the word of God through his reading directly from scripture.[27] This underscores the clear sense of many Christians that the *lectio* represented in effect God speaking to those assembled – as the following words of Ambrose attest:

> Why do you not use the time that you have free from church affairs for reading? Why not visit Christ, speak with Christ, listen to Christ? We speak with him when we pray, we listen to him when we read the divine words [lit.: "oracles"].[28]

For the Patristic tradition of the early Church, the liturgy of the word was understood to stand alongside, not in subordination to, the Eucharist.[29] Thus Jerome could compare scripture to the body of Christ "in expressions which sound extravagant to modern readers."[30] If Jerome's dictum, "ignorance of the scriptures is ignorance of Christ,"[31] expressed a widespread attitude among the church fathers, Augustine offers a good example of the heights to which knowledge of the scriptures could soar. Always first and foremost a preacher of the Word, he (like most of the fathers) saw that Word as a unity, a single whole comprising both the "books" of the Hebrew scriptures and those of the New Covenant. This whole was to be drawn upon in explaining any particular part thereof, and his immense memory allowed him to do just this: "In one sermon, he could move through the whole Bible, from Paul to Genesis and back again, *via* the Psalms, piling half-verse on half-verse."[32]

It would be possible to pursue at great length how psalmody, *lectio,* and sermon reflect the active presence of the spoken word of Holy Writ in the early church. Certainly these phenomena deserve separate study as significant chapters in the history of the Bible's role in Christian piety.[33] I want, however, to pass instead to the later third century and the particular context of early Christian monasticism, where we can see with unusual clarity the dynamic role of the spoken word of the sacred *biblia* among some of the earliest "athletes" of Christian spirituality – those persons who took their faith so seriously as to devote their entire life in all its details to God. Since the early desert monks of Egypt and Syria–Palestine placed such strong and exclusive emphasis upon scripture as the source of authority for all that they did, their piety and practice offer an especially rich context in which to examine the oral aspects of scripture in early Christian history.

CHAPTER 11

God's Word in the Desert

And these words which I command you this day shall be upon your heart; and you shall teach them diligently to your children, and shall talk of them when you sit in your house, and when you walk by the way, and when you lie down, and when you rise. You shall therefore lay up these words of mine in your heart and in your soul.

– Deut. 6.6-7; cf. Deut. 11.18-19

The wellsprings of Christian monastic life, East and West – and of a considerable portion of Christian spirituality more broadly – are to be found in the practices of the desert ascetics of Egypt and Palestine between the closing decades of the third and the end of the fourth century C.E.[1] Two of the "saints of the desert", both of them Egyptians, stand out here: Antony and Pachomius. Although neither has any claim to having initiated the Christian ascetic pursuit of a life of retreat, each became the symbolic father of a particular style of ascetic discipline. Because of their renowned piety and eventual influence (both direct and indirect) on diverse monastic movements elsewhere, both have occupied special places in the early history of Christian spirituality virtually since their own lifetimes. Saint Antony (d. ca. 356), who became widely known in Christendom through Athanasius' *Life of Antony,* has in the past commonly been viewed as the father of Christian eremitic or anchoritic monachism – the solitary withdrawal from society to pursue devotions and ascetic discipline as a hermit – even though he had many predecessors in such practice. Similarly, Saint Pachomius (d. ca. 347) has been widely regarded as the founder of cenobitic, or communal, monachism in Christendom, even though many desert monks had lived in at least loose association with one another before his time. His claim to this distinction rests both upon the strong impress made by his formal monastic Rule on the ensuing organization of Christian monastic communities and upon his subsequent recognition as the first organizer of a true community, or "monastery-church", of monks.[2] It is Pachomius and his community of disciples who are our primary concern in what follows.

The Pachomian *Koinonia*

Pachomius was born about the year 292. The principal early Coptic and Greek biographies tell us that as a young man he was conscripted and served as a Roman soldier until about 314. At this time, he became a Christian convert, and for some years after his conversion he pursued an ascetic and anchoritic existence devoted to charity under the tutelage of an older hermit of upper Egypt named Palamon.[3]

Some time before the year 320, Pachomius received a call to an expanded vocation arising from but going beyond the eremitic existence he had thus far led. With the help of his brother, he set up a monastic retreat community, a *koinonia,* at Tabennesi (whence the later common name, "Tabennesiots", for the Pachomian monks). Tabennesi was situated in the Thebaid, the region of upper Egypt around the sharp bend of the Nile below ancient Thebes (some four hundred miles south of Alexandria).[4] Here, under his leadership and guidance, and after him that of his two major disciples, Horsiesius (d. between 386 and 412?)[5] and Theodore (d. 368), a new kind of communal piety developed. Those Christians who sought retreat from the spiritual anarchy and religious persecutions of the troubled fourth-century Mediterranean world came together in increasing numbers to submit their lives to the discipline of the Pachomian community and its Rule. They formed first one, then a number of monastic communities (including at least two convents for women) in the Thebaid. Although these communities were basically Coptic-speaking, at least one Greek-speaking *koinonia* had been established well before Pachomius' death.[6] All of these monasteries were dedicated to an extremely simple way of life, devoid of luxuries and distractions and devoted to love of one's neighbor and the constant mindfulness and worship of God. The basic disciplines of this life were asceticism, especially fasting; daily handiwork and other simple labor; and almost continual worship and meditation involving principally scripture recitation or chanting and other forms of prayer.

Continuities in Pachomian and Later Monachism

The lines of continuity that connect the Pachomian *koinonia* and later Christian monastic institutions are undisputed, however one assesses the specific degree of "influence" of Pachomian ideals and practices on later forms relative to that of other early models, such as the monastic practice of lower Egypt or

Syria–Palestine. Certainly Pachomianism came to be seen in the Christian monastic tradition of the late patristic and early medieval periods as a, if not the, major precursor of subsequent monasticism East and West. This occurred both because the Pachomian Rule was so often taken as a model for the formulation, or a standard for evaluation, of later monastic institutions, and also because of the persistent influence of Pachomian ideals on those of later monasticism.[7]

The spread of the Pachomian Rule was particularly evident in the East. It took hold early in Ethiopia and, according to tradition, reached Mesopotamia and Persia in the mid-fourth century.[8] As late as the twelfth century a Pachomian monastery of some five hundred monks is said to have survived in Constantinople. Even though in the Eastern world the Pachomian Rule was subsumed in the tradition initiated by Basil the Great (d. 379), it still retained great popularity as a spiritual guide to the monastic life.[9] Furthermore, the work and thought of Basil were themselves influenced to an as yet not fully understood, but apparently significant degree by Pachomian cenobitic ideals.[10]

Pachomian influence filtered into the West by several identifiable routes: through the two sojourns in Western Europe[11] of the Alexandrian bishop, Athanasius (d. 373), who held the Tabennesiots and other desert ascetics in high esteem (as evidenced especially in his *Life of Antony*); through the Pachomian Rules and writings themselves, particularly as they became known in the Latin translations of Jerome (d. 420);[12] and through the Latin works of John Cassian (d. ca. 435)[13] and Palladius (d. 425),[14] not to mention the actual monastic communities set up under Cassian's regulation in France. Benedict knew and used the Pachomian Rule, along with various other earlier works on monastic life such as those of Cassian and Basil.[15] Thus, there is considerable justification for seeing in Pachomian monachism a significant model for, as well as a temporal precursor of later Christian monastic practice and piety.

Scripture and the Monastic Life

If the Pachomian tradition itself did not survive as an active order, its spirit did, and nowhere more clearly than in the principle that scripture is the ultimate basis for every facet of the monastic life. Monasticism, as much as, and usually more than other modes of Christian spirituality, has always been rooted firmly in the word of God as contained for Christians in holy scripture. This rootedness begins with the monk's adherence to the command of Jesus (Matt. 19.21) to "go, sell what you possess and give to the poor, . . . and come, follow me." It continues in the active role played by the scriptures, which historically have consistently provided the basis for monastic devotion, liturgy, discipline, theology, order, and values. Indeed, the *lectio divina,* or "sacred reading", was uniquely associated with monks and their way of life from the earliest days of Christian monastic piety.[16] As a saying of one of the fourth-century desert fathers has it: "The asceticism of the monk [is] meditation of the scriptures and realization of God's precepts. . . ."[17] The fundamental importance of the biblical word in all forms of Christian monachism, not least the many Western institutions developed under the influence of the Benedictine Rule, is striking and widely recognized, however much the later tendency was to use other Christian texts alongside the Bible as the material of the *lectio divina*.[18]

The centrality of scripture was if anything even more pronounced in the Pachomian tradition than in its successors.[19] In even the most cursory reading of the Pachomian sources, one is struck by the often almost seamless web of scriptural allusions and citations that runs through nearly every document written by or about Pachomius and his disciples.[20] These writings also reflect the daily role of scripture in the chanting of psalms, the special gatherings for instruction on the meaning of scripture, and the reading or recitation during daily work and night vigils. The Rule developed by Pachomius was itself viewed as a kind of digest and explanation of those scriptural precepts most applicable to the life of the monk.[21]

If, however, the Pachomian emphasis upon scripture is unusually explicit, it cannot be seen as an anomaly or aberration within the larger world of Christian monasticism. It would be surprising if any later arbiters of monastic rules in East or West would not have claimed the same consciousness of intent in basing their own institutions on scripture that is so evident in the Pachomian case. They, too, would have agreed with the Pachomian dictum that the scriptures "are the main thing and the breath of God."[22] It is well as we turn to the particular case of Pachomian treatment of scripture to keep in mind that it is the original seedbed from which all later Christian monasticism and its scriptural orientation have sprung, early or late.

Scripture in the Pachomian *Koinonia*

The Rules and other writings that provide us with our primary sources for Pachomian monasticism testify not only to the presence of scripture in every facet of the life of Pachomius and his disciples; they also reflect the high degree to which that scriptural presence was primarliy an oral and aural one in the daily and yearly round of the *koinonia*. When Pachomius' disciple Theodore says in his *Instructions*,[23] "let us then pay heed to what we hear in the Holy Scriptures," "hear" is not simply a metaphor for silent reading of a written book, but a literal expression of the vocal character of reading and recitation among the Tabennesiots.

To be sure, the monasteries of fourth-century Egypt had collections of books, even if we cannot compare the probable extent of these with that of, say, the large medieval monastic libraries in Western Europe.[24] There is a reasonable possibility, for example, that the invaluable Gnostic collection of manuscripts found in the late 1940s at Nag Hammadi came originally from the library of a Pachomian monastery in the vicinity.[25] As that part of the *Rules (Praecepta)* of Pachomius that deals with reception of the novice monk makes clear, learning to read from books was an obligation imposed upon everyone who entered the *koinonia:*

> . . . if he [the newcomer] is illiterate, he shall go at the first, third, and sixth hours to someone who can teach and has been appointed for him. He shall stand before him and learn very studiously with all gratitude. Then the fundamentals of a syllable, the verbs, and nouns shall be written for him, and even if he does not want to, he shall be compelled to read.
>
> There shall be no one whatever in the monastery who does not learn to read and does not memorize something of the Scriptures. [One should learn by heart] at least the New Testament and the Psalter.[26]

References to the borrowing, use, and treatment of books are common enough in the Pachomian *Rules* and other sources to indicate that they were a visible and important part of *koinonia* life,[27] as were letters between the Pachomian abbots and outside figures such as Athanasius, Ammon, or the holy Antony.[28] Furthermore, use of the standard Jewish and Christian phrase, "[as] it is written", or the like, to introduce a quotation from scripture is a common formula that occurs throughout the sources – a reminder of how fundamental was the concept of God's Word as Holy Writ, as well as how strong was its authority as proof text and guide.[29]

Nevertheless, if writing and reading were common enough in the Pachomian daily round, they served primarily as vehicles for the far more crucial task of memorizing and internalizing ("learning *by heart*" in the fullest sense of the phrase) the words of scripture in order literally to live them and, through their constant reading and recitation, in effect to breathe them each moment of the day.[30] The provisions of Pachomius and his successors for both reading aloud and recitation of the scriptures from memory were as explicit as they were fundamental. In the "Instruction Concerning a Spiteful Monk" of Pachomius, the monks are told to "Recite constantly the words of God."[31] Similarly, Horsiesius admonishes his fellow monks:[32]

> Let us devote ourselves to reading and learning the Scriptures, reciting them continually,[33] aware of the text, "A man shall be filled with the fruit of his own mouth [Prov. 13.2], and he will be paid the price of his labors" [Wis. 10.17]. These are the [words] which lead us to eternal life, the [words] our father handed down to us and commanded us continually to recite,[34] that what was written might be fulfilled in us . . . .[35]
>
> Consider by how many testimonies the word of the Lord urges us to recite[36] the holy Scriptures that we may possess through faith what we have repeated with our mouth[37] . . . .

Theodore declares matter-of-factly at one point, "We read from the Scriptures every day and we recite them."[38] This is if anything an understatement. The very first prerequisite for entry into and participation in the communal life of the monastery, even for the illiterate, was memorization of a minimum of scripture. Rule 49 of the *Praecepta* says of the person who asks to join the community: "he shall remain outside at the door [of the monastery] a few days and be taught the Lord's prayer and as many psalms as he can learn."[39] Once inside, the novice monk would have found that very little went on *without* the accompaniment of recitation from the Psalms or other passages of scripture. The sources reflect the intensity of the preoccupation with the divine word: We find substantial references to memorization of scripture; to recitation/meditation as a major preoccupation in its own right; to liturgical recitation, including both communal worship and funeral rites; to the chanting of psalms and other scriptural passages while walking, weaving, baking, gathering rushes, and welcoming special visitors; and to scripture reading and recitation during the communal meals and as the basis of all teaching and preaching in the community. In what follows, we shall look briefly at each of these in order to form some idea of how pervasive the sound of the scriptural word was within the *koinonia*.

Memorization

Memorization was a basic discipline for the Pachomian monks, as it had been originally for Pachomius at the start of his own ascetic training. While striving to emulate his teacher Palamon's piety, he is said to have devoted himself "more and more to important exercises, to a great and intensive *ascesis*, and to lengthy recitations of the books of Holy Scripture. He had his heart set on reciting them in order [and] with great ease."[40] In the monasteries, monks assembled each evening after their "modest meal", at which time it was the practice for "each one to pronounce what he knew of the holy Scriptures. . . . when they were seated, each one brought forth the saying he had learned or that he had heard from the lips of others."[41] Repeated allusions in the sources to learning and reciting the scriptures by heart reflect how fundamental a feature of Pachomian monachism memorization was.[42] Indeed, in characterizing the Tabennesiots, Palladius notes that, along with the various kinds of manual labor required of them, "they learn all the scriptures by heart."[43]

Although it is unlikely that more than a few monks really memorized "all the scriptures by heart", it does appear that all of them learned at least a minimum number of biblical verses, above all from the Psalms. As we saw above, entry into the community in the first place required one to learn enough psalms and other scriptural passages by heart in order to participate in at least the basic routine of the monastery. Thus memorization was the first labor demanded of a monk, whether lettered, semiliterate, or completely illiterate: ". . . they will also be given psalms [to learn] by heart; and moreover they shall learn from the books of holy Scripture."[44] One of the *Rules* of Horsiesius specifies this general demand in terms of a practical minimum required of even those least adept at memorization: "Let us be wealthy in texts learned by heart. Let him who does not memorize much memorize at least ten sections along with a section of the psalter."[45]

Just how important knowing the words of God by heart was in the context of the monastic life is difficult to grasp for most of us today, at least for those of us outside those contemporary monastic communities in which the meditative tradition is still alive. The word of God was quite simply the chief and singularly most effective weapon against all temptation and error – what St. Paul called "the sword of the Spirit" (Eph. 6.17).[46] Paul's military metaphor is echoed in Theodore's admonition to his fellow monks:

> I assure you, my brothers, that if we do not keep watch at all times with the words of the holy Scriptures, the enemy will take from us the fear of the Lord and make us fear him. Then we will do evil works and provoke God, our creator.[47]

Reciting or reading scripture was thus the first step to realizing its guidance and protection in one's life and action as well as one's speech. One may speculate about the quasi-magical character of this faith in the efficacy of the recited scriptural word, but however that may be, the religious sense of the power of the divine word (and of the recitative discipline) was strong among the Tabennesiots. One of the Sahidic fragments attributes the following words to Pachomius:

> If then an impure thought rises up in your heart, or hatred . . . . and if you want all these thoughts to diminish in you and not to have power over you, then recite in your heart without ceasing every fruit that is written in the Scriptures, having in yourself the resolution to walk in them, as it is written in Isaiah [33.18], "Your heart shall meditate on the fear" of the Lord, and all these things shall cease from you, little by little . . . .[48]

Memorization provided the first line of access to the word of God, and it was an access that allowed for recitation (i.e., *meditatio:* see below, "Meditation") of scripture at times when reading from a book was not possible or difficult: for example, in night vigils, while walking, during manual labor, or in teaching and discussion. It was presumably this immediate accessibility of the memorized word of which Theodore speaks in these words ascribed to him in the Bohairic life of Pachomius:

> Now then, my brothers, I assure you before God and his Christ that a single psalm is possibly enough to save us if we understand it well, act on it, and observe it. But, above all, we have always at hand the holy Gospels of our Lord Jesus Christ and all the rest of the holy Scriptures and their thoughts.[49]

"At hand" here means "in the memory", ready to be called forth at any and every moment. The discipline of learning and being able to quote at will from the scriptures was, however, not aimed ultimately at achieving technical expertise in memorization,[50] but rather at transforming the total thought and speech of the individual monk, so that ". . . if one of the faithful is seized by a thought, he produces only the sweetness of the words of God written in the Scriptures."[51]

"Meditation"

An almost ceaseless practice of recitation was enjoined upon all the members of the *koinonia,* and this recitation and constant internalization of scripture were the overriding goals of memorization. "The Pachomians spent most of their time reciting, and for that purpose they had to learn a great part of the Scripture by heart."[52] Memorization of scripture made possible sustained recitation of sacred texts, or, more precisely, "meditation" of those texts, since the words for recitation in the sources are the Latin *meditatio* or Greek [and Coptic] *meletē.* Before we consider specific ways and contexts in which recitation and reading aloud from the scriptures were carried on, the activity of recitation/meditation itself bears a closer look.

When we examine the meanings of the words that correspond to "meditation" and "meditate" in either the biblical text itself or the Pachomian and other early and medieval Christian sources, it becomes rapidly apparent how easily modern usage can mislead us.[53] Today these words carry almost exclusively the sense of a wholly internal, abstract, and soundless process of mental reflection or focusing of consciousness on a particular theme or idea. They convey neither the close connection of "meditation" specifically to a scriptural text nor the physical dimension of audible recitation and repetition and of training and exercising that the corresponding Hebrew, Greek, and Latin terms can render.[54]

In early Christian piety the act of "meditating" was closely linked to a passage or book of scripture. This direct tie to a scriptural text continued strong into the high Middle Ages, although with time not only scriptural texts but also later Christian writings became appropriate objects of meditation in monastic, clerical, and lay devotional use: The writings of the Church Fathers, for example, became "classics" of Christian spirituality worthy of being learned and "meditated" in their own right in the *lectio divina.*[55] However, even in later medieval times, whatever the precise focus of "meditation" might be, it was still a *text,* not a problem or theme that one "meditated", and that text was normally, if not necessarily, a scriptural passage. In the Patristic age this was even more exclusively the case: While "meditation" suggested contemplation or study aimed at realizing the full meaning of a text, it did not mean simply "contemplation" or "reflection" as an abstract activity that could be divorced from the confrontation with a concrete portion of the scriptural word.[56]

Nor was it a silent, interior act of mind and heart alone: The tongue had also to be involved. The Hebrew *hāgāh,* like the Latin *meditare* and the Greek (and Coptic, which uses the Greek) *meletan,* denoted in the first instance an oral activity, namely "to murmur, recite or repeat aloud (from memory)." From this developed the extended meanings, "to recite or go over internally, in one's heart" and "to practice assiduously, study, take care with". Reflection on a text, like reading a text, was an audible and vocal, not a silent and purely mental activity.[57] Heinrich Bacht, Jean Leclercq, and a number of other modern scholars have underscored this active, physical, vocal dimension of *meditatio* in Pachomian and other patristic use, as well as in later medieval use, especially in the monastic context.[58] Leclercq describes this aspect of meditation as follows:

> For the ancients, to meditate is to read a text and to learn it "by heart" in the fullest sense of this expression, that is to say, with one's whole being: with the body, since the mouth pronounces it, with the memory which fixes it, with the intelligence which understands its meaning, and with the will which longs to put it into practice.[59]

The other major classical sense, especially in Latin usage, of *meditare/meletan* was also decidedly physical and concrete: "to exercise or train oneself in, to practice diligently"; accordingly, *meditatio* also denoted "preparation, exercise, practice, training", and *meletē* "care, attention, practice, exercise", as well as reflective recitation.[60] This "practitional" sense can be also be documented in Patristic usage,[61] and it occurs at least as late as the twelfth century in the Latin West alongside the increasing use of *meditatio/meditari* in a "reflective" or internalized sense.[62]

Accordingly, meditation in the Pachomian, and indeed in all early (and much of later) monasticism, is to be understood as an exercise that includes contemplation of a (scriptural) text, but always a contemplation grounded in repeated recitation of the scriptural word viva voce. Such recitation is most commonly from memory, but it can also be from a written text. The key idea seems to have been the "rumination" (*ruminatio*) that is explicitly used in medieval sources as a descriptive metaphor for the meditative act: one moves one's mouth vigorously, "chewing" the words of the text, savoring and resavoring them, working through them diligently and actively to extract all of their spiritual nourishment.[63] Meditation here is not abstract contemplation but determined "exercise" in the word of God: What the mouth repeats, the heart should experience, the mind grasp, and the whole being translate into practice. The taking of the Holy Scriptures in one's mouth was as basic for the Pachomian monk as the taking and eating of bread from the Lord's table.[64]

For these reasons, it is preferable to do as many translators of the Pachomian and other monastic texts do – namely, to translate *meletan, meditare,* and related words not as "to meditate", but rather as "to recite"; or, if "to meditate" be retained, to keep it as a transitive verb, the object of which is a scriptural or other text. The idea of "meditating scripture" must be understood in its fullest sense as a mindful recitation aimed at focusing the mind and heart on the word of God. Therefore, I have chosen to use the unfamiliar but accurate usages, "to meditate scripture" and "meditation of scripture" rather than "to meditate *on* scripture" or "meditation *on* scripture", to which we are more accustomed, and which signal to most of us a silent, mental cogitation far removed from the kind of meditation the Pachomians and many Christian contemplatives, both monastics and others, have cultivated.

Recitation in the Daily Round

Meditation or recitation of scripture provided the Pachomian monk with a physical and mental discipline that set the deeply religious tone of every aspect of life in the *koinonia.* This is most vividly evident in the clear intention of Pachomius and his successors to integrate scriptural meditation in all of the monks' daily occupations. The Psalms and other scriptural passages that the monks were required to learn by heart were chanted, sung, or murmured aloud not only in formal devotions and communal worship (see below, "Liturgy and Instruction"), but during work and leisure, while walking within the monastic compound or traveling abroad, and on special occasions. Such repeated recitation during even the most commonplace activities joined with liturgical recitation to form what amounted to "continuous recitation night and day"[65] that was meant to fufill the biblical injunction to "pray without ceasing" (1 Thess. 5.17; Eph. 6.18).[66]

The vocal meditation of scripture was especially important in the varied daily labors of the monks: farming, gardening, blacksmithing, baking, carpentry, fullering, basketweaving, tanning, cobblery, calligraphy, or whatever.[67] "At work, they shall talk of no worldly matter, but either recite holy things or else keep silent."[68] While many of the particular kinds of manual labor undertaken by the monks are treated in the Pachomian sources, the latter give greatest attention to the daily work of baking bread.[69] Not least among the specific rules for monks working in the bakery are those delineating how they are to combine scriptural meditation with their work. Punishment was meted out for disobeying these rules.[70] One of Horsiesius' regulations reveals the larger religious purpose of meditating scripture during the baking – presumably a purpose that held for all such meditation during any kind of work or activity:

When the time has come to make our small quantity of bread, all of us, great and little, must work at making bread in the fear of God and with great understanding, reciting[71] the word of God with gravity, without pride, boasting, or respect of persons.[72]

To this end, the rules of both Pachomius and Horsiesius are very specific about how the meditation of scripture during baking and kneading was to be carried out:

No one shall speak when the kneading is done in the evening, nor shall those who work at the baking or at the [kneading] boards in the morning. They shall recite together[73] until they have finished.[74]

... Let all of us in the kneading room recite, not shouting, but softly .... We shall not knead without reciting: we may recite or pause; and if we so desire, we may recite in our heart. If we need a bit of water, we shall strike the trough without saying anything, and those who have charge of supplying water will quickly bring it along. Nor will these cease to recite, and they will take care not to spill water on the feet of those who are kneading.[75]

Beyond their involvement in the more specialized crafts and bread-baking, all monks were expected also to engage in the weaving of rushes, palm fiber, or the like as a regular pasttime – both alone in their cells during free time and in company in the twice-daily prayer gathering of the *synaxis*[76] and the regular catechetical, or instructional sessions.[77] This plaiting of mats and ropes was a handiwork practiced by Pachomius and his teacher Palamon even before the founding of the Tabennesi community.[78] It was used especially as a nocturnal labor joined to recitation to help the monks keep the night vigils, probably since it, like recitation from memory, could be carried on in darkness.[79] Just as the meditation of God's word fought off sleep and idle thoughts by occupying the mind and mouth with divine things, weaving rushes occupied the hands productively and kept the body awake and alert through the long hours of darkness or other hours of free time in the individual monk's cell.[80]

While Pachomian meditation of scripture sought to realize "a unity of prayer-life and daily work",[81] recitation of scripture was by no means limited to the monks' manual labor alone. The sources reflect the virtually constant recourse to meditation that the Pachomian discipline encouraged – not only during the fulfillment of special tasks in the routine of the community,[82] but for most other occasions as well. All walking and traveling, whether simply between one's cell and the *synaxis* or other common gathering,[83] between the monastery and the fields or river,[84] or entering or leaving one of the monasteries,[85] was accompanied by the chanting or singing of psalms and other segments of scripture. Similarly, whenever Pachomius or Theodore or any special visitor arrived at one of the monasteries, he would be met by the brothers there singing or chanting psalms or reciting other scriptural texts.[86] The monks' reception of the archbishop Athanasius of Alexandria, on occasions when he visited upper Egypt, is recorded in several of the sources.[87] The first part of the account of one of Athanasius' visits in Theodore's time is especially vivid:

> Apa Theodore and the brothers went north. They found the archbishop in the northern part of the diocese of Shmoun. He was mounted on a donkey and countless people were following him, including bishops, innumerable clerics with lamps and candles, and also monks from various places who were preceding him chanting psalms and canticles. Apa Theodore quickly put into shore in front of the monasteries of the diocese of Shmoun. He took with him, too, all the brothers of those monasteries and, reciting all together from the words of the holy Scriptures and the Gospels of our Lord Jesus Christ, they went north on foot to meet him. . . . [After meeting him, Theodore took the donkey's bridle, and] then the brothers, a hundred men strong, preceded him singing psalms. . . .[88]

Liturgy and Instruction

Liturgy and instruction are the last, but by no means least important, arenas of Pachomian life in which the oral/aural role of scripture was significant. The recitation of scripture provided the fundamental content of formal prayer and worship as well as the core of preaching and teaching in the *koinonia.* In concert with the meditative practices already described, scriptural *meditatio* in prescribed worship and *catēchēsis* assured the constant presence of the word of God in the mouths and ears of the monks.

Assiduousness in prayer was one of the major marks, if not the major mark, of Pachomian piety. All prayer was rooted in meditation of scripture, or, to put it in another way, meditation of scripture was the basic form of prayer. Prayer and recitation/meditation are even interchangeable terms: In descriptions of the night vigils, it is sometimes difficult to tell where scriptural recitation or singing of psalms ends and private, personal prayer begins. At other times a slight distinction is suggested, as in references to how the monks kept vigil over the body of Pachomius before his burial "with readings and prayers" or, immediately after this, how the monk Petronios was buried "with prayers and psalms".[89] Similarly, a distinction between scriptural meditation and personal prayer is suggested by a reference to how Theodore, while "sitting in his cell plaiting ropes and reciting passages of the holy Scriptures he had learned by heart, . . . would get up and pray every time his heart urged him to do so . . . ."[90] Nevertheless, the overall impression given in the sources is that scriptural meditation/recitation was a major part of the "unceasing prayer" toward which the monastic life was fundamentally directed.

Recitation was certainly the key liturgical exercise of the Tabennesiots, whether practiced in solitude or semisolitude, as in the night vigils observed by the monks, or in company, as in the twice-daily collective prayer of the *synaxis,* or assembly. The morning assembly (Copt.: *sôouh,* "collect, assembly") was apparently held in the common hall with the entire community present, whereas the evening gathering (Copt.: *soou ensop,* "six sections") was held in each house within the compound. The basic form of the *synaxis* in the evening, and probably in the morning as well, seems to have been repeated rounds of recitation and free, personal prayer. In each assembly, several monks, in order of seniority, took turns reciting six "prayers", or "sections" (Copt.: *ensop;* sing.: *sop*), of scripture before the assembly, after which all stood and recited the *Pater noster* in unison before prostrating themselves in silent, penitential prayer, returning finally to their seats before the next recitation.[91]

In liturgical use, as in other contexts already mentioned, the Psalms held a special place in the scriptural recitation and reading of the Pachomian communities – a preeminence they also enjoyed, of course, in the wider Christian usage of both the Eastern and the Western church.[92] Although they do not seem to have had a formal place in the daily asssemblies of the *synaxis,* the Psalms seem to have been especially important in two particular liturgical contexts: (1) the special communal assemblies on Saturdays, Sundays, and the other days of the liturgical calendar on which the Eucharist was celebrated; and (2) at all vigils and burial services for deceased monks or nuns. In the former services on weekends and holy days, the usual round of scriptural recitation, *Pater noster,* and personal prayer was replaced by antiphonal recitation of psalms led by the abbots and housemasters in the monasteries. In the latter services associated with burials, the monks recited psalms in unison through a night of vigil and during the procession of the corpse to its place of burial.[93]

In Pachomian liturgical life generally, there was apparently little distinction made in liturgical practice between private, "personal" prayer and communal, "public" prayer. Modern separation of the two should not be projected anachronistically back upon the Pachomians, for whom there was only personal prayer to and personal contact with God, whether expressed in secret, alone, or publicly, in communion with other monks.[94] The sources suggest that the major purpose of the Pachomian *koinonia* was to be a liturgical community, that is, one that encouraged a life of continual worship and prayer, both solitary and communal.[95]

Closely allied to the formal worship of the *synaxis* were the five sessions each week designated as "instruction", or *catēchēsis,* in scripture, a practice traced to Pachomius, who with his first community of monks "spoke the word of God to them, commenting on the Scriptures."[96] Three of these preaching/teaching sessions were held by the superior of the monastery for the whole community: one on Saturday and two on Sunday. The remaining two evening sessions were held on Wednesdays and Fridays (the two special days of fasting and prayer each week) by the housemasters in the separate houses of the monastic compound.[97] The homilies of the superiors and housemasters were followed by discussion and sharing of scriptural passages or by individual reflection by the brothers.[98] The subject of these sessions was Holy Scripture, its interpretation and implementation in the lives of those present. Thus it is said of Theodore that "whenever he spoke to the brothers from the holy Scriptures of the Lord, he would recite the passages for them and also explain their spiritual significance to them."[99] The homiletic Testament of Horsiesius reflects the degree to which the words of scripture formed the basis of not only the texts interpreted but also the very language of interpretation itself.[100] These sessions were occasions to strengthen the monks' knowledge of the scriptural texts as well as their interpretation; the two were hardly separable. In this, as in every other aspect of Pachomian life, the basis of everything was the scriptural word that was supposed to live in the minds and on the lips of the monks who made its meditation and implementation their chief occupation.

In this monastic discipline, the life of faith striven for was envisioned as a scriptural life pure and simple: This meant a life permeated and paced, as well as directed and governed, by the living, lively words of scripture. The sources indicate that sacred writings were primarly oral in function and aural in impact, rather than written or visual. In these writings, God spoke through the voices of the biblical writers in the timeless and transforming speech of divine revelation. Literalism does not seem to have been the necessary corollary of scripturalism among the Tabennesiots. Their oral citation of scriptural passages appears to have been an effort to capture allusively the correct sense without adhering word for word to one particular linguistic or textual version of those writings from Old and New Testament books that were at this time generally recognized as authoritative. The important fact for these persons was that God spoke to them through the voices of the biblical writers in the timeless speech of divine inspiration or revelation. The total commitment of the life they chose to pursue and their visceral sense of the immediacy of the divine presence were mirrored in the intensity of their preoccupation with scripture and the vividness with which they heard God's voice in its words.

For the Pachomians, the lifeline of faith was whatever exercise could keep the speech of the scriptures constantly ringing in their hearts and minds. Although the historian of religion may see elements of a magical faith in the talismanic efficacy of such constant repetition, this cannot diminish the deep religious intent in the monks' dogged allegiance to the daily round of scriptural recitation. These ascetics sought quite simply and explicitly to fill their minutes, hours, and days with divine speech and thought rather than their own negligent and flawed, all-too-human words and ideas, in order thereby to be transformed and, ultimately, to be saved. For them, the scriptural word has always an overt, symbolic, or allusive meaning, as their constant, if not always perfectly appropriate, proof-texting demonstrates. However, beyond specific verbal meaning there is simple comfort as well as efficacy merely in the repetitive act of reciting the sacred texts in chant or song, alone or collectively. Any conception of scripture that is adequate to the study of religion more generally has to be able to do justice to this kind of scriptural piety and textual presence.

CHAPTER 12

Hearing and Seeing: The Rhetoric of Martin Luther

. . . in the new law all these infinite burdens of ceremonies – that is, dangers of sins – have been removed. God now requires neither the feet nor the hands nor any other member except the ears. To this degree, all has been reduced to an easy way of life. For if you ask a Christian what work renders him worthy of the name Christian, he will not be able to give any answer at all except the hearing of the word of God, that is, faith. Therefore the ears alone are the organs of the Christian person, who is justified and judged a Christian not by the works of any member, but through faith.

– Martin Luther

The Medieval Background

Like the early Christian centuries, the Western Middle Ages could provide ample material for one or more separate studies of oral aspects of Christian holy writ. In this period in Christendom East and West, the oral roles of sacred texts took precedence over the written as much as, and probably more than, they had in late antiquity in the Mediterranean. As we have seen, illiteracy was the norm among the masses of the Christian laity and scarcely unknown even among monks and lower clerics.[1] In medieval chirographic culture, even literate Christians (including those in monasteries, cathedral schools, or universities) had limited opportunity for living with a Bible to hand (let alone other books) in the casual way that their modern Western counterparts do. In literate as well as illiterate circles, reading was essentially an oral activity, and the act of writing a letter or copying a manuscript was also an oral process, as we have seen in Chapter 4. Just as monastic scribes sounded their text aloud as they wrote, so most medieval Christians, even highly educated ones, conceived of and treated the written word as something that speaks with an audible voice to reader and listener. Gregory the Great (d. 604), for example, could speak quite un-self-consciously of catastrophes "of which we heard in the sacred pages" (*quae in sacris paginis audiebamus*) coming to pass in his day, a time which marks for many the onset of the "medieval" period.[2]

Wholly aside from the question of the oral dimensions of the written word in general, the most common means of access to the Bible specifically were aural ones. For the great majority of premodern Christians – monk, cleric, and layperson alike – the primary contact with scripture was in the liturgy. The chanting and singing of psalms; the repetition of scriptural or scripturally derived prayers, litanies, and hymns; and the preaching of scripturally based sermons – all of these perpetuated the vocal presence of the biblical word. If, for both clerics and laypersons, the Bible took a backseat as immediate religious authority to the church that had canonized it and to the exegetical tradition of the church, it remained still the cornerstone of the imposing edifice of Christian tradition and faith. The importance of the Bible's direct or indirect presence among Christians throughout the medieval period is not open to question, however much the later Protestant reformers found to criticize about the church's limitation of direct and personal access to holy writ.[3]

Nor did the increasing inaccessibility of the Latin text to the majority of Christians in the centuries after the barbarian migrations and decline of the Western Christian empire mean that the scriptural word was silenced. Architecture and art came to serve as primary sources of Christian scriptural education, supplying to literate and illiterate alike vivid visual images drawn primarily from the Bible. The oft-remarked and massively important pictorial orientation of the medieval Christian world – whether in Byzantium, Bohemia, or Bologna – is indisputable. Nevertheless, we should not forget that without the oral reading, reciting, chanting, and singing of the biblical word in liturgical and devotional life, not to mention the biblically tinged popular lore of story and song, the images on the walls and windows of churches and in the pages of books would not have been intelligible – or at least only imperfectly so. "Sermons in stone" could only be "preached" on a cathedral façade or an altarpiece after they had been preached in catechism and worship, in public or private reading, and in homiletic recapitulation and elaboration. The notion that very low literacy among the populace meant that scripture was only or even primarily communicated pictorially betrays both a naïve understanding of how independently visual art can function socially and a misjudgment of how effectively books can function as oral texts in a largely illiterate world. This is an issue that bears further investigation by scholars who would describe adequately the piety of Christians of whatever rank in medieval European society, West or East.

The Reformation and the Spoken Word of Scripture

The functional orality of Christian scripture did not end with the waning of the Middle Ages in Europe. The great Protestant reformers themselves evidenced a profoundly aural sensibility to the scriptural word that they raised up, under the banner of *sola scriptura,* as their ultimate authority. The biblical word to which their theology and piety gave pride of place over church tradition and papal authority was emphatically not the "dead letter" of the written text. For all of the reformational emphasis on the need for better texts of the scriptures and closer adherence to scriptural authority, scripture was less a document than a lively vocal presence in their lives and thought. In Calvin's words, "all of Scripture is to be received as if God were speaking."[4] The reformers' emphasis upon scripture as the word of God lent itself readily to identification of Holy Writ with the spoken word of the gospel message. A sensibility to the transformative power of God's word provided one excellent basis for the common reformational emphasis on bringing the word through vernacular scripture and sermon not only to the *literati* (those who were schooled in Latin) but also to the *idiotae* (those unlettered in Latin). In this effort, Luther and others focused upon the "liturgy of the Word" (*Wortgottesdienst*) as a "liturgy of Scripture" (*Schriftgottesdienst*), for which the point of departure was "the reading of the word of God".[5]

Within the liturgy of the Word, the Protestant sermon (not unlike the traditional sermon, but with new emphasis) was especially closely tied to the text of scripture. In a tract of the Strasbourger reformer Tilman von Lyn, for example, the double theme of the necessity of preaching the word of God and grounding all preaching in the scriptural word predominates.[6] It was assumed that the preacher's primary duty was to elaborate, explain, and communicate the Christian message as found first and foremost in the Bible and to make his congregation conversant with the biblical text. Preaching of the gospel was never intended to stray far from the Gospels and other sacred books of scripture, in which God speaks to his people. Luther, Zwingli, and other reformers worked their way through entire biblical books in their preaching much as Augustine and Chrysostom had done. The clear reading aloud of a scriptural text is the first of the four elements of proper homiletic method listed in William Perkins's *Art of Prophesying,* a work popular in England throughout the seventeenth century.[7] The Bible belonged to the sermon, and the sermon to the Bible.

Similarly, the learning and study of God's word in scripture, directly from the written or printed text itself, or indirectly in catecheses and hymnbooks, became a basic element of Protestant education.[8] In the new world of German Protestantism, for example, the only books that approached the Bible in influence were the Catechism and the Hymnal; "the first . . . was taken in part from Luther's Bible and reflected throughout the same spirit and the same language, [and] the same held true for the Hymnal."[9] The importance of Bible study and reliance on the biblical word was a common theme even of popular Protestant propaganda and preaching.[10] Godfrey Davies notes that in the early seventeenth century, "Englishmen studied the Bible with an intensity probably never equalled, and it is hardly possible to read a speech or writing of any length without perceiving its indebtedness to the Authorized Version."[11]

Memorization of the vernacular (and sometimes the Latin, Greek, or Hebrew) Bible was commonplace for the great figures of the Reformation and subsequent Protestantism and also proceeded apace among the wider clergy, as anyone who reads their sermons or tracts will readily recognize. It is remarkable how completely a Martin Luther, Martin Bucer, John Calvin, or John Bunyan speaks a scripturally saturated language – that is, thinks, speaks, and writes in the vocabulary, stylistic modes, thought-world, and imagery of the Bible (a phenomenon already common, to be sure, among educated Christian laypersons, clerics, and monks for many centuries). In its degree of permeation by the scriptural word, this kind of discourse mirrors that of a figure such as Horsiesius, discussed in Chapter 11. Such persons do not so much quote scripture or use it for proof-texting as they simply "speak scripture" – a scripture in which they are literally and spiritually, linguistically and theologically "at home"; one that they can and do recite largely if not wholly by heart, often to the point of mixing its words and phrases almost unconsciously with their own expression, and always to such a degree that their own vocabulary and manner of speech are resonant with the idiom and cadences of the Bible. In this regard, Gerhard Ebeling's dictum about the Bible-consciousness of earlier generations applies above all to the Reformers and a substantial number of subsequent Protestant preachers and writers down to very recent times: "To our forefathers, the Bible was a linguistic home, even if with varying intensity and controversial understanding; and therefore God was to a certain extent the linguistic center . . . ."[12]

Luther and Scripture

There is no better example of this kind of scripture-consciousness than that to be found in the work of Martin Luther – the man who represents for many the epitome of Protestant scripturality, or "book religion". In what follows, I want to focus specifically upon Luther's emphasis on the oral and aural aspects of God's word in scripture. His understanding and treatment of the vocal character of the biblical word offers a variation on the theme of the orality of written scripture that is especially revealing for those immersed in or only conversant with a silent, visual orientation to holy writ. It is a variation of particular interest because it lies at the heart of the strongest "book" tradition that Christian history has produced.

The pivotal role of scripture in Martin Luther's thought needs even less elaboration than did its similar centrality in early Christian monasticism. Volumes have been written on Luther's concept of scripture, the role of scripture in the larger scheme of his thought, and his exegesis of the biblical text.[13] Luther's understanding of the word of God, that most central theme of Reformation thought, was indissolubly bonded to the role of scripture as the tangible embodiment of the Word. If he commonly juxtaposed "the spirit" (*spiritus/der Geist*) and "the letter" (*littera/der Buchstabe*) of scripture, to the advantage of the former as the ultimate source of Christian faith and life, this in no way lessened his concern with the written word of scripture as the palpable authority for that faith and life. Throughout Luther's voluminous writings, the presence of biblical texts and a concern with their specific words and meanings are everywhere in evidence. Not only his many specifically exegetical works but his unstinting allusion to and quotation from the Bible as authority in all of his writings testify to this. By any standards, he was a man with a "stupendous grounding in the Bible" (*stupende Bibelfestigkeit*).[14]

For Luther, just as for virtually all previous luminaries of the church, scripture was the Christian's fundamental resource – a resource, however, that he and other Reformers felt had been excessively subordinated over time to church traditionalism and papal authority. This indispensable resource represented for Luther the word of God in its most explicit and complete form. He could even affirm, "we have no word [from God] except Scripture."[15] For him, God spoke not only in the Gospels and other writings of the New Testament, but also, and often preeminently, in the Hebrew scriptures. The Old Testament was to Luther *the* Scripture par excellence, whereas the New was first and foremost the spoken Christian gospel, the proclamation, or *kerygma,* of the Christ.[16] Quite apart from his keen awareness of the unique historicity of every book of the Bible, both testaments were for him at once scripture and kerygma, for both were essentially the timeless word of God. As such, he conceived of both as a unity, an indissoluble, consistent whole, the ultimate purpose of which was to proclaim and to disclose the Christ.[17]

If Luther's motives were not only theological but also pragmatic in their concentration upon the weaknesses of European Christianity at the time, he could not have chosen a more potent and flexible authority than scripture to emblazon upon the banners of reform. In practical terms, his emphasis upon the gospel message and its scriptural expression was ideally suited to his age. Its concomitant emphases on preaching and teaching, on vernacular translations of the Bible and scriptural hymnody, and on straightforward exegesis and comprehension of scripture, were perfect responses to existing circumstances. These included general Latinate illiteracy, not to mention widespread inability to read or write any language, as well as a growing thirst among Christian laity for a different kind of religious participation and community than that offered by the church of the times. These circumstances were coupled with changing social and economic conditions that increased the practical need and demand for literacy among the populace. Here the religious concerns and programs of Luther and other Reformers before and after him meshed well with other kinds of interests that a *sola scriptura* principle could meet.

We cannot, however, speak here of a fixation on biblical literalism as a new absolutist principle of religious authority. For all of Luther's stress upon the centrality of scripture, and for all of his concern for its meaning, his work shows a remarkable lack of literalist attachment either to the immutable words of the text or to the fixed canonical boundaries of holy writ. Yet this freedom vis-à-vis the literal word does not weaken the character of scripture as God's authoritative word. Nor does it stem from any lack of awareness of the problem of textual variance among Septuagint, Hebrew scripture, Greek New Testament, and the Vulgate. It comes instead from Luther's focus on the word of scripture as the unitary and consistent word of God, when understood as a whole and read diligently in any of its parts.

Although he was utterly committed to a close exegesis of the text, an abiding concern with its overall message and content dominated Luther's relationship to scripture. Even in his first lectures on the Psalms (1513–15), he could point to differences between "our version", meaning the Vulgate, and that of the Hebrew text without feeling that these posed theological problems.[18] Similarly, while he held scripture to be the word of God, Luther was prepared to recognize that some books of scripture are of less value than others (as in the case of the last four books of the New Testament) or do not really belong in the scriptural canon (as in the case of the book of Esther). Similarly, although he was convinced of the unusual religious value of an apocryphal book such as 1 Maccabees, he did not try to make it a part of the canon. In general, while he did not attempt to alter the generally recognized canon of the church, neither did he see it as something set in stone nor did he view it as a uniform list that implies an equal valuation of all biblical books.[19]

The central importance of scripture for Luther was its place at the heart of the Christian life – the practical life of faith and action. In his eyes, this life demands that one keep constant company with scripture and use it as one's fundamental guide and support. He admonishes the Christian accordingly:

> . . . keep watch, study, pay attention to the lection; truly, you cannot read too much in scripture; and what you read, you cannot read too well; and what you read well, you cannot understand too well; what you understand well, you cannot teach too well; and what you teach well, you cannot live too well.[20]

It follows from this that scripture is in itself completely clear and intelligible to everyone who will make the effort to read it,[21] so long as one does so in the proper spirit.[22] One has only to avoid straying from its clear words, "for we can be certain that no simpler speech has appeared on earth than that [which]

God has spoken."[23] On the other hand, scripture is simultaneously so rich and deep, that "when one thinks one has learned it all, then one must first begin."[24] This latter aspect of scripture – its depth, subtlety, and difficulty – is reflected in the importance Luther attached to the learning of Latin, Greek, and Hebrew, both by preachers and by those young boys who are able, as a means of preventing at least some avoidable errors in the interpretation of scriptural texts.[25]

On balance, Luther emphasized the clarity and accessibility of scripture over its obscurity and difficulty – at least for the reader of sincerity and faith who is assisted by the spirit.[26] In the end, however, neither the inherent clarity of scripture nor the intellectual tools of any interpreter are ever adequate in themselves for true understanding of scripture. Rather, the Holy Spirit alone can give meaning to the reading of scripture, however easy or difficult the text in question and however learned or unlearned the reader: "no one can understand God or God's word rightly unless he receives it directly [lit.: 'without mediation'] from the Holy Spirit."[27] The special *claritas* of scripture comes, therefore, ultimately through the Holy Spirit, which "can be found nowhere more immediately and livelier than in its [the Spirit's] own holy letters [*sacris literis*], which it wrote."[28]

Luther and the Spoken Word of Scripture

For our purposes, what is of particular interest in Luther's treatment of scripture is his emphasis upon the vocal aspect of the biblical word. This emphasis has been often noted, perhaps most strikingly by Emanuel Hirsch:

> In the church of Jesus Christ, according to Luther, all writing and printing are only make-shift means . . . . *Word* in the true sense is never merely something written and printed. The gospel is "living voice" [*lebendige Stimme*]. The Bible was for him not so much a "reading book" [*Lesebuch*], but much more a "listening-book" [*Hörebuch*].[29]

We find in his writings many indications of his own lively aural sense of the word of God in scripture. As learned and "bookish" as he certainly was, and as much as he can be said to have been the first truly prolific and widely read author of the printed word in the West, Martin Luther was a man for whom the written (or printed) page was still far from being a silent piece of paper. Books "spoke" in the audible tones of the author or reader to him, as presumably to most of his contemporaries. "To read and to hear" was a natural pairing of words expressing the oral/aural nature of the written text in his experience and usage.[30] The idea of "hearing a letter [*Buchstabe*] from God's word" came easily to him.[31] Like many Christians before and since, he seems to have understood the biblical text almost literally as God speaking, as audible words addressed to human ears.[32] The gripping immediacy with which he heard the voice of God in scripture is so powerfully evident in virtually everything he wrote as to be either utterly compelling or else largely incomprehensible to anyone who reads much of his work. To Luther's way of thinking, only "the hearing of the word of God" [*das Hören des Wortes Gottes*] can bring true joy such that the heart finds peace in the presence of God.[33] "It is after all not possible to comfort a soul, unless it hear the word of its God. But where is God's word in all books except scripture? . . . No book can comfort save Holy Scripture."[34]

Memorizing and Meditating Scripture

Luther's aural sense of God's word in scripture was in one respect solidly grounded in his own practical experience and that of his age: Knowing scripture by heart was something if not assumed, then hardly remarkable for the serious theologian. Luther recognized clearly the importance of memorizing and retaining the biblical text. God's word should not only be heard, but "also learned and retained."[35] He himself had the words of scripture by heart in the Latin of the Vulgate – presumably as a product of his own Augustinian monastic training.[36] Thus he could remark almost in passing, "then I ran through the scriptures as I had them in memory."[37] Furthermore, in addition to his phenomenal command of the Latin text, he developed considerable knowledge of the other available versions, working ever more seriously with the Hebrew and then the Greek text as his mastery of these languages grew in the period after 1516.[38]

In addition to knowing the text of scripture intimately and extensively, true understanding of it required, in Luther's view, assiduous and sustained effort. This means that "if you know Holy Scripture, nevertheless it must be read and reread,"[39] above all in frequent and concentrated meditation.[40] God revealed His word in order "that we might hear it and use it actively; and learn from it what we do not know by nature."[41] This is largely to be achieved through meditation of that word. As an active *engagement* with God's word, meditation of scripture was for Luther "the highest, most effective, and most concise erudition."[42] Thus he names *meditatio* as one of the three "rules" that comprise the way of true religious inquiry:

> I will show you a proper way to study theology, for I have trained myself in it. . . . And that is the way that the holy king David teaches in Psalm 119 (doubtless all the Patriarchs and Prophets also followed it). Therein you will find three rules abundantly set forth through the whole psalm, and they are: *oratio, meditatio, tentatio*.[43]

With regard to *meditatio*, Luther stands in the long tradition of Christian spirituality in which, as we have seen earlier, meditation on scripture means physical as well as mental labor: The lips as well as the mind and heart are necessarily engaged. To the Christian he says:

. . . you should meditate. That is, always repeat the oral speech and the literal word in the Book and compare them with each another, not only in your heart, but also outwardly, read them and reread them with diligent attentiveness and reflection, [to see] what the Holy Spirit means by them.[44]

"Seeing" and "Hearing"

Luther's stress upon the hearing of the word is most striking in the frequent contrast that he employs between using one's ears and relying only on one's eyes, that is, between (merely) seeing the word of God written on the page and (truly) hearing it spoken (by God) in the reading of the text directly to the listener. While these contrasts would seem to be perfect grist for the mill of the present project, there is more to them than at first appears. As a result, a few caveats are in order.

There is a danger that the visual–oral dichotomy, which Luther used frequently and vividly to didactic and rhetorical ends, may be taken too literally.[45] With regard to using this dichotomy as supporting evidence for the importance of the aural dimension of scripture to Luther, this danger is primarily twofold: that the "word" (of God) in Luther's usage may be identified only with the literal biblical text as read or recited, and that "hearing" the word may be associated only with physical listening to the reading aloud of scripture. Both of these are possible misreadings that would give an inaccurate picture of Luther's usage.

First, much of Luther's rhetoric of the Word reflects not so much his identification of the oral speech of God with the revealed text of scripture as his stress on preaching and sharing, by one's witness, the word of God in the sense of God's acts in history (especially the culminating act of redemption) and the word of God as the living proclamation of these acts.[46] What he preached was "the oral gospel" (*das mündliche Euangelion*), which is "a divine power that blesses all who have faith in it."[47] This oral gospel "is actually intended not as writing, but oral word. . . . [It] should not be proclaimed with the pen, but with the mouth."[48] Ultimately, the gospel is the content or message conveyed more than the particular words of the concrete biblical text itself. In other words, every reference to the Word is by no means to be taken as a literal reference to the verbatim text of scripture. More often, for Luther, "[the] Gospel is not really that which is in books and composed in letters, but rather an oral preaching and living word, and a voice which resounds through the whole world and is shouted forth abroad."[49]

A second possible misinterpretation is to read Luther's contrast between ear and eye, and between hearing and seeing, as a literal, rationalistic choice of the ear over the eye and hearing over seeing as the preferable organ and sense to be employed by the Christian. Often he does use "hearing" to describe an act of faith in contrast to a mere "seeing", which seems more certain simply because we "doubting Thomases" are inclined to trust only what is visible and tangible. Yet Luther is talking primarily in such contexts neither about ears as better sense organs and hearing as a better sense perception for spiritual development, nor about devotion to oral learning at the expense of visual learning. If he seems to denigrate the visual, it is in large part to emphasize, as David Steinmetz points out, that "the work of God is . . . not visible to sight" and that "everything the eye sees provides impressive grounds for distrusting the promises of God."[50] (In this sense, it would be consonant with his approach to call faith "blind".) Thus when Luther calls the ears "the organs of the Christian", he is speaking largely metaphorically: The true Christian needs to listen truly and well to the message of scripture rather than let himself or herself be led astray by the appearances of this world. In this sense faith is by hearing, not by seeing.[51] Hearing is not the external work of the ears, but the internal work of the Holy Spirit in the human heart.[52]

Nevertheless, despite these important caveats, Luther's emphasis on the aural perception and reception of God's word in scripture is still a consequential one for our concern with the significance of the vocal dimension of Christian scripture. The metaphorical emphasis upon ear versus eye should not be allowed to obscure the fact that it was an emphasis based upon physical experience – not only that of Luther personally, but of any of his contemporaries who would also have been far more attuned to the sound than the look of a text. There can be little question but that in the "book religion" of the greatest Reformer, the scriptural text was very much an aurally perceived and orally used book even while it was also a written and printed one. Luther's frequent use of oral/aural imagery to characterize the preaching, reading, and reception of the word was rooted in reality: It reflected his own predisposition to conceive of *both* the gospel message of God's word and the holy writ or "letters" of that word as vocal speech directed at him and every Christian. If for no other reason, his own ability to "run through" much if not all of the Bible from memory would have given him this predisposition. For Luther the written word of the Bible was not simply a manuscript, but a manuscript with a voice – or, still better, a manuscript that was the medium for God's voice. It was the most natural thing in the world for him to talk, as we have seen, of God *speaking* in what He *wrote*.

Recognition of how closely the spoken word of scripture was linked or even identified in Luther's thinking with the spoken word of Christian preaching removes much of the necessity for splitting hairs over what Luther may have meant by "word" in a given instance. It is often a fool's errand in reading Luther to try to distinguish the "word of God" as preached message or kerygma from the "word of God" as biblical text. The scriptural text itself is naturally identified with the spoken word of the gospel message, just as the kerygma is naturally perceived as a spoken proclamation of both the word of God and the biblical text. To say that when Luther speaks of God's word, he means the preached word, is finally no different from saying that he means the word of scripture, which is the essence and basis of the preached word.[53] This natural identification of the two can be clearly seen in his discussion of the star at Christ's birth in Matt. 2:

> Now what is the star? It is nothing else but the new light, the preaching and Gospel, orally and publicly preached [*die predigt und Euangelium, mundlich und offentlich predigt*]. Christ has two witnesses to His birth and His dominion. One is the scripture or word comprehended in the letters [i.e., literally]. The other is the voice or the word called out by the mouth. . . . Now scripture is not to be understood before the light appears, for the prophets are explained through the Gospel. Therefore the star has first to rise and be seen, for, in the New Testament, preaching should take place orally with lively voice, publicly, and that which was previously hidden in the letters and secretly seen should be presented in speech and hearing.[54]

The New Testament here is not simply a book but the new dispensation that fulfilled the old. Scripture, the word of God, and the preaching of the word flow together here and become effectively inseparable. As Luther puts it a little later in the same passage: "We also see in the Apostles, how all their preaching was nothing but a presentation of scripture and a building upon it. Therefore Christ himself also did not write down his teaching, as Moses did his, but gave it orally . . . ."[55]

Similarly, when Luther talks of the Holy Spirit's speaking through scripture, he is talking both about the literal letter of the biblical text and about the Christian "good news" to which the text bears witness. The contrast between the "letter" and the "spirit", which is equivalent to that between the "law" of the Old Testament and the "gospel" of the New, should not be carried over and applied literally to Luther's contrast between the spoken word of the gospel with the written word of holy writ. Rather, where he speaks of hearing the word with the ears as the only way to faith, one must recognize that he is not denigrating the reading of God's word in the scriptures, but speaking metaphorically about how that word is to be revered, repeated, and taken to heart as a living voice of truth:

> He [Christ] takes here in particular the two members, ears and tongue, for you know that the Kingdom of Christ is founded upon the word, which one can neither grasp nor comprehend other than through these two members, ears and tongue. And [the kingdom] is ruled alone through the word and the faith [that is] in the hearts of men. The ears grasp the word, and the heart has faith in it.[56]

Book, Writ, and Word

A final, telling angle on Luther's vividly aural sense of the word of scripture is to be found in his description of the Bible as "the Holy Spirit's own special book, writ, and word."[57] In his juxtaposition of these three terms – the German *Buch, Schrift, Wort* – to describe scripture, Luther reaches (perhaps) unconsciously for a complex of words rather than a single one to express what he understands scripture to be. It is a book (*Buch*), to be sure, but a book that is both a writ (*Schrift*) and a word (*Wort*), a written document and oral speech or spoken message. It is as if he begins by identifying it simply as "book", then expands on this basic, generic characterization by specifying its "book" character as both written text and spoken word. In doing so, Luther presents an intentional or unintentional circumlocution of "scripture" or "Bible" by three possible synonyms or overlapping ideas, which, taken together, comprehend the richness and complexity of the scriptural word. I read this sentence as vivid evidence that "book" and "writ" were not wholly synonymous for Luther, any more than were "book" and "word", or "writ" and "word". The wording of his statement suggests that "book" for him was a larger, more encompassing concept than that of "writ", which designates the tangible copy of the Bible and its authoritativeness as a text fixed and preserved by tradition. Similarly, "book" was a different kind of concept from that of "word", which is the message of the Spirit – what it says, presumably in the human heart. Therefore I would gloss the passage to read that the Bible is the Spirit's own special book, namely as both the written, literal text and the spoken message or divine word that the literal text carries (and, when read or preached, embodies). In other words, the Bible is the book of the Holy Spirit, both as writ and as word.

Consideration of Luther's aural sense of scripture could easily occupy an entire volume. It might, for example, even be possible to document some development or shift in his treatment of ear, hearing, and the like through his long career – something that I feel is not evident, based on my own admittedly selective readings in various parts of the massive Luther corpus. Even then, my own point would remain the same: His language and imagery belong to a world in which the written word is simultaneously the word spoken and heard in full immediacy. It is also a world in which the word spoken and heard is primary. It can stand alone, but not so the written word, which is inseparable from it, and not, as in our world, an independent, silent notation that may but need not be read aloud. Luther's world is one in which the book's contents are not so many printed sheets of paper but living pages that "speak" to the reader and, in the case of the scriptures, speak God's word to the reader. Here holy writ and holy word are one and the same holy book, just as the preached "good news" and the text of scripture are one and the same gospel.

Luther's statements about the word of God, if understood as I am suggesting here, take on a concreteness and immediacy that most of us today are able to grasp only with difficulty, if at all. Even where we find them metaphorically compelling and rhetorically powerful, their literal sense eludes us. Nevertheless, if it was natural to him and his audience for the written word of scripture to be experienced and conceived of as an oral word, it was also much more natural to them than to us today to conceive of and perhaps to experience God's direct speech in the reading of scripture (or in the preaching of a sermon). A recognition of the fundamental orality of written texts in Luther's world of discourse gives us one key to entrance into the thought-world of this now distant age. It suggests that we not presume only metaphorical intent in every reference to "hearing" and "seeing" or other "physical" language, but ask always how such references might have been understood in a society in which books did speak with lively voices and the written letters of a text could carry the audible voice of God. Correspondingly, it necessitates a reevaluation of the constraints that our own views of scripture specifically, and books in general, place upon not only our historical understanding of this or other distant eras and places, but also the character of our individual relationships to whatever we ourselves may recognize as scripture.

Taken together with a case such as that of the Pachomian fathers, Luther's rhetoric and thought underscore the central reality of the audible word of the sacred book in important sectors of Christian piety. To the desert monks or the European reformers, a scholarly study of the oral dimension of the written word would have seemed strange at best, for orality was simply an organic part of what a text is in its very essence. Yet we today rarely think of Christian "book religion" as a significantly oral phenomenon. Indeed, we have enough trouble recognizing the even more pronounced oral aspects of the Qur'ān or Veda in societies that are by and large still far more significantly oral than our own.

The issue, however, is not a matter of an opposition between the spoken and the written or printed word. Rather, it is a matter of the interpenetration of the two and the indispensability of both to any adequate picture of scripture in the Christian, just as in any other scriptural tradition. Luther stands at the very heart of the "back to the Book" movement of Western Protestantism, just as the Pachomians are a model as well as important source of scripture-based monastic discipline in East and West. What both remind us of is the need to recognize that the book of holy scripture for reformers and monks alike was a living word above all else, and that a substantial element of its living quality consisted in the ringing words of its message as proclaimed from lectern and pulpit, recited in psalms and prayers, and meditated upon and memorized in loving devotion. It was a speaking book, just as it has been for countless other Christians, and just as Veda, Qur'ān, Torah, or any other scripture has been for its faithful readers and reciters.

Conclusion

What are given are always expressions of life; occurring in the world of the senses they are always expressions of a mind which they help us understand.

– Wilhelm Dilthey

. . . scriptures are collections of symbols. Their peculiar characteristic is a kind of magical elasticity. To successive generations of believers they mean things that would be paraphrased in utterly different words. Yet for century upon century they continue to satisfy the wants of mankind; they are "a garment that need never be renewed".

– Arthur Waley

Neglect of the oral dimension of scripture leads not only to excessive emphasis on the documentary text: Implicit in the loss of the fundamental orality of the written word is also the loss of an important perspective on the functional aspect of scripture. The relationship to the spoken word of the text is inherently dynamic and personal in a way that the relationship to the printed word alone is not, or is only rarely and with difficulty, at least in the present day. The significance of the spoken scriptural word does not stem from some primordial, mystical, or inherent psychological power that sets it apart from the written or printed word, nor is the oral dimension clearly the most fascinating aspect of scripture. The oral dimension is, however, the one most intimately bound up with the major personal and communal roles of scripture in religious life, especially those that move not only in the intellectual or ideational realm, but also in that of the senses – as, for example, in ritual or devotional use.

More than this: The spoken word of scripture has been overwhelmingly the most important medium through which religious persons and groups throughout history have known and interacted with scriptural texts. Most of those myriad persons who have claimed a sacred text at all have received, known, and transmitted its message orally, not in writing. Any simple extrapolation from the Western literacy data cited in Chapter 3 will suggest that, in terms of percentages, even in the Western world only a fraction of Christians and Jews before the nineteenth century were able to read for themselves any part of their holy scriptures; and only a tiny fraction of all people around the world, from the beginning of history to the present day, who have lived in any community with a sacred scripture, have ever been able to read a word of their holy writ. On this ground alone, it is manifest that to understand the phenomenon of scripture in any fashion that is remotely faithful to historical realities, we must look to its function as a text that above all has been read and recited aloud, repeated and memorized, chanted and sung, quoted and alluded to in the oral and aural round of daily life.

The Oral–Written Dichotomy

For the most part, the written text and the spoken word are seen as opposed, or at most only complementary, verbal phenomena in religious contexts. This kind of contrast is mirrored, for example, in the old saw, *vox audita perit, littera scripta manet,* "the voice heard perishes, the written letter endures." Especially in the study of authority structures in the history of particular religious communities, this contrast is often expressed in terms of the "scripture–tradition" dichotomy. One example of this dichotomy is the confessional divergence between Protestant and Roman Catholic or Orthodox Christians over the relative authority of scripture and tradition (often formulated as a "book–church" tension). Another is the theological distinction between Qur'ān and Ḥadīth as sources of authority that has been elaborated by Muslim scholars.

A scripture–tradition distinction of a different kind has also served in religious studies and anthropology to distinguish, often in crassly evolutionary fashion, the progressive, "major" religious traditions (those with written sacred books) from the "archaic" or "primitive" traditions (those of preliterate oral societies). Anthropologists as well as phenomenologists of religion have used this distinction to assign opposite values to written texts and oral traditions. For example, one may emphasize the power or adaptability of the oral word as opposed to the tendency to literalism and legalism associated with a written text, or, conversely, the authority and permanence of the written word as opposed to the personalist and fluid character of oral tradition.

The Spectrum of Scriptural Expression

In this study, I have sought to move beyond this kind of dichotomization in order to highlight the *interpenetration* of the written and the spoken word.

Rather than argue for the importance of oral texts over written texts, I have sought to emphasize the oral aspects of written texts themselves and the relative neglect of these aspects in both modern scholarship and popular usage.

From a theoretical standpoint, however, such a dichotomy can have its uses. If we postulate a spectrum of religious discourse, with pure oral tradition and the vocal expressions of myth or prayer at one pole, and the written pages of sacred texts at the other, a wide variety of *Mischbildungen,* or intermediate combinations of oral and written word, intervene across the postulated spectrum. In general, this spectrum of expression represents a continuum of textuality that ranges from that of "primary oral" or preliterate cultures to that of the most highly literate, typographic cultures. Thus it could be seen as evolutionary in accordance with the common valuation of civilizational and cultural indices discussed in Chapter 1: Evolutionary "progress" correlates with increasing reliance on the written word.

This postulated spectrum need not, however, be seen in terms of cultural evolution; instead, its range can represent the different psychological and social needs and the different modes of expression characteristic of divergent religious and cultural contexts. Thus the vocal word conveys with peculiar force a sense of spontaneity, participation, or personal involvement for the individual and the group through the emotional, sensual impact of hymnody and prayer, litany and praise, formulaic chant, ritual dicta, and texts read or recited aloud. Such *engagement* is characteristic of religious sensibilities at the oral end of the spectrum. On the other hand, delight in the authoritative fixity, solidity, beauty, and powerful presence of the written codex, and pleasure in the intricacies of textual study, commentary, and interpretation – whether in search of symbolic and allegorical meanings, or of literal or prescriptive meanings – are but two of the many factors that have caused the holy writ of scripture after scripture to be both venerated and studied and also treated as a bearer of *mana*-like or talismanic power. A predominance of this kind of visual sensibility would characterize the script/print end of the spectrum.

This theoretical spectrum can also be used in yet a different way, to describe and compare particular historical traditions or subtraditions of religion in terms of their respective emphases upon certain kinds of verbal discourse. This would be a continuum whose two extremes correspond in many ways to Siegfried Morenz's "cult religion" and "book religion".[1] Thus we might postulate at the oral end a pole at which the most highly oral and, in Morenz's term, "cultic" communities of history stand. Here would come above all the Vedic tradition of Indian Brahmanic religion, but not far from this would lie also some forms of Muslim Qur'ān-piety. At the opposite pole would be the starkest traditions of "book religion" or bibliolatry: Protestant Christian literalism, Sikh veneration of the Guru Granth Sahib, some forms of Jewish Torah-piety, and the like.

Nonetheless, even as one postulates such a spectrum, however purely heuristically it is intended, exceptions within each major scriptural tradition begin to intrude on any simplistic set of divisions among the "great religions". For example, Vedic manuscript traditions, however young, do still exist in the orally oriented world of Brahmanic piety, just as veneration of the physical copy of the sacred text as an icon can even be readily demonstrated in Hindu contexts.[2] Muslim veneration of the written Qur'ān exemplar, or *muṣḥaf,* and delight in the elaborately calligraphed qur'anic word have been prominent parts of the highly oral Islamic milieu. Protestant memorization of scripture, as well as oral proof-texting in preaching and witnessing, belie any too narrow emphasis upon the written word as an essential characteristic of Protestant religiousness. Sikh chanting of the Ādi Granth accompanies the veneration of the physical text as guru. Finally, Jewish memorizing, reading aloud, and cantillation of the Torah balances the primary emphasis in Judaic tradition upon reading and study of the written Torah.

Inconsistencies and crossovers thus abound in the schema, and I would argue even that most traditions fall finally closer to the midpoint of the spectrum than to either pole. This should not be surprising. Most forms of scriptural piety involve interplay, or even interpenetration, of oral and visual elements, rather than exclusive dominance of either. This holds true in a wider sense for most religious practice with regard to the interpenetration of all the sensual elements of religious experience. A particularly vivid example for me is a Russian Orthodox service that I attended quite by chance in the city of Smolensk over twenty years ago. Before and during the service, the kissing and touching of icons, the antiphonal chanting and singing of liturgy and hymns, the smells and sounds of the swinging, lighted censers, and the interplay of light through the cathedral windows all seemed clearly designed to produce for the small congregation of regular worshipers what I can only describe as a "synaesthetic" experience.

Even if this is an atypical example, virtually any instance of worship in most traditions, including even the sparse and elegant performance of the Muslim *ṣalāt* ritual, would still yield some degree of interaction if not interpenetration between visual and auditory, and often also tactile and olfactory, stimuli. This is so obvious that we are inclined to pass over it as unworthy of mention; yet in doing so, we risk losing much that is of importance in religious practice, even if we gain an apparent clarity of description unclouded by mention of the intangible or hard-to-describe experiences of the participants.

When we return to the particular matter of scripture and the interplay of oral and visual experience in its use, it is important to keep both aspects and their typical reciprocity in mind. This reciprocity extends beyond the specific context of public worship in which, for example, the holy book may be carried in procession, held aloft, or kissed, as well as recited or read aloud. It is also evident in many private forms of reading and study of scripture, and it is present in diverse ways even in those traditions that seem most exclusively "oral" or "literate" in orientation.

In all of this, I offer no new, fixed schema for the categorization of sacred texts. Mine is, rather, an attempt to throw light on some of the complexity of so apparently simple and straightforward a phenomenon as scripture. I have sought to explore those cases in particular in which strong orality coexists with a strong tradition of holy writ – a state of affairs that I am convinced is characteristic of every scriptural tradition with few exceptions – these being, most prominently, certain Christian and, to a lesser degree, Jewish communities in very recent times in the modern West, where the oral presence of scripture has greatly dwindled. Writtenness and orality are not finally antithetical, but complementary; the absence or loss of either is significant.

Implications of Orality

With these points in mind, we come back finally to the problem of scriptural orality itself. It is bound up with a number of issues that are important for the general history of religion as well as for the study of the role of sacred texts in religion. At least three such issues merit individual mention at the close of these inquiries: those related directly to the oral function of written sacred texts; those concerned with what I have termed the "sensual" dimension of religion; and those concerned more broadly with the place of scripture in a culturally pluralistic world that is still working out the consequences of the revolutionary impact of Western-style "modernity".

Even if my general point about the importance of the oral dimension of even the clearest examples of scriptural books is conceded, we have to ask how important this orality is. Does it really matter that our modern Western experience of texts may not be normative (and may even be genuinely aberrant) when seen in a larger historical perspective? Does it matter, so long as we doff the appropriate scholarly caps to the oral function of texts in semiliterate contexts, if we continue to rely on our standard treatment of texts (that is, as silent repositories of visual "data") as a model for understanding texts in other ages and other places?

I believe that it does matter, and that it matters considerably for any adequate understanding of scripture as a major religious datum. At the most obvious level, the dominance of oral/aural interaction with sacred texts has been the rule rather than the exception for the vast majority of persons and communities throughout history. A treatment of scripture that ignores or slights this fact is historically anachronistic, culturally biased, or both. It matters also, however, because an increased focus upon the oral dimension of scriptural texts encourages a vivid sense of how important all of the functional aspects of scripture are to any adequate history of religion and, correlatively, how important it is to approach scripture and other phenomena in relational rather than objectivist or reductionist terms.

Recognition of these points will greatly enrich not only our understanding of scripture, but also our grasp of individual and collective religiousness. Adequate comprehension of the multiple functions of scripture might lead, for example, to clearer recognition of the functions of other apparently "simple" religious phenomena, from icons to saints' shrines. Like scripture, such matters cannot be studied only in reductionist fashion as mere objects or artifacts. Their significance stems from their appropriation by, and relation to, religious persons and communities. This is hardly a revolutionary idea, but it is a perception all too easily obscured in the drive to identify, categorize, and label the myriad phenomena of religious life. Greater attention to the auditory immediacy of sacred texts at the very least underscores the functional immediacy of any important religious "object" in the experience and perception of the faithful. It shows the active relation between perceiver and perceived that is essential to meaningful experience.

If sensitivity to the oral functions of scripture does matter, what are some possible ramifications of orality in the preservation, transmission, and use of a scriptural text? More specifically: (1) Do oral reading and recitation of the text lead to greater intimacy with the sacred word than mere silent reading normally allows? (2) Does such focus typically go hand-in-hand with religious reform or revitalization movements? (3) Is it usually associated with an emphasis on liturgy? (4) Does it work against literalism in the understanding and interpretation of a text? These are not questions that can be answered simply. All are in some measure implicitly present throughout the present study, but since none save the first is addressed directly, a few remarks on each are in order.

1. *Oral recitation versus silent reading.* The very act of learning a text "by heart" internalizes the text in a way that familiarity with even an often-read book does not. Memorization is a particularly intimate appropriation of a text, and the capacity to quote or recite a text from memory is a spiritual resource that is tapped automatically in every act of reflection, worship, prayer, or moral deliberation, as well as in times of personal and communal decision or crisis. It is hard to conceive of a highly oral relationship to a scriptural text that does not greatly reinforce scriptural piety. We do not have to go to the extreme of maintaining that oral mastery of scripture is the ideal form of scriptural piety to note the apparent fact (at least in Western experience) that the waning of memorization and recitation of a sacred text has historically gone hand in hand with a decline of scriptural piety, however we may wish to assign cause and effect. Conversely, many of the most intense mystical and spiritual traditions of religious piety – most of which have been movements of spiritual interiorization and renewal, from Sufism to Nichiren Buddhism – have been rooted in the recitation and meditation of scriptural texts or formulas. It seems both

reasonable and potentially productive of new insights to investigate the oral and written functions of religious texts, especially scriptures, as factors or indicators in changing trends of religious piety.

2. *Reform and revitalization.* We can also ask if there may be a correlation between highly oral use of scripture and religious reform movements. The "back to the book" emphasis of many reform movements is well known, especially in Christian and Islamic contexts, but also in traditions and contexts as diverse as that of folk Buddhism in Sung China and the Ārya Samāj in nineteenth-century India. In these cases, most participants have had to know the "book" orally, if only because of the limitations of literacy. We need to know more about the ways in which memorization and recitation of scriptural texts are related to movements of revival and reform. In addition to any connection between the upsurge in reading, recitation, and memorization of scripture and the renewed stress on the authority and meaning of scripture, other factors also deserve attention. For example, the "internalizing" of important texts through memorization and recitation can serve as an effective educational or indoctrinational discipline. Nor should we overlook the importance of publicly bolstering piety and faith and increasing personal and group enthusiasm by providing for constant reading and reciting of a community's authoritative scripture in every aspect of its life, from ritual to instruction. A shared text – one that can be chanted in unison and constantly referred to as a proof text common to an entire community – is a powerful binding factor in any group, and especially in a minority group at odds with and bent on reforming or converting the larger society around it. Such issues lie well beyond the scope of this work, but all deserve more attention.

3. *Liturgy.* Johannes Leipoldt and Siegfried Morenz, in their classic study of scripture in the Mediterranean, pointed to the liturgical reading of a text as the surest index of its scriptural status.[3] Liturgical use of sacred texts is clearly the most common and often the most important context for the oral use of scripture, even though liturgy does not always focus principally upon scriptural texts, and sacred texts commonly play important oral roles outside of formal worship and ritual. Even within the sphere of liturgy, there are substantial differences in how scripture functions. For example, the Bible is omnipresent in Christian communal worship, and the readings are closely correlated with the liturgical calendar (the particular text should fit the particular context). In the Islamic case, however, the Qur'ān figures even more centrally in virtually all acts of worship, but little attention is paid to *which* qur'anic texts are recited on a given occasion (the particular text matters much less than the sheer vocal presence of some portion of the sacred word). In the Hindu case, the ancient Brahmanic rituals that use the Vedas are unthinkable without the Vedic texts; yet for the vast majority of Hindus, these rituals have not been a part of their active liturgical life for well over two thousand years, even though the recitation of Vedic mantras has been central to personal

devotion and, through the offices of Brahman priests, communal worship as well. Wherever the Vedic word is used, however, perfection of form and precision of expression are always central, and questions of content almost irrelevant. On the other hand, recitation of the popular, vernacular texts that are the living scriptures of the masses of Hindus may involve great attention to content as well as beauty and perfection of performance.

Thus we need to be very clear about *which* scriptural piety is under discussion. If there is any shared characteristic of liturgical uses of scripture across the spectrum of piety in the major traditions, it lies more in the simple psychological and theological necessity for the scriptural word – read or recited – to be proclaimed and heard in public than in any specific role it may play in communal worship.

4. *Scriptural literalism.* Regardless of the supposed "inexactness" of oral transmission, emphasis upon the oral text of a scriptural book does not appear to have worked against scriptural literalism. Literalism has more to do with the perception of a scripture's authority than with its primary form of expression. Indeed, scrupulous attention to the syllables of the recited word often matches or exceeds attention to the "letter" of the written word, something epitomized in the Vedic recitative tradition. While intimacy with an entire sacred text may lead to a certain freedom in the use of the text and produce what I have called "speaking scripture" (as opposed to quoting it consciously and verbatim), it can also produce a spirit of literalism such as the literalism that developed in the tradition of qur'anic memorization. This literalism has at times led Muslims to stress the exact pronunciation of every syllable and also to insist on the revealed, divine or transcendent character of every word of the sacred text.

These are only some of the most obvious questions concerning the implications of orality in the use of scripture. If the answers seem less than clear-cut, we may have to look less for the regularity of specific consequences or effects of the oral uses of sacred texts and more for what the oral dimensions of scripture reveal of its role as a linchpin of religious piety and community – what I have termed its relational function. Furthermore, this relational function will necessarily differ from tradition to tradition. Even when there are similarities, the oral role of a sacred text will have a different meaning and serve different ends depending on the historical and cultural context and the groups or individuals involved.

The Sensual Dimension of Religion

Perhaps the most important result of attention to the oral dimension of scripture is to make more vivid the intensely personal engagement of a community with its sacred text. Sacred books are not just authoritative documents or sources of doctrinal formulas; they are living words that produce a variety of responses – emotional and physical as well as intellectual and spiritual. Moreover, at no point in the life of a sacred book is it likely to elicit more varied responses than when it is being chanted, sung, or recited in some meaningful context such as that of worship or meditation.

To speak of scripture as more than authoritative documents or sources of doctrines poses questions of methodology as well as content. In particular, how do we discern the ways in which scripture has penetrated into those sectors of religious life that lie outside the more or less élitist domains of the literati or intellectuals – the preachers, theologians, scholars, mystics, monks, or priests who function as interpreters of scripture and dogma? Is it possible, wholly apart from consideration of the literate, often scholastic, "book" tradition, to understand the impact of a scriptural book in highly oral, largely nonliterate or semiliterate segments of a larger community? How do we abandon the prejudice that persons who encounter the word of scripture only through hearing it read, recited, or sung, or by seeing its stories portrayed in visual images, are somehow less "scriptural" than those who read the silent pages for themselves? How do we recognize that, even for someone who is highly literate, scriptural words that are spoken, sung, or chanted have an impact different from that of the written text read in privacy and silence?

Such questions are particularly difficult and may allow no definitive answers. They plunge us into a consideration of the affective role of texts in everyday life – a role that poses considerable problems of meaning and understanding. It is no simple task to pin down the impact of chanted texts as part of the multisensory, sometimes synaesthetic experience of communal worship, or the impact of sacred-language texts in linguistically "foreign" contexts, where the holy text must be inculcated by teaching the bare rudiments, or only the sounds, of its language. What's more, because every historical tradition is unique, it will present different problems and require different formulation of common questions. In a case such as Hindu India, understanding scripture involves understanding a textual tradition, the Vedic, that is the province of only a small élite yet still dominates symbolically the thinking of much wider circles. In Islamic contexts, we have to ask what it means for countless Muslims who can neither read nor speak Arabic to exert immense energies in the effort to learn part or all of the Qur'ān in order to recite it by heart. In Christian contexts, the problem is to investigate the diverse modes, in addition to individual reading and study, by which the biblical word has been communicated to and by the faithful – whether these involve hymnody, liturgy, prayer, preaching, or whatever. In Jewish contexts, we must try to grasp the relationship between knowing Torah by heart as Law or Scripture and living Torah as the righteous way of life. In Buddhist contexts, a major task is to understand the link between the word of the Buddha chanted from the Sūtras and the aquisition of merit on the one hand or the attainment of enlightenment on the other.

In considering such questions, we move rapidly beyond the narrow confines of scripture into much more general theoretical issues. In particular, we must ask ourselves as historians of religion if we have not seriously short-changed both ourselves and our field of study by ignoring or minimizing the "sensual" aspects of religious life – the sensory and sensible stimuli and responses that figure so fundamentally in religious practice of all kinds, from pilgrimage to rites of passage and from public worship and ceremonial to ablutions, private prayer, and meditation. It is not only in adequately conceptualizing scripture and its oral dimensions that we as students of religion have fallen down. In general, the physical, material world of religious objects, ritual actions, and musical sounds and their roles in the multisensory domain of even the most "everyday" religious activity have too often been left to art historians, sociologists, anthropologists, musicologists, or psychologists without serious support from scholars primarily concerned with interpreting religious thought and practice.

Even in the specific domain of scripture, not only the oral, but also the overtly physical aspects of sacred books have not been given their due. A nonreductionist study of the uses of the written or printed text – the bound volume, the calligraphed scroll, the illuminated page, the scriptural amulet, the phylactery, the prayer-wheel – could shed considerable light on the functional nature of scripture. Once we are able to get beyond our inclination to dismiss many of the roles of the physical text as magical or superstitious and strive instead to see the continuities and congruities between phenomena as diverse as, on the one hand, the holding up or kissing of a scriptural text in ritual, the touching of it for its power or blessing, or the divinatory use of it for guiding decision, and, on the other, the reading, chanting, preaching, proof-texting, or theologizing from that same text, we shall be better able to deal with scripture in all of its multifaceted, relational quality and to do some justice to its importance in varied sectors of religious life.

The oral uses of scripture do provide especially clear examples of the important sensory roles of sacred texts. By paying scant attention to the vocal dimensions of sacred texts, we have missed something essential both to an understanding of scripture and to better comprehension of religious sensibility and praxis. A focus on the written text has encouraged us to look at scripture in isolation from its community of faith or else to concentrate far too exclusively upon its interpretation and use in doctrinal matters. Often, those scholars most concerned with religious texts have done least to explore the contextual meanings of such texts in their typically vocal use by persons and communities of faith. Why, for example, do we not have more serious studies of mnemonic mastery and meditation of religious texts, or of the roles of scripture in homiletics, chant, and hymnody, when these are so basic in almost every major tradition of religious life?

To take only memorization as a case in point, we know very little about the differences between groups or persons who know their scripture utterly by heart and those (often in the same tradition) who know too little of theirs to repeat it without the printed page before them. Yet simple logic would indicate that such "by-heart" knowledge must make a great deal of difference in how a person understands and uses scripture. Certainly the historical witness of those religious groups and persons whose intense piety has been inseparable from intimate and often complete knowledge of their holy book or books bears this out. It is a vastly different thing to read and revere a text as an authoritative *document* than to *internalize* it in memory and meditation until it permeates the sensual as well as the intellectual sphere of consciousness. This internalization, or "having the text by heart", leads the person of faith to accept so naturally the guidance of the text that its word becomes effectively absolute, quite apart from any dogmatic principle of scriptural authority or the reassuring presence of any physical text we might point to and handle as a sacred object.

The major Christian thinkers – and the major thinkers of the Muslim, Indian, Jewish, and other scriptural traditions – have been characterized by the aforementioned capacity to (or rather the *incapacity not* to) "speak scripture" when they write or utter any words at all. They have known scripture so intimately that it has passed into the fabric of their thinking and discourse and provided the conceptual matrix as well as the inner linguistic content of that thinking and discourse. Such thorough familiarity with scripture goes beyond, even though it includes, the venerable practice of proof-texting with scriptural citations at every opportunity. It determines mental constructs no less than rhetorical constructs.

This kind of "scripturality" is patently a major matter for the historian who is trying to probe and describe spirituality in a particular context, just as it is a matter of concern for anyone interested in the psychology and sociology of religion. Might we not, for example, learn a great deal from thorough study of the scriptural dimensions of the language of a John Donne, al-Ghazālī, Rāmānuja, or Shinran? Or the roles of scriptural texts in the liturgy and devotional practice of the Sanūsīyah, the English Puritans, the Dādupanth, or the Unification Church?

Scripture and Modern Culture

I have emphasized throughout this study that the modern West appears to be historically anomalous in its understanding of scripture, largely because of its general loss of a significant oral/aural relationship to the scriptural word and, indeed, the written word altogether. I have tried to document some of the reasons why I believe this sweeping generalization to be a reasonable one, especially with respect to the peculiar character of our relation to books, writing, and reading. It will undoubtedly need further testing to be sustained in specific contexts, but if it be admitted at least as a provisional thesis, it also raises questions of the relationship between the changing role of scripture and other changes in the modern world in which we live.

Two of these changes are of special importance here: first, the linked phenomena of the "typographic" revolution of print culture and the literacy revolution for which it prepared the way; second, what is commonly referred to as the "secularization" of the modern world.

It would be hard to deny that the spread of at least minimal literacy among the majority of the population and a high degree of reliance upon the printed page have been hallmarks of Western "modernity". As such, they deserve recognition alongside more obvious processes such as industrialization, technologization, and increased professional specialization. What some have called a "typographic" society has been realized up to now only in the context of modernization in the West or on the Western model. Be that as it may, there can be little dispute about the significance of both the printed word and mass literacy in making the "modernity" of the modern West what it has been up to the present time. This significance is not diminished even if we are now in the process of passing beyond the high-print-literacy, typographic culture of the last one hundred years into a new age of electronic communications – one in which visual images and audiovisual media are beginning to replace visual texts, and visual-literacy skills are being superseded by oral/aural skills quite different from those of preliterate oral culture.[4]

An even more obvious component of Western modernity has been the secularization of sectors of life previously controlled by religious considerations and comprehensible only within a religious worldview. The importance of this does not negate the importance of frequent movements of religious revival such as those growing out of present-day American fundamentalism, or the widespread attempts to find new spiritual paths based on Eastern models. Rather, it underscores the widespread Western estrangement from organized religion and the overall loss of consensus on the religious values that can be acknowledged as bases of communal existence. To put it slightly differently, the modern society that has come into being in the nineteenth and especially the twentieth century in the predominantly Christian West is one unprecedented in its pluralism. Overall, the secularization or pluralization of the European–American world has fostered a progressive objectification of "religion" as one among many elements of social life rather than as a key dimension of all of the others. For better or worse, religious norms have become less and less dominant as the bases of societal ethics, individual morality, political order, and cultural standards.[5]

These "modern" facts of mass literacy and print culture on the one hand and secularization or pluralization of culture on the other have had significant consequences for the role of scripture in the present-day West. The capacity for mass production, widespread distribution, and increased reading of scripture has been inherent in the typographic and literacy revolutions. This has worked in many ways to increase familiarity with the Bible and to place the Bible more squarely in the accessible sphere of ordinary objects and everyday reality. However, putting a Bible in everyone's hands has had mixed consequences for the status of the Bible in the culture as a whole. With regard to its functional roles, the printed Bible has become the chief medium of contact with scripture where once the text read or recited aloud was dominant; but with increased availability has come increased familiarity, which has always a negative as well as a positive side. A book does not have to be opened, after all; therefore its physical availability is not necessarily a replacement for the loss of the high-density vocal presence of scripture in public discourse. At the least, we can observe in the past century or more that, just as availability of the biblical text has greatly increased through growth of literacy and the ubiquitous presence of printed Bibles, the strong biblical saturation of Western culture has sharply decreased.[6]

On the other hand, any decline in the public presence of scripture in Western culture must be ascribed in the first instance to the wider social processes summed up under the catchword of "secularization". The secularization of Western society has worked against a traditional scriptural orientation as well as a unitary traditional religious orientation more generally. The Bible has lost much of its earlier widely recognized stature as the only textual authority transcending national boundaries, sectarian divisions, ethnic or cultural diversities, and differences of socioeconomic or intellectual class. Both it and the "classics" have ceased to be cornerstones of Western education, and it is evident that scripture can no longer be the central symbol of authority, values, and truth that it once was, even in the social and political arenas. Its authority, like that of many other traditional absolutes, has patently diminished for Western society at large, however central and supreme it may yet be for many particular groups and still countless individuals. Whether this is viewed as a desirable or a deplorable development will depend upon the person consulted, but the fact of the development itself is hard to deny.

Many of the corollaries of these changes in the perception, use, and status of scripture are obvious. Once a generally recognized locus of contact with things transcendent, the Bible has undergone a "leveling" in which its mythopoëic discourse is commonly taken by the modern secularist as mere legendarizing and speculative moralizing or, equally lamentably, by the biblical fundamentalist as a text reporting literal truths analogous to those of modern scientific inquiry. Even the fact that our modern historical consciousness allows scholars today to look with greater dispassion upon the Bible as but one among many holy scriptures of human history is, for all of its intellectually positive dimensions, also a symptom of a significant diminution in the preeminent importance of scripture in Western society.

The present study suggests, however, that these developments with respect to scripture in modern Western culture result at least in part from changed attitudes to and uses of texts as well as from overt processes of secularization. It bears repeating that our documentary, text-critical orientation in contemporary scriptural studies reflects a wider conception of scripture as merely a particular kind of written text – perhaps special because of its historical importance, but ultimately one among other genres of written or printed matter. The emphasis on the centrality of the written text, whether in scholarly biblical criticism, in fundamentalist literalism, or in popular attitudes, must be seen in the wider context of the diminution of scripture's role in Western Christian culture and religion as a whole. The biblical text formerly "lived" in good part by being internalized in memory and vocabulary by the faithful, and even to some degree by the marginally or less than committed, if only because of its permeation of the schoolroom and the public arena. Modern times have seen it too easily become an object – whether a closed book on the shelf of the secularized or a ready-to-hand, "black and white" proof text for the literal-minded.

These considerations may have implications for societies outside the modern West as well. If the rise of typographic, mass-literacy culture and the concomitant decline of scriptural orality and of textual orality in general can be linked to the secularization and the diminished visible importance of scriptural and other "classical" texts in the West, are similar developments in other cultures with respect to their central scriptural texts also closely linked to secularization? In trying to answer such questions, and to grapple with changes or potential changes in other forms of "book religion", the Western experience may provide a point of departure. However unique it may be in strict historical terms, this experience may well offer a useful, legitimate, and important source of reference – whether for contrast or comparison – for the study of scripturality in other traditions only now (or still now) experiencing forces of modernization and change similar to those that have already been at work in the West for between one and two centuries, if not longer.

Today almost every other culture and religious tradition is undergoing, usually in highly compressed form and with much greater rapidity, and consequently with greatly reduced reaction and adjustment time, the same kinds of modernizing processes that we in the West have experienced. It seems inevitable that they are also becoming, or will become, print-dominated and perhaps high-literacy societies as well. Secularization is already perceived as a threat to traditional religious sensibilities wherever modernization of any degree has taken hold in the non-Western world. Whether secularization will mean the demise of the dominance of the Qur'ān in Muslim societies, for example, is a question of moment for Muslims as well as for scholars interested in the contemporary Muslim world and the future course of Islam.

Postscript

This cannot, however, be the final word. The printed scriptures in the Western world have still not passed from the religious, much less the wider cultural, scene even in this highly secular age. If, for example, the Bible no longer commands center stage in Western culture, it is even today demonstrably much more than simply one among other members of the genus "book", both for the religious and the nonreligious person. This has much to do with the formative role of Christian religion and morality in Western civilization. If the Bible is no longer our universal, visible authority, it has passed nonetheless into the constitutive fabric of our value structures, our language, our art, and our entire imaginative framework, or *Weltanschauung* – what Northrop Frye has appositely termed our "mythological universe". Originally its specifically religious character and function for the vast majority put it at the heart of our entire tradition and made it the touchstone of public morality and discourse. Today its many subtler and more hidden functions, which extend far beyond the specifically confessional or liturgical realm, continue to give it a cultural significance, even if one that is reduced, or at least less overt and conscious than previously. Diminished in its oral presence for most, as well as in its spiritual authority for many, the Bible continues to be prominent as both a literary and linguistic, and not seldom as a moral and ethical, resource of our larger society.

NB

This suggests in turn other, more specific questions about the present and future roles of other scriptures in other contexts. Is, for example, the Qur'ān on its way to becoming more and more a broadly cultural and less and less what we would describe as a specifically religious force in Islamic societies? This is a question worth asking and exploring, however superfluous it may seem to the devout Muslim and, for different reasons, the avowed secularist. The oral factor may well be a significant indicator in this instance: The sustained or diminished importance of the recited Qur'ān will likely be crucial in gauging, if not determining, whether or not this occurs. Similarly, how Buddhist *sūtra*s are being used or not used in modern Śri Lankan or Japanese society, or how the oral performance of the Bhāgavata Purāṇa is being affected by changing patterns of life in urban areas of India, may be questions whose answers have significance beyond the narrow realm of scriptural or ritual studies. Likewise of considerable moment for the future of Chinese culture is the decline or potential loss of the Chinese literati's intimate, often verbatim knowledge of their "scriptures", the classics (*ching*), which have been the lifeblood of China's existence for well over two millennia. We may wonder also whether the eventual transition in most non-Western societies from illiteracy to high literacy will affect materially how such societies and their religious traditions deal with scriptural and other important texts. If diminished oral intimacy with texts means diminished intimacy and traffic with or dependence on scriptural texts, it may follow that an increased print orientation will make it difficult to use scripture as a basis for more than a narrowly sectarian revival of religious sensibilities.

Thus questions of the relationship of persons and communities to scripture extend beyond theological issues of authority and revelation, or literalism and esoteric interpretation, into the sociological and social-psychological arenas of cultural, moral, and political norms and the relationship of these to scriptural texts that have been historically important or central to a given society. Even if its visible manifestations are diminished and its scope restricted by secularization and other change, the power of scriptural formulas, diction, vocabulary, images, motifs, and allusions in secular public use, let alone secular literary use, persists in a society. This fact needs serious study and elucidation not only in the heydays of traditional religion and culture, but perhaps especially in posttraditional eras, or transitional ones somewhere between the two. The rhetoric of scriptural language has often a ring and a resonance that outlast as well as outstrip its specifically religious applications, and we know far too little about these and their functions in most cultural contexts.

If such matters seem to lie far afield from the inquiries pursued in this book, it may be in good part because of our own entrapment in the modern dichotomization of the religious and the secular. Understanding the scriptural images and language of a great religious personage in any tradition is finally not so different an endeavor – although it may be an easier one – from understanding those of a modern public figure or writer who, consciously or unconsciously, draws upon these images and language in wholly secular contexts. The line between the study of the history of religion and the history of culture and ideas is hardly a clear one – and is often a specious one. The scriptural rhetoric of the American civil rights movement of the 1960s and 1970s would, for example, make a fascinating study in scripture in one sector of the contemporary West. However, scriptural language operates at much less dramatic levels of oral discourse as well – often in echoes so faint as to go unremarked.

In this regard, I still remember an otherwise unmemorable incident of nearly twenty years ago now, hearing a speech given in classical Arabic on a civic occasion by the rather modestly educated mayor of an Arab Christian village in the mountains of the Lebanon. I had been studying the Qur'ān for several months at the time, and I was amazed to hear qur'anic phrases and, at least as I perceived it, even some cadences of qur'anic diction, in this modern Christian's sometimes grammatically awkward but often lyric attempts at eloquence in the traditional, inflected style of formal classical Arabic. As he stood in the afternoon heat, wiping his brow in a kind of visual punctuation of the somewhat labored flow of his rhetoric, and spoke of things like honor, hospitality, and friendship, I was fascinated by the obvious aural presence in his mind's ear of what was to him a religiously, but clearly not a linguistically, alien text. The qur'anic echo was distinctly if mutedly evident in the consciously "elevated" discourse toward which he aspired that hot summer's day.

As I have worked in recent years on the oral aspects of scripture, I have thought of that speech from time to time, and in some ways it is for me a peculiarly telling, if somewhat banal, example of the importance of the vocal scriptural word for an entire *linguistic* rather than just a single *religious* tradition. It reminds also of the persistent presence, the peculiar staying power, of scripture in verbal, and especially oral, discourse. We have seen or could think of more vivid examples of scriptural presence in the spoken word, ranging from the proof-texting of the Muslim *ḥāfiẓ* or the fundamentalist Christian preacher to public recitations of Qur'ān or *Devī Māhātmya,* the prose of a John Bunyan or Martin Bucer, and the rhetoric of a Sam Erwin or a Martin Luther King; yet this ironical instance of "cross-religious" oral scriptural presence is a vivid reminder for me that the ring of the scriptural word echoes at all levels of experience and sophistication and not only in the narrowly defined "religious" or the highly literate sphere. Thus it may serve with the muted eloquence of simplicity and the immediacy of everyday experience to point at the end of these inquiries toward all the unexplored but enduring oral dimensions of scripture, which, however closely tied they may be to it, always extend well beyond the written word alone.

Notes

Introduction

1. Even a modern comparative scholar such as the late S. G. F. Brandon could remark that ". . . the Bible at once appears as the supreme example of a Holy Book" ("The Holy Book, the Holy Tradition and the Holy Ikon," p. 2). The major curiosity of such a statement is the apparently complete willingness to ignore the striking role of the Qur'ān in the Islamic tradition – a role that would easily make this scripture at least a viable contender for the place of "supreme example of a holy book."
2. The most significant and sophisticated general study to date is that done over thirty years ago by Johannes Leipoldt and Siegfried Morenz, *Heilige Schriften. Betrachtungen zur Religionsgeschichte der antiken Mittelmeerwelt* (1953). Even though its scope is limited to sacred books in the world of late antiquity, the work has much to offer anyone interested in generalizing about scripture. Leipoldt and Morenz make a serious attempt to look at the various characteristics and uses of sacred texts in the Mediterranean area, treating topics such as the origin of scripture; its unity, text, and translation; and its public and private reading, interpretation, and magical use. Phenomenological discussions and surveys of various aspects of scripture worldwide are found in: Friedrich Heiler, *Erscheinungsformen und Wesen der Religion,* pp. 266–364; Geo Widengren, *Religionsphänomenologie,* pp. 546–93; Gerardus van der Leeuw, *Phänomenologie der Religion,* pp. 457–509 [Eng. trans. pp. 403–46]; and Gustav Mensching, *Das heilige Wort.* A survey of the scriptures of the major world religious traditions is found in Günter Lanczkowski, *Heilige Schriften.* Two volumes of articles by different contributors on the scriptures of selected individual traditions are F. F. Bruce and E. G. Rupp, eds., *Holy Book and Holy Tradition* (1968), and Wendy D. O'Flaherty, ed., *The Critical Study of Sacred Texts* (1979). A recent (1985) collective volume, *The Holy Book in Comparative Perspective,* edited by Frederick M. Denny and Rodney L. Taylor, also offers an interesting if somewhat uneven series of articles describing and discussing sacred texts in particular traditions. Although this volume is mistitled (little comparative perspective is offered), most of the contributors do attempt consciously to pay attention to the functional roles of holy books in the traditions treated.
3. The aforementioned Denny and Taylor volume (n. 2) gives some evidence of this concern. It has been articulated most forcibly by Wilfred Cantwell Smith in several publications: "The Study of Religion and the Study of the Bible," "The True

Meaning of Scripture," and "Scripture as Form and Concept," the last of these an as yet unpublished article in a forthcoming work edited by Miriam Levering, *Rethinking Scripture* (scheduled for 1987 publication). The other contributors to the latter volume, most of whom, like the present author, have worked with Smith and share his concern with the ongoing roles of scriptural texts in religious life, also point in their contributions to significant uses and meanings of scripture in particular traditions such as the Jain, Chinese Buddhist, Indian, Islamic, Jewish, and Christian. Note especially the previously published articles of one contributor, Thomas B. Coburn: "The Study of the Purāṇas and the Study of Religion," and "'Scripture' in India." Much remains to be done on sacred texts in Hindu life, but see J. F. Staal, *Nambudiri Veda Recitation* and other works mentioned in Chapter 6 below. The concern with the role of the Qur'ān as a living force in Muslim life has been the subject of a number of studies by scholars such as J. Jomier, Frederick M. Denny, Kristina Nelson, and the present author; see Chapters 8 and 9. The role of the Bible in various periods and sectors of Christian history has been treated in an even greater number of studies, many of them of book length (see n. 4 below and Part IV, passim). Of recent work, note especially the work of several younger historians of American religion, some of whom are represented in Nathan O. Hatch and Mark A. Noll, eds., *The Bible in America.*

4. Besides the many specialized studies in diverse traditions, note for only the Christian and Muslim traditions such works as: Beryl Smalley, *The Study of the Bible in the Middle Ages;* Hans Frei, *The Eclipse of Biblical Narrative;* Robert M. Grant, with David Tracy, *A Short History of the Interpretation of the Bible;* Ignaz Goldziher, *Die Richtungen der islamischen Koranauslegung;* and Paul Nwyia, *Exégèse coranique et langage mystique.*
5. This paragraph and several of the following ones on the problem of the generic study of scripture are substantially the same as portions of the present author's article, "Scripture," in Mircea Eliade et al., eds., *The Encyclopedia of Religion,* 16 vols. (New York: Macmillan, 1987), s.v.
6. Roger Lapointe, "Classicisme et canonicité"; Ernst Robert Curtius, *Europäische Literatur und lateinisches Mittelalter,* chap. 14; cf. Wilfred C. Smith, "Scripture as Form and Concept."
7. Edward Gibbon, *Miscellaneous Works* (London, 1814) 4: 358. Also cited below, p. 57.
8. The clearest and most succinct discussion of the varying enumerations of the "canon" of "classics" in Chinese culture is that found in *EB*[15], s.v. "Confucian Texts, Classical" (Wing-Tsit Chan).
9. On nonliterate oral tradition generally, see Jan Vansina, *Oral Tradition;* Albert B. Lord, *The Singer of Tales;* Ruth Finnegan, *Oral Poetry;* id., *Oral Literature in Africa;* and Jack Goody, ed., *Literacy in Traditional Societies;* id., *The Domestication of the Savage Mind;* M. T. Clanchy, "Remembering the Past and the Good Old Law." See especially the bibliographies in the works of Finnegan and Goody for some of the vast specialized literature in this domain. See also Chapter 1 in the present volume. On the dichotomy between oral and written tradition more generally, see Bruce and Rupp; Walter J. Ong, *Orality and Literacy;* Edward Shils, *Tradition* (esp. pp. 91–94). On specific historical contexts and traditions, see Birger Gerhardsson, *Memory and Manuscript;* Eduard Nielsen, *Oral Tradition;* Geo Widengren, *Literary and Psychological Aspects of the Hebrew Prophets;* Werner Kelber, *The Oral and the Written Gospel;* H. Bacht et al., *Die mündliche Überlieferung;* Eric Havelock, *The Literate Revolution in Greece and Its Cultural Consequences.*

Part I. Of Written and Spoken Words

1. G. S. Brett, *Psychology Ancient and Modern* (London: Longmans, 1928), pp. 36–37, as cited in Marshall McLuhan, *The Gutenberg Galaxy,* p. 74.
2. Eric A. Havelock, *The Literate Revolution in Greece and Its Cultural Consequences,* p. 50. Cf. Ferdinand de Saussure, *Cours de linguistique générale:* ". . . la langue étant le dépôt des images acoustiques, et l'écriture la forme tangible de ces images" (p. 32, =Eng. trans. p. 15); ". . . le mot écrit se mêle si intimement au mot parlé dont il est l'image, qu'il finit par usurper le rôle principal; on en vient à donner autant et plus d'importance à la représentation du signe vocal qu'à ce signe lui-même" (p. 45, =Eng. trans. p. 24); ". . . le mot écrit tend à se substituer dans notre esprit au mot parlé . . . " (p. 48, =Eng. trans. p. 26). Similarly, Walter J. Ong, *Orality and Literacy,* p. 8: "Written texts all have to be related somehow, directly or indirectly, to the world of sound, the natural habitat of language, to yield their meanings. 'Reading' a text means converting it to sound . . . . Writing can never dispense with orality." Cf. also Walter J. Ong, *Interfaces of the Word,* pp. 21–25. For a somewhat different approach to the relationship between spoken and written language, see Michael Stubbs, *Language and Literacy,* esp. pp. 10–14, 21–42, 103–15.
3. One of the most cogent statements of some psycholinguistic reasons for this tendency can be found in de Saussure, *Cours de linguistique,* pp. 46–47 (=Eng. trans. p. 25), where he underscores (1) the sense of permanence, stability, and unity of language over time fostered by writing, which makes us think it rather than speech to be the primary linguistic form; (2) the preference for visual rather than aural impressions because they are "sharper and more lasting"; (3) the influence of the literary language and schooling through books and the fixed "code" of orthography, which "adds to the undeserved importance of writing"; and (4) the fact that when language and orthography disagree, it is simply easier to rely on the written form for the solution: "thus writing assumes undeserved importance."
4. H. J. Chaytor, *From Script to Print,* p. 6.

Chapter 1. Writing and Written Culture

1. *OED* 1: 989a; cf. 988c; David Diringer, *The Book Before Printing,* pp. 24–25. The book and writing itself are, of course, much older than Germanic culture. For readable and comprehensive overviews of their history and development before the advent of moveable-type printing, see (on book): Diringer, ibid.; Helmut Presser, *Das Buch vom Buch,* esp. chaps. 1–2; Wilhelm Schubart, *Das Buch bei den Griechen und Römern;* (on writing): I. J. Gelb, *A Study of Writing;* Hans Jensen, *Die Schrift in Vergangenheit und Gegenwart.*
2. See Liddell and Scott, s.v. "byblos", "biblion".
3. As Elizabeth L. Eisenstein, *The Printing Press as an Agent of Change,* p. 9, n. 18, has pointed out, we lack a common descriptive term for the preprint literate culture based on handwritten communications. Like her, I find "chirographic", as Walter J. Ong uses it, to be the most accurate parallel term to "typographic" (for print culture), but somewhat too abstruse to adopt uniformly. "Scribal" (Eisenstein's choice) may be best, although its association with the work of professional scribes who write by hand can make it occasionally misleading. As a rule, I use "scribal", "chirographic", "script" (the last by analogy with "print [culture]"), and occasionally even "written", interchangeably to refer to periods and institutions characterized by the presence of writing but not yet by moveable-type printing.

4. Cf. Jack Goody and Ian Watt, "The Consequences of Literacy," p. 27; Gelb, *Study of Writing*, pp. 221–23. Note also Eric Havelock's comment on the negative side of our attitudes about this: "It is a curious kind of cultural arrogance which presumes to identify human intelligence with literacy. . . . Language for communication . . . . is the foundation of all human cultures. These have existed as oral systems from prehistoric times. The age of script, of the successive stages of a growing literacy, is by comparison a mere moment in the history of our species" (*Literate Revolution*, pp. 44–45). Robert Pattison's *On Literacy* is an extended argument along much the same lines, stressing that literacy is not merely reading and writing in traditional terms, but ability to use language discriminately. The Western view that has "associated literacy with a variety of civic and moral benefits, as if it were the indispensable correlate of civilization," goes back at least to the seventeenth century in England and America, according to David Cressy, "The Environment for Literacy," p. 23. Cf. Thomas Carlyle's hyperbole concerning the "civic" benefits of printing and writing: "Printing, which comes necessarily out of Writing, I say often, is equivalent to Democracy: invent Writing, Democracy is inevitable." (*On Heroes, Hero-Worship, and the Heroic in History*, p. 258).
5. Cited passages, in order of occurrence, as follows: Gardiner, *Egypt of the Pharaohs* (1961; New York: Oxford University Press, Galaxy Books, 1966), p. 19; Spengler, *The Decline of the West*, trans. Charles Francis Atkinson (1928; 8th repr. ed., New York: Alfred A. Knopf, 1950), 2: 150; Redfield, *The Primitive World and Its Transformations* (Ithaca, N.Y.: Cornell University Press, 1953), p. 7; Jensen, *Die Schrift*, p. 9 (cf. Eng. trans., p. 15); McLuhan, *Gutenberg Galaxy*, p. 27 (cf. pp. 18, 45, 48); Carl L. Becker, "The Sword and the Pen," in *Progress and Power* ([Palo Alto, Calif.]: Stanford University Press; London: Humphrey Milford, Oxford University Press, 1936), p. 41. Cf. David R. Olson, "From Utterance to Text," p. 257 ("Speech makes us human and literacy makes us civilized"); Hilda H. Golden, "Literacy," p. 416b. See also J. C. Carothers, "Culture, Psychiatry, and the Written Word."
6. As Herbert Grundmann noted already in 1958 ("Litteratus – illitteratus," p. 2, n. 3), there has been a recent (postwar, presumably) countertrend toward recognizing that "preliterate" societies can have quite advanced levels of cultural complexity. The tenor of the "cultural relativist" movement in modern anthropology has been one conducive to skepticism about the easy assumption that lack of writing necessarily makes a society "primitive"; but in many areas of life, from administration to religion to art, the effective differences, wholly apart from value judgments, between even partially literate and preliterate, wholly oral cultures are pronounced. Furthermore, recent research by Sylvia Scribner and Michael Cole suggests, albeit very tentatively, that although literacy does convey major new abilities, it may not be the source of more generalized capacities such as abstract thinking ("Literacy without Schooling"; *The Psychology of Literacy*). See below, Chapters 2 and 3.
7. On the historian's need for writings to supplement anonymous archaeological data, and on the study of nonliterate societies both with and without writings about them from neighboring literate cultures, see Stuart Piggott, *Approach to Archaeology* (Cambridge, Mass.: Harvard University Press, 1959), chap. 5, pp. 101–25. Cf. pp. 76–81 and J. Vansina, R. Mauny, and L. V. Thomas, eds., *The Historian in Tropical Africa*, pp. 2–19 (in French; =Eng. trans. pp. 60–75).
8. Steiner, *After Babel*, p. 29. Cf. V. H. Galbraith, *Studies in the Public Records*, p. 26.
9. *Book Before Printing*, p. 16. This view, albeit not so baldly stated and without expression of such total confidence in the accuracy of written sources, was in recent

years well represented in deliberations at Harvard in the faculty committee that oversees the recently implemented undergraduate Core Curriculum. It proved difficult to get courses in archaeological anthropology into the Core program because the subcommittee on the Core area of "Historical Studies" was loathe to endorse a course under a "historical studies" rubric in which no written documents were available to study the ancient cultures or periods under discussion.

10. Cf. Rüdiger Schott, "Das Geschichtsbewußtsein schriftloser Völker," esp. pp. 171–86, 199–201, and the extensive literature cited therein; Vansina, Mauny, and Thomas, *Historian in Tropical Africa,* pp. 2–7 ("Les traditions orales"; =Eng. trans. pp. 60–65), 165–76 (H. Deschamps, "Traditions orales au Gabon"), 305–21 (Roland Oliver, "Reflections on the Sources of Evidence for the Pre-Colonial History of East Africa").
11. Cf. Schott, "Geschichtsbewußtsein," p. 196. See Michael T. Clanchy, "Remembering the Past and the Good Old Law," for an excellent survey of the nature of oral traditions (including references to recent anthropological literature) and the problems they pose for the historian. Cf. Goody and Watt, "Consequences of Literacy," esp. pp. 28–34. On oral tradition generally, see the classic work of Jan Vansina, *Oral Tradition.* Cf. Vansina, Mauny, and Thomas, *Historian in Tropical Africa;* and Schott, "Geschichtsbewußtsein."
12. Cf. Tela Zaslof, "Readings on Literacy," p. 155, where she remarks of the diverse literature surveyed, "No matter what the authors' special concerns about literacy, they concur on its cultural significance: the manner in which social groups rely on written language reflects and modifies the structure of their thought processes, the nature of their self-expression, and their dialogue with others." On such changes, see Jacques Derrida, *Of Grammatology,* pp. 92–93, 299–302, inter alia. On the other hand, the study of literacy among the Vai in Liberia by Scribner and Cole (see above, n. 8), for all the tentativeness and occasional obscurity of its results (in what is in any case a very particular – e.g., trilingual – situation), seems to argue that the psychological effects of literacy as opposed to preliteracy in terms of a shift in modes of consciousness may be less sweeping or uniform than many writers have postulated (*Psychology of Literacy,* esp. Part IV, "Testing Consequences," pp. 163–260; cf. id., "Literacy without Schooling").
13. This term is Eric A. Havelock's: See his *Literate Revolution,* esp. pp. 23–24. Cf. id., *Preface to Plato,* pp. 166–90, esp. pp. 180ff., on the oral as opposed to the literate relationship between knower and knowledge. See also Walter J. Ong, *The Presence of the Word,* p. 45; V. H. Galbraith, "The Literacy of the Medieval English Kings," pp. 6–7.
14. "Remembering the Past," p. 176.
15. On poetry as an "encyclopedic" mnemonic device, see Havelock, *Preface to Plato,* chaps. 3–5, pp. 36–96. For a somewhat different aspect of aurally oriented verse forms as mnemonic aids, cf. the highly oral mnemonics of Veda or Qur'ān recitation (see Chapters 6–9). On the classic Western visual-image mnemonic systems, see Helga Hajdu, *Das mnemotechnische Schrifttum des Mittelalters;* Frances A. Yates, *The Art of Memory;* Jonathan D. Spence, *The Memory Palace of Matteo Ricci.* On the psychology of memory, which seems to have been studied remarkably little from the standpoint of mnemonic devices, see F. C. Bartlett, *Remembering,* and Alan D. Baddeley, *The Psychology of Memory* (on mnemonics, esp. pp. 347–69).
16. This appears to have been the case, for example, in the relationship between the original oral reports and the eventually dominant written transmission of the Ḥadīth, or Tradition literature, in Islam. Cf. the comments of the sinologist Arthur Waley,

trans., *The Way and Its Power,* p. 101: "The earliest use of connected writing . . . was as an aid to memory. That is, its purpose was to help people not to forget what they knew already; whereas in more advanced communities the chief use of writing is to tell people things that they have not heard before." See also Jensen, *Die Schrift,* p. 14 (=Eng. trans. p. 20); Olson, "From Utterance to Text," pp. 264, 266.

17. *The Domestication of the Savage Mind,* p. 37. Cf. "The Writer's Audience is Always a Fiction," chap. 2 of Ong, *Interfaces of the Word,* esp. pp. 80–81; Spengler, *Decline of the West* 2: 150; Goody and Watt, "Consequences of Literacy," pp. 53, 62; Carothers, "Culture, Psychiatry, and the Written Word," p. 311; Ong, *Presence of the Word,* p. 114; McLuhan, *Gutenberg Galaxy,* p. 27; Olson, "From Utterance to Text," esp. pp. 257–62; Marcel Jousse, *L'anthropologie du geste,* p. 30; Patricia M. Greenfield, "Oral or Written Language," esp. pp. 169–71; Patricia Marks Greenfield and Jerome S. Bruner, "Culture and Cognitive Growth," p. 104; Paul Ricoeur, *Hermeneutics and the Human Sciences,* pp. 146–47. See also Brian Stock, *The Implications of Literacy,* p. 84.

18. J. Læssøe, "Literary and Oral Tradition in Ancient Mesopotamia," pp. 210–12, drawing on Samuel N. Kramer, "The Epic of Gilgameš and Its Sumerian Sources: A Study in Literary Evolution," *JAOS* 64 (1944): 7–23, and Alexander Heidel, *The Gilgamesh Epic and Old Testament Parallels* (1946; 2nd ed. 1949; Chicago and London: University of Chicago Press, 1963), esp. pp. 13–16, which see. Læssøe's general thesis is that "the perfection of writing and the advance of literacy may be said to walk hand in hand in Mesopotamia, for the great creations of literary endeavour did not come into existence in that country until writing had provided the facilities to deal with intricate and manifold notions" (p. 212). See also Thorkild Jacobsen, *The Treasures of Darkness* (New Haven and London: Yale University Press, 1976), pp. 193–219, esp. pp. 208–15.

19. Goody and Watt, "Consequences of Literacy," pp. 56–57, 62, 64. Cf. Havelock, "Literate Revolution," p. 8, on the advent of literacy in Greece: "Nonliterate speech had favored discourse describing action; the postliterate altered the balance in favor of reflection. The syntax of Greek began to adapt to an increasing opportunity offered to state propositions in place of describing events. This was the 'bottom line' of the alphabetic legacy to postalphabetic culture."

20. *Orality and Literacy,* pp. 8–9. Cf. p. 15: "Literacy . . . is absolutely necessary for the development not only of science but also of history, philosophy, explicative understanding of literature and of any art . . . ."

21. Clanchy, "Remembering the Past," offers a brief survey of evidence from modern anthropological studies that underscores the different nature of written as opposed to oral history records. See also the examples cited in Goody and Watt, "Consequences of Literacy," esp. pp. 31–33, and the discussion of Schott, "Geschichtsbewußtsein," pp. 195–201.

22. Goody and Watt, "Consequences of Literacy," p. 67. Cf. Franz Bäuml's comment, which, while disconcertingly categorical about what "characterizes preliterate society", still underscores significant differences in historical consciousness between the worlds of primary orality and written communication: "The independent existence of a fixed text eliminates the possibility – and the necessity – for a homœostatic, 'pastless' view of the past, of the sort which characterizes preliterate societies and which can be assumed, on the basis of the evidence offered by medieval [European] epics originating in the oral tradition, to characterize illiterate subcultures in a literate society as well" ("Varieties and Consequences of Medieval Literacy and Illiteracy," p. 249).

23. Cf. Bruno Gentili and Giovanni Cerri, "Written and Oral Communication in Greek Historiographical Thought," pp. 139–40, esp. p. 140, n. 24. The often-quoted passage in question is from Thucydides 1.22.4 (cf. 1.21), cited by Gentili and Cerri in the trans. of Charles Forster Smith. Cf. John Finley's translation: "My work has been composed, not for the applause of today's hearing, but as a possession forever" (*Thucydides*, p. 291). Gentili and Cerri go on (pp. 141–49) to give other examples from classical writers (esp. Duris of Samos and Polybius) that highlight differences between oral and written orientations in writing history.
24. On this point, see Goody, *Domestication*, especially his comments on "ethnocentric dichotomies" and "the material concomitants of the process of mental 'domestication'" of the "savage mind" (pp. 9ff.). Cf. Greenfield and Bruner, "Culture and Cognitive Growth," p. 90: "intelligence is to a great extent the internalization of 'tools' provided by a given culture . . . ." See also Galbraith, "Literacy of English Kings," pp. 6–7; Carothers, "Culture, Psychiatry, and the Written Word"; Olson, "From Utterance to Text," p. 263; Scribner and Cole, *Psychology of Literacy;* id., "Literacy without Schooling."
25. *Domestication*, pp. 109–10. Goody's whole book is an attempt to point out the effects of literacy on "modes of thought" - an attempt to reformulate the "primitive/civilized" and other dichotomies used as organizing schemes for categorizing human societies on a "we–they" basis. See also the excellent discussion of Goody's and others' ideas about differences between literate, semiliterate, and nonliterate cultures in Marilyn R. Waldman, "Primitive Mind/Modern Mind."
26. *On Literacy*, pp. 40–41. See esp. pp. 40–60 for Pattison's rejection of some of the ideas of Goody, McLuhan, Havelock, etc. (which he interprets in the most categorical and extreme way possible, whereas Havelock in particular is much more cautious than Goody, McLuhan, or Ong; cf., for example, n. 19 above). See also nn. 6, 25 above.

Chapter 2. The Print Textuality of Modern Culture

1. *Dialogues of Alfred North Whitehead*, p. 153.
2. Michael T. Clanchy, *From Memory to Written Record;* id., "Looking Back from the Invention of Printing"; Brian Stock, *The Implications of Literacy;* V. H. Galbraith, *Studies in the Public Records;* id., "The Literacy of the Medieval English Kings." For a different evaluation of the importance of continuities between late medieval and post-Gutenberg literacy, see Elizabeth L. Eisenstein, *The Printing Press as an Agent of Change*, esp. pp. 25ff.
3. Rolf Engelsing, *Analphabetentum und Lektüre*, p. 20; Carlo M. Cipolla, *Literacy and Development in the West*, pp. 42, 50.
4. The standard treatments of Chinese printing remain those of Thomas Francis Carter, *The Invention of Printing in China and Its Spread Westward* (1925; 2nd rev. ed., 1955), and Paul Pelliot, *Les débuts de l'imprimerie en Chine* (1953). These works do not, however, deal at any length with the social and cultural consequences of the new invention. On pre-Sung and early Sung block printing, see esp. Pelliot. On the invention of moveable type, but character rather than letter type (and clay rather than metal type) by the commoner Pi Sheng in the 1040s, see Carter, pp. 211–22. Cf. Denis Twichett, *Printing and Publishing in Medieval China* (1983), pp. 74–76; Otto W. Fuhrmann, "The Invention of Printing," pp. 243–45. On the development of moveable-, cast-metal-type (but also character, not alphabetic-letter) printing in Korea even before the end of the fourteenth century, see Carter, pp. 223–37; but see also Twitchett, pp. 78–79, and esp. Fuhrmann, "Invention," pp. 245–48, who suggests

that the Korean bronze type castings may have been imported from China. On the progress of Gutenberg's technology over these earlier types of printing, see James Moran, *Printing Presses*, chap. 1, esp. pp. 16–19.

5. Eisenstein, *Printing Press;* Marshall McLuhan, *The Gutenberg Galaxy;* Harold A. Innis, *Empire and Communications*, pp. 141–70 (chap. 7). Cf. Walter J. Ong, *Orality and Literacy*, pp. 117–38 (chap. 5); Miriam Usher Chrisman, *Lay Culture, Learned Culture*, pp. 59–75 (for the specific case of Strasbourg).
6. Walter J. Ong, "Ramist Method and the Commercial Mind," p. 167; McLuhan, *Gutenberg Galaxy*, pp. 124–25.
7. *Orality and Literacy*, p. 10.
8. Paul Ricoeur, *Hermeneutics and the Human Sciences*, p. 145, where at the outset of his essay, "What is a Text," Ricoeur begins: "Let us say that a text is any discourse fixed in writing."
9. See Lewis and Short, s.v. "textus"; *OED*, s.v. "text". For other examples of limitation of "text" to writing, see David Olson, "From Utterance to Text," in which "utterance" refers to oral "texts" of all kinds and "text" to written or printed ones alone; and Stock, *Implications of Literacy*, p. 91, where he uses "oral" in contrast to "textual" and "text" as "written text", even though he has just spoken (p. 90) of "a written version of a text" being inessential to a "textual community", whereas a person who had "mastered" a text and used it as a basis for reform was indispensable. There is nothing particularly problematic about such semantically ambiguous usage, since we are accustomed to it, but it makes clear our general inclination to revert to the use of "text" to refer fundamentally to "written text". It also reminds us how fundamental the written word is to our objectification of a body of discourse as a "text".
10. "Resurrection and Insurrection," pp. 1, 5.
11. Steiner, *Language and Silence*, pp. 18, 19; John U. Nef, *Cultural Foundations of Industrial Civilization*, p. 7; Eisenstein, *Printing Press*, pp. 602–03, 628–31, 685–87. Of particular interest is Nef's emphasis on the huge growth and increased status of statistics in the modern world. Cf. his entire discussion, "Towards Quantitative Precision," pp. 6–17, and that of Eugene S. Ferguson, "The Mind's Eye."
12. *Man: His First Million Years*, p. 150. Also cited in McLuhan, *Gutenberg Galaxy*, p. 76. Cf. Eric A. Havelock, *The Literate Revolution in Greece and Its Cultural Consequences*, p. 289: "Language uttered and remembered has no corporeal existence. . . . Language written and read becomes an object, a thing, separated from the consciousness that creates it, and immobilized in a condition of physical survival." See also Olson, "From Utterance to Text," esp. p. 278.
13. The comment of Franz Bäuml, "Varieties and Consequences of Medieval Literacy and Illiteracy," p. 248, with reference to the handwritten word, applies a fortiori to the printed word: "the written word . . . exists independently of the writing writer and the reading reader; all or any part of a written text is available in any sequence to anyone with access to it; its arrangement is spatial, lending itself to organization in terms of symbolic systems extraneous to its content, such as the alphabet or numbers." Cf. Ferguson, "Mind's Eye," esp. pp. 828–31.
14. Rudolf Hirsch, *Printing, Selling and Reading, 1450–1550*, p. 6.
15. This is one of the recurring points made in Eisenstein, *Printing Press;* see, for example, pp. 532–33, 588, 612, 698. Cf. George Sarton, *The Appreciation of Ancient and Medieval Science during the Renaissance (1450–1600)*, pp. xi–xii, 89–95; Ferguson, "Mind's Eye," pp. 828, 830–31; Ong, *Orality and Literacy*, pp. 126–27.

16. From *Boke Called the Gouvernour* (1531), as cited by Foster Watson, *The Beginnings of the Teaching of Modern Subjects in England,* p. 138 (also cited from Watson, but with incorrect page citation and differing punctuation, in Eisenstein, *Printing Press,* p. 698). Cf. Sarton, *Appreciation of Science,* pp. 89–95; Ferguson, "Mind's Eye," esp. p. 835.
17. "Culture, Psychiatry, and the Written Word," p. 311.
18. Ong, *Orality and Literacy,* p. 118. Cf. id., *Presence of the Word,* p. 114.
19. Cf. Eisenstein, *Printing Press,* pp. 131–33, esp. p. 132: "To hear an address delivered, people have to come together; to read a printed report encourages individuals to draw apart. 'What the orators of Rome and Athens were in the midst of a people *assembled,*' said Malesherbes in an address of 1775, 'men of letters are in the midst of a *dispersed* people.' . . . The wide distribution of identical bits of information provided an impersonal link between people who were unknown to each other." See also n. 13 above.
20. Cf. A. Lloyd James, *Our Spoken Language,* p. 30: "The invention of printing broadcast the printed language and gave to print a degree of authority that it has never lost." (Also cited by H. J. Chaytor, *From Script to Print,* pp. 7–8).
21. Josef Balogh, "'Voces paginarum.'"; Ong, *Orality and Literacy,* pp. 108–12. On rhetoric, see the section "The Passing of Rhetoric" below. Cf. the comment (in the 1920s) of G. L. Hendrickson: "Almost within the memory of men now living the printed page has brought about the decline, if not the death, of oratory, whether of the parliament, the bar, or the pulpit; the newspaper and the review, anticipating every subject of comment, have killed conversation and debate; the learned archive or scientific journal renders the gatherings of scholars insignificant for purposes other than convivial; and books have in large degree displaced the living voice of the teacher" ("Ancient Reading," p. 183).
22. David Riesman, "The Oral and Written Traditions," p. 25; Ong, "Ramist Method," p. 167; McLuhan, *Gutenberg Galaxy,* pp. 124–25 (passage cited as epigraph to the present chapter).
23. Of interest would be, for example, the history of indexes, use of alphabetization, chapter and section divisions, footnotes, title pages, and other reference aids or "finding devices" that came into their own with the advent of printing. This is not, to be sure, to say that they had not existed earlier: In Western Europe, the human memory was already being augmented by artificial reference aids (indexing, alphabetization, etc.) from about the second half of the twelfth century; for example, even though alphabetization as a principle of order for a sizeable dictionary had already been used in the eleventh century by Papias, it found few imitators until after the twelfth century. (Richard H. Rouse and Mary A. Rouse, "*Statim invenire,*" pp. 202–05 and ff., including further references in the notes).
24. H. I. Marrou, *A History of Education in Anquity,* pp. 52–54, 79–91 (the quotation is from p. 80); George A. Kennedy, *Classical Rhetoric and Its Christian and Secular Tradition from Ancient to Modern Times,* pp. 3–9, 15–40; Ernst Robert Curtius, *Europäische Literatur und lateinisches Mittelalter,* chap. 4, esp. sect. 4.2; Moses Hadas, *A History of Greek Literature,* pp. 159–76.
25. Peter Dronke, "Mediaeval Rhetoric," p. 315.
26. Kennedy, *Classical Rhetoric,* p. 77, 96–99, inter alia; Curtius, *Europäische Literatur,* chap. 4.3. On memory and the significant but little-known technical tradition that grew up around it and throve for over fifteen hundred years in the West, see Frances A. Yates, *The Art of Memory;* Helga Hajdu, *Das mnemotechnische Schrifttum.* Cf. Jonathan D. Spence, *The Memory Palace of Matteo Ricci.*

27. *Classical Rhetoric,* p. 109; cf. pp. 5, 110–19.
28. Ibid., p. 111.
29. "Rhetoric," pp. 801b–02a.
30. Kennedy, *Classical Rhetoric,* p. 240.
31. Sloan and Perelman, "Rhetoric," p. 802a. This article is also the principal source for the developments discussed in the preceding paragraph. Cf. also Kennedy, *Classical Rhetoric,* pp. 220–41, esp. 240–41.
32. On the older meaning of "encyclopedia" (Gr. *enkuklopaideia,* from *enkuklios paideia,* "circle [i.e., complete system] of learning"), see Ulrich Dierse, *Enzyklopädie,* esp. pp. 1–8; Robert L. Collison, *Encyclopaedias,* chap. 1; id., "Encyclopaedia," pp. 779–80; [Wilhelm-Traugott?] Krug, "Encyklopädie," p. 204b. On the history of the encyclopedia as a written or printed compendium, see esp. Collison's book and article already cited and the masterly article of S. H. Steinberg, "Encyclopaedias," as well as Ulrich Dierse, *Enzyklopädie;* Maurice de Gandillac et al., *La pensée encylopédique au moyen âge;* Werner Lenz, *Kleine Geschichte großer Lexika.*
33. Walter J. Ong speaks, for example of a "secondary orality" in modern communications, and such seems to be the essential and not entirely farfetched message beneath the jargon of recent popular prophets of "information technology" and "compunications" who speak of a "New Literacy", or "the bundle of information skills that may be required to function" in society in coming years (Benjamin M. Compaine, "Information Technology and Cultural Change," p. i). One (serious) suggestion, for example, is that the "New Literacy" may bring new forms of imagination, based on "the ability to think holistically and intuitively rather than sequentially and logically" (ibid., p. ii).
34. This is not by any means to deny the material factors that allowed encyclopedic works to flourish in typographic society. One was certainly the growth of vernaculars and their use from about the seventeenth century on in encyclopedic compendia. Another was the reduced cost of books because of printing: "only when printing was introduced into Europe did the cost of production drop by any large amount; this development in turn helped to stimulate the growth of readership. A notable feature at the time of the early printing press was the sudden growth in the popularity of some of the older encyclopaedias as a result of the tendency to ensure a ready market by printing works of which many manuscript copies were in circulation" (Collison, "Encyclopaedia," p. 787b).
35. This does not obviate the legitimate distinctions that have received so much attention in recent years between oral traditional culture and chirographic culture. Cf. Jack Goody, ed., *Literacy in Traditional Societies;* Jan Vansina, *Oral Tradition;* Ruth Finnegan, *Oral Literature in Africa;* id., *Oral Poetry.* Nor is it to deny the visual orientation of the medieval West or the apparent present-day shift from words to images/signs in the communications industry and more widely – a shift usually thought of as moving to communication methods that are "visual" in a way that printed text is not.
36. See Ong, *Orality and Literacy,* esp. pp. 117–38, 157–79; Carothers, "Culture, Psychi-atry, and the Written Word," esp. p. 310; Chaytor, *From Script to Print,* pp. 1, 7–8.
37. It is perhaps not so farfetched as it may at first seem to see with Eric Havelock "Western" or "European" science and thought as more accurately described by the term "alphabetic" than by "Western" – the use of alphabetic script, Latin or Greek or Cyrillic, being a characteristic separating them still today from the thought worlds of Arabic, Sanskritic, Chinese, or even Japanese cultures in the modern world (*Origins*

of Western Literacy, pp. 82-86). This becomes ever more difficult to maintain, however, as Japan develops more and more into a giant of modern scientific, technological, and literate culture that can more than hold its own with the "alphabetic" West.

Chapter 3. Books, Reading, and Literacy in the Premodern West

1. Some of the more notable of these: Josef Balogh, "'Voces paginarum'"; G. L. Hendrickson, "Ancient Reading"; H. J. Chaytor, *From Script to Print;* J. C. Carothers, "Culture, Psychiatry, and the Written Word"; Marshall McLuhan, *The Gutenberg Galaxy;* Walter J. Ong, *The Presence of the Word;* id., *Orality and Literacy;* Harold A. Innis, *Empire and Communications;* Elizabeth L. Eisenstein, *The Printing Press as an Agent of Change* (cf. her article, "The Advent of Printing and the Protestant Revolt," which is essentially a resumé of her book's arguments). Cf. Eric A. Havelock, *Origins of Western Literacy,* pp. 68–86. Balogh's article is the most extreme in arguing that silent reading was all but unknown in antiquity, a claim thoroughly refuted by Bernard M. W. Knox, "Silent Reading in Antiquity." Yet even Knox notes that reading aloud was apparently the norm throughout antiquity, at least for literary texts (e.g., pp. 421, 435).
2. Frederic G. Kenyon, *Books and Readers in Ancient Greece and Rome,* pp. 24–25; Moses Hadas, *Ancilla to Classical Reading,* pp. 21–22 (quoting the *locus classicus* on the subject, Strabo 13.1.54); Jack Goody and Ian Watt, "The Consequences of Literacy," p. 55; Eric A. Havelock, *The Literate Revolution in Greece and Its Cultural Consequences,* p. 11.
3. See Chapter 2, n. 2.
4. *Literate Revolution,* p. 167. Cf. the citation from Whitehead at the beginning of Chapter 2. For Havelock's range of ideas on this point, see, in addition to the essays collected in *Literate Revolution,* both *Origins of Western Literacy,* pp. 53–86, and *Preface to Plato,* esp. pp. 36–60. G. S. Kirk's analysis of the orality of the Homeric epic in *Homer and the Oral Tradition* supports Havelock at least insofar as Kirk recognizes that "the differences between oral and literate expression, although considerable, are not necessarily so profound as is widely assumed" (p. 69). Both scholars implicitly or explicitly argue that too sharp a distinction between oral and written composition is a misapplication or misguided extension of the Millman Parry–Albert Lord thesis about oral formulaic composition (see n. 16). Frederic Kenyon's and Moses Hadas's studies of books and readers in the ancient world affirm also the lasting orality of reading and "publishing" long after a literate élite had developed, as do the works of other classical historians that we shall encounter in what follows.
5. Cf. McLuhan, *Gutenberg Galaxy,* pp. 90, 124–27, 130–33. In my opinion, McLuhan does not sufficiently recognize how long the tension between oral and written modes of expression persists after the coming of printing, at least among the vast majority of a population. See below, "After the Advent of Printing."
6. Havelock, *Literate Revolution,* p. 9.
7. My trans. from the German trans. of the original Egyptian text from Chester Beatty Papyrus IV, by Emma Brunner-Traut, p. 8 of "Die Weisheitslehre des Djedef-Hor," *Zeitschrift für ägyptische Sprache und Altertumskunde* 76 (1940): 3–9.
8. Ruth Finnegan, *Oral Poetry,* p. 29. Cf. Balogh, "'Voces paginarum,'" pp. 84–87.
9. Ong, *Orality and Literacy,* p. 8. Cf. Ferdinand de Saussure, *Cours de linguistique*

générale, p. 32 (=Eng. trans. p. 15); Havelock, *Literate Revolution*, p. 50; Arthur Lloyd James, *Our Spoken Language*, esp. chap. 1.

10. Balogh, "'Voces paginarum'"; Hendrickson, "Ancient Reading." But see also the refutation of Balogh's more extravagant claims by Knox, "Silent Reading."
11. *On Heroes, Hero-Worship, and the Heroic in History* (1842), p. 251.
12. Rudolf Pfeiffer, *History of Classical Scholarship from the Beginnings to the End of the Hellenistic Age*, pp. 17–32; H. Curtis Wright (largely following Pfeiffer), *The Oral Antecedents of Greek Librarianship*, pp. 149–69; James Westfall Thompson, *Ancient Libraries*, pp. 17–19; Kenyon, *Books and Readers*, pp. 22–24.
13. William Chase Greene, "The Spoken and the Written Word," esp. p. 40.
14. *Preface to Plato*, pp. 36–60, esp. p. 40; *Literate Revolution*, pp. 185–207 ("The Preliteracy of the Greeks"), esp. pp. 185–88, 201–03; also pp. 261–313 ("The Oral Composition of Greek Drama"), esp. pp. 261–63, 286ff. See also Kenyon, *Books and Readers*, p. 22.
15. On the probable limits of the dispersion of reading, see, for example, Kenyon, *Books and Readers*, pp. 21–22. Whenever it came, "general" literacy in Athens would presumably have been limited in any case almost exclusively to Athenian citizens, themselves a minority of the total population. On the orthographic difficulties of reading early Greek manuscript texts, see ibid., pp. 67–68; Wilhelm Schubart, *Das Buch bei den Griechen und Römern*, pp. 80ff., 136ff.; H. I. Marrou, *A History of Education in Antiquity*, pp. 165–66.
16. On which, see the classic studies by Milman Parry and Albert Lord: Parry, *The Making of Homeric Verse* (posthumously collected works); Lord, *The Singer of Tales*. Cf. Finnegan, *Oral Poetry*, esp. pp. 30–51, 58–72.
17. The best discussion of the often-remarked Greek aversion to "bookishness" and the written word that I have seen is that of Pfeiffer, *History of Classical Scholarship*, pp. 16–32, esp. pp. 31–32 (see also the refs. given in the notes). Cf. Kenyon, *Books and Readers*, pp. 24–25; Ernst Robert Curtius, *Europäische Literatur und lateinisches Mittelalter*, pp. 308–14 (=Eng. trans. pp. 304–10); Karl Kerényi, *Apollon*, p. 166.
18. *Ancilla*, p. 50 (cf. pp. 51–60 for numerous instances of oral reading and recitation of different genres of literary works). Cf. John E. B. Mayor, ed. and comm., *Thirteen Satires of Juvenal*, pp. 173–81; George A. Kennedy, *Classical Rhetoric and Its Christian and Secular Tradition from Ancient to Modern Times*, p. 111; Erwin Rohde, *Der griechische Roman und seine Vorläufer*, pp. 304–06, n. 1 (to p. 304); Kenyon, *Books and Readers*, pp. 20–21.
19. Ruth Crosby, "Oral Delivery in the Middle Ages," p. 88 (source refs. in n. 3); Kenyon, *Books and Readers*, p. 20; Rohde, *Griechische Roman*, p. 305 (note); Hadas, *Ancilla*, p. 51, 59–60. But for a more skeptical approach to the impeccability of the sources on public readings by Herodotus and other early Greek historians, see Arnaldo Momigliano, "The Historians of the Classical World and Their Audiences," pp. 195–98.
20. *Phaedrus* 274c–77a. Cf. *Protagoras* 329a.
21. As recounted in Satyrus, *Life of Euripides* 39.19 (Graziano Arrighetti, ed. *Satiro, Vita di Euripide*, Studi classici e orientali, vol. 13 [Pisa: Goliardica, 1964], pp. 75–76 [Greek text; =Ital. trans. p. 90]). I owe the Satyrus ref. to Philip Whaley Harsch, *A Handbook of Classical Drama* ([Palo Alto, Cal.]: Stanford University Press; London: Humphrey Milford, Oxford University Press, 1944), p. 157, n. 5, which see. Several other scholars mention this story also but cite Harsch, each other, or no one, instead of the classical source: e.g., F. W. Hall, *A Companion to Classical*

Texts (Oxford: Clarendon Press, 1913), pp. 27–28 (no ref.); Greene, "Spoken and Written Word," p. 39 (ref. to Harsch and Hall); Alfred North Whitehead, *Dialogues of Alfred North Whitehead as Recorded by Lucien Price*, p. 170 (no ref.); and Frits Staal, *Nambudiri Veda Recitation*, p. 14 (citing Whitehead).

22. Strabo's account (13.1.54) is translated in Hadas, *Ancilla*, pp. 21–22. On the probable accuracy of the reported later discovery in Skepsis of Aristotle's own copies of some of his works, see Wolfgang Speyer, *Bücherfunde in der Glaubenswerbung der Antike*, pp. 142–43. Hadas feels that "with Aristotle the use of books changed to something like their function in our own day" (ibid., p. 21). Although this is an exaggeration (given the expanded functions of books after printing), even if applied only to a tiny élite, it does indicate the consensus that, at least from this time forward, books (at this time in the form of scrolls) were common in the Mediterranean world. Cf. Kenyon, *Books and Readers*, pp. 24–27; Thompson, *Ancient Libraries*, pp. 19ff.; Pfeiffer, *History of Classical Scholarship*, p. 67; Wright, *Oral Antecedents*, pp. 167–73; Havelock, *Literate Revolution*, pp. 11, 48, 329–36; Goody and Watt, "Consequences of Literacy," p. 55; L. D. Reynolds and N. G. Wilson, *Scribes and Scholars*, pp. 5–6. On the teaching of writing in Greece and Rome, see F. David Harvey, "Greeks and Romans Learn to Write."
23. On memorization: M. L. W. Laistner, *Christianity and Pagan Culture in the Later Roman Empire*, p. 11; Marrou, *History of Education*, pp. 150–57, esp. p. 154. On dictation: Eduard Norden, *Die antike Kunstprosa vom VI. Jahrhundert v. Chr. bis in die Zeit der Renaissance*, p. 538, n. 2, with source refs.
24. Momigliano, "Historians of the Classical World," p. 195. Many examples are given on p. 196. For the Roman republican period in particular, see the ample discussion of the public *lectiones* in Jérôme Carcopino, *Daily Life in Ancient Rome*, pp. 193–201 (=Fr. orig. pp. 226–34).
25. Others who make reference to such public readings or recitations are Martial, Juvenal, Pliny, Lucian, and Tacitus. See the sources cited in Hadas, *Ancilla*, pp. 60–64; Mayor, *Thirteen Satires*, pp. 173–81, 282–83; Carcopino, *Daily Life*, pp. 193–201 (=Fr. orig. pp. 226–34); Kenyon, *Books and Readers*, pp. 83–85, nn. 2, 3; Balogh, "'Voces paginarum,'" pp. 88–92, 98, 100–02; Crosby, "Oral Delivery," pp. 88–89, esp. 89, nn. 1–4; William Nelson, "From 'Listen, Lordings' to 'Dear Reader,'" p. 111; Rohde, *Griechische Roman*, p. 304–06 (n. 1 to p. 304).
26. *Daily Life*, p. 199 (=Fr. orig. p. 232). Carcopino goes on to argue that the desire of every scribbler to have his work heard in society, and the pressure on better writers to read from their latest works, however trivial, contributed to a substantial drop in literary standards (pp. 199–201; =Fr. orig. pp. 232–34). Cf. Mayor, *Thirteen Satires*, pp. 173–81.
27. Nietzsche, *Werke* (Leipzig: Kröner, 1912) 8: 248, as cited in Balogh, "'Voces paginarum,'" p. 231, to the effect "daß die eigentliche Prosa des Altertums durchaus Widerhall der lauten Rede ist und an deren Gesetzen sich gebildet hat; während unsere Prosa immer mehr aus dem Schreiben zu erklären ist . . ."; Norden, *Antike Kunstprosa*, p. 6. Cf. also Hadas, *Ancilla*, pp. 51–52.
28. "Sed cum legebat, oculi ducebantur per paginas et cor intellectum rimabatur, uox autem et lingua quiescebant. . . ." (*Confessionum libri XIII*, p. 75^{15-16}). Cf. also the Eng. trans. of Edward B. Pusey, in *The Confessions of Saint Augustine*, p. 98.
29. Above, n. 1.
30. *Literate Revolution*, p. 29. Cf. pp. 331–36. Nevertheless, as Hadas points out, it was in the Alexandrian age that it became common for poets like Apollonius or

Lycophron, writing more for each other than a public at large, to compose their works to be read alone by a single reader rather than heard by an audience (*Ancilla*, pp. 54–55).

31. Crosby, "Oral Delivery"; Franz H. Bäuml, "Varieties and Consequences of Medieval Literacy and Illiteracy," p. 245 (with further refs. in n. 21). Cf. Chaytor, *Script to Print*, esp. pp. 10–13; Nelson, "'Listen, Lordings,'" p. 112; Mayor, *Thirteen Satires*, pp. 181–82.
32. M. T. Clanchy, *From Memory to Written Record*, p. 217.
33. Chaytor, *Script to Print*, p. 14.
34. As translated in Appendix I to John William Adamson, "The Illiterate Anglo-Saxon," p. 18.
35. Norden, *Antike Kunstprosa*, p. 6; Balogh, "'Voces paginarum,'" p. 88.
36. Balogh, "'Voces paginarum'"; Crosby, "Oral Delivery."
37. ". . . quorum nomina recitamus et quorumcumque non recitamus sed a te recitantur in libro vitae" [trans. mine], as cited in Leo Koep, *Das himmlische Buch in Antike und Christentum*, p. 109, quoting from an *oratio super oblata* cited by F. E. Warren, *The Liturgy and Ritual of the Celtic Church* (Oxford, 1881), pp. 232f. [Eng. trans. mine].
38. "Homo erat eloquens, Gallice et Latine, . . . Scripturam Anglice scriptam legere nouit elegantissime . . . ." (*The Chronicle of Jocelin of Brakelond*, ed. and trans. H. E. Butler [London, etc., 1949], p. 40). I prefer and follow the translation of this passage in Clanchy, *Memory to Written Record*, p. 159, rather than that of Butler.
39. "Seignurs, oi avez le[s] vers del parchemin . . . " (*The Romance of Horn by Thomas*, ed. Mildred K. Pope, Anglo-Norman Texts, 9–10; 2 vols. [Oxford: Basil Blackwell, for the Anglo-Norman Text Society, 1955]), 1: 1; the Eng. trans. is that of Clanchy, *Memory to Written Record*, p. 164. Cf. Gregory the Great's mention of "that which we hear in the sacred pages" (see p. 142 below).
40. Benedict of Nursia, *Regula monachorum* 48.5: "Post Sextam autem surgentes a mensa pausent in lecta sua cum omni silentio, *aut forte qui voluerit legere sibi sic legat, ut alium non inquietet*" (italics mine).
41. "'Voces paginarum,'" pp. 237–38.
42. "Tres digiti scribunt, duo oculi vident. Una lingua loquitur. totum corpus laborat. . . ." W. Wattenbach, *Das Schriftwesen im Mittelalter*, p. 495. Also cited in Chaytor, *From Script to Print*, p. 14, n. 1. Umberto Eco, with his uncanny sensitivity to historical detail, picks up in his historical novel, *The Name of the Rose* (trans. William Weaver [San Diego: Harcourt, Brace Jovanovitch, 1983], p. 184) on the close connection among speaking, reading, and writing in medieval times when he describes the Benedictine "scribe-monk imagined by our sainted founder [Benedict of Nursia]," as one "capable of copying without understanding, surrendered to the will of God, writing as if praying, and praying inasmuch as he was writing."
43. Cf. Brian Stock, *The Implications of Literacy*, p. 13: ". . . the evidence, such as it is, suggests that at no point in the subsequent three centuries [after the millennium] was a significant percentage of laymen able to read and to write. . . . there was a tiny minority who were truly literate and a much larger majority for whom communication could take place only by word of mouth. Down to the age of print and in many regions long afterwards, literacy remained the exception rather than the rule. Despite primary schools, cheap paper, spectacles, and the growing body of legal and administrative material, the masses of both town and countryside as late as the Reformation remained relatively indifferent to writing."
44. James Westfall Thompson's *The Literacy of the Laity in the Middle Ages* (1939) is the classic refutation of the older theory of virtually total lay illiteracy throughout

the medieval period. Thompson's work points to the evidence of variable Latinate literacy according to time, place, and circumstance over the long sweep of the "Middle Ages", to reading versus writing literacy, and to the important distinction between Latinate and vernacular literacy in later times. Adamson's "Illiterate Anglo-Saxon" (1946) supports Thompson's thesis with reference to the pre-Norman English context, just as V. H. Galbraith, "The Literacy of the Medieval English Kings" (writing in 1935, before Thompson's work), stresses that not all royalty were illiterate, even before the twelfth century in England, let alone thereafter. The literacy debate has not abated in more recent literature. While even as late as 1958, Grundmann ("Litteratus - illitteratus") could stress the relatively uniform illiteracy (i.e., ignorance of Latin, and hence of reading and writing altogether), at least into the twelfth century, of all classes of laypersons, other scholars have more recently demonstrated the greater complexity of the Medieval situation, especially after the eleventh century. They point both to the existence of a variety of types of literacy: e.g., "professional", "cultivated", and "pragmatic" (occupational), to use M. B. Parkes's distinctions ("Literacy of the Laity", p. 555) and to the relatively greater literacy rates that would result, at least for the late Middle Ages, from inclusion in the equation of vernacular literacy and ability simply to read. See also Bäuml, "Varieties and Consequences"; Stock, *Implications of Literacy;* Clanchy, *Memory to Written Record,* esp. pp. 175–201; John William Adamson, "Literacy in England in the Fifteenth and Sixteenth Centuries."

45. Bäuml, "Varieties and Consequences," pp. 246ff. Cf. Parkes, "Literacy of the Laity."
46. E.g., Crosby, "Oral Delivery," pp. 98–100; Chaytor, *Script to Print,* p. 10.
47. *Memory to Written Record,* p. 150.
48. *Implications of Literacy,* p. 16. Stock goes on to remark that writing was often used for notes or lists set down to help one recall what was memorized and used orally (pp. 16–17). Cf. Parkes, "Literacy of the Laity"; V. H. Galbraith, *Studies in the Public Records,* pp. 27–28, 48–49, 64–65
49. Thompson, *Literacy of the Laity,* pp. 141–42; Grundmann, "Litteratus - illitteratus," p. 10; cf. n. 28; Parkes, "Literacy of the Laity," p. 556; Carlo M. Cipolla, *Literacy and Development in the West,* p. 40, n. 11, citing Lambertus, "Hist. Com. Ghinensium," chap. 80, in *Monumenta germaniae historica: Scriptorae* 24: 598. Grundmann also notes that Baldwin, in turn, recited for his cleric readers the vernacular poems that he learned from players - a further support for the fact emphasized by Grundmann (see esp. pp. 3ff., 13–14, 24–25) that in medieval times one did not have to be literate in Latin to be educated.
50. Thompson, *Literacy of the Laity,* p. 95, citing from the *Monumenta germaniae historica: Scriptores* 27: 366.
51. See examples in Chaytor, *Script to Print,* pp. 11–13; Clanchy, *Memory to Written Record,* pp. 216–17; Nelson, "'Listen, Lordings,'" p. 112; Roger M. Walker, "Oral Delivery or Private Reading?," esp. pp. 39–42. Many Carolingian book dedications expressly state that they are meant to be read aloud to the king: Grundmann, "Litteratus - illiteratus," pp. 42–43. Cf. pp. 47–48 for a case from about 1190 in which the Welsh writer Giraldus Cambrensis laments that his Latin works do not find many readers by comparison with less good vernacular writings, but that he would prefer to have them translated into French by an able person in order to find hearers, rather than to have them translated ad hoc by a lector as he reads them aloud (cf. Clanchy, p. 214). Chaytor and Nelson note also that Cambrensius read his Latin work, *Topographia hiberniae,* "before a public meeting at Oxford for three days in succession to different audiences" (Chaytor, p. 11; Nelson, p. 112); however, such an

extended reading seems by this time (1188) to have been unusual (see Clanchy, pp. 217–18).

52. Parkes, "Literacy of the Laity," p. 563. Cf. Stock, *Implications of Literacy,* pp. 17–18, 557–65 and ff.; M. T. Clanchy, "Looking Back from the Invention of Printing," esp. pp. 16–20. On the increased popular literacy in this period, see Adamson, "Literacy in England"; Margaret Aston, "Lollardy and Literacy"; H. S. Bennett, *English Books & Readers 1475 to 1557,* pp. 19–29, 54–64.

53. Balogh, "'Voces paginarum,'" pp. 234–36. Cf. William J. Bouwsma, "The Culture of Renaissance Humanism," pp. 8–17, 23–26, 34–36, 40, esp. p. 9: "The peculiarity of the renaissance that began in the fourteenth century lay in its special emphasis on rhetoric, in the particular value it attached to graceful, persuasive, and effective verbal communication, both orally and in writing. For the first time since antiquity, rhetoric came fully into its own." For a specific case (Strasbourg), see Miriam Usher Chrisman, *Lay Culture, Learned Culture,* pp. 196–98.

54. Aston, "Lollardy and Literacy," p. 353. Aston notes (ibid.) also that "groups of fervent readers, listeners and learners attending scriptural meetings, are characteristic of the Lollards from the the days when their translated text first became available." She points out, too, how important memorizing and reciting scripture were among the Lollards (p. 355).

55. Ibid., p. 368; Natalie Z. Davis, "Printing and the People," p. 203.

56. "Lollardy and Literacy," p. 370.

57. *Gutenberg Galaxy,* p. 250. See id., "The Effect of the Printed Book on Language in the 16th Century"; Chaytor, *From Script to Print,* esp. pp. 6–8; Balogh, "'Voces paginarum,'" pp. 237–38; Ong, *Orality and Literacy,* p. 118. Cf. *Gutenberg Galaxy,* pp. 124–25, 141; Carothers, "Culture, Psychiatry, and the Written Word," p. 310.

58. *The Memory Palace of Matteo Ricci* p. 22 (translating from Ricci's *Li Madou ti baoxiang tu,* sec. 2, pp. 1b–2). Another part of the same passage of Ricci is also noteworthy here: "Those who live one hundred generations after us are not yet born, and I cannot tell what sort of people they will be. Yet thanks to the existence of written culture even those living ten thousand generations hence will be able to enter into my mind as if we were contemporaries. As for those worthy figures who lived a hundred generations ago, although they too are gone, yet thanks to the books they left behind we who come after can hear their modes of discourse, observe their grand demeanor, and understand both the good order and the chaos of their times, exactly as if we were living among them."

59. Cipolla, *Literacy and Development,* pp. 51, 61; Rolf Engelsing, *Analphabetentum und Lectüre,* pp. 25–41, esp. 39–40; Robert W. Scribner, *For the Sake of Simple Folk,* p. 2; Helen Sullivan, "Literacy and Illiteracy," pp. 516a–17a; Davis, "Printing and the People," pp. 203–05, 214. On the interrelations between the Reformation and books, reading, education, and literacy, cf. also Lawrence Stone, "Literacy and Education in England, 1640–1900," pp. 76–83; Lucien Febvre and H.-J. Martin, *L'apparition du livre,* pp. 432–77; Gerald Strauss, *Luther's House of Learning,* esp. pp. 193–202; Eisenstein, "Advent of Printing," p. 248–50 (emphasizing the use of printing by the Reformers more than the role of the Reformers in spreading literacy).

60. Engelsing, *Analphabetentum,* pp. 26–32; Cipolla, *Literacy and Development,* p. 52. Cf. Chrisman, *Lay Culture,* pp. 37–75.

61. *The Age of Reform 1250–1550: An Intellectual and Religious History of Late Medieval and Reformation Europe* (New Haven and London: Yale University Press, 1975), p. 204. Cf. Aston, "Lollardy and Literacy," pp. 348–49, 368; Scribner, *For the Sake of Simple Folk,* p. 2; Engelsing, *Analphabetentum,* pp. 21–24.

62. Davis, "Printing and the People," p. 189.
63. R. S. Schofield, "The Measurement of Literacy in Pre-Industrial England," p. 313. Also cited in Aston, "Lollardy and Literacy," p. 368.
64. *For the Sake of Simple Folk,* p. 2.
65. Robert M. Kingdon, "Patronage, Piety, and Printing in Sixteenth-Century Europe," pp. 27-36. Kingdon estimates that perhaps 100,000 copies of thc Huguenot psalter were run off at Beza's behest by a Lyons–Geneva syndicate headed by the printer Antoine Vincent around 1561-62 (pp. 28-29), whereas the Genevan printer Plantin alone "sold at least twenty-two thousand breviaries during the first eight years of his production of them." Because Plantin was but one, although by far the largest, of "dozens of printers who were publishing this volume . . . , it becomes clear that the Roman breviary, like the Huguenot psalter, was one of the best sellers of the century" (p. 34).
66. Davis, "Printing and the People," p. 214.
67. Nelson, "'Listen, Lordings.'"
68. McLuhan, *Gutenberg Galaxy,* p. 84.
69. Nelson, "'Listen Lordings,'" pp. 114–17, and the references cited in the notes there. The citation itself is from p. 113.
70. David Cressy, "The Environment for Literacy," p. 34 (describing specifically the situation in England and New England). Cf. p. 28: "despite the evangelical insistence on reading, the church in England continued to stress the oral elements of liturgical worship and catechetical instruction. Psalms could be sung and sermons could be heard without the complications of print. The Protestant revolution notwithstanding, it was not necessary to be literate to be devout, and entry into the Kingdom of Heaven was not conditional on being able to read." Cf. Schofield, "Measurement of Literacy," pp. 312–13.
71. On the circulation of the pamphlets of *La bibliothèque bleue,* and their dissemination among the poorest village groups through evening readings, see Robert Mandrou, *De la culture populaire aux XVIIe et XVIIIe siècles,* pp. 17–26, esp. 18–19.
72. Davis, "Printing and the People," pp. 194–209, 212–15.
73. Mayor, *Thirteen Satires,* pp. 181–82.
74. Cipolla, *Literacy and Development,* pp. 51, 61, and the other refs. cited above, n. 59.
75. Cressy, "Environment for Literacy," esp. pp. 33–40. Cressy stresses in general the socioeconomic factors resulting in practical need for literate skills as much more important than the Protestant emphasis on literacy education in determining who actually learned to read and write. See esp. pp. 37–39. Note the similar emphasis on the socially determined bases for differing kinds of literacy by Stone, "Literacy and Education," pp. 69–76; and, for an earlier period, the emphasis on "the growth of literacy for practical purposes" by Clanchy, *From Memory to Written Record* (see esp. chap. 10, "Practical Literacy").
76. In Sweden, a sustained church- and state-sponsored, family-based literacy campaign brought reading literacy from about 20–50 percent in 1680 to between 65 and 98 percent in 1750 and 90–98 percent in 1850, a level generally reached elsewhere in Western Europe only in the present century (Egil Johansson, *The History of Literacy in Sweden in Comparison with Some Other Countries,* esp. p. 64, fig. 15). In Scotland, Presbyterian zeal for Bible reading stimulated a call for a national system of education in 1560 and put through legislation in 1646 and 1696 to carry out such a plan; as a result, literacy for adult males climbed from about 15 percent in 1600 or 33 percent in 1675 to about 74 percent in 1750 and 88 percent in 1800 (Stone, "Literacy

and Education," pp. 80–81, 96, 120–21 [Table V, Graph 3], 126–27, 135–36). On the influence of nonconformism and puritanism on literacy rates in England, see ibid., pp. 101–02.

77. Cf., for example, Natalie Davis's comments about widespread illiteracy in rural France in the sixteenth century: "Printing and the People," pp. 194–209.
78. Schofield, "Measurement of Literacy," p. 313, citing R. K. Webb, *The British Working Class Reader, 1790–1848* (London, 1955), pp. 33–34.
79. On these points, see Cipolla, *Literacy and Development,* pp. 51, 56–60, 75–77; but cf. pp. 72–73.
80. Cipolla, *Literacy and Development,* pp. 55, 60, 64, 74–75, 85–86. For more specific statistics and judgments on urban-rural and male-female variations, see: (on England) Thomas W. Laqueur, "Toward a Cultural Ecology of Literacy in England, 1600–1850," p. 46; Cressy, "Environment for Literacy," pp. 35–40; (on France) Davis, "Printing and the People"; François Furet and Jacques Ozouf, *Lire et écrire;* Furet and Wladimir Sachs, "La croissance de l'alphabétisation en France (XVIIIe–XIXe siècle)." The latter two French studies are the most detailed and carefully documented, yet wide-ranging, studies of European literacy from the seventeenth through the nineteenth century. They are especially interesting for their attempt to delineate regional variation, as well sex-linked variance and rates in towns as opposed to country. Their careful, statistically based distinctions among different kinds of literacy and the correlation of various indicators for each with signature evidence (the usual measure in modern European historiography) is also important and illuminating.
81. Engelsing, *Analphabetentum,* chaps. 6, 8, 10, provides useful, brief statistical overviews of book production in each of these centuries.
82. Stone, "Literacy and Education," p. 120, table V; Sullivan, "Literacy and Illiteracy," p. 516. Cf. Cipolla, *Literacy and Development,* p. 63. For a breakdown of the French statistics on increases in literacy in this period by *département,* see Cipolla, pp. 20–22, and, in much greater detail, but without overall averages for France as a whole, Furet and Sachs, "Croissance de l'alphabétisation," esp. pp. 723 (Map 1), 731–33 (Table 1); Furet and Ozouf, *Lire et écrire* 1: 13–68, esp. pp. 58–59 (=Eng. trans. pp. 48–49).
83. Stone, "Literacy and Education," p. 120.
84. Cf. Johansson, *History of Literacy,* pp. 71–75, esp. p. 74, fig. 20.
85. Cipolla, *Literacy and Development,* p. 102. This estimate is still very high from a global perspective, since as recently as 1957 some 44 percent of the world's adult (15 and over) population was estimated to be illiterate, and 50 percent of the world's nations judged to have more than 50 percent illiteracy (UNESCO, *L'analphabétisme dans le monde au milieu du xxe siècle,* p. 12). If anything, the last figure would be much more than 50 percent of today's nations, since so many new nations have been carved from the areas of highest illiteracy in the past thirty years. All gross figures for Western Europe cloak huge regional divergences: Some Scandinavian or German countries had reached the 90 percent level more than a century earlier, whereas areas of the Balkans and southern Italy, Spain, or Greece are still far below such a level today (see, e.g., ibid., pp. 88–125).
86. Cipolla, *Literacy and Development,* pp. 55, 71, 115.
87. Stone, "Literacy and Education," pp. 99–101; Laqueur, "Toward a Cultural Ecology," pp. 45–46, citing for the signature statistics William A. Sargent, "On the Progress of Elementary Education," *Journal of the Royal Statistical Society* 30, pt. 1 (March, 1867). On the reliability of signatures as measures of literacy, see Schofield,

"Measurement of Literacy," pp. 319–24; Furet and Ozouf, *Lire et écrire,* pp. 20ff.; Furet and Sachs, "Croissance de l'alphabétisation," esp. p. 731.

88. Laqueur estimates that 20–30 percent more persons could read than could read and write ("Toward a Cultural Ecology," pp. 45–46).
89. Cipolla, *Literacy and Development,* p. 115.
90. Furet and Ozouf, *Lire et écrire,* p. 58 (=Eng. trans. p. 47). Cf. Cipolla, *Literacy and Development,* p. 126, who gives figures of 86 and 81 percent literacy for French males and females, respectively, but includes those aged ten and over in these totals.
91. Cipolla, *Literacy and Development,* pp. 73, 127. Cf. Johansson, *History of Literacy,* p. 74, fig. 20.
92. Ong, *Presence of the Word,* pp. 63, 64, 71–72.
93. In his poem "Der Spaziergang." The lines in which this phrase occurs are cited in full as the epigraph to the present chapter.
94. "Nachdem die Rede aus dem Gebiet des Ohrs in das Gebiet des lesenden Auges, nachdem sie aus dem Gebiete der Stimme in den Wirkungskreis der schreibenden Hände einmal höchst unnatürlicherweise versetzt worden, so erstirbt sie nun auch, schrumpft zusammen, vertrocknet mehr und mehr: Das Wort schwindet ineinander und wird mehr und mehr zur Zahl" (*Zwölf Reden über die Beredsamkeit und deren Verfall in Deutschland,* p. 69). Also cited in Balogh, "'Voces paginarum,'" p. 220.

Part II. Of Written and Spoken Scripture

1. George Steiner, "After the Book?" in Robert Disch, ed., *The Future of LIteracy,* p. 154.
2. "Die Entstehung eines heiligen Schrifttums bedeutet einen tiefen Einschnitt in der Geschichte der Religionen: über die schriftlosen Religionen erheben sich hoch die Schriftreligionen" (*Erscheinungsformen und Wesen der Religion,* p. 343).
3. See the controversial and somewhat overdrawn but telling critique of the exclusivity of this orientation by Wilfred Cantwell Smith, "The Study of Religion and the Study of the Bible." Cf. id., "The True Meaning of Scripture." Cf. the analogous comments of Northrup Frye, *The Great Code: The Bible and Literature,* p. xvii, on the textual study of critical biblical scholarship as "lower criticism", and the remarks on the written-text scholarly bias in the study of religion by Sam D. Gill, "Nonliterate Traditions and Holy Books," esp. pp. 230–33. For a biblical scholar's critique of the historical-critical approach (in favor of a "canonical" approach) to the Hebrew scriptures, see Brevard S. Childs, *Introduction to the Old Testament as Scripture,* esp. pp. 49–106. The "postcritical" approach called for by Childs results from his perception that there is "something fundamentally wrong with the foundations of the biblical discipline" (p. 15). But see the thoroughgoing critique of Child's agendum for "canonical criticism" in James Barr, *Holy Scripture,* esp. pp. 130–71. James A. Sanders, *Torah and Canon,* has also argued for a shift in earlier text-critical emphases toward a canonical criticism focused upon the function rather than the form of the canon (see also id., *Canon and Community*). For all their differences, what Childs, Barr, and Sanders share is a feeling that historical-critical work has sometimes lost a sense of proportion, and that more work on the history of the understanding of scripture is in order, not necessarily as a replacement but rather as a supplement to the former (e.g., Barr, pp. 84ff.). On the history of biblical studies in the modern West, see Hans-Joachim Kraus, *Geschichte der historisch-kritischen Erforschung des Alten Testaments;* Herbert F. Hahn, *The Old Testament in Modern Research;* Werner Georg Kümmel, *Das Neue Testament.* Shorter summaries are available in Childs, *Intro-*

duction, pp. 30–39, 89–94 (for the Hebrew Bible only) and the following *RGG*[3] articles: "Bibelkritik: AT" (F. Baumgärtel), 1: 1184–88; "Bibelkritik: NT" (E. Dinkler), 1: 1188–90; "Bibelwissenschaft des AT" (C. Kuhl), 1: 1227–36; "Bibelwissenschaft: NT" (W. G. Kümmel), 1: 1236–51. A survey of modern scholarship on other scriptural texts of the world is harder to find, but some impression can be gleaned from Jacques Waardenburg, *Classical Approaches to the Study of Religion: Aims, Methods and Theories of Research,* 2 vols. (The Hague and Paris: Mouton, 1973–74); Eric Sharpe, *Comparative Religion: A History* (New York: Charles Scribner's Sons, 1975). Cf. Charles J. Adams, ed., *A Reader's Guide to the Great Religions* (1965; 2nd rev. ed., New York: Free Press [Macmillan]; London: Collier Macmillan, 1977).

Chapter 4. Scripture in Judeo-Christian Perspective

1. While it is difficult to speak of both the Chinese "classics" and Western "scriptures" as "holy writ", there are solid grounds for doing so, if one takes into account the cultural differences involved as well as the respective authoritativeness of the texts in each case. See Rodney L. Taylor, "Confucianism," esp. pp. 181–82, 191–92; Laurence G. Thompson, "Taoism," p. 204. Cf. the comments of Roger Lapointe, "Classicisme et canonicité," p. 333.
2. A point brought out clearly and eloquently by Harry Y. Gamble, Jr., "Christianity."
3. Leo Koep, *Das himmlische Buch in Antike und Christentum;* Geo Widengren, *The Ascension of the Apostle and the Heavenly Book,* esp. pp. 11, 20–21, 27–28, 38–39, 47, 74–75; id., *Muhammad, the Apostle of God, and His Ascension,* pp. 115–39. See also the refs. in n. 5 below.
4. On both the book of wisdom and the book of destiny, see Widengren, *Ascension of the Apostle,* and *Muhammad, the Apostle of God,* esp. pp. 115–39. The most concise overview of Widengren's ideas can be found in the chapter, "Heiliges Wort und Heilige Schrift," pp. 543–76 of his *Religionsphänomenologie,* and in his article "Holy Book and Holy Tradition in Islam," in Bruce and Rupp, esp. pp. 210–16.
5. On the concept of the book of works or judgment, see esp. *ERE,* s.v. "Fate (Jewish)" (A. E. Suffrin); *ERE,* s.v. "Book of Life" (Alfred Jeremias); *CBTEL,* s.v. "Book"; *TRE,* s.v. "Buch/Buchwesen I: Religionsgeschichtlich" (Gunter Lanczkowski). Specifically on the Islamic notion, see the Qur'ān, Sūrahs 17.13–14,71; 69.25–26; 84.10; further references and discussion in: Julius Augapfel, "Das *Kitāb* im Qurân," pp. 390–92; Frants Buhl, "'Die Schrift' und was damit zusammenhängt im Qurân," pp. 370–73; Johannes Pedersen, review of Eduard Meyer, *Ursprung und Geschichte der Mormonen,* p. 115.
6. Koep, *Das himmlische Buch,* pp. 31–39, 72–127 (esp. 72–85). Cf. *TRE,* s.v. "Buch/Buchwesen II:2: Das Buch des Lebens" (Peter Welten) (with further refs.); S. G. F. Brandon, *The Judgment of the Dead: The Idea of Life after Death in the Major Religions* (New York: Charles Scribner's Sons, 1967), pp. 65, 103. See also the Jeremias and Suffrin articles cited above in n. 5.
7. *Das himmlische Buch,* pp. 68–127.
8. "Entstehung und Wesen der Buchreligion."
9. Brevard S. Childs, *Introduction to the Old Testament as Scripture,* pp. 132–35; the three citations are from pp. 133, 135, and 134, respectively.
10. Leipoldt and Morenz, *Heilige Schriften;* Morenz, "Entstehung und Wesen."
11. Smith, "Scripture as Form and Concept." The bulk of the general interpretation that follows in this and the next paragraph is based on Smith's arguments.

12. *Ancilla to Classical Reading*, pp. 137, 142.
13. Childs, *Introduction*, p. 50; Theodor Zahn, *Grundriss der Geschichte des Neutestamentlichen Kanons*, pp. 1–11 (on *kanōn*), 59–61 (on Athanasius); Gunnar Östborn, *Cult and Canon*, pp. 12–13 (with further refs. regarding Athanasius and his "list"). Origen, *De principiis* 4.33, had, however, previously used the adjectival form of the word in the term *scripturae canonicae* (ibid.). On the probable derivation of "canon" of scriptures from "canon" as "list", not "canon" as "rule" or "standard", see the comments of James Barr, *Holy Scripture*, p. 49, n. 1 (pace the arguments of Östborn, ibid., that "canon" applied to scripture meant orginally what is "correct" or a "standard"). Note also that the relatively quite late use of "canon" indicates that as a concept it was of little if any significance for fixing even the Christian notion of scripture, and of none except ex post facto significance for that of the Jews. For a concise but illuminating survey of the development of the major modern theories about Jewish and Christian notions of canon, see Albert C. Sundberg, Jr., *The Old Testament of the Early Church*.
14. See n. 11 above.
15. Plato, *Laws* 11.934c; 1 Chron. 15.15. On *graphē* in general, see Liddell and Scott, s.v. *graphē; Theol. Begriffslex.*, s.v. "Schrift" (R. Mayer).
16. E.g., Exod. 32.16, Tob. 8.24, Ps. 86.6: cf. *Theol. Begriffslex.*, s.v. "Schrift" (R. Mayer).
17. E.g., *Epistle of Barnabas* 4.7, 5.4; Irenaeus, *Adversus Haereticos* 2.24.3, 2.27.1 (=*PG* 7: 793, 802).
18. "Ē ouk oidate en Ēlia ti legei hē graphē . . . ." Cf. John 10.35.
19. E.g., Matt. 4.4,6, 21.13; Rom. 1.17, 2.24, 1 Cor. 2.9.
20. *DBS* 2: 460 ("Écriture sainte: Le nom"); *JE* 3: 140b–41a, s.v. "Bible Canon"; *RGG*^{3} 1: 1123a, s.v. "Bibel"; *Theol. Begriffslex*, s.v. "Buch" (U. Becker); *Sacramentum Verbi*, ed. Johannes B. Bauer (New York: Herder and Herder, 1970) 3: 817 (s.v. "Scripture"); *CBTEL*, s.v. "Scripture", p. 477b.
21. Hans von Campenhausen, *Aus der Frühzeit des Christentums*, pp. 152–96. See Chapter 10 below.
22. Adolf von Harnack, "Über das Alter der Bezeichnung 'die Bücher' ('die Bibel') für die H. Schriften in der Kirche."
23. *DBS* 2: 461 ("Écriture sainte: Le nom"), citing, for example, references to *The Imitation of Christ* and Saint Bonaventure.
24. E.g., Rom. 1.2, 2 Tim. 3.15; Origen, *In Ioannem* 5.4 (*PG* 14); 1 Macc. 12. Further references in *DBS* 2: 459–60 ("Écriture sainte: Le nom").
25. *EJ* 4: 816 ("Bible"); *JE* 3: 141a ("Bible Canon"); *DBS* 2: 459 ("Écriture sainte: Le nom"). Note that *kitvê* and *sifrê* are construct plural forms of *k^{e}tūb* and *sēfer*, the regular plurals of which are *k^{e}tūbîm* and *sefārîm*, respectively.
26. Lewis and Short, s.v. "scriptura"; *Med. lat. lex.*, s.v. "scriptura".
27. *OED*, s.v. "Scripture".
28. In his *Summa totius hæresis saracenorum*, ed. James Kritzeck, in Kritzeck's *Peter the Venerable and Islam* (Princeton: Princeton University Press, 1964), p. 206.
29. "Ipsi non credunt Scripturis, si vos narretis unum, et ipsi narrabunt aliud" (Rubroek, *Itinerarium*, p. 294). I owe my notice of Rubroek's debate to R. W. Southern, *Western Views of Islam in the Middle Ages*, pp. 47–52.
30. See, for example, the Qur'ān, Sūrah 2.285 or 4.136, which refers to faith or lack of faith in God, His angels, His "books" (*kutub*), and His prophets.
31. Raymond Schwab, *La renaissance orientale* (Paris: Payot, 1950; Eng. trans. Gene

Patterson-Black and Victor Reinking, *The Oriental Renaissance* [New York: Columbia University Press, 1984]), esp. chaps. 1-3.

32. "A Preliminary Discourse," introduction to Sale's translation (the first from the original Arabic into English), *The Koran*, p. 43 (beginning of sect. III). The *OED* does not give this occurrence and can cite no instance of "scripture" used for non-Christian religious texts before Gibbon three decades later (see n. 33).
33. Edward Gibbon, *Miscellaneous Works* (1814) 4: 358, as cited in *OED*, s.v. "scripture". Cited also above, p. 3.
34. Some examples from book titles (with dates of publication) give an impression: *The World's Great Scriptures*, ed. Lewis Browne (New York, 1946); *The Scriptures of Mankind: An Introduction*, [ed.] Charles Samuel Braden (New York, 1952); *Hindu Scriptures: Hymns from the Rigveda, Five Upanishads, The Bhagavadgītā*, ed. Nicol Macnicol (London and New York, 1938); Johannes Leipoldt and Siegfried Morenz, *Heilige Schriften* (1953); Gunter Lanczkowski, *Heilige Schriften* (1956).
35. *Religious Thought and Life in India: An Account of the Religions of the Indian Peoples, Based on a Life's Study of Their Literature and on Personal Investigations in Their Own Country*, vol. I (London: John Murray, 1883), p. 8.
36. Preface to F. Edgerton, trans., *The Bhagavad Gītā, or Song of the Blessed One* (Cambridge, Mass., 1944; repr. ed., New York: Harper & Row, 1964), p. vii; Dwight Goddard, ed., *A Buddhist Bible* (1938; Boston, 1970). Cf. also book titles such as *The Ramayan of Tulsidas, or the Bible of Northern India*, by John M. Macfie (Edinburgh, 1930), and *The Bible of the World*, ed. Robert O. Ballou (New York, 1939).

Chapter 5. Holy Writ and Holy Word

1. On ancient Greek mistrust of writing and books, see Johannes Leipoldt and Siegfried Morenz, *Heilige Schriften*, pp. 12–14; Frederic G. Kenyon, *Books and Readers in Ancient Greece and Rome*, pp. 24–25; Karl Kerényi, *Apollon*, p. 166; Carl Schneider, *Kulturgeschichte des Hellenismus* 2: 228; and the refs. cited above in Chapter 3, n. 17. The *locus classicus* for the negative Greek attitude is Socrates' disquisition on the harmful effect of writing on the memory, in Plato's *Phaedrus* 274–75. On the Indian attitudes, see Chapter 6 below.
2. Gustav Mensching, *Das heilige Wort*, pp. 80–81, 85–87; Friedrich Heiler, *Erscheinungsformen und Wesen der Religion*, pp. 342–43, 354–55; Leo Koep, *Das himmlische Buch in Antike und Christentum*, pp. 3 (n. 2), 4–6; Kurt Goldammer, *Die Formenwelt des Religiösen*, p. 252; Alfred Bertholet, "Die Macht der Schrift in Glauben und Aberglauben," pp. 43-46; Geo Widengren, *Religionsphänomenologie*, pp. 566ff.
3. Ernest Gellner, *Muslim Society*, Cambridge Studies in Social Anthropology, ed. Jack Goody, vol. 32 (Cambridge: Cambridge University Press, 1981), p. 22.
4. *Apollon*, pp. 165–66. Cf. Leipoldt and Morenz, *Heilige Schriften*, p. 11; Goldammer, *Formenwelt*, p. 250; Heiler, *Erscheinungsformen*, p. 342.
5. Heiler, *Erscheinungsformen*, p. 342. Cf. Hans Jensen, *Die Schrift in Vergangenheit und Gegenwart*, p. 3.
6. Siegfried Morenz, *Ägyptische Religion*, pp. 230–33; Leipoldt and Morenz, *Heilige Schriften*, p. 11. Cf. Kerényi, *Apollon*, p. 161: "Ägypten ist ein positives Beispiel dafür, daß das Verhältnis einer Kultur zu ihrer schriftlichen Ausdrucksform für das Wesen der betreffenden Kultur bezeichnend ist."

7. Robert Will, *Le culte* 2: 363; RGG^2 5: 266, s.v. "Schriften, heilige" (Alfred Bertholet); Heiler, *Erscheinungsformen,* pp. 354–57; Gustav Mensching, *Die Religion,* pp. 328–29.
8. See Morenz, *Ägyptische Religion,* pp. 224–43.
9. Wm. Theodore de Bary, Wing-tsit Chan, and Burton Watson, comps., *Sources of Chinese Tradition,* Records of Civilization: Sources and Studies, no. 55 (New York and London: Columbia University Press, 1960), p. 6; Edwin O. Reischauer and John K. Fairbank, *East Asia: The Great Tradition,* A History of East Asian Civilization, vol. 1 (Boston: Houghton Mifflin, 1958), p. 72; Y. Chu Wang, "Ideas and Men in Traditional China," *Monumenta Serica* 19 (1960): 213.
10. See Leipoldt and Morenz, *Heilige Schriften,* pp. 57–58. On the probable antiquity of writing down not only the formal, "scriptural" Torah but also the "oral Torah" of Halakhic and other traditions, see J. Weingreen, "Oral Torah and Written Records." On the "canon" of Hebrew scripture, see G. W. Anderson, "Canonical and Non-Canonical"; *JE* 3: 140b–54a, s.v. "Bible Canon" (Nathaniel Schmidt); Gunnar Östborn, *Cult and Canon.* Cf. James Sanders, *Torah and Canon,* pp. 1-9, 91ff. But note that our evidence for any legally formal "canonization" at a particular time is weak: Jonathan Rosenbaum, "Judaism," pp. 16–17; Albert C. Sundberg, Jr., *The Old Testament of the Early Church,* esp. pp. 51-79, 102–03, 107–28; Harry Y. Gamble, Jr., "Christianity," p. 38.
11. Above, Chapter 4. See also Leipoldt and Morenz, *Heilige Schriften,* pp. 41-52; Ernst Robert Curtius, *Europäische Literatur und lateinisches Mittelalter,* pp. 254-61 (=Eng. trans. pp. 256–60).
12. On the "canonizing" of the Judaic scriptures, see refs. in n. 10 above. On the "canonizing" of the Tripiṭaka, see André Bareau, Walter Schubring, and Christoph von Fürer-Haimendorf, *Die Religionen Indiens, III: Buddhismus–Jinismus–Primitivvölker,* Die Religionen der Menschheit, ed. Christel Matthias Schröeder, vol. 13 (Stuttgart: W. Kohlhammer, 1964), pp. 23–32 (further literature, p. 23, n. 1). Cf. A. K. Warder, *Indian Buddhism* (Delhi, Patna, Varanasi: Motilal Banarsidass, 1970), pp. 4–14; Reginald A. Ray, "Buddhism."
13. ". . . die normgebende, das feste Vorbild, denn sie ist die Schrift als Urkunde für die göttliche Offenbarung, ein Exemplar des heiligen Buches, das der Offenbarungsbringer von der Gottheit selbst empfangen hat" (*Religionsphänomenologie,* p. 566 [trans. mine]).
14. See Chapter 4 and the following: Koep, *Das himmlische Buch,* esp. pp. 1–2, 127–28; Curtius, *Europäische Literatur,* p. 315, n. 3; Mensching, *Das heilige Wort,* pp. 73–75.
15. Heiler, *Erscheinungsformen,* pp. 350–52; Mensching, *Das heilige Wort,* pp. 72–73; Leipoldt and Morenz, *Heilige Schriften,* pp. 29–36. For specific examples, see, for India, Chapter 6 below; for China, the affirmation of the divine origins of the Taoist "Three Caverns" (*San Tung*) groupings of scriptural texts by Chang Chün-fang, cited in Laurence G. Thompson, "Taoism," p. 211 (cf. the discussion by the editors of the Ming edition of the Taoist canon of its transcendent origins, cited in ibid., pp. 212–14); and, for Japan, the statement about the superhuman nature of the Lotus Sūtra by Nichiren, cited in Masaharu Anesaki, *Nichiren, the Buddhist Prophet,* p. 16.
16. RGG^2 10: 264, s.v. "Schriften, heilige" (A. Bertholet) [trans. mine]; van der Leeuw, *Religion in Essence,* pp. 435–36 (=*Phänomenologie,* p. 495). For general statements on belief in the magical power of writing, see Franz Dornseiff, *Das Alphabet in Mystik und Magie,* p. 1; Leipoldt and Morenz, *Heilige Schriften,* p. 11; Koep, *Das himmlische Buch,* p. 3. Examples, most from living traditions, can be found in

HwDA, s.v. "Schreiben, Schrift, Geschriebenes" (Karl-Albrecht Tiemann); *JE* 3: 202–05, s.v. "Bibliomancy" (M. Grunwald and Kaufmann Kohler); Jack Goody, "Restricted Literacy in Northern Ghana," pp. 201–02; Maurice Bloch, "Astrology and Writing in Madagascar," pp. 283, 285; Ivor Wilks, "The Transmission of Islamic Learning in the Western Sudan," pp. 192–93; Curtius, *Europäische Literatur,* p. 323.

17. See, for example, Bertholet, "Macht der Schrift," pp. 18–32; *ERE* 2: 616b–17a, s.v. "Bibliolatry" (A. Dorner); *JE* 3: 202–05, s.v. "Bibliomancy"; "Bibel" (Oskar Rühle), *HwDA* 1: 1208b–19a; *HwDA* 9: 379–81; Edward W. Lane, *An Account of the Manners and Customs of the Modern Egyptians,* pp. 247–49, 253–54, 282; Edward Westermarck, *Ritual and Belief in Morocco* 1: 208–18, 312, 493, 512–13, 566; 2: 318–19, 399 inter alia; Goody, "Restricted Literacy," pp. 201, 211, 230–31, 237; Piet Zoetmulder, "Die Hochreligionen Indonesiens," p. 289. My Harvard colleague, Ali S. Asani, has kindly pointed out to me the common use of *ginān* texts for divinatory or oracular purposes in popular Ismāʻīlī circles. (On the *ginān* literature generally, see Azim Nanji, *The Nizārī Ismāʻīlī Tradition in the Indo-Pakistan Subcontinent,* pp. 7–24.) On the many talismanic and protective powers of copying and reciting Buddhist *sūtras* in Japan (and China), see M. W. de Visser, *Ancient Buddhism in Japan,* esp. chaps. 1, 5, 10–16.
18. *HwDA* 1: 1212b–15a, s.v. "Bibel" (Oskar Rühle).
19. *Epistolae* 55.20.37, as cited in *TRE* 6: 57 (in Heinrich Karpp, "Die Funktion der Bibel in der Kirche," pt. IV of art. "Bibel"). On such oracular use in European folk practice, see *HwDA* 1: 1215a–15b, s.v. "Bibel."
20. Curtius, *Europäische Literatur,* p. 307; cf. p. 323.
21. Gregory Schopen, "The Phrase *'sa pṛthivīpradeśaś caityabhūto bhavet'* in the *Vajracchedikā.*"
22. Concerning the Torah scrolls, see, for example, the comments of Jacob Neusner, *The Life of Torah,* pp. 26–30. For a recent instance of the continuing Jewish emphasis on the special, strictly scribal calligraphic preparation of Torah scrolls, cf. "A new Torah . . . an old Tradition," *The Boston Globe* (May 3, 1982), pp. 13–14. Concerning the Tibetan *sūtra* ritual, I am indebted to my Harvard colleague, M. David Eckel, for a description of the Dharmsala practice (pers. commun., November, 1983). For general comment on the "ungeheure Verehrung" of the Tibetan canonical collections in Tibet, see Günter Lanczkowski, *Heilige Schriften,* p. 124. On faith in the miraculous nature of the Lotus Sūtra (*Hoke-kyō*) and the sacred task of copying it, see Kyoko Motomochi Nakamura, trans., *Miraculous Stories from the Japanese Buddhist Tradition,* pp. 33–34, 86–88, 230, 235–36, 238–39, 245–46, 248–49, 250–51, etc.; Yoshiko K. Dykstra, "Miraculous Tales of the Lotus Sutra," pp. 189–98 passim. On Nichiren practice, see Anesaki, *Nichiren,* pp. 15ff., 80–86; Helen Hardacre, *Lay Buddhism in Contemporary Japan,* pp. 29, 136, 151. For examples of special Muslim treatment of the Qur'ān, see, for example, Lane, *Account of Manners and Customs,* pp. 514; Wilks, "Transmission of Islamic Learning," p. 193.
23. Gerhard Ebeling, "Wort Gottes und Hermeneutik," p. 327.
24. "Mᵉṭammᵉ'îm 'et-ha-y-yādayîm." See Anderson, "Canonical and Non-Canonical," p. 114; *JE,* 3: 141b, s.v. "Bible Canon."
25. T. C. Skeat, "Early Christian Book-Production"; Colin H. Roberts and T. C. Skeat, *The Birth of the Codex,* pp. 38–66, esp. 54–61.
26. Erich Bethe, *Buch und Bild im Altertum,* p. 103; Jean Leclercq et al., *La spiritualité du moyen âge,* p. 110; Ernst von Dobschütz, *Die Bibel im Leben der Völker,* pp. 82ff., 123f.; David Leistle, "Über Klosterbibliotheken des Mittelalters," pp. 215–24, 225ff.; Francis Wormald, "Bible Illustration in Medieval Manuscripts."

27. Concerning Manichaean books, see Hans-Joachim Klimkeit, "Vom Wesen manichäischer Kunst," esp. pp. 201–04; id., *Manichaean Art and Calligraphy*, pp. 20–23. On the background for Muslim focus upon qur'anic calligraphy, see Anthony Welch, "Epigraphs as Icons." For fine examples of the magnificence of qur'anic manuscripts, see Martin Lings and Yasin Hamid Safadi, *The Qur'ān*. On Tibetan collections, see, for example, David Snellgrove and Hugh Richardson, *A Cultural History of Tibet* (Boulder, Colo.: Prajña, 1980), pp. 160, 170; Lanczkowski, *Heilige Schriften*, p. 124. On veneration of the Granth: W. Owen Cole and Piara Singh Sambhi, *The Sikhs*, pp. 43ff., esp. 54–55, 58–66, 107, 112–35 passim. Cf. W. H. McLeod, "The Sikh Scriptures," pp. 98–105.
28. E.g., Martin Luther, *WA* 10: 625-627, passim. Cf. Will, *Le culte* 2: 335, 365; *TRE*, 6: 71, 73, s.v. "Bibel". The identity of the gospel "word" that is "heard" with scripture that is "heard" is, however, by no means a straightforward issue in Luther or other reformers' usage. See Chapter 12 below.
29. *WA* 10.i.2: 74^{32}–75^{4}: "Es ist yhe nicht muglich eyn seele zu trosten, sie hore denn yhres gottis wortt. Wo is aber gottis wortt ynn allen buchernn außer der heyligen schrifft? . . . trosten mag keyn Buch, denn die heyligen schrifft."
30. E.g., Heiler, *Erscheinungsformen*, pp. 275, 277–79, 283–86; Mensching, *Das heilige Wort*, esp. pp. 71–72; van der Leeuw, *Religion in Essence*, pp. 422–34 (=*Phänomenologie*, pp. 480–94); Jack Goody, *The Domestication of the Savage Mind;* Robert H. Lowie, *Primitive Religion* (1924; New York: Liveright, 1948), pp. 321-29; Bronislaw Malinowski, "Myth in Primitive Psychology," in *"Magic, Science and Religion" and Other Essays* (1948; Garden City, NY: Doubleday, Anchor Books, 1954), pp. 93–148.
31. *Das heilige Wort*, p. 71. Cf. id., *Die Religion*, p. 327; F. Max Mueller, Preface to *The Upanishads. Part I*, p. xiii.
32. Stanley Tambiah, "The Magical Power of Words"; van der Leeuw, *Religion in Essence*, p. 403–12 (=*Phänomenologie*, pp. 457–68); W. Brede Kristensen, *The Meaning of Religion*, pp. 224–26 (cf. pp. 86–87); Mensching, *Das heilige Wort*, pp. 112–17; Lorenz Dürr, *Die Wertung des göttlichen Wortes im Alten Testament und im antiken Orient*, pp. 2–19, 22–32. Cf. Northrop Frye, *The Great Code*, p. 6.
33. On the distinction between *legomenon* and *drōmenon*, see Jane Ellen Harrison, *Themis: A Study of the Social Origins of Greek Religion* (Cambridge, 1912; 2nd rev. ed., [1927]; repr. ed. London: Merlin, 1963), pp. 42–45, 328–31. Cf. Heiler, *Erscheinungsformen*, p. 266. On speech as act from a philosophical perspective, see J. L. Austin, *How to Do Things with Words*.
34. Van der Leeuw, *Religion in Essence*, p. 405 (=*Phänomenologie*, p. 460).
35. Hermann Usener, *Götternamen. Versuch einer Lehre von der religiösen Begriffsbildung* (Bonn: Friedrich Cohen, 1896), pp. 279–301; Ernst Cassirer, *Sprache und Mythos. Ein Beitrag zum Problem der Götternamen*, Studien der Bibliothek Warburg, ed. Fritz Saxl, no. 6 (Leipzig and Berlin: B. G. Teubner, 1925), pp. 14–20 (=Eng. trans. Susanne K. Langer, *Language and Myth* [1946; repr. ed., New York: Dover, 1953], pp. 33–43).
36. Heiler, *Erscheinungsformen*, p. 276. Cf. Barbara Stoler Miller, ed. and trans., *Love Song of the Dark Lord: Jayadeva's "Gītagovinda"* (New York: Columbia University Press, 1977), p. 18.
37. *Nambudiri Veda Recitation*, p. 16.
38. Morenz, *Ägyptische Religion*, pp. 172–74. The Memphite narrative is translated in John A. Wilson, trans., *The Ancient Near East: An Anthology of Texts and Pictures* (Princeton: Princeton University Press, 1958), pp. 1–2.

39. E.g., *Ṛg Veda* 1.164, 10.125, 10.82.3, 10.71.1; *Atharva Veda* 4.30. See W. Norman Brown, *Man in the Universe: Some Continuities in Indian Thought* (1966. Berkeley, Los Angeles, London: University of California Press, 1970), p. 28; id. "Theories of Creation in the Ṛg Veda," p. 44; id., "The Creative Role of the Goddess Vāc in the Rig Veda." See also Louis Renou, "Les pouvoirs de la parole dans le Ṛgveda," esp. p. 8; Albrecht Weber, "Vâc und λόγοσ"; id., "Die Hoheit der vâc," esp. pp. 121–25 [trans. of and commentary on *Atharva Veda* 4.30]; Vidya Niwas Misra, "*Vāk* Legends in the *Brāhmaṇa* Literature," pp. 109–10.
40. On the Witoto: Konrad Theodor Preuss, *Religion und Mythologie der Uitoto. Textaufnahmen und Beobachtungen bei einem Indianerstamm in Kolumbien, Südamerika* (Göttingen: Vandenhoeck & Ruprecht; Leipzig: J. C. Hinrichs, 1921–23), pp. 633–34 (quoted inexactly by Heiler, *Erscheinungsformen,* p. 332). On the Dogon: Marcel Griaule, *Conversations with Ogotemmeli* (Oxford: Oxford University Press, 1975), pp. 16–40; also reprinted in Barbara C. Sproul, ed., *Primal Myths: Creating the World* (San Francisco: Harper & Row, 1979), pp. 49–66.
41. Concerning Torah: Leipoldt and Morenz, *Heilige Schriften,* p. 25; Dürr, *Wertung des göttlichen Wortes,* pp. 22–32. A detailed survey of the idea of Torah as primordial wisdom and the instrument of creation, summed up in the Rabbinic dictum, "Torah is from Heaven" (*Torāh min ha-sh-shāmayîm*), is given by Barbara A. Holdrege, "The Bride of Israel," pp. 4–12 (this material will find a place also in Ms. Holdrege's Harvard doctoral dissertation, currently in preparation [expected completion: 1987]). Concerning the Qur'ān, see the credal statements of the *Waṣīyat Abī Ḥanīfah* (art. 9) and the *Fiqh Akbar II* (art. 3), trans. in A. J. Wensinck, *The Muslim Creed: Its Genesis and Historical Development.* (Cambridge, 1932; repr. ed. London: Frank Cass, 1965), pp. 127, 189. Cf. Harry Austryn Wolfson, *The Philosophy of the Kalam* (Cambridge, Mass., and London: Harvard University Press, 1976), pp. 235–44; cf. pp. 244–303.
42. This can be seen in the Buddhist case in the shift from the more literal understanding of the Buddha-word (*buddhavacana*) as transmitted in the Pali "canonical" texts of the Tripiṭaka (but cf. George D. Bond, "Two Theravada Traditions of the Meaning of 'the Word of the Buddha'") to the Mahāyāna notion of the cosmic teaching of the eternal Buddha. Cf. the Buddha's statements in chap.16 of the Lotus Sūtra (*Scripture of the Lotus Blossom of the Fine Dharma,* pp. 237–44). See also Sukumar Dutt, *Buddhist Monks and Monasteries of India: Their History and their Contribution to Indian Culture* (London: George Allen and Unwin, 1962), pp. 261–64. Concerning the Veda's eternal character, see Chapter 6.
43. Geo Widengren, *The Ascension of the Apostle and the Heavenly Book,* pp. 45, 59–62; id., *Muhammad, the Apostle of God, and His Ascension,* p. 129.
44. Heiler, *Erscheinungsformen,* p. 281.
45. William G. Boltz, "The Religious and Philosophical Significance of the 'Hsiang erh' *Lao tzu* in the Light of the *Ma-wang-tui* Silk Manuscripts," *BSOAS* 45 (1982): 101–02, n. 17; Rodney L. Taylor, "Confucianism," pp. 183–84; Arthur Waley, "Introduction" to id., trans., *The Analects of Confucius,* p. 51. Cf. Thompson, "Taoism." On *śruti,* see Chapter 6.
46. Cf. Heiler, *Erscheinungsformen,* pp. 339ff.
47. On the Synagogue and early Christian church, see Chapter 10; Ismar Elbogen, *Der jüdische Gottesdienst in seiner geschichtlichen Entwicklung,* chap. 3; Paul Glaue, *Die Vorlesung heiliger Schriften im Gottesdienste.* However, cf. Walter Bauer, *Der Wortgottesdienst der ältesten Christen.* On Hellenistic cults, see Leipoldt and Morenz, *Heilige Scriften,* p. 96.

48. On the Pāṭimokkha, see Ñāṇamoli, trans., *The Pāṭimokkha: 227 Fundamental Rules of a Bhikkhu* (Bangkok: Social Science Association Press of Thailand, for Maha Makut Academy, 1966); Michael Carrithers, *The Forest Monks of Sri Lanka: An Anthropological and Historical Study* (Delhi, Bombay, etc.: Oxford University Press, 1983), pp. 142–47. On the *Paritta*s, see L[ynn] A. de Silva, *Buddhism: Beliefs and Practices in Sri Lanka* (Colombo, Sri Lanka, private publ.), pp. 81–90. On the Blue Sūtra, see Helen Hardacre, *Lay Buddhism in Contemporary Japan,* chap. 4, esp. pp. 148–52.
49. Geo Widengren, *Die Religionen Irans,* pp. 245–59.

Chapter 6. Scripture as Spoken Word: The Indian Paradigm

1. Johannes Leipoldt and Siegfried Morenz, *Heilige Schriften,* pp. 15–17; Gustav Mensching, *Die Religion,* p. 327; Friedrich Heiler, *Erscheinungsformen und Wesen der Religion,* pp. 298, 351–52; F. Max Müller, ed., Preface to *The Upanishads. Part I,* p. xiii. Cf. Walter J. Ong, *Orality and Literacy,* pp. 96–101 (drawing heavily upon M. T. Clanchy, *From Memory to Written Record,* esp. pp. 230–41, which see). For an extreme statement of the relationship between truth and the spoken word, with special reference to the Indian context, see David Frawley, *The Creative Vision of the Early Upaniṣads,* pp. 3–9 ("The Question of Language").
2. This characterization of scripture is that of Basil Hall, "Biblical Scholarship," p. 39.
3. J. F. Staal, *Nambudiri Veda Recitation,* p. 15. The beginning of writing in India cannot be precisely dated, but the use of writing likely was introduced (or "reintroduced", if one takes account of the still undeciphered Indus script) from Mesopotamia sometime in the early to middle part of the first millennium B.C. An epigraphically certain *terminus post quem* in the third century B.C. is provided by the inscriptions of the great Buddhist Mauryan king Aśoka (r. ca. 269–ca. 232 B.C.). The classical treatments of the problem are the nineteenth-century discussions of Albrecht Weber, "Über den semitischen Ursprung des indischen Alphabets," and Georg Bühler, *Indische Palaeographie,* pp. 1–19. Cf. T. W. Rhys Davids, *Buddhist India* (1903; 3rd Indian repr. ed., Calcutta: Susil Gupta, 1957), p. 119, on the possibility that Buddhists were the first to make use of writing in India. However, contrary to Bühler's conservative dating of the earliest Indian writing only back to the 4th C. B.C., see Theodor Goldstücker, *Pāṇini,* pp. 66–75, who sees writing as perhaps as old as the Ṛg Vedic hymns; so also others critical of Bühler's conclusions who rather boldly date writing many centuries earlier, e.g., D. R. Bhandarkar, "The Indian Alphabet"; Shyâmajî Krishṇavarmâ, "The Use of Writing in Ancient India." For more moderate, but still earlier, estimates of likely dates for writing's introduction, generally in the first half of the first millennium B.C., see R. Otto Franke, "Mudrâ = Schrift (oder Lesekunst)?"; Auguste Barth, *Bulletins des religions de l'Inde,* pp. 317-24. Cf. the summary remarks of Bimal Kumar Datta, *Libraries and Librarianship of Ancient and Medieval India,* pp. 13–16. A. L. Basham, *The Wonder That Was India* (1954; 2nd rev. ed., New York: Hawthorn Books, 1963), pp. 396–98, maintains that by Aśoka's time the Brāhmī script had already had years, perhaps centuries, of prior development. D. D. Kosambi, *Ancient India: A History of Its Culture and Civilization* (New York: Random House, Pantheon Books, 1965), p. 88, argues for a date of no later than 700 B.C. as a *terminus post quem* for the introduction of writing from Mesopotamia to India. A useful, if brief summary of some of these and other arguments about the antiquity of writing in India can be found in V. M. Apte, "The 'Spoken Word' in Sanskrit Literature," pp. 270–76.

4. Krishna Sivaraman, "The Word as a Category of Revelation," p. 46.
5. J. Brough, "Some Indian Theories of Meaning," p. 161. Cf. Bühler, *Indische Palaeographie*, pp. 3–4.
6. Bühler, *Indische Palaeographie*, pp. 3–4; Winternitz, *Geschichte der indischen Litteratur* 1: 29–31 (=Eng. trans. 1: 31–34); Renou, *Le destin du Véda dans l'Inde*, pp. 37–39 (cf. Renou, Jean Filliozat, et al., *L'Inde classique* 1: 270–71); van Buitenen, in *EB*[15], Macropaedia 8: 933b ("Hindu Sacred Literature"); Gonda, *Vedic Literature*, pp. 43–54; id., *Die Religionen Indiens* 1: 9, 21–26.
7. Staal, *Nambudiri Veda Recitation*, pp. 11–17; id., "The Concept of Scripture in the Indian Tradition"; Eidlitz, *Der Glaube und die heiligen Schriften der Inder*, pp. 7–29; Coburn, "'Scripture' in India," pp. 435–59.
8. For the discussion of Hindi usages in this paragraph, I am indebted principally to a personal communication from Philip Lutgendorf, 13 February 1985. The citation concerning *pūjā-pāṭha* is taken from a draft of his important forthcoming Chicago Ph.D. dissertation [late 1986], "The Life of a Text: Tulsīdās' *Rāmacaritamānasa* in Performance," draft chap. II, pp. 2 (citation), 75 n. 98 (on *kaṇṭhastha* and the *hṛdaya* idiom). See n. 48 below. On the Sanskrit root *paṭh*, for recitation, cf. Giorgio Bonazzoli, "Composition, Transmission and Recitation of the Purāṇa-s," p. 259.
9. Cf. Jan C. Heesterman, "Die Autorität des Veda," p. 31; Staal, *Nambudiri Veda Recitation*, p. 11; Francis X. D'Sa, *Śabdaprāmāṇyam in Śabara and Kumārila*, esp. chaps. 8, 15. My Harvard colleague, Gary Tubb, has pointed out to me with particular clarity the common mistranslation of *apauruṣeya* as "of nonhuman origin"; the point at issue in the Mīmāṁsā schoolmen's use of the term was that the Veda was eternal and uncreated – it had no origin, either with human beings or with gods or any other being. As P. V. Kane puts it in discussing the Mīmāṁsā position, "it is this theory that the Veda has existed from all eternity, was not created by any person, human or divine, that is the point of the whole system" (*A Brief Sketch of the Pūrva-Mīmāṅsā System* [Pune, India: Pandurang Vaman Kane, 1924], p. 19). Cf. the following statement from the Mīmāṁsā treatise known as the *Āpadevī*: "For the Veda is not the work of any person," "vede tu puruṣābhāvāl lināḍiśabdaniṣṭha eva" (Franklin Edgerton, ed. and trans., *The Mīmāṅsā Nyāya Prakāśa, or Āpadevī: A Treatise on the Mīmāṅsā System by Āpadeva* (New Haven: Yale University Press, 1929), pp. 194 (=Eng. trans. p. 40). For the full Mīmāṁsā argument about the beginningless chain of teaching/transmission by which the Veda has come down to the present, see also the entire passage in which this statement occurs. I am grateful to Professor Tubb for the preceding references.
10. "Yasmāt pakvād amṛtaṃ sambabhūva yo gāyatryāḥ adhipatir babhūva/ yasmin vedāḥ nihitāḥ viśvarūpas tenaudanenāti tarāmi mṛtyum": "I overpass death by means of that oblation, from which, when cooked, ambrosia [or: immortality (*amṛta*)] was produced, which became the lord of the Gāyatri, and in which the omniform Vedas are comprehended" (text and trans. in John Muir, *The Vedas*, p. 4).
11. "'Scripture' in India," p. 442. The prime expressions are ones suggesting visionary experience on the part of the inspired Vedic poet-seers, as the superb study of Jan Gonda, *The Vision of the Vedic Poets*, has shown; but the poets' experiences issued in and were inseparable from hymnody – the only medium of expression remotely adequate to these experiences being the word, the poem, the song (see ibid., esp. pp. 13–18, 29–30, 36–39, 42, 58–61, inter alia). Cf. Carl Anders Scharbau, *Die Idee der Schöpfung in der vedischen Literatur*, pp. 123–24: "[Es] lagen in alter Zeit die Funktionen des Sehens und Hörens so nahe beieinander, daß die Sprache nur ein

gemeinsames Wort (svar, bhā) für sie hatte. Das bedeutet, daß ganz sensitiv alle Erscheinung, alles Sichtbare zugleich erlebt, gehört wurde als Wort. . . . Die Weisheit wurde gehört, nicht gelesen!"

12. For a trans. of this hymn, see Wendy Doniger O'Flaherty, trans., *The Rig Veda,* pp. 34–35.
13. See W. Norman Brown, "The Creative Role of the Goddess Vāc in the Rig Veda," p. 393; Vidya Niwas Misra, "*Vāk* legends in the *Brāhmaṇa* Literature," p. 111; Schabau, *Idee der Schöpfung,* pp. 123–31, 135–38. Cf. Bénard Essers, *Vāc,* pp. 45–110.
14. Brown, "Creative Role of Vāc," p. 394. For a translation of the entire hymn, with useful commentary and explanatory notes, see O'Flaherty, trans., *Rig Veda,* pp. 71–83.
15. "yám kāmáye tám̩-tam ugrám kr̥ṇomi tám brahmā́ṇam̩ tám ŕ̥ṣim̩ tám̩ sumedhā́m" (Brown, "Creative Role of Vāc," p. 397). Brown has a complete translation of 10.125 in his article, "Theories of Creation in the R̥g Veda," pp. 51–52. Note that the whole hymn is in the first person, the speaker being Vāc herself. Cf. the translation of the same line of this hymn by O'Flaherty: "[Whom I love, I make] awesome; . . . a sage, a wise man, a Brahmin" (*Rig Veda,* p. 63). This hymn occurs in only slightly modified form in the Atharva Veda (4.30) as well. See *Atharva Veda Saṁhitā,* p. 69 (text; =trans. pp. 200–01).
16. O'Flaherty translates *vāc* in this hymn as "speech" (*Rig Veda,* pp. 61–62), whereas Frits Staal interprets it as "language" more generally (see his translation, discussion, and reproduction of the Sanskrit text in "R̥gveda 10.71 on the Origin of Language"). Cf. Otto Strauss, "Altindische Spekulationen über die Sprache und ihre Probleme," pp. 100–02.
17. See Misra, "*Vāk* Legends," pp. 112–18, where he adduces numerous examples and includes the relevant Sanskrit passages in his notes.
18. "Vāg akṣaram prathamajā r̥tasya vedānām mātā amr̥tasya nābhiḥ": "Speech is an imperishable thing, and the firstborn of the rite, the mother of the Vedas, and the centerpoint of immortality" (Muir, *The Vedas,* p. 10; cf. his slightly different trans.). For a somewhat different use of "mother of the Vedas" in relation to the "four Vedas", cf. *Harivaṃśa* 11.516, as cited in ibid., p. 12.
19. *Satapatha Brāhmaṇa* 2.1.4.10 is cited in Heiler, *Erscheinungsformen,* p. 333. In *Br̥hadāranyaka Upaniṣad* 4.1.2, the relevant statement is "vāg vai samrāṭ paramaṃ brahma": "Speech, O Emperor, is the supreme Brahman" (*The Br̥hadāraṇyaka Upaniṣad,* ed. and trans. Mādhavānanda, p. 571; cf. the trans. in id., p. 572).
20. "Yāvad brahma viṣṭhitaṃ tāvatī vāg iti yatra ha kva ca brahma tad vāg yatra vā vāk tad vā brahmety etat tad uktaṃ bhavati" (*Aitareya Āraṇyaka,* ed. Arthur Berriedale Keith, pp. 93^{2-3} [=Eng. trans. p. 186]). See also id., p. 163, n. 8, for further references to similar statements in other classical texts. Cf. André Padoux, *Recherches sur la symbolique et l'énergie de la parole dans certains textes tantriques,* p. 22.
21. Paul Thieme, "Bráhman," esp. pp. 102–08, 112–26. On specifically Vedic usages, cf. Louis Renou and Liliane Silburn, "Sur la notion de *brahman.*"
22. Bruno Liebich, "Über den Sphoṭa," pp. 214–15; Gonda, *Vision,* p. 338–39; Eidlitz, *Glaube und Schriften der Inder,* p. 12. The term *śabda-brahman* is not a new one among the grammarians: It is found, for example, in *Maitri Upaniṣad* 6.22.
23. On the extensive and involved Indian discussions of *śabda, sphoṭa, śabda-brahman,* and other concepts related to the idea of the eternity of speech or word, see Madeleine Biardeau, *Théorie de la connaissance et philosophie de la parole dans le brahmanisme classique,* esp. pp. 35–43, 177–91, 211–28, 265–71, 358–84, 394ff.;

T. R. V. Murti, "The Philosophy of Language in the Indian Context," esp. pp. 357–69; Krishna Sivaraman, "The Word as a Category of Revelation," esp. pp. 48–54; Gaurinath Sastri, *The Philosophy of Word and Meaning,* esp. chaps. 1, 5, 6; Liebich, "Über den Sphoṭa"; Prabhat Chandra Chakravarti, *The Philosophy of Sanskrit Grammar,* esp. chap. IV, "Theory of Sphoṭa"; E. Frauwallner, "Mimāmsāsūtram I, 1, 6–23"; Strauss, "Altindische Spekulationen," pp. 125–36; Emil Abegg, "Die Lehre von der Ewigkeit des Wortes bei Kumārila"; D'Sa, *Śabdaprāmāṇyam,* esp. chaps. 5, 6, 10, 11; Richard V. De Smet, "Language and Philosophy in India"; Gopika Mohan Bhattacharya, "A Study on the Eternity of Sound"; "Dr." Ballantyne, "The Eternity of Sound"; Padoux, *Recherches,* esp. pp. 77–78, 85ff., 105–07.

24. Frits Staal, "The Concept of Scripture in the Indian Tradition," pp. 121–22; Wayne Howard, *Sāmavedic Chant,* pp. 2–8.
25. Louis Renou, in Renou, Filliozat, et al., *L'Inde classique* 1: 270–71 (citing al-Bīrūnī's eleventh-century report of the consignment in Kashmir of some Vedic texts to writing as the oldest evidence of written Vedic documents). For an instance of how reliance on a written text without the oral recitative guidance of a qualified teacher can lead to errors in Vedic transmission, see [V. Raghavan], "Present Position of Vedic Chanting and its Future," pp. 67–68.
26. Cf. J. L. Mehta, "The Hindu Tradition," pp. 44–45.
27. On which, see Staal, *Nambudiri Veda Recitation;* Wayne Howard, *Sāmavedic Chant;* [Raghavan], "Present Position of Vedic Chanting"; id., "Vedic Chanting"; N. A. Jairazbhoy, "Le chant védique," esp. p. 144ff.; id., "Vedic Chant."
28. For lists and descriptions of the various modes and the general mnemonic system sketchily indicated here, see the introduction to K. V. Abhyankar and G. V. Devasthali, *Vedavikṛtilakṣaṇa-Saṁgraha,* esp. pp. xviiff.; Jairazbhoy, "Chant védique," pp. 144–61; Staal, *Nambudiri Veda Recitation,* esp. pp. 21–30, 40–52. I am also indebted to Mr. V. O. Manjul, Dr. R. N. Dandekar, and other members of the Bhandarkar Institute in Pune for their helpful discussions of these modes and techniques of recitation during my visit there in March 1983. Probably the most ancient mention of the three basic mnemonic modes of Veda memorization is found in the *Aitareya Āraṇyaka* 3.1.3 (Keith ed., pp. 128–29 [=Eng. trans. pp. 241–42]).
29. "Vedam est, quidquid ad religionem pertinet, vedam non sunt libri" (Theodor Zachariae, review of W. Caland, *De Ontdekkingsgeschiedenis van den Veda,* p. 160). Cf. Leipoldt and Morenz, *Heilige Schriften,* p. 13. It is certainly the case, as Zachariae's discussion makes clear, that Vedic manuscripts did exist by the time the first Europeans tried to find out about the Vedas, but the valid vehicle of the text, then as always, was the oral recitative tradition.
30. "Hindu Tradition," p. 50. "*Devattam brahma*" would presumably be "*devāttam brahma*" if diacriticals were supplied.
31. Chakravarti, *Philosophy of Sanskrit Grammar,* p. 3. Cf. *Laws of Manu* 2.156: "A man is not therefore (considered) venerable because his head is gray; him who, though young, has learned the Veda, the gods consider to be venerable" (Georg Bühler, trans., *The Laws of Manu,* p. 59).
32. E.g., 2.76–107; 4.93, 125 (Bühler trans., pp. 44–49, 143, 149).
33. E.g., according to Śaṅkara's commentary on *Brahma Sūtra* 1.3.34–38, as cited and translated by Muir, *The Vedas,* pp. 292–300. An exception is women's presence at *śrauta* (sacrificial) rites. On the prohibition of the unauthorized acquisition of the Veda from someone else's recitation, see *Laws of Manu* 2.117,172 (Bühler trans., pp. 51, 61).

34. One such has been reported to me by Gary Tubb. After a Maratha wedding ceremony in Pune not long ago, there was considerable agitation on the part of some Brahmans because the public address system for broadcasting the celebration to the neighborhood was accidentally left on during the recitation of Vedic mantras by one of the Brahman priests – the result being that anyone in the vicinity could have heard the sacred words.
35. As reported by Albrecht Weber, "Eine angebliche Bearbeitung des Yajurveda," p. 235, citing G. A. Franke's edition of "Die dänischen Missionsberichte aus Ostindien," vol. 4 (Halle, 1742), pp. 1251–56.
36. 5.3.3 (the trans. is that of Keith, pp. 301–02).
37. Winternitz, *Geschichte* 1: 31 (my trans., =*History* 1: 33). Winternitz's term is *merkwürdig* (cf. id. 1: 28, =*History* 1: 31); F. Max Müller, *My Autobiography* (New York: Scribner's, 1901), p. 193. Cf. Winternitz's further remarks (*Geschichte* 1: 31; =*History* 1: 34): ". . . noch heute gründet sich der ganze litterarische und wissenschaftliche Verkehr in Indien auf das mündliche Wort. Nicht aus Manuskripten oder Büchern lernt man die Texte, sondern nur aus dem Munde des Lehrers – heute wie vor Jahrtausenden. Der geschriebene Text kann höchstens als Hilfsmittel beim Lernen, als eine Gedächtnisstütze benutzt werden, aber es kommt ihm keine Autorität zu."
38. "Pustakasthā tu yā vidyā parahastagataṃ dhanam/ kāryakāle samutpanne na sā vidyā na tad dhanam" (Text supplied by Gary A. Tubb).
39. 2.146 (=Bühler trans., p. 57). Cf. 2.144 (=Bühler trans., p. 56). On the immense importance and authority of the teacher in Hindu tradition generally, see, e.g., the discussion of Harry M. Buck, "Saving Story and Sacred Book," pp. 86–87. Cf. Vibhuti Bhushan Mishra, *Religious Beliefs and Practices of North India during the Early Mediaeval Period,* Handbuch der Orientalistik, ed. B. Spuler, 2nd div., supp. vol. 3 (Leiden and Cologne, E. J. Brill, 1973), pp. 81–82.
40. Ananda K. Coomaraswamy, "The Bugbear of Literacy," p. 41.
41. On the traditional Hindu system of oral teaching and learning, see, inter alia, Radha Kumud Mookerji, *Ancient Indian Education,* esp. pp. 26–29, 67–68, 88–95, 173–202, 211–19; A. S. Altekar, *Education in Ancient India,* esp. pp. 47–81; K. G. Ghurye, *Preservation of Learned Tradition in India,* esp. pp. 12–22; F. E. Keay, *Indian Education in Ancient and Later Times,* pp. 1–47.
42. *EB*[15], pp. 933, 940b ["Hindu Sacred Literature" (van Buitenen)]; J. A. B. van Buitenen, "On the Archaism of the Bhāgavata Purāṇa," p. 24.
43. On the relatively small contact of most Hindus with the Veda, see, inter alia, Zachariae, review of Caland, *Ontdekkingsgeschiedenis,* p. 160 ("Die Purāṇas sind an die Stelle des Veda getreten."); Renou, *Destin du Véda,* p. 2; Heesterman, "Autorität des Veda," pp. 29, 33; id., "Veda and Dharma," esp. pp. 80–81, 92–94.
44. *EB*[15], p. 933b.
45. "Composition of the Purāṇa-s," p. 269.
46. "Purānapaṭhanaṃ yatra tatra saṁnihito hariḥ," as cited and trans. in ibid., p. 258. See also pp. 258–59 for other examples.
47. Bonazzoli, "Composition of the Purāṇa-s," pp. 259–73. The citations are from ibid., pp. 273 and 272, respectively.
48. "The Life of a Text . . . in Performance." I am much indebted to Mr. Lutgendorf for a copy of portions of a draft of the thesis, as well as of an earlier, unpublished paper ("The Life of a Text: Tulasīdāsa's *Rāmacaritamānasa* in Oral Exposition") delivered at the American Academy of Religion annual meeting in December 1984, and for his permission to use and quote from these. In what follows concerning the *Mānasa*'s

recitation, I depend exclusively upon material contained in chap. II ("The Text in Recitation and Song") of his study and in his paper.

49. "Life of a Text . . . in Performance," draft chap. II, p. 24.
50. Ibid., draft chap. II, pp. 14–19. See esp. p. 18, n. 37.
51. Ibid., draft chap. II, pt. 4 (on the *māhāyajña*) and pt. 5 (on *Mānas* -singing).
52. See, for example, the description of the festive ninefold *path,* or recitation (in nine days) of the *Srī Durga Saptaśatī* in the household of a prominent Raipur businessman by Lawrence A. Babb, *The Divine Hierarchy,* pp. 39–46; cf. pp. 218–26. Note that this recitation, from beginning to end, as is commonly the case, is an act of worship (under the direction of a Brahman priest and accompanied by substantial ritual activities) and not simply a pious form of entertainment.
53. Interesting material on the popular recitation of the *Bhāgavata Purāṇa* will be available when the doctoral dissertation of James Nye at the University of Wisconsin is completed. I am grateful to him for discussions of his work on the recitation of this and other *upapurāṇā*s on which he was working during several days together in Banaras in 1983 at the Institute of Indian Studies guest house.
54. See Coburn, "'Scripture' in India."

Part III. "An Arabic Reciting": Qur'ān as Spoken Book

1. See above, Chapter 4. See also *Kor. Unters.,* p. 65.
2. Stanley Lane-Poole, as quoted without source ref. by Samuel M. Zwemer, "Translations of the Koran," p. 82.
3. The appellation is that of Sydney E. Ahlstrom, *A Religious History of the American People* (New Haven and London: Yale University Press, 1972), p. 92. Cf. pp. 128–30

Chapter 7. Revelation and Recitation

1. All subsequent qur'anic references are prefaced by "S.", for *Sūrah,* the Arabic term used to designate the 114 chapter divisions of the text. The first number in each reference refers to the *sūrah,* and the second to the verse, or *āyah,* within the *sūrah.* The references accord with the *āyah* divisions of the standard Cairo text. All translations from the Qur'ān are my own, since no single translation is equally satisfactory at all points. I have, however, consulted and relied often upon the following translations (each of which has both special virtues and particular shortcomings) in formulating my wording: George Sale, *The Koran* (1734); Richard Bell, *The Qur'ān* (1937–39); Régis Blachère, *Le coran* (1949–50); Arthur J. Arberry, *The Koran Interpreted* (1955); and Rudi Paret, *Der Koran* (1962).
2. Wilfred Cantwell Smith, *The Meaning and End of Religion,* pp. 95–96. On Manichaean scriptures, see Geo Widengren, *Mani and Manichaeism,* trans. from the German orig. (1961) by Charles Kessler, History of Religion Series, ed. E. O. James (New York: Holt, Rinehart and Winston, 1965), pp. 74–94, 107–13; G. Haloun and W. B. Henning, "The Compendium of the Doctrines and Styles of the Teaching of Mani, the Buddha of Light," *Asia Major,* n.s., 3 (1953): 184–211, esp. 204–11; Albert Henrichs, "The Cologne Mani Codex Reconsidered," *Harvard Studies in Classical Philology* 83 (1979): 339–67, esp. 362–63. On Manichaeism more generally, see Geo Widengren, *Die Religionen Irans,* pp. 299–308; id., *Mani and Manichaeism.*

3. The work of Richard Bell and his student, W. Montgomery Watt, has focused attention on evidence supporting a gradual evolution in the Qur'ān of the idea of scripture, one in which "book" (*kitāb:* on which, see the following subsection, "Scripture as a Generic Idea") gradually becomes more prominent as a generic concept as well as a term for the revelations given Muhammad. According to this view, *qur'ān* as the original name of the specific revelation given by God to Muhammad is slowly replaced or supplemented by *kitāb* in the course of Muhammad's prophetic career. See esp. Watt, ed., *Bell's Introduction to the Qur'ān,* pp. 137–44. More recently, a student of Watt's, Alford T. Welch, *EI*^{2}, s.v. "Ḳur'ān" (esp. pp. 400–03), and especially Tilman Nagel, "Vom 'Qur'ān' zur 'Schrift'," have attempted to refine somewhat this evolution, focusing principally on the shift of *kitāb* into the foreground in the middle and later periods of qur'anic revelation. In agreement with John Bowman, "Holy Scriptures, Lectionaries and Qur'an," pp. 33–34, I feel that too sharp a contrast between *qur'ān* and *kitāb* is a misreading of the Qur'ān – one that rests, in my view, on an attempt to push hypothetical chronologization of the qur'anic materials well beyond the limits of any "development" we can actually reconstruct from the text itself.
4. For a detailed discussion of *nabī* (=Heb. *nābī';* Aram. *n*^{e}*bī'ā;* cf. Gk. *prophētēs*) and *rasūl* (cf. Gk. *apostolos;* Aram. *š*^{e}*līḥā*) and ideas of prophethood in Islam, see Arendt Jan Wensinck, "Muhammed und die Propheten"; Arthur Jeffery, *The Qur'ān as Scripture,* pp. 19–31; *Kor. Unters.,* pp. 44–53. The elaboration of stories about the previous prophets came to play a large role in Muslim folklore in the literary genre known as "tales of the prophets" (*qiṣaṣ al-anbiya'*). See, e.g., the well-known collection of this title by Abū Ja'far Muḥammad b. 'Abd Allāh al-Kisā'ī (fl. 11th or 12th C.?), *Vita [sic] prophetarum auctore Muḥammad Ben Abdallah al-Kisa'i . . .,* ed. Isaac Eisenberg (2 vols., Leiden, 1922–23); Eng. trans. W[heeler] M. Thackston, Jr., *The Tales of the Prophets of al-Kisa'i,* Library of Classical Arabic Literature, ed. Ilse Lichtenstadter, vol. 2 (Boston: Twayne, 1978). On the whole genre, see the doctoral dissertation of Tilman Nagel, "Die Qiṣaṣ al-Anbiyā'. Ein Beitrag zur arabischen Literaturgeschichte" (Bonn, 1967).
5. "Wa-hādhā kitāb^{un} anzalnāhu mubārak^{un} muṣaddiq^{u} lladhī bayn^{a} yadayhi . . . ." Cf. S. 2.97, 3.3, 3.81, 5.48, 5.59, 35.31, 46.12, inter alia.
6. Note that I give both the Hijrah ("Hegira") date of the Muslim lunar calendar (always first) and the Julian or Gregorian date of the Christian solar calendar (always second) in references to events in Islamic history, as well as in all bibliographic references to Hijrah-dated Arabic publications.
7. It is surprising in many ways that the generic notion of scripture present from the start in Islam has played no evident role in determining our modern Western scholarly use of "scripture" as a generic term – or is it only that such a role has never been traced? It would be interesting to investigate the degree to which, even as far back as the Western Middle Ages, contact with and awareness of Islamic thought – however limited – suggested to European minds an analogy between Muslims' possession of a Book (however false or "nefarious" [see Chapter 4, section on "Generalization of the Concept"] it may have appeared to Christians and Jews). Given the historical contacts and early translations of the Qur'ān (e.g., that of Robert of Ketton in 1143), it would seem logical that Muslim concern with scripture would have impinged upon Western consciousness even before awareness of Indian scriptural texts, although the greater antiquity of Indian, as of Chinese, sacred texts seems to have been what piqued Western interest in these early on.

8. Some passages, however, do suggest that all apostles were not precisely equal: e.g., S. 2.253: "These are the apostles; some of them We have preferred over others [in what we have given them] . . . ."
9. *OED*, s.v. "Scripture," meaning 4. See Chapter 4, section on "The Semantic Background."
10. On the problem of the meanings of *kitāb* in the Qur'ān, see the refs. given in n. 3 above and nn. 11, 12, 15 below; the suggestive discussions of Ary A. Roest Crollius, *Thus Were They Hearing,* pp. 89–108, 133–43 (with many references to earlier literature); and also the two brief summaries of the pertinent issues in *EI*² 5: 401b–02a, 403, s.v. "Ḳur'ān" (A. T. Welch).
11. E.g., Qurān, S. 2.179: "Fasting is prescribed for/made incumbent upon you" (*kutiba 'alaykum aṣ-ṣawm*). See *WKAS* 1: 37b (s.v. "KaTaBa"), 42a (s.v. "KiTāB"); Lane, *Lexicon* (citing the *Tāj al-'arūs*), 2590a, 2590c, s.v. "K-T-B"; *Lisān* 1 : 699b, s.v. "K-T-B" (where the meaning of *kitāb* as "prescription" or "duty" is apparently derivative of the Qur'ān's authority as *kitāb Allāh:* "wal-kitābᵘ: al-farḍᵘ, wal-ḥukmᵘ, wal-qadarᵘ"). Cf. *EI* 2: 1044b, s.v. "Kitāb" (F. Krenkow). See also n. 12.
12. This is the sense of *kataba shayᵃⁿ 'alá fulānⁱⁿ,* "to make something incumbent upon someone", "to impose s.th. upon s.o.," or "to decree s.th. for s.o." Although *kitāb* is most commonly associated with the idea of writing, this other sense of the root verb (with the preposition *'alá*) is also an important one: writing and fixing, impressing, or laying down something are closely linked ideas; a *kitāb* is both something written and something laid down, fixed, or "decreed"; hence its use also to mean "(divine) prescription or order", as in S. 2.235, 4.24,103, or a "fixed term or destiny", as in S. 3.145. See the refs. in n. 11.
13. Cf. S. 12.1-2, 43.2-3, and 56.7-8 (cited in the epigraph to this chapter). On the heavenly book idea in Islam and, earlier, in the ancient Near East more generally, see Jeffery, *Qur'ān as Scripture,* pp. 12–18; Frants Buhl, "'Die Schrift' und was damit zusammenhängt"; and the references to the work of Leo Koep and Geo Widengren cited in n. 3 of Chapter 4 (where cf. nn. 4–6).
14. *Umm al-kitāb* also occurs once, in S. 3.7, in a different sense, namely as those verses of the Qur'ān whose sense is "distinct", or "clear" (*āyāt muḥkamāt*), rather than "ambiguous" (*āyāt mutashābihāt*). On these designations, see *Itqān* 2: 2–13.
15. E.g., Ṭabarī 25: 48 (on S. 43.4); cf. ibid. 13:169 (on S. 13.39). Concerning *al-kitāb, ahl al-kitāb,* and *umm al-kitāb,* see Johannes Pedersen, review of Eduard Meyer, *Ursprung und Geschichte der Mormonen; Kor. Unters.,* pp. 65–67; Buhl, "'Die Schrift'"; *EI* 2: 1044b–45a, s.v. "Kitāb" (F. Krenkow); Dawid Künstlinger, "Kitāb und Ahlu-l-kitāb"; Julius Augapfel, "Das *Kitāb* im Qurân"; Geo Widengren, *Muhammad,* esp. pp. 115–39; Nagel, "Vom 'Qur'ān' zur 'Schrift'," esp. pp. 150–65. Roest Crollius has put forward a different interpretation of these terms, as well as of *lawḥ maḥfūẓ,* in the passages usually interpreted as referring to the heavenly book. He argues with some cogency (*Thus Were They Hearing,* pp. 81–143, esp. 133–43) that *kitāb* refers not to a heavenly book, but to scripture as a genus – as the divine communication given to previous messengers and peoples and hence the sign of divine revelation generally. In the light of this reading, *umm al-kitāb* is still to be seen, he believes, as the source of scripture given to humankind [N.B. erroneous qur'anic citations for two of the three passages in question, p. 140], but (ibid., pp. 83–84, 141) the *lawḥ maḥfūẓ* is to be understood in the light of its function as a common symbol of religious authority among various peoples – preeminently Jews and Christians. The *lawḥ* thus refers to the written scriptures of other communities as they appear in their place of honor, as "a tablet conserved" on the lectern in worship,

or even the lectern for scripture reading itself. His arguments seem to me to offer a plausible alternative interpretation of the usages in question, and certainly one in consonance with many of the unambiguous occurrences of *kitāb* and especially *kutub* in a generic sense. However, I do not see that they are sufficient as they stand to refute the "heavenly book" interpretation conclusively. This is clearly a topic that needs yet another thorough investigation, despite all the ink already spilled on it.

16. See Ismar Elbogen, *Der jüdische Gottesdienst in seiner geschichtlichen Entwicklung*, pp. 186–94.
17. Little has been written on this issue, but see *EI*^{2} 5: 428a–32b, s.v. "Ḳur'ān" [sect. 9, "Translations of the Kur'ān" (J. D. Pearson)]; Samuel Zwemer, "Translations of the Koran," esp. pp. 80–83, 92–99. As Pearson notes (p. 429a) the Ḥanafī school, unlike the other three major legal schools in Sunnī Islam, has been willing to admit the permissability of translation, so opposition to it has not been unanimous among the *'ulama'*. For examples of twentieth-century Muslim arguments against translation of the Qur'ān, see the two articles from the journal of the Azhar in Cairo, *al-Manār*, cited in Zwemer's work, p. 98 – esp. that which objects to "translation of the Qur'ān into Turkish and the call of the Turks to do without the Arabic Qur'ān in favor of what they call 'the Turkish Qur'ān'." The writer goes on to say that if the Turks can do without the Qur'ān, they can do still better without other books such as those of Ḥadīth, *tafsīr*, jurisprudence (*fiqh*), and the rest of the Arabic sciences (*al-Manār* 17, pt. 2 (1332/1913): 160$^{10-13}$).
18. On *i'jāz* and *'ismah*, see Tor Andrae, *Die Person Muhammeds in Lehre und Glauben seiner Gemeinde*, chaps. 3–4; *EI*^{2} 3: 1018a–20b, s.v. "I'djaz" (G. von Grünebaum); ibid. 4: 182b–84a, s.v. "'Iṣma" (W. Madelung); Muḥammad 'Alī al-Tahānawī, *Kashshāf iṣṭilāḥāt al-funūn*, ed. Muḥammad Wajīh et al. (Calcutta, 1862; 6 vol. repr. ed., Beirut: Khayyat, 1966), s.v. "mu'jizah" (4: 975ff.), "iṣmah" (4: 1047f.); *Itqān*, 2: 116–25 (*i'jāz*); Ibn Hazm, *al-Faṣl fī l-milal wal-ahwā' wal-nihal*, 5 vols. (Cairo, 1317–21/1899–1903) 4: 29–30, 46–56; Muḥammad al-Bāqillānī, *I'jāz al-Qur'ān* (Cairo, 1349/1930). See also Hermann Stieglecker, *Die Glaubenslehren des Islam* (Paderborn, Munich, Vienna: F. Schöningh, 1962), pp. 158–69, 185–88, 371–408, 472–87.
19. On the attitudes of the Roman Catholic church to vernacular translation of the Bible, see *CE* 8: 640, s.v. "Scripture" (A. J. Maas), sect. VI.
20. Note, however, that the Muslim view of the history of the collection and codification of the written Qur'ān under the first three caliphs, as well as the general modern Islamicist agreement with the basic outlines, if not the specifics, of this view, has been radically questioned by some scholars. John Wansbrough in particular, in *Quranic Studies* (1977), argues that several different styles of explanatory gloss and "exegesis" (all based on Jewish antecedents) are discernible in the qur'anic text itself. His conclusion, based on literary and rhetorical analysis, but unsupported by corroborating historical evidence, is that there was a long process of "canonization" (at least two centuries) in the Islamic as in the Jewish and Christian cases. Cf. the similar skepticism about the traditions surrounding the 'Uthmānic redaction and its variant traditions on the part of John Burton, in *The Collection of the Qur'ān* (1977). Burton, however, reaches virtually opposite conclusions. He sees the traditional accounts as a smokescreen hiding the fact that the *textus receptus* had already been fixed under Muhammad's personal direction, well before 'Uthmān's caliphate, and thus represents in fact the codex of the Prophet himself. While both of these interpretations, especially Wansbrough's, place the issue of "canonization" in a novel light, neither can be said to be proven at present. In addition, even if accepted, neither offers

a picture of a canonization process for the Qur'ān that is very similar to that of Judaic or Christian history.

21. As does Wilfred Cantwell Smith, "Some Similarities and Differences between Christianity and Islam," pp. 56–58. On the analogy between Qur'ān and Christ, see Chapter 10, section on "The Word of God and Holy Writ," esp. n. 3.
22. Clifford Geertz, "Art as a Cultural System," p. 1490.
23. On this point, see the succinct remarks of S. D. Goitein, *Studies in Islamic History and Institutions* (Leiden: E. J. Brill, 1966), p. 88.
24. On the meaning and derivation of *qur'ān,* see my article, "The Earliest Meaning of 'Qur'ān'," p. 364.
25. An exception to this is the title *Qur'ān karīm* (instead of *al-Qur'ān al-karīm*), which appears on many editions, especially but not exclusively those published outside the Arab world. This is used apparently as a quotation from S. 56.77: "Truly, it is a noble Recitation" ("Innahu la-qur'ān^{un} karīm^{un}").
26. But see n. 20 above.
27. The most commonly cited names of the "scribes of Revelation" are those of Ubayy b. Ka'b, Zayd b. Thābit, 'Abd Allāh b. Abī Sarḥ, 'Uthmān, and Mu'āwiyah. See refs. below, n. 31; *GdQ* 1: 46; 2: 1–5; *GAS* 1: 3; Watt, *Bell's Introduction,* pp. 37–38. Note that the first two of these are mentioned in the traditions recording those who "collected" (*jama'a*) the Qur'ān during Muhammad's lifetime (Ibn Sa'd 2: 112–15). Whether *qurrā'* from the beginning always meant "reciters" (sing.: *qāri',* from *Q-R-'*), or in some contexts rather "villagers" (sing.: *qārī,* from *Q-R-Y,* as in *qaryá,* "village") has been a matter of debate. On the side of "reciters", see G. Martin Hinds, "Kûfan Political Alignments and their Background in the Mid-Seventh Century A.D." On the side of "villagers", see M. A. Shaban, *Islamic History* 1: 22–23, 50–55, 67–78; and, building on Shaban's work, G. H. A. Juynboll, "The Qurrā' in Early Islamic History." The use of the term for Qur'ān reciters in at least some early contexts is undisputed, and in later times exclusive: See id., "The Position of Qur'ān Recitation in Early Islam." On the possible role of the "early readers" of the second century in developing a fully inflected reading of the Qur'ān that had not originally existed, see Paul E. Kahle, "The Qur'ān and the 'Arabīya," pp. 180–82; id., "The Arabic Readers of the Koran," pp. 70–71.
28. "Mā bayn al-daffatayn" (e.g., Bukhārī 66.16; *Musnad* 1: 415); also "mā bayn al-lawḥayn" and "mā bayn lawḥay al-muṣḥaf" (e.g., Bukhārī 65 on S. 59.4. [further refs.: Arendt Jan Wensinck, *Concordance et indices de la tradition musulmane* 6: 152, s.v. "lawḥ"]).
29. *EI* 2: 1063b, s.v. "Ḳoran" (Frants Buhl). Buhl's summary discussion of this point is the clearest in the literature. See also *GdQ* 1: 31–34.
30. E.g., *qalam,* "pen"; *suḥūf,* "pages" or "writings"; *asāṭīr,* "written documents"; *zubūr,* "writings" or "psalms"; and *kitāb* itself (cf. S. 6.7, cited as an epigraph to this chapter). On the oldest evidence of Arabic writing, see Frants Buhl, *Das Leben Muhammeds,* pp. 52–56; *EI*^{2} 1: 564b–65b, s.v. "'Arabiyya," sect. ii.: "The Literary Language: Classical Arabic" (C. Rabin).
31. See *EI*^{2} 4: 1113a–22b, esp. 1119–20, s.v. "Khaṭṭ," sect. i: "In the Arab World" (J. Sourdel-Thomine). On the writing down of the revelations in Muhammad's lifetime and immediately thereafter, see Bukhārī 65 on S. 4.19; ibid., 66.3 (on the collection of the Qur'ān); Ibn Sa'd 3.2: 59 (Ubayy b. Ka'b); Bukhārī 56.31 (Zayd b. Thābit); Labīb al-Sa'īd, *The Recited Koran,* pp. 19–22. Cf. *GdQ* 2: 1–5, 8–27; Ibn Sa'd 2: 112–15. On Muhammad's writings to the tribes and nations, see Ibn Sa'd 1.ii: 15–38 (=J. Wellhausen, ed. and trans., "Die Schreiben Muhammads und die Gesandtschaften an

ihn," pp. 97–135 [Arabic text pp. 1–28]); and, for a critical look at their authenticity, Buhl, *Leben Muhammeds,* pp. 294–98; W. Montgomery Watt, "Muḥammad's Letters to the Princes," Excursus D of *Muhammad at Medina,* pp. 345–47.

32. Cf. Rudi Paret, *Mohammed und der Koran,* pp. 59–60.
33. E.g., the readings of one of the first Muslims, the famous Companion of the Prophet, 'Abd Allāh ibn Mas'ūd (d. 32/652–53), who knew by heart major portions of the qur'anic revelations learned directly from Muhammad. A pietist, possibly with 'Alid (Shī'ī) leanings, Ibn Mas'ūd did not prevail as the chief authority on the final recension. His only mildly variant version of the Qur'ān was not followed as the basis of the "official" codex prepared under the Caliph 'Uthmān – perhaps on political rather than text-critical grounds. On his life, see esp. Ibn Sa'd 3.i: 106–14; *GdQ* 3: 312 (index refs.); and *EI*[2], s.v. "Ibn Mas'ūd" (J.-C. Vadet), the last of which includes further sources in its bibliography.
34. *GdQ* 3: 78–83, 118.
35. "Earliest Meaning of 'Qur'ān'."
36. R. Payne Smith, *Thesaurus Syriacus,* 2 vols. (Oxford, 1883–1901) 2: 3716b, citing several occurrences in the first sense from sources as early as St. Cyril's commentary on Luke; Bowman, "Holy Scriptures." The latter provides a convincing argument for the influence of *qeryānā*'s use as a common technical term in Syriac Christian liturgical contexts. This usage can be documented at least as early as the sixth and seventh centuries in lectionary manuscripts with rubrics such as *qeryānā d-yōm bā'awwātā,* "Reading for the Day of Supplications," and *qeryānā d-sulāqeh d-māran,* "Reading for the Ascension of Our Lord" (pers. commun. from Alford T. Welch, 26 March 1980, citing discussion with Sebastian Brock; oral confirmation by Brock, Oxford, England, Oct. 1982). For previous discussions of *qeryānā* and the often-suggested linkage with *qur'ān,* see the references given in my article, "Earliest Meaning of 'Qur'ān'," p. 365, n. 18. To these add Th. W. Juynboll, *Handbuch des islāmischen Gesetzes nach der Lehre der schāfi'itischen Schule* (Leiden: E. J. Brill; Leipzig: Otto Harrossowitz, 1910), p. 2.
37. "Holy Scriptures," pp. 33–35.
38. Josef Horovitz, "Qurān," p. 67, does not distinguish between the two closely related Hebrew terms, calling both "Schriftverlesung". Cf. *GdQ* 1: 32, where it is noted that *miqrā'* can be used for part as well as the whole of scripture. Arthur Jeffery, *The Foreign Vocabulary of the Qur'ān,* p. 234, notes that Marracci and Geiger long ago argued for the Hebrew as the source of *qur'ān,* but he still prefers a Syriac Christian derivation. Cf. *JE* 3: 141a, s.v. "Bible Canon". Judith Wegner, formerly of the Harvard Law School, has also stressed the functional as well as semantic similarity of *miqrā'* in Jewish usage to that of *qur'ān* in Muslim use (pers. commun., Nov. 1979). Note that whatever the similarities in the Hebrew or the Syriac usages to those of the Qur'ān, we do not apparently have in *qur'ān* a case of direct borrowing of a Hebrew or Syriac term. The Syriac would be the closest, yet *qeryānā* should have yielded the perfectly good Arabic verbal noun form *qiryān,* had it been taken over directly (see my "Earliest Meaning of 'Qur'ān'," p. 365, n. 20).
39. *EJ* 4: 816. Cf. Künstlinger, "Kitāb und Ahlu-l-kitāb," p. 239; id., "Die Namen der 'Gottes-Schriften' im Qurān," p. 76, n. 2; *GdQ* 1: 32. On Torah reading in the synagogue, see Elbogen, *Der jüdische Gottesdienst,* pp. 155–74 (cf. 174–86).
40. Cf. Tor Andrae, *Mohammed,* pp. 78–79 (=Eng. trans. p. 96 [which, however, is a wholly unsatisfactory rendering of this important summary passage]). See also John Bowman, "Holy Scriptures." On the use of Syriac terminology by Arab Christians, see J. Spencer Trimmingham, *Christianity among the Arabs in Pre-Islamic Times*

(London and New York: Longman; Beirut: Librairie du Liban, 1979), pp. 266–67; on the presence of Christians in Arabia more generally, see also ibid., chaps. 7, 8, and the index references under "Syriac-language Christianity" and "Syriac", as well as Richard Bell, *The Origin of Islam in Its Christian Environment,* esp. chaps. 1, 2. On the probable Christian influences on Muhammad and early Islam, see John Bowman, "The Debt of Islam to Monophysite Syrian Christianity," and the still basic studies of Bell, *Origin of Islam,* chaps. 3–7, and Tor Andrae, "Der Ursprung des Islams und das Christentum," esp. 23: 155–206 (see also 24: 277–92, 25: 45–112, for discussion of the possible influence of Syriac Christian piety on the qur'anic worldview).

41. Widengren, *Religionen Irans,* p. 197; id., "Holy Book and Holy Tradition in Iran," esp. pp. 40, 45–52; H. S. Nyberg, *Die Religionen des alten Iran,* chap. 8, "Die Sassanidenzeit: der awestische Kanon"; Stig Wikander, *Feuerpriester in Kleinasien und Iran,* Skrifter utgivna av Kungl. Humanistiska Vetenskapssamfundet i Lund, no. 40 (Lund: C. W. K. Gleerup, 1946), pp. 28–35; cf. 125–91, esp. 159ff.; cf. H. W. Bailey, *Zoroastrian Problems in the Ninth-Century Books* (Oxford: Clarendon Press, 1943), chap. 5, "Patvand."
42. On the excellence of reciting S. 112, cf. Muslim 6.259–63; on the obligation to recite S. 1 in every performance of *ṣalāt,* see ibid. 4.34–46 (cf. 6.254–56).
43. *Yatlū* is the imperf. third sing. of *talā.* Cf. S. 2.129,151; 3.164; 28.59; 65.11; 98.2. The repeated linkage of apostle and reciting in these passages indicates how closely are linked the notions of revelation through a messenger and recitation of what God reveals.
44. *Ḥaqq*^{a} *tilāwat*^{i}*hi* is used here not as a simple nominal construct phrase, but as a true adverbial accusative to intensify the finite form of the verb *talā:* Literally, the phrase transliterated in the text reads, "[those who] recite it [scripture] with/like a true recitation" –.in other words, recite it in the clearest or best recitative fashion (as it should be recited).
45. Concerning which, see my "Earliest Meaning of 'Qur'ān'," esp. pp. 367–73.
46. "Wa-mā takūnu fī sha'n^{in} wa-mā tatlū minhu min qur'ān^{in} wa-lā ta'malūna min 'amal^{in} illā kunnā 'alaykum shuhūd^{an} idh tufīḍūna fīhi."
47. I.e., gets up in the night from sleep to perform extra, supererogatory devotions, a common practice among the pietists and mystics of Islam, as in many other mystical or ascetic traditions. See *SEI,* s.v. "Tahadjdjud" (A. J. Wensinck).
48. *Mabānī,* p. 58: "yuqaṭṭi' al-layl^{a} taṣbīḥ^{an} wa-qur'ān^{an}." Also in Ṭabarī^{2} 1: 97 (where *qur'ān* is glossed as *qirā'ah,* which is the more common verbal-noun form of *qara'a*). Also cited in *Kor. Unters.,* p. 74, and *GdQ* 1: 34.
49. *Musnad* 4: 159: "kāna rajul^{an} kathīr^{a} l-dhikr^{i} lillāh fī l-qur'ān."
50. Bukhārī 66.11; Tirmidhī 46.25. Cf. Muslim 6.240–42. This is clearly an instance in which *sakīnah* cannot be translated as "tranquillity", as is often done. On the meaning of *sakīnah,* see my discussion and the references given in *Divine Word and Prophetic Word in Early Islam,* p. 21, n. 13.
51. Muslim 2.285: "wa-fī kull^{i} ṣalāt^{in} qur'ān^{un}." Cf. Muslim 4.42, in which this is put negatively: "there is no *ṣalāt* without a recitation [*qirā'ah*]."
52. Bukhārī 64.35.27, 65 on S. 48.1, 66.12.1; *Musnad* 6: 11.
53. Bukhārī 67.80.2. Cf. *Musnad* 2: 62; Ibn Mājah 6.65.6. In these two latter occurrences, *al-qur'ān* is used to refer to the feared revelation, whereas Bukhārī's version has only the indefinite "something" [*shay'*] [that would be revealed].
54. "Inna . . . qad unzila 'alayhi al-laylat^{a} qur'ān^{un}," Bukhārī 65.on S. 2.14 (cf. 15,16). For other refs. to particular *qur'ān*s being revealed, see Bukhārī 96.5.6; *Musnad* 1: 237; 2: 307, 337; 3: 255 (=Muslim 5.297). See also Wensinck, *Concordance* 5:

349b, s.v. "qur'ān", for further examples of *qur'ān* as an indefinite singular referring to one unit of the revelation.

55. "Ḥasibat hādhā qur'ān[an]": *Lisān* 7: 183ab. I owe this reference to Wolfhart Heinrichs.
56. *Al-Faṣl* (above, n. 18), 3: 143[14]. I am indebted to Wilfred Cantwell Smith for this reference.
57. *Al-Fuṣūl fī l-uṣūl,* art. 45, p. 64 of pt. 2 of Richard M. Frank, ed. and trans., "Two Short Dogmatic Works of Abū l-Qāsim al-Qushayrī," *MIDEO* 15 (1982): 53–74 (pt. 1); 16 (1983): 59–94 (pt. 2). I am indebted to Professor Frank for a prepublication copy of the Arabic text. Cf. his trans. of art. 45 in ibid. 16: 81.
58. *Musnad* 3: 215. Cf. n. 51 above.
59. Tirmidhī 2.110.
60. Muslim 4.145; cf. 4.149,154; 6.232-37. There are conflicting Prophetic traditions on whether and when one should recite loudly in *ṣalāt.* Cf. inter alia Bukhārī 10.96,97,108; Muslim 4.47-49,146. For many further references in Ḥadīth, see A. J. Wensinck, *A Handbook of Early Muhammadan Tradition,* p. 132a.
61. E.g., Bukhārī 66.17,20,21,23,26,36; 40.9; Muslim 6.202-04,224-31,243; *Musnad* 4: 103, 121–22, 283, 285; Nasā'ī 42.21,22.
62. Tirmidhī 46.17.2.
63. "Sa-atlū 'alayk[a] bi-dhālika qur'ān[an]": Tirmidhī 44.(S. 63).5. Cf. *Musnad* 5: 30.
64. Witness, for example, the most famous story of the conversion of 'Umar b. al-Khaṭṭāb, later the second caliph, but at first a bitter Meccan opponent of the Prophet: According to tradition, it was hearing his sister reading aloud a *qur'ān* and then his reading it himself that led him to become a Muslim. Ibn Isḥāq 1: 367–71 (=Eng. trans. pp. 156–57).

Chapter 8. Muslim Scripture as Spoken Word

1. See Chapter 7, n. 50.
2. There is some lack of clarity in the sources available to me as to whether the Cairo edition appeared publicly for the first time in 1337, 1342, 1343, or 1344 (i.e., the range of dates 1919-26 C.E.). Gotthelf Bergsträsser, "Koranlesung in Kairo," p. 2, gives A.H. 1343 as the date on the title page of a copy of this text that he owned, but notes in his description of the publication information given in the afterword to the text that the names of the editors of the text appear with a date of 10 Rabī' II, 1337 [=13 Jan. 1919] (this is the exact information given in the appended material to the 1974 reprint edition that I own), with a printing date of 1342 [=1923–24] at the Official Printing House in Būlāq, Cairo. Arthur Jeffery, "Progress in the Study of the Qur'ān Text," p. 6, gives 1923 [=1341–42] as the date of issue. The *Encyclopaedia Britannica* (1966 ed.), s.v. "Koran" (Wilfred C. Smith) prefers the 1919 [=1337] date given in the original afterword material. However, in *GdQ* 3: 273, Otto Pretzl cites Bergsträsser's article and still gives 1344/1925 as the date of the first edition. *SEI,* s.v. "Ḳur'ān" (Frants Buhl) gives 1342; *EI*[2], p. 426a, s.v. "Ḳur'ān" (A. Welch), has 1344/1924, which is an error all around, as the first day of A.H. 1344 was 22 July 1925. Thus 1342/1923–24 seems the most probable year of the initial printing (or the first public printing).
3. "Koranlesung in Kairo," pp. 10–12. On the "official" Qur'ān, see Bergsträsser's entire discussion, ibid., pp. 1–13. Cf. also the brief comments in *GdQ* 3: 273–74, where Otto Pretzl says further of this Muslim edition, and not with any intentional condescension, "Die mit ungemein grosser Sorgfalt hergestellte Ausgabe ist eine

vom wissenschaftlichen Standpunkt aus erstaunliche Leistung orientalischer Koran-gelehrter."

4. *EI*[2] 5: 126a–28a, s.v. "Ḳirā'a" (Rudi Paret); Régis Blachère, *Introduction au Coran*, p. 103; *GdQ* 3: 160–90. On particular "readings" of individuals, see Gotthelf Bergsträsser, "Die Koranlesung des Hasan von Basra"; Edmund Beck, "Die b. Mas'ūd-varianten bei al-Farrā'."
5. On the science of *qirā'ah* generally, with primary emphasis on the *qirā'āt*, see *GdQ*, vol. 3 ("Die Geschichte des Korantexts"); Blachère, *Introduction*, pp. 103–35, 199–210; Otto Pretzl, "Die Wissenschaft der Koranlesung," esp. pp. 1–47; Ignaz Goldziher, *Die Richtungen der islamischen Koranauslegung*, pp. 1–54; Frederick M. Denny, "Exegesis and Recitation," esp. pp. 109ff. Further literature may be found in *EI*[2], s.v. "Ḳirā'a," p. 128a. The traditional Muslim source is Ibn al-Jazarī, *al-Nashr fī l-qirā'āt al-'ashr*. See also Labīb al-Sa'īd, *The Recited Koran*, pp. 15–60.
6. Al-Sa'īd, *Recited Koran*, pp. 19–50. This is not, however, to deny that the early specialists in Qur'ān recitation worked with the 'Uthmānic text orthography in devising or defending variant readings: See, e.g., the comments of Bergsträsser on the Qur'ān readings of al-Ḥasan al-Baṣrī, "Koranlesung des Hasan," p. 54.
7. Ibid., pp. 53–55; cf. p. 25.
8. Ibn al-Jazarī, *al-Nashr* 1: 9^{12-14}. Cf. *GdQ* 3: 118–29; Arthur Jeffery, *The Qur'ān as Scripture*, p. 98; Kristina Nelson, *The Art of Reciting the Qur'an*, pp. 2–3.
9. Bukhārī 44.4, 59.6, 66.5, 88.9, 97.53. For other occurrences of this *ḥadīth* in the classical collections, see Arendt Jan Wensinck et al., *Concordance et indices de la tradition musulmane* 1: 448b. Cf. al-Jazarī, *al-Nashr* 1: 19–22; Goldziher, *Richtungen*, 3ff., 36ff.; *GdQ* 1: 48–52; Nelson, *Art of Reciting*, App. B ("The Seven *Aḥruf* and the *Qirā'āt*"), pp. 199–201.
10. *GAS* 1: 4–13; *EI*[2], s.v. "Ḳirā'a," pp. 127b–28a; Pretzl, "Wissenschaft der Koranlesung," pp. 4ff.
11. *GAS* 1:14; Blachère, *Introduction*, pp. 127–29.
12. That this recognition did not come without struggle is indicated by the public hearing on the personal *qirā'āt* preferences of Ibn Miqsam (d. 354/965) and his subsequent forced disavowal of these, not to mention the trial and flogging of Ibn Shanabūdh (d. 328/939), which led to a similar recantation of his variant readings of even the 'Uthmānic *written* text. On Ibn Miqsam and his hearing before the sultan, see Ibn al-Jazarī, *Ghāyat al-nihāyah fī ṭabaqāt al-qurrā'* 2: 123–25; *GdQ* 3: 122–23. See also Arthur Jeffery, "The Qur'ān Readings of Ibn Miqsam." On Ibn Shanabūdh and his trial at the hands of the vizier Ibn Muqlah, see Ibn al-Jazarī, ibid. 2: 52–56; *GdQ* 3: 110–12; *EI*[2], s.v. "Ibn Sh̲anabūd̲h̲" (Rudi Paret), with further bibliography.
13. On the "seven", "ten", and "fourteen" *qirā'āt*, see Abū 'Amr 'Uthmān al-Dānī, *al-Taysīr fī l-qirā'āt al-sab'*, esp. pp. 4–16; Blachère, *Introduction*, pp. 116–32; *GdQ* 3: 186–89; al-Sa'īd, *Recited Koran*, pp. 53–56, 127–30. On actual variations on particular passages, see esp. Goldziher, *Richtungen*, pp. 4–32; Arthur Jeffery, ed., *Materials for the History of the Text of the Qur'ān;* al-Dānī, *Taysīr;* Bergsträsser, "Koranlesung des Hasan." On other variant readings, see id., ed., *Ibn Ḫālawaih's Sammlung nichtkanonischer Koranlesarten;* Edmund Beck, "Der 'ut̲mānische Kodex in der Koranlesung des zweiten Jahrhunderts." Further literature in *EI*[2], s.v. "Ḳirā'a."
14. See Nelson, *Art of Reciting*, chap. 2; Frederick M. Denny, "The *Adab* of Qur'an Recitation." Cf. Bergsträsser (and Huber), "Koranlesung in Kairo," pp. 110–34.
15. Cf. S. 25.32. *Tartīl*[an] is hard to translate adequately here; it intensifies the verb *rattala*, of which it is the verbal noun (*maṣdar*) used as a cognate accusative. On the

sense of *tartīl* as measured or slow, distinctly uttered chant, see Lane, *Lexicon,* 1028; Nelson, *Art of Reciting,* pp. 83–87; Lamyā' al-Fārūqī, "Tartīl al-Qur'ān al-Karīm," esp. pp. 106–07; *EI* 4: 601, s.v. "Tadjwīd" (Moh. Ben Cheneb).

16. Cf. Nelson, *Art of Reciting,* pp. 86–87.
17. For a detailed discussion of *murattal* and *mujawwad* styles, see Nelson, *Art of Reciting,* chap. 5, pp. 101–35. Cf. also pp. 14–18, 83–100. Note that the terminology – not only with respect to *tajwīd* but also *tartīl* – can vary in meaning from context to context: Cf. also Habib Hassan Touma, "Die Koranrezitation," pp. 87–88; M. Talbi, "La qirā'a bi-l-alhān." For a good practical understanding of the common distinction between *tartīl* (i.e., *murattal* recitation) as the accurate and measured, but less musically modulated and embellished form of recitation, and *tajwīd* (i.e., *mujawwad* recitation) in the special sense of artistically embellished, highly euphonic cantillation, see Denny's description of two different recitation sessions in modern Cairo: "*Adab* of Qur'an Recitation," pp.149–58. Denny's exclusive use of the terms *tartīl* and *tajwīd* in this article is somewhat at odds with Kristina Nelson's description of the terms used in the same environment; his article equates without further explanation *tartīl* with *murattal* and *tajwīd* with *mujawwad,* as is often done.
18. Nelson, *Art of Reciting,* esp. chap. 4, pp. 52–100. Cf. pp. 184–87. As a whole, Nelson's fine study shows how a variety of skills and disciplines, as well as more intangible qualities of mind and feeling, are involved, both in theory and practice, in *tajwīd* (esp. chaps. 2–5, 7).
19. See above, nn. 5, 13. Of works on *tajwīd,* see esp. the two standard and best-known Muslim works (to which Denny, "*Adab* of Qur'an Recitation," provides good brief descriptive introductions, pp. 145–49): Abū Zakarīyā al-Nawawī (d. 676/1277), *al-Tibyān fī ādāb ḥamalat al-Qur'ān* ("Exposition of the Proper Modes of Transmitting the Qur'ān"), and Muḥammad al-Ghazālī (d. 505/1111), "Ādāb tilāwat al-qur'ān" ("On the Proper Modes of Reciting the Qur'ān"), chap. 1.8 of his *Iḥyā' 'ulūm al-dīn* (=Ghazālī 1: 272–93; Eng. trans. by Muhammad Abul Quasem, *The Recitation and Interpretation of the Qur'an*). Of modern scholarly study of *tajwīd,* besides the recent work of Nelson and Denny, note esp. Bergsträsser, "Koranlesung in Kairo," which includes a discussion and musical settings of sample recitations by Karl Huber, pp. 113–31; Pretzl, "Wissenschaft der Koranlesung"; Jean Cantineau and Léo Barbès, "La récitation coranique à Damas et à Alger"; M. Talbi, "La qirā'a bi-l-alḥān"; Touma, "Koranrezitation"; Si Hamza Boubakeur, "Psalmodie coranique." Cf. the less adequate article by Henry George Farmer, "The Religious Music of Islām."
20. The groundwork was already laid by Gotthelf Bergsträsser, Otto Pretzl, and Arthur Jeffery as early as the 1920s and 1930s. After their deaths and the destruction of much of Pretzl's materials in Munich in World War II, such studies lapsed except for Jeffery's final work in the 1950s. More recently, several studies long and short have appeared that have supplemented the earlier, more philologically and *qirā'āt*-oriented work with material on *tajwīd,* e.g., the earlier-cited works: al-Sa'īd, *Recited Koran;* Nelson, *Art of Reciting;* Denny, "Exegesis and Recitation"; id., "*Adab* of Qur'ān Recitation"; id., "Types of Qur'ān Recitation Sessions in Contemporary Cairo." I am particularly grateful to Professor Denny for providing me with a manuscript of this last paper. Another scholar currently working on roles of the Qur'ān in Muslim piety, and interested in recitation, is Richard C. Martin. See his essay concerning the oral force and symbolic character of the text in specific societal contexts, to which he suggests application of modern hermeneutical and speech-act modes of analysis:

"Understanding the Qur'an in Text and Context." Cf. also his art. "Tilāwah," in *The Encyclopedia of Religion*, ed. Mircea Eliade et al., 16 vols. (New York: Macmillan, 1987), s.v.

21. Today the practical application of the science of recitation extends also to the careful preparation of artistically and technically correct recordings of the qur'anic text for use on radio and otherwise. See Bernard Weiss, "Al-Muṣḥaf al-Murattal"; al-Sa'īd, *Recited Koran*, pp. 65–125.
22. Cited and translated without page reference from *Munājāt Sayyidinā Mūsā* (Damascus, Cairo, n.d.) by Constance Padwick, *Muslim Devotions*, p. 114 (altered slightly to correct translator's error in rendering the Arabic definite article).
23. On *ḥifẓ*, see below, section "Muslim Education." Note that both *qirā'ah* and *tilāwah* are used to refer to recitation of the Qur'ān in general, but *qirā'ah* is the term used in compounds referring to a particular style (e.g., *al-qirā'ah bil-alḥān*), while *tilāwah* "is always general" (Nelson, *Art of Reciting*, p. 73; cf. examples in pp. 72–77). Cf. al-Fārūqī, "Tartīl al-Qur'ān", pp. 106–07. Note especially the ethical dimension lent to *tilāwah* by its double sense, "to follow" and "to recite": Cf. S. 2.121, 35.29, 27.91, and Ghazālī 1.8.introd. (=1: 272[21–22]).
24. For example, Padwick (*Muslim Devotions*, p. xxii) calls the Qur'ān "the psalter as well as the lectionary of Muslim worship."
25. *Mabānī*, p. 57. On the dating of this anonymous text, see Jeffery's preface to his edition. Note that the translation of the following passage corrects and supersedes my rendering of the phrase "sā'ir al-Qur'ān" some years ago in my *Divine Word and Prophetic Word in Early Islam*, p. 56, line 4, on which see Lane, *Lexicon*, 1282c.
26. Padwick, *Muslim Devotions*, p. 108. Cf. Ghazālī on *qirā'ah* in *ṣalāt:* 1.4.2 (=1: 153–54).
27. Bukhārī 10.94; Muslim 6.254-56; Tirmidhī 2.69; Dārimī 2.36. Cf. Ghazālī 1.4.2 (=1: 154).
28. Ghazālī, ibid.
29. For specific examples of traditional funeral recitation practices, see the description of Moroccan usage at the end of the nineteenth century by Budgett Meakin, *The Moors*, pp. 377–86 (chap. 21, "Funeral Rites"), and that of funerary practices in nineteenth-century Cairo by Edward William Lane, *An Account of the Manners and Customs of the Modern Egyptians*, pp. 511–28 (chap. 28, "Death and Funeral Rites").
30. S. 12.2, 20.113, 39.28, 41.3, 42.7, 43.3.
31. M[elchior] Yvan, *Voyages et récits*, 2 vols. (Brussels and Leghorn: Meline, Cans; Leipzig: J. P. Meline, 1853–55), vol. 2 (*Six mois chez les Malais*), p. 76. The entire anecdote is found on pp. 75–76. The translation is my own, as I have been unable to obtain a copy of the English translation apparently published in London in 1855. I am grateful to William Roff (pers. commun., 14 July 1980) for the reference to the English translation and a citation of part of the passage in question (from which it appears that the English translation is in any case rather free).
32. On traditional Muslim education, see the fine article "Education (Muslim)" in *ERE* 5:198–207 (Ignaz Goldziher), as well as the works cited in the ensuing notes to the present chapter, especially those of Dale Eickelman. Cf. also, on Moroccan education: Eduard Michaux Bellaire, "L'enseignement indigène au Maroc"; the interesting description of late-nineteenth-century education in Morocco in Meakin, *The Moors*, pp. 325; and the brief general survey of Bayard Dodge, *Muslim Education in Medieval Times* (Washington: Middle East Institute, 1962).
33. "Min a'ẓam al-balīyah tashyīkh al-ṣaḥīfah" (al-Sa'īd, *Recited Koran*, p. 54).

34. Cf. Daniel A. Wagner and Abdelhamid Lotfi, "Traditional Islamic Education in Morocco," pp. 241–42; id., "Learning to Read by 'Rote'," pp. 112–15; Dale F. Eickelman, "The Art of Memory," pp. 492–93.
35. *al-Muqaddimah* 3: 260. "Signs of (the) religion" is *sha'ā'ir al-dīn* here. On memorization and recitation as the heart of Islamic education, see also the excellent article by Dale F. Eickelman, "The Art of Memory," and chap. 3 of the same author's recent book, *Knowledge and Power in Morocco,* pp. 57–71. On the technique of teaching the Qur'ān in the traditional elementary school, see *EI* 3: 177b–80a, esp. 178a–79a, s.v. "Maktab" (L. Brunot); Ja'far Sharīf, *Islam in India, or the "Qānūn-i-Islām",* pp. 51–52; Lamin Sanneh, *The Jakhanke,* pp. 154–71. Cf. id., "The Islamic Education of an African Child."
36. "Le musulman ne met pas l'enfant à l'école coranique pour l'instruire, mais pour le former selon la tradition immuable, qui fut celle de ses propres parents et celle de ses proches," as cited from Haut Comité méditerranéen et de l'Afrique du Nord, *l'Islam dans les colonies françaises,* p. 32, by Renaud Santerre, *Pédagogie musulmane d'Afrique noire,* p. 13.
37. Santerre, *Pédagogie musulmane,* p. 145 ("un méchanisme de formation totale"). See esp. pp.13–17, 111–14, 122ff., 145–50, and passim. Cf. esp. Santerre's comment (p. 123): "L'enfant jadis était confié au *mallum* [the Qur'ān teacher] pour être initié non seulement au Coran, mais aussi à l'ensemble de la vie sociale. Le maître devait se charger de le socialiser et d'en faire un homme."
38. Eickelman, *Knowledge and Power,* pp. 62–63.
39. *al-Ayyām,* vol. 1 ([first publ. 1926–27.] Cairo: Dār al-Ma'ārif, n.d.), chaps. 5–11, pp. 28–72 (=Eng. trans. E. H. Paxton, *An Egyptian Childhood: The Autobiography of Taha Hussein* [London, 1932; repr. ed., London: Heinemann; Washington, D.C.: Three Continents, 1981], pp. 13–33). Cf. the portrait of the West African Qur'ān teacher in the autobiographical novel of Cheikh Hamidou Kane, *Ambiguous Adventure,* trans. from the French original (1962) by Katherine Woods (New York: Walker and Co., 1963), chap. 1, pp. 3–12.
40. For concrete examples from the Yemen and Senegal, see Wagner and Lotfi, "Learning to Read"; from Morocco, see id., "Traditional Islamic Education," pp. 240–44, 249–51.
41. See Denny, "Types of Qur'ān Recitation Sessions," for interesting examples from Cairo.
42. See the comments of Eickelman, *Knowledge and Power,* p. 64, on the question of "understanding" the recited text and on the development of an ability to cite contextually appropriate passages from the Qur'ān by listening to one's seniors.
43. Dārimī, sect. 18, *ḥadith* 8 of the "Muqaddimah".
44. Cited by Ghazālī 1.8.1 (=1: 273^{2-3}). This tradition is also found in the classical sources (see, e.g., Wensinck, *Concordance* 1:275b, for examples). The editorial note in my copy of Ghazālī labels this *ḥadīth* "weak" and says that it is cited in Abū Nu'aym's *Faḍā'il al-qur'ān* as well.
45. Or in each night of any month: Cf. Ghazālī 1.8.2 (=1: 276^{4}). The thirtieths, or "parts" (*ajzā';* pl. of *juz'*), are not, certainly, the only divisions of the Qur'ān used for recitative purposes: See ibid., the entire section 1.8.2(3) on divisions of the text for recitation (=1: 276^{12-19}). Cf. Edward Sell, *The Faith of Islam,* App. A.
46. Such retreats in Ramaḍān are known as *i'tiqāf;* lit.: "withdrawing, retreating". See *SEI,* s.v. "I'tikaf" (Th. W. Juynboll); *Kitāb al-fiqh 'alá l-madhāhib al-arba'a: qism al-'ibādāt* (Cairo: Wizārat al-Awqāf wal-Shu'ūn al-Ijtimā'īyah, 1387/1967), section "al-I'tiqāf," pp. 551–60.

47. *The Faith Movement of Mawlānā Muḥammad Ilyās*, p. 81. The term *khatmah*, or "completion" (lit.: "sealing") is used formally to designate the conclusion of the recitation of the entire qur'anic text from begining to end, or from any point back to the same point of the text. Muslims often recite, or attend recitation of, the entire Qur'ān during the single night of the *laylat al-qadr*. Cf. Sharīf, *Islam in India*, pp. 206–08. For another testimony (from West Africa) to the importance of Ramaḍān recitation, especially on the *laylat al-qadr*, see Santerre, *Pédagogie musulmane*, p. 108.
48. *EI*², s.v. "Dhikr" (Louis Gardet); art. "Zikr," Hughes, *Dictionary*, s.v.; Kōjirō Nakamura, *Ghazali on Prayer*, Supplement to the Bulletin of the Institute of Oriental Culture (Tokyo: University of Tokyo, 1973), pp. 10–18 (further lit., p. 11, n. 4). Cf. Haq, *Faith Movement*, pp. 54–55, 58, 63, 81.
49. Denny, "*Adab* of Qur'an Recitation," and esp. "Types of Qur'ān Recitation Sessions." There is also much information on public recitation in contemporary Cairo in Nelson, *Art of Reciting*, esp. pp. 157–73.
50. Nelson, *Art of Reciting*, pp. 167ff.
51. On the importance of *tajwīd* for accurate transmission of the text, see the comments of Nelson, ibid., pp. 114–15.
52. For an extremely informative survey of such popular use of qur'anic terms and phrases, see J. Jomier, "La place du Coran dans la vie quotidienne en Égypte." Cf. M. Piamenta, *Islam in Everyday Arabic Speech*, passim (e.g., pp. 10, 73, 75, 86; see also the index, pp. 263–64, s.v. "Qur'ān"); Padwick, *Muslim Devotions*, pp. 108ff.
53. Christian Snouck Hurgronje, *Mekka in the Latter Part of the 19th Century*, p. 29; Hughes, *Dictionary*, pp. 45–46; *EI*², s.v. "Fātiḥah" (Rudi Paret); Jomier, "Place du Coran," pp. 141, 149; Piamenta, *Islam in Everyday Speech*, p. 87.
54. See Jomier, ibid., esp. pp. 148–65, and Bess A. Donaldson, "The Koran as Magic," for diverse examples of the popular use of particular *sūrah*s and verses. See also Padwick, *Muslim Devotions*, pp. 109–20, and esp. 117ff., and Piamenta, *Islam in Everyday Speech*, p. 114, on *Yā Sīn*. On the *laylat al-barā'ah*, the 15th of the month of Sha'bān, see ibid., pp. 117–18; Hughes, *Dictionary*, p. 570 (s.v. "Shab-i-barāt"); "Mrs. Meer Hasan Ali," *Observations on the Musulmans of India*, 2 vols. (London: Parbury, Allen, 1832), pp. 300–03; Sharīf, *Islam in India*, pp. 203–04; Snouck Hurgronje, *Mekka*, p. 61.
55. Ghazālī 1.8.introd. (=1: 272^{17-18}).
56. Padwick, *Muslim Devotions*, p. 119.

Chapter 9. Voicing the Qur'ān: Questions of Meaning

1. *EI* 3: 178, s.v. "Maktab" (L. Brunot). Cf. the similar remarks of Geoffrey Parrinder about Qur'ān schools in Africa: "The Qur'ān is learnt by heart, in Arabic. . . . The children have no knowledge of what they learn, as it is entirely mechanical and alien. Perhaps it might be justified as a discipline, or a soporific, but it certainly is not education" (*Religion in an African City* [London, New York, Toronto: Oxford University Press, Geoffrey Cumberlege, 1953], p. 66). Good correctives to such views about the uselessness of pure memorization are the discussions of the "rote" character of memorization in Daniel A. Wagner and Abdelhamid Lotfi, "Learning to Read by 'Rote'" and Dale F. Eickelman, *Knowledge and Power in Morocco*, pp. 63–65.
2. James, *The Varieties of Religious Experience: A Study in Human Nature*, The Gifford Lectures on Natural Religion, Edinburgh, 1901–02 (1902; repr. ed., New York: Random House, Modern Library, n.d.), p. 53; Otto, *Das Heilige. Über das*

Irrationale in der Idee des Göttlichen und sein Verhältnis zum Rationalen (1917; repr. ed., Munich: C. H. Beck, 1963), p. 13 (cf. chaps. 1–4); Friedrich Schleiermacher, *Über die Religion. Reden an die Gebildeten unter ihren Verächtern* (Berlin, 1799; repr. in the critical ed. of R. Pünjer, Braunschweig, 1879, with original pagination of 1st ed.), pp. 52–53. These are definitions of the religious sensibility with which I can work, for they are recognizable to me in the religiousness of persons in both my own and other traditions – not least the Islamic.

Part IV. "The Lively Oracles of God": Bible as Spoken Word

Chapter 10. The Spoken Word of Christian Holy Writ

1. See Franz H. Bäuml, "Varieties and Consequences of Medieval Literacy and Illiteracy," pp. 237–39, 244; James Westfall Thompson, *The Literacy of the Laity in the Middle Ages,* esp. chap. 1; M. B. Parkes, "The Literacy of the Laity," pp. 555–56; M. L. W. Laistner, *Christianity and Pagan Culture in the Later Roman Empire,* p. 9. On literacy and textuality in medieval Europe, see Chapter 3 above. See also n. 25 below. Cf. Peter Brown, *The World of Late Antiquity, AD 150–750,* pp. 174–82.
2. For a brief, clear summary of the German and Swiss reformers' understanding of "the scripture principle", and the implications of this principle for interpretation and even communal (both ecclesial and municipal) authority, see Steven E. Ozment, *The Reformation in the Cities,* pp. 145–51. Note especially Ozment's observation that "wherever the Reformation succeeded officially, the test of scripture was its quasi-legal justification. Once subjected to this test the traditional concept, practices, and institutions of religion became vulnerable to Protestant and magisterial assault" (p. 150). On the ambiguity of meaning in the formula *sola scriptura,* see Bernd Moeller, "The German Humanists and the Beginnings of the Reformation" [Ger. orig., 1959], in *Imperial Cities and the Reformation: Three Essays,* ed. and trans. H. C. Erik Midelfort and Mark U. Edwards, Jr. (Philadelphia: Fortress Press, 1972), p. 29.
3. The parallelism between Christ and Qur'ān rather than Bible and Qur'ān has been noted by many scholars. The earliest mention of it of which I am aware is by Heinrich Frick, in his *Vergleichende Religionswissenschaft* (Berlin and Leipzig: Walter de Gruyter, 1928), pp. 16, 68–73, who, however, quotes Nathan Söderblom, without giving a specific reference, on the comparision of Christ to Qur'ān and Buddhist Dharma. Söderblom, in *The Living God: Basal Forms of Personal Religion* (London, Oxford University Press, Humphrey Milford, 1933), pp. 326–37, does discuss this analogy. Later observations on the Christ–Qur'ān analogy can be found in Wilfred Cantwell Smith, "Some Similarities and Differences between Christianity and Islam," pp. 52–53, and implicitly in Marshall G. S. Hodgson, *The Venture of Islam: Conscience and History in a World Civilization,* ed. Reuben Smith, 3 vols. (Chicago: University of Chicago Press, 1974), 2: 338.
4. For examples of Jesus' reliance upon the Hebrew scriptures, according to the Gospel authors, see Matt. 4.10, 5.17ff., 11.10, 12.3-5, 13.14-15, 15.7-9, 19.17-19, 21.16,42, 22.29; Mark 12.24,28-34, 14.49; Luke 4.4,8,12,16-21, 7.27, 19.46, 20.17,42-43; John 5.39, 7.38. On the complex nature of Paul's reliance upon these scriptures (and for a comprehensive list of Pauline allusions to or citations from scripture), see Adolf von Harnack, "Das Alte Testament in den Paulinischen Briefen und in den Paulinischen Gemeinden," in which he argues for the primacy always of the Christian gospel as *the* authority for Paul, but notes how differentially the apostle used Hebrew scripture

citations and allusions to bolster his message. Note esp. Harnack's summary statement (p. 141): "Paulus hat die Buchreligion des A.T. für die Christenheit nicht gewollt und nicht geschaffen; aber indem er neben seiner grundlegenden Konzeption von Gesetz und Evangelium, Werke und Glauben, Knechtschaft und Freiheit, die typologische Betrachtung des A.T. nicht nur bestehen ließ, sondern auch selbst übte, und indem er in einigen Fällen für Evangelisches einfach die Autorität des A.T. anrief, hat er doch die bedenklichen Entwicklungen [of 'book religion' in a negative, literalistic sense] mitverschuldet, die in den Gemeinden sich vollzogen."

5. Hans von Campenhausen, *Aus der Frühzeit des Christentums*, pp. 152–96 ("Das Alte Testament als Bibel der Kirche"), esp. pp. 154–55. See also R. P. C. Hanson, "Biblical Exegesis in the Early Church," pp. 414–16; Adolf von Harnack, *Über den privaten Gebrauch der heiligen Schriften in der alten Kirche*, pp. 28, n. 1 (=Eng. trans. p. 40, n. 1). Cf. Ferdinand Hahn, "Das Problem 'Schrift und Tradition' im Urchristentum." On the versions of the Hebrew scriptures available in the early Christian centuries, see Bleddyn J. Roberts, "The Old Testament: Manuscripts, Text and Versions."
6. E.g., *1 Clement* 4.1, 14.4, 36.3, 39.3, 48.2, 50.4,6; Ignatius, *Epistle to the Ephesians* 5.3, where citations of Hebrew scripture are introduced by *gegraptai*, "it is written". Cf. *1 Clement* 45.1, 53.1, 56.3, where the Hebrew scriptures are called "holy scriptures" (*hieras graphas*) or "holy word" (*hagios logos*). *1 Clement* alone has between 70 and 120 citations of or allusions to passages of Hebrew scripture (Campenhausen, *Aus der Frühzeit*, p. 160, n. 29). The equally early *Epistle of Barnabas* (end of 1st C.? Cf. Helmut Köster, *Einführung in das Neue Testament*, p. 715) uses Hebrew scriptural citations extensively, and, like *1 Clement* also (23.5, 34.6), introduces some of these citations as coming from "the scripture" (*hē graphē: Barnabas* 4.7, 6.12, 13.2). For an apparent reference (mid-second century) to Hebrew scripture as "the books" (="bible"), see Adolf von Harnack's argument to this effect regarding *ta biblia* in *2 Clement* 14.2, where it occurs alongside *hoi apostoloi* for the Gospels, or possibly Gospels and Epistles. Not all of the other examples discussed by Harnack are as clear. ("Über das Alter der Bezeichnung 'die Bücher' ('die Bibel') für die H. Schriften in der Kirche," pp. 339–40).
7. See the previous note and references given there, and Campenhausen, *Aus der Frühzeit*, pp. 157–62. The words of Arthur Darby Nock are apposite here: "From the beginning Christians were in a situation which made for a greater emphasis on the prophets and a smaller or qualified emphasis on the Pentateuch" (cited among the *obiter dicta* presented in Nock's *Essays on Religion and the Ancient World*, ed. Zeph Stewart, 2 vols. [Cambridge, Mass.: Harvard University Press, 1972], p. 965).
8. Cf. the connection of sacred writings and divine authority in what Ernst Robert Curtius calls the "Buchmetaphorik" already to hand in the Hebrew scriptures (refs. in his *Europäische Literatur und lateinisches Mittelalter*, pp. 314–15 [=Eng. trans. pp. 310–11]; but see the following note).
9. On the Jewish influence, with special regard to the liturgy and the reading from scripture in particular, see: W. O. E. Oesterley, *The Jewish Background of the Christian Liturgy*, pp. 38–40, 84–100, 111–21; Paul Glaue, *Die Vorlesung heiliger Schriften im Gottesdienste*, pp. 1–20, 38–40, inter alia; J. A. Lamb, "The Place of the Bible in the Liturgy," pp. 563–65; Gregory Dix, *The Shape of the Liturgy*, pp. 37–40. Wilhelm Bousset, *Kurios Christos. Geschichte des Christusglaubens von den Anfängen des Christentums bis Irenaeus* ([1914?]; 2nd rev. ed., Göttingen: Vandenhoeck & Ruprecht, 1921), pp. 297–98, notes especially the Jewish background of scripture reading, sermon, and prayer, the three major elements in the early

Christian liturgy of the Word (*Wortgottesdienst*). But see also D. Walter Bauer, *Der Wortgottesdienst der ältesten Christen* (esp. pp. 5, 18–20, 37–38), where it is argued that the synagogue had little or no influence on Christian worship before the third century at the earliest, especially not (pace Glaue) on the regular reading of Hebrew scripture, which Bauer holds to have been impossible (if only because of the cost and size of a codex) for the first two Christian centuries (pp. 39–48). If Glaue's arguments push meager evidence too far on some points, Bauer's skepticism, at least about the second century, seems hardly better justified. Although the general influence of Judaic traditions on Christian origins is indisputable, it would seem that the actual direct influence of synagogal Judaism in particular came to bear only after the first century or so. See Gerhard Delling, *Worship in the New Testament*, pp. 6–7, 42–43, 92–103 (=Ger. ed. pp. 18–19, 50–51, 89–98), who argues more persuasively than Bauer for a rejection of synagogal influence on worship in the primitive Christian community, but recognizes the later (2nd C.?) adoption by the emerging Church of Jewish patterns of worship (see esp. p. 43, n. 5).

10. Johannes Leipoldt and Siegfried Morenz, *Heilige Schriften*, p. 118. Cf. Curtius's comment (p. 314; =Eng. trans. p. 310): "Seine höchste Weihe wurde dem Buch durch das Christentum zuteil. Es war eine Religion des heiligen Buches. Christus ist der einzige Gott, den uns die antike Kunst mit einer Buchrolle darstellt." Neither Curtius nor Leipoldt and Morenz commit themselves on the date by which this occurred. Von Campenhausen notes that primitive Christianity is not to be understood as a "religion of the Book", citing Celsus in the late second century as one for whom it was still not such (*Aus der Frühzeit*, pp. 156–57), but noting also how much the development of a "scripture-principle" in Christianity is to be associated with Justin Martyr (ibid., pp. 180–91). On this question, see what follows, esp. nn. 14, 15 below.
11. Walter J. Ong, *The Presence of the Word*, p. 14. The greatly increased number of papyri from the early Christian centuries that have become available through finds in Palestine and especially Egypt tend to support Ong's rather hyperbolic (and wholly undocumented) characterization. See the excellent overview of T. C. Skeat, "Early Christian Book-Production," and the works cited there and also in the bibliography (*Camb. Hist. Bib.* 2: 512–13).
12. Harnack, *Über privaten Gebrauch*, pp. 33–37 (=Eng. trans. pp. 48–53). Harnack's book as a whole attempts to document by detailed reference to the sources just how widespread the reading of scripture by private individuals was in the first Christian centuries – in marked contrast to the mystery religions in which holy texts were commonly kept secret and withheld from all save the initiated. See also Leipoldt and Morenz, *Heilige Schriften*, pp. 88–114 ("Vorlesung und Geheimhaltung"), esp. pp. 110 (on "apocrypha"), 115–22 ("Das häusliche Lesen"). This evidence may offer some of the best arguments for the "book" orientation of the tradition that developed in the second and third centuries.
13. Glaue, *Vorlesung heiliger Schriften*, esp. pp. 14–20, 22–27; Oscar Cullmann, *Urchristentum und Gottesdienst*, pp. 26–27 (=Eng. trans pp. 24–25); Leipoldt and Morenz, *Heilige Schriften*, pp. 108–14; Lamb, "Place of the Bible," pp. 565–72; Eric Werner, *The Sacred Bridge*, pp. 58–63. Cf. nn. 15, 17 below.
14. *Apolog.* 67.3; *2 Clement* 2.4. See also n. 15 below. Cf. the importance ascribed to to the scriptures in 2 Timothy 3.15-17: "all scripture is inspired by God [*theopneustos*] and profitable for teaching, for reproof, for correction, and for training in righteousness." On the generally accepted dating of these texts to a period no later than the middle of the second century C.E., see Köster, *Einführung*, pp. 670–73

(*2 Clement*), 744 (the Pastoral Epistles), 779–80 (Justin's *First Apology*); cf. Edgar J. Goodspeed, *A History of Early Christian Literature,* rev. Robert M. Grant (Chicago: University Press, Phoenix Books, 1966), pp. 87–90 (*2 Clement*), 101–05 (Justin).

15. Justin (*Apolog.* 67.3) says that on Sundays "the memoires [called "gospels" in 66.7] of the Apostles and the writings of the prophets are read" ("ta apomnēmoneumata tōn apostolōn ē ta suggrammata tōn prophētōn anaginōsketai"). See Glaue, *Vorlesung heiliger Schriften,* pp. 62–71, for a detailed discussion of this passage; he argues on pp. 67–68 that for Justin the "prophets" included Moses, David, Solomon, etc., and hence the term refers to the Hebrew scriptures in general (on possible confirmation of this in *2 Clement,* see chap. 14.2 [discussed in n. 6 above] and cf. Glaue, ibid., pp. 71–78). It may, of course, be that the reference to the prophets here is only to the *n^e^vī'îm* and *k^e^tūvîm* as distinguished from the Pentateuch (see Werner, *Sacred Bridge,* p. 96, n. 27). The earliest clear and detailed description of the lesson in the early church is in the *Apostolic Constitutions* (probably of late 4th C. Syrian origin, but containing much older traditions), which lists two lessons from the Hebrew scriptures, one from the Acts of the Apostles, one from the Epistles, and one from the Gospels (*Apost. Const.* 2) and, in another passage, five pericopes for the lesson: from the Law, Prophets, Epistles, Acts, and Gospels (*Apost. Const.* 8; cited in Werner, *Sacred Bridge,* pp. 58–59). See also Egeria, *Diary of a Pilgrimage,* chaps. 24–26 (on the dating of this famous pilgrimage account, see the trans.'s introduction, pp. 12–15). On the general problem of the scripture *lectio* in the early church liturgy, see Werner, *Sacred Bridge,* pp. 58–101; Leipoldt and Morenz, *Heilige Schriften,* pp. 106–14; Oesterley, *Jewish Background,* pp. 111–21; Glaue, *Vorlesung heiliger Schriften* (and the same author's sequel studies, "Die Vorlesung heiliger Schriften bei Cyprian," and "Die Vorlesung heiliger Schriften bei Tertullian,"). Note that Glaue's emphasis upon the importance of the reading from the Hebrew scriptures in the early Christian community has been contested by Bauer, *Wortgottesdienst,* pp. 39–48; Bauer does not, however, deny the importance of these scriptures for the earliest (apostolic) period apart from their use or nonuse in public worship, nor apparently the possible later influence of Torah reading on Christian worship after ca. 100–150 C.E.

16. Glaue, "Vorlesung bei Tertullian," pp. 148-49; cf. Lamb, "Place of the Bible," pp. 571-72. Concerning specifically the Pauline letters, see Eduard Norden, *Die antike Kunstprosa vom VI. Jahrhundert v. Chr. bis in die Zeit der Renaissance,* p. 538, who notes that stylistically Paul's letters themselves were, like many other letters of the period, written to be read aloud. He describes them as for the most part nothing but "ein notwendiger Ersatz für die mündliche Rede." That Paul himself clearly intended them to be read to the congregation is evident from Col. 4.16 and 1 Thess. 5.27.

17. I.e., in the often-cited passage that explains why the writer of the "Canon" excludes the prophetic-apocalyptic *Shepherd of Hermas* from his list of scriptural books. After indicating that it is to be excluded primarily because of its recent (i.e., postapostolic) authorship, the writer notes: "Therefore it must indeed be read, but cannot be publicly recited to the people in church – neither among the prophets, whose number is filled, nor among the apostles, who taught at the end of the times" ("et ideo legi eum quidem oportet, se publicare vero in ecclesia populo neque inter prophetas completo numero neque inter apostolos in fine temporum potest"). Cited from Hans von Campenhausen, *The Formation of the Christian Bible,* p. 257 (discussion of the passage, pp. 256–59) [=Ger. orig. ed. pp. 298, 297–300, respectively]. This Muratorian passage is referred to and quoted in numerous other discussions of the canon issue: e.g., Glaue, *Vorlesung heiliger Schriften,* pp. 81–82; Leipoldt and

Morenz, *Heilige Schriften*, p. 27; Carl Andresen, *Die Kirchen der alten Christenheit*, pp. 156–57 (where the author also notes [p. 156] that, still earlier, Marcion's "canon" of Christian scripture had been formulated with a view to communal worship: "man bezeichnete als 'kanonisch', was vor der Gemeinde verlesen werden durfte"). Concerning the "Muratorian Canon" more generally, see von Campenhausen, *Entstehung*, pp. 282–303 (=Eng. trans. pp. 243–62); Köster, *Einführung*, p. 439. Cf. the warning of Cyril of Jerusalem (d. 386) that Christians should not read for themselves any writings not read publicly in worship (*Catecheses* 4.33,36, as cited in Leipoldt and Morenz, *Heilige Schriften*, p. 110).

18. Adolf von Harnack, "Über den Ursprung des Lectorats und der anderen niederen Weihen"; Andresen, *Kirchen der alten Christenheit*, p. 209; Lamb, "Place of the Bible", pp. 574–75; Glaue, "Vorlesung bei Cyprian," pp. 208–13; cf. id., "Vorlesung bei Tertullian," pp. 151–52; *CE* 9: 111 (s.v. "Lector"); Leipoldt and Morenz, *Heilige Schriften*, p. 114; Werner, *Sacred Bridge*, pp. 121–22. Early (e.g., mid-3rd C.) mention of the lector can be found in *2 Clement* 19.1 (=*Apost. Fathers* 1: 158); *Apost. Const.* 8.22. A clear testimony to the presence of lectors responsible for the copies of scripture from which they read to the congregation is found in an official account of a local imperial proceeding against a Christian bishop and his church in Cirta (modern Constantine, Algeria), on May 19, 303, during the persecution of Diocletian. The text is translated *in extenso* in Dix, *Shape of the Liturgy*, pp. 24–26. According to Dix (p. 35), the "minor orders", including that of lector, were already in existence as appointive offices by 200 C.E.

19. As, e.g., in Carthage: Glaue, "Vorlesung bei Cyprian," p. 204. Even nearly a century earlier, Justin Martyr (d. ca. 165 C.E.) describes an instance in which the liturgy of the Word, or *synaxis*, and the Eucharist were celebrated together (*Apolog*. 67.1). Dix, *Shape of the Liturgy*, pp. 36–37, citing Justin and other evidence, sees the *synaxis* and the Eucharist as the two originally separate parts of Christian worship that were often joined between the second and fourth centuries, after which they "were gradually fused, until they came everywhere to be considered inseparable parts of a single rite." Lamb, "Place of the Bible," p. 568, also cites Justin and, pace Cullmann (*Urchristentum und Gottesdienst*, pp. 32–34; =Eng. trans. pp. 30–32), agrees with Dix (p. 566), citing Tertullian's statement that in his time (mid-3rd C.) it was still the case that "'either the sacrifice is offered, or the word of God is ministered' (*De Cult. Fem.* II, xi, 2)." Beryl Smalley, *The Study of the Bible in the Middle Ages*, pp. 11–12 (citing H. de Lubac and J. Daniélou), remarks that, in discussing the sacraments, Origen (d. ca. 251/254) "puts more emphasis on Scripture than on the Eucharist; [for him] the Logos was incarnate in the flesh of the holy text." Certainly Origen's well-known emphasis upon the scriptural word would have fitted well with a church order in which that word played a major part alongside the Eucharistic celebration.

20. Dobschütz, "Bible in the Church," p. 603; "Preaching (Christian)" (J. Stalker), *ERE* 10: 215a; Lamb, "Place of the Bible," pp. 575–77. Cf. the statement of Egeria about the Sunday dawn service on Golgotha in Jerusalem (presumably in the early 5th C.): "These sermons are given every Sunday so that the people may be instructed in the Scriptures and the love of God" (*Diary*, chap. 25).

21. Egeria, *Diary*, chaps. 24–25; Werner, *Sacred Bridge*, pp. 129–33; Dobschütz, "Bible in the Church," p. 605; Oesterley, *Jewish Background*, pp. 148–49; Dix, *Shape of the Liturgy*, pp. 39–40; Lamb, "Place of the Bible," pp. 568–70, with many primary-source references. On the evident inclination to hymnody in the time of Paul, see Col. 3.16 and other references given in Leipoldt and Morenz, *Heilige Schriften*, p. 118.

22. Emmanuel von Severus, "Das Wort 'Meditari' im Sprachgebrauch der Heiligen Schrift," pp. 370–71: "Kein Buch der Heiligen Schriften wurde in der Liturgie der Kirche häufiger verwandt, von den Kirchenvätern eifriger und eingehender erklärt, als das Buch der Psalmen. Noch für Gregor d. Gr. galt die Kenntnis der psalmen als Maßstab des theologischen Wissens. Nur solche Kandidaten sollten die Priesterweihe erhalten, die den Wortlaut der Psalteriums beherrschten. Diese Psalmverse waren so sehr Eigentum der Prediger geworden, daß sie immer wieder zitiert und geradezu ein Bestandteil ihrer Sprache wurden. Das bedeutet nicht Geringeres, als daß mit der Zeit auch der Bedeutungsinhalt zahlreicher in den Psalmen verwendeter Wörter in den dort bestimmten Gebrauch in die theologische und aszetische Literatur überging." Cf. Aidan Kavanagh, *Elements of Rite* (New York: Pueblo, 1982), p. 36. The major role of the Psalms in history, especially in the West, has been repeatedly studied. The classic survey is that written by Rowland E. Prothero at the beginning of this century: *The Psalms in Human Life* (extensive bibliography in his App. A).
23. Friedrich Heiler, *Die Ostkirchen*, pp. 197, 199–204, 213; Andresen, *Kirchen der alten Christenheit*, pp. 237–40 (cf. p. 660); "Brevier" (J. Pascher), *LTK* 2: 679a–84b; *CE*, s.v. "Lectionary"; "Evangeliaria"; "Breviary"; *ODCC*^{2}, s.v. "Lectionary"; "Evangeliary"; "Epistolary"; "Hymnary"; "Breviary"; *The New Schaff–Herzog Encyclopaedia of Religious Knowledge* (Grand Rapids, Mich., 1952), s.v. "Evangeliarium"; *RGG*^{3}, s.v. "Stundenbuch", "Stundengebet".
24. Laistner, *Christianity and Pagan Culture*, pp. 9, 29; Ernst von Dobschütz, *Die Bibel im Leben der Völker*, p. 29; Leipoldt and Morenz, *Heilige Schriften*, p. 120 (citing as their main authority Eusebius [d. ca. 340]). Cf. the words of *1 Clement* to the congregations to whom the author writes: "You know [*epístasthe*] the holy scriptures well" (53.1). The percentage of Christians who could not read probably grew in size from the latter days of the Western Roman Empire to Carolingian times, even though the wholesale illiteracy of laypersons, including the nobility, was exaggerated by earlier medieval scholarship: See Thompson, *Literacy of the Laity*, esp. chap. 1 (on literacy and textuality in early and medieval Christianity, see Chapter 3 of the present volume; cf. n. 1 above). Bauer, *Wortgottesdienst*, pp. 42–43, stresses the cost factor as a major obstacle to even an entire church purchasing a copy of the Septuagint text. More recent scholarship takes a much more optimistic view of the wide distribution and use of papyri codices of scripture (Skeat, "Early Christian Book-Production," esp. pp. 54–55, 59, 65–69, 71). A dearth of literacy would of course still not have prevented the Christians' being unusually "book-bound", either in their emphasis upon the liturgical and instructional use of scripture, or in their reverence for and attachment to it – an attachment negatively attested by the concerted attempts to destroy Christian books (=scriptural codices) in the imperial persecutions, notably that of Diocletian beginning in 303. Cf. Dobschütz, *Bibel im Leben*, pp. 28, 44–47; for an example, see the incident quoted in Dix, *Shape of the Liturgy*, pp. 24–26 (cited above, n. 18).
25. Leipoldt and Morenz, *Heilige Schriften*, p. 120. Cf. Dobschütz, *Bibel im Leben*, p. 29; Hans Rost, *Die Bibel im Mittelalter*, p. 17. On the memorization of scripture by the Christian child, cf. *Apost. Const.* 4.11.
26. ". . . quam erat omnium sensibus memoriaeque inveteratum, et tot aetatum successionibus decantatum" (Letter 71, =*PL* 33: 242–43); cited in W. Schwarz, *Principles and Problems of Biblical Translation*, p. 38. On pre-Jerome Latin translations of the Hebrew scriptures, see Harnack, *Über privaten Gebrauch*, pp. 32–33 (=Eng. trans. pp. 46–47); Roberts, "The Old Testament", pp. 24–25. On Latin translations of New Testament writings in the same period, see C. S. C. Williams, "The History of the Text and Canon of the New Testament to Jerome," pp. 36–39.

27. "Et ego legere volo. Plus enim me delectat hujus verbi esse lectorem, quam verbi mei disputatorem" (Sermon 355.1; =*PL* 39: 1574; cited also by Denys Gorce, *La lectio divina*, p. X).
28. *De officiis ministrorum* 1.20.88 (ed. Georg Krabinger, Tübingen, 1857, p. 62; also in *PL* 16: 50): "Cur non illa tempora, quibus ab ecclesia vacas, lectioni impendas? Cur non Christum revisas, Christum adloquaris, Christum audias? Illum adloquimur, cum oramus, ilum audimus, cum divina legimus oracula." For a German trans. of this passage, see Gerhard Schneider, "Bibel und Meditation," p. 25. On scripture as God speaking, see also Leipoldt and Morenz, *Heilige Schriften*, p. 53, n. 1 (citing Harnack, *Über privaten Gebrauch*, p. 46, n. 1); Robert Will, *Le culte*, II: 81–82; and Peter Brown's comment about Augustine's sense of the scriptural word in n. 32 below.
29. Cf. above, esp. n. 13, and Kavanagh, *Elements of Rite*, p. 36.
30. Smalley, *Study of the Bible*, p. 1, note 2. Cf. her remarks about such comparison (ibid., p. 1): "Claudius of Turin sums up the patristic tradition as it had reached the scholars of Charlemagne's day. The Word is incarnate in Scripture, which like man has a body and soul. The body is the words of the sacred text, the 'letter', and the literal meaning; the soul is the spiritual sense. To explain the literal sense is to expound *litteraliter vel carnaliter; littera* is almost interchangeable with *corpus*."
31. "Ignoratio scripturarum ignoratio Christi est" (*In Isaiam*, prol. 1, =*PL* 24: 17). This and similar dicta of Jerome are also cited in *Dict. spir*. 4.1: 153a (s.v. "Écriture sainte et vie spirituelle" [sect. author: Paul Antin]). On the church fathers' command of the holy scriptures and sense of their importance, see Rost, *Bibel im Mittelalter*, pp. 16–17. For numerous patristic citations illustrative of this point, see the rather uncritical study of Louis Leloir, "La lecture de l'Écriture selon les anciens Pères."
32. Peter Brown, *Augustine of Hippo*, p. 254. Note also Brown's characterization (p. 259) of Augustine as preacher-teacher: ". . . even the world of nature was only God's 'dumb show': what interested him far more was the spoken word, the speech of god committed to a book, 'an eloquence, teaching salvation, perfectly adjusted to stir the hearts of all learners' [*Confessions* XII, xxvi, 36]."
33. A history nicely sketched in its general outlines by Dobschütz, *Bibel im Leben*, and, in greater detail (if not always very critically) for the medieval West by Rost, *Bibel im Mittelalter*.

Chapter 11. God's Word in the Desert

1. For a lively and succinct overview of the origins of desert monasticism, see the early chapters of Derwas Chitty, *The Desert a City*, esp. chaps. 1 and 2 for Antonian and Pachomian monasticism. The classical treatment is that of Stephan Schiwietz [Siwiec], in vol. 1 of *Das morgenländische Mönchtum*, pp. 48–224. See also the systematic treatment of Karl Heussi, *Der Ursprung des Mönchtums*, esp. 69–131 on Antony and the Pachomian tradition, as well as the brief but informative summary of "the transition from asceticism to monasticism" by Bernhard Lohse, *Askese und Mönchtum in der Antike und in der alten Kirche*, pp. 173–77 (see also pp. 183–210).
2. Armand Veilleux, *La liturgie dans le cénobitisme pachômien au quatrième siècle*, pp. 167–97, esp. 167–81 ("monastère-église" and "koinonia ecclésiale" are Veilleux's terms: see pp. 181–95). Cf. Owen Chadwick, *John Cassian*, p. 6. On the comparison of the ascetic "styles" of these two desert saints, see Heinrich Bacht, "Antonius und Pachomius." Cf. Lohse, *Askese und Mönchtum*, pp. 190–204, esp. 202–04; J. Gribomont, "Obéissance et Évangile selon saint Basile le Grand," pp.

192-93. On Pachomius and the general history and character of the Pachomian movement, see Fidelis Ruppert, *Das pachomianische Mönchtum und die Anfänge klösterlichen Gehorsams*, pp. 11-365, esp. pp. 11-103, 159-281; Heinrich Bacht, "Pakhôme et ses disciples," in *Théol. vie mon.*, pp. 39-71; Paulin Ladeuze, *Étude sur le cénobitisme Pakhomien pendant le IVe siècle et la primière moitié du Ve*, pp. 155-305; Heussi, *Ursprung*, pp.115-31.

3. For the traditional account of Pachomius' early life, conversion, and anchoritic apprenticeship, see *PK* 1: 24-38, 298-304 (=*SBo* 2-15; G^1 2-11).
4. On the beginnings of Pachomius' communities according to the traditional sources, see *PK* 1: 39-43, 305-07, 427-30 (=*SBo* 17-19; G^1 12-15; S^1 6-10).
5. The precise death date of Horsiesius, who served as Pachomius' successor as abbot at Tabennesi from 346 to 351 and again after Theodore's death in 368, is uncertain. The dating of his death in the patriarchate of Theophilos of Alexandria (385-412) follows the deductions from references in two early manuscripts offered by Heinrich Bacht in "Studien zum 'Liber Orsiesii'," pp. 107-10, and *Vermächtnis* 1: 24-28.
6. *PK* 1: 361-62 (=G^1 95).
7. On the question of demonstrable influence, see, e.g., Charles De Clercq, "L'influence de la règle de saint Pachôme en Occident," which focuses on translations of Pachomian rules and parallels between these rules and major later rules. The epochal character of Pachomius' organization of cenobitic communities for the general history of Christian monasticism was recognized as early as the first half of the fifth century by the Greek Church historian Sozomen (*Historia ecclesiastica* [ed. Hussey, 3 vols., Oxford, 1860], 3.14.5 [p. 266], as cited and quoted in O. Grützmacher, *Pachomius und das älteste Klosterleben*, p. 96). A very brief overview of the transmission of Pachomian, Antonian, and other Eastern monastic influence from Egypt and Syria-Palestine to Europe and elsewhere is given by David Knowles in his *Christian Monasticism*, pp. 15-33. On the later influence of what Heinrich Bacht calls the "Eigenart" of the "pachomianisches Mönchsideal", see his "Die Rolle der Heiligen Schrift bei Horsiesius", p. 191 (further lit. in n. 3).
8. Friedrich Heiler, *Die Ostkirchen*, pp. 255-56; cf. W. H. Mackean, *Christian Monasticism in Egypt to the Close of the Fourth Century*, p. 150.
9. Heiler, *Ostkirchen*, p. 256. Heiler notes that, even in relatively recent times, one of the most famous Russian monks and saints, Seraphim of Sarow [d. 1833], used the Pachomian *Praecepta* as his daily reading (p. 256).
10. For a discussion of significant differences from, as well as continuities with and possible influences of Pachomian monasticism upon Basilian/Cappadocian forms, see Emmanuel Amand de Mendieta, "Le système cénobitique basilien comparé au système cénobitique pachômien," esp. pp. 33-34, 37-39, 47-50, 52-54, 62-65, 69-71; see also id. ["David Amand"], *L'ascèse monastique de saint Basile*, pp. 45-52.
11. In 335-37 at Trier and in 339-46 at Rome (Knowles, *Christian Monasticism*, p. 25). Cf. De Clercq, "L'influence de la règle," p. 171.
12. On how Jerome came to undertake this translation (from Greek translations of the original Coptic texts), see *Vermächtnis* 1: 9-12; and Armand Veilleux 's Introduction to *PK* 2, esp. pp. 7-13. The texts translated by Jerome include the rules and institutes of Pachomius, Theodore, and Horsiesius, as well as letters of all three and the "Testament" of Horsiesus, often known as the *Liber Orsiesii*. The Latin texts in Jerome's translation have been collected and edited by Amand Boon in his *Pachomiana Latina*. They are included among the texts translated into English by Armand Veilleux in *PK* 2 and *PK* 3.
13. I.e., the "Cenobitic Institutions", *De institutis coenobiorum*, and the "Conferences",

Conlationes. See Chadwick, *John Cassian,* esp. chaps. II and VI; cf. Julien Leroy, "Le cénobitisme chez Cassien." Cassian's influence extended also to Eastern monasticism; a Greek translation of his works must have been in circulation as early as the fifth century (Chadwick, p. 157).

14. Palladius treats Pachomian monasticism in a few brief passages and the connected narrative of chaps. 32-34 of his *Historia Lausiaca* (*Hist. Laus.* 2: 26, 48, 52-53, 87-100; =*PK* 2: 123-32). On the problems of using Cassian's and Palladius' reports on Pachomian life as sources for accurate information about the Pachomian monasteries and their history, see the excellent discussion by Armand Veilleux in his excursus, "La valeur de Pallade et de Cassien pour la connaissance du monachisme pachômien," in *La liturgie,* pp. 138–54.
15. On parallel passages in, and comparison of, the Rules of Benedict and Pachomius, see De Clercq, "L'influence de la règle," pp. 175–76; Placide Deseille, "Eastern Christian Sources of the Rule of Saint Benedict," esp. pp. 109–16.
16. Denys Gorce, *La lectio divina,* pp. xvi-xxix, 63-80. Cf. Jean-Marie Leroux, "Monachisme et communauté chrétienne d'après saint Jean Chrysostome," in *Théol. vie mon.,* p.156; Jean Leclercq, "La lecture divine"; René Draguet, trans., *Les pères du désert,* pp. XL–XLIII. On *lectio divina* generally, see Jean Leclercq, *L'amour des lettres et le désir de dieu,* pp. 19–23, 71–73 (=Eng. trans. pp. 13–16, 72–73). For a modern interpretation, see Robert McGregor, "Monastic Lectio Divina," 54–56.
17. *PG* 79: 1473 (Saying/Apophthegma no. 4): *aschēsis monachou, meletē Graphōn, kai poiēsis entolōn tou theou.* Hyperechios apparently lived at the beginning of the fourth century - where (lower Egypt or Syria–Palestine?) is not clear (Ferdinand Poswick, "Les apophtegmes d'Hyperechios. L'ascèse du moine, méditation des écritures," *Coll. cist.* 32 (1970), pp. 232–33; see ibid., p. 245 for text and French translation of the cited saying). On the translation of *meletē graphōn* with "meditation *of* the scriptures" instead of the more familiar "meditation *on* the scriptures," see below, section "Meditation."
18. On the key role of the scriptures in Christian monasticism generally, and for further references to relevant literature, see esp. Claude Peifer, "The Biblical Foundations of Monasticism". Cf. Gorce, *Lectio divina,* pp. xvi–xxix. See also James McMurray, "The Scriptures and Monastic Prayer". On Cassian's emphasis on scripture: Franz Bauer, "Die Heilige Schrift bei den Mönchen des christlichen Altertums"; *Dict. spir.* 4.1: 163–64 ("Écriture sainte et vie spirituelle," sect. II.A.4.3: "Cassien" [Jean-Claude Guy]); Chadwick, *John Cassian,* pp. 101–02. On the Benedictines: Sigismund Pawlowsky, *Die biblischen Grundlagen der Regula Benedicti,* esp. pp. 10–11 (further lit.), 34–102; Peifer, "Biblical Foundations," pp. 17–19 (see p. 17, n. 36, for further lit.); Emmanuel von Severus, "Zu den biblischen Grundlagen des Mönchtums"; *Dict. spir.* 4.1: 167–69 ("Écriture sainte et vie spirituelle," sect. II.A.4.6: "Saint Benoît" [Jean Gaillard]). For Basilian, or Cappadocian, monasticism, see Margaret Gertrude Murphy, *St. Basil and Monasticism,* pp. 35–42; Amand de Mendieta, "Le système cénobitique basilien," pp. 35 (esp. n. 2), 44–45; id., *L'ascèse monastique,* pp. 82–85, 265, 326–33; J. Gribomont, "Les Règles Morales de saint Basile et le Nouveau Testament"; id., "Obéissance et Évangile," esp. pp. 202–03, 213–15.
19. On the crucial place of scripture in Pachomian and other early monasticism, see: Heinrich Bacht, "Vom Umgang mit der Bibel im ältesten Mönchtum"; id., "Rolle der Heiligen Schrift," pp.191–212; id., "Pachôme et ses disciples," in *Théol. vie mon.,* pp. 40, 42–47, 71; Ruppert, *Das pachomianische Mönchtum,* pp. 128–58 ("Die Heilige Schrift als Norm"); P. Resch, *La doctrine ascétique des premiers maîtres égyptiens du quatrième siècle,* pp. 138–67, esp. 157–67; Corbinian Gindele, "Die

Schriftlesung im Pachomiuskloster"; Veilleux, *La liturgie*, chap. 5: "L'Écriture sainte dans la Koinonia pachômienne," pp. 262–75 [trans., with some omissions, but with some additional English refs., as: "Holy Scripture in the Pachomian Koinonia"; Gorce, *Lectio divina*, pp. 63–80 ("L'étude et la méditation des Écritures d'après les fondateurs du monachisme oriental et la Régle de Pakhôme"); *Dict. spir.* 4.1: 160–61 ("Écriture sainte et vie spirituelle," sect. II.A.4.1: "Le cénobitisme pachômien" [Jean-Claude Guy]); G. M. Columbas, "La Biblia en la espiritualidad del monacato primitivo"; Hermann Dörries, "Die Bibel im ältesten Mönchtum"; Adalbert de Vogüé, "*Sub Regula uel Abbate*," pp. 31–35; Murphy, *St. Basil and Monasticism*, pp. 35–44. Note that a few scholars have raised some questions about the degree of "scriptural awareness" that is actually to be found in the earliest monasticism. See Wilhelm Bousset, *Apophthegmata*, pp. 82–83; cf. 90–93; Heussi, *Ursprung des Mönchtums*, pp. 276–80; and esp. Dörries, "Bibel im ältesten Mönchtum." However, as Bacht has noted ("Vom Umgang mit der Bibel," p. 557), these scholars have concentrated upon the eremitic "desert fathers" rather than upon the earlier Pachomian sources.

20. As Ruppert points out, "Manche Schriften der Pachomianer bilden gleichsam ein Mosaik aus Schrifttexten" (*Das pachomianische Mönchtum*, p. 128). Cf. the Preface of Veilleux to *PK* 1: xxvii, where the same point is stressed. (Veilleux also notes that the rather free quotations typical of the Pachomian sources are evidently based on a Sahidic Coptic version of the scriptures or on the Septuagint rather than upon the Hebrew scriptures or the Greek New Testament.) The massive presence of scriptural references and citations throughout the Pachomian corpus is readily apparent. See, for example, the careful annotations in the text editions of Louis Théodore Lefort (*PVSS*, *PVBS* 1, *OPD* 1), Amand Boon (*Pach. lat.*), and François Halkin (*PVG*, *Corp. Ath.*). Biblical references are similarly well identified (and, because of the margin-reference format, visually still more vivid) in Veilleux's superbly annotated translation of all the major Pachomian documents, *Pachomian Koinonia (PK)*. See also the "Biblical Index" in *PK* 3: 237–96. The most profuse and continual use of scriptural allusions and citations in the Pachomian corpus is to be found in the writings attributed to Horsiesius: his *Letters* and his *Instructions* (*PK* 3: 135–65; =*OPD* 1: 63–80), his *Regulations* (*PK* 2: 197–220; =*OPD* 1: 82–99), and most of all, his *Testament* (*PK* 3: 171–215; =*Pach. lat.*, pp. 109–47). The frequency of Biblical citations in Horsiesius' writings specifically has been studied in some detail by Pio Tamburrino in his article, "Bibbia e vita spirituale negli scritti di Orsiesi," and, more especially with regard to the "Testament" (or "Liber"), by Bacht, "Rolle der Heiligen Schrift," esp. pp. 192–95.
21. Peifer, "Biblical Foundations of Monasticism," p. 14.
22. *PK* 1: 117 (=*SBo* 88). Cf. n. 30 below.
23. *PK* 3: 118 (=*Theod. Instr.* 43).
24. On medieval monastic libraries, see David Leistle, "Über Klosterbibliotheken des Mittelalters," esp. pp. 367–77; Émile Lesne, *Les livres, "scriptoria" et bibliothèques du commencement du VIIIe à la fin du XIe siècle*, pp. 465–804, esp. pp. 767–69.
25. There has been considerable debate as to the original source and *Sitz im Leben* of the Nag Hammadi library. An overview of the debate and the basic theories proposed can be gleaned from three articles in particular: Torgny Säve-Söderbergh, "Holy Scriptures or Apologetic Documentations? The 'Sitz im Leben' of the Nag Hammadi Library," in *Les Textes de Nag Hammadi. Colloque du Centre d'Histoire des Religions (Strasbourg, 23–25 octobre 1974)*, ed. Jacques-É. Ménard, Nag Hammadi Studies, 7 (Leiden: E. J. Brill, 1975), p. 3–14; Frederik Wisse, "Gnosticism and Early Monasticism in Egypt," in *Gnosis. Festschrift für Hans Jonas*, ed. Barbara

Aland et al. (Göttingen: Vandenhoeck & Ruprecht, 1978), pp. 431–40; and Charles W. Hedrick, "Gnostic Proclivities in the Greek *Life of Pachomius* and the *Sitz im Leben* of the Nag Hammadi Library," *Novum Testamentum* (1980), pp. 78–94. Säve-Söderbergh proposes that the Nag Hammadi Mss were part of a Pachomian collection of diverse Gnostic texts assembled for purposes of refuting heresies (including some Gnostic teachings) in favor of an emerging "orthodoxy". Wisse and Hedrick argue that within the Pachomian monasteries there was a probable diversity of theological points of view and certain affinities for Gnostic ideas consonant with asceticism, both of which allowed easily for possession of Gnostic texts such as those found at Nag Hammadi (buried perhaps after the moves against "heretical" works in the second half of the fourth century defined such texts as unacceptable). Both of these views diverge from those originally put forward by Jean Doresse, in *The Secret Books of the Egyptian Gnostics: An Introduction to the Gnostic Coptic Manuscripts Discovered at Chenoboskion*, trans. Philip Mairet and rev. by the author (London: Hollis & Carter, 1960 [Fr. orig., 1958]), pp. 134–40, 249–309, esp. 249–63: that the Nag Hammadi Mss were cached by a group of Sethian Gnostics under pressure from the "orthodox" Pachomians of the late fourth century, probably after the promulgation of the antiheretical decree of Athanasius in 367. See also Dwight W. Young, "The Milieu of Nag Hammadi: Some Historical Considerations," *Vigilae Christianae* 24 (1970): 127–37. More recently, Tito Orlandi, "A Catechesis against Apocryphal Texts by Shenute and the Gnostic Texts of Nag Hammadi," *HTR* 75 (1982): 85–95; see esp. pp. 93–95) has argued for the presence of an Evagrian group in upper Egypt in the early fifth century, perhaps in Shenutian and Pachomian monasteries, who might have owned these texts.

26. *PK* 2: 166 (=*Pr.* 139b–40). This passage is missing in the Coptic fragments collected in *OPD* 1 and the Greek *Excerpta* fragments collected in the Appendix to *Pach. lat.;* Latin text in *Pach. lat.*, p. 50^{1-10}, as follows: "Et si litteras ignorabit, hora prima et tertia et sexta uadet ad eum qui docere potest et qui ei fuerit delegatus, et stabit ante illum, et discet studiosissime cum omni gratiarum actione. Postea uero scribentur ei elementa syllabae, uerba ac nomina, et etiam nolens legere compelletur [139b]. Et omnino nullus erit in monasterio qui non discat litteras et de scripturis aliquid teneat: qui minimum usque ad nouum testamentum et psalterium [140]." According to Bacht, this insistence that all monks learn to read "gehört mit zu den erstaunlichen Besonderheiten des Instituts der Pachomianer. . . . Eine derartige Forderung wird beispielsweise bei BENEDIKT nicht mehr durchgehalten" (*Vermächtnis* 1: 179, n. 234).
27. E.g., *PK* 2: 29, 52, 82–83, 149, 162, 170, 182 (=*Paral.* 7, 27; *Am. Letter* 15; *Pr.* 25, 101–02; *Pach. inst.* 2; *Pach. leg.* 7); *PK* 1: 231 (=*SBo* 189).
28. *PK* 1: 230 (=*SBo* 189); *PK* 2: 98–99, 101–02 (=*Am. Letter* 29, 32). Such references suggest that letters were also exchanged regularly among at least the abbots, if not other monks, of the separate monasteries.
29. E.g., *PK* 1: 228, 336, 356, 447, 452 (=*SBo* 187; G^1 56, 87; S^2 7–8; S^{10} 2); *PK* 2: 62, 63, 75, 216 (=*Paral.* 38, 39; *Am. Letter* 6; *Hors. Reg.* 52); *PK* 3: 23, 25, 69, 70, 129, 153–65 passim (=*Pach. Instr.* 24, 26; *Pach. Letter* 7:1, 7:2; *Theod. Letter* 2:4; *Hors. Letter*, passim).
30. The image, "breathing" scripture, is not simply rhetorical excess: First, because the continual murmured recitation of Psalms or other scriptural texts was incumbent upon all the monks (see the discussion of meditation and recitation below, sections "Meditation" and "Recitation in the Dailiy Round"); and, second, because one of the most common epithets used for the scriptures in the Pachomian sources is "the

breath of God" (Sahidic: ^{e}*nnife* ^{e}*ntepnoute*): e.g., *PK* 3: 105, 114, 115 (=*Theod. Instr.* 19, 35, 38; *OPD* 1: 49^{19-20}, 56^{21}, 57^{22}). Cf. *PK* 1, p. 117 (=*SBo* 88 [*PVBS* 1: 101^{20-21}]).

31. *PK* 3: 17 (=*Pach. Instr.* 14).
32. *PK* 3: 210 (=*Hors. Test.* 51–52, in *Pach. lat.*, pp. 143^{19}–44^{8}).
33. "In earum semper meditatione versemur."
34. "Iugiter meditanda praecepit." See also *PK* 2: 145, 146, 150, 151, 156 (=*Pr.* 3, 6, 28, 36–37, 59–60).
35. There follows at this point citation of Deut. 11.18-20 and 4.10. The paragraph closes with a reference to Solomon's words of Prov. 3.3, "Write them across your heart."
36. "Considerate quantis testimoniis ad meditationem sanctarum scripturarum nos sermo Domini cohortetur."
37. "Quae ore volvimus." Boon, *Pach. lat.*, p. 144^{7}, reads "quae ore volumus." Both Bacht, *Vermächtnis* 1: 181 (n. 240), and Veilleux, *PK* 3: 223 (n. 1 to *Hors. Test.* 52), prefer the reading *volvimus* (also attested in one of the Ms codices): i.e., "we have repeated, turned over, pondered" (<*volvo*) instead of "we have desired, intended" (<*volo*).
38. *PK* 1: 218 (=*SBo* 183).
39. *PK* 2: 153 (=*Pr.* 49); Greek (*Excerpta* A): "psalmous auton meletan poiēsousin" (*Pach. lat.*, p. 174^{15-16}). The *Excerpta* B passage has only "psalms" (*psalmous: Pach. lat.*, p. 174^{15}). Veilleux, in a note to *Pr.* 49, says that "the Greek *Excerpta* have simply 'psalms'," in support of his view that "as many . . . as he can learn [*quantos potuerit discere: Pach. lat.*, p. 25^{14}]" may be Jerome's gloss (*PK* 2: 187) of the original. However, pace Veilleux, I would read the *Excerpta* A version as a support for Jerome's translation.
40. *PK* 1: 38 (=*SBo* 15).
41. *PK* 1: 52–53 (=*SBo* 29).
42. E.g., *PK* 1: 58, 338, 340, 357 (=*SBo* 34; G^{1} 58, 61, 88); *PK* 2: 54, 59, 146, 156, 166, 202 (=*Paral.* 29, 35; *Pr.* 6, 59–60, 139–40; *Hors. Reg.* 17); *PK* 3: 97, 117 (=*Theod. Instr.* 8, 42).
43. "Apostēthizousi de pasas tas graphas." *PK* 2: 129 (=*Hist. Laus.* 2: 96^{5}). Even if Palladius' statement is unlikely to have been true of all Pachomian monks, it does appear from this and other references in the sources that, as Gindele maintains, it must not have been at all unusual for some of the brothers eventually to memorize the whole New Testament and the Psalter for their use in meditation ("Schriftlesung," p. 115).
44. *PK* 1: 451–52 (=S^{10} 2). Cf. the passage from *Hors. Test.* 51–52 (*PK* 3: 210) cited above, section "Scripture in the Pachomian *Koinonia*.".
45. *PK* 2: 202 (=*Hors. Reg.* 16). "Section" here translates the Coptic *sôp*, lit. "time" (Fr.: *fois*), which Veilleux has convincingly shown to be equivalent in this kind of context to the Greek *meros*/Coptic *mers* "section", "part", "piece", "segment", and linked to the Greek *apostēthizomenos* and Coptic *apostēthous* (aptly trans. as "par-coeur" by Lefort, *OPD* 2: 85–86), all of which are used to refer to sections of the Psalter [and other books of scripture?] learned by heart for the purposes of prayer and meditation/recitation (Veilleux, *La liturgie*, pp. 309–15; cf. id., *PK* 2: 191 [n. 1 to *Pr.* 121]). See below, sections "Meditation" and "Liturgy and Instruction."
46. Eph. 6.16-17 is cited at least once to this effect in the Pachomian sources: *Hors. Test.* 19 (=*PK* 3: 184).
47. *PK* 1: 224–225 (=*SBo* 186). Cf. one of Theodore's "Instructions", in which he reminds the monks that, as a result of God's love, "salvation and fervor come to us in proportion to the haste each of us makes to be renewed in 'the fruits of the

Spirit', . . . and in proportion to the heat of the flame of our continuous recitation night and day" (*PK* 3: 108; =*Theod. Instr.* 26).

48. *PK* 1: 453 (=S^{10} 4).
49. *PK* 1: 231-32 (=*SBo* 189).
50. Yet it does appear that the memorization of the scriptures provided a model for and training in learning everything that Pachomius and his successors sought to teach the monks. It is said of Pachomius' instruction of the brothers that "he gave them laws and traditions; some were committed to writing, some others were learned by heart, after the manner of the holy Gospels of Christ." (*PK* 1, p. 145; =*SBo* 104).
51. *PK* 1: 228 (=*SBo* 187).
52. Veilleux, *PK* 1: 414 (n. 1 to G^1 58).
53. Cf. Gerhard Schneider, "Bibel und Meditation," p. 14: "Es gibt . . . kein biblisches Wort - weder im Hebräischem noch im Griechischen - , das unserem 'meditieren' unmittelbar entspräche."
54. On the meaning of Hebrew *hāgāh,* Greek [and Coptic] *meletan/meletê,* and Latin *meditari/meditatio* in Biblical usage, see the detailed and informative study of Emmanuel von Severus, "Das Wort 'Meditari' im Sprachgebrauch der Heiligen Schrift," and the other references given in n. 58 below.
55. See, for a specific instance, Roger D. Ray, "Orderic Vitalis and His Readers," esp. pp. 20, 21, 24–25, 32 (further refs. in n. 48). Cf. the explanation of *meditatio* in the *Rule* of St. Benedict given by Benno Linderbauer in his commentary (*RB*, p. 228): "Unter meditatio ist das Auswendiglernen der Psalmen, die Einübung des Lesens der Lektionen und des Gesanges zu verstehen. Diese Erklärung is auch mit der sonstigen Bedeutung des Wortes, sowohl in der klassischen als auch in der späteren Zeit im Einklang."
56. This is underscored for the Pachomian context by Heinrich Bacht ("'Meditatio' in den ältesten Mönchsquellen," p. 255): "Dem Inhalt nach hat diese Weise des Meditierens fast ausschließlich die Heilige Schrift zum Gegenstand." Bacht goes on to note that this is almost always explicitly stated in Jerome's trans. of the *Rule,* seldom so in the few Coptic parallels that we have, and sometimes so, sometimes not, in the Bohairic Coptic *Life.* On balance, he argues that even where the scriptures are not explicitly named, the sources presume that they are understood to be the objects of meditation/recitation (ibid., pp. 255-56).
57. Severus, "Das Wort 'Meditari'", esp. pp. 366–69. See also Koehler and Baumgartner, p. 224a, s.v. "H-G-H"; *OLD,* p. 1090a-b, s.v. "meditatio", "meditor"; Lewis and Short, p. 1124b-c, s.v. "meditatio", "meditor"; Liddell and Scott, pp. 1096b-97a, s.v. "meletainō"; *Thes. ling. lat.* 8: 574-81, s.v. "meditor" (Wolfgang Buchwald), esp. 575-76, 579-80.
58. Bacht, "'Meditatio'"; Leclercq, *L'amour des lettres,* pp. 22-23, 72-73 (Eng. trans. pp. 15-17, 72-74); id., "Liturgy and Contemplation," pp. 81-83; id., "Meditation as a Biblical Reading"; id., "De Saint Grégoire à Saint Bernard," part I of Jean Leclercq, François Vandenbroucke, and Louis Bouyer, *La spiritualité du moyen âge,* p. 113; Adalbert de Vogüé, "Les deux fonctions de la méditation dans les Règles monastiques anciennes," pp. 4, 9, 10-16. Further refs. in Veilleux, *La liturgie,* pp. 267-69; id., *PK* 1: 414 (n. 1 to G^1 58). See also Gindele, "Schriftlesung," pp. 114-15; Fidelis Ruppert, "Arbeit und geistliches Leben im pachomianischen Mönchtum," pp. 8-12; id., "*Meditatio - Ruminatio*"; Emmanuel von Severus, "Das Wesen der Meditation und der Mensch der Gegenwart," pp. 108-13; id., "Der heilige Ignatius als Lehrer des betrachtenden Gebetes," pp. 278-80; Hans Wolter, "Meditation bei Bernhard von Clairvaux," esp. pp. 208-14. Cf. Josef Sudbrack, "Zum Thema: Betrachtung oder

Meditation?", pp. 95–97; Modestus Van Assche, "'Divinae vacare lectioni'," pp. 21–22; Irénée Hausherr, *Noms du Christ et voies d'oraison*, Orientalia Christiana Analecta, 157 (Rome: Pont. Institutum Orientalium Studiorum, 1960), pp. 167–75.

59. *L'amour des lettres*, p. 23 (my trans. of the French follows that of the Eng. ed., p. 17, with minor emendations/corrections). Cf. Bacht, "'Meditatio'", p. 254, on the act of meditation: "Dem Akt nach handelt es sich – an den meisten Stellen – nicht um einen rein geistigen, innerlichen Vorgang, sondern um ein vernehmbares Aufsagen von Texten und Formeln, dem sich die Mönche allein oder in Gemeinschaft hingeben, wobei sie die Texte entweder auswendig hersagen oder vor sich hinlesen." Leclercq, "Meditation as a Biblical Reading," p. 562, argues further that meditation, "according to [Benedictine] tradition" demands that "our mind be in accord with our voice" (or "with what the lips pronounce"): "mens nostra concordet voci nostrae." However, as Giles Constable has pointed out to me (pers. commun., 2 July 1985), the exact sources and original sense of this oft-cited phrase from the Benedictine Rule are by no means utterly clear.
60. See nn. 57–59.
61. See, e.g., Emmanuel von Severus, "'Silvestrum tenui musam meditaris avena'," pp. 27–29, where Ambrose's use of *meditari* as an equivalent of *exerceri* in the Roman military sense of "training" or "exercise" is discussed and documented. Cf. Assche, "'Divinae vacare lectioni'," pp. 21–22.
62. Joseph MacCandless, "'Meditation' in Saint Bernard," pp. 279–82.
63. Leclercq, *L'amour des lettres*, pp. 72–73 (=Eng. trans. p. 73); Ruppert, "*Meditatio – Ruminatio*."
64. Gindele, "Schriftlesung," p. 115. Cf. his further observation on the importance of this scripture meditation, which expresses well the intent if not perhaps the actual result of the exercise for everyone: "Sich die hl. Texte fortwährend wiederholend, vorstellend, einübend, lebt der Pachomianer in einer Vergegenwärtigung, in einer 'Anschauung Gottes', die jedem erreichbar war."
65. *PK* 3: 108 (=*Theod. Instr.* 26). Cf. Bacht's observation ("'Meditatio'", pp. 249–50) that this constant meditation is "keineswegs als ein 'geistiges Mattenflechten' ohne innere Teilnahme gedacht. . . . All die asketischen Bemühungen, zu denen die Mönche verpflichtet sind, haben nur den einen Sinn, den inneren Menschen zu dieser ständigen Gottzuwendung zu läutern." Cf. Ruppert, "Arbeit und geistliches Leben," pp. 12–14.
66. Bacht, "'Meditatio'", p. 256, characterizes "diese Weise des monotonen bzw. singenden Hersagens von Schrifttexten" as "eine sehr schlichte Form des Betens (richtiger: der Gebetszurüstung)." The Pachomian sources themselves commend "unceasing prayer", together with fasting and purity of body and heart, as the fundamentals of monastic life: e.g., *PK* 3: 31–32 (=*Pach. Instr.* 39); cf. *PK* 2: 33 (=*Paral.* 11). The way in which the Pachomians carried this out, however, should not be confused with the practices of the anchorites of lower Egypt or Syria–Palestine. The Pachomian practice of prayer and Scripture meditation does not seem to have been the same kind of "unceasing" prayer lauded by Cassian in books 2 and 3 of the *Institutes* as the one form of prayer cultivated by the Egyptian monks: namely, observance of a literal *laus perennis* and wholesale rejection of observance of particular "hours" (*horae*) of prayer. See Veilleux's incisive critique of the uncritical acceptance by scholars such as Anton Baumstark (*Nocturna Laus*, pp. 105–23) of Cassian's descriptions as an accurate depiction of Pachomian usage (*La liturgie*, pp. 277–87). On the particular ways in which the Pachomians sought to "pray without ceasing", see ibid., pp. 287–92.
67. *PK* 2: 129 (=*Hist. Laus.* 2: 96^{1-5}). On the kinds of labor in which the Tabennesiots engaged, see Ruppert, "Arbeit und geistliches Leben," esp. pp. 3–7; see also Excursus

3, "Das Armutsverständnis des Pachomius und seiner Jünger," in *Vermächtnis* 1, esp. pp. 230–35. Note that Jerome in his Preface to the *Praecepta* of Pachomius says that the brothers in each monastic community were organized into houses according to their special crafts. He makes specific mention of linen-weavers, mat-weavers, tailors, carriage makers, fullers, and shoemakers (*PK* 2: 143; =*Pach. lat.*, pp. 7–8). From the Pachomian sources themselves, taken as a whole, it would appear that perhaps most if not all of the brothers shared some of the work in the fields, the cutting of rushes, and the baking of bread, even if they had other, specific craft specialities. I have found, however, no explicit confirmation of my interpretation in the secondary literature. See also n. 69 below.

68. *PK* 2: 156 (=*Pr*. 60): "Operantes nihil loquentur saeculare, sed aut meditabuntur ea quae sancta sunt, aut certe silebunt" (*Pach. lat.*, p. 91[6–7]). Greek *Excerpta* A: "ergazomenōn dé, mēdeis lalēsē dia tēs hulēs, alla meletēsōsin ē hēsuchsaōsin"; *Excerpta* B: "mēdeis ergazomenōn lalēsē dia tas hulas, alla meletēsōsin ē hēsuchasōsin" (*ibid.*, p. 177[1–3]).
69. This may be only because of the fragmentary nature of some of the relevant sections of the particularly detailed *Rules* of Horsiesius (see *PK* 2: 207–20 passim (=*Hors. Reg.* 27–64ff.), but in the sources generally the baking of bread does seem be singled out for special mention – as evidenced by such apparently innocuous statements such as that in *PK* 2: 216 (=*Hors. Reg.* 53): "During every occupation and in the kneading room, let us perform the prayers with zeal . . . ." Note also the sizeable sections of the *Rules* of Pachomius and especially those of Horsiesius given over to the bakery: *Pr*. 116–17; *Hors. Reg.* 39–50 (=*PK* 2: 210–16).
70. *PK* 1: 100–01 (=*SBo* 77). Cf. p. 97 (=*SBo* 74) and p. 358 (=*G*[1] 89).
71. Coptic: *enmeleta* (*OPD* 1: 92[23]).
72. *PK* 2: 210 (=*Hors. Reg.* 39; =*OPD* 1: 92[20–25]).
73. Coptic: *eunameleta* (*OPD* 1: 32[31]); Greek: *meletēsōsin* (*Excerpta* B); *Excerpta* A reads *meletēsōsin homou*, "let them recite together" (*Pach. lat.*, p. 181[14–15]). In his Latin trans. (*Pach. lat.*, p. 44), Jerome has "simile habebunt silentum et tantum de psalmis et de scripturis aliquid decantabunt": "they shall also keep silence and only sing something from the psalms or from [other parts of] the Scriptures." Cf. *PK* 1: 100 (=*SBo* 77), which describes how Pachomius instituted such rules for the bakery, including "the commandment that no man should speak in the bakery, but all should recite [[e]*ntouermeletan*: *PVBS* 1: 82[11]] God's word together. . . ."
74. *PK* 2: 163 (=*Pr*. 116).
75. *PK* 2: 212–13 (=*Hors. Reg.* 44–45): In the original (*OPD* 1: 94[18,24,25,26], 95[3]), all of the Coptic verbs translated here in English by "recite", "reciting", etc., are compound forms of the verb *meleta*, a loanword from the Greek *meletan*. Cf. also *PK* 2: 213–14 (=*Hors. Reg.* 46–47: *OPD* 1: 95[4–18]). Note that this rule seems to allow for silent recitation/mediation ("in our heart"), whereas the preceding one of Pachomius (*Pr*. 116) and the apparent paraphrase of it cited above in n. 73 (*PK* 1: 100; =*SBo* 77) refer only to vocal, unison recitation.
76. *PK* 2: 145146 (= *Pr*. 4–5). Cf. n. 79 below.
77. Which apparently occurred regularly five times a week. See Veilleux, *PK* 2: 186, n. 1 to *Pr*. 20 (includes the major primary-source refs.); Ruppert, "Arbeit und geistliches Leben," pp. 5, 7.
78. *PK* 1: 35 (=*SBo* 14): "Another day, while they were seated on either side of a burning fire, working together at their manual labor and reciting the holy Scripture by heart, a brother . . . appeared . . . ."
79. *PK* 1: 31 (=*SBo* 10) [attributed to Palamon]: "The rule of monastic life, according to

what we have learned from those who went before us, is as follows: We always spend half the night, and often even from evening to morning, in vigils and the recitation of the words of God, also doing manual work with threads, hairs, or palm-fibres, lest we be overcome by sleep. . . ."

80. *PK* 2: 54 (=*Paral.* 29): Of one of the pious monks, a gardener, it is said: "During the day he worked out in the garden, and, taking his food toward sunset, he entered his cell and sat on a stool in the middle of the cell, plaiting ropes until the night *synaxis.* And so, if it happened that the needs of nature compelled him to snatch a little sleep, he would sleep sitting and holding in his hands the ropes he was plaiting. He did not plait the ropes by the light of a lamp, but sitting in darkness, while reciting the Scriptures by heart." Cf. the practices of Theodore described in *PK* 1: 58, 133 (=*SBo* 34, 96).
81. "Eine Einheit von Gebets- und Arbeitsleben" (Ruppert, "Arbeit und geistliches Leben," p. 12).
82. *PK* 2: 151 (=*Pr.* 36): "The one who strikes the signal to assemble the brothers for meals shall recite while striking [*meditetur in percutiendo: Pach. lat.*, p. 22^{4}]"; *PK* 2: 151 (=*Pr.* 37): "The one who dispenses sweets to the brothers at the refectory door as they go out shall recite something from the Scriptures while doing so [*in tribuendo meditetur aliquid de scripturis: Pach. lat.*, p. 22^{6-7}]."
83. *PK* 2: 145 (=*Pr.* 3): "As soon as he hears the sound of the trumpet calling [the brothers] to the *synaxis*, he shall leave his cell, reciting something from the Scriptures [*de scripturis aliquid meditans* (*Pach. lat.*, p. 14^{3}); Greek *Excerpta* A version (ibid., p. 170^{10}) has only *meletōn*] until he reaches the door of the *synaxis*"; *PK* 2: 201–02 (=*Hors. Reg.* 13–14): "When the *synaxis* is dismissed, let us recite [^{e}*nt*^{e}*nmeleta: OPD* 1: 85^{33}] until we reach our houses. . . . Let us recite [^{e}*nt*^{e}*nmeleta: OPD* 1: 86^{15}] also both going to and returning from the *synaxis.*" See also *PK* 2: 150 (=*Pr.* 28), 213–14 (=*Hors. Reg.* 47); *PK* 1: 161, 255, 264, 338 (=*SBo* 108, 204, 209; G^{1} 58).
84. Going out to the fields or off to gather rushes, or returning from such tasks, the brothers marched as a group and chanted psalms or other scriptures in unison. See *PK* 1: 86–87 (=*SBo* 66, 108); *PK* 2: 156 (=*Pr.* 58–59); cf. *PK* 1: 159 (=*SBo* 108).
85. *PK* 1: 161 (=*SBo* 108): ". . . As for our father Pachomius, he left [Tabennesi] too with the brothers who had come with him to gather his rushes. They recited the word of God until they came north to Phbow." Cf. *PK* 1: 195, 204 (=*SBo* 138, 143).
86. *PK* 1: 159, 204 (=*SBo* 108, 143).
87. *PK* 1: 51, 249–54, 317, 401 (=*SBo* 28, 201–04; G^{1} 30, 143).
88. *PK* 1: 249–50 (=*SBo* 201). The account of this visit to upper Egypt by Athanasius continues in *PK* 1: 251–54 (=*SBo* 201–04) and includes other instances of festive welcoming processions accompanied by the singing of psalms.
89. *PK* 1: 380 (=G^{1} 116, 117).In the Coptic account of the burial of Petronios, the brothers are said to have "spent the whole night reading and praying around him" (*PK* 1: 187; =*SBo* 130). Cf. the Pachomian precept that the monk "shall not neglect the times of prayer and psalmody [*orandi et psallendi tempora*], whether he is on a boat, in the monastery, in the fields, or on a journey, or fulfilling any service whatever" (*PK* 2: 166; =*Pr.* 142; *Pach. lat.*, pp. 50–51).
90. *PK* 1: 58 (=*SBo* 34). See also Ruppert, "Arbeit und geistliches Leben," pp. 10–11.
91. *PK* 2: 145–47 (=*Pr.* 3–14); *PK* 2: 198–200 (=*Hors. Reg.* 6–11); Veilleux, *La liturgie*, pp. 307–08. Note that the Greek term *synaxis* is used both for the building in the monastery in which the monks assembled and for the gathering itself: Cf. Jerome's use of both *collecta* and *conventiculum* in the same passage to translate *synaxis: Pr.* 3 (=*PK* 2: 145); cf. *Pach. lat.*, p. 14^{1-3}, and the Greek of *Excerpta* A

(ibid., p. 170[7–11]). In my description of the content of the *synaxis* gatherings, I follow the detailed and convincing arguments of Veilleux in *La liturgie*, pp. 292–315, where he includes references to and/or discussion of all of the critical passages for this problem in the sources.

92. The place of the Psalms as the most frequently used texts for recitation among the Tabennesiots is clearly attested in the narratives of the various Pachomian *Lives*, even though the frequently used Lat. *psallere*/ Gk. [>Copt.] *psallō* of the sources may sometimes refer to "singing" or "chanting" generally rather than specifically to "singing psalms" in these narratives (Veilleux, *PK* 2: 186, n. 1 to *Pr*. 17). The central role of the Psalms in Pachomian piety is also indicated by their relative frequency of citation in the major Pachomian sources taken as a whole. In the texts collected and translated in *PK*, there are 328 citations of the Psalms as opposed to 252 of Matthew (i.e., 30% more), and Matthew is by far the other most heavily cited biblical or apocryphal book, the next most frequently cited books being Proverbs (136 times), Isaiah (130), Luke (125), and Romans (120) (calculations based on the list of citations provided by Veilleux in his "Biblical Index," *PK* 3: 236–96). On the general importance of the Psalter in the patristic period, see for example Severus, "Das Wort 'Meditari'," pp. 370–71 (esp. the passage cited above in Chapter 10, n. 22, which see).

93. *PK* 2: 147–48 (=*Pr*. 15–18); *PK* 1: 40, 50, 123, 178–79, 187, 257, 260, 320, 368, 380, 405 (=*SBo* 18, 27, 92, 123, 130, 181, 205, 207; G^1 32, 103, 116–17, 149). See Veilleux, *La liturgie*, pp. 313–15; cf. pp. 233–37.

94. Veilleux, *La liturgie*, p. 276, with references to supporting sources on this point in nn. 1 and 2.

95. Note the words ascribed to Horsiesius: "Let us give heed with exactness to the canons of prayer, with a fear of the Lord that is worthy of Him, whether at the *synaxis* or at the Six Sections, or in our houses, or anywhere, whether in the fields or in the community. Wherever we are, even while walking along the road, we must pray to God with our whole heart, being attentive to prayer alone . . . ." (*PK* 2: 198–99; =*Hors. Reg*. 6). This interpretation follows Veilleux, *La liturgie*, pp. 161–66, 195–97, pace the views of scholars who see the Pachomian tradition as one opposed to the Christian liturgical life (e.g., Eligius Dekkers, "Were the Early Monks Liturgical?" esp. pp. 124, 130–31, 133–35, 137). Veilleux argues strongly against the views of Dekkers and others and for the importance of liturgy (and ecclesial concerns generally) in the Pachomian scheme. It is important in any case not to confuse possible antiliturgical strains in early Christian eremitism with the cenobitic and ecclesial ideals of the Pachomian rule: Cf. André Louf, "The Word Beyond the Liturgy," 6: 360–64; 7: 63–66.

96. *PK* 1: 52, 62 (=*SBo* 29, 39). Cf. *PK* 1: 117 (=*SBo* 88): "From that day on when our father Pachomius assembled the brothers for the instruction, he spoke to them first on the Scriptures because they are the main thing and the breath of God. . . ." Cf. also *PK* 1: 365 (=G^1 99).

97. *PK* 1: 316 (=G^1 28); *PK* 1: 49 (=*SBo* 26). Cf. Veilleux, *La liturgie*, pp. 270–73. See also *PK* 2: 166, 171 (=*Pr*. 138; *Pach. inst*. 15 [esp. Jerome's text, *Pach. lat*., p. 57]). Cf. *PK* 2: 163 (=*Pr*. 115) and Veilleux's discussion of this apparent reference to *three* weekly lessons given by the housemasters, *La liturgie*, pp. 271–72.

98. *PK* 1: 338, 385 (=G^1 58, 125); *PK* 1: 52–53 (=*SBo* 29); *PK* 2: 164 (=*Pr*. 122). Cf. Gindele, "Schriftlesung," p. 116, on the monks' discussion of scripture.

99. *PK* 1: 233 (=*SBo* 190). Cf. also *PK* 1: 135–36, 203–24, 237, 255 (=*SBo* 98, 143, 193, 204–05); *PK* 2: 89 (=*Am. Letter* 21).

100. *PK* 3: 171–215; cf. n. 20 above.

Chapter 12. Hearing and Seeing: The Rhetoric of Martin Luther

1. See Chapter 3, section "The Medieval West." Cf. Franz Bäuml, "Varieties and Consequences of Medieval Literacy and Illiteracy," p. 237: "At all levels of society, the majority of the population of Europe between the fourth and the fifteenth centuries was, in some sense, illiterate."
2. Cited by J. de Ghellinck, "'Pagina' et 'Sacra Pagina'," p. 33. The phrase occurs in the following context (the plague referred to being presumably that during which Gregory took office as Pope in 590): "Iam mundi huius omnia perdita conspicimus quae in sacris paginis audiebamus peritura, eversae urbes, castra directa, . . . ecclesiae dirutae, . . . quasi paginae nobis codicum factae sunt iam ipsae plagae terrarum."
3. Beyond the monastic and clerical milieu, this presence was generally indirect, but from the tenth or eleventh century, growth of literacy, especially vernacular literacy, seems to have increased direct contact. See, e.g., the instances of lay knowledge of, use of, and influence from the scriptures in late-medieval Mainz cited in Franz Falk, *Bibelstudien, Bibelhandschriften und Bibeldrucke in Mainz vom achten Jahrhundert bis zur Gegenwart*, pp. 76–86.
4. Cited by Roland H. Bainton, "The Bible in the Reformation," p. 12 (with no ref. to the original text quoted). Cf. Calvin's expression of similar ideas: *Institutes* 1.6.1, 1.7.4–5, 1.9.3 (John Calvin, *Institutes of the Christian Religion*, trans. Henry Beveridge, 1845; photogr. repr., 2 vols. [Grand Rapids, Mich.: Wm. B. Eerdmans, 1983] 1: 64, 71–72, 86).
5. Friedrich Heiler, *Katholischer und evangelischer Gottesdienst*, p. 43.
6. Transcribed in Marc Lienhard and Jean Rott, "Die Anfänge der evangelischen Predigt in Straßburg und ihr erstes Manifest," pp. 65–66 (cf. esp. pp. 72–73 of von Lyn's text, reproduced on pp. 68–73 of Lienhard and Rott, as well as the discussion of the further example of Mattheus Zell's tract, "Christliche Verantwortung," ibid., p. 66).
7. S. L. Greenslade, "Epilogue," pp. 491–92.
8. See, for the early German reformation, Gerald Strauss, *Luther's House of Learning*, pp. 151–75 (esp. 152–55, 170–71), 230–36. On the often less than happy results of such learning, see ibid., p. 224. Cf. Wilhelm Walther's comments on how Luther's Bible was taken as the basis of Protestant German school curricula, in *Luthers Deutsche Bibel*, p. 186.
9. Walther, *Luthers Deutsche Bibel*, p. 186 (trans. mine).
10. R. W. Scribner, *For the Sake of Simple Folk*, esp. pp. 196–97, 204–06.
11. *The Early Stuarts* (1937), p. 404, as cited by S. L. Greenslade, "Epilogue," p. 492.
12. "Unsern Vorvätern war die Bibel Sprachheimat, wenn auch mit wechselnder Intensität und in strittigem Verständnis; und deshalb war Gott gewissermaßen Sprachzentrum . . . ." (Gerhard Ebeling, *Gott und Wort*, p. 13).
13. E.g., Heinrich Bornkamm, *Luther und das Alte Testament* (1948); Jaroslav Pelikan, *Luther the Expositor* (1959); Johannes Preuss, *Die Entwicklung des Schriftprinzips bei Luther bis zur Leipziger Disputation* (1901); Otto Scheel, *Luthers Stellung zur heiligen Schrift* (1902); Karl Thimme, *Luthers Stellung zur Heiligen Schrift* (1903); Paul Schempp, *Luthers Stellung zur Heiligen Schrift* (1929); Gerhard Ebeling, *Evangelische Evangelienauslegung* (1942; 2nd ed., 1962); Harald Østergaard-Nielsen, *Scriptura sacra et viva vox* (1957); Friedrich Beisser, *Claritas scripturae bei Martin Luther* (1966). See also sect. I of the brief bibliography to Bainton, "The Bible in the Reformation," in *Camb. Hist. Bib.* 3: 536.
14. Karl August Meissinger, *Der katholische Luther*, p. 82. *Bibelfestigkeit*, literally "biblical solidity" or "Bible-strength", expresses here the high degree of verbatim

familiarity with the text of scripture that Luther possessed, and out of which he worked. In this regard, Meissinger points out that in the early, "pre-Reformation" lectures, Luther apparently cited almost all biblical passages from memory, since his quotations are generally exact, whereas his chapter-numbering in identifying the citations is often imprecise (ibid.). (The utter unconcern with, or inexactitude about, chapter and verse numbers seems to be characteristic of memorizers of lengthy scriptural texts, if my own experience with Muslims who know the Qur'ān by heart is any indication.) Although one can test effectively the saturation of Luther's work with biblical references simply by reading almost any one of his myriad works, some representative statistics based on a sample segment of Luther's writings are given and discussed by Ebeling, *Evangelische Evangelienauslegung*, pp. 39–40.

15. *WA* 10.ii: 108.
16. Pelikan, *Luther*, p. 85; Bornkamm, *Luther*, pp. 71–72; Karl Gerhard Steck, *Lehre und Kirche bei Luther*, p. 155.
17. See, for example, *WA* 54: 88^{10-12}: "Und sonderlich ists Gott zu thun umb die offenbarung und erkentnis seines Sons, durch die gantze Schrifft, Alts und Newen Testaments, Alles gehets auff den Son . . . ." Cf. *WA* 24: 17^{11-13}. On the unity of scripture in Luther, see Steck, *Lehre und Kirche*, pp. 147–68; Ebeling, *Evangelische Evangelienauslegung*, pp. 402–04; Heinrich Bornkamm, *Das Wort Gottes bei Luther*, pp. 23–24; id., *Luther*, pp. 69–74, 151–84, esp. 169–76. Note Bornkamm's statement (*Luther*, p. 73): "Die Einheit [der beiden Testamente] liegt darin, daß der Gesamtinhalt des göttlichen Wortes, Gesetz und Evangelium, beide umfaßt und in beiden enthalten ist." See also Pelikan, *Luther*, p. 60.
18. E.g., *WA* 3: 590–91, 601, 648; 4: 26, 29, 30–31.
19. Bornkamm, *Luther*, pp. 159–64. Cf. Pelikan, *Luther*, pp. 86–88. Note the subtitle given by Luther in his German Bible to the Apocrypha: "Bücher, so der heiligen Schrift nicht gleich gehalten, und doch nützlich und gut zu lesen sind" – so the text in my edition of the Lutherbibel: *Die Bibel, oder die ganze Heilige Schrift des Alten und Neuen Testaments nach der Übersetzung Martin Luthers* (Stuttgart: Württembergische Bibelanstalt, 1963).
20. *WA* 53: 218^{19-23}. The passage begins: "Wache, studire, Attende lectioni . . . ."
21. *WA* 8: 236^{14-28}, 239^{16-21}. On Luther's concept of the fundamental "clarity of scripture", see Beisser, *Claritas scripturae*. Cf. Gerhard Ebeling, "Wort Gottes und Hermeneutik," pp. 321–22; Østergaard-Nielsen, *Scriptura sacra*, pp. 120–25.
22. Namely, one in which it is handled "with fear and humility" (*in timore und humilitate*), and penetrated more through "reverent prayer" (*piae orationis*) than "acuity of the intellect" (*acumine ingenii*) (*WA* 1: 507^{25-29}).
23. *WA* 24: 19^{30-31}: "Denn wir müssen des sicher seyn, das kein einfeltiger rede auff erden komen sey denn das Gott geredt hat."
24. *WA* 49: 223^{8-9}: ". . . wen man meinet, man habs ausgelernet, so mus man erst anfahen."
25. *WA* 11: 455^{27-34}. Further references in Kurt Aland, ed., *Lutherlexikon* (supp. vol. 3 [1957] to *Luther Deutsch*), pp. 308–09, s.v. "Sprachen, Sprachkenntnisse."
26. Ebeling, "Wort Gottes und Hermeneutik," pp. 321–22. On Luther's emphasis upon the necessity of faith for the understanding and interpretation of the "letter" of scripture according to the "spirit", see Beisser, *Claritas scripturae*, e.g., pp. 19–20, 24, 26, 28, inter alia.
27. *WA* 7: 546^{24-25}: "Denn es mag niemant got noch gottes wort recht vorstehen, er habs denn on mittel von dem heyligen geyst." See also *WA* 16: 68^{22-24}; 30.i: 218^{10-12}. On Luther's concept of the necessity for God's grace (through inspiration

by the Holy Spirit) in order to understand and interpret scripture, see W. Schwarz, *Principles and Problems of Biblical Translation,* pp. 167–212, esp. 169–72 (the passage quoted above in the present note is also cited and trans. on p. 171). On the central importance of the Holy Spirit in the communication and understanding of the word of God, see Regin Prenter, *Spiritus creator,* pp. 107–32, esp. pp. 107–08. Prenter notes that for Luther, "das äußere Wort ist nur das Werkzeug, das Gott benutzt, wenn er sein eigenes lebendiges Wort in die Herzen der Menschen schreibt" (p. 108) and cites several passages from Luther's lectures on the Psalms (*WA* 3: 256^{10}, 259^{13}, 250^{4}, inter alia) in support of this.

28. *WA* 7: 97^{2-3}: ". . . nusquam praesentius et vivacius quam in ipsis sacris suis, quas scripsit, literis inveniri potest."
29. *Luthers Deutsche Bibel* (Munich, 1928), pp. 69–70, as cited in Schempp, *Luthers Stellung,* p. 32.
30. E.g., *WA* 46: 62.
31. *WA* 16: 41^{18-21}: "Denn ich hab es zuvor offt gesagt und sag es noch, das es ein theuer und köstlich ding ist, wenn man Gottes Wort höret, Und man solt alle Land durchlauffen, das man wirdig sein möchte, einen buchstaben von Gottes wort zu hören . . . ."
32. See the citation from his lecture on Hebrews quoted in part above as the epigraph to the present chapter. The original Latin is as follows: ". . . in nova lege omnia illa ceremoniarum infinita onera id est peccatorum pericula ablata sunt nec iam pedes aut manus nec ullum aliud membrum deus requirit praeter aures. adeo sunt omnia in facilem vivendi modum redacta. Nam si quaeras ex Christiano quodnam sit opus quo dignus fiat nomine Christiano, nullum prorsus respondere poterit poterit nisi auditum verbi dei, id est fid. ideo solae aures sunt organa Christiani hominis, quia non ex ullius membri operibus sed de fide iustificatur et Christianus iudicatur." (*Luthers Vorlesung über den Hebräerbrief nach der vatikanischen Handschrift,* ed. Emanuel Hirsch and Hanns Rückert, Arbeiten zur Kirchengeschichte, no. 13 [Berlin and Leipzig: Walter de Gruyter, 1929], p. 250; cf. *WA* 37: 512^{16-17}–13^{9} [Lat.], 512^{36}–13^{19-29} [Ger.]).
33. *WA* 40.ii: 409^{23-26}.
34. *WA* 10.i.2: 74^{32}–75^{4}: "Es ist yhe [=ja] nicht muglich, eyn seele zu trosten, sie hore denn yhres gottis wortt. Wo ist aber gottis wortt ynn allen buchernn außer der heyligen schrifft? . . . trosten mag keyn Buch, denn die heyligen schrifft . . . ."
35. *WA* 30.i: 146: "Darümb wisse, das nicht alleine umb hören zuthuen ist, sondern auch sol gelernet und behalten werden."
36. Luther's Augustinian mentor, Staupitz, had written as follows about the importance of memorizing scripture for the monastic novice: "Der Novize soll die Heilige Schrift begierig lesen, andächtig hören, und eifrig lernen" (cited in Thimme, *Luthers Stellung zur Heiligen Schrift,* p. 7). On Luther's knowledge of scripture, see also n. 14 above.
37. *WA* 54:186^{10-11}: "Discurrebam deinde per scripturas, ut habebat memoria."
38. See Schwarz, *Principles and Problems,* pp. 187–95, 206–11; Ebeling, *Evangelische Evangelienauslegung,* pp. 205–06; Walther, *Luthers Deutsche Bibel,* pp. 39–45.
39. *WA* 25: 27^{5-6}: "Si sanctam scis scripturam, tamen semper relegendum . . . ."
40. *WA* 9: 440^{19-24}. N.B. esp. 440^{20}: "Predicari sive quecumque meditatio seu lectio, non enim refert." For other examples, see David C. Steinmetz, *Luther and Staupitz,* p. 53, Ebeling, *Evangelische Evangelienauslegung,* pp. 435–39, and the passages from Luther's work cited in the notes to both.
41. *WA* 43: 314^{36-37}: ". . . ut audiamus et tractemus, et ea, quae nobis natura ignota sunt, discamus."

42. *WA* 3: 539^{23-24}: "Meditatio enim est summa, efficacissima et brevissima eruditio." Cited also in Steinmetz, *Luther and Staupitz*, p. 53.
43. *WA* 50: 658^{29}–59^{4}: "Uber das wil ich dir anzeigen eine rechte weise in der Theologia zu studirn, denn ich mich geübet habe . . . . Und ist das die weise, die der heilige König David (on Zweivel [haben sie] auch alle Patriarchen und Propheten gehalten) leret im 119. Psalm. Da wirstu drey Regel innen finden, durch den gantzen Psalm furgestellet. Und heissen also: Oratio, Meditatio, Tentatio."
44. *WA* 50: 659^{22-25}: "Nicht allein im hertzen, sonder auch eusserlich die mündliche rede und buchstabische wort im Buch imer treiben und reiben, lesen und widerlesen, mit vleissigem auffmercken und nachdencken, was der heilige Geist damit meinet." On the trans. of "treiben und reiben" in this context as "repeat and compare", see editorial notes 3, 4 (ibid.). Cf. *WA* 32: 64^{24}–65^{6}.
45. Steinmetz, *Luther and Staupitz*, p. 57; cf. John Dillenberger, *God Hidden and Revealed: The Interpretation of Luther's "Deus absconditus" and Its Significance for Religious Thought* (Philadelphia: Muhlenberg Press, 1953), p. xiv.
46. Cf. the statement of Hanns Rückert: "Luther versteht unter dem Wort Gottes immer die viva vox evangelii, das lebendig in der Kirche verkündigte Wort, so daß damit die Geschichte dieser Kirche mit umgriffen ist als das Element, in dem Verkündigung und Weitergabe erfolgen" (as quoted in R. J. Geiselmann, "Das Konzil von Trient über das Verhältnis der Heiligen Schrift und der nicht geschriebenen Traditionen," p. 126).
47. *WA* 18: 136^{21-23}: "Und das mündliche Euangelion ist eyne göttliche Krafft, die do selig mache alle die dran glauben."
48. *WA* 10.i.1: 17^{7-12}: "Und Euangeli eygentlich nitt schrifft, sondern mundlich wort seyn solt . . . . [Euangeli,] das nitt mit der feddernn, sondern mit dem mund soll getrieben werden."
49. *WA* 12: 259^{10}: "Euangelion ist eygentlich nicht das, das in ynn büchern stehet und ynn buchstaben verfasset wirtt, sondern mehr eyn mundliche predig und lebendig wortt, und eyn stym, die da ynn die gantz wellt erschallet und offentlich wirt aussgeschryen." Cf. *WA* 10.i.2: 204^{20}: "Auffs erst, ists eyne rufende stym, nicht eyne schrifft: denn das gesetz und allte testament ist eyne todte schrifft ynn bucher verfasset. Aber das Euangelion soll eyn lebendige stymme seyn." Both passages are quoted by Schemmp, *Luthers Stellung*, pp. 33–34, n. 4, among others (cf. Bainton, "Bible in the Church," p. 20).
50. *Luther and Staupitz*, p. 57.
51. This line of imagery is neither original nor unique to Luther, although it was a strong theme of his work. Cf. Rom. 10.17: "ara hē pistis ex akoēs, hē de akoē dia hrēmatos Christou": "So faith is from hearing, and hearing [comes] through the word of Christ" [RSV: "So faith is from what is heard, and what is heard comes by the preaching of Christ"]. Cf. the citation of this verse by Luther's contemporary, Tilman von Lyn of Strassbourg (Lienhard and Rott, "Anfänge der evangelischen Predigt," p. 72).
52. Cf. Prenter refs. in n. 27 above.
53. Luther's concept of the "word of God" is certainly much more complex than this indicates, but for present purposes this question cannot be pursued further here. On this concept see Bornkamm, *Wort Gottes;* Schempp, *Luthers Stellung*, chaps. 1, 4, 6; Pelikan, *Luther*, esp. pp. 48–70.
54. *WA* 10.i.1: 625^{12}–26^{2}.
55. *WA* 10.i.1: 626^{5-9}: "Auch sehen wyr ynn den Apostoln, wie alle yhre predigett nichts anders geweßenn ist, denn die schrifft erfurbringen und sich drauff bawen.

Darumb hatt auch Christus selbs seyn lere nitt geschrieben, wie Moses die seine, ßondern hatt sie mundlich than . . . ."

56. *WA* 37: 512^{36}–13^{19}; cf. ibid. 4: 9–11.
57. *WA* 54: 474^{4}: "Des heiligen Geists eigen, sonderlich Buch, Schrifft und Wort."

Conclusion

1. "Entstehung und Wesen der Buchreligion."
2. A point emphasized to me with special vigor by Wendy Doniger O'Flaherty (pers. commun., March 1986) and also remarked upon in a forthcoming work of hers provisionally entitled *The Cave of Echoes: Other Peoples' Myths* (in the chapter "Oral and Written Gratification in the East," according to the preliminary draft Ms generously shared with me by the author).
3. *Heilige Schriften,* p. 17.
4. See, e.g., Benjamin M. Compaine's discussion of the recent ideas (e.g., of Anthony Oettinger) about a "New Literacy" that will result from the new developments in information technologies ("Information Technology and Cultural Change"; cf. Chapter 3, n. 33).
5. None of this is intended as a value judgment; these developments can be judged as positive or negative according to one's concerns and viewpoint. Certainly the results of such developments have been diverse. For example, in historical perspective, the "infamy" of religious intolerance, persecution, obscurantism, and authoritarianism that Voltaire and other prophets of the Enlightenment so excoriated has indeed been "erased" by comparison with, say, their presence on the sixteenth-century European scene. Yet Enlightenment rationalism and scientific and materialistic determinism have also failed to establish a sure basis of humanistic norms for social and individual life to replace those of traditional religion – hence, perhaps, the recurring revival of religious interest and fervor. "Secularization" as I use the term refers less to a process in which religion somehow disappears, and much more to one in which religious considerations no longer are easily agreed upon or widely recognized even as ideally important, let alone as factors of primary importance, in most sectors of life.
6. For some striking and interesting documentation of this specifically in American society, see the articles in Nathan O. Hatch and Mark A. Noll, *The Bible in America.* Note, e.g., Grant Wacker's observation in his article on the late nineteenth century: ". . . the Bible gradually ceased to be regarded as Scripture and came instead to be regarded as a mixture of Scripture and literature. Or, put another way, the Bible came to be seen as a human as well as a divine document" ("The Demise of Biblical Civilization," p. 124).

Abbreviations

This list includes encyclopedias, dictionaries, and other standard reference works not listed in the Bibliography. Full bibliographic information on all other entries can be found in the Bibliography under the names or titles given in bold type below, or in the notes, which are referenced in the Index of Names.

Abū Dāwūd	**Abū Dāwūd**, Sulaymān b. al-Ash'ath. *al-Sunan.* (4 vols. in 2)
Am. Letter	*Letter of Bishop Ammon* (Gk. text of Florence Ms [1021 C.E.] ed. F. **Halkin**, in *PVG,* pp. 97–121; text of Athens Ms [ca. 1000 C.E.] ed. F. **Halkin**, in *Corp. Ath.,* pp. 99–115)
Apolog.	**Justin** Martyr. *First Apology,* ed. Edgar J. Goodspeed
Apost. const.	F. X. **Funk**, ed. *Didascalia et Constitutiones apostolorum* (2 vols.)
Apost. Fathers	*The* ***Apostolic*** *Fathers* [Gk. and Lat. texts] (2 vols.)
ARG	*Archiv für Reformationsgeschichte*
BP	Hans **Quecke**, ed. *Die Briefe Pachoms*
Bruce and Rupp	F. F. **Bruce** and E. G. Rupp, eds. *Holy Book and Holy Tradition*
Bukhārī	al-**Bukhārī**. *al-Jāmi' al-ṣaḥīḥ* (9 vols.)
Camb. Hist. Bib.	*The* ***Cambridge*** *History of the Bible* (3 vols.)
CBTEL	*Cyclopædia of Biblical, Theological, and Ecclesiastical Literature,* comp. John McClintock and James Strong (10 vols. New York, 1867–86)
CE	*The Catholic Encyclopedia* (15 vols. + index. New York, 1900–13)
Coll. cist.	*Collectanea cisterciensia. Revue de spiritualité monastique* (Vols. 1–26 entitled *Collectanea ordinis Cisterciensium reformatorum*)

Corp. Ath.	F. **Halkin**, ed.; A.-J. Festugière, trans. *Le corpus athénien de saint Pachôme*
CSCO	*Corpus Scriptorum Christianorum Orientalium*
Dārimī	al-**Dārimī**. *al-Sunan* (2 vols.)
DBS	*Dictionnaire de la Bible, Supplément,* gen. ed. Louis Pirot (10 vols. to date. Paris, 1928–)
Denny and Taylor	F. M. **Denny** and R. L. Taylor, eds., *The Holy Book in Comparative Perspective*
Dict. spir.	*Dictionnaire de spiritualité, ascetique et mystique, doctrine et histoire,* ed. M[arcel] Viller et al. (11 vols. to date. Paris, 1932–)
EB[15]	*The New Encyclopædia Britannica* (15th ed. 30 vols., 1974)
EI	*The Encyclopaedia of Islam* (4 vols. + Supp. 1913–38)
EI[2]	*The Encyclopaedia of Islam. New Edition.* (1954–)
EJ	*Encyclopaedia Judaica* (16 vols. Jerusalem, 1971–72)
Encl. mus. sacr.	J. **Porte**, ed. *Encyclopédie des musiques sacrées.*
ERE	*Encyclopaedia of Religion and Ethics,* ed. J. Hastings (12 vols. + index. Edinburgh, 1908–26)
G[1]	*First Greek Life of Pachomius* (Gk. text of Florence Ms [1021 C.E.] ed. F. **Halkin**, in *PVG,* pp. 1-96 [photogr. repr. in *LifePG*[1]]; text of Athenian Ms [ca. 1000 C.E.] ed. F. **Halkin**, in *Corp. Ath.,* pp. 11–72)
GAS	Fuat Sezgin, *Geschichte des arabischen Schrifttums,* vol. 1 (Leiden, 1967)
GdQ	Th. **Nöldeke**, et al. *Geschichte des Qorāns* (3 vols.)
Ghazālī	al-**Ghazālī**. *Iḥyā' 'ulūm al-dīn* (5 vols.)
Goldziher Mem.	S. **Löwinger** and J. Somogyi, eds. *Ignace Goldziher Memorial Volume* (2 vols.)
Goody, *Literacy*	J. **Goody**, ed. *Literacy in Traditional Societies*
HDB	James Hastings, ed. *Dictionary of the Bible* (rev. ed. F. C. Grant and H. H. Rowley. New York, 1963)
HER	*Harvard Educational Review*
Hist. Laus.	C. **Butler**, ed. *The Lausiac History of Palladius*
Hors. Letter	*Letters* of Horsiesius (Copt. texts of Letters I and II ed. L. T. **Lefort**, in *OPD* 1: 63–65; III and IV only in Ms [not consulted], Chester Beatty Library)
Hors. Reg.	*Regulations* of Horsiesius (Copt. text ed. L. T. **Lefort**, in *OPD* 1: 82–99)
Hors. Test.	*Testament ["Book"] of Horsiesius* ["Liber Orsiesii"] (Lat. text ed. A. **Boon**, in *Pach. lat.,* pp. 109–47)
HTR	*Harvard Theological Review*
Hughes, *Dict.*	Thomas Patrick Hughes, *A Dictionary of Islam* (1885; expurgated repr. ed., Lahore, n.d.)
HwDA	*Handwörterbuch des deutschen Aberglaubens,* ed. Hans Bächthold-Stäubli (10 vols. Berlin, 1927–42)

Ibn Isḥāq	**Ibn Isḥāq**, *al-Sīrah al-nabawīyah* (4 vols.)
Ibn Sa°'d	**Ibn Sa'd**, *Kitāb al-ṭabaqāt al-kabīr* (8 vols.)
IJMES	*International Journal of Middle Eastern Studies*
Itqān	al-**Suyūṭī**, *al-Itqān fī 'ulūm al-Qur'ān*
JAAR	*Journal of the American Academy of Religion*
JAOS	*Journal of the American Oriental Society*
JAS	*Journal of Asian Studies*
JE	*The Jewish Encyclopedia,* ed. Isadore Singer et al. (12 vols. New York and London, 1901–06)
Johns, *ICSQ*	A. H. **Johns**, ed., *International Congress for the Study of the Qur'an*
Koehler and Baumgartner	Ludwig Koehler and Walter Baumgartner, eds., *Lexicon in Veteris Testamenti libros* (Leiden, 1953)
Kor. Unters.	J. **Horovitz**, *Koranische Untersuchungen*
Lane, *Lexicon*	E. W. Lane, *An Arabic–English Lexicon* (8 vols. London and Edinburgh, 1863–93)
Leg.	The *Precepts and Laws* of Pachomius (Latin text ed. A. **Boon** in *Pach. lat.,* pp. 71–74)
Lewis and Short	Charlton T. Lewis and Charles Short, eds. *A Latin Dictionary* (1879; repr. ed. Oxford, 1969)
Liddell and Scott	H. G. Liddell and Robert Scott, eds. *A Greek–English Lexicon* (1843; 9th rev. ed. H. S. Jones, with R. McKenzie, 1940; repr. with supp., 1968. Oxford, 1983)
LifePG[1]	A. N. **Athanassakis**, trans., *The Life of Pachomius (Vita prima graeca)*
Lisān	Ibn Manẓūr, *Lisān al-'arab* (15 vols. Beirut, 1374/1955)
LTK	*Lexikon für Theologie und Kirche* (2nd rev. ed. 10 vols. Freiburg i. Breisgau, 1957–65)
Mabānī	***Muqaddimat kitāb al-mabānī***, ed. Arthur Jeffery
Med. lat. lex.	*Mediae latinitatis lexicon minus,* comp. J. F. Niermeyer (Leiden, 1976)
MIDEO	*Mélanges de l'Institut Dominicain d'Études Orientales du Caire*
MLN	*Modern Language Notes*
Muslim	**Muslim** ibn al-Hajjāj, *Ṣaḥīḥ* (4 vols. + indexes)
Musnad	**Ibn Ḥanbal**, *al-Musnad* (6 vols.)
Musnad[2]	**Ibn Ḥanbal**, *al-Musnad* (ed. Aḥmad Shākir, 15 vols.)
MW	*The Muslim World* (formerly *The Moslem World*)
Nasā'ī	**al-Nasā'ī**, *al-Sunan* (8 vols.)
ODCC[2]	*The Oxford Dictionary of the Christian Church* (2nd rev. ed. F. L. Cross and E. A. Livingstone, 1974; repr. ed. Oxford, etc., 1983)
OED	*The Oxford English Dictionary* (Compact, micrographically reproduced ed., Oxford, etc., 1971)

OLD	*Oxford Latin Dictionary,* ed. P. G. W. Glare (Oxford, 1982 [fascicles publ. 1968–82])
OPD	L. T. **Lefort**, ed. *Oeuvres de S. Pachôme et de ses disciples* (2 vols.: 1= *CSCO* 159 [Copt.]; 2= *CSCO* 160 [Fr. trans.])
Pach. inst.	*Precepts and Institutes* of Pachomius (Copt. text ed. L. T. **Lefort** in *OPD* 1: 80, 33–36)
Pach. Instr.	*Instructions* of Pachomius (Copt. text ed. L. T. **Lefort** in *OPD* 1: 1–26)
Pach. lat.	A. **Boon**, ed. *Pachomiana Latina*
Pach. leg.	*Precepts and Laws* of Pachomius (Lat. text ed. A. **Boon** in *Pach. lat.,* pp. 71–74)
Pach. Letter	*Letters* of Pachomius (Gk. and Copt. texts ed. H. **Quecke** in *BP,* pp. 99–118; Lat. text ed. A. **Boon** in *Pach. lat.,* pp. 75–101)
Paral.	Pachomian *Paralipomena* (Gk. text of Florence Ms [A.D. 1021] ed. F. **Halkin** in *PVG,* pp. 122–65; text of Athenian Ms [ca. 1000 C.E.] ed. F. **Halkin**, in *Corp. Ath.,* pp. 73–93)
PG	J. P. Migne, ed. *Patrologia graeca* (Paris, 1857–)
PK (1,2,3)	A. **Veilleux**, trans. *Pachomian Koinonia* (vols. 1, 2, 3)
PL	J. P. Migne, ed. *Patrologia latina* (Paris, 1844–)
Pr.	*Precepts (Praecepta)* of Pachomius (Lat. text ed. A. **Boon**, in *Pach. lat.,* pp. 13–52; partial Copt. text ed. L. T. **Lefort**, in *OPD* 1)
PVBS	L. T. **Lefort**, ed. *S. Pachomii vita bohairice scripta* (2 vols.: 1= *CSCO* 89; 2=*CSCO* 107)
PVG	F. **Halkin**, ed. *Sancti Pachomii vitae graecae*
PVSS	L. T. **Lefort**, ed. *S. Pachomii vitae sahidice scriptae*
RB	**Benedict** of Nursia, *Regula Monachorum* (ed. and comm. B. Linderbauer)
Resnick, *Literacy*	D. P. **Resnick**, ed. *Literacy in Historical Perspective*
*RGG*²	*Die Religion in Geschichte und Gegenwart* (2nd rev. ed. 5 vols. + indexes. Tübingen, 1927–32)
*RGG*³	*Die Religion in Geschichte und Gegenwart* (3rd rev. ed. 6 vols. + indexes. Tübingen, 1957–65)
RHR	*Revue de l'Histoire des Religions*
S^1, S^2, S^{10}	The (first, second, tenth) Sahidic *Life of Pachomius,* fragments (Copt. texts ed. L. T. **Lefort**, in *PVSS*)
SBo	The Bohairic *Life of Pachomius* (Copt. text ed. L. T. **Lefort**, in *PVBS* 1, pp. 1–215)
SEI	*Shorter Encyclopaedia of Islam,* ed. H. A. R. Gibb and J. H. Kramers (1953; repr. ed., Leiden and London, 1961)
Ṭabarī	al-**Ṭabarī**, *Jāmi' al-bayān 'an ta'wīl āy al-Qur'ān* (30 vols.)

Ṭabarī[2]	al-**Ṭabarī**, *Jāmiʿ al-bayān* . . . (ed. Shākir, 16 vols. to date)
Theod. Instr.	*Instructions* of Theodore (Copt. text ed. L. T. **Lefort**, in *OPD* 1: 37–60)
Theod. Letter	*Letters* of Theodore (Lat. text ed. A. **Boon** in *Pach. lat.*, pp. 105–06)
Theol. Begriffslex.	*Theologisches Begriffslexikon zum Neuen Testament,* ed. Lothar Coenen, E. Beyreuther, and H. Bietenhard (2 vols. in 3 [1; 2.1; 2. 2] Wuppertal, 1967–71)
Théol. vie mon.	***Théologie*** *de la vie monastique*
Thes. ling. lat.	*Thesaurus linguae latinae* (Leipzig, 1900–)
Tirmidhī	Muḥammad al-**Tirmidhī**, *al-Jāmiʿ al-ṣaḥīḥ* (5 vols.)
TLZ	*Theologische Literaturzeitung*
TRE	*Theologische Realenzyklopädie* (12 vols. to date. Berlin and New York, 1977–)
Vermächtnis 1	H. **Bacht**, *Das Vermächtnis des Ursprungs,* vol. 1
WA	Martin **Luther**, *Werke* (Weimarer Ausgabe)
WKAS	*Wörterbuch der klassischen arabischen Sprache,* ed. M. Ullman, with A. Spitaler (J. Kraemer and H. Gätje, founding eds.; 2 vols. to date. Wiesbaden, 1970–)
WZKM	*Wiener Zeitschrift für die Kunde des Morgenlandes*
ZDMG	*Zeitschrift der Deutschen Morgenländischen Gesellschaft*
ZNTW	*Zeitschrift für die neutestamentliche Wissenschaft und die Kunde der älteren Kirche*

Bibliography

The following is a bibliography of the most relevant and frequently cited works consulted in the present study. Works relevant only to very specific or ancillary issues and most works cited only once are not included; these are cited in full in the notes in which they occur and listed in the index. Dictionaries, encyclopedias, and other standard reference works have normally been omitted from the Bibliography and instead cited in brief in the list of abbreviations (e.g., *The New Encyclopaedia Britannica, The Encyclopaedia of Islam*). Three kinds of additional, bracketed information may follow some bibliographic entries: (1) the abbreviation used throughout this book for the work; (2) a cross reference to another entry; and (3) reprint or other editions that were *not* consulted directly. For translated works, usually both the original and its English translation are cited in the same entry, the original first, followed by the translation. (In the text, the original is normally the source relied upon, except where the English version represents not only a translation, but also a revision of the original, in which case it precedes the original and is the version referred to in the text.) Otherwise, where multiple versions or editions of a work are cited in a bibliographic entry, all references in the book are to the last cited version or edition. Note that diacritical marks do not affect alphabetization (e.g., "ü" is treated as "u", "ø" as "o").

Abegg, Emil. "Die Lehre von der Ewigkeit des Wortes bei Kumārila." In *ANTIΔΩPON. Festschrift Jacob Wackernagel . . . gewidmet von Schülern, Freunden und Kollegen.* Göttingen: Vandenhoeck & Ruprecht, 1923, pp. 255–64.

Abhyankar, K. V., and G. V. Devasthali, comp. and ed. *Vedavikṛtilakṣaṇa-Saṁgraha: A Collection of Twelve Tracts on Vedavikṛtis and Allied Topics.* Research Unit Publications, 5. Poona: Bhandarkar Oriental Research Institute, 1978.

Abū Dāwūd, Sulaymān b. al-Ash'ath al-Sijistānī. *al-Sunan.* Ed. Muḥammad Muḥyī l-Dīn 'Abd al-Ḥamīd. 4 vols. in 2. Cairo: Dār al-Fikr, n.d. [Abū Dāwūd]

Adamson, John William. "The Illiterate Anglo-Saxon." In *"The Illiterate Anglo-Saxon" and Other Essays on Education, Medieval and Modern.* Cambridge: Cambridge University Press, 1946, pp. 1–20.

———. "Literacy in England in the Fifteenth and Sixteenth Centuries." In *"The Il-*

literate Anglo-Saxon" and Other Essays on Education, Medieval and Modern. Cambridge: Cambridge University Press, 1946, pp. 38–61.

____. "Medieval Education." In *"The Illiterate Anglo-Saxon" and Other Essays on Education, Medieval and Modern.* Cambridge: Cambridge University Press, 1946, pp. 62–76.

Adler, Israël. "Histoire de la musique religieuse juive." In *Encl. mus. sacr.*, pp. 469–93.

Aitareya Āraṇyaka, The. Ed. and trans. Arthur Berriedale Keith. Anecdota Oxoniensia, Aryan Series, pt. 9. Oxford: Clarendon Press, 1909.

Aland, Kurt, ed. *Luther Deutsch.* [**See** Luther, Martin.]

____, ed. *Lutherlexikon.* Luther Deutsch, supp. vol. 3. Stuttgart: Ehrenfried Klotz, 1957.

____, ed., with Ernst Otto Reichert and Gerhard Jordan. *Hilfsbuch zum Lutherstudium.* Gütersloh: Carl Bertelsmann Verlag, n.d. [1957?]. 3rd rev. ed. Witten: Luther-Verlag, 1970.

Altekar, A. S. *Education in Ancient India.* Banaras: The Indian Book Shop, 1934.

Amand, David. [**See** Amand de Mendieta, Emmanuel.]

Amand de Mendieta, Emmanuel ["David Amand"]. *L'ascèse monastique de saint Basile. Essai historique.* Maredsous: Éditions de Maredsous, 1949.

____. "Le système cénobitique basilien comparé au système cénobitique pachômien." *RHR* 152 (1957): 31–80.

Anderson, G. W. "Canonical and Non-Canonical." In *Camb. Hist. Bib.* 1: 113–59.

Andrae, Tor. *Mohammed. Sein Leben und sein Glaube.* Göttingen: Vandenhoeck & Ruprecht, 1932. Eng. trans. Theophil Menzel. *Mohammed: The Man and His Faith.* New York: Charles Scribner's Sons, 1936. Rev. ed. 1955. New York and Evanston, Ill.: Harper & Row, Harper Torchbooks, 1960.

____. *Die Person Muhammeds in Lehre und Glauben seiner Gemeinde.* Archives d'études orientales, ed. J.-A. Lundell, vol. 16. Stockholm: P. A. Norstedt & Söner, 1918.

____. "Der Ursprung des Islams und das Christentum." *Kyrkohistorisk Årsskrift* 23 (1923): 149–206; 24 (1924): 213–92; 25 (1925): 45–112.

Andresen, Carl. *Die Kirchen der alten Christenheit.* Die Religionen der Menschheit, ed. Christel Matthias Schröder, vol. 29. Stuttgart, etc.: W. Kohlhammer, 1971.

Anesaki, Masaharu. *Nichiren, the Buddhist Prophet.* 1916. Repr. ed. Gloucester, Mass.: Peter Smith, 1966.

Antes, Peter. "Schriftverständnis im Islam." *Theologische Quartalschrift* 161 (1981): 179–91.

Anwarul Haq. [**See** Haq, M. Anwarul.]

Apostolic Constitutions. [**See** Funk, Franciscus Xaverius, ed.]

Apostolic Fathers, The. Gk. texts with an Eng. trans. by Kirsopp Lake. 2 vols. The Loeb Classical Library. London: William Heinemann: New York: G. P. Putnam's Sons, 1912–13. [*Apost. Fathers*]

Apte, V. M. "The 'Spoken Word' in Sanskrit Literature." *Bulletin of the Deccan College Research Institute* 4 (1943): 269–80.

Arberry, Arthur J., trans. [**See** Qur'ān, al-.]

Assche, Modestus Van. "'Divinae vacare lectioni'. De 'ratio studiorum' van Sint Benedictus." *Sacris erudiri* 1 (1948): 13–34.

Aston, Margaret. "Lollardy and Literacy." *History* 62 (1977): 347–71.

Athanassakis, Apostolos N., trans. *The Life of Pachomius (Vita prima graeca).* Society of Biblical Literature Texts and Translations, 7 (Early Christian Literature Series, 2). Missoula, Mont.: Scholars Press, 1975. [*Life PG*[1]]

[*Atharva Veda Saṁhitā* .] Ed. R. Roth and W. D. Whitney, as: *Atharva Veda Sanhita.* Vol. 1: Text. Berlin, 1856. Eng. trans. William Dwight Whitney. Rev. and trans. Charles Rockwell Lanman, as *Atharva-Veda Saṁhitā.* 2 pts. Cambridge, Mass.: Harvard University Press, 1905.

Augapfel, Julius. "Das *Kitāb* im Qurân." *WZKM* 29 (1915): 384–93.

Augustine of Hippo, [Saint] Aurelius. *Confessionum libri XIII.* Ed. Lucas Verheijen. Corpus Christianorum, Ser. Latina, 27. Turnhout, Belgium: Brepols, 1981. Eng. trans. Edward B. Pusey. *The Confessions of Saint Augustine.* New York: Random House, Modern Library, 1949.

Austin, J. L. *How to Do Things with Words.* The William James Lectures Delivered at Harvard University in 1955. Cambridge, Mass.: Harvard University Press, 1962.

Babb, Lawrence A. *The Divine Hierarchy: Popular Hinduism in Central India.* New York and London: Columbia University Press, 1975.

Bacht, Heinrich. "Antonius und Pachomius. Von der Anachorese zum Cönobitentum." In *Antonius Magnus Eremita, 356–1956. Studia ad antiquum monachismum spectantia,* ed. Basilius Steidle. Studia Anselmiana, 38. Rome, 1956, pp. 66–107.

———. "'Meditatio' in den ältesten Mönchsquellen." *Geist und Leben* 28 (1955): 360–73. Rev. version published as Excursus 4 of Bacht, *Vermächtnis* 1: 244–64.

———. "Pakhôme et ses disciples." In *Théol. vie mon.,* pp. 39–71.

———. "Die Rolle der Heiligen Schrift bei Horsiesius." Excursus 1 of Bacht, *Vermächtnis* 1: 191–212.

———. "Studien zum 'Liber Orsiesii'." *Historisches Jahrbuch* 77 (1958): 98–124.

———. *Das Vermächtnis des Ursprungs. Studien zum frühen Mönchtum I.* Studien zur Theologie des geistlichen Lebens, ed. Friedrich Wulf and Josef Sudbrack, vol. 5. Würzburg: Echter Verlag, 1972. [*Vermächtnis* 1]

———. *Das Vermächtnis des Ursprungs. Studien zum frühen Mönchtum II. Pachomius – Der Mann und sein Werk.* Studien zur Theologie des geistlichen Lebens, ed. Friedrich Wulf and Josef Sudbrack, vol. 8. Würzburg: Echter Verlag, 1983.

———. "Vom Umgang mit der Bibel im ältesten Mönchtum." *Theologie und Philosophie* [formerly *Scholastik*] 41 (1966): 557–66.

——— [misspelled on title p. as "H. Bracht"], H. Fries, and R. J. Geiselmann. *Die mündliche Überlieferung: Beiträge zum Begriff der Tradition.* Ed. Michael Schmaus. Munich: Max Hueber, 1957.

Baddeley, Alan D. *The Psychology of Memory.* Basic Topics in Cognition Series, ed. Sam Glucksberg. New York: Basic Books, 1976.

Bainton, Roland H. "The Bible in the Reformation." In *Camb. Hist. Bib.* 3: 1–37 (text), 536 (Bibliog.).

Ballantyne, "Dr." "The Eternity of Sound: A Dogma of the Mi´ma´nsa´." *The Pandit* (Banaras) 1 (1866): 68–71, 86–88.

Balogh, Josef. "'Voces paginarum'. Beiträge zur Geschichte des lauten Lesens und Schreibens." *Philologus* 82 (1926–27): 83–109, 202–40.

Barbès, Léo. [**See** Cantineau, Jean, and Léo Barbès.]

Barr, James. *Holy Scripture: Canon, Authority, Criticism.* Philadelphia: The Westminster Press, 1983.

Barrier, N. Gerald, ed. [**See** Juergensmeyer, Mark, and N. Gerald Barrier, eds.]

Barth, Auguste. *Bulletins des religions de l'Inde (1889–1902).* Œuvres de Auguste Barth, recueillies à l'occasion de son quatre-vingtième anniversaire, vol. 2. Paris: Ernest Leroux, 1914.

Bartlett, F. C. *Remembering: A Study in Experimental and Social Psychology.* New York: Macmillan; Cambridge: Cambridge University Press, 1932.

Bauer, D. Walter. *Der Wortgottesdienst der ältesten Christen.* Tübingen: J. C. B. Mohr (Paul Siebeck), 1930.

Bauer, Franz. "Die Heilige Schrift bei den Mönchen des christlichen Altertums. Nach den Schriften des Johannes Cassianus." *Theologie und Glaube* 17 (1925): 512–32.

Bäuml, Franz H. "Varieties and Consequences of Medieval Literacy and Illiteracy." *Speculum* 55 (1980): 237–65.

Baumstark, Anton. *Nocturna Laus. Typen frühchristlicher Vigilienfeier und ihr Fortleben vor allem im römischen und monastischen Ritus.* Ed. P. Odilo Heiming. Liturgiewissenschaftliche Quellen und Forschungen, vol. 32. Münster (Westphalia): Aschendorff, 1957.

Beck, Edmund. "Der 'ut̠mānische Kodex in der Koranlesung des zweiten Jahrhunderts." *Orientalia* 14 (1945): 355–73.

____. "Die b. Mas'ūdvarianten bei al-Farrā'." *Orientalia* (Rome) 25 (1956): 353–83; 28 (1959): 186–205, 230–56.

Becker, C. H. "Zur Geschichte des islamischen Kultus." *Der Islam* 3 (1912): 374–99. Repr. in C. H. Becker, *Islamstudien. Vom Werden und Wesen der islamischen Welt.* 2 vols. Leipzig: Quelle & Meyer, 1924–32. Photo-repr. ed. Hildesheim: Georg Olms, 1967. 1: 472–500.

Beisser [Beißer], Friedrich. *Claritas scripturae bei Martin Luther.* Forschungen zur Kirchen- und Dogmengeschichte, vol. 18. Göttingen: Vandenhoeck & Ruprecht, 1966.

Bell, Richard. *Introduction to the Qur'ān.* [**See** Watt, William Montgomery, ed.]

____. *The Origin of Islam in its Christian Environment.* The Gunning Lectures, Edinburgh University, 1925. London: Macmillan, 1926.

____, trans. [**See** Qur'ān, al-.]

Bellaire, Michaux. "L'enseignement indigène au Maroc." *Revue du Monde Musulman* 15 (1911): 422–52.

[Benedict of Nursia, Saint.] *S. Benedicti Regula monachorum.* Ed. and comm. Benno Linderbauer. Metten: Benediktinerstift, 1922. [*RB*]

Bennett, H. S. *English Books & Readers 1475 to 1557: Being a Study in the History of the Book Trade from Caxton to the Incorporation of the Stationers' Company*. Cambridge: Cambridge University Press, 1952.

Berger, Morroe. *Islam in Egypt Today: Social and Political Aspects of Popular Religion*. Cambridge: Cambridge University Press, 1970.

Bergsträsser [Bergsträßer], G[otthelf]. "Die Koranlesung des Hasan von Basra." *Islamica* 2 (1926): 11–57.

____. "Koranlesung in Kairo." *Der Islam* 20 (1932): 1–42; 21 (1933): 110–40 (incl. sect. by K. Huber, "Koranrezitationen," pp. 113–33).

____. [**See** Nöldeke, Theodor, et al.]

____, ed. [**See** Ibn Khālawayh.]

Bertholet, Alfred. "Die Macht der Schrift in Glauben und Aberglauben." *Abhandlungen der Deutschen Akademie der Wissenschaften zu Berlin*. Philos.-hist. Klasse. 1948, no. 1 (48 pp.).

____. "Wortanklang und Volksetymologie in ihrer Wirkung auf religiösen Glauben und Brauch." *Abhandlungen der Preußischen Akademie der Wissenschaften* (Berlin). 1940, no. 6 (24 pp.).

Besse, J.-M. *Les moines d'orient antérieurs au concile de Chalcédoine (451)*. Paris and Poitiers: H. Oudin, 1900.

Bethe, Erich. *Buch und Bild im Altertum*. Comp. and ed. Ernst Kirsten. Leipzig and Vienna: Otto Harrassowitz, 1945.

Bhandarkar, D. R. "The Indian Alphabet." *Calcutta Review*, n.s., 29 (1920): 21–39.

Bhattacharya, Gopika Mohan. "A Study on the Eternity of Sound." *Calcutta Review* 142 (1957): 61–71.

Biardeau, Madeleine. *Théorie de la connaissance et philosophie de la parole dans le brahmanisme classique*. Le monde d'outre-mer passé et présent, ser. 1, Études, 23. Paris and the Hague: Mouton, 1964.

Bischoff, Bernhard. "Elementarunterricht und Probationes Pennae in der ersten Hälfte des Mittelalters." *Mittelalterliche Studien. Ausgewählte Aufsätze zur Schriftkunde und Literaturgeschichte*. Vol. 1. Stuttgart: Anton Hiersemann, 1966, pp. 74–87.

Bizer, Ernst. *Fides ex auditu. Eine Untersuchung über die Entdeckung der Gerechtigkeit Gottes durch Martin Luther*. 3rd rev. ed. Neukirchen/Vluyn: Neukirchener Verlag, 1966.

Blachère, Régis. *Introduction au Coran*. Islam d'hier et d'aujourd'hui, ed. E. Lévi-Provençal, vol. 3. Paris: G.-P. Maisonneuve, 1947.

____, trans. [**See** Qur'ān, al-.]

Bleeker, C. J. "Religious Tradition and Sacred Books in Ancient Egypt." In Bruce and Rupp, pp. 20–35.

Bloch, Maurice. "Astrology and Writing in Madagascar." In Goody, *Literacy*, pp. 278–97.

Bonazzoli, Giorgio. "Composition, Transmission and Recitation of the Purāṇa-s (A Few Remarks)." *Purāṇa* 25 (1983): 254–80.

Bond, George D. "Two Theravada Traditions of the Meaning of 'the Word of the Buddha'." *The Maha Bodhi* 83 (1975): 402–13.

Boon, Amand, ed. *Pachomiana Latina. Règle et épitres de S. Pachôme, épitre de S. Théodore et "Liber" de S. Orsiesius. Text latin de S. Jérôme.* Bibliothèque de la Revue d'histoire ecclésiastique, no. 7. Louvain: Bureaux de la Revue, 1932. [*Pach. lat.*]

Bornkamm, Heinrich. *Luther und das Alte Testament.* Tübingen: J. C. B. Mohr (Paul Siebeck), 1948.

____. *Das Wort Gottes bei Luther.* Schriftenreihe der Luthergesellschaft, no. 7. Munich: Chr. Kaiser, 1933.

Boubakeur, Si Hamza. "Psalmodie coranique." *Encl. mus. sacr,* pp. 388–403.

Bousset, Wilhelm. *Apophthegmata. Studien zur Geschichte des ältesten Mönchtums.* Ed. Theodor Hermann and Gustav Krüger. Tübingen: J. C. B. Mohr (Paul Siebeck), 1923.

Bouwsma, William J. "The Culture of Renaissance Humanism." 1959, 1966. Rev. ed. AHA Pamphlets, 401. Washington, D.C.: American Historical Association, 1973.

Bowman, John. "The Debt of Islam to Monophysite Syrian Christianity." In *Essays in Honour of Griffithes Wheeler Thatcher, 1863–1950,* ed. E. C. B. MacLaurin. Sydney: Sydney University Press, 1967, pp. 191–216.

____. "Holy Scriptures, Lectionaries and Qur'an." In Johns, *ICSQ,* pp. 29–37.

Boyd, James W. "Zoroastrianism: Avestan Scripture and Rite." In Denny and Taylor, pp. 109–25.

Brandon, S. G. F. "The Holy Book, the Holy Tradition and the Holy Ikon." In Bruce and Rupp, pp. 1–19.

[Bṛhadāraṇyaka Upaniṣad.] *The Bṛhadāraṇyaka Upaniṣad, with the Commentary of Śaṅkarācārya.* Trans. Swāmī Mādhavānanda. [1934?] 4th ed. Calcutta: Advaita Ashrama, 1965.

Brough, John. "Some Indian Theories of Meaning." *Transactions of the Philological Society* (London and Oxford), 1953, pp. 161–76.

Brown, Peter. *Augustine of Hippo: A Biography.* Berkeley and Los Angeles: University of California Press, 1969.

____. *The World of Late Antiquity,* A.D.*150–750.* London: Thames and Hudson, 1971. Repr. ed. [New York:] Harcourt Brace Jovanovich, 1976.

Brown, W. Norman. "The Creative Role of the Goddess Vāc in the Rig Veda." In *Pratidānam: Indian, Iranian and Indo-European Studies Presented to F. B. J. Kuiper . . . ,* ed. J. C. Heesterman, G. H. Schokker, and V. I. Subramoniam. Janua linguarum, Series maior, no. 34. The Hague and Paris: Mouton, 1968, pp. 393–97. [Repr. in W. Norman Brown. *India and Indology: Selected Articles.* Ed. Rosane Rocher. Delhi, etc.: Motilal Banarsidass, 1978, pp. 75–78.]

____. "Theories of Creation in the Ṛg Veda." *JAOS* 85 (1965): 23–34. Repr. in W. Norman Brown. *India and Indology: Selected Articles.* Ed. Rosane Rocher. Delhi, etc.: Motilal Banarsidass, 1978, pp. 40–52.

Bruce, F. F. *History of the Bible in English, from the Earliest Versions.* New York: Oxford University Press, 1978.

____, and E. G. Rupp, eds. *Holy Book and Holy Tradition.* Grand Rapids, Mich.: William B. Eerdmans, 1968. [Bruce and Rupp]

Buck, Harry M. "Saving Story and Sacred Book: Some Aspects of the Phenomenon of Religious Literature." In *Search the Scriptures: New Testament Studies in Honor of Raymond T. Stamm,* ed. J. M. Myers, O. Reimherr, and H. N. Bream. Gettysburg Theological Studies, no. 3. Leiden: E. J. Brill, 1969, pp. 79–94.

Buhl, Frants. *Das Leben Muhammeds.* Trans. from the Danish by Hans Heinrich Schaeder. Leipzig: Quelle & Meyer, 1930.

____. "'Die Schrift' und was damit zusammenhängt im Qurân." In *Oriental Studies Published in Commemoration of . . . Paul Haupt,* ed. Cyrus Adler and Aaron Ember. Baltimore: Johns Hopkins Press; Leipzig: J. C. Hinrichs, 1926, pp. 364–73.

Bühler, G[eorg]. *Indische Palaeographie von circa 350 a. Chr. - circa 1300 p. Chr.* Grundriß der indo-arischen Philologie und Altertumskunde, ed. Georg Bühler, vol. 1, pt. 2. Strasbourg: Karl J. Trübner, 1896.

____, trans. [**See** *Mānavadharmaśāstra.*]

Buitenen, J. A. B. van. "On the Archaism of the Bhāgavata Purāṇa." In *Krishna: Myths, Rites, and Attitudes,* ed. Milton Singer. 1966. Chicago and London: University of Chicago Press, Phoenix Books, 1968, pp. 23–40.

Bukhārī, Muḥammad b. Ismāʿīl al-. *al-Jāmiʿ al-ṣaḥīḥ.* Ed. Ḥasūnah al-Nawāwī. 9 vols. Cairo: Muṣṭafá al-Bābī al-Ḥalabī wa-Awlāduhu, [1378/1958?]. Repr. ed. Beirut: Dār Iḥyā' al-Turāth al-ʿArabī, n.d. [Bukhārī]

Bulgakov, Sergius. *The Orthodox Church.* Trans. from the Russian by Elizabeth [C.] Cram. Ed. by Donald A. Lowrie. New York and Milwaukee: Morehouse; London: Centenary Press, n.d. [1935?].

Burdach, Konrad. "Die nationale Aneignung der Bibel und die Anfänge der germanischen Philologie." In *Festschrift Eugen Mogk zum 70. Geburtstag, 19 Juli 1924.* Halle/Saale: Max Niemeyer, 1924, pp. 231–334.

Burton, John. *The Collection of the Qur'ān.* Cambridge, etc.: Cambridge University Press, 1977.

Butler, Cuthbert, ed. *The Lausiac History of Palladius: A Critical Discussion together with Notes on Early Egyptian Monachism.* 2 vols. Texts and Studies, Contributions to Biblical and Patristic Literature, ed. J. Armitage Robinson, vol. 6.1–2. Cambridge, 1898–1904. [*Hist. Laus.*]

Caland, W[illem]. "De Ontdekkingsgeschiedenis van den Veda." *Verslagen en Mededeelingen der Koninklijke Akademie van Wetenschappen.* Afdeeling Letterkunde. Ser. 5, pt. 3 [vol. 51] (1918): 261–334.

The Cambridge History of the Bible. Vol. 1: From the Beginnings to Jerome, ed. P. R. Ackroyd and C. F. Evans (1970); Vol. 2: The West from the Fathers to the Reformation, ed. G. W. H. Lampe (1969); Vol. 3: The West from the Reformation to the Present Day, ed. S. L. Greenslade (1963). Cambridge: Cambridge University Press, 1963–70. [*Camb. Hist. Bib.*]

Campenhausen, Hans von. *Aus der Frühzeit des Christentums. Studien zur Kirchengeschichte des ersten und zweiten Jahrhunderts.* Tübingen: J. C. B. Mohr (Paul Siebeck), 1963.

____. *Die Entstehung der christlichen Bibel.* Tübingen: J. C. B. Mohr (Paul

Siebeck), 1968. Eng. trans. J. A. Baker. *The Formation of the Christian Bible.* Philadelphia: Fortress, 1972.

Cantineau, Jean, and Léo Barbès. "La récitation coranique à Damas et à Alger." *Annales de l'Institut d'Études Orientales* (Algiers) 6 (1942–47): 66–91.

Carcopino, Jérôme. *Daily Life in Ancient Rome: The People and the City at the Height of the Empire.* Ed. Henry T. Rowell. Trans. E. O. Lorimer. New Haven: Yale University Press, 1940. [Fr. orig.: *La vie quotidienne à Rome à l'appogee de l'Empire.* Paris: Hachette, 1939.]

Carlyle, Thomas. *On Heroes, Hero-Worship, and the Heroic in History: Six Lectures.* [1840]. 2nd ed. London: Chapman and Hall, 1842.

Carothers, J. C. "Culture, Psychiatry, and the Written Word." *Psychiatry* 22 (1959): 307–20.

Carter, Thomas Francis. *The Invention of Printing in China and Its Spread Westward.* 1925. Rev. ed. 1931. 2nd rev. ed. L. Carrington Goodrich. New York: Ronald Press, 1955.

Cassian, John. *Conlationes.* Ed. and trans. into Fr. by E. Pichery as: Jean Cassien. *Conférences.* 3 vols. Sources chrétiennes, nos. 42, 54, 64. Paris: Éditions du Cerf, 1955–59.

——. *De institutis coenobiorum.* Ed. and trans. into Fr. by Jean-Claude Guy as: Jean Cassien. *Institutions cénobitiques.* Sources chrétiennes, no. 109. Paris: Éditions du Cerf, 1965.

Cerri, Giovanni. [**See** Gentili, Bruno, and Giovanni Cerri.]

Chadwick, Owen. *John Cassian: A Study in Primitive Monasticism.* 1950. 2nd ed. [without subtitle]. Cambridge: Cambridge University Press, 1968.

Chakravarti, Prabhat Chandra. *The Philosophy of Sanskrit Grammar.* Calcutta: University of Calcutta, 1930.

Chaytor, H. J. *From Script to Print: An Introduction to Medieval Vernacular Literature.* Cambridge: W. Heffer & Sons, 1945.

Childs, Brevard S. *Introduction to the Old Testament as Scripture.* Philadelphia: Fortress, 1979.

Chitty, Derwas J. *The Desert A City: An Introduction to the Study of Egyptian and Palestinian Monasticism under the Christian Empire.* Crestwood, N.Y.: St. Vladimir's Seminary Press, 1966.

Chrisman, Miriam Usher. *Lay Culture, Learned Culture: Books and Social Change in Strasbourg, 1480–1599.* New Haven and London: Yale University Press, 1982.

Cipolla, Carlo M. *Literacy and Development in the West.* Harmondsworth, UK, Baltimore, Md., and Victoria, Austral.: Penguin, 1969.

Clanchy, M. T. *From Memory to Written Record: England, 1066–1307.* Cambridge, Mass.: Harvard University Press, 1979.

——. "Looking Back from the Invention of Printing." In Resnick, *Literacy,* pp. 7–22.

——. "Remembering the Past and the Good Old Law." *History* 55 (1970): 165–76.

Clement, First Epistle of. In *Apost. Fathers* 1: 1–121.

Clement, Second Epistle of. In *Apost. Fathers* 1: 123–63.

Clercq, Charles de. [**See** De Clercq, Charles.]

Coburn, Thomas B. " 'Scripture' in India: Towards a Typology of the Word in Hindu Life." *JAAR* 52 (1984): 435–59.

____. "The Study of the Purāṇas and the Study of Religion." *Religious Studies* 16 (1980): 341–52.

Cole, Michael. [**See** Scribner, Sylvia, and Michael Cole.]

Cole, W. Owen, and Piara Singh Sambhi. *The Sikhs: Their Religious Beliefs and Practices.* London, Henley, and Boston: Routledge & Kegan Paul, 1978.

Collison, Robert L. "Encyclopaedia." *EB*[15], Macropædia 6: 779b–99b.

____. *Encyclopaedias: Their History Throughout the Ages.* New York and London: Hafner, 1964.

Columbas, G. M. "La Biblia en la espiritualidad del monacato primitivo." *Yermo* 1 (1963): 3–20, 149–70, 271–86; 2 (1964): 3–14, 113–29.

Compaine, Benjamin M. "Information Technology and Cultural Change: Toward a New Literacy?" Publication of the Program on Information Resources Policy. Cambridge, Mass.: Harvard University, Center for Information Policy Research, 1984.

Confucius. [**See** Waley, Arthur, trans.]

Constable, Giles. *Medieval Monasticism: A Select Bibliography.* Toronto Medieval Bibliographies, ed. John Leyerle, no. 6. Toronto and Buffalo: University of Toronto Press, 1976.

Coomaraswamy, Ananda K. "The Bugbear of Literacy." In *The Bugbear of Literacy.* 1949. Rev. ed. Bedfont, Middlesex, England: Perennial Books, 1979, pp. 33–49.

____. "Recollection, Indian and Platonic." In Supp. no. 3 (April–June, 1944), to *JAOS* 64 (1944), pp. 1–18.

Corless, Roger. "The Meaning of *Ching (Sūtra?)* in Buddhist Chinese." *Journal of Chinese Philosophy* 3 (1975): 67–72.

Cressy, David. "The Environment for Literacy: Accomplishment and Context in Seventeenth-Century England and New England." In Resnick, *Literacy,* pp. 23–42.

____. *Literacy and the Social Order: Reading and Writing in Tudor and Stuart England.* Cambridge, etc.: Cambridge University Press, 1980.

Crollius, Ary A. Roest. [**See** Roest Crollius, Ary A.]

Crosby, Ruth. "Oral Delivery in the Middle Ages." *Speculum* 11 (1936): 88–110.

Cullmann, Oscar. *Urchristentum und Gottesdienst.* 1944. 2nd rev. ed. Zürich: Zwingli-Verlag, 1950. Eng. trans. A. Stewart Todd and James B. Torrance [with an extra chapter, "Jesus and the Day of Rest," trans. from the Fr. ed. of Part 2 (Paris, 1951)]. *Early Christian Worship.* Studies in Biblical Theology, no. 10. London: SCM Press, 1953.

Curtius, Ernst Robert. *Europäische Literatur und lateinisches Mittelalter.*1948. 2nd rev. ed. Bern: A. Francke, 1954. Eng. trans. [of 1st ed.] by Willard R. Trask. *European Literature and the Latin Middle Ages.* Bollingen Series, no. 36. 1953. Princeton: Princeton University Press, 1973.

Dānī, Abū 'Amr 'Uthmān b. Sa'īd al-. *al-Taysīr fī l-qirā'āt al-sab'.* Ed. Otto Pretzl as *Das Lehrbuch der sieben Koranlesungen.* Bibliotheca Islamica, ed.

Hellmut Ritter, vol. 2. Leipzig: F. A. Brockhaus; Istanbul: Matba'at al-Dawlah, 1930.

Danzel, Th[eodor] W[ilhelm]. *Die Anfänge der Schrift.* Diss., Leipzig, 1912.

Dārimī, 'Abd Allāh b. 'Abd al-Raḥmān al-. *al-Sunan.* Ed. Muḥammad Aḥmad Dahmān. 2 vols. in 1. [Cairo?]: Dār Iḥyā' al-Sunnah al-Nabawīyah, n.d. [Dārimī]

Datta, Bimal Kumar. *Libraries and Librarianship of Ancient and Medieval India.* Delhi, etc.: Atma Ram & Sons, 1970.

Davis, Natalie Zemon. "Printing and the People." Chap. 7 of *Society and Culture in Early Modern France.* Stanford, Calif.: Stanford University Press, 1975.

De Clercq, Charles. "L'influence de la règle de saint Pachôme en Occident." In *Mélanges d'histoire du moyen âge dédiés à la mémoire de Louis Halphen.* Paris: Presses universitaires de France, 1951, pp. 169–76.

Dekkers, Eligius. "Moines et liturgie." *Coll. cist.* 22 (1960): 329–40.

____. "Were the Early Monks Liturgical?" *Coll. cist.* 22 (1960): 120–37. (Rev. version of orig. Fr. article: "Les anciens moines cultivaient-ils la liturgie?" In *Vom christlichen Mysterium. Gesammelte Arbeiten zum Gedächtnis von Odo Casel O.S.B.,* ed. Anton Mayer, Johannes Quasten, and Burkhard Neun-heuser. Düsseldorf: Patmos-Verlag, 1951, pp. 97–114.) [Rev. versions also appeared in Fr., in *Maison-Dieu* 51 (1957): 31–54, and in Ger., in *Liturgie und Mönchtum* 22 (1958): 37–58.]

Delling, Gerhard. *Worship in the New Testament.* Trans. Percy Scott, with minor revisions by the author. Philadelphia: Westminster, 1962. [Ger. orig.: *Der Gottesdienst im Neuen Testament.* Göttingen: Vandenhoeck & Ruprecht, 1952.]

Denny, Frederick M[athewson]. "The *Adab* of Qur'an Recitation: Text and Context." In Johns, *ICSQ,* pp. 143–60.

____. "Exegesis and Recitation: Their Development as Classical Forms of Qur'ānic Piety." In *Transitions and Transformations in the History of Religions. Essays in Honor of Joseph M. Kitagawa,* ed. Frank E. Reynolds and Theodore M. Ludwig. Leiden: E. J. Brill, 1980, pp. 91–123.

____. "Types of Qur'ān Recitation Sessions in Contemporary Cairo." Unpublished paper delivered at the annual meeting of the American Research Center in Egypt, Detroit, Michigan, 1 May 1977.

____, and Rodney L. Taylor, eds. *The Holy Book in Comparative Perspective.* Studies in Comparative Religion, ed. Frederick M. Denny. Columbia: University of South Carolina Press, 1985. [Denny and Taylor]

Derrida, Jacques. *Of Grammatology.* Trans. Gayatri Chakravorty Spivak. Baltimore and London: Johns Hopkins University Press, 1976. [Fr. orig.: *De la grammatologie.* Paris: Éditions de Minuit, 1967.]

Deseille, Placide. "Eastern Christian Sources of the Rule of Saint Benedict." *Monastic Studies* 11 (1975): 73–122. [Trans. Stephen Leahy from the Fr. orig.: "Regards sur la tradition monastique," *Vie monastique* (Abbaye de Bellefontaine) 3 (1974): 83–168.]

De Smet, Richard V. "Language and Philosophy in India." In *Proceedings of the*

XIIth International Congress of Philosophy. Vol. 10: Eastern Philosophies and Western Thought. Florence: Sansoni, 1960, pp. 47–54.

Devasthali, G. V., comp. and ed. [**See** Abhyankar, K. V.]

de Visser, M. W. [**See** Visser, M. W. de.]

de Vleeschauwer, H. J. [**See** Vleeschauwer, H. J. de.]

de Vogüé, Adalbert. [**See** Vogüé, Adalbert de.]

Dictionary of the Bible, ed. James Hastings. Rev. ed. F. C. Grant and H. H. Rowley. New York: Scribner's, 1963.

Dierse, Ulrich. *Enzyklopädie. Zur Geschichte eines philosophischen und wissenschaftstheoretischen Begriffs.* Archiv für Begriffsgeschichte, Supp. no. 2. Bonn: Bouvier Verlag Herbert Grundmann, 1977.

Dijk, S. J. P. van. "The Bible in Liturgical Use." In *Camb. Hist. Bib.* 2: 220–52.

Diringer, David. *The Book Before Printing: Ancient, Medieval and Oriental.* 1953. Repr. ed. New York: Dover, 1982.

Disch, Robert, ed. *The Future of Literacy.* Englewood Cliffs, N.J.: Prentice-Hall, Spectrum Books, 1973.

Dix, Gregory. *The Shape of the Liturgy.* 1945. 2nd ed. Westminster, UK: Dacre Press, 1945.

Dobschütz, Ernst von. *Die Bibel im Leben der Völker.* 3rd rev. ed. by Alfred Adam. Witten/Ruhr: Luther-Verlag, [1954].

____. "Bible in the Church," *ERE* 2: 579–615.

Donaldson, Bess Allen. "The Koran as Magic." *MW* 27 (1937): 254–66.

Dornseiff, Franz. *Das Alphabet in Mystik und Magie.* 1922. 2nd ed. ΣΤΟΙΧΕΙΑ. Studien zur Geschichte des antiken Weltbildes und der griechischen Wissenschaft, ed. Franz Boll, no. 7. Leipzig and Berlin: B. G. Teubner, 1925.

Dörries, Hermann. "Die Bibel im ältesten Mönchtum." *TLZ* 72 (1947): 215–22.

Draguet, René, trans. *Les pères du désert.* Bibliothèque spirituelle du chrétien lettré. Paris: Librairie Plon, 1949.

Driver, G. R. *Semitic Writing: From Pictograph to Alphabet.* The Schweich Lectures of the British Academy, 1944. London: Oxford University Press, 1948.

Dronke, Peter. "Mediaeval Rhetoric." In *The Mediaeval World,* ed. David Daiches and Anthony Thorlby. Literature and Western Civilization, [2]. London: Aldus Books, 1973, pp. 315–45 (chap. 9).

D'Sa, Francis X. *Śabdaprāmāṇyam in Śabara and Kumārila: Towards a Study of the Mīmāṃsā Experience of Language.* Publications of the De Nobili Research Library, ed. Gerhard Oberhammer, vol. 7. Vienna: Gerold & Co., 1980.

Dürr, Lorenz. *Die Wertung des göttlichen Wortes im Alten Testament und im antiken Orient. Zugleich ein Beitrag zur Vorgeschichte des neutestamentlichen Logosbegriffes.* Mitteilungen der Vorderasiatisch-Ägyptischen Gesellschaft, vol. 42 (1937), no. 1. Leipzig: J. C. Hinrichs, 1938.

Dykstra, Yoshiko K. "Miraculous Tales of the Lotus Sutra: *The Dainihonkoku Hokkegenki.*" *Monumenta Nipponica* 32 (1977): 189–210.

Ebeling, Gerhard. *Evangelische Evangelienauslegung. Eine Untersuchung zu Luthers Hermeneutik.* Munich: Chr. Kaiser, 1942. Repr. ed. with corrections. Darmstadt: Wissenschaftliche Buchgesellschaft, 1962.

____. *Gott und Wort.* Tübingen: J. C. B. Mohr (Paul Siebeck), 1966.

____. "Wort Gottes und Hermeneutik." In *Wort und Glaube.* Tübingen: J. C. B. Mohr (Paul Siebeck), 1960, pp. 319–48. [Repr. from *Zeitschrift für Theologie und Kirche* 56 (1959): 224–51.]

"Écriture sainte et vie spirituelle." [numerous contributors] *Dict. spir.* 4.1: 128–278.

Egeria. *Diary of a Pilgrimage.* Trans. George E. Gingras. Ancient Christian Writers, no. 38. New York and Paramus, N.J.: Newman Press, 1970.

Eickelman, Dale F. "The Art of Memory: Islamic Education and its Social Reproduction." *Comparative Studies in Society and History* 20 (1978): 485–516.

____. *Knowledge and Power in Morocco: The Education of a Twentieth-Century Notable.* Princeton, N.J.: Princeton University Press, 1985.

Eidlitz, Walther. *Der Glaube und die heiligen Schriften der Inder.* Olten and Freiburg: Walter–Verlag, 1957.

Eisenstein, Elizabeth L. "The Advent of Printing and the Protestant Revolt: A New Approach to the Disruption of Western Christendom." In *Transition and Revolution: Problems and Issues of European Renaissance and Reformation History,* ed. Robert M. Kingdon. Minneapolis: Burgess, 1974, pp. 235–70.

____. *The Printing Press as an Agent of Change: Communications and Cultural Transformations in Early–Modern Europe.* 2 vols. 1979. One-vol. repr. ed. (continuous pagination). Cambridge, etc.: Cambridge University Press, 1980.

Elbogen, Ismar. *Der jüdische Gottesdienst in seiner geschichtlichen Entwicklung.* Leipzig, 1913. 4th ed. (photo–repr. of 3rd ed., Frankfurt/Main, 1931). Hildesheim: Georg Olms, 1962.

Engelsing, Rolf. *Analphabetentum und Lektüre. Zur Sozialgeschichte des Lesens in Deutschland zwischen feudaler und industrieller Gesellschaft.* Stuttgart: J. B. Metzlersche Verlagsbuchhandlung, 1973.

____. "Die Perioden der Lesergeschichte in der Neuzeit." *In Zur Sozialgeschichte deutscher Mittel- und Unterschichten.* Kritische Studien zur Geschichtswissenschaft, ed. Helmut Berding et al., vol. 4. Göttingen: Vandenhoeck & Ruprecht, 1973, pp. 112–54.

Essers, Bénard. "Vāc: Het Woord als Godsgestalte en als Godgeleerdheid in de Veda, in het bijzonder in de Ṛgveda-Saṃhitā en in de Atharvaveda-Saṃhitā." Diss., Groningen (Netherlands), 1952.

Faddegon, B. "Het menschelijke en het eeuwige Woord volgens de oude indische Wijsbegeerte." In *De Nieuwe Gids* 36 (1921): 854–77.

Falk, Franz. *Bibelstudien, Bibelhandschriften und Bibeldrucke in Mainz vom achten Jahrhundert bis zur Gegenwart.* Mainz: Franz Kirchheim, 1901.

Farmer, Henry George. "The Religious Music of Islām." *Journal of the Royal Asiatic Society* (1952), pp. 60–65.

Fārūqī, Lamyā' al-. "Tartīl al-Qur'ān al-Karīm." In *Islamic Perspectives: Studies in Honour of Mawlānā Sayyid Abul A'lā Mawdūdī,* ed. Khurshid Ahmad and Zafar Ishaq Ansari. Leicester: The Islamic Foundation; Jeddah: Saudi Publishing House, 1979, pp. 105–19.

Febvre, Lucien, and Henri-Jean Martin. *L'apparition du livre.* L'évolution de l'humanité, 49. Paris: Albin Michel, 1958.

Ferguson, Eugene S. "The Mind's Eye: Nonverbal Thought in Technology." *Science* 197 (1977): 827–36.

Finley, John H., Jr. *Thucydides.* Cambridge, Mass., 1942. Repr. ed. Ann Arbor, Mich.: University of Michigan Press, 1963.

Finnegan, Ruth. *Oral Literature in Africa.* Oxford: Clarendon Press, 1970.

____. *Oral Poetry: Its Nature, Significance and Social Context.* Cambridge, etc.: Cambridge University Press, 1977, 1979.

Franke, R. Otto. "Mudrâ = Schrift (oder Lesekunst)?" *ZDMG* 46 (1892): 731–34.

Frauwallner, E. "Mīmāmsāsūtram I, 1, 6–23." *Wiener Zeitschrift für die Kunde Süd- und Ostasiens* 5 (1961): 113–24.

Frawley, David. *The Creative Vision of the Early Upaniṣads: Udgītha Ādityasya, the Exalted Song of the Sun.* Madras (private publ., Rajsri Printers), 1982.

Frei, Hans W. *The Eclipse of Biblical Narrative: A Study in Eighteenth and Nineteenth Century Hermeneutics.* New Haven and London: Yale University Press, 1974.

Frick, Heinrich. "Ideogramm, Mythologie und das Wort." In Heinrich Frick, ed. *Rudolf Otto Festgruß.* Marburger Theologische Studien. Gotha: Leopold Klotz, 1931. No. 3, pp. 1–20.

Friedländer, Paul. *Platon.* Vol. 1 (of 3): Seinswahrheit und Lebenswirklichkeit. 2nd rev. ed. Berlin: Walter de Gruyter, 1954.

Frye, Northrop. *The Great Code: The Bible and Literature.* San Diego, New York, and London: Harcourt Brace Jovanovich, Harvest/HBJ Books, 1981.

Fuhrmann, Otto W. "The Invention of Printing." In *Reader in the History of Books and Printing,* ed. Paul A. Winckler. Readers in Librarianship and Information Science, no. 26. Englewood, Colo.: Information Handling Services, 1978, pp. 237–83.

Funk, Franciscus Xaverius, ed. *Didascalia et Constitutiones apostolorum.* 2 vols. Paderborn: Ferdinand Schoeningh, 1905. [*Apost. Const.*]

Furet, François, and Jacques Ozouf. *Lire et écrire. L'alphabétisation des français de Calvin à Jules Ferry.* Vol 1. Paris: Les Éditions de Minuit, 1977. Eng. trans. [of vol. 1 only]: *Reading and Writing: Literacy in France from Calvin to Jules Ferry.* Cambridge Studies in Oral and Literate Culture, ed. Peter Burke and Ruth Finnegan, [no. 5]. Cambridge, etc.: Cambridge University Press; Paris: Éditions de la Maison des Sciences de l'Homme, 1982.

Furet, François, and Wladimir Sachs. "La croissance de l'alphabétisation en France (XVIIIe–XIXe siècle)." *Annales* 29 (1974): 714–37.

Galbraith, V. H. "The Literacy of the Medieval English Kings." The Raleigh Lecture on History, British Academy, 1935. London: Humphrey Milford, [1935].

____. *Studies in the Public Records.* London, Edinburgh, etc.: Thomas Nelson and Sons, 1948.

Gamble, Harry Y., Jr. "Christianity: Scripture and Canon." In Denny and Taylor, pp. 36–62.

Gandillac, Maurice de, et al. *La pensée encyclopédique au moyen âge.* Cahiers d'Histoire Mondiale, vol. 9, no. 3. Neuchâtel: Éditions de la Baconnière, for UNESCO, 1966.

Gandz, Solomon. "Oral Tradition in the Bible." In *Jewish Studies in Memory of George A. Kohut,* ed. Salo W. Baron and Alexander Marx. New York: Alexander Kohut Memorial Foundation, 1935, pp. 248–69.

Geertz, Clifford. "Art as a Cultural System." *MLN* 91 (1976): 1473–99.

Geiselmann, R. J. "Das Konzil von Trient über das Verhältnis der Heiligen Schrift und der nicht geschriebenen Traditionen." In H[einrich] Bacht [misspelled on title p. as "H. Bracht"], H. Fries, and R. J. Geiselmann. *Die mündliche Überlieferung: Beiträge zum Begriff der Tradition.* Ed. Michael Schmaus. Munich: Max Hueber, 1957, pp. 123–206.

Gelb, I. J. *A Study of Writing.* 1952. 2nd rev. ed. Chicago and London: University of Chicago Press, Phoenix Books, 1963.

Gentili, Bruno, and Giovanni Cerri. "Written and Oral Communication in Greek Historiographical Thought." In *Communication Arts in the Ancient World,* ed. Eric A. Havelock and Jackson P. Hershbell. Humanistic Studies in the Communication Arts, ed. G. N. Gordon. New York: Hastings House, 1978, pp. 137–55.

Gerhardsson, Birger. *Memory and Manuscript: Oral Tradition and Written Transmission in Rabbinic Judaism and Early Christianity.* Trans. Eric J. Sharpe. Acta seminarii neotestamentici upsaliensis, 22. Uppsala and Lund: C. W. K. Gleerup; Copenhagen: Ejnar Munksgaard, 1961.

Geyer, R. "Zur Strophik des Qurâns." *Wiener Zeitschrift für die Kunde des Morgenlandes* 22 (1908): 265–86.

Ghazālī, Muḥammad b. Muḥammad al-. ["Ādāb tilāwat al-qur'ān," Book 8 of *Iḥyā' 'ulūm al-dīn*]. Eng. trans. Muhammad Abul Quasem. *The Recitation and Interpretation of the Qur'an: Al-Ghazālī's Theory.* Bangi, Selangor, Malaysia: private publ., 1979.

____. *Iḥyā' 'ulūm al-dīn.* 5 vols. Beirut: Dār al-Ma'rifah lil-Ṭabā'ah wal-Nashr, n.d. [Ghazālī]

____. *Jawāhir al-qur'ān.* Cairo: Maṭba'at Kurdistān al-'Ilmīyah, 1329/1911. Eng. trans. Muhammad Abul Quasem. *The Jewels of the Qur'ān: Al-Ghāzālī's Theory.* Bangi, Selangor, Malaysia: private publ., 1977.

Ghellinck, Joseph de. "'Pagina' et 'Sacra Pagina'. Histoire d'un mot et transformation de l'objet primitivement désigné." In *Mélanges Auguste Pelzer. Études d'histoire littéraire et doctrinale de la Scolastique médiévale offertes à Monseigneur Auguste Pelzer à l'occasion de son soixante-dixième anniversaire.* Recueil de travaux d'histoire et de philologie, 3rd ser., no. 26. Louvain: Bibliothèque de l'université and Éditions de l'Institut supérieur de philosophie, 1947, pp. 23–59.

Ghurye, K. G. *Preservation of Learned Tradition in India.* Bombay: Popular Book Depot, 1950.

Gill, Sam D. "Nonliterate Traditions and Holy Books: Toward a New Model." In Denny and Taylor, pp. 224–39.

Gindele, Corbinian. "Die Schriftlesung im Pachomiuskloster." *Erbe und Auftrag* 41 (1965): 114–22.

Ginzberg, Carlo. *The Cheese and the Worms: The Cosmos of a Sixteenth-Century Miller.* Trans. John and Anne Tedeschi. Baltimore and London: Johns

Hopkins University Press, 1980. [Ital. orig.: *Il formaggio e i vermi: Il cosmo di un mugnaio del '500* (Turin, 1976).]

Glaue, Paul. "Die Vorlesung heiliger Schriften bei Cyprian." *ZNTW* 23 (1924): 201–13.

____. "Die Vorlesung heiliger Schriften bei Tertullian." *ZNTW* 23 (1924): 141–52.

____. *Die Vorlesung heiliger Schriften im Gottesdienste. 1. Teil. Bis zur Entstehung der altkatholischen Kirche.* Berlin: Alexander Duncker, 1907.

Goehring, James Ernst. "The Letter of Ammon and Pachomian Monasticism." Ph.D. diss., Claremont Graduate School, 1981.

Goldammer, Kurt. *Die Formenwelt des Religiösen. Grundriß der systematischen Religionswissenschaft.* Stuttgart: Alfred Kröner, 1960.

Golden, Hilda H. "Literacy." *International Encyclopedia of the Social Sciences* 9: 412b–17b.

Goldstücker, Theodor. *Pāṇini: His Place in Sanskrit Literature.* London, 1860. Repr. ed. Surendra Nath Shastri. Chowkhamba Sanskrit Series, vol. 48. Varanasi [Banaras]: Chowkhamba Sanskrit Series Office, 1965.

Goldziher, Ignaz. *Die Richtungen der islamischen Koranauslegung. An der Universität Upsala gehaltene Olaus-Petri-Vorlesungen.* Veröffentlichungen der "de Goeje-Stiftung", no. 6. 1920. Photo-repr. ed. Leiden: E. J. Brill, 1952, 1970.

Gonda, Jan. *Die Religionen Indiens, I: Veda und älterer Hinduismus.* Die Religionen der Menschheit, ed. Christel Matthias Schröder, vol. 11. Stuttgart: W. Kohlhammer, 1960.

____. *Vedic Literature (Saṃhitās and Brāhmaṇas).* A History of Indian Literature, ed. Jan Gonda, vol. 1, pt. 1. Wiesbaden: Otto Harrassowitz, 1975.

____. *Vedic Ritual: The Non-Solemn Rites.* Handbuch der Orientalistik, ed. B. Spuler et al. Division 2: Indien, ed. J. Gonda, vol. 4, pt. 1. Leiden and Cologne: E. J. Brill, 1980.

____. *The Vision of the Vedic Poets.* Disputationes Rheno-Trajectinae, ed. J. Gonda, vol. 8. The Hague: Mouton, 1963.

Goody, Jack [John Rankine]. *The Domestication of the Savage Mind.* Cambridge, etc.: Cambridge University Press, 1977.

____. "Restricted Literacy in Northern Ghana." In Goody, *Literacy,* pp. 199–264.

____, ed. *Literacy in Traditional Societies*.Cambridge, etc.: Cambridge University Press, 1968. [Goody, *Literacy*]

____ and Ian Watt. "The Consequences of Literacy." *Comparative Studies in Society and History* 5 (1963): 304–45. Repr. in Goody, *Literacy,* pp. 27–68.

Gorce, Denys. *La lectio divina, des origines du cénobitisme à Saint Benoît et Cassiodore, I: Saint Jerôme et la lecture sacrée dans le milieu ascétique romain.* Wépion-sur-Meuse, Belgium: Monastère du Mont-Vierge, and Paris: Auguste Picard, 1925. (only one volume published)

Gough, Kathleen. "Implications of Literacy in Traditional China and India." In Goody, *Literacy,* pp. 70–84.

____. "Literacy in Kērala." In Goody, *Literacy,* pp. 133–60.

Graham, William A. *Divine Word and Prophetic Word in Early Islam: A Reconsideration of the Sources, with Special Reference to the Divine Saying or*

"Ḥadīth Qudsī". Religion and Society, ed. Leo Laeyendecker and Jacques Waardenburg, vol. 7. The Hague and Paris: Mouton, 1977.

____. "The Earliest Meaning of 'Qur'ān'." *Die Welt des Islams,* n.s., 23/24 (1984): 361–77.

____. "*Qur'ān* as Spoken Word: An Islamic Contribution to the Understanding of Scripture." In *Approaches to Islam in Religious Studies,* ed. Richard C. Martin. Tucson: University of Arizona Press, 1985, pp. 23–40.

____. "Scripture." *The Encyclopedia of Religion.* Ed. Mircea Eliade et al. 16 vols. + index vol. New York: Macmillan, 1987. S.v.

Grant, Robert M., with David Tracy. *A Short History of the Interpretation of the Bible.* 1963. 2nd rev. ed. Philadelphia: Fortress, 1984.

Greene, William Chase. "The Spoken and the Written Word." *Harvard Studies in Classical Philology* 60 (1951): 23–59.

Greenfield, Patricia M[arks]. "Oral or Written Language: The Consequences for Cognitive Development in Africa, the United States and England." *Language and Speech* 15 (1972): 169–78.

____, and Jerome S. Bruner. "Culture and Cognitive Growth." *International Journal of Psychology* 1 (1966): 89–107.

Greenslade, S. L. "Epilogue." In *Camb. Hist. Bib.* 3: 476–519.

Gribomont, J. "Obéissance et Évangile selon saint Basile le Grand." *La vie spirituelle.* Supp. vol. 6, no. 20 (1952): 192–215.

____. "Les Règles Morales de saint Basile et le Nouveau Testament." In *Studia Patristica, vol. II: Papers presented to the Second International Conference on Patristic Studies held at Christ Church, Oxford, 1955.* Pt. 2. Edited by Kurt Aland and F. L. Cross. Texte und Untersuchungen zur Geschichte der altchristlichen Literatur, vol. 64 (ser. 5, vol. 9). Berlin: Akademie-Verlag, 1957, pp. 416–26.

Grundmann, Herbert. "Litteratus - illitteratus. Der Wandel einer Bildungsnorm vom Altertum zum Mittelalter." *Archiv für Kulturgeschichte* 40 (1958): 1-65.

Grützmacher, O. *Pachomius und das älteste Klosterleben. Ein Beitrag zur Mönchsgeschichte.* Freiburg (Breisgau) and Leipzig: J. C. B. Mohr (Paul Siebeck), 1896.

Hackmann, H. *Religionen und heilige Schriften. Antrittsvorlesung . . . an der Universität Amsterdam.* Berlin: Karl Curtius, 1914.

Hadas, Moses. *Ancilla to Classical Reading.* 1954. New York: Columbia University Press, 1961.

____. *A History of Greek Literature.* New York: Columbia University Press, 1950.

____. *A History of Latin Literature.* New York: Columbia University Press, 1952.

Hahn, Ferdinand. "Das Problem 'Schrift und Tradition' im Urchristentum." *Evangelische Theologie* 30 (1970): 449–68.

Hahn, Herbert F. *The Old Testament in Modern Research.* 1954. Expanded ed. Philadelphia: Fortress, 1966.

Hajdu, Helga. *Das mnemotechnische Schrifttum des Mittelalters.* Vienna, Amsterdam, and Leipzig: Franz Leo, 1936.

Hajnal, I[stván]. "À propos de l'enseignement de l'écriture dans les universités médiévales." *Scriptorium* 11 (1957): 3–28.

____. "Universities and the Development of Writing in the XIIth–XIIIth Centuries." *Scriptorium* 6 (1952): 177–95.

Halkin, François, ed. *Le corpus athénien de saint Pachôme avec une traduction française par André-Jean Festugière.* Cahiers d'orientalisme, 2. Geneva: Patrick Cramer, 1982. [*Corp. Ath.*]

____, ed. *Sancti Pachomii vitae graecae.* Subsidia hagiographica, 19. Brussels: Société des Bollandistes, 1932. [*PVG*]

Hall, Basil. "Biblical Scholarship: Editions and Commentaries." In *Camb. Hist. Bib.* 3: 38–93.

Hanson, R. P. C. "Biblical Exegesis in the Early Church." In *Camb. Hist. Bib.* 1: 412–33.

Haq, M. Anwarul [M. Anwār al-Ḥaqq]. *The Faith Movement of Mawlānā Muḥammad Ilyās.* London: George Allen & Unwin, 1972.

Hardacre, Helen. *Lay Buddhism in Contemporary Japan: Reiyūkai Kyōdan.* Princeton, N.J.: Princeton University Press, 1984.

Harnack, Adolf von. "Das Alte Testament in den Paulinischen Briefen und in den Paulinischen Gemeinden." *Sitzungsberichte der Preussischen Akademie der Wissenschaften.* Philos.-Hist. Klasse (Berlin, 1928), pp. 124–41.

____. "Heilige Scriften." In *Reden und Aufsätze.* N.s., vol. 4: Erforschtes und Erlebtes. Giessen: Alfred Töpelmann, 1923, pp. 65–67.

____. "Über das Alter der Bezeichnung 'die Bücher' ('die Bibel') für die H. Schriften in der Kirche." *Zentralblatt für Bibliothekswesen* 45 (1928): 337–42.

____. *Über den privaten Gebrauch der heiligen Schriften in der alten Kirche.* Beiträge zur Einleitung in das Neue Testament, vol. 5. Leipzig: J. C. Hinrichs, 1912. Eng. trans. J. R. Wilkinson. *Bible Reading in the Early Church.* New York: G. P. Putnam's Sons; London: Williams and Norgate, 1912.

____. "Über den Ursprung des Lectorats und der anderen niederen Weihen." 2nd part of *Die Quellen der sogenannten apostolischen Kirchenordnung nebst einer Untersuchung über den Ursprung des Lectorats und der anderen niederen Weihen.* Texte und Untersuchungen zur Geschichte der altchristlichen Literatur, ed. Oscar von Gebhardt and Adolf Harnack, vol. 2, no. 5. Leipzig: J. C. Hinrichs, 1886, pp. 57–103.

Harvey, F. David. "Greeks and Romans Learn to Write." In *Communication Arts in the Ancient World,* ed. Eric A. Havelock and Jackson P. Hershbell. Humanistic Studies in the Communication Arts, ed. G. N. Gordon. New York: Hastings House, 1978, pp. 63–78.

____. "Literacy in the Athenian Democracy." *Revue des études grecques* 79 (1966): 585–635.

Hatch, Nathan O., and Mark A. Noll, eds. *The Bible in America: Essays in Cultural History.* New York and Oxford: Oxford University Press, 1982.

Havelock, Eric A. *The Literate Revolution in Greece and Its Cultural Consequences.* Princeton, N.J.: Princeton University Press, 1982.

____. *Origins of Western Literacy.* Monograph Series, no. 14. [Toronto]: Ontario Institute for Studies in Education, 1976.

____. *Preface to Plato.* A History of the Greek Mind, vol. 1. Cambridge, Mass.: Harvard University Press, Belknap Press, 1963.

____. "The Psychology of Rhythmic Memorization." Chap. 3 of *The Greek Concept of Justice: From Its Shadow in Homer to Its Substance in Plato.* Cambridge, Mass., and London: Harvard University Press, 1978, pp. 38–54.

____ and Jackson P. Hershbell, eds. *Communication Arts in the Ancient World.* Humanistic Studies in the Communication Arts, ed. G. N. Gordon. New York: Hastings House, 1978.

Heesterman, Jan C. "Die Autorität des Veda." In *Offenbarung, Geistige Realität des Menschen. Arbeitsdokumentation eines Symposiums zum Offenbarungsbegriff in Indien,* ed. Gerhard Oberhammer. Publications of the De Nobili Research Library, ed. Gerhard Oberhammer, vol. 2. Vienna: [Indologisches Institut der Universität Wien], 1974, pp. 29–40.

____. "Veda and Dharma." In *The Concept of Duty in South Asia,* ed. Wendy Doniger O'Flaherty and J. Duncan M. Derrett. N.p.: South Asia Books (for School of Oriental and African Studies), 1978, pp. 80–95.

Heiler, Friedrich. *Erscheinungsformen und Wesen der Religion.* 1961. 2nd rev. ed. Die Religionen der Menschheit, ed. Christel Matthias Schröder, vol. 1. Stuttgart, etc.: W. Kohlhammer, 1979.

____. *Katholischer und evangelischer Gottesdienst.* 2nd. rev. ed. Munich: Ernst Reinhardt, 1925.

____. *Die Ostkirchen.* [Rev. version of *Urkirche und Ostkirche* (1937)] Ed. Anne Marie Heiler and Hans Hartog. Munich and Basel: Ernst Reinhardt, 1971.

Hendrickson, G. L. "Ancient Reading." *The Classical Journal* (Cedar Rapids, Iowa) 25 (1929): 182–96.

Heussi, Karl. *Der Ursprung des Mönchtums.* Tübingen: J. C. B. Mohr (Paul Siebeck), 1936.

Hinds, [G.] Martin. "Kûfan Political Alignments and their Background in the Mid-Seventh Century A.D." *IJMES* 2 (1971): 346–67.

Hirsch, Rudolf. *The Printed Word: Its Impact and Diffusion (Primarily in the 15th–16th Centuries).* London: Variorum Reprints, 1978.

____. *Printing, Selling and Reading, 1450–1550.* Wiesbaden: Otto Harrassowitz, 1967.

Hodgson, Marshall G. S. "Islâm and Image." *History of Religions* 3 (1964): 220–60.

Holdrege, Barbara A. "The Bride of Israel: The Ontology of the Torah in the Jewish Tradition." Unpublished article (typescript). Forthcoming in *Rethinking Scripture,* ed. Miriam Levering. Albany, N.Y.: SUNY Press, [1987].

Horner, Winifred Bryan, ed. *Composition and Literature: Bridging the Gap.* Chicago and London: University of Chicago Press, 1983.

Horovitz, Josef. "Bemerkungen zur Geschichte und Terminologie des islamischen Kultus." *Der Islam* 16 (1927): 249–63.

____. *Koranische Untersuchungen.* Studien zur Geschichte und Kultur des islamischen Orients, ed. C. H. Becker, no. 4. Berlin and Leipzig: Walter de Gruyter, 1926. [*Kor. Unters.*]

____. "Qurān." *Der Islam* 13 (1923): 66–69.

Howard, Wayne. *Sāmavedic Chant.* New Haven and London: Yale University Press, 1977.

Huber, K. [**See** Bergsträsser, Gotthelf.]

Hume, Robert Earnest, trans. *The Thirteen Principal Upanishads.* 2nd rev. ed. London, etc.: Oxford University Press, 1931.

Hurgronje, Christian Snouck. [**See** Snouck Hurgronje, Christian.]

Hurvitz, Leon, trans. [**See** Lotus Sūtra.]

Ibn Ḥanbal, Aḥmad b. Muḥammad. *al-Musnad.* Ed. Muḥammad al-Zuhrī al-Ghamrāwī [with the commentary of al-Muttaqī, *Muntakhab kanz al-'ummāl,* on the margins]. 6 vols. Cairo, 1313/1895. [*Musnad*]

____. *al-Musnad.* Ed. Aḥmad Muḥammad Shākir. 15 vols. to date. Cairo, 1949-. [*Musnad*[2]]

Ibn Isḥāq, Muḥammad. *al-Sīrah al-nabawīyah* [in the recension of 'Abd al-Malik ibn Hishām]. Ed. Muṣṭafá al-Saqqā, Ibrāhīm al-Abyārī, and 'Abd al-Hafīẓ Shalabī. 4 vols. Cairo, 1355/1937. Repr. ed. Beirut: Iḥyā al-Turāth al-'Arabī, 1391/1971. Eng. trans. Alfred Guillaume. *The Life of Muhammad.* 1955. Lahore, Karachi, Dacca: Oxford University Press, 1967. [Ibn Isḥāq]

Ibn al-Jazarī, Abū l-Khayr Muḥammad b. Muḥammad al-Dimashqī. *Ghāyat al-nihāyah fī ṭabaqāt al-qurrā'.* Ed. Gotthelf Bergsträsser and Otto Pretzl as *Das biographische Lexikon der Koranlehrer von Samsaddin Muhammad ibn al-Gazari.* 2 vols. Cairo, 1351–52/1932–33.

____. *al-Nashr fī l-qirā'āt al-'ashr.* Ed. 'Alī Muḥammad al-Dabbā'. 2 vols. Cairo: Matba'at Muṣṭafá Muḥammad, n.d.

Ibn Khālawayh. *Mukhtaṣar fī shawādhdh al-Qur'ān min kitāb al-badī'.* Ed. G. Bergsträsser as *Ibn Ḫālawaih's Sammlung nichtkanonischer Koranlesarten.* Bibliotheca Islamica, ed. Hellmut Ritter, vol. 7. Leipzig: F. A. Brockhaus; Cairo: Matba'ah al-Raḥmānīyah, 1934.

Ibn Khaldūn, 'Abd al-Raḥman b. Muḥammad. *al-Muqaddimah . . . wa-hiya al-juz' al-awwal min kitāb al-'ibar.* Ed. M. Quatremère. 3 vols. Paris: Benjamin Duprat, 1858. Eng. trans. Franz Rosenthal. *The Muqaddimah: An Introduction to History.* 3 vols. New York: Bollingen Foundation; London: Routledge & Kegan Paul, 1958.

Ibn Sa'd, Muḥammad, Kātib al-Wāqidī. *Kitāb al-Ṭabaqāt al-kabīr.* 8 vols. Cairo: Dār al-Taḥrīr, 1388-90/1968-70. [Ibn Sa'd]

Ihde, Don. *Listening and Voice: A Phenomenology of Sound.* Athens, Ohio: Ohio University Press, 1976.

Innis, Harold A. *Empire and Communications.* Oxford, 1950. Rev. ed. Mary Q. Innis. Toronto: University of Toronto Press, 1972.

Jaeger, Werner. *Paideia: the Ideals of Greek Culture.* Trans. Gilbert Highet (vol. 1 from 2nd Ger. ed. [1935]; vols. 2, 3, from the Ger. Ms). 3 vols. 1939 (vol. 1; 2nd ed. 1945); 1943 (vol. 3); 1944 (vol. 2). Repr. ed. New York: Oxford University Press, 1960.

Jairazbhoy, N. A. "Le chant védique." In *Encl. mus. sacr.,* pp. 135–61.

James, Arthur Lloyd. [**See** Lloyd James, Arthur.]

Jan, Yün-hua. [**See** Yün-hua Jan.]

Jeffery, Arthur. *The Foreign Vocabulary of the Qur'ān.* [Gaekwad's Oriental Series, vol. 74.] Baroda: Oriental Institute, 1938.

____. "Progress in the Study of the Qur'ān Text." *MW* 25 (1935): 4–16.

____. *The Qur'ān as Scripture.* New York: Russell F. Moore, 1952.

____. "The Qur'ān Readings of Ibn Miqsam." In *Goldziher Mem.* 1: 1–38.

____, ed. *Materials for the History of the Text of the Qur'ān: The Old Codices.* "Printed for the Trustees of the 'de Goeje Fund'," no. 11. Leiden: E. J. Brill, 1937.

____, ed. [**See** *Muqaddimat kitāb al-mabānī.*]

Jeffries, Charles. *Illiteracy: A World Problem.* London: Pall Mall, 1967.

Jensen, Hans. *Die Schrift in Vergangenheit und Gegenwart* (Glückstadt and Hamburg: J. J. Augustin, [1935]. 2nd rev. ed. Berlin: VEB Deutscher Verlag der Wissenschaften, 1958. Eng. trans. (3rd rev. ed.) by George Unwin. *Sign, Symbol and Script: An Account of Man's Efforts to Write.* New York: G. P. Putnam's Sons, 1969.

Johansson, Egil. *The History of Literacy in Sweden in Comparison with Some Other Countries.* Educational Reports Umeå, no. 12. Umeå, Sweden: Umeå University and Umeå School of Education, 1977.

Johns, A[nthony] H. *International Congress for the Study of the Qur'an, Australian National University, Canberra, 8–13 May 1980.* Ser. 1. 2nd ed. Canberra: Australian National University [1981]. [Johns, *ICSQ*]

Jomier, J. "La place du Coran dans la vie quotidienne en Égypte." *Institut des Belles Lettres Arabes* (Tunis), 15th year, no. 58 (1952), pp. 131–65.

Jones, Sidney. "Arabic Instruction and Literacy in Javanese Muslim Schools." *International Journal of the Sociology of Language* 42 (1983): 83–94.

Jousse, Marcel. *L'anthropologie du geste.* Voies ouvertes, ed. Jean Sulivan. Paris: Gallimard, 1974.

Juergensmeyer, Mark, and N. Gerald Barrier, eds. *Sikh Studies: Comparative Perspectives on a Changing Tradition.* Berkeley Religious Studies Series. Berkeley, Calif.: Graduate Theological Union, 1979.

Justin Martyr. *Apologia* ("First Apology"). In *Die ältesten Apologeten. Texte mit kurzen Einleitungen.* Ed. Edgar J. Goodspeed. Göttingen: Vandenhoeck & Ruprecht, 1914, pp. 24–77. [*Apolog.*]

Juvenal. *Satires.* [**See** Mayor, John E. B., ed. and comm.]

Juynboll, G. H. A. "The Position of Qur'ān Recitation in Early Islam." *Journal of Semitic Studies* 19 (1974): 240–51.

____. "The Qurrā' in Early Islamic History," *Journal of the Economic and Social History of the Orient* 16 (1973): 113–29.

Kahle, Paul E. "The Arabic Readers of the Koran." *Journal of Near Eastern Studies* 8 (1949): 65–71.

____. "The Qur'ān and the 'Arabīya." In *Goldziher Mem.* 1: 163–82.

Keay, F. E. *Indian Education in Ancient and Later Times: An Inquiry into Its Origin, Development and Ideals.* London, etc.: Oxford University Press, Humphrey Milford, 1938.

Keith, Arthur Berriedale, ed. and trans. [**See** *Aitareya Āraṇyaka.*]

Kelber, Werner H. *The Oral and the Written Gospel: The Hermeneutics of Speaking and Writing in the Synoptic Tradition, Mark, Paul, and Q.* Philadelphia: Fortress Press, 1983.

Kennedy, George A. *Classical Rhetoric and Its Christian and Secular Tradition from Ancient to Modern Times.* Chapel Hill: University of North Carolina Press, 1980.

Kenyon, Frederic G[eorge]. *Books and Readers in Ancient Greece and Rome.* 1932. 2nd rev. ed. Oxford: Clarendon Press, 1951.

Kerényi, Karl. *Apollon. Studien über antike Religion und Humanität.* 1937. [3rd?] rev. ed. Düsseldorf: Eugen Diederichs, 1953.

Kingdon, Robert M. "Patronage, Piety, and Printing in Sixteenth-Century Europe." In *A Festschrift for Frederick B. Artz,* ed. David H. Pinkney and Theodore Ropp. Durham, N.C.: Duke University Press, 1964, pp. 19–36.

Kirk, G. S. *Homer and the Oral Tradition.* Cambridge, etc.: Cambridge University Press, 1976.

Klimkeit, Hans-Joachim. *Manichaean Art and Calligraphy.* Iconography of Religions, ed. Th. P. van Baaren et al. Leiden: E. J. Brill, 1982.

____. "Vom Wesen manichäischer Kunst." *Zeitschrift für Religions- und Geistesgeschichte* 34 (1982): 195–219.

Knowles, David. *Christian Monasticism.* New York and Toronto: McGraw–Hill, World University Library, 1969.

Knox, Bernard M. W. "Silent Reading in Antiquity." *Greek, Roman and Byzantine Studies* 9 (1968): 421–35.

Koep, Leo. *Das himmlische Buch in Antike und Christentum. Eine religionsgeschichtliche Untersuchung zur altchristlichen Bildersprache.*Theophaneia. Beiträge zur Religions- und Kirchengeschichte des Altertums, 8. Bonn: Peter Hanstein, 1952.

Köster, Helmut. *Einführung in das Neue Testament im Rahmen der Religionsgeschichte und Kulturgeschichte der hellenistischen und römischen Zeit.* Berlin and New York: Walter de Gruyter, 1980.

Kraus, Hans-Joachim. *Geschichte der historisch-kritischen Erforschung des Alten Testaments.* 2nd ed., Zurich: Neukirchener Verlag, 1969.

Kṛishṇavarmâ, Shyâmajî. "The Use of Writing in Ancient India." *Actes du sixième Congrès International des Orientalistes tenu en 1883 à Leide.* Pt. 3, sect. 2: "Aryenne." Leiden: E. J. Brill, 1885.

Kristensen, W. Brede. *The Meaning of Religion: Lectures in the Phenomenology of Religion.* Trans. John B. Carman. The Hague: Martinus Nijhoff, 1960.

Krug, [Wilhelm–Traugott?]. "Encyklopädie." *Allgemeine Encyklopädie der Wissenschaften und Künste,* ed. J. S. Ersch and J. G. Gruber. Leipzig: Gleditsch/ Brockhaus, 1818–89. S.v.

Kümmel, Werner Georg. *Das Neue Testament. Geschichte der Erforschung seiner Probleme.* Freiburg and Munich: Karl Alber, 1958, 1970.

K'ung Fu–tzu. [**See** Waley, Arthur, trans.]

Künstlinger, Dawid. "Kitāb und Ahlu-l-Kitāb." *Rocznik Orientalistyczny* 4 (1928): 238–47.

____. "Die Namen der 'Gottes-Schriften' im Qurān." *Rocznik Orientalistyczny* 13 (1937): 72–84.

Ladeuze, Paulin. *Étude sur le cénobitisme Pakhomien pendant le IVe siècle et la première moitié du Ve.* Louvain: J. van Linthout, and Paris: A. Fontemoing, 1898.

Læssøe, J. "Literacy and Oral Tradition in Ancient Mesopotamia." In *Studia orientalia Ioanni Pedersen septuagenario . . . dicata.* Copenhagen: Einar Munksgaard, 1953, pp. 205–18.

Laistner, M. L. W. *Christianity and Pagan Culture in the Later Roman Empire, Together with an English Translation of John Chrysostom's "Address on Vainglory and the Right Way for Parents to Bring Up Their Children."* Ithaca, N.Y., and London: Cornell University Press, 1951. Repr. ed. Cornell Paperbacks, 1967, 1978.

Lake, Kirsopp, trans. [**See** *Apostolic Fathers.*]

Lamb, J. A. "The Place of the Bible in the Liturgy." In *Camb. Hist. Bib.* 1: 563–86.

Lanczkowski, Günter. *Heilige Schriften. Inhalt, Textgestalt und Überlieferung.* Stuttgart: W. Kohlhammer, Urban-Bücher, 1956.

Lane, Edward William. *An Account of the Manners and Customs of the Modern Egyptians.* London, 1836. 5th (standard) ed. 1860. Ed. Edward Stanley Poole. Repr. ed. (with corrections). New York: Dover, 1973.

Lanman, Charles Rockwell. [**See** *Atharva Veda Saṁhitā.*]

Lao-Tzu. [**See** Waley, Arthur, trans.]

Lapointe, Roger. "Classicisme et canonicité." *Science et ésprit* 33 (1981): 323–34.

Laqueur, Thomas W. "The Cultural Origins of Popular Literacy in England 1500–1850." *Oxford Review of Education* 2 (1976): 255–75.

____. "Toward a Cultural Ecology of Literacy in England, 1600–1850." In Resnick, *Literacy,* pp. 43–57.

Leclercq, Jean. *L'amour des lettres et le désir de dieu. Initiation aux auteurs monastiques du moyen âge.* Paris: Éditions du Cerf, 1957. Eng. trans. Catharine Misrahi. *The Love of Learning and the Desire for God: A Study of Monastic Culture.* 1961. 3rd ed. New York: Fordham University Press, 1982.

____. "La lecture divine." *La Maison-Dieu* (1946), no. 1, pp. 21–33.

____. "Liturgy and Contemplation." *Monastic Studies* 10 (1974): 71–86. [Trans. Steven P. Manning from the Sp. orig.: "Oracion privada y oracion publica," *Cuadernos Monásticos* 20 (1972): 79–110.]

____. "Meditation as a Biblical Reading." *Worship* 33 (1958–59): 562–69.

____, François Vandenbroucke, and Louis Bouyer. *La spiritualité du moyen âge.* Histoire de la spiritualité chrétienne, ed. Louis Bouyer et al., vol. 2. [Paris]: Aubier, 1961.

Leeuw, G[erardus] van der. *Phänomenologie der Religion.* Neue theologische Grundrisse, ed. Rudolf Bultmann. 1933. 2nd rev. ed. Tübingen: J. C. B. Mohr (Paul Siebeck), 1956. Eng. trans. J. E. Turner with Appendices . . . incorporating the additions of the 2nd Ger. ed. by Hans H. Penner. *Religion in Essence and Manifestation.* New York and Evanston, Ill.: Harper and Row, Harper Torchbooks, 1963.

Lefort, L[ouis] Th[éodore], ed. and trans. *Oeuvres de S. Pachôme et de ses disciples.* 2 vols. Scriptores Coptici, vols. 23, 24 (Copt. texts: *CSCO,* 159; Fr. trans.: *CSCO,* 160). Louvain: L. Durbecq, 1956. [*OPD* 1,2]

——, ed. and trans. *S. Pachomii vita bohairice scripta.* Scriptores Coptici, ser. 3, vol. 7 [2 vols. in 1]. Copt. text: *CSCO,* 89. Paris: "E Typographeo Reipublicae," 1925. Lat. trans.: *CSCO,* 107. Louvain: "Ex Officina Orientali et Scientifica," 1936. [*PVBS* 1,2]

——, ed. *S. Pachomii vitae sahidice scriptae.* 1 vol. in 2 pts. Scriptores Coptici, ser. 3, vol. 8 (*CSCO,* 99/100). Paris: "E Typographeo Reipublicae," 1933–34. [*PVSS*]

——, trans. *Les vies coptes de saint Pachôme et de ses premiers successeurs.* Bibliothèque du *Muséon,* vol. 16. Louvain: Bureaux du *Muséon,* 1943.

Leipoldt, Johannes. "Zur Geschichte der Auslegung." *TLZ* 75 (1950): 229–34.

——, and Siegfried Morens. *Heilige Schriften. Betrachtungen zur Religionsgeschichte der antiken Mittelmeerwelt.* Leipzig: Otto Harrassowitz, 1953.

Leistle, David. "Über Klosterbibliotheken des Mittelalters." *Studien und Mitteilungen zur Geschichte des Benediktiner-Ordens und seiner Zweige* 36 [n.s., 5] (1915): 197–228, 357–77.

Leloir, Louis. "La lecture de l'Écriture selon les anciens Pères." *Revue d'ascetique et de mystique* (Paris) 47 (1971): 183–99.

Lenz, Werner. *Kleine Geschichte großer Lexika. Ein Beitrag zum "Internationalen Jahr des Buches".* Gütersloh, Berlin, etc.: Bertelsmann, 1972.

Leroux, Jean-Marie. "Monachisme et communauté chrétienne d'après saint Jean Chrysostome." In *Théol. vie mon,* pp. 143–90.

Leroy, Julien. "Le cénobitisme chez Cassien." *Revue d'ascétique et de mystique* 43 (1967): 121–58.

Lesne, Émile. *Les livres, "scriptoria" et bibliothèques du commencement du VIIIe à la fin du XIe siècle.* Vol. 4 of *Histoire de la propriété ecclésiastique en France* (6 vols. Lille and Paris/Lille, 1910–43). Mémoires et travaux publiés par des professeurs des facultés catholiques de Lille, no. 46. Lille: Facultés Catholiques, 1938.

Lewis, I. M. "Literacy in a Nomadic Society: The Somali Case." In Goody, *Literacy,* pp. 266–76.

Liebermann, Saul. "The Publication of the Mishnah." In *Hellenism in Jewish Palestine.* Texts and Studies of the Jewish Theological Seminary of America, vol. 18. New York: Jewish Theological Seminary of America, 1962.

Liebich, Bruno. "Über den Sphoṭa (Ein Kapitel über die Sprachphilosophie der Inder)." *ZDMG* 77 [n.f., 2] (1923): 208–19.

Lienhard, Marc, and Jean Rott. "Die Anfänge der evangelischen Predigt in Straßburg und ihr erstes Manifest: der Aufruf des Karmeliterlesemeisters Tilman von Lyn (Anfang 1522)." In *Bucer und seine Zeit. Forschungsbeiträge und Bibliographie,* ed. Marijn de Kroon and Friedhelm Krüger. Veröffentlichungen des Instituts für europäische Geschichte Mainz (Abteilung für abendländische Religionsgeschichte, ed. J. Lortz), vol. 80. Wiesbaden: Franz Steiner, 1976, pp. 54–73.

Linderbauer, B. [**See** Benedict of Nursia.]

Lings, Martin, and Yasin Hamid Safadi. *The Qur'ān. Catalogue of an Exhibition of Qur'ān Manuscripts at the British Library, 3 April–15 August 1976.* London: World of Islam Publishing Co., 1976.

Lloyd James, A[rthur]. *Our Spoken Language.* London, Edinburgh, etc.: Thomas Nelson and Sons, 1938.

Lohse, Bernhard. *Askese und Mönchtum in der Antike und in der alten Kirche.* Religion und Kultur der alten Mittelmeerwelt in Parallelforschungen, ed. Carsten Colpe and Heinrich Dörrie, vol. 1. Munich and Vienna: R. Oldenbourg, 1969.

Lord, Albert B. *The Singer of Tales.* Harvard Studies in Comparative Literature, 24. Cambridge, Mass.: Harvard University Press, 1960.

Lotfi, Abdelhamid. [**See** Wagner, Daniel, and Abdelhamid Lotfi.]

[Lotus Sūtra (Saddharmapuṇḍarīkasūtra)]. *Scripture of the Lotus Blossom of the Fine Dharma, Translated from the Chinese of Kumārajīva.* Trans. Leon Hurvitz. Records of Civilization: Sources and Studies, ed. W. T. H. Jackson et al., no. 94. New York: Columbia University Press, 1976.

Louf, André. "The Word Beyond the Liturgy." *Cistercian Studies* 6 (1971): 353–68; 7 (1972): 63–76.

Löwinger, Samuel, and Joseph Somogyi, eds. *Ignace Goldziher Memorial Volume.* 2 vols. Budapest, 1948. [*Goldziher Mem.*]

Lüling, Günter. *Über den Ur-Qur'ān. Ansätze zur Rekonstruktion vorislamischer christlicher Strophenlieder im Qur'ān.* Erlangen: H. Lüling, 1974.

Lutgendorf, Philip. "The Life of a Text: Tulsīdās' *Rāmacaritamānasa* in Performance." Draft of forthcoming Ph.D. diss., University of Chicago [1986].

____. "The Life of a Text: Tulasīdāsa's *Rāmacaritamānasa* in Oral Exposition." Unpublished paper delivered at the American Academy of Religion annual meeting, Chicago, December 1984.

Luther, Martin. *D. Martin Luthers Werke. Kritische Gesamtausgabe.* Weimar: Hermann Böhlau, 1883–. [*WA*]

____. *Luther Deutsch. Die Werke Martin Luthers in neuer Auswahl für die Gegenwart.* Ed. Kurt Aland. 10 vols. + index. Stuttgart: Ehrenfried Klotz; Göttingen: Vandenhoeck & Ruprecht, 1959–81.

MacCandless, Joseph. " 'Meditation' in Saint Bernard." *Coll. cist.* 26 (1964): 277–93.

McGregor, Robert. "Monastic Lectio Divina." *Cistercian Studies* 6 (1971): 54–56.

Mackean, W[illiam] H. *Christian Monasticism in Egypt to the Close of the Fourth Century.* Studies in Church History. London: Society for Promoting Christian Knowledge; and New York: Macmillan, 1920.

McLeod, W. H. "The Sikh Scriptures: Some Issues." In *Sikh Studies: Comparative Perspectives on a Changing Tradition,* ed. Mark Juergensmeyer and N. Gerald Barrier. Berkeley, Calif.: Graduate Theological Union, Berkeley Religious Studies Series, 1979, pp. 97–111.

McLuhan, Marshall. "The Effect of the Printed Book on Language in the 16th Century." In *Explorations in Communication: An Anthology,* ed. Edmund Carpenter and Marshall McLuhan. Boston: Beacon Press, 1960, pp. 125–35.

____. *The Gutenberg Galaxy: The Making of Typographic Man.* Toronto: University of Toronto Press, 1962.

McMurray, James. "The Scriptures and Monastic Prayer." *Cistercian Studies* 2 (1967): 15–37.

Mādhavānanda, Swāmī, trans. [**See** Bṛhadāraṇyaka Upaniṣad.]

Mahārāj, B. H. Bon. "The Uniqueness of Vedic Reading." *Śāradā Piṭha Pradīpa: A Bi-Annual Journal of Indological Research Institute, Dwarka* 7 (1967): 1–13.

Makkī, Abū Ṭālib Muḥammad b. ʿAlī al-Hārithī al-. *Qūt al-qulūb fī muʿāmalat al-maḥbūb.* 2 vols. [1310/1892–93]. Cairo: Muṣṭafá al-Bābī al-Ḥalabī wa-Awlāduhu, 1381/1961.

[*Mānavadharmaśāstra*] *The Laws of Manu.* Trans. Georg Bühler. The Sacred Books of the East, vol. 25. Oxford: Clarendon, 1886. Repr. ed. New York: Dover, 1969.

Mandrou, Robert. *De la culture populaire aux XVIIe et XVIIIe siècles: La bibliothèque bleue de Troyes.* [Paris:] Stock, 1964.

Marrou, H. I. *A History of Education in Antiquity.* Trans. George Lamb. New York: Sheed and Ward, 1956. [Fr. orig.: *Histoire de l'éducation dans l'antiquité.* 3rd. ed. Paris: Éditions du Seuil, 1948.]

Martin, Henri-Jean. [**See** Febvre, Lucien, and Henri-Jean Martin.]

Martin, Richard C. "Understanding the Qur'an in Text and Context." *History of Religions* 21 (1982): 361–84.

Mauk, Fred[erick H.] "Resurrection and Insurrection." *Journal of Aesthetics and Art Criticism* 45, no. 2 (Winter 1986): 1–7.

Mayor, John E. B., ed. and comm. *Thirteen Satires of Juvenal, with a Commentary.* 2 vols. 4th rev. ed. London: Macmillan, 1886.

Meakin, Budgett. *The Moors: A Comprehensive Description.* London: Swan Sonnenschein, 1902.

Meggitt, M. [J.]. "Uses of Literacy in New Guinea and Melanesia." In Goody, *Literacy,* pp. 300–09.

Mehta, J. L. "The Hindu Tradition: The Vedic Root." In *The World's Religious Traditions: Current Perspectives in Religious Studies, Essays in Honour of Wilfred Cantwell Smith,* ed. Frank Whaling. Edinburgh: T. & T. Clark, 1984, pp. 33–54.

Meinhold, Peter. *Luthers Sprachphilosophie.* Berlin: Lutherisches Verlagshaus, 1958.

Meissinger, Karl August. *Der katholische Luther.* Ed. Otto Hiltbrunner. Munich: Leo Lehnen, 1952.

Mendieta, Emmanuel Amand de. [**See** Amand de Mendieta, Emmanuel.]

Mensching, Gustav. *Das heilige Wort. Eine religionsphänomenologische Untersuchung.* Untersuchungen zur allgemeinen Religionsgeschichte, ed. Carl Clemen, vol. 9. Bonn: Ludwig Röhrscheid, 1937.

____. *Die Religion. Erscheinungsformen, Strukturtypen und Lebensgesetze.* Stuttgart: Curt E. Schwab, 1959.

Michaux Bellaire, E. "L'enseignement indigène au Maroc." *Revue du Monde Musulman* 15 (1911): 422–52.

Miller, Jeanine. *The Vedas: Harmony, Meditation and Fulfilment.* London: Rider, 1974.

Misra, Vidya Niwas. "*Vāk* Legends in the *Brāhmaṇa* Literature." In *Proceedings of the Twenty-Sixth International Congress of Orientalists, New Delhi, January 4–10, 1964.* Vol. 3, pt. 1. Poona: Bhandarkar Oriental Research Institute, 1969, pp. 109–18.

Mizuno, Kōgen. *Buddhist Sutras: Origin, Development, Transmission.* Tokyo: Kōsei, 1982.

Moeller, Bernd. "Frömmigkeit in Deutschland um 1500." *ARG* 56 (1965): 5–31.

Momigliano, Arnaldo. "The Historians of the Classical World and Their Audiences." *American Scholar* 47 (1977–78): 193–204.

Montagu, Ashley. *Man: His First Million Years.* 1957. New York: New American Library, Mentor Books, 1958.

Mookerji, Radha Kumud. *Ancient Indian Education.* London: Macmillan, 1947.

Moran, James. *Printing Presses: History and Development from the Fifteenth Century to Modern Times.* Berkeley and Los Angeles: University of California Press, 1973.

Morenz, Siegfried. *Ägyptische Religion.* Die Religionen der Menschheit, ed. Christel Matthias Schröder, vol. 8. Stuttgart: W. Kohlhammer, 1960.

____. "Entstehung und Wesen der Buchreligion." *TLZ* 75 (1950): 709–16.

Müller, Adam. *Zwölf Reden über die Beredsamkeit und deren Verfall in Deutschland.* [1816?]. Repr. ed. Frankfurt/M.: Insel, 1967.

Müller, David Heinrich. *Die Propheten in ihrer ursprünglichen Form. Die Grundgesetze der ursemitischen Poesie erschlossen . . . in Bibel, Keilinschriften und Koran . . . .* 2 vols. Vienna: Alfred Hölder, 1896.

Müller, F[riedrich] Max. Preface to *The Upanishads. Part I.* Trans. F. Max Müller. The Sacred Books of the East Translated by Various Oriental Scholars, ed. F. Max Müller (50 vols. Oxford, 1879–1910), vol. 1. Oxford: Clarendon Press, 1879, pp. ix–xlvii.

Müller, Friedrun R. *Untersuchungen zur Reimprosa im Koran.* Bonner Orientalistische Studien, n.s., ed. Otto Spies, vol. 20. Bonn: Selbstverlag des Orientalischen Seminars der Universität, 1969.

Muir, J[ohn], comp. and trans. *The Vedas: Opinions of Their Authors and of Later Indian Writers on Their Origin, Inspiration, and Authority.* Original Sanskrit Texts on the Origin and History of the People of India, Their Religion and Institutions, comp. and trans. J. Muir, vol. 3. [London: Trübner, 1868.] 2nd rev. ed. 1874. Repr. ed. Amsterdam: Oriental Press, 1967.

Muqaddimat kitāb al-mabānī [author unknown]. In Arthur Jeffery, ed. *Two Muqaddimahs to the Qur'ānic Sciences.* Cairo, 1375/1954, pp. 1–250. [*Mabānī*]

Murphy, James J. *Rhetoric in the Middle Ages: A History of Rhetorical Theory from Saint Augustine to the Renaissance.* Berkeley, Los Angeles, and London: University of California Press, 1974.

Murphy, Margaret Gertrude. *St. Basil and Monasticism.* The Catholic University of America Patristic Studies, vol. 25. Washington, D.C.: Catholic University of America, 1930.

Murti, T[iruppattur] R. V. "The Philosophy of Language in the Indian Context." In *Studies in Indian Thought: Collected Papers of Prof. T. R. V. Murti,* ed.

Harold G. Coward. Delhi, etc.: Motilal Banarsidass, 1983, pp. 357–76. [Orig. publ. in *Proceedings of the 37th Session, Indian Philosophical Congress*, 1963.]

Muslim ibn al-Ḥajjāj, Abū l-Ḥusayn. *al-Ṣaḥīḥ*. Ed. Muḥammad Fu'ād 'Abd al-Bāqī. 4 vols. and indices. Cairo, 1374–75/1975–76. Repr. ed. Beirut: Dār Iḥyā' al-Turāth al-'Arabī, n.d. [Muslim]

Nagel, D. William. *Geschichte des christlichen Gottesdienstes*. 2nd rev. and expanded ed. Sammlung Göschen, vol. 1202/1202a. Berlin: Walter de Gruyter, 1970.

Nagel, Tilman. "Vom 'Qur'ān' zur 'Schrift' – Bells Hypothese aus religionsgeschichtlicher Sicht." *Der Islam* 60 (1983): 143–65.

Nakamura, Kōjirō. "A Structural Analysis of *Dhikr* and *Nembutsu*." *Orient* (Tokyo) 7(1971): 75–96.

Nakamura, Kyoko Motomochi, trans. *Miraculous Stories from the Japanese Buddhist Tradition: The "Nihon ryōiki" of the Monk Kyōkai*. Harvard–Yenching Monograph Series, vol. 20. Cambridge, Mass.: Harvard University Press, 1973.

Nanji, Azim. *The Nizārī Ismā'īlī Tradition in the Indo-Pakistan Subcontinent*. Monographs in Islamic Religion and Theology, ed. Richard Frank et al. Delmar, N.Y.: Caravan Books, 1978.

Nasā'ī, Aḥmad b. 'Abd al-Raḥmān b. Shu'ayb al-. *al-Sunan*. 8 vols. Cairo: Muṣṭafá al-Bābī al-Ḥalabī wa-Awlāduhu, 1383/1964. [Nasā'ī]

Nawawī, Abū Zakarīyā Yaḥyá b. Sharaf al-. *Riyāḍ al-ṣāliḥīn*. Ed. 'Abd al-'Azīz Ribāḥ and Aḥmad Yūsuf al-Daqqaq, with Shu'ayb al-Arna'ūṭ. Damascus: Dār al-Ma'mūn li-l-Turāth, [1976?].

———. *al-Tibyān fī ādāb ḥamalat al-Qur'ān*. Ed. Juma'ah 'Alī al-Khuwalī. Cairo: al-Maktabah al-Tawfīqīyah, 1397/1977.

Nef, John U. *Cultural Foundations of Industrial Civilization*. Cambridge: Cambridge University Press, 1958.

Nelson, Kristina. *The Art of Reciting the Qur'an*. Modern Middle East Series, no. 11. Austin, Tex.: University of Texas Press, 1985.

Nelson, William. "From 'Listen, Lordings' to 'Dear Reader'." *University of Toronto Quarterly* 46 (1976–77): 110–24.

Neusner, Jacob. *The Life of Torah: Readings in the Jewish Religious Experience*. Encino and Belmont, Calif.: Dickenson, 1974.

Neuwirth, Angelika. *Studien zur Komposition der mekkanischen Suren*. Studien zur Sprache, Geschichte und Kultur des islamischen Orients. Beihefte zur Zeitschrift "Der Islam", ed. Bertold Spuler. N.s., vol. 10. Berlin and New York: Walter de Gruyter, 1981.

———. "Zur Struktur der *Yūsuf*-Sure." In *Studien aus Arabistik und Semitistik. Anton Spitaler zum siebzigsten Geburtstag von seinen Schülern überreicht*, ed. Werner Diem and Stefan Wild. Wiesbaden: Otto Harrassowitz, 1980, pp. 123–52.

Nielsen, Eduard. *Oral Tradition: A Modern Problem in Old Testament Introduction*. London: SCM Press, 1954.

Nöldeke, Theodor, Friedrich Schwally, Gotthelf Bergsträsser, and Otto Pretzl.

Geschichte des Qorāns. 2nd rev. ed. Vol. 1 (Nöldeke and Schwally): Über den Ursprung des Qorāns; vol. 2 (Nöldeke and Schwally): Die Sammlung des Qorāns; vol. 3 ([Nöldeke,] Bergsträsser, and Pretzl): Die Geschichte des Korantexts. Leipzig: Dieterich'sche Verlagsbuchhandlung, 1909–38. [*GdQ*]

Noll, Mark A. [**See** Hatch, Nathan O., and Mark A. Noll, eds.]

Norden, Eduard. *Die antike Kunstprosa vom vi. Jahrhundert v. Chr. bis in die Zeit der Renaissance.* Leipzig, [1898?]. 5th ed. 1 vol. in 2 pts. (continuous pagination). Darmstadt: Wissenschaftliche Buchgesellschaft, 1958.

Notopoulos, James A. "Mnemosyne in Oral Literature." *Transactions and Proceedings of the American Philological Association* 69 (1938): 465–93.

Nwyia, Paul. *Exégèse coranique et language mystique: Nouvel essai sur le lexique technique des mystiques musulmans.* Recherches publiées sous la direction de l'Institut de Lettres Orientales de Beyrouth, ser. 1: Pensée arabe et musulmane, vol. 49. Beirut: Dar el-Machreq, 1970.

Nyberg, H. S. *Die Religionen des alten Iran.* Mitteilungen der Vorderasiatisch–Aegyptischen Gesellschaft, vol. 43. 1938. Repr. ed. Osnabrück: Otto Zeller, 1966.

Oberhammer, Gerhard. "Die Überlieferungsautorität im Hinduismus." In *Offenbarung, Geistige Realität des Menschen. Arbeitsdokumentation eines Symposiums zum Offenbarungsbegriff in Indien,* ed. Gerhard Oberhammer. Publications of the De Nobili Research Library, ed. Gerhard Oberhammer, vol. 2. Vienna: [Indologisches Institut der Universität Wien], 1974, pp. 41–92.

Oesterley, W. O. E. *The Jewish Background of the Christian Liturgy.* Oxford, 1925. Repr. ed. Gloucester, Mass.: Peter Smith, 1965.

O'Flaherty, Wendy Doniger, ed. *The Critical Study of Sacred Texts.* Berkeley: Graduate Theological Union, Berkeley Religious Studies Series, 1979.

____, trans. *The Rig Veda: An Anthology.* Harmondsworth (G.B.), New York, etc.: Penguin Books, 1981.

Olson, David R. "From Utterance to Text: The Bias of Language in Speech and Writing." *HER* 47 (1977): 257–81.

Ong, Walter J. *Interfaces of the Word. Studies in the Evolution of Consciousness and Culture.* Ithaca and London: Cornell University Press, 1977.

____. "Literacy and Orality in Our Times." In *Composition and Literature: Bridging the Gap,* ed. Winifred Bryan Horner. Chicago and London: University of Chicago Press, 1983, pp. 126–40.

____. *Orality and Literacy: The Technologizing of the Word.* London and New York: Methuen, 1982.

____. *The Presence of the Word: Some Prolegomena for Cultural and Religious History.* New Haven, 1967. 2nd ed. Minneapolis: University of Minnesota Press, 1981.

____. "Ramist Method and the Commercial Mind." *Studies in the Renaissance* 8 (1961): 155–72.

Östborn, Gunnar. *Cult and Canon: A Study in the Canonization of the Old Testament.* Uppsala Universitets Årsskrift, 1950, 10 (Uppsala: A.-B. Lundequistska; Leipzig: Otto Harrossowitz, [1950]).

Østergaard-Nielsen, H[arald]. *Scriptura sacra et viva vox. Eine Lutherstudie.* Forschungen zur Geschichte und Lehre des Protestantismus, ed. Ernst Wolf, 10th ser., vol. 10. Munich: Chr. Kaiser, 1957.

Overmyer, Daniel L. *Folk Buddhist Religion: Dissenting Sects in Late Traditional China.* Cambridge, Mass., and London: Harvard University Press, 1976.

Ozment, Steven E. *The Reformation in the Cities: The Appeal of Protestantism to Sixteenth-Century Germany and Switzerland.* New Haven and London: Yale University Press, 1975.

Ozouf, Jacques. [**See** Furet, François, and Jacques Ozouf.]

Pachomius/Pachomian Texts. [**See** Athanassakis, Apostolos N.; Boon, Armand; Cranenburgh, H. van; Halkin, François; Lefort, Louis Th.; Veilleux, Armand.]

Padoux, André. *Recherches sur la symbolique et l'énergie de la parole dans certains textes tantriques.* Publications de l'Institut de Civilisation Indienne, no. 21. Paris: E. de Boccard, 1963.

Padwick, Constance E. *Muslim Devotions: A Study of Prayer-Manuals in Common Use.* London: SPCK, 1961, 1969.

Palladius. [**See** Butler, Cuthbert, ed.]

Paret, Rudi. "Besonderheiten alter Koranhandschriften." In *Studien zur Geschichte und Kultur des Vorderen Orients. Festschrift für Bertold Spuler zum siebzigsten Geburtstag,* ed. Hans R. Roemer and Albrecht Noth. Leiden: E. J. Brill, 1981, pp. 310–20.

____. *Grenzen der Koranforschung.* Bonner Orientalistische Studien, ed. R. Paret and W. Kirfel, no. 27. Stuttgart: W. Kohlhammer, 1950.

____. *Mohammed und der Koran.* 1957. 5th rev. ed. Stuttgart, Berlin, etc.: W. Kohlhammer, Urban-Taschenbücher, 1980.

____, trans. [**See** Qur'ān, al-.]

Parkes, M. B. "The Literacy of the Laity." In *The Mediaeval World,* ed. David Daiches and Anthony Thorlby. Literature and Western Civilization, [2]. London: Aldus Books, 1973, pp. 555–77 (chap. 16).

Parry, Milman. *The Making of Homeric Verse: The Collected Papers of Milman Parry.* Ed. Adam Parry. Oxford: Clarendon Press, 1971.

Pattison, Robert. *On Literacy: The Politics of the Word from Homer to the Age of Rock.* Oxford, New York, etc.: Oxford University Press, 1982.

Pawlowsky, Sigismund. *Die biblischen Grundlagen der Regula Benedicti.* Wiener Beiträge zur Theologie, vol. 9. Vienna: Verlag Herder, 1965.

Pedersen, Johannes. "The Islamic Preacher." In *Goldziher Mem.* 1: 226–51.

____. Review of Eduard Meyer, *Ursprung und Geschichte der Mormonen* (1912). *Der Islam* 5 (1914): 110–15.

Peifer, Claude. "The Biblical Foundations of Monasticism." *Cistercian Studies* 1 (1966): 7-31.

Pelikan, Jaroslav. *Luther the Expositor: Introduction to the Reformer's Exegetical Writings.* Luther's Works: Companion Volume. St. Louis: Concordia, 1959.

Pelliot, Paul. *Les débuts de l'imprimerie en Chine.* Œuvres posthumes de Paul Pelliot, vol. 4. Paris: Imprimerie Nationale, Adrien-Maisonneuve, 1953.

Perelman, Chaim. [**See** Sloan, Thomas O., and Chaim Perelman.]

Pfeiffer, Rudolf. *History of Classical Scholarship from the Beginnings to the End of the Hellenistic Age.* Oxford: Clarendon Press, 1968.

Piamenta, M. *Islam in Everyday Arabic Speech.* Leiden: E. J. Brill, 1979.

Plato. [*Complete Works,* Gk. text and Eng. trans.] Vols. 1, 2 (of 12). The Loeb Classical Library. Vol. 1: *Euthyphro, Apology, Crito, Phaedo, Phaedrus.* Trans. Harold North Fowler. 1914. Vol. 2: *Laches, Protagoras, Meno, Euthydemus.* Trans. W. R. M. Lamb, 1924. Cambridge, Mass.: Harvard University Press; London: William Heinemann, 1966 (vol. 1), 1967 (vol. 2).

Porte, Jacques, ed. *Encyclopédie des musiques sacrées.* 4 vols. Paris: Labergerie, 1968–70. Vol. 1 (1968). [*Encl. mus. sacr.*]

Prenter, Regin. *Spiritus creator. Studien zu Luthers Theologie.* 1944 [orig., Danish ed.]. 3rd, Ger. ed. Trans. W. Thiemann. Forschungen zur Geschichte und Lehre des Protestantismus, ed. Ernst Wolf, 10th ser., vol. 6. Munich: Chr. Kaiser, 1954.

Presser, Helmut. *Das Buch vom Buch. 5000 Jahre Buchgeschichte.* 2nd rev. ed. Hannover: Schlütersche Verlagsanstalt und Druckerei, 1978.

Pretzl, Otto. "Die Wissenschaft der Koranlesung (*'Ilm al-Qirā'a*). Ihre literarischen Quellen und ihre Aussprachegrundlagen (*Uṣūl*)." *Islamica* 6 (1933–34): 1–47, 230–46, 290–331.

____. [**See** Nöldeke, Theodor, et al.]

____, ed. [**See** Dānī, Abū 'Amrū 'Uthmān b. Sa'īd al-.]

Preuss, Johannes [Hans]. *Die Entwicklung des Schriftprinzips bei Luther bis zur Leipziger Disputation. Im Zusammenhang mit der Stellung Luthers zu den andern theologischen Autoritäten seiner Zeit dargestellt.* Leipzig: Chr. Herm. Tauchnitz, 1901.

Price, Lucien. [**See** Whitehead, Alfred North.]

Prothero, Rowland E. *The Psalms in Human Life.* [1903/4?]. New York: E. P. Dutton, Everyman's Library, n.d.

Quecke, Hans, ed. *Die Briefe Pachoms. Griechischer Text der Handschrift W. 145 der Chester Beatty Library eingeleitet und herausgegeben von Hans Quecke.* Textus patristici et liturgici, 11. Regensburg: Friedrich Pustet, 1975. [*BP*]

[Qur'ān, al-]. *Le Coran.* Trans. Régis Blachère. 2 vols. 1949–50. Repr. ed. (1 vol.): *Le Coran (al-Qor'ân).* Paris: G.-P. Maisonneuve–Max Besson, 1957.

____. *Der Koran.* Trans. Rudi Paret. Stuttgart, Berlin, etc.: W. Kohlhammer, 1962.

____. *The Koran; Commonly Called, The Alcoran of Mohammed.* Trans. George Sale. 1734. London: Orlando Hodgson, n.d.

____. *The Koran Interpreted.* Trans. Arthur J. Arberry. 2 vols. London, 1955. 2nd impression. London: George Allen & Unwin; New York: Macmillan, 1963.

____. *The Qur'ān: Translated, with a Critical Re-Arrangement of the Surahs.* Trans. Richard Bell. 2 vols. Edinburgh: T. & T. Clark, 1937–39.

Raghavan, V. "Vedic Chanting; Music, Dance and Drama." In *International Seminar on Traditional Cultures in South-East Asia* (Bombay, etc.: Orient Longmans, 1960), pp. 168–77.

[Raghavan, V., et al.] "Present Position of Vedic Chanting and Its Future." *Bulletin of the Institute of Traditional Cultures, Madras* (1957), pp. 48–69.

Ray, Reginald A. "Buddhism: Sacred Text Written and Realized." In Denny and Taylor, pp. 148–80.

Ray, Roger D. "Orderic Vitalis and His Readers." *Studia Monastica* 14 (1972): 15–33.

Reitzenstein, Richard. *"Historia monachorum" und "Historia lausiaca". Eine Studie zur Geschichte des Mönchtums und der frühchristlichen Begriffe Gnostiker und Pneumatiker.* Forschungen zur Religion und Literatur des Alten und Neuen Testaments, 24 [n.s., 7]. Göttingen: Vandenhoeck & Ruprecht, 1916.

Renou, Louis. *Le destin du Véda dans l'Inde.* Études védiques et pāṇinéennes, vol. 6. Publications de l'Institut de Civilisation Indienne, no. 10. Paris: E. de Boccard, 1960. Eng. ed. and trans. Dev Raj Chanana. *The Destiny of the Veda in India.* Delhi, etc.: Motilal Banarsidass, 1965.

____. "Les pouvoirs de la parole dans le Ṛgveda." In *Études védiques et pāṇinéennes,* vol. 1. Publications de l'Institut de Civilisation Indienne, no. 1. Paris: E. de Boccard, 1955, pp. 1–27.

____. *Sanskrit et culture. L'apport de l'Inde à la civilisation humaine.* Paris: Payot, 1950.

____, Jean Filliozat, et al. *L'Inde classique. Manuel des études indiennes.* 3 vols. Paris: Payot, 1947–49 (vol. 1); Paris: Imprimerie Nationale, 1953 (vol. 2).

____, and Liliane Silburn. "Sur la notion de *bráhman.*" *Journal Asiatique* (1949), pp. 7–46.

Resch, P. *La doctrine ascétique des premiers maîtres égyptiens du quatrième siècle.* Études de théologie historique. Paris: Gabriel Beauchesne, 1931.

Resnick, Daniel P., ed. *Literacy in Historical Perspective.* Washington: Library of Congress, 1983. [Resnick, *Literacy*]

____, and Lauren B. Resnick. "The Nature of Literacy: An Historical Exploration." *HER* 47 (1977): 370–85.

Reu, M. *Luther's German Bible: An Historical Presentation Together with a Collection of Sources.* Columbus, Ohio: Lutheran Book Concern, 1934.

Reynolds, L. D., and N. G. Wilson. *Scribes and Scholars: A Guide to the Transmission of Greek and Latin Literature.* Oxford, London, etc.: Oxford University Press, 1968.

Ricoeur, Paul. *Hermeneutics and the Human Sciences: Essays on Language, Action and Interpretation.* Ed. and trans. John B. Thompson. Cambridge, etc.: Cambridge University Press; Paris: Editions de la Maison des Sciences de l'Homme, 1981.

Riesman, David. "The Oral and Written Traditions." *Explorations:. Studies in Culture* 6 (1956): 22–28.

Roberts, Bleddyn J. "The Old Testament: Manuscripts, Text and Versions." In *Camb. Hist. Bib.* 2: 1–26.

Roberts, Colin H., and T. C. Skeat. *The Birth of the Codex.* London: Oxford University Press (for the British Academy), 1983.

Robson, James. "The Magical Use of the Koran." *Transactions of the Glasgow University Oriental Society* [1929–33] 6 (1934): 51–60.

Roest Crollius, Ary A. *Thus Were They Hearing: The Word in the Experience of Revelation in Qur'ān and Hindu Scriptures.* Documenta missionalia, 8. Rome: Università Gregoriana Editrice, 1974.

Rohde, Erwin. *Der griechische Roman und seine Vorläufer.* Leipzig: Breitkopf und Härtel, 1876.

Rosenbaum, Jonathan. "Judaism: Torah and Tradition." In Denny and Taylor, pp. 10–35.

Rost, Hans. *Die Bibel im Mittelalter. Beiträge zur Geschichte und Bibliographie der Bibel.* Augsburg: M. Seitz, 1939.

Roth, R. [**See** *Atharva Veda Saṁhitā.*]

Rouse, Richard H., and Mary A. Rouse. "*Statim invenire:* Schools, Preachers, and New Attitudes to the Page." In *Renaissance and Renewal in the Twelfth Century,* ed. Robert L. Benson and Giles Constable, with Carol D. Lanham. Cambridge, Mass.: Harvard University Press, 1982, pp. 201–25.

Rubroek, William of ["Fr. Guillelmus de Rubruc"]. *Itinerarium.* In *Itinera et relationes fratrum minorum saeculi XIII et XIV.* Comp. and ed. Anastasius van den Wyngaert. *Sinica franciscana* (8 vols. in 11. 1929–75), vol. 1. Florence, 1929, pp. 147–332.

Rupp, E. G., ed. [**See** Bruce, F. F., and E. G. Rupp, eds.]

Rupp, Gordon. "Word and Spirit in the First Years of the Reformation." *ARG* 49 (1958): 13–25.

Ruppert, Fidelis. "Arbeit und geistliches Leben im pachomianischen Mönchtum." *Ostkirchliche Studien* 24 (1975): 3–14.

____. "*Meditatio – Ruminatio.* Zu einem Grundbegriff christlicher Meditation." *Erbe und Auftrag* 53 (1977): 83–93.

____. *Das pachomianische Mönchtum und die Anfänge klösterlichen Gehorsams.* Münsterschwarzacher Studien, vol. 20. Münsterschwarzach: Vier–Türme–Verlag, 1971.

Sa, Francis X. D'. [**See** D'Sa, Francis X.]

Sachs, Wladimir. [**See** Furet, François, and Wladimir Sachs.]

Saddharmapuṇḍarīkasūtra. [**See** Lotus Sūtra.]

Sa'īd, Labīb al- ["Labib as-Said"]. *The Recited Koran: A History of the First Recorded Version.* Trans. and adapted by Bernard Weiss, M. A. Rauf, and Morroe Berger. Princeton, N.J.: The Darwin Press, 1975.

Sale, George. "A Preliminary Discourse." In George Sale, trans. *The Koran; Commonly Called the Alcoran of Mohammed.* 1734. London: Orlando Hodgson, n.d, pp. 1–143.

____, trans. [**See** Qur'ān, al-.]

Sambhi, Piara Singh. [**See** Cole, W. Owen, and Piara Singh Sambhi.]

Sanders, James A. *Canon and Community: A Guide to Canonical Criticism.* Philadelphia: Fortress, 1984.

———. *Torah and Canon.* Philadelphia: Fortress, 1972.

Sanneh, Lamin O. "The Islamic Education of an African Child: Stresses and Tensions." In *Conflict and Harmony in Education in Tropical Africa,* ed. Godfrey N. Brown and Mervyn Hiskett. London: George Allen & Unwin, 1975, pp. 168–86.

———. *The Jakhanke: The History of an Islamic Clerical People of the Senegambia.* London: International African Institute, 1979.

Santerre, Renaud. *Pédagogie musulmane d'Afrique noire: L'école coranique peule du Cameroun.* Montréal: Presses de l'Université de Montréal, 1973.

Sarton, George. *The Appreciation of Ancient and Medieval Science during the Renaissance (1450–1600).* Philadelphia: University of Pennsylvania Press, 1955.

Sastri, Gaurinath. *The Philosophy of Word and Meaning: Some Indian Approaches with Special Reference to the Philosophy of Bhartṛhari.* Calcutta: Sanskrit College, 1959.

Saussure, Ferdinand de. *Cours de linguistique générale.* Ed. Charles Bally and Albert Sechehaye, in collaboration with Albert Riedlinger. [1915?]. 3rd ed. Paris: Payot, 1967. Eng. trans. Wade Baskin. *Course in General Linguistics.* 1959. New York, Toronto, London: McGraw–Hill, 1966.

Scharbau, Carl Anders. *Die Idee der Schöpfung in der vedischen Literatur. Eine religionsgeschichtliche Untersuchung über den frühindischen Theismus.* Veröffentlichungen des orientalischen Seminars der Universität Tübingen, ed. E. Littmann and J. W. Hauer, no. 5. Stuttgart: W. Kohlhammer, 1932.

Scheel, Otto. *Luthers Stellung zur heiligen Schrift.* Sammlung gemeinverständlicher Vorträge und Schriften aus dem Gebiet der Theologie und Religionsgeschichte, 29. Tübingen und Leipzig: J. C. B. Mohr (Paul Siebeck), 1902.

Schempp, Paul. *Luthers Stellung zur Heiligen Schrift.* Forschungen zur Geschichte und Lehre des Protestantismus, ed. Paul Althaus, Karl Barth, and Karl Heim, 2nd. ser., vol. 3. Munich: Chr. Kaiser, 1929.

Schiwietz [Siwiec], Stephan. *Das morgenländische Mönchtum.* 3 vols. Mainz: von Kirchheim (vols. 1, 1904; 2, 1913), and Mödling (nr. Vienna): Missionsdruckerei St. Gabriel (vol. 3, 1938), 1904–38.

Schneider, Carl. *Kulturgeschichte des Hellenismus.* 2 vols. Munich: C. H. Beck, 1967–69.

Schneider, Gerhard. "Bibel und Meditation. Hinweise zum meditativen Umgang mit der Heiligen Schrift." *Geist und Leben* 38 (1965): 13–38.

Schofield, R. S. "Dimensions of Illiteracy, 1750–1850." *Explorations in Economic History* 10 (1973): 437–54.

———. "The Measurement of Literacy in Pre-Industrial England." In Goody, *Literacy,* pp. 311–25.

Schopen, Gregory. "The Phrase *'sa pṛthivīpradeśaś caityabhūto bhavet'* in the *Vajracchedikā:* Notes on the Cult of the Book in Mahāyāna," *Indo-Iranian Journal* 17 (1975): 147–81.

Schott, Rüdiger. "Das Geschichtsbewußtsein schriftloser Völker." *Archiv für Begriffsgeschichte* 12 (1968): 166–205.

Schubart, Wilhelm. *Das Buch bei den Griechen und Römern. Eine Studie aus der berliner Papyrussammlung.* Handbücher der Königlichen Museen zu Berlin. Berlin: Georg Reimer, 1907. [2nd rev. ed. Berlin and Leipzig: Walter de Gruyter, 1921.]

Schubert-Christaller, Else. *Der Gottesdienst der Synagoge. Sein Aufbau und sein Sinn.* Giessen: Alfred Töpelmann, 1927.

Schwally, Friedrich. [**See** Nöldeke, Theodor, et al.]

Schwarz, W. *Principles and Problems of Biblical Translation: Some Reformation Controversies and Their Background.* Cambridge: Cambridge University Press, 1955.

Scribner, R[obert] W. *For the Sake of Simple Folk: Popular Propaganda for the German Reformation.* Cambridge Studies in Oral and Literate Culture, ed. Peter Burke and Ruth Finnegan, no. 2. Cambridge, etc.: Cambridge University Press, 1981.

Scribner, Sylvia, and Michael Cole. "Literacy without Schooling: Testing for Intellectual Effects." *HER* 48 (1978): 448–61.

____. *The Psychology of Literacy.* Cambridge, Mass., and London: Harvard University Press, 1981.

Sell, Edward. "'Ilmu't-tajwíd," Appendix A of *The Faith of Islam.* [1880]. 3rd rev. ed. Madras: SPCK Depôt, 1907, pp. 376–405.

Severus, Emmanuel von. "Der heilige Ignatius als Lehrer des betrachtenden Gebetes." *Geist und Leben* 29 (1956): 277–83.

____. "'Silvestrem tenui musam meditaris avena.' Zur Bedeutung der Wörter meditatio und meditari beim Kirchenlehrer Ambrosius." In *Perennitas. Beiträge zur christlichen Archäologie und Kunst, zur Geschichte der Literatur, der Liturgie und des Mönchtums sowie zur Philosophie des Rechts und zur politischen Philosophie. P. Thomas Michels OSB zum 70. Geburtstag,* ed. Hugo Rahner and Emmanuel von Severus. Beiträge zur Geschichte des alten Mönchtums und des Benediktinerordens, supp. vol. 2. Münster: Aschendorff, 1963, pp. 25–31.

____. "Das Wesen der Meditation und der Mensch der Gegenwart." *Geist und Leben* 29 (1956): 108–16.

____. "Das Wort 'Meditari' im Sprachgebrauch der Heiligen Schrift." *Geist und Leben* 26 (1953): 365–75.

____. "Zu den biblischen Grundlagen des Mönchtums." *Geist und Leben* 26 (1953): 113–22.

Shaban, M. A. *Islamic History: A New Interpretation I: A.D. 600–750 (A.H. 132).* Cambridge, etc.: Cambridge University Press, 1971, 1976.

Sharīf, Ja'far. *Islam in India, or the "Qānūn-i-Islām": The Customs of the Musalmāns of India.* "Composed under the direction of" and trans. G. A. Herklots. 1832. Rev. ed. William Crooke. 1921. Repr. ed. New Delhi: Oriental Books Reprint Corporation, 1972.

Shiloah, Amnon. "L'Islam et la musique." In *Encl. mus. sacr,* pp. 414–21.

Shils, Edward. *Tradition.* Chicago: University of Chicago Press, 1981.

Silburn, Liliane. [**See** Renou, Louis, and Liliane Silburn.]

Sivaraman, Krishna. "The Word as a Category of Revelation." In *Revelation in Indian Thought: A Festschrift in Honour of Professor T. R. V. Murti,* ed. Harold Coward and Krishna Sivaraman. Emeryville, Calif.: Dharma Publishing, 1977, pp. 45–64.

Siwiec, Stephan. [**See** Schiwietz, Stephan.]

Skeat, T. C. "Early Christian Book-Production: Papyri and Manuscripts." In *Camb. Hist. Bib.* 2: 54–79.

Sloan, Thomas O., and Chaim Perelman. "Rhetoric." *EB*[15]. Macropædia 15: 798b–805b.

Smalley, Beryl. *Historians in the Middle Ages.* London: Thames and Hudson, 1974.

____. *The Study of the Bible in the Middle Ages.* Oxford: Clarendon, 1941. 2nd ed. Oxford: Basil Blackwell, 1952. Repr. of 2nd ed. Notre Dame, Ind.: University of Notre Dame Press, 1964.

Smet, Richard V. De. [**See** De Smet, Richard V.]

Smith, D. Moody, Jr. "The Use of the Old Testament in the New." In *The Use of the Old Testament in the New and Other Essays: Studies in Honor of William Franklin Stinespring,* ed. James M. Efird. Durham, N.C.: Duke University Press, 1972, pp. 3–65.

Smith, Wilfred Cantwell. *The Meaning and End of Religion: A New Approach to the Religious Traditions of Mankind.* New York: Macmillan, 1962.

____. *Questions of Religious Truth.* New York: Charles Scribner's Sons, 1967.

____. "Scripture as Form and Concept. Their Emergence for the Western World." Unpublished article (typescript). Forthcoming in *Rethinking Scripture,* ed. Miriam Levering. Albany, N.Y.: SUNY Press, [1987].

____. "Some Similarities and Differences between Christianity and Islam: An Essay in Comparative Religion." In *The World of Islam: Studies in Honour of Philip K. Hitti,* ed. James Kritzeck and R. Bayly Winder. London: Macmillan; New York: St. Martin's Press, 1959, pp. 47–59.

____. "The Study of Religion and the Study of the Bible." *JAAR* 39 (1971): 131–40.

____. "The True Meaning of Scripture: An Empirical Historian's Nonreductionist Interpretation of the Qur'an." *IJMES* 11 (1980): 487–505.

Snell, Bruno. *The Discovery of the Mind: The Greek Origins of European Thought.* Trans. T. G. Rosenmeyer. 1953. New York and Evanston, Ill.: Harper & Row, Harper Torchbooks, 1960.

Snouck Hurgronje, C[hristian]. *Mekka in the Latter Part of the 19th Century.* Trans. from the German by J. H. Monahan. [Orig. Ger. ed., 1889.] Leiden and London, 1931. Photo-repr. ed. Leiden: E. J. Brill, 1970.

____. "Une nouvelle biographie de Mohammed" [review of H. Grimme, *Mohammed* (1892–95)]. *Revue de l'histoire des religions* 30 (1894): 48–70, 149–78.

Southern, R. W. *Western Views of Islam in the Middle Ages.* Cambridge, Mass., and London: Harvard University Press, 1962, 1978.

Spence, Jonathan D. *The Memory Palace of Matteo Ricci.* New York: Viking, Elisabeth Sifton Books, 1984.

Speyer, Wolfgang. *Bücherfunde in der Glaubenswerbung der Antike.* Hypomnemata. Untersuchungen zur Antike und zu ihrem Nachleben, no. 24. Göttingen: Vandenhoeck & Ruprecht, 1970.

Spolsky, Bernard. "Triglossia and Literacy in Jewish Palestine of the First Century." *International Journal of the Sociology of Language* 42 (1983): 95–109.

Staal, J[ohan] F[rederik] ["Frits"]. "The Concept of Scripture in the Indian Tradition." In *Sikh Studies: Comparative Perspectives on a Changing Tradition,* ed. Mark Juergensmeyer and N. Gerald Barrier. Berkeley Religious Studies Series. Berkeley, Calif.: Graduate Theological Union, 1979, pp. 121–24.

____. *Nambudiri Veda Recitation.* Disputationes Rheno–Trajectinae, ed. J. Gonda, vol. 5. The Hague: Mouton, 1961.

____. "Ṛgveda 10.71 on the Origin of Language." In *Revelation in Indian Thought: A Festschrift in Honour of Professor T. R. V. Murti,* ed. Harold Coward and Krishna Sivaraman. Emeryville, Calif.: Dharma Publishing, 1977, pp. 3–14.

____. "Sanskrit and Sanskritization." *JAS* 22 (1962-63): 261–75.

Steck, Karl Gerhard. *Lehre und Kirche bei Luther.* Forschungen zur Geschichte und Lehre des Protestantismus, ed. Ernst Wolf, 10th ser., vol. 27. Munich: Chr. Kaiser, 1963.

Steinberg, S. H. "Encyclopaedias." *Signature* (London), n.s., 12 (1951): 3-22.

____. *Five Hundred Years of Printing.* 1955. 2nd rev. ed. Harmondsworth, UK, Baltimore, Md., and Victoria, Austral.: Penguin, 1961.

Steiner, George. *After Babel: Aspects of Language and Translation.* 1975. London, Oxford, New York: Oxford University Press, 1976, 1981.

____. "After the Book?" In Robert Disch, ed. *The Future of Literacy.* Englewood Cliffs, N.J.: Prentice-Hall, Spectrum Books, 1973, pp. 145–57.

____. *Language and Silence: Essays on Language, Literature, and the Inhuman.* New York: Atheneum, 1982.

Steinmetz, David C. *Luther and Staupitz: An Essay in the Intellectual Origins of the Protestant Reformation.* Duke Monographs in Medieval and Renaissance Studies, no. 4. Durham, N.C.: Duke University Press, 1980.

Stock, Brian. *The Implications of Literacy: Written Language and Models of Interpretation in the Eleventh and Twelfth Centuries.* Princeton, N.J.: Princeton University Press, 1983.

Stone, Lawrence. "Literacy and Education in England, 1640–1900." *Past and Present* 42 (1969): 69–139.

Strauss, Gerald. *Luther's House of Learning: Indoctrination of the Young in the German Reformation.* Baltimore, Md., and London: Johns Hopkins University Press, 1978.

Strauss [Strauß], Otto. "Altindische Spekulationen über die Sprache und ihre Probleme." *ZDMG* 81 [n.s., 6] (1927): 99–151.

Stubbs, Michael. *Language and Literacy: The Sociolinguistics of Reading and Writing.* London, Boston, and Henley: Routledge & Kegan Paul, 1980.

Sudbrack, Josef. "Zum Thema: Betrachtung oder Meditation?" *Erbe und Auftrag* 48 (1972): 95–101.

Sudhaus, Siegfried. "Lautes und leises Beten." *Archiv für Religionswissenschaft* 9 (1906): 185–200.

Sullivan, Helen. "Literacy and Illiteracy." *Encyclopaedia of the Social Sciences* 9: 511b–23b.

Sundberg, Albert C., Jr. *The Old Testament of the Early Church.* Harvard Theological Studies, no. 20. Cambridge, Mass.: Harvard University Press, 1964.

____. "The Old Testament of the Early Church (A Study in Canon)." *HTR* 51 (1958): 205–26.

Suyūṭī, Jalāl al-Dīn ʻAbd al-Raḥmān. *al-Itqān fī ʻulūm al-Qur'ān* [with Abū Bakr al-Bāqillānī, *I'jāz al-Qur'ān,* on the margins]. 2 vols. in 1. 2nd ed. Cairo: Muṣṭafá al-Bābī al-Ḥalabī wa-Awlāduhu, 1370/1951. [*Itqān*]

Ṭabarī, Abū Jaʻfar Muḥammad b. Jarīr al-. *Jāmiʻ al-bayān ʻan ta'wīl āy al-Qur'ān.* 30 vols. Cairo, 1321/1903. 3rd repr. ed. Cairo: Muṣṭafá al-Bābī al-Ḥalabī wa-Awlāduhu, 1388/1968. [Ṭabarī]

____. *Jāmiʻ al-bayān ʻan ta'wīl āy al-Qur'ān.* Ed. Maḥmūd Muḥammad Shākir and Aḥmad Muḥammad Shākir. 16 vols. to date. Cairo, [1954?]ff. [Ṭabarī^2]

Talbi, M. "La qirā'a bi-l-alḥān." *Arabica* 5 (1958): 183–90.

Tambiah, S[tanley] J. "Literacy in a Buddhist Village in North-East Thailand." In Goody, *Literacy,* pp. 86–131.

____. "The Magical Power of Words." *Man,* n.s., 3 (1968): 175–208.

Tamburrino, Pio. "Bibbia e vita spirituale negli scritti di Orsiesi." In C. Vagaggini et al., *Bibbia e spiritualità.* Biblioteca di cultura religiosa, 2nd ser., no. 79. Rome: Edizioni Paoline, 1967, pp. 83–119.

Tao Tê Ching. [**See** Waley, Arthur, trans.]

Taylor, Rodney L. "Confucianism: Scripture and the Sage." In Denny and Taylor, pp. 181–203.

____, ed. [**See** Denny, Frederick M., and Rodney L., eds.]

Théologie de la vie monastique. Études sur la tradition patristique. Théologie. Études publiées sous la direction de la faculté de théologie S. J. de Lyon-Fourvière, 49. Paris: Aubier, 1961. [*Théol. vie mon.*]

Thieme, Paul. "Bráhman." *ZDMG* 102 [n.s., 27] (1952): 91–129.

Thimme, Karl. *Luthers Stellung zur Heiligen Schrift.* Gütersloh: C. Bertelsmann, 1903.

Thompson, James Westfall. *Ancient Libraries.* Berkeley, Calif.: University of California Press, 1940.

____. *The Literacy of the Laity in the Middle Ages.* University of California Publications in Education, vol. 9. Berkeley, Calif.: University of California Press, 1939. Repr. ed. New York: Burt Franklin, 1960.

Thompson, Laurence G. "Taoism: Classic and Canon." In Denny and Taylor, pp. 204–23.

Tirmidhī, Muḥammad b. ʻIsá al-. *al-Jāmiʻ al-ṣaḥīḥ [Kitāb al-Sunan].* Ed. Aḥmad Muḥammad Shākir, Muḥammad Fu'ād ʻAbd al-Bāqī, and Ibrāhīm ʻAṭwah ʻŪḍ. 5 vols. Cairo: Muṣṭafá al-Bābī al-Ḥalabī wa-Awlāduhu, 1356/1937–1395/1975. [Tirmidhī]

Touma, Habib Hassan. "Die Koranrezitation: Eine Form der religiösen Musik der

Araber." *Baessler-Archiv: Beiträge zur Völkerkunde* 48 [n.s., 23] (1975): 87–120.

Tracy, David. [**See** Grant, Robert M., and David Tracy.]

Turner, E. G. *Greek Papyri: An Introduction.* Oxford: Clarendon Press, 1968.

Twitchett, Denis. *Printing and Publishing in Medieval China.* New York: Frederic C. Beil, 1983.

[UNESCO]. *L'analphabétisme dans le monde au milieu du xxe siècle. Étude statistique.* N.p.: UNESCO, 1957.

Van Assche, Modestus. [**See** Assche, Modestus Van]

van Buitenen, J. A. B. [**See** Buitenen, J. A. B. van.]

Vansina, Jan. *Oral Tradition: A Study in Historical Methodology.* Trans. H. M. Wright [Fr. orig. ed.: *De la tradition orale: Essai de methode historique,* 1961]. Chicago: Aldine, 1965.

____, R. Mauny, and L. V. Thomas, eds. *The Historian in Tropical Africa: Studies Presented. . . at the University of Dakar, Senegal, 1961.* London, Ibadan, Accra: Oxford University Press, for the International African Institute, 1964.

Veilleux, Armand. "Holy Scripture in the Pachomian Koinonia." *Monastic Studies* 10 (1974): 143–53. [Partial trans. of chap. 5 of *La liturgie* (see below) from the Fr. by "monks of Mount Melleray Abbey, Ireland".]

____. *La liturgie dans le cénobitisme pachômien au quatrième siècle.* Studia Anselmiana, 57. Rome: "I. B. C." Libreria Herder, 1968.

____, trans. *Pachomian Koinonia: The Lives, Rules, and Other Writings of Saint Pachomius and His Disciples.* 3 vols. [1: The Life of S. Pachomius and His Disciples; 2: Pachomian Chronicles and Rules; 3: Instructions, Letters, and Other Writings of S. Pachomius and His Disciples]. Cistercian Studies Series, 45, 46, 47. Kalamazoo, Mich.: Cistercian Publications, 1980–82. [*PK*]

Visser, M. W. de. *Ancient Buddhism in Japan: Sūtras and Ceremonies in Use in the Seventh and Eighth Centuries A.D. and Their History in Later Times.* 2 vols. Leiden: E. J. Brill; Paris: Paul Geuthner, 1935.

Vleeschauwer, H. J. de (and H. Curtis Wright, ed. and trans.). "Origins of the Mouseion of Alexandria." In *Toward a Theory of Librarianship: Papers in Honor of Jesse Hauk Shera,* ed. Conrad H. Rawski. Metuchen, N.J.: Scarecrow Press, 1973, pp. 87–113. Repr. in H. Curtis Wright. *The Oral Antecedents of Greek Librarianship.* Provo, Utah: Brigham Young University Press, 1977, pp. 175–201.

Vogüé, Adalbert de. "Les deux fonctions de la méditation dans les Règles monastiques anciennes." *Revue d'histoire de la spiritualité* 51 (1975): 3–16.

____. "*Sub Regula uel Abbate:* A Study of the Theological Significance of the Ancient Monastic Rules." In *Rule and Life: An Interdisciplinary Symposium,* ed. M. Basil Pennington. Cistercian Studies Series, 12. Spencer, Mass.: Cistercian Publications, 1971, pp. 21–63.

Wagner, Daniel A., and Abdelhamid Lotfi. "Learning to Read by 'Rote'." *International Journal of the Sociology of Language* 42 (1983): 111–21.

____. "Traditional Islamic Education in Morocco: Sociohistorical and Psychological Perspectives." *Comparative Education Review* 24 (1980): 238–51.

Waldman, Marilyn R. "Primitive Mind/Modern Mind: New Approaches to an Old Problem Applied to Islam." In *Approaches to Islam in Religious Studies*, ed. Richard C. Martin. Tucson: University of Arizona Press, 1985, pp. 91–105.

Waley, Arthur, trans. *The Analects of Confucius.* London: George Allen & Unwin, 1938. New York: Alfred A. Knopf and Random House, Vintage Books, n.d.

____, trans. *The Way and Its Power: A Study of the Tao Tê Ching and Its Place in Chinese Thought.* [London, 1934]. New York: Grove Press, Evergreen Books, 1958.

Walker, Roger M. "Oral Delivery or Private Reading? A Contribution to the Debate on the Dissemination of Medieval Literature." *Forum for Modern Language Studies* 7 (1971): 36–42.

Walther, Wilhelm. *Luthers Deutsche Bibel. Festschrift zur Jahrhunderfeier der Reformation.* 1917. 2nd ed. Berlin: Ernst Siegfried Mittler, 1918.

Wansbrough, John. *Quranic Studies: Sources and Methods of Scriptural Interpretation.* London Oriental Series, vol. 31. Oxford: Oxford University Press, 1977.

Watson, Foster. *The Beginnings of the Teaching of Modern Subjects in England.* London: Isaac Pitman and Sons, 1909.

Watt, Ian. [**See** Goody, Jack, and Ian Watt.]

Watt, W[illiam] Montgomery, ed. *Bell's Introduction to the Qur'ān, completely revised and enlarged by W. Montgomery Watt.* Islamic Surveys, 8. Edinburgh: The University Press, 1970.

____. *Muhammad at Mecca.* Oxford: Clarendon Press, 1953.

____. *Muhammad at Medina.* Oxford: Clarendon Press, 1956.

Wattenbach, W. *Das Schriftwesen im Mittelalter.* 1871. 4th ed. (photo-repr. of 3rd rev. ed. Leipzig: S. Hirzel, 1896). Graz: Akademische Druck- u. Verlagsanstalt, 1958.

Webb, R. K. *The British Working Class Reader 1790–1848: Literacy and Social Tension.* London: Allen & Unwin, 1955. New York: Augustus M. Kelley, 1971.

Weber, Albrecht. "Eine angebliche Bearbeitung des Yajurveda." *ZDMG* 7 (1853): 235–48.

____. "Die Hoheit der vâc." *Indische Studien* (Leipzig) 18 (1898): 117–25.

____. "Über den semitischen Ursprung des indischen Alphabets." *ZDMG* 10 (1856). Repr. in *Indische Skizzen. Vier bisher in Zeitschriften zerstreute Vorträge und Abhandlungen.* Berlin: Ferdinand Dümmler, 1857, pp. 125–50.

____. "Vâc und λογοσ." *Indische Studien* (Leipzig) 9 (1865): 473–80.

Weingreen, J. "Oral Torah and Written Records." In Bruce and Rupp, pp. 54–67.

Weiss, Bernard. "*al-Muṣḥaf al-Murattal:* A Modern Phonographic 'Collection' (*Jam'*) of the Qur'ān." *MW* 64 (1974): 134–40.

Welch, Anthony. "Epigraphs as Icons: The Role of the Written Word in Islamic

Art." In *The Image and the Word: Confrontations in Judaism, Christianity and Islam,* ed. Joseph Gutmann. Religion and the Arts, ed. Anthony Yu and Joseph Gutmann, no. 4. Missoula, Mont.: Scholars Press, 1977, pp. 63–74.

Wellhausen, J[ulius]. "Die Composition des Hexateuchs." *Jahrbuch für deutsche Theologie* 21 (1876): 392–450, 531–602; 22 (1877): 407–79. Repr. ed.: *Skizzen und Vorarbeiten II. Die Composition des Hexateuchs.* Berlin: Georg Reimer, 1882. Repr. in *Die Composition des Hexateuchs und der historischen Bücher des Alten Testaments.* 2nd ed. Berlin: Georg Reimer, 1889, pp. 1–210.

Wensinck, A[rendt] J[an]. *A Handbook of Early Muhammadan Tradition.* Leiden: E. J. Brill, 1971.

____. "Muhammed und die Propheten." *Acta Orientalia* 2 (1923): 168–98.

____, et al. *Concordance et indices de la tradition musulmane.* 7 vols. Leiden: E. J. Brill, 1936–69.

Werner, Eric. *The Sacred Bridge: Liturgical Parallels in Synagogue and Early Church.* New York: Schocken, 1970. ["This volume comprises Part I of *The Sacred Bridge,* originally published by Columbia University Press in 1959."]

____. *A Voice Still Heard: The Sacred Songs of the Ashkenazic Jews.* University Park, Penn., and London: Pennsylvania State University Press, 1976.

Westermarck, Edward. *Ritual and Belief in Morocco.* 2 vols. London: Macmillan, 1926. Photo-repr. ed. New Hyde Park, N.Y.: University Books, 1968.

Whitehead, Alfred North. *Dialogues of Alfred North Whitehead as Recorded by Lucien Price.* Boston: Little, Brown, and Co., 1954.

Whitney, William Dwight. [**See** *Atharva Veda Saṁhitā*]

Widengren, Geo. *The Ascension of the Apostle and the Heavenly Book.* King and Saviour, 3. Uppsala Universitets Årsskrift, 1950, 7. Uppsala: A.-B. Lundequistska; Leipzig: Otto Harrassowitz, 1950.

____. "Holy Book and Holy Tradition in Iran: The Problem of the Sassanid Avesta." In Bruce and Rupp, pp. 36–53.

____. "Holy Book and Holy Tradition in Islam." In Bruce and Rupp, pp. 210–36.

____. *Literary and Psychological Aspects of the Hebrew Prophets.* Uppsala Universitets Årsskrift, 1948, 10. Uppsala: A.-B. Lundequistska; Leipzig Otto Harrassowitz, 1948.

____. *Muhammad, the Apostle of God, and His Ascension.* King and Saviour, 5. Uppsala Universitets Årsskrift, 1955, 1. Uppsala: A.-B. Lundequistska; Wiesbaden: Otto Harrassowitz, 1955.

____. *Die Religionen Irans.* Die Religionen der Menschheit, ed. Christel Matthias Schröder, vol. 14. Stuttgart: W. Kohlhammer, 1965.

____. *Religionsphänomenologie.* Berlin: Walter de Gruyter, 1969.

Wilks, Ivor. "The Transmission of Islamic Learning in the Western Sudan." In Goody, *Literacy,* pp. 162–97.

Will, Robert. *Le culte. Étude d'histoire et de philosophie religieuses.* 3 vols. Strasbourg and Paris: Librairie Istra, 1925; Paris: Librairie Félix Alcan, 1929, 1935.

Williams, C. S. C. "The History of the Text and Canon of the New Testament to Jerome." In *Camb. Hist. Bib.* 2: 27–53.

Wilson, N. G. [**See** Reynolds, L. D., and N. G. Wilson.]

Winckler, Paul A., ed. *Reader in the History of Books and Printing.* Readers in Librarianship and Information Science, no. 26. Englewood, Colo.: Information Handling Services, 1978.

Winternitz, M[oriz]. *Geschichte der indischen Litteratur.* 2nd ed. 3 vols. Leipzig: C. G. Amelangs, 1909. Eng. trans. "Mrs. S. Ketkar" and H. Hohn, rev. by the author. *A History of Indian Literature.* 2 vols. Calcutta, 1927–33. 2nd ed. New Delhi: Oriental Books Reprint Corp., 1972.

Wolter, Hans. "Meditation bei Bernhard von Clairvaux." *Geist und Leben* 29 (1956): 206–18.

Wormald, Francis. "Bible Illustration in Medieval Manuscripts." In *Camb. Hist. Bib.* 2: 309–37.

Wright, H. Curtis. *The Oral Antecedents of Greek Librarianship.* Provo, Utah: Brigham Young University Press, 1977.

Yates, Frances A. *The Art of Memory.* Chicago: University of Chicago Press, 1966.

Yün-hua Jan. "The Power of Recitation: An Unstudied Aspect of Chinese Buddhism." *Studi Storico Religiosi* 1 (1977): 289–99.

Zachariae, Theodor. Review of W. Caland, *De Ontdekkingsgeschiedenis van den Veda* (Amsterdam, 1918). In *Göttingische gelehrte Anzeigen* (Königliche Gesellschaft der Wissenschaften) 183 (1921): 148–65.

Zahn, Theodor. *Grundriss der Geschichte des Neutestamentlichen Kanons. Eine Ergänzung zu der Einleitung in das Neue Testament.* Leipzig, 1901. 2nd rev. ed. Leipzig: A. Deichert (Georg Böhme), 1904.

Zaslof, Tela. "Readings on Literacy: A Bibliographical Essay." In Resnick, *Literacy,* pp. 155–70.

Zoetmulder, Piet. "Die Hochreligionen Indonesiens." In Waldemar Stöhr and Piet Zoetmulder. *Die Religionen Indonesiens.* Die Religionen der Menschheit, ed. Christel Matthias Schröder, vol. 5,1. Stuttgart: W. Kohlhammer, 1965, pp. 223–345.

Zwemer, Samuel M. "Translations of the Koran." In *Studies in Popular Islam: A Collection of Papers dealing with the Superstitions and Beliefs of the Common People.* London: Sheldon; New York: Macmillan, 1939.

Index of Names

'Abd Allāh b. Abi Sarḥ, 208n27
'Abd Allāh b. Rawāḥah, 94
Abegg, Emil, 202n23
Abhyankar, K. V., 202n28
Abū Nu'aym, 215n44
Adams, Charles S., 192n3
Adams, John Quincy, 26
Adamson, J. W., 186n34, 187n44, 188n52
Ādi Granth (Guru Granth Sahib), 3, 53, 62, 157, 158, 197n27
Ahlstrom, Sydney E., 204n3
Alambert, Jean le Rond d', 26
Aland, Barbara, 226–27n25
Aland, Kurt, 235n25
Alexander the Great, 52
Alfred, King, 36
"Ali, Mrs. Meer Hasan", 216n54
Amand, David, 224n10
Ambrose, 36, 125, 230n61
Ammon (Egyptian bishop), 130
Anderson, G. W., 195n10, 196n24
Andrae, Tor, 207n18, 209–10n40
Andresen, Carl, 221nn17,18, 222n23
Anesaki, Masaharu, 195n15, 196n22
Antin, Paul, 223n31
Antony, Saint (of Egypt), 126, 130
Apocrypha, *see* Index of Subjects, s.v.
Apollonius (of Rhodes, 3rd cent. B.C.), 185n30
Apostolic Constitutions, 220n15, 221n18
Apte, V. M., 199n3
Arberry, Arthur J., 204n1
Aristotle, 24, 31, 34, 36, 52, 185n22
Arrighetti, Graziano, 184n21
Ārya Samāj, *see* Index of Subjects, s.v.
Asani, Ali S., 196n17
Aśoka, 199n3
Assche, Modestus Van, 230nn58,61
Aston, Margaret, 39, 188nn52,54,61, 189n63
Athanasius (bishop of Alexandria), 53, 126, 128, 130, 136, 193n13, 227n25, 232n88
Augapfel, Julius, 192n5, 206n15
Augustine of Hippo, Saint, 24, 35, 36, 61, 124, 125, 143, 223nn28,32
Austin, J. L., 197n33
Avesta, 66; *see also* Index of Subjects, s.v.

Babb, Lawrence A., 204n52
Bacht, Heinrich, 134, 174n9, 223n2, 224nn2,5,7, 225–26n19, 226n20, 227n26, 228n37, 229nn56,58, 230nn59,65,66
Baddeley, Alan D., 177n15
Bahā'ullāh (Bahā'ī founder, d. 1892), 5
Bailey, H. W., 210n41
Bainton, Roland H., 234nn4,13, 237n49
Baldwin II, Duke of Guines, 38, 187n49
Ballantyne, "Dr.", 202n23
Ballou, Robert O., 194n36
Balogh, Josef, 33, 35, 36, 37, 181n21, 183nn1,8, 184n10, 185nn25,27, 186nn35,36, 188nn53,57, 191n94
Bāqillānī, Muḥammad al-, 207n18
Barbès, Léo, 213n19
Bareau, André, 195n12
Barnabas, Epistle of, 122, 218n6
Barr, James, 191n3, 193n13
Barth, Auguste, 199n3
Bartlett, F. C., 177n15
Bary, Wm. Theodore de, 195n9

Basham, A. L., 199n3
Basil the Great, Saint, 128
Bauer, D. Walter, 198n47, 219n9, 220n15, 222n24
Bauer, Franz, 225n18
Bauer, Johannes B., 193n20
Baumgärtel, F., 192n3
Bäuml, Franz, 178n22, 180n13, 186n31, 187nn44,45, 217n1, 234n1
Baumstark, Anton, 230n66
Bayle, Pierre, 26
Beck, Edmund, 212nn4,13
Becker, Carl L., 12, 176n5
Becker, U., 193n20
Beisser, Friedrich, 234n13, 235nn21,26
Bell, Richard, 204n1, 205n3, 210n40
Bellaire, Eduard Michaux, 214n32
Benedict of Nursia, Saint, 37, 128, 186nn40,42, 227n26, 229n55
Bennett, H. S., 188n52
Bergsträsser, Gotthelf, 97, 211nn2,3, 212nn4,6,13,14, 213nn19,20
Bertholet, Alfred, 61, 194n2, 195nn7,16, 196n17
Bethe, Erich, 196n26
Beveridge, Henry, 234n4
Beza, Theodore, 189n65
Bhagavadgītā, 3, 57, 75
Bhāgavata Purāṇa, 77, 169, 204n53
Bhandarkar, D. R., 199n3
Bhartṛhari, 71
Bhattacharya, Gopika Mohan, 202n23
Biardeau, Madeleine, 201n23
Bible, *see* Index of Subjects, s.v.
Bibliothèque bleue de Troyes, 41, 189n71
Bīrūnī, Abū al-Rayḥān al-Khwārizmī al- (d. ca. 1050), 202n25
Blachère Régis, 204n1, 212nn4,5,11,13
Bloch, Maurice, 196n16
Bloomfield, Maurice, 67
Blue Sūtra, *see* Index of Subjects, s.v.
Boltz, William G., 198n45
Bonaventure, Saint (Giovanni di Fidanza), 193n23
Bonazzoli, Giorgio, 75-76, 200n8, 203n47
Bond, George D., 198n42
Boon, Amand, 224n12, 226n20, 228n37
Bornkamm, Heinrich, 234n13, 235nn16,17,19, 237n53
Boubakeur, Si Hamza, 213n19
Bousset, Wilhelm, 218n9, 226n19
Bouwsma, William J., 188n53
Bouyer, Louis, 229n58
Bowman, John, 90, 205n3, 209n36, 209-10n40
Braden, Charles Samuel, 194n34
Brahman (as supreme deity, in India), 71; *see also* Index of Subjects, s.v. *brahman*
Brandon, S. G. F., 173n1, 192n6
Brett, G. S., 175n1
Brock, Sebastian, 209n36
Brough, John, 200n5
Brown, Peter, 217n1, 223nn28,32
Brown, W. Norman, 198n39, 201nn13-15
Browne, Lewis, 194n34
Bruce, F. F., 173n2, 174n9, 192n4
Brunot, L., 215n35, 216n1
Bucer, Martin, 144, 171
Buchwald, Wolfgang, 229n57
Buck, Harry M., 203n39
Buhl, Frants, 192n5, 206nn13,15, 208nn29,30, 209n31, 211n2
Bukhārī, Muḥammad b. Ismā'īl al-, 208nn28,31, 210nn50,52-54, 211nn60,61, 212n9, 214n27
Bunyan, John, 144, 171
Bruner, Jerome S., 178n17, 179n24
Brunner-Traut, Emma, 183n7
Buddhaghosa, 4
Bühler, Georg, 69, 199n3, 200nn5,6, 202nn31-33, 203n39
Buitenen, J. A. B. van, 69, 200n6, 203n42
Burton, John, 207n20
Butler, H. E., 186n38

Caland, Willem, 202n29, 203n43
Calvin, John [Jean], 121, 143, 144
Cambrensis, Giraldus, 187n51
Campenhausen, Hans von, 193n21, 218nn5-7, 219n10, 220n17
Cantineau, Jean, 213n19
Carcopino, Jérome, 35, 185nn24-26
Carlyle, Thomas, 33, 176n4
Carothers, J. C., 22, 176n5, 178n17, 179n24, 182n36, 183n1, 188n57
Carrithers, Michael, 199n48
Carter, Thomas Francis, 179n4
Cassian, John, 128, 225nn13,14,18, 230n66
Cassirer, Ernst, 64, 197n35
Celsus, 219n10
Cerri, Giovanni, 179n23
Chadwick, Owen, 223n2, 225nn13,18
Chakravarti, Prabhat Chandra, 202nn23,31
Chambers, Ephraim (author of *Cyclopaedia* of 1728), 26

Chan, Wing-Tsit, 174n8, 195n9
Chang Chün-fang, 195n15
Charlemagne, 223n30
Chaytor, H. J., 175n4, 181n20, 182n36, 183n1, 186nn31,33,42, 187nn46,51, 188n57
Cheneb, Mohammed Ben, 213n15
Cheng Dayue [Ch'eng Ta-yüeh], 39
Childs, Brevard, 52, 191n3, 192n9, 193n13
Chitty, Derwas, 223n1
Chrisman, Miriam Usher, 180n5, 188nn53,60
Chrysostom, 143,
Cicero, 24
Cipolla, Carlo M., 179n3, 187n49, 188nn59–60, 189n74, 190nn79,80,82,85, 191nn89–91
Clanchy, M. T., 14, 19, 38, 174n9, 177n11, 178n21, 179n2, 186nn32,38,39, 187n44, 187–88n51, 188n52, 189n75, 199n1
Claudius of Turin, 223n30
Clement, First Epistle of, 122, 218n6
Clement, Second Epistle of, 123, 219n14, 220nn14,15, 221n18
Clercq, Charles de, *see* De Clercq, Charles
Coburn, Thomas B., 67, 69, 174n3, 200n7, 204n54
Cole, Michael, 176n6, 177n12, 179n24
Cole, W. Owen, 197n27
Collison, Robert L., 182nn32,34
Columbas, G. M., 226n19
Compaine, Benjamin M. 182n33, 238n4
Conlationes (of John Cassian), 225n13
Constable, Giles, 230n59
Coomaraswamy, Ananda K., 203n40
Cressy, David, 176n4, 189nn70,75, 190n80
Crosby, Ruth, 36, 184n19, 185n25, 186nn31,36, 187n46
Cullman, Oscar, 219n13, 221n19
Curtius, Ernst Robert, 174n6, 181nn24,26, 184n17, 195nn11,14, 196nn16,20, 218n8, 219n10
Cyril of Jerusalem (bishop of Jerusalem), 221n17
Cyril, Saint (bishop of Alexandria), 209n36

Dādupanth, *see* Index of Subjects, s.v.
Dandekar, R. N., 202n28
Dānī, Abū ʻAmr ʻUthmān al-, 212n13
Daniélou, Jean, 221n19
Dārimī, ʻAbdallāh b. ʻAbd al-Raḥmān al-, 214n27, 215n43
Datta, Bimal Kumar, 199n3
Davids, T. W. Rhys, 199n3
Davies, Godfrey, 144
Davis, Natalie Z., 188n55,59, 189nn62,66,72, 190nn77,80
De Clercq, Charles, 224nn7,11, 225n15
Dekkers, Eligius, 233n95
Delling, Gerhard, 219n9
Denny, Frederick M., 108, 173nn2,3, 174n3, 212nn5,14, 213nn17,19,20, 215n41, 216n49
Derrida, Jacques, 11, 177n12
Deschamps, H., 177n10
Deseille, Placide, 225n15
Devasthali, G. V., 202n28
Devī Māhātmya, 171
Dickens, Charles, 41
Diderot, Denis, 26
Dierse, Ulrich, 182n32
Dillenberger, John, 237n45
Dilthey, Wilhelm, 155
Dinkler, E., 192n3
Diocletian, Emperor, 221n18, 222n24
Diringer, David, 14, 175n1
Disch, Robert, 191n1
Dix, Gregory, 218n9, 221nn18,19,21, 222n24
Dobschütz, Ernst von, 196n26, 221nn20,21, 222nn24,25, 223n33
Dodge, Bayard, 214n32
Dogon, 64, 198n40
Donaldson, Bess Allen, 216n54
Donne, John, 165
Doresse, Jean, 227n25
Dorner, A., 196n17
Dornseiff, Franz, 195nn16
Dörries, Hermann, 226n19
Draguet, René, 225n16
Dronke, Peter, 181n25
D'Sa, Francis X., 200n9, 202n23
Dürr, Lorenz, 197n32, 198n41
Dutt, Sukumar, 198n42
Dykstra, Yoshiko K., 196n22

Ebeling, Gerhard, 144, 196n23, 234nn12,13, 235nn14,17,21,26, 236nn38,40
Eckel, Malcolm David, 196n22
Eco, Umberto, 186n42
Edgerton, Franklin, 57, 194n36, 200n9
Edwards, Mark U., Jr., 217n2
Egeria (Jerusalem pilgrim, late 4th cent.), 220n15, 221nn20,21
Eickelman, Dale, 105, 214n32, 215nn34,35,38,42, 216n1

Eidlitz, Walther, 69, 200n7, 201n22
Eisenberg, Isaac, 205n4
Eisenstein, Elizabeth L., 22, 175n3, 179n2, 180nn5,11,15, 181nn16,19, 183n1, 188n59
Elbogen, Ismar, 198n47, 207n16, 209n39
Eliade, Mircea, 16, 174n5, 214n20
Elyot, Thomas, 22
Encyclopaedia Britannica, or Dictionary of Arts and Sciences, 26
Engelsing, Rolf, 179n3, 188nn59–61, 190n81
Erasmus, 38
Erwin, Sam, 171
Essers, Bénard, 201n13
Euripides, 34
Eusebius, 222n24
Evagrians, 227n25

Fairbank, John K., 195n9
Falk, Franz, 234n3
Farmer, Henry George, 213n19
Fārūqī, Lamyā' al-, 213n15, 214n23
Febvre, Lucien, 188n59
Ferguson, Eugene S., 180nn11,13,15, 181n16
Filliozat, Jean, 200n6, 202n25
Finnegan, Ruth, 174n9, 182n35, 183n8, 184n16
Frank, Richard, 211n57
Franke, G. A., 203n35
Franke, R. Otto, 199n3
Frauwallner, E., 202n23
Frawley, David, 199n1
Frick, Heinrich, 58, 217n3
Frye, Hans, 174n4
Frye, Northrop, 9, 191n3, 197n32
Fuhrmann, Otto W., 179n4
Fürer-Haimendorf, Christoph von, 195n12
Furet, François, 190nn80,82, 191nn87,90

Gaillard, Jean, 225n18
Galbraith, V. H., 176n8, 177n13, 179nn24,2, 187nn44,48
Gamble, Harry, Y., Jr., 192n2, 195n10
Gandillac, Maurice de, 182n32
Gardet, Louis, 216n48
Gardiner, Alan, 12, 176n5
Geertz, Clifford, 208n22
Geiger, Abraham, 209n38
Geiselmann, R. J., 237n46
Gelb, I. J., 175n1, 176n4
Gellner, Ernest, 194n3
Gentili, Bruno, 179n23
Gerhardsson, Birger, 174n9
Gervase of Tilbury, 38
Ghazālī, Abū Ḥamid Muḥammad al-, 109, 165, 213n19, 214nn23,26,27,28, 215nn44,45, 216n55
Ghellinck, J. de, 234n2
Gibbon, Edward, 3, 57, 174n7, 194n33
Gilgamesh, 15
Gill, Sam D., 191n3
Gindele, Corbinian, 225n19, 228n43, 229n58, 230n64, 233n98
Gītagovinda, 75
Glaue, Paul, 198n47, 218n9, 219nn9,13, 220nn15–17, 221nn18,19
Goddard, Dwight, 194n36
Goitein, S. D., 208n23
Goldammer, Kurt, 194nn2,4
Goldstücker, Theodor, 199n3
Goldziher, Ignaz, 174n4, 212nn5,9,13, 214n32
Gonda, Jan, 69, 200nn6,11, 201n22
Goodspeed, Edgar, J., 220n14
Goody, Jack, 15, 174n9, 176nn4,5, 177n11, 178nn17,19,21,22, 179nn24–26, 182n35, 183n2, 185n22, 194n3, 196nn16,17, 197n30
Gorce, Denys, 223n27, 225nn16,18, 226n19
Gorgias of Leontini, 24
Grant, Robert M., 174n4, 220n14
Greene, William C., 184n13, 185n21
Greenfield, Patricia M., 178n17, 179n24
Greenslade, S. L., 234nn7,11
Gregory the Great (Pope Gregory I), 142, 186n39, 222n22, 234n2
Griaule, Marcel, 198n40
Gribomont, J., 223n2, 225n18
Grundmann, Herbert, 176n6, 187nn44,49,51
Grünebaum, Gustav von, 207n18
Grunwald, M., 196n16
Grützmacher, O., 224n7
Gutenberg, Johannes, 26, 31
Guy, Jean-Claude, 225n18, 226n19

Hadas, Moses, 34, 52, 181n24, 183nn2,4, 184n19, 185nn22,25,27,30
Ḥadīth, *see* Index of Subjects, s.v.
Hadju, Helga, 177n15, 181n26
Hahn, Ferdinand, 218n5
Hahn, Herbert F., 191n3
Ḥajjāj b. Yūsuf, al-, 88
Halkin, François, 226n20
Hall, Basil, 199n2

Hall, F. W., 184n21
Haloun, G., 204n2
Hanson, R. P. C., 218n5
Haq, M. Anwarul, 107, 216n48
Hardacre, Helen, 196n22, 199n48
Harnack, Adolf von, 193n22, 217–18n4, 218nn5,6, 219n12, 221n18, 222n26, 223n28
Harrison, Jane Ellen, 197n33
Harsch, Philip W., 184n21
Harvey, F. D., 185n22
Ḥasan al-Baṣrī, al-, 212n6
Ḥassān b. Thābit, 93
Hatch, Nathan O., 174n3, 238n6
Hausherr, Irénée, 230n58
Havelock, Eric A., 17, 31, 34, 35, 174n9, 175n2, 176n4, 177nn13,15, 178n19, 179n26, 180n12, 182n37, 183nn1,2,4,6, 184n9, 185n22
Hedrick, Charles W., 227n25
Heesterman, Jan C., 200n9, 203n43
Heidel, Alexander, 178n18
Heiler, Friedrich, 47, 173n2, 194nn2,4,5, 195nn7,15, 197nn30,33,36, 198nn44,46, 199n1, 201n19, 222n23, 224nn8,9, 234n5
Heinrichs, Wolfhart, 211n55
Hendrickson, G. L., 33, 35, 181n21, 183n1, 184n10
Henning, W. B., 204n2
Henrichs, Albert, 204n2
Herodotus, 34, 184n19
Hesiod, 52
Heussi, Karl, 223n1, 224n2, 226n19
Hinds, G. Martin, 208n27
Hirsch, Emanuel, 147, 236n32
Hirsch, Rudolf, 180n14
Hodgson, Marshall G. S., 217n3
Holdrege, Barbara A. 198n41
Homer, 3, 31, 52, 57, *see also Iliad, Odyssey*
Horace, 35
Horovitz, Josef, 209n38
Horsiesius (Pachomian disciple and abbot), 117, 127, 130, 132, 135, 224n5, 226n20; *see also* Index of Subjects, s.v.
Howard, Wayne, 202nn24,27
Huber, Karl, 212n14, 213n19
Hughes, Thomas Patrick, 216nn48,53,54
Ḥusayn, Ṭaha, 105
Hyperechios, 225n17

Ibn ʻAbbās (Companion of the Prophet Muḥammad), 95
Ibn al-ʻArabī, Muḥyī l-Dīn, 108
Ibn Ḥanbal, Aḥmad (Muslim legist, scholar, d. 241/855), 110
Ibn Ḥazm, 94, 207n18
Ibn Isḥāq, Muḥammad, 211n64
Ibn al-Jazarī, Abū l-Khayr Muḥammad, 212nn5,8,9,12
Ibn Khaldụn, 105
Ibn Mājah, Muḥammad b. Yazīd, 210n53
Ibn Masʻūd, ʻAbd Allāh, 99
Ibn Miqsam, 212n12
Ibn Mujāhid, Abū Bakr, 99
Ibn Muqlah (ʻAbbasid vizier), 212n12
Ibn Saʻd, Muḥammad, 208n31, 209n33
Ibn Shanabūdh, 212n12
Ibn ʻUmar (Companion of the Prophet Muḥammad), 93
Ignatius of Antioch, 122, 218n6
Iliad, 3, 9, 16; *see also* Homer
Ilyās, Muhammad, 107
Imitation of Christ, The (by Thomas à Kempis), 193n23
Innis, Harold A., 180n5., 183n1
institutis coenobiorum, De, 224n13
Irenaeus, Bishop of Lyons, 193n17
Isis (Egyptian deity), 65
Isocrates (Athenian orator), 24

Jacobsen, Thorkild, 178n18
Jairazbhoy, N. A., 202nn27,28
James, A. Lloyd, 181n20, 184n9
James, E. O., 204n2
James, William, 113, 216n1
Jeffery, Arthur, 205n4, 206n13, 209n38, 211n2, 212nn8,12,13, 213n20
Jensen, Hans, 12, 175n1, 176n5, 178n16, 194n5
Jeremias, Alfred, 192nn5,6
Jerome, Saint (Eusebius Hieronymus), 53, 124, 125, 128, 222n26, 223n31, 224n12, 228n39, 229n56, 231nn67,73, 232n91, 233n97
Jesus of Nazareth, 82; attitude of, toward Hebrew scripture, 122, 217n4; *see also* Index of Subjects, s.v. Christ
Jocelin of Brakelond, 36
Johansson, Egil, 189n76, 190n84, 191n91
Johnson, Samuel, 11
Jomier, J., 174n3, 216nn52–54
Josephus, Flavius, 54, 55
Jousse, Marcel, 178n17

Justin Martyr, 123, 219n10, 220nn14,15, 221n19
Juvenal, 185n25
Juynboll, G. H. A., 208n27
Juynboll, Theodor W., 209n36, 215n46

Kabīr, 3
Kahle, Paul E., 208n27
Kane, Cheikh Hamidou, 215n39
Kane, Pandurang Vaman, 200n9
Karpp, Heinrich, 196n19
Kavanagh, Aidan, 222n22, 223n29
Keith, Arthur Berriedale, 201n20, 202n28, 203n36
Kelber, Werner, 174n9
Kennedy, George A., 25, 181nn24,26, 182nn30,31, 184n18
Kenyon, Frederic George, 183nn2,4, 184nn12,14,15,17,18, 185nn22,25, 194n1
Kerényi, Karl, 184n17, 194nn1,6
Kessler, Charles, 204n2
Khan, The Great (leader of the Mongols), 56
King, Martin Luther, 171
Kingdon, Robert M., 189n65
Kirk, G. S., 183n4
Kisā'ī, Abū Ja'far Muḥammad b. 'Abd Allāh al- 205n4
Kitāb al-Mabānī, see Mabānī, Kitāb al-
Klimkeit, Hans-Joachim, 197n27
Knowles, David, 224nn7,11
Knox, Bernard M. W., 183n1, 184n10
Koep, Leo, 51, 186n37, 192nn3,6, 194n2, 195nn14,16, 206n13
Kohler, Kaufmann, 196n16
Kojiki [Records of Ancient Matters], 3
Kosambi, D. D., 199n3
Köster, Helmut, 218n6, 219n14, 221n17
Krabinger, Georg, 223n28
Kramer, Samuel N., 178n18
Kraus, Hans Joachim, 191n3
Krenkow, F., 206nn11,15
Krishṇavarmâ, Shyâmajî, 199n3
Kristensen, W. Brede, 197n32
Kritzeck, James, 193n28
Krug, [Wilhelm Traugott?], 182n32
Kuhl, C., 192n3
Kümmel, Werner Georg, 191–92n3
Künstlinger, Dawid, 206n15, 209n39

Ladeuze, Paulin, 224n2
Laessøe, J., 178n18
Laistner, M. L. W., 185n23, 217n1, 222n24
Lamb, J. A., 218n9, 219n13, 221nn18–21
Lambertus, 187n49
Lanczkowski, Günter, 173n2, 192n5, 194n34, 196n22, 197n27
Lane, Edward W., 196nn17,22, 206n11, 213n15, 214nn25,29
Lane-Poole, Stanley, 204n2
Langer, Suzanne K., 197n35
Lapointe, Roger, 174n6, 192n1
Laqueur, Thomas W., 190nn80,87, 191n88
Leclercq, Jean, 134, 196n26, 225n16, 229n58, 230nn59,63
Leeuw, Gerardus van der, 61, 173n2, 195n16, 197nn30,32,34
Lefort, Louis Théodore, 226n20
Leipoldt, Johannes, 52, 161, 173n2, 192n10, 194nn1,4,6,34, 195nn10,11,15,16, 198nn41,47, 199n1, 202n29, 219nn10,12,13, 220nn15,17, 221nn17,18,21, 222nn24,25, 223n28
Leistle, David, 196n26, 226n24
Leloir, Louis, 223n31
Lenz, Werner, 182n32
Leroux, Jean-Marie, 225n16
Leroy, Julien, 224n13
Lesne, Émile, 226n24
Levering, Miriam, 174n3
Lichtenstadter [Lichtenstädter], Ilse, 205n4
Liebich, Bruno, 201n22, 202n23
Lienhard, Marc, 234n6, 237n51
Linderbauer, Benno,229n55
Lings, Martin, 197n27
Lohse, Bernhard, 223nn1,2
Lord, Albert B., 174n9, 183n4, 184n16
Lotfi, Abdelhamid, 215nn34,40, 216n1
Lotus Sūtra, *see* Index of Subjects, s.v.
Louf, André, 233n95
Lowie, Robert H., 197n30
Lubac, H. de, 221n19
Lucian, 185n25
Lutgendorf, Philip, 76–77, 200n8, 203n48
Luther, Martin, 63, 117, 118, 121, 141–54, 197n28, 234n8, 235nn14,17,19,21,26, 235–36n27, 236nn36,40, 237nn51,53; *see also* Index of Subjects, s.v.
Lycophron of Chalcis, 186n30
Lyn, Tilman von, 143, 234n6, 237n51

Mabānī, Kitāb al-, 102, 210n48, 214n25
MacCandless, Joseph, 230n62
Macfie, John M., 194n36
McGregor, Robert, 225n16
MacKean, W. H., 224n8

McLeod, W. H., 197n27
McLuhan, Marshall, 12, 17, 19, 29, 30, 39, 175n1, 176n5, 178n17, 179n26, 180nn5,6,12, 181n22, 183n5
McMurray, James, 225n18
Macnicol, Nicol, 194n3
Madelung, Wilferd, 207n18
Mādhavānanda, Swāmī, 201n19
Mahābhārata, 3
Mairet, Philip, 227n25
Malesherbes, 181n19
Malinowski, Bronislaw, 197n30
Mandrou, Robert, 189n71
Mani, 52, 62, 82, 197n27
Manjul, V. O., 202n28
Mann, Thomas, 113
Marcion, 221n17
Marracci, Ludovico, 209n38
Marrou, H. I., 181n24, 184n15, 185n23
Martial, 185n25
Martin, Henri-Jean, 188n59
Martin, Richard C., 213n20
Mauk, Frederick H., 21
Mauny, R., 176n7, 177nn10,11
Mayer, R., 193nn15,16
Mayor, John E. B., 184n18, 185nn25,26, 186n31, 189n73
Meakin, Budgett, 214nn29,32
Mehta, J. L., 73, 202n26
Meissinger, Karl August, 234n14, 235n14
Ménard, Jacques-Émile, 226n25
Mendieta, Emmanuel Amand de, 221n10, 225n18
Mensching, Gustav, 63, 173n2, 194n2, 195nn7,14,15, 197nn30,32, 199n1
Meyer, Eduard, 192n5, 206n15
Midelfort, H. C. Erik, 217n2
Miller, Barbara Stoler, 197n36
Mīmāṁsā, *see* Index of Subjects, s.v.
Mishnah, *see* Index of Subjects, s.v.
Mishra, Vibhuti Bhushan, 203n39
Misra, Vidya Niwas, 198n39, 201nn13,17
missal, Roman, *see* Index of Subjects, s.v.
Moeller, Bernd, 217n2
Momigliano, Arnaldo, 184n19, 185n24
Monier Williams, M., 57
Montagu, Ashley, 22
Moran, James, 180n4
Morenz, Siegfried, 51, 52, 157, 161, 173n2, 192n10, 194nn1,4,6,34, 195nn8,10,11,15,16, 197n38, 198nn41,47, 199n1, 202n29, 219nn10,12,13, 220n15, 221nn17,18,21, 222nn24,25, 223n28
Moses, 50, 51, 52, 82, 151
Mu'āwiyah b. Abī Sufyān (first Umayyad Caliph), 208n27
Muḥammad b. 'Abd Allāh, the Prophet, 50, 56, 57, 88, 89, 91, 94, 95, 110, 208n27, *see also* Index of Subjects, s.v.
Muir, John, 200n10, 201n18, 202n33
Müller, Adam, 43–44
Müller, Friedrich Max, 1, 57, 72, 74, 197n31, 199n1, 203n37
Murphy, Margaret Gertrude, 225n18, 226n19
Murti, T. R. V., 202n23
Muslim b. al-Ḥajjāj, 210nn42,50,51,54, 211nn60,61, 214n27
Musnad, al- (of Ibn Ḥanbal), 208n28, 210nn49,53,54, 211n58

Nag Hammadi, *see* Index of Subjects, s.v.
Nagel, Tilman, 205nn3,4
Nakamura, Kōjirō, 216n48
Nakamura, Kyoko Motomochi, 196n22
Ñāṇamoli, 199n48
Nanji, Azim, 196n17
Nasā'ī, Aḥmad b.'Abd al-Raḥmān al-, 211n61
Nawawī, Abū Zakarīyā al-, 213n19
Nef, John U., 22, 180n11
Nelson, Kristina, 108, 174n3, 212nn8,9,14, 213nn15–20, 214n23, 216nn49–51
Nelson, William, 40, 185n25, 186n31, 187n51, 189nn67,69
Nestorians, *see* Index of Subjects, s.v.
Neusner, Jacob, 196n22
New Testament, *see* Index of Subjects, s.v.
Nichiren, 4, 62, 195n15, 196n22; *see also* Index of Subjects, s.v.
Nielson, Eduard, 174n9
Nietzsche, Friedrich, 35, 185n27
Nihongi [Chronicles of Japan], 3
Nock, Arthur Darby, 218n7
Noll, Mark A., 174n3, 238n6
Norden, Eduard, 35, 185n23, 185n27, 186n35, 220n16
Nwyia, Paul, 174n4
Nyberg, H. S., 210n41
Nye, James, 104n53

Odyssey, 3; *see also* Homer
Oesterley, W. O. E., 218n9, 220n15, 221n21
O'Flaherty, Wendy Doniger, 173n2, 201nn12,14–16, 238n2

Oliver, Roland, 177n10
Olson, David R., 176n5, 178n16,17, 179n24, 180nn9,12
Ong, Walter J., 15, 21, 30, 174n9, 175n2, 177n13, 178n17, 179n26, 180nn5,6,15, 181nn18,21,22, 182nn33,36, 183nn1,9, 191n92, 199n1, 218n11
Origen, 54, 193nn13,24, 221n19
Orlandi, Tito, 227n25
Östborn, Gunnar, 193n13, 195n10
Østergaard-Nielsen, Harald, 234n13, 235n21
Otto, Rudolf, 12, 113, 216n1
Otto IV, 38
Ozment, Steven E., 40, 217n2
Ozouf, Jacques, 190nn80,82, 191nn87,90

Pachomius, Saint, 126–27, 129, 131, 132, 137, 224nn2–5,7,12, 232n85, 233n96; *see also* Index of Subjects, s.v. Pachomius, Rule of
Padoux, André, 201n20, 202n23
Padwick, Constance, 214nn22,24,26, 216nn52,54,56
Palladius (bishop of Helenopolis and author of *Historia lausica*), 128, 131, 225n14, 228n43
Palomon (teacher of Pachomius), 127, 131, 136, 231n79
Papias, 181n23
Paret, Rudi, 204n1, 209n32, 212nn4,12, 216n53
Parkes, M. B., 187nn44,45,48,49, 188n52
Parrinder, Geoffrey, 216n1
Parry, Milman, 183n4
Pascher, J., 222n23
Patañjali (d. ca. 150 C.E.), 71
Pater Noster, 138
Pāṭimokkha, see Index of Subjects, s.v.
Pattison, Robert, 17, 176n4, 179n26
Paul, the Apostle, 51, 119, 132; *see also* Index of Subjects, s.v.
Pawlowsky, Sigismund, 225n18
Paxton, E. H., 215n39
Pearson, J. D., 207n17
Pedersen, Johannes, 192n5, 206n15
Peifer, Claude, 225n18, 226n21
Pelikan, Jaroslav, 234n13, 235nn16,17,19, 237n53
Pelliot, Paul, 179n4
Pentateuch, *see* Index of Subjects, s.v.
Perelman, Chaim, 25, 182n31
Perkins, William, 143
Peter the Venerable (Abbot of Cluny), 56
Petrarch, 38
Petronius (Pachomian monk), 137, 232n89
Pfeiffer, Rudolf, 184nn12,17, 185n22
Philo of Alexandria, 54, 55
Pi Sheng, 179n4
Piamenta, M., 216nn52–54
Piggot, Stuart, 176n7
Plantin, Christophe (printer, d. 1589), 189n65
Plato, 24, 34, 53, 193n15, 194n1
Pliny, 185n25
Pope, Mildred K., 186n39
Poswick, Ferdinand, 225n17
Prenter, Regin, 236n27, 237n52
Presser, Helmut, 175n1
Pretzl, Otto, 211nn2,3, 212nn5,10, 213nn19,20
Preuss, Johannes, 234n13
Preuss, Konrad Theodor, 198n40
Prothero, Rowland E., 222n22
Psalms, *see* Index of Subjects, s.v.
psalter, Huguenot, *see* Index of Subjects, s.v.
Ptah (ancient Egyptian God), 64
Pünjer, R., 217n2
Purāṇa(s), *see* Index of Subjects, s.v.

Quasem, Muhammad Abul, 213n19
Quintilian, 24
Qur'ān, *see* Index of Subjects, s.v.
Qushayrī, Abu l-Qāsim 'Abd al-Karīm, 94

Rabin, C., 208n30
Raghavan, V., 202nn25,27
Rāmacaritamānasa, 76–77, 203n48, 204n51
Rāmānuja, 165
Rāmāyaṇa, 3, 75–77
Ramus, Peter, 26; *see also* Index of Subjects, s.v. rhetoric, Ramist
Ray, Reginald A., 195n12
Ray, Roger D., 229n55
Redfield, Robert, 12, 176n5
Reischauer, Edwin O., 195n9
Renou, Louis, 69, 198n39, 200n6, 201n21, 202n25, 203n43
Resch, P., 225n19
Reynolds, L. D., 185n22
Rhetorica ad herennium, 24
Ricci, Matteo, 39, 188n58
Richardson, Hugh, 197n27
Ricoeur, Paul, 15, 21, 178n17, 180n8
Riesman, David, 181n22
Robert of Ketton, 205n7

Roberts, Bleddyn J., 218n5, 222n26
Roberts, Colin H., 196n25
Roest Crollius, Ary A., 206nn10,15
Roff, William, 214n31
Rohde, Erwin, 184nn18,19, 185n25
Rosenbaum, Jonathan, 195n10
Rost, Hans, 222n25, 223nn31,33
Rott, Jean, 234n6, 237n51
Rouse, Mary A. and Richard H., 181n23
Rousseau, Jean-Jacques, 9
Rückert, Hanns, 236n32, 237n46
Rühle, Oskar, 196nn17,18
Rupp, E. G., 173n2, 174n9, 192n4
Ruppert, Fidelis, 224n2, 225n19, 226n20, 229n58, 230nn63,65,67, 231n77, 232nn81,90

Sachs, Wladimir, 190nn80,82, 191n87
Sacred Books of the East, The (ed. F. Max Müller), 1, 57
Safadi, Yasin Hamid, 197n27
Sa'īd, Labīb al-, 208n31, 212nn5,6,13, 213n20, 214nn21,33
Sale, George, 57, 194n32, 204n1
Sambhi, Piara Singh, 197n27
Samson, Abbot, 36
Sanders, James A., 191n3, 195n10
Śaṅkara, 202n33
Sanneh, Lamin, 215n35
Santerre, Renaud, 105, 215nn36,37, 216n47
Sargent, William A., 190n87
Sarton, George, 180n15, 181n16
Sastri, Gaurinath, 202n23
Satyrus, 184n21
Saussure, Ferdinand de, 9, 175nn2,3, 183n9
Säve-Söderbergh, Torgny, 226–27n25
Saxl, Fritz, 197n35
Scharbau, Carl Anders, 200n11, 201n13
Scheel, Otto, 234n13
Schemp, Paul, 234n13, 236n29, 237nn49,53
Schiller, Friedrich, 30, 43
Schiwietz, Stephan, 223n1
Schleiermacher, Friedrich, 112, 113, 217n2
Schmidt, Nathaniel, 195n10
Schneider, Carl, 194n1
Schneider, Gerhard, 223n28, 229n53
Schofield, R. S., 189nn63,70, 190nn78,87
Schopen, Gregory, 196n21
Schott, Rüdiger, 177nn10,11, 178n21
Schröder, Christel Matthias, 195n12
Schubart, Wilhelm, 175n1, 184n15
Schubring, Walter, 195n12
Schwab, Raymond, 193n31
Schwarz, W., 222n26, 236nn27,38
Scribner, Robert W., 40, 188nn59,61, 234n10
Scribner, Sylvia, 176n6, 177n12, 179n24
Sell, Edward, 215n45
Septuagint, *see* Index of Subjects, s.v.
Seraphim of Sarow, 224n9
Severus, Emmanuel, von, 222n22, 225n18, 229nn54,57,58, 230n61, 233n92
Sévigne, Madame de, 41
Shaban, M. A., 208n27
Shakespeare, William, 61
Sharīf, Ja'far, 215n35, 216nn47,54
Sharpe, Eric, 192n3
Shepard of Hermas, 220n17
Sheridan, Thomas, 25
Shils, Edward, 174n9
Shinran Shonin, 165
Siddhartha Gautama (the Buddha), 86
Silburne, Liliane, 201n21
Silva, A. de, 199n48
Sivaraman, Krishna, 200n4, 202n23
Skeat, T. C., 196n25, 218n11, 222n24
Skepsis [place], 185n22
Sloan, Thomas O., 25, 182n31
Smalley, Beryl, 174n4, 221n19, 223n30
Smet, Richard V. de, 202n23
Smith, R. Payne, 209n36
Smith, Reuben, 217n3
Smith, Wilfred Cantwell, 52, 53, 173n3, 174n3,6, 191n3, 192n11, 204n2, 208n21, 211nn2,56, 217n3
Snell, Bruno, 17
Snellgrove, David, 197n27
Snouck Hurgronje, Christian, 216nn53,54
Socrates, 34, 194n1
Söderblom, Nathan, 217n3
Sourdel-Thomine, J., 208n31
Southern, R. W., 193n29
Sozomen (church historian), 224n7
Spence, Jonathan D., 39, 177n15, 181n26
Spengler, Oswald, 12, 176n5, 178n17
Speyer, Wolfgang, 185n22
Sproul, Barbara C., 198n40
Spuler, Berthold, 203n39
Staal, Johan Frederik, 64, 69, 174n3, 185n21, 199n3, 200nn7,9, 201n16, 202nn24,27,28
Stalker, J., 221n20
Staupitz (Luther's Augustinian mentor), 236n36
Steck, Karl Gerhard, 235nn16,17
Steinberg, S. H., 182n32

Steiner, George, 13, 19, 22, 176n8, 180n11, 191n1
Steinmetz, David, 150, 236n40, 237nn42,45
Stewart, Zeph, 218n7
Stieglecker, Hermann, 207n18
Stock, Brian, 38, 178n17, 179n2, 180n9, 186n43, 187nn44,48, 188n52
Stone, Lawrence, 188n59, 189nn75,76, 190nn82,83,87
Strabo, 34, 183n2, 185n22
Strauss, Gerald, 188n59, 234n8
Strauss, Otto, 201n16, 202n23
Stubbs, Michael, 175n2
Sudbrack, Josef, 229n58
Suetonius, 35
Suffrin, A. E., 192nn5,6
Sullivan, Helen, 188n59, 190n82
Sundberg, Albert C., Jr., 193n13, 195n10

Ṭabarī, Muḥammad b. Jarīr al-, 206n15, 210n48
Tabennesi (Pachomian "mother" community), 127, 136, 224n5, 232n85
Tabennesiots, *see* Index of Subjects, s.v.
Tacitus, 185n25
Tahānawī, Muḥammad 'Alī al-, 207n18
Talbi, M., 213nn17,19
Tambiah, Stanley, 197n32
Tamburrino, Pio, 226n20
Tantras, *see* Index of Subjects, s.v.
Targum, *see* Index of Subjects, s.v.
Taylor, Rodney L., 173nn2,3, 192n1, 198n45
Tertullian, 221n19
Thackeray, William Makepeace, 41
Thackston, Wheeler M., Jr., 205n4
Theodore (Pachomian leader), 127, 129, 131, 132, 136, 139, 224nn5,12, 228n47, 232n80
Theophilos of Alexandria, 224n5
Thieme, Paul, 201n21
Thimme, Karl, 234n13, 236n36
Thomas, L. V., 176n7, 177nn10,11
Thomas, Master (author of *Romance of the Horn*), 37, 186n39
Thompson, James Westfall, 184n12, 185n22, 186n44, 187nn44,49,50, 217n1, 222n24
Thompson, Laurence G., 192n1, 195n15, 198n45
Thoreau, Henry David, 49
Thucydides, 16, 34, 179n23
Tiemann, Karl-Albrecht, 196n16
Tirmidhī, Muḥammad al-, 210n50, 211nn59,62,63, 214n27
Torah, *see* Index of Subjects
Touma, Habib Hassan, 213nn17,19
Tracy, David, 174n4
Trimmingham, J. Spencer, 209n40
Tubb, Gary A., 200n9, 203nn34,38
Tulsīdās, 76, 203n48
Twitchett, Denis, 179n4

Ubayy b. Ka'b, 208nn27,31
'Umar b. al-Khaṭṭāb (second caliph of Islam), 211n64
UNESCO, 190n85
Usener, Hermann, 64, 197n35
'Uthmān b. 'Affān (third caliph of Islam), 88, 89, 98, 207n20, 208n27, 209n33

Vadet, J.-C., 209n33
Vandenbroucke, François, 229n58
Vansina, Jan, 174n9, 176n7, 177nn10,11, 182n35
Veda(s), *see* Index of Subjects, s.v.
Vielleux, Armand, 223n2, 224n12, 225n14, 226nn19,20, 228nn37,39,45, 229nn52,58, 230n66, 231n77, 232n91, 233nn91–95,97
Vincent, Antoine (16th-cent. printer), 189n65
Viśvakarman (Vedic creator deity), 70
Visser, M. W. de, 196n17
Vogüé, Adalbert de, 226n19, 229n58
Voltaire, 238n5

Waardenburg, Jacques, 192n3
Wacker, Grant, 238n6
Waley, Arthur, 155
Walther, Wilhelm, 234nn8,9, 236n38
Wagner, Daniel A., 215nn34,40, 216n1
Wajīh, Muḥammad, 207n18
Wakeham, William, of Devizes, 39
Waldman, Marilyn R., 179n25
Waley, Arthur, 177n16, 198n45
Walker, Roger M., 187n51
Wang, Y. Chu, 195n9
Wansbrough, John, 207n20
Warder, A. K., 195n12
Warren, F.E., 186n37
Watson, Burton, 195n9
Watson, Foster, 181n16
Watt, Ian, 176n4, 177n11, 178nn19,21,22, 183n2, 185n22
Watt, William Montgomery, 205n3, 208n27, 209n31

Wattenbach, W., 37, 186n42
Webb, R. K., 190n78
Weber, Albrecht, 198n39, 199n3, 203n35
Wegner, Judith, 209n38
Weingreen, J., 195n10
Weiss, Bernard, 214n21
Welch, Alford T., 205n3, 206n10, 209n36, 211n2
Welch, Anthony, 197n27
Wellhausen, Julius, 208n31
Welton, Peter, 192n6
Wensinck, Arendt Jan, 198n41, 205n4, 208n28, 210nn47,54, 211n60, 212n9, 215n44
Werner, Eric, 219n13, 220n15, 221nn18,21
Westermarck, Edward, 196n17
Whitehead, Alfred North, 9, 19, 183n4, 185n21
Widengren, Geo, 45, 50, 60, 173n2, 174n9, 192nn3,4, 194n2, 198n43, 199n49, 204n2, 206nn13,15, 210n41
Wikander, Stig, 210n41
Wilks, Ivor, 196nn16,22
Will, Robert, 195n7, 197n28
William of Rubroek, 56, 193n29
Williams, C. S. C., 222n26
Wilson, John A., 197n38
Wilson, N. G., 185n22
Winternitz, Moriz, 69, 74, 200n6, 203n37
Wisse, Frederik, 226–27n25
Witoto, *see* Index of Subjects, s.v.
Wolfson, Harry Austryn, 198n41
Wolter, Hans, 229n58
Woods, Katherine, 215n39
Wormald, Francis, 196n26
Wright, H. Curtis, 184n12, 185n22
Wyclif, John, 38

Yates, Francis A., 177n15, 181n26
Young, Dwight W., 227n25
Yvan, Melchior, 214n31

Zachariae, Theodor, 202n29, 203n43
Zahn, Theodor, 193n13
Zand, *see* Index of Subjects, s.v.
Zaslof, Tela, 177n12
Zayd b. Thābit, 208nn27,31
Zedler, Johann Heinrich (author of *Universal-Lexicon* of 1732–50), 26
Zell, Matthew, 234n6
Zend Avesta, 3
Zoetmulder, Piet, 196n17
Zwemer, Samuel M., 204n2, 207n17
Zwingli, Ulrich, 121, 143

Index of Subjects
(including technical and foreign terms)

abhyāsa [Skt.: "repeating, tossing over"], 73
ācārya [Skt.: "master, teacher"], *see guru*
ahl al-kitāb [Ar.: "people of scripture/the Book"], 51, 57, 83, 206n15
aḥruf [Ar.: "letters; modes"], 99
'ālim (pl. *'ulamā'*) [Ar.: "learned (person)"], 106, 114
alphabetic literacy, *see* literacy, alphabetic
alphabetic thought, *see* Western thought, as alphabetic
anagignōskonta [Gk.: "reader, lector"], 124
anagnōsis [Gk.: "lection, lesson, (public) reading"], 123; as synonym for Syr. *qeryānā,* 90
anagnōsma [Gk.: "what is read, lection"], as synonym for Syr. *qeryānā,* 90
anagnōstēs [Gk.: "reader, lector"], 124
apauruṣeya [Skt.: "not of personal origin"], 70, 200n9
Apocrypha, 55, 121
Apostolic Fathers, 122
apostolos [Gk.], *see* epistolary
Arabic: as language of revelation, 84–85; qur'anic, as standard of literacy, 106; sacrality of qur'anic recitation in, 103–04
art and architecture, as sources of scriptural education, 142
Ārya Samāj, and oral use of scripture, 161
asāṭīr [Ar.: "written documents"], 208n30
aṣl al-kitāb [Ar.: "the root of scripture; the original Scripture"], 84
Augenblicks-gott [Ger.: "momentary deity"], 64
Avesta, compared to Qur'ān, 83
balāghah [Ar.: "eloquence; rhetoric"], 98
Baqarah, al- (Sūrah 2: "The Cow"), 109
barakah [Ar.: "blessing"], 104, 112
basmalah [Ar.], *see bism allāh al-raḥmān al-raḥīm*
Benedictine Rule, 129, 225n15
Bhakti hymns, 77
Bibelfestigkeit [Ger.: "Bible-solidity"], 145, 234n14
Bible, 39, 40; as aurally accessible, 142; Authorized ("King James") Version, 85, 144; Christian, 1, 49, 55, 57; in Christian history, 174n3; commitment to original language of, 85; contrasted with Qur'ān as to liturgical use, 102; critical study of, 191n3; as documentary text, 46; English, 40; as "listening-book" (*Hörebuch),* 147; Hebrew, 3, 53; as holy book, 173n1; as holy object/icon, 62, 119–20; Jewish, 1, 57; Jewish and Christian use of, 88; Latin Vulgate, 53, 146, 148 (and Latin as sacred liturgical language, 85); linguistic derivation of word, 54–55; magical use/power of, 61, 119, 157; "of mankind", 49; and memorization, 43; orality of, 118, 123–25; place of, in the modern West, 167, 169; and preaching, during Reformation, 143; Protestant study of, 144; role in Christian liturgy, 161; role in Christian piety, 125; as scripture, 45; as scripture and literature, 238n6; as scripture vis-à-vis Qur'ān, 56; as speaking book, 154; as spoken word,

117–54; as "Sprachheimat", 144, 234n12; as tangible book, 48; as unified whole, for Luther, 145, 146, 235n17; in vernacular translation, 41, 121, 143, 145, 207n19; vocal aspect of, for Luther, 147–54, 237nn48,49; as word of God, 119–20, 147
Bible-consciousness, 144
biblia, ta [Gk.: "the books"], 122, 218n6
biblical storytelling, 120
biblically inspired art, 120
bibliolatry, *see* Bible, magical use of
bibliomancy, *see* Bible, magical use of
bism allāh al-raḥmān al-raḥīm [Ar.: "In the name of God, the Merciful, the Compassionate"], 108
Blue Sūtra, in Japanese Reiyukai ritual, 66, 199n48
book(s): as *aide mémoire*, 39; Buddhist reverence for, 61; as central fact of modern life, 19; concepts of, 9, 30, 40; development of reference aids for, 181n23; differences between manuscript and printed, 31–32; embellishment and ornamentation of, 86; etymology of the term, 11; Greek mistrust of, 194n1; heavenly, 50–51, 60, 65, 83–84, 206n15, 207n15; history and development of, 175n1; as icon, 119–20; importance of, for historical inquiry, 14; increase of, during 17th cent., 40; intended for ears, 38; as mass-produced, impersonal, 22; not synonymous with "writ", for Luther, 152; Pachomian use of, 130; permanence of, 188n58; printed, 1, 40; production statistics 42, 190n81; and Puritans, 80; religion(s) of the, 51–53, 79, 81; as revealed authority, 51–53; role in Judaic, Christian, and Muslim piety, 79; sacramental character of, in Islam, 109; in seventh-century Arabia, 91; as silent, physical document, 20, 44, 45; as voices, 39; *see also ahl al-kitāb;* printed word; printing; Qur'ān, calligraphy of; religion of the book
book culture, *see* script culture; print culture
book religion/*Buchreligion*, 51, 52, 157, 168; *see also* religion of the book
Brahman [Skt.: *brāhmaṇa*, member of highest Indian class/caste group], 71, 72, 73, 74, 76
brahman (as Skt. term), earliest meaning of, 71
Brāhmī script, 199n3
breviarium, *see* breviary
breviary: and recitation, 66; Roman, 40, 124, 189n65
"Buchmetaphorik" [Ger.: "book-metaphorics"], 218n8
Buchstabe [Ger.: "letter (of alphabet)"], 147, 236n31, 237nn44,49; *see also literis, sacris*
buddhavacana/word of the Buddha [Skt., Pali: "word of the Buddha, Buddha-word"], 4, 65, 68, 86, 163, 198n42; *see also Lotus Sūtra*
Buddha-word, *see buddhavacana*

"Cairo text" (of Qur'ān), *see* Qur'ān, standard text of
canon: according to Luther, 146; as authoritative book, 48, 60; of biblical books, 121, 220n17; as body of writings, 53, 193n13; Buddhist (Tripiṭika), 195n12, 198n42; as communal process, 86; comparison of Buddhist, with Qur'ān, 86; of Hebrew scriptures, 51–52, 195nn10,12; in Judaic, Christian, and Muslim tradition, 86, 207n20; of Marcion, 221n17; Muratorian, 221n17; Taoist, 195n15; witness of, 52
canonization, in Islam, 207n20, 208n20
cantillation, *see tajwīd*
catechetical instruction, 120, 142, 143; in Pachomian *koinonia*, 136, 137–38
chant, 164
Chester Beatty Papyrus IV, Egyptian text from, 183n7
ching [Chin.: "classics"], 3, 169; and Chinese culture, 174n8; considered as scripture, 57, 60, 192n1
chirographic culture, *see* script culture
Christ: analogy of, to Qur'ān, 121, 217n3; as incarnate Word, 121; *see also* Index of Names, s.v. Jesus of Nazareth
clarity (of scripture), *see* scripture, clarity of, according to Luther
"classic": as authoritative text, 52; in western Culture, 167, 168
"classics", Chinese, *see ching*
collecta [Lat.], *see synaxis*
conventiculum [Lat.], *see synaxis*
Council of Trent, 121
criticism, biblical, *see* Bible, critical study of

Dādupanth (Hindu group, followers of Dādu), 165
Dharma, Buddhist, 217n3
dhikr [Ar.: "reminder"], 107–08, 113; as name for the Qur'ān, 90; among ṣūfīs, 107
dictation: in ancient world, 185n23; in script culture, 35
dictionaries, in 17th and 18th cent. Europe, 26
"Divine Saying" (Ar.: *ḥadīth qudsī*), distinguished from Qur'ān, 102–03
documents, increased use of in post-12th-cent. Europe, 38
drōmenon [Gk.: "what is done"], contrasted to *legomenon*, 64, 197n33

education: in ancient Greece, 34; in Indian culture, 74–75, 203nn39,41; Muslim, 104–06, 214n32, 215nn35–42, 216n1; Protestant, 143, 147
Egypt (New Kingdom period), attitude to written word in, 32
"Egyptian text" (of Qur'ān), *see* Qur'ān, standard text of
electronic media, 166; related to alphabetic print, 21
encyclopedia(s): and democratization of literacy, 27; development and success of, in the West, 26, 182n34; history of, 182n32; as index of Western modernity, 27; older meaning of the term, 182n32; and print culture, 28; as printed reference tool, 23; as substitute for memorization, 27
epistolarē [Gk.]/*epistolarium* [Lat.], *see* epistolary
epistolary, 124
euangelion [Gk.]/*evangeliarium* [Lat.], *see* evangeliary
Eucharist: compared with Qur'ān recitation, 87; in Patristic age, 125, 221n19
evam me sutaṃ [Pali: "thus have I heard" (Skt.: *evaṃ mayā śrutam*)], 69
evangeliary, 66, 124
exegesis: Christian, 120, 124, 145, 146; Muslim, 98, 101, 112, 113, 207n17

Fātiḥah, al- (Sūrah 1: "The Opening"), 103, 109
fiqh [Ar.: "understanding; jurisprudence"], 207n17
folklore, Muslim, 205n4
funerals: Muslim, 103, 113, 214n29; in Pachomian *koinonia,* 131
furqān [Ar.: "criterion"], as name for the Qur'ān, 90

Gāyatrī (or Sāvitrī) verse (Ṛg Veda 3.62.10), 73, 200n10
ginan (Ismā'īlī text attributed to a *dā'ī,* or missionary-preacher), 61, 196n17
Gnostic texts, 129–30, 227n25
Gnosticism, Sethian, 227n25
gospel: as "living voice", for Luther, 147, 237n49; sent to Jesus, in Muslim view, 82; as word of God, 120–21
guru [Skt.: "teacher, master"], 74, 203n39
guruparamparā [Skt.: "succession of teachers"], 74

Ḥadīth, 4, 51, 79, 94, 96, 106, 107, 156, 177n16, 207n17, 211n60, 212n9, 215nn43,44; contrasted to Qur'ān, 102–03; nature of, 93
ḥadīth qudsī, see Divine Saying
ḥāfiẓ (fem.: *ḥāfiẓah*) [Ar.: "one who has (the Qur'ān) by heart"], *see* memorization, of Qur'ān
hāgāh [Heb.], *see* meditation
ḥamalat al-qur'ān [Ar.: "transmitters of the recitation"], 88
ḥamalat al-waḥy [Ar.: "transmitters of the revelation"], 88
ḥamdu lillāh, al- [Ar.: "praise be to God!"], 109
Ḥanafī school (of Islamic legal interpretation), 207n17
Harappan civilization, 13
hearing: and seeing, distinction between, according to Luther, 149–51; the word of God, 148
Hebrew: as language of revelation, 84–85; as source for Arabic use of *qur'ān,* 209n38
Hebrew scriptures: authority of, 122, 218nn4,8; and Luther, 145, 146; role in early Christian church, 122, 123, 218nn4–6, 226n20; translated into Latin, 222n26
Heilsgeschichte, and successive revelation, in Islam, 82–83
ḥifẓ [Ar.: "memorizing, memorization (esp. of Qur'ān)"], *see* memorization, of Qur'ān

history: dependence upon written documents, 14; as written narrative, 13, 16
holy book, holy writ, *see* scripture
Holy Spirit, its role in understanding scripture, 147, 150–52, 235n27, 236n27, 238n57
homiletics, 164; method of, in Reformation, 143
Horsiesius: rule of, 136, 139, 224nn5,12, 231n69, 233n95; use of scripture by, 226n20; *see also* Index of Names, s.v.
hymnal, in Protestantism, 143–44
hymnody, 157, 163, 164; Protestant, 145; in time of Paul, 221n21; *see also* hymnal, in Protestantism

'ibādah [Ar.: "devotion, worship"], 107; *see also 'ibādāt*
'ibādāt [Ar.: "(prescribed) acts of worship"], 95
idiotae [Lat.], *see literacy*
i'jāz [Ar.: "inimitability" of the Qur'ān], 5, 85, 101, 103, 207n18
illitteratus [Lat.], *see* literacy
'ilm al-qirā'āt [Ar.: "science of readings"], 97
'ilm al-qirā'āt wal-tajwīd [Ar.: "science of readings and recitation"], 98
'ilm al-tajwīd [Ar.], *see tajwīd*
Islam, as book-oriented, 81
"islamization" of individual through Muslim education, 105
'iṣmah [Ar.: "protection from error"], 85, 207n18
istighfār [Ar.: "asking for forgiveness"], 109
i'tiqāf [Ar.: "withdrawal, retreat" to mosque, in Ramaḍān], 107, 215n46

Ju Chiao (Chin.: Confucian tradition), 60
juz' ["part, portion" (esp. of Qur'ān, as recitative division)], 107, 215n45

kalām Allāh [Ar.: "the speech of God"], 89, 110, 121
kanōn [Gk.: "rule, measure; list"], *see* canon
kaṇṭhastha [Hindi: "memorized"], 69
kerygma, 122, 145, 151; as word of God, 120, 121
khatmah (Ar.: pl.: *khatamāt*) ["sealing, completion", of full recitation of the Qur'ān], 107, 216n47
kitāb [Ar.: "book, scripture"], 51, 53, 57, 80, 81, 82, 83, 84, 88, 89, 91, 96, 205n3, 206nn10–12, 207n15
"knowledge explosion", in 20th cent., 27
ktābā d'qeryānā [Syr.: "lectionary"], 90
kuttāb (Ar.: Qur'ān school), 105, 106, 112, 215n36, 216n1
kuttāb al-waḥy [Ar.: "scribes of the revelation"], 88, 208n27

language: modern notion of, 33; and revelation, 84–86; scripturally saturated, 144
Latin: increasing inaccessibility of, throughout medieval period, 142; as language of liturgy and Bible, 120; translations of Hebrew scriptures prior to Jerome, 222n26; translations of New Testament, 222n26
lawḥ maḥfuẓ [Ar.: "preserved tablet"], 84, 89, 206n15
laylat al-barā'ah [Ar.: "Night of Quittance"], 109, 216n54
laylat al-qadr [Ar.: "Night of Power"], 107, 216n47
lectio [Lat.: "lection, (public) reading; pericope"], 123–24, 125; in early Christian worship, 220nn15,16; Jewish influence upon, 218n19; synonymous with Syriac *qeryānā,* 90
lectio divina [Lat.: "sacred reading, lection"], 128–29, 133
lection(es), see reading, public
lectionary, 66, 124, 221n18, 229n55
lector [Lat.: "reader"], 32, 36
legomenon [Gk.: "what is said"], *see drōmenon*
letteraturizzazione [Ital.], 25
letter-writing, in Pachomian *koinonia,* 130, 227n28
letters, sacred, *see literis, sacris*
libraries: in the ancient world, 35; in 4th-cent. monasteries, 129; of medieval monasteries, 129, 226n24
literacy: alphabetic, 19; in ancient Greece, 34; changes the uses of and attitudes to texts, 17; church-driven, 42; and clergy, 37; close to preliteracy, 31; defining, 37, 187n44; and definition of *litteratus* and *illitteratus,* 37; demographics of, 42–43, 190nn80,82,85,87, 189n76; and development of abstract thinking, 178n20; in early Christianity, 123,

literacy *(cont.)*
124; élite vs. mass, 43; in Hellenistic-Roman culture, 120; and increase of written records, 38; as index of modernity, 20; Latinate, 37, 145, 187nn44,49; lay, 28, 31; limited nature of, in late medieval Europe, 186n43; linked to perfection of writing, 178n18; as measure of civilization, 12, 176nn5,6; in medieval West, 37, 120, 141, 217n1, 222n24; minimal, 20, 23; in modern West, 33, 166, 168; the "New Literacy", 182n33, 238n4; in 19th-cent. Europe, 41; "nonreading", 37–38; and objective study, 15; oral, 31, 38; popular, 188n52; practical, 189n75; in premodern West, 156; and Protestantism, 42, 189nn75,76; and the Reformation, 40, 188n59; taken as sign of intelligence, 176n4; and transmission of tradition, 16; typographic, 22; and the understanding of history, 16–17; varieties of, 187n44; vernacular, 37–38, 40, 234n3; visual, 31; *see also* writing
literalism, 160, 162, 170; biblical, 145
literate culture, *see* literacy, script culture
literis, sacris [Lat.: "holy, sacred letters"], referring to scripture, 147
litteratus [Lat.], *see* literacy
liturgy: Jewish influence on Christian, 218n9, 220n15; and oral use of scripture, 160, 161–62, 163; Pachomian, 131, 137–40, 233n95; in Patristic age, 125, 222n22; as primary contact with scripture in medieval Christianity, 142; Syriac Christian, 90
"liturgy of the Word", 123–24, 143, 219n9, 221n19
"liturgy of Scripture", *see* "liturgy of the Word"
logos [Gk.: "word"], 121, 218n6, 221n19
Lollards, 38–39, 188n54
Lotus Sūtra, 3, 4; and *buddhavacana,* 198n42; in Japanese Buddhism, 62, 196n22; and Nichiren, 195n15, 196n22; and recitation, 66
lughah [Ar.: "language; philology"], 98
Luther, Martin: attitudes of, toward Old and New Testaments, 145, 151; German Bible of, 144; and scripture, 144–54, 235nn17,21,26, 235-36n27, 236n36; and spoken word of scripture, 147–54; *see also* Index of Names, s.v.

magic, 112
māhātmya (Skt.: Hindu poem of praise), 7
Mahāyāna Buddhism, problem of scripture in, 4
maktab [Ar.: "place of writing, school"], *see kuttāb*
mantra, *see* recitation, of mantras
maqra' [Ar.: "recitation session"], 108, 113
mā shā' llāh [Ar.: "whatever God wills!"], 108–09
meaning: discursive and nondiscursive, 111–15; and scripture, 110–15; *see also* memory, and meaning
meditare/meditatio [Lat.], *see* meditation, recitation
meditation, 164, 165; as basic form of prayer in Pachomian praxis, 137, 230n66; in Benedictine tradition, 230n59; as exercise, 134, 148–49, 230n61; in Luther's thought, 148–49; as oral activity, 134–37, 230nn65,66; in Pachomian tradition, 131, 132, 133–40, 228n45, 229nn54–57, 230nn59,64–66, 231n75, 232n83; of the scriptures, 129, 135, 137, 225n17
meletan/meletē [Gk., Copt.], *see* meditation
memorization, 164, 165, 235n14; as access to word of God, 132; importance of, in preprint culture, 124; in Pachomian tradition, 130–33, 228n43, 229n50; of Qur'ān, 102, 106, 171, 162, 163, 214n23; in Reformation and Protestantism, 144, 148–49; of scripture, 158, 160, 161
memory: in ancient education, 35, 185n23; importance among the illiterate, 43; and meaning, 114; in medieval reading, 36; in Muslim education, 104–06, 215n35; psychology of, 177n15; in rhetoric, 25; and "rote" learning, 216n1; versus written record, 14–16; *see also* mnemonic systems
Mīmāṁsā (one of six major "schools" of Indian thought), 71, 200n9
miqrā' [Heb.: "reading, scripture lesson; Scripture"], 90, 92, 209n38
mi'rāj [Ar.: "ascension" of Muḥammad], 50
Mishnah, 4
missal, Roman, 40

mnemonic systems, 15, 181n26; and poetry, 177n15; and Qur'ān, 177n15; and Veda, 72, 177n15, 202n28
modernity/modernization, 159, 165–71; *see also* secularization
monastery: medieval, 37; of 4th-cent. Egypt, 129
"monastery-church" ("monastère-église"), 127, 223n2; *see also* monasticism/monachism
monastic discipline, 127
monasticism/monachism: Antonian, 223n1, 224n7; Basilian/Cappadocian, 224n10; Benedictine, 225n18; cenobitic, 126, 224nn7,13, 233n95; Christian, 122, 125, 126–27, 128, 224n7; continuities between Pachomian and later, 127–28, 129; desert, 223n1; eremitic/anchoritic, 126, 226n19, 230n66, 233n95; as rooted in the word of God, 128; Pachomian, 118, 126–40; 223n1, 225n14, 226nn19,20; Shenutian, 227n25; and transition from asceticism, 223n1; and women, 127
Mu'awwidhatān, al- (Sūrahs 113, 114: "The two that protect, deliver from evil"), 109
Muḥammad b. 'Abd Allāh, the Prophet: Christian influences on, 210n40; and Ḥadīth, 93; and revelation, 82, 205n3, 208nn27,31, 209n33; the "seal of the prophets", 82; *see also* Index of names, s.v.
mujawwad [Ar.: "ornamented"], 100–01, 213n17
mu'jiz [Ar.: "inimitable, miraculous"], *see i'jāz*
Muratorian canon, *see* canon, Muratorian
murattal [Ar.: "chanted in measured and clear fashion"], 100–01, 213n17
muṣḥaf (pl.: *maṣāḥif*) [Ar.: "codex, exemplar" of the Qur'ān], 89, 93, 98, 99, 103, 158
mysterium tremendum [Lat.], 113
myth, as oral phenomenon, 16

nabī [Ar.: "prophet"], *see* prophet, in Islam
nadwah [Ar.: "gathering"], 108
Nag Hammadi, 130; *Sitz im Leben* of, 226n25, 227n25
nahw [Ar.: "grammar"], 98
Nestorians, 56
New Testament, 5, 53–55; and Hebrew scripture, 122; in Latin, 222n26; and Luther, 145, 146, 151; use of, in Pachomian tradition, 130, 226n20, 228n43; *see also* Bible
Nichiren Buddhism, role of recitation in, 160
Numinose, das [Ger.], 113

Old Testament, 53, 55; as "law", 151; typological interpretation of, 218n4
oral communication: contextual nature of, 15; immediacy of, 123; in modern, secular culture, 45; as momentary performance, 16; as personally engaging, 157; power and adaptability of, 156
oral culture: continuities with script culture, 17; diversities within, 14; in late antiquity, 35; as "primitive", 156; transmission of tradition in, 16
oral formulaic composition, *see* Parry–Lord thesis
"oral gospel, the" ("das mündliche Euangelion"), in Luther, 149
oral society, *see* oral culture
oral tradition, 7; contrasted with written tradition, 14, 47, 174n9, 191n2; nature of, 177n11; nonliterate, 174n9
oral transmission, 14; of Christian scripture, 120; in Indian culture, 67–77, 203n37; in Islam, 79–80; as means of preserving sacred texts, 66
oral–written dichotomy, 15, 58–59, 156, 175n2
orality: of Bible, 118, 143; of holy writ, 141; implications of, 159–62; importance in the West, through 17th cent., 41; of Indian texts, 69; of language, 9; of Muslim scripture (Qur'ān), 81, 90ff.; the norm in ancient Greece, 34; primary, 7; as quality of literate, "scriptural" forms of religious life, 111; of reading, 9; within script culture, 18; of scripture, 155–71; of scripture, in Pachomian tradition, 129, 137, 139; secondary, 182n33; vestiges of, 41; of written word, 155
oratory, *see* rhetoric

Pahlavi, *see* writing, of Middle Persian texts
Pachomian *koinonia,* 127, 135, 153, 224nn4,7,10, 227n25; centrality of scripture in, 129; and reading of books, 130; role of scripture in, 129–40

Pachomius, Rule of, 128, 129, 130, 136, 224nn7,9,12, 225n15, 231nn67,69,73,75; *see also* Index of Names, s.v. Pachomius, Saint
pamphlets, popular, dissemination in France of, 41, 189n71
parā vāk [Skt.: "supreme Word"], 71
Paritta (or "Pirit", Buddhist recitative text) [Pali], 66
Parry–Lord thesis, 34, 183n4
pāṭha [Skt.: "recitation, recital, study"], 69, 72
Pāṭimokkha and recitation, 66, 199n48
Paul, the Apostle: authority of Hebrew scripture for, 122, 217n4, 218n4; role of his letters in early Christian worship, 220n16; *see also* Index of Names, s.v.
Pentateuch, 52, 53, 54, 218n7, 220n15; *see also* Torah
periochē [Gk.: "passage, selection (from a text), lection"], as synonym for Syriac *qeryānā,* 90
pictorial orientation of medieval world, 142
piety: biblical, 118; communal, 127; Muslim, 117; Pachomian, 137–40, 233n92; scriptural, 140
Pirit, see Paritta
pluralism, in modern West, 166
poetry: and public reading, 35; as mnemonic device, 177n15
pointing, of Arabic consonantal texts, 98
prayer, 157, 163; Jewish background of Christian, 218n9; and liturgy, in medieval Christianity, 142; in Pachomian *koinonia,* 135, 136, 137, 138, 228n45, 230n66, 232n89; "personal" and "public" not separated by Pachomians, 138
preaching, 158; Christian, 121, 123, 163; Luther's stress on, 149–51, 237nn49, 237–38n55; in medieval period, 142; in Pachomian *koinonia,* 131, 137; quotation of scripture in, 120
preliteracy, *see* literacy
preliterate culture/society, 157, 166; view of history in, 178n22
preprint literate culture, *see* script culture
print culture, 9, 113, 157; assumptions of, about oral communication, 63; development of, in West, 19; distance from oral and script culture, 29; identification of text with printed word in, 21; typographic attitudes in, 20–24; typographic revolution, literacy, and, 166
print-dominated society, *see* print culture
print revolution in modern West, 18, 20
print textuality, 23
printed page, as symbol of authority, 46
printed word/printed book: affect on reader, 19; characteristics of, 32; and displacement of orality, 21; less ambiguous than written word, 23; as living page, 152; and objective, "scientific" scholarship, 21, 23; objectivity of, 22, 180nn12,13; and scripture, in Reformation, 120–21; as source of authority, 23; and typographic revolution, 30; as visual documentation, 21; and visual experience, 10
printing: changes wrought by, 22; in China, 20, 179n4; and continuing orality, 40; in Europe, 17, 39; of Hindu devotional literature, 77; in Korea, 179n4; moveable type, 12, 20, 28
progress, correlated with reliance on written word, 157; *see also* modernity/modernization
propaganda, Protestant, 144
prophet, in Islam, 82, 205n4
protoscripture, 65
psalmody, *see* Psalms
Psalms, 82; Luther's lectures on, 146; role of, in Christian liturgy, 124, 125, 142, 222n22; use of, in Pachomian tradition, 130, 131, 132, 135, 136, 137, 138, 227n30, 228nn43,45, 229n55, 231n73, 232nn84,89, 233n92; *see also* psalter
psalter: compared to Qur'ān as to role in liturgy, 102, 214n24; Huguenot, 40, 189n65; liturgical use of, 88; and recitation, 66; *see also* Psalms
pūjā [Skt.: "worship"], 69
pūjā-pāṭha [Hindi: "worship"], 69, 200n8; *see also pāṭha*
Purāṇas, 4, 75–77; recitation of, 75–76; rooted in oral tradition, 75
Puritans, 165

Qadr, al- (Sūrah 96: "The Decree [or Power]"), 107
qalam [Ar.: "pen"], 208n30
qara'a [Ar.: "to read (aloud), recite"], 97
qāri' (pl.: *qurrā'*) [Ar.: "reciter"], 88, 101, 208n27

qerī'ā [Heb.: "reading, lection (from Scripture)"], 90, 92, 209n38
qeryānā [Syr.: "lection, reading"], 90, 92, 209nn36,38
qirā'ah (pl.: *qirā'āt*) ["recitation; reading, lection" (of the Qur'ān)], 96–102, 212nn5,12,13, 213n20, 214nn23,26; *bil-alḥān* [melodic recitation], 100; crystallization of, as a formal science, 99
qiṣaṣ al-anbiyā' [Ar.: "tales of the prophets"], 205n4
qul [Ar.: "say!"], in the Qur'ān, 91
qur'ān [Ar.: "reciting, recitation"]: in relation to *kitāb,* in the Qur'ān, 205n3; use of the term, 80, 81, 88–95; use of, in a generic sense, 92; use of, to denote an activity, 92–94; use of, for a unit of text, 92–94; *see also* Qur'ān
Qur'ān, 3, 4, 5, 57, 156, 170, 171; 235n14; as analogue of Christ, 121, 217n3; calligraphy of, 86, 97, 110, 158, 197n27; central role of, in Islam, 117; and the creative power of speech, 65, 198n41; distinguished from Divine Sayings, 102–03; as divine presence, 87; effects of modernization upon, 168, 169; as embodiment of revelation, 121; as heavenly book, 50, 53, 192n5; as holy book, 173n1; liturgical centrality of, 88, 102–03, 214n24; magical use of, 61, 216n54; in Muslim life and practice, 102–09, 110–11, 114, 174n3, 213n20, 216nn52,54; in Muslim worship, 161; as *nefaria scriptura,* 56; oral mnemonics of its recitation, 177n15; orality of, 111, 157; original Muslim understanding of, 88–95; popular use of, 216nn52,54; as prayerbook, lectionary, and hymnal, 102; and problems of meaning, 111–15; as prototypical "book of scripture", 79; and question of canonization process, 207n20, 208n20; recitation of, as art and science, 96–102; recitation of, as music, 101; reverential treatment of, 62; sacrality of recitation of, 103–04; sacrality of text of, 101, 103, 114; as speaking book, 154; as spoken and written word, 80; standard text of, 96–97, 211n2; transmission of, as recited, phonetic text, 98; Turkish, 207n17; variant readings in, 89, 97, 99, 209n33, 212n13; veneration of, 196n22; and vernacular translation, 85, 103, 207n17; writing down of, 110; *see also qur'ān;* education, Muslim

raḥmah [Ar.: "mercy"], 109
Ramaḍān, 117; Qur'ān recitation during, 107, 113, 215n46, 216n47
rasm [Ar.: "form; orthography"], 98
rasūl [Ar.: "apostle, messenger"], 82, 205n4, 210n43
reader, as *lector,* 32
reading: in ancient Greece, 184n15; liturgical, 120; modern, contrasted with ancient, 32; orality of, 9, 33, 141; in Pachomian *koinonia,* 130; public, 35, 42, 123, 185nn24,25; of scripture, in private, 218n12; silent, 32–33, 36, 38, 41, 43, 45–46, 160; in vernacular, 38; vocal, 37, 123, 142
recitation, 65–66, 160, 161; as accompaniment to monks' labors, 135–36; in ancient Greece, 34; as chief mark of being Muslim, 95; at funerals, in Islam, 214n29; in Hindu ritual life, 69–77; in Islamic education, 215n35; as key liturgical exercise in Pachomian praxis, 137; in Pachomian tradition, 130, 131, 132, 133–40, 228n45, 231n75, 232n82; magical aspects of, 132, 139; Muslim talismanic use of, 109; of mantras, 77; of non-Vedic texts, 75–77, 204n52; of Old-Persian Zoroastrian texts, 66; permeation of Muslim life by, 106–09, 215n35; of Qur'ān, 79–95, 96–109, 210n42; role of, in Muslim society, 101–09; Vedic, 64, 70–75; as science in Islam, 96–102; of scripture, in Protestant Reformation, 144; *see also* breviary; Lotus Sūtra; *Paritta, pāṭha; Pāṭimokkha;* Qur'ān; revelation, and Qur'ān recitation
reform movements, *see* revitalization movements
Reformation, Protestant, 118, 120, 122; in Germany and Switzerland, 143, 217n2, 234n8; and spoken word of scripture, 143–54
reformers, Protestant, 142, 143
religion: objectification of, 166; scriptural vs. scriptureless, 47; sensual aspects of, 112–13, 159, 162–65

religion of the book, 51–52, 118, 120, 122, 144, 150, 218n4, 219nn10,12
revelation: original and successive, in Islam, 82; and Qur'ān recitation, 210n43; and sacrality of language, 86
revitalization movements, 160, 161
rhetoric, 24–26; applied to written literature, 25; Augustine's treatment of, 24; decline in modern West, 23–26, 181n21; in education, 24, 25, 35; five divisions of, 24; history of, 24–26; importance for literate culture, 24, 25; influence on writing, 37; of Martin Luther, 141–54; in modern secular culture, 45; Ramist, 25; in Renaissance, 188n53; scriptural, 170; *see also balāghah*
rhētōr (s) [Gk.], 24
riwāyah (pl.: *riwāyāt*) [Ar.: "tradition, report"], 99, 100
ṛṣi (s) [Skt.: "seer(s)"], 70, 73, 200n11; in Vedas, 65
ruminatio [Lat.: "chewing, rumination"], as key aspect of monastic meditation, 134; *see also* meditation

śabda [Skt.: "sound, word"], 70–71, 201n23
śabda-brahman [Skt.: "sound-Brahman"], 71, 201nn22,23
sacred writings, *see* scripture
sakīnah, al- [Ar.: "tranquility, (divine) presence"], 93, 96, 210n50
salafī [Ar.: "traditionalist"], 107
ṣalāt [Ar.: "worship"], 85, 92, 93, 94, 100, 102–03, 109, 113, 117, 158, 210nn42,51, 211n60, 214n26
saṁhitā (s) [Skt.: "compilation(s), collection(s)"], 70, 72, 74
saṃpradāya [Skt.: "handing down"], 74
San Tung [Chin.: "Three Caverns"], 195n15
Sanūsīyah, 165
śāstra [Skt.: "precept, treatise"], 74
Schriftgottesdienst [Ger.: "liturgy of scripture"], *see "liturgy of the Word"*
scribal culture, *see* script culture
scribes, monastic, 141
script culture, 12; Aristotle and the transition from oral to, 34; continuities with oral culture, 17, 183n4; developing a descriptive term for, 175n3; in Egyptian New Kingdom, 32; as first stage in decline of spoken word, 31; illiteracy the rule in, 31; and libraries, 35; and new types of consciousness, 17; orality of, 18, 31, 33, 141
scripturality, Protestant, 144
scripture: auditory immediacy of, 160; as authoritative, 49, 156; in Benedictine monasticism, 225n18; as "book, writ, and word", in Luther, 152–54, 238n57; as "breath of God", 129, 227n30, 228n30; centrality of, in Pachomian tradition, 129, 225n19, 227n30; characteristics of, 68; as chief authority for Christian preaching, 120; citation of, in early Christian sources, 218n6; citation of, in Pachomian corpus, 226n20; clarity of, according to Luther, 147, 235n21; comparisons with the Islamic concept of, 84–88; and divine authority, 218n8; in early Christian church, 122–25; as focus of meditation, in monastic tradition, 133; functional aspect of, 155; generalization of the concept, 55–57; general notion of, in Basilian/Cappadocian monasticism, 225n18; general notion of, in Hindu tradition, 68–77; as generic concept in Islam, 82–84, 205n7, 206n15; as "holy writ", 59–63; in Islam, 81–88; in Judaic, Christian, and Islamic tradition, 87; Manichaean, 204n2; memorization and recitation of, 133–37, 158, 222n5, 229n50; and modern culture, 165–71; and monastic life, 128–40, 225nn18,19; as oral in function and aural in impact, 139; orality of, 155–71; orality of, among Pachomians, 129; physical aspects of, 164; private reading of, in early Christianity, 218n12; quotation from, in sermons, 120; relational quality of, 5–6; and reluctance to translate, 85; Sahidic coptic version of, 226n20; semantics of the term, 53–55; sensual dimension of, 6–7, 164; as spoken word in Reformation, 143–54, 237nn48,49; in vernacular, 143; as word of God, 121, 223n28; "writtenness" of, 60
scripture-consciousness, *see* Bible-consciousness
scripture-principle, 219n10
scripture–tradition dichotomy, 156
secularization, 166, 167, 168, 170, 238n5; *see also* modernity/modernization

Septuagint, 53, 54, 146, 222n24, 226n20
sermon: in Christian worship, 124, 125; Jewish background of Christian, 218n9; Protestant, 143–44, 145; *see also* preaching
shaykh [Ar.: "master, teacher"], 106
shu [*"Chin.: books"* (classics)], 3
śiṣya [Skt.: "student, pupil"], 74
smṛti [Skt.: "what is remembered"], 65, 71, 75
sola scriptura [Lat.: "scripture alone"], 120, 143, 146, 217n2
speech, *see* language
sphoṭa [Skt.: "(essence of) word, speech"], 71, 201n23
spirit and letter, 145, 237n44
spoken word: as act, 64–65; as creative, 64–65; as sacred, 62–66; scriptural presence in, 171; as truth, 67–68, 71, 199n1
śruti [Skt.: "what is heard"], 4, 65, 71, 75, 198n45
Stundenbuch, see breviary
successive revelation, in Islam, *see Heilsgeschichte*
Sufism, and recitation, 160
ṣuḥuf [Ar.: "pages; writings"], 208n30
sūtra(s), Buddhist, 163, 169; magical use of, 61, 196n17
svādhyāya [Skt.: "study, going over by oneself"], 72, 73
synagogue, influence of, on Christian worship, 219n9
synaxis [Gk.: "gathering, assembly"], 136, 138, 232nn80,83, 232–33n91, 233n95; *see also "liturgy of the Word"*
Syriac: as source for Ar. *qur'ān,* 209n38; used among Arab Christians, 209n40
Syriac Christianity, possible influences of, on Qur'ānic worldview, 210n40

Tabennesiots (Pachomian monks), 127–39 passim, 230n67, 233n92
tafsīr [Ar.: "exegesis"], *see* exegesis, Muslim
tajwīd [Ar.: "cantillation, recitation"], 98, 102, 106, 108, 213nn17–20, 216n51; art of, 100–01; as reenactment of revelation, 100
talā [Ar.: "to recite; follow"], 91, 210nn43,44
Tantras (as Indian scriptural texts), 75
tanzīl [Ar.: "sending down, revelation"], 81
Targum, used to convey meaning of Hebrew scriptures, 85
tartīl [Ar.: "measured chanting"], 100–01, 213nn15,17
ta'wīl [Ar.: "esoteric, allegorical exegesis"], 113
teacher, role in transmission of Vedas, 74–75; *see also guru*
text: affective role of, 163; as focus of meditation in monastic life, 133; as icon, 158; limitation of term to written documents, 180n9; and textual presence, 140; and textuality in medieval Europe, 217n1, 222n24; as written or printed document, 21; *see also* printed word/printed book
theopneustos ["inspired by God"], 219n14
tilāwah [Ar.: "reciting, recitation"], 102, 107, 108, 109, 214n23
Torah, 4, 46, 47, 51, 52, 53, 60, 82, 85, 87, 163, 195n10, 209n39; and "book religion"; cantillation of, 158; and creative power of speech, 198n41; influence on Christian worship, 220n15; and recitation, 66; as speaking book, 154; veneration of, 61, 196n22
trivium [Lat.], 25
typographic culture, *see* print culture

'ulamā', see 'ālim
umm al-kitāb [Ar.: "the mother of scripture"], 84, 89, 206nn14,15
Unification Church, 165
'Uthmānic consonantal text of Qur'ān, 97, 98, 99, 212nn6,12
'Uthmānic redaction of Qur'ān, 207n20, 209n33

vāc [Skt.: "speech"], 70, 201n16
Vāc [Skt.: "Speech"]: equated with Brahman, 71; as goddess, "mother of the Vedas", 70, 201nn15,17; personified as deity, 64
Vācaspati [Skt.: "Lord of Speech"], 70
Veda(s), 4, 5, 154; as authoritative and holy, 56; and Brahmanic ritual, 161–62; compared to Qur'ān, 80, 83, 102; considered as "scripture", 57; and creative word, 64–65; hymnody, 200n11; magical elements in, 74; memorization of, 72; as model for recitation of popular texts, 75, 77; oral mnemonics of, 177n15; as *scriptura abscondita,* 75; transmission of, 72–75

Vedic tradition, 163; orality of, 157; respect for written word within, 158
Vedic word, sacrality of, 73–74
vikṛti (s) [Skt.: "alteration(s)"], 72
Vulgate, *see* Bible, Latin Vulgate

Western thought, as "alphabetic", 182n37
Westminster Confession, 121
Witoto (South American native tribe), 64, 198n40
word of the Buddha, *see buddhavacana*
word of God: centrality in Christian liturgical tradition, 120; in Christianity, 119–22; functional complexity and multiple meanings of, 121; as kerygma and as text, 151; as scripture, 121, 130; as synonym for Bible, 119; transformative power of, 143
work, united with prayer, in Pachomian tradition, 135–36
worship, Christian, *see* liturgy; "liturgy of the Word"
Wortgottesdienst [Ger.], *see* "liturgy of the Word"
writing: as aid to memory, 178n16; alphabetic, 50; Arabic, 89, 208n30; and autonomy of written word, 15; as basis for historical inquiry, 13–14, 176n7, 177n9; in Indian culture, 68, 203n37; introduced to India from Mesopotamia, 199n3; as measure of civilization, 12; of Middle Persian (Pahlavi) texts, 66; as new technology, 17; as oral process in script culture, 141; orality of, 37; in Pachomian *koinonia,* 130; permanence of, 16, 175n3; phonetic, 11; and rhetoric, 37; as ritually polluting, 74; as taught in ancient Greece and Rome, 185n22; and textuality, 11; and thought processes, 14–17; visual quality of, 175n3; *see also* literacy; script culture
written culture, *see* script culture
written text: centrality of, in modern West, 168; compared to oral text, 15; importance in Islam, 79; as oral phenomenon, 123, 142, 144, 147, 153; as secondary in Islam, 98; *see also* writing; written word
written language, compared to oral language, 175n2
written tradition, 7; contrasted with oral tradition, 14, 174n9
written word: as authoritative and permanent, 156, 157; authoritativeness of, in Judaism and early Christianity, 122, 123; functional orality of, 36, 155, 157; as magical, 61, 157, 164; objectivity of, 180nn12,13; permanence and authority of, 59; as something that speaks, 142

Yā Sīn (Sūrah 36), 109, 216n54

Zand (Zoroastrian commentaries), 66
Zoroastrians, in Arabia, 91
zubūr [Ar.: "writings; psalms"], 208n30